Leon County, Florida Heritage Book;

Historical Stories of Events, Places & People that Shaped Tallahassee

© 2012
Compiled by:
The Leon County Heritage Book Committee

Of The
Tallahassee Genealogical Society, Inc.

Published by
Southern Yellow Pine (SYP) Publishing
4351 Natural Bridge Rd.
Tallahassee, FL 32305

All Rights reserved. No part of this publication may be reproduced, stored in a retrieval system or transmitted in any form or by any means, electronic, mechanical, photocopying, recording, scanning or otherwise, without the prior written permission of the Publisher. For permission or further information contact SYP Publishing, LLC. 4351 Natural Bridge Rd. Tallahassee, FL 32305.

www.syppublishing.com
The contents and opinions expressed in this book do not necessarily reflect the views and opinions of Southern Yellow Pine Publishing or , Tallahassee Genealogical Society, Inc. nor does the mention of brands or trade names constitute endorsement.

Credit to Florida State Archive- *Florida Photographic Collection* for various photos provided within. Each is credited.
All other photos remain the property of the individuals that submitted them

Copyright Compiled Text – Tallahassee Genealogical Society, Inc.
Copyright Individual Articles – Each article is the sole property of the author noted at the end of each story

Front Cover photograph by; Beatrice Queral, *Florida's State Capitol*
Back cover photograph by; Amy Tison Hutson, *Florida's Prime Meridian Marker*

ISBN-10: 098570621X

ISBN-13: 978-0-9857062-1-0

Printed in the United States of America
First Edition
September 2012

DEDICATION

**The Leon County Heritage Book is dedicated to
TGS Charter Members
and those who served as its first
officers and directors.**

Cliff Burkhart
Mavis Day
Barbara Boykin
Mary Elizabeth Black
Eleanor Cotton
Clinita Ford
Ed Mims
Florida Parker

Original logo designed by John Lane Mims

Contents

ACKNOWLEDGEMENTS ....

FORWARD ....

LEON COUNTY ARTS & ENTERTAINMENT 1

LEON COUNTY BUSINESSES 9

LEON COUNTY COMMUNITIES 27

LEON COUNTY SCHOOLS AND UNIVERSITIES 35

LEON COUNTY LOCAL LANDMARKS 46

LEON COUNTY ORGANIZATIONS 54

RELIGIOUS COMMUNITIES/CEMETERIES 60

LEON COUNTY SPECIAL EVENTS 68

LEON COUNTY REMINISCENCES 72

LEON COUNTY FAMILIES 85

ACKNOWLEDGEMENTS

Heritage Book Committee Volunteers

Rubie Butterworth	Jay P. Collins	Diane Dittgen
Julianne Hare	Donna Heald	Pat Herold
Amy Hutson	Carol Johnson	Susie Lamb
Jane Madelon	Mary J. Marchant	Dr. Lynn McLarty
Miriam McLarty	Lynn McWhorty	Deanna Ramsey
Robert Ramsey	Dick Sherwin	Robert Sneed
Laurie Wishmeier		

Additional Thanks and Recognition

To the Florida Department of State, State Library and Archives Photographic Collection – The Florida Memory Project – for facilitating the use of some of the images included here.

FORWARD

The history of Leon County, Florida is as diverse as its people. Native Americans lived, worshipped, and battled in these rolling hills for over 10,000 years. When Europeans discovered the area's spring-fed waterways, fertile soil, and rich hunting and fishing grounds; they helped themselves to the land. Spain, Great Britain, France, and those who called themselves Americans set off a series of political and often bloody conflicts as they fought to seize control.

In the end, Florida became a vital part of the expanding United States. Waves of land speculators, plantation builders, slaves, merchants, and free farmers moved in. They represented a multitude of cultures, races, and religions. They were wealthy; they were dirt poor. Many came willingly; others came because they had no choice. Some folks settled in, some took what they could and moved on, but all of them contributed to the rich heritage that is today's Tallahassee.

Numerous books have been written about this place we call home, but – until now – most of our story has been told through the eyes of historians rather than those who actually lived it. The Tallahassee Genealogical Society (incorporated in 1981-1982) wanted to preserve our history in a simpler format.

In 2008, the organization formed a partnership agreement with Heritage Publishing Consultants and encouraged our members to submit their family stories and their recollections of life in Tallahassee during the recent past. The effort to compile these accounts turned out to be more exciting – and challenging – than any of us could imagine. What started as a less-than-a-year work plan grew into a multi-year series of meetings, work sessions, material handling, filing, typing, scanning and photo-copying. The partnership with HPC was terminated and a contract was signed with a new publisher, SYP Publishing of Tallahassee, FL to complete the project. Stories remain the sole property of the submitters, and the committee is grateful to all who took time to write down and submit their stories.

Committee members came and went over the full course of the project. Leadership changed. Good friends were lost and new friendships were forged. It is difficult to acknowledge the contributions of time, talent, materials, and financial support that went into this effort and our sincerest apologies if we omitted anyone from our list of volunteers.

LEON COUNTY ARTS & ENTERTAINMENT

The Artist Series

The Artist Series of Tallahassee, Fl. was founded by Waldie Anderson in 1995.

The purpose of the Artist Series of Tallahassee, Inc., is to develop, foster, and promote the arts as experiences central to the lives of the citizens of Leon County and the surrounding region. Toward this end, it will undertake the following activities:

1. Present a yearly concert series, hosting diverse programming by performing artists of national and international stature; 2. Provide an opportunity for area residents to participate in the musical activities of the Big Bend Community Orchestra; 3. Seek and apply for state, federal and private funds available in support of the arts; 4. Engage in any other activities that will enhance the arts and cultural life in Leon County and the surrounding region.

Submitted by: Ginny Densmore, 9713 Waters Meet Drive, Tallahassee, FL 32312

The Big Bend Community Orchestra

The Big Bend Community Orchestra (BBCO) provides opportunities for community musicians to learn and play together, encourages school age children to become interested in music through educational programs, and performs, orchestral music for the public. The BBCO consists of more than 50 volunteer musicians and includes professionals, homemakers, music teachers, and students. Waldie Anderson, conductor from Feb. 1994 until 2004, co-founded the orchestra with Ginny Densmore. Dr. James Croft led the organization from 2004-2007 and Dr. Shelby Chipman has directed since the fall of 2007. BBCO is affiliated with Tallahassee Community College and students there can receive credit with the permission of the instructor.

BBCO has presented more than 68 concerts and played over 300 compositions by a variety of composers spanning four centuries, including lighter classics and "pops." Local talent of all ages has been showcased from the community as well as orchestra members. A "Young Artist Competition" is held each spring and the winners have a chance to perform a solo with the orchestra.

Concerts are given on Saturday afternoons at 4:00 so that senior citizens and families with children can attend. Children in the audience are given the opportunity to come on stage to see and hear the instruments "up close and personal."

Membership in the orchestra is open to all capable musicians on a space available basis with first priority given to adult community members and non-music major university students who are not eligible for school groups.

Our Artistic Director, Dr. James Croft and Waldie Anderson are Emeritus Conductors. For more information, consult the website: wwwBBCOrch.org

Submitted by: Ginny Densmore, 9713 Waters Meet Drive, Tallahassee, FL 32312

Bruce Cook's River-Wood Studio

Bruce Cook is a self taught folk artist who lived in South Florida for over thirty years. He has created and exhibited his unique art work for several years across the southeast areas of Florida. Bruce recently moved to the Suwannee Valley with his wife, Dottie, and they have shown their art work in Tallahassee for many years.

The mixed media bas reliefs and sculptures used are from natural materials with non-toxic stains and durable epoxy finishing. Most of Bruce's work features Marine life, Flora and Fauna of North Florida, and the cultural traditions of South Carolina and Georgia.

Mr. Bruce Cook at the 2010 Marketplace in Tallahassee, Florida

His work is in three museums' permanent collections, has been accepted at the Princeton University Medical Center spring 2009 exhibition, and is on display in the State of Florida Capitol building collection.

Bruce has completed several public commissions and is a Program Presenter and Artist in Residence for the "VSA of Florida." In 2006 he was adjudicated to the Southern Artists Federation. This group is comprised of 600 nominated artists from nine southern states. The winners are posted in 2010 "Who's Who in American Art."

Bruce's rare talent is for demonstrating and producing the ancient, traditional and vanishing Folk Art form of the "Hex signs" from the rural "Pennsylvania Dutch" countryside. The originality in his work has been very well received and can be seen at shows, galleries, and public buildings throughout Florida, including the Florida panhandle. Mr. Cook is also "2009 Volunteer of the Year" award-recipient.

Written-Submitted by: Bruce Cook, Live Oak, Florida 386-842-5814 bdcookdesign@aol.com

Capital City Band of TCC

The Capital City Band was organized in 1922 and performed in Tallahassee until the mid-forties. In 1966 the band was reorganized as the Tallahassee Community Band by Jayne Marsh Standley, now music therapy professor at Florida State University, as a project for a graduate course in music therapy at FSU. In 1971, the band became affiliated with Tallahassee Community College and changed its name to The Capital City Band of TCC.

The band provides a musical outlet for area musicians and is made up of people with various levels of playing proficiency. Auditions are not required, but regular attendance and responsible musicianship are expected. The band is open to adult community members and is also available for college credit to students enrolled at Tallahassee Community College. High school students may participate with the permission of the director. The band performs several concerts a year and has made their services available for community-sponsored events such as Veterans Day, July 4th Celebrations, Springtime Tallahassee, and the Winter Festival as well as performing in area retirement homes and the senior center. In the early years, performances were given every Christmas at Sunland Hospital. For the first several years of Springtime Tallahassee, the Tallahassee Community Band was the only band that participated in the parade, riding on the back of a flat-bed truck.

Gary Coates has been the director of the Jazz Band at TCC since 1994, and became the director of the Capital City Band in 1996.

The Capital City Band meets in Room 165 in the Communications & Humanities wing Monday nights, 7:15- 9:15 when TCC is in session.

Submitted by: Ginny Densmore, 9713 Waters Meet Drive, Tallahassee,

The Drive-In Theatres

The Capital Drive-In at Four Points and the Perry Highway Drive-In at the Truck Route (east) and Perry Highway provided newsreels, cartoons, and movies. The acreage was covered with speakers next to which cars parked. A snack bar, rest rooms, and the projection building were behind the cars.

Speakers were pulled into cars and hung on windows. If mosquitoes were bad, it was doubly hot because windows would be rolled up to keep them outside. Spiral mosquito repellants were burned inside the car, but the odor was awful.

The McPhersons lived on Bass Street northward of the fairgrounds and the Capital Drive-In. Without television, Dotty and Elmer went to the drive-in every time the movie changed, at least 3 times a week.

On weekends, they took Dotty's girlfriends. Dotty's mother, Thelma, would not go, because she would not tolerate the discomfort of sitting in the car so long and in the heat or cold, and needed her beauty sleep.

When Dotty got older, she and her friends went to the drive-ins. The Capital Drive-In had seats at the front of the parking lot. Sometimes they sat in those seats. For one of Dotty's birthdays, they went to the Capital Drive-In and sat in those seats. One gift was a beautiful beaded wallet, with royal blue, red, and green beads shaped into a flower. She lost it there. It was the most beautiful wallet she ever saw. When she thinks about the Capital Drive-In, she always remembers her lost beaded wallet.

The Perry Highway Drive-In came and doubled the entertainment opportunities. Both are now gone and only the memories remain.

Written and Submitted by Dorothy Lee "Dotty" McPherson, 24236

Early Theaters in Tallahassee

A history of Florida's capital city shows the first theatrical entertainment for its citizens began in 1857, when Tallahassee became a regular stop in the schedules of various road shows, usually circuses and minstrel shows.

The first theater in Tallahassee was built in 1874 on the northeast corner of Adams and Jefferson Streets, and was known as Gallie's Hall, later named the Tallahassee Opera House. In 1890, the building was sold to James Munro and renamed Munro's Opera House.

Ending the 36-year monopoly of the Opera House was the plan when a 1,200 seat auditorium was constructed at Leon High School. This plan was dashed in 1911 when the courts ruled that public school buildings could not be leased for amusement purposes. Governor Albert W. Gilchrist was a strong supporter of theater. In 1910, he acted the title role in "The Reverie of a Bachelor," a fund-raising project to build the Woman's Club and, in 1912, dedicated the Capital City Theater (later known as Daffin's Theater) on the site of the city's only cotton warehouse (the north side of College Avenue between Monroe and Adams Streets).

The first play in Tallahassee to include the name "Little Theater" was probably the 1928 Business and Professional Woman's Club production of "Lightnin" which included future Governor LeRoy Collins in the cast. Another effort to establish a community theater in Tallahassee came in 1937, when the Tallahassee Little Theater Guild was organized on February 1st.

Gallie's Hall at Adams and Jefferson Streets

Shortly after the group was formed, Tallahassee's mayor proclaimed the first week of May as "Little Theater Week" for the purpose of officially encouraging and increasing the membership of the Little Theater Group, and for stimulating public interest in the activity of "Tallahassee's Little Theater."

In its first season, the group presented three evenings of one-act plays. Its first full-length play, "Post Road," ran for one evening (April 19, 1938) at the Augusta Conradi Little Theater on the FSU campus. Later that year, "Aaron Slick from Punkin' Crick" and "Cradle Song" each received two performances. In 1939, future Governor Farris Bryant was featured in the play "Fresh Fields." When he was re-elected as governor, his daughter Adair was an active member of Tallahassee Little Theater.

After 1940, the community theater in Tallahassee was relatively dormant until a reorganized Tallahassee Little Theater presented "Star Bound" on March 26, 1945 at the Leon High School auditorium. The play was sponsored by the city recreation department and benefited the Red Cross. "Star Bound" would be the last play produced under the old Tallahassee Little Theater banner. The cash balance from this one activity was later transferred to the current Tallahassee Little Theatre which was organized in 1949.

Submitted by: Richard R. Sherwin, 616 Acorn Grove Court, Tallahassee, FL 32312 risher@aol.com

The Tallahassee Bach Parley

The Tallahassee Bach Parley was incorporated not-for profit in the State of Florida in September 1981, following its first concert in August of that year. From its inception, the Parley has been a community-based organization.

The Parley's purposes are to present vital, interesting, and informative performances of primarily Baroque music, with special sensitivity to style and other traditions, using period instruments as much as possible. For many years, a choir auditioned from the community presented Bach choral works in programs that also featured solo and ensemble works. Some of the early dress

Bach Parley Monogram, based on J.S. Bach's personal seal

rehearsals were open to the public; and educational commentary on the musical works and the instruments has always been an important feature of Parley concerts.

In the first decade, most musicians on the regular season concerts performed without remuneration. It is to their dedication, and the faithfulness of our audience and supporters, that we owe our existence. The Parley is supported by memberships and donations; and the Division of Cultural Affairs and the Florida Arts Council of Florida's Department of State have supported many of our efforts through grants.

Submitted by: Mary J. Marchant, 2901 Springfield Drive, Tallahassee, FL 32309; Source: Karyl Louwenaar Lueck; August 2008

Tallahassee Community Chorus

The Tallahassee Community Chorus began in 1988 as a collaborative effort between the Florida State University School of Music and 37 community singers. Over 20 years the group has grown to be Florida's Premiere Chorus and one of the leading community choruses in the country. Much of the momentum for this growth and development has been provided by the Artistic Director, Dr. Andre Thomas, whose energy, skill and musical talents are known and respected throughout the choral world. The Chorus continues to enjoy an excellent relationship with the Florida State University College of Music.

The Tallahassee Community Chorus

The current 250-member chorus includes singers representing all walks of life. Age is no restriction, with members being of high school age up to senior citizens. The mission of the Chorus is to enjoy the experience of promoting choral music through excellence of performance and to reach out into the schools and community.

Large masterworks with orchestra are the focus of the repertoire of the Chorus. Each season consists of 3 major concerts. Recent performances include works by Handel, Beethoven, Brahms, Haydn, and several others. The Chorus has had the privilege of performing under the baton of the late Robert Shaw and several other renowned choral directors.

The Chorus has performed at Carnegie Hall (2004); The Kennedy Center (2008); and in China at the First International Bejing Choral Festival (2007).

During the month of July, 2011, The Chorus represented the State of Florida and Tallahassee in the Prague Choral Festival at the historic Smetana Hall. Future plans include another trip to Carnegie Hall.

Submitted by: Mary J. Marchant 2901 Springfield Drive, Tallahassee, FL 32309; Source: Internet: "Our History" from The Tallahassee Community Chorus, Florida's Premier Community Chorus; Andre Thomas, Artistic Director

Tallahassee Little Theatre

This volunteer organization began 60 years ago with a production of "Boy Meets Girl" at a military movie theater at Dale Mabry Field, a World War II Army post located west of the city. The building had been donated by the City of Tallahassee and served as the production space for Tallahassee Little Theatre (TLT) from 1949 until 1954. A nearby airplane hangar was used to construct and store sets for upcoming plays

Despite its humble beginnings, TLT expanded its

Tallahassee Little Theatre

efforts to produce three or four plays each season and eventually moved its shows to Alfriend Hall at St. John's Episcopal Church. Sets had to be erected there after Sunday services and removed before the following Sunday services began. During the summers from 1950 through 1955, melodramas, including "The Drunkard", "Only an Orphan Girl", and "A Fate Worse Than Death", were performed at the American Legion Hall.

Alfriend Hall served TLT for nearly ten years until a permanent site was donated at the corner of Betton and Thomasville Roads.

Construction began in 1961 and the first production in the new building, "Separate Tables", opened in 1964. After air conditioning was added in 1974, TLT was able to offer summer productions in its building. During the next 35 seasons, patrons could enjoy comedies, dramas, musicals, melodramas, and children's theater.

TLT secured funding from grants and private donations in 1991 and began to expand the 141-seat building into its current structure, which includes 259 permanent seats, two lobbies, and a set construction and storage area. The new building was dedicated on May 1, 1994.

Drawing from the community and its universities, TLT is fortunate to be able to fill its need for actors, production crews, front-of-house personnel, and administrative help with volunteer help. Several actors have followed their experiences on the TLT stage with careers on the Broadway stage.

One of the oldest community theatres in Florida, TLT has produced nearly 400 plays in 60 seasons and has expanded its mission of furthering and promoting a community understanding of the dramatic arts by providing workshops, summer activities for children, and senior citizen acting opportunities. Its members travel throughout the community entertaining with mystery dinner theatres and visiting churches and senior citizen locations with short selections.
Submitted by: Dick Sherwin, 616 Acorn Grove Court, Tallahassee, FL 32312 Risher1@aol.com

Tallahassee Music Guild

The Tallahassee Music Guild celebrates its 47th anniversary this year (2011). Its organization was announced on October 2, 1964. Charter members felt the need to have an organized group of music lovers who would be interested in enriching the community through music. These interested supporters were Eloise Berry, Ramona Beard, Irene Bergman, Jeannette Humphress, Elena Nickolaidi an Corinne Gridley, who served as the first President of the Guild.

One month later, the Tallahassee Music Guild awarded the first scholarship to a student of Mme. Elena Nickolaidi, Professor of Voice at Florida State University. As of 2009, the Guild has awarded 453 scholarships.

The object of the Guild is to present scholarships based on genuine need of financial assistance and excellence in study and potential, and to promote interest in music in the community. The scholarships are funded through members' dues, donations, fund raising, and an endowment fund which was established in response to members wishing to give a memorial in honor or in memory of a loved one or friend.

THE TALLAHASSEE MUSIC GUILD

2009-2010

Membership in the Guild is by invitation and is limited to seventy-five members. Meetings are held monthly, September through May. The Guild's business is conducted by an Executive Board comprised of elected officers and appointed committee chairpersons. Each active member is encouraged to serve on at least one committee.
"There's a difference between interest and commitment. When you're interested in doing something, you do it only when circumstances permit. When you're committed to something, you accept no excuses, only results."
From the 2009-2010 The Tallahassee Music Guild Yearbook www.TallahasseeMusicGuild.org
Submitted by: Mary J. Marchant, 2901 Springfield Drive, Tallahassee, FL 32309

Tallahassee Swing

Over thirty years ago, Hal Friensehner, Alan Nelson, and Dick Drennon got a group of musicians together at the home of Margaret and Sam Moorer to enjoy playing big band swing music. Others who enjoyed playing the music soon joined the group. Under the leadership of Hal Friensehner, the band began to play in public as *SwingStyle Tallahassee*. Several years later, the band was reorganized and renamed, with Elliot Toole as leader and Pat Cook as business manager. *Tallahassee Swing* started performing in public at the Governor's Square Mall and the Tallahassee Senior Center, and soon was playing for parties, weddings, and concerts in North Florida, South Georgia, (and on occasion Lake City and Orlando). Tallahassee Swing has played for weekly Tuesday night dances (7:30-10 p.m.) at the American Legion Hall at Lake Ella for over 21 years.

Some original musicians are no longer with us. Sam Moorer (trumpet) and Phil Leamon (piano) had played during the big band era. They mentored and inspired the "newer" musicians. Several of the members of the original band still play with Tallahassee Swing. The band continues to attract talented musicians (former FSU Marching Chiefs, state employees, business owners, students, and others). Over the years, several other bands have spun off from Tallahassee Swing, and musicians who have performed with Tallahassee Swing have gone on to play with the Glenn Miller, Count Basie, and Duke Ellington bands. The longevity of Tallahassee Swing is due to dedication of the musicians in the band, the lasting appeal of the music, and the continued support of people who appreciate live big band dance music.

Submitted by: Pat Cook, Business Manager Tallahassee Swing

Tallahassee Symphony Orchestra

The Tallahassee Symphony Orchestra evolved from a 1979 performance of Handel's Messiah, presented by Maestro Nicholas Harsanyi and area professionals. According to notes in the 1990-1991 program book, "...enthusiasm for a resident orchestra grew at the same time that the new Civic Center was nearing completion. It was decided that the grand celebration to open the Tallahassee/Leon County Civic Center should include a symphony performance by Tallahassee's own orchestra. With volunteers handling promotion, ticket sales, and fundraising, Maestro Harsanyi conducted the premiere performance on September 14, 1981."

After the death of Maestro Harsanyi in 1987, the TSO was led by a series of guest conductors under the supervision of Phillip Spurgeon, Artistic Advisor. After one season under David S. Z. Pollitt, David Hoose took over the baton in 1993 and led the Orchestra to new artistic heights. Maestro's Hoose's resignation after eleven years led us into an exciting conductor search during the 2005-2006 season, culminating in the appointment of Miriam Bums as the new Music Director in June 2006.

The Tallahassee Symphony Orchestra is governed by a volunteer board. The Board is a group of hardworking volunteers who are committed to providing the Tallahassee area with the cultural, educational and economic enrichment that a professional orchestra provides. They contribute drive and vision for continuing excellence in the arts for our community.

TSO continues to achieve its mission of "producing musical performances of the highest quality," presenting works of both classic and contemporary composers. The musicians come from varied backgrounds.

It is the only professional orchestra in the region, and is a cultural jewel for Tallahassee.

Submitted by: Mary J. Marchant, 2901 Springfield Drive Tallahassee, FL 32309; Source: Excerpts taken directly from program book notes.

The Tallahassee Symphony Society

In the fall of 1992, while serving as Chair of the Board of Directors of the Tallahassee Symphony Orchestra, Dot Hinson organized a Christmas Tour of Homes as a major fund raiser to support the orchestra. Ruth McDonald chaired this initial Tour of Homes and its success suggested the need for an organization to make it an annual event and to perform other activities supportive of the Tallahassee Symphony Orchestra. So, in March of 1993, Dot Hinson founded the Tallahassee Symphony Society. Irene Kogan was elected as the Society's first President. The mission of the Society was simple - to conduct an annual Holiday Tour of Homes and to promote other activities to support the orchestra.

To date, through the efforts of many men and women, the Tallahassee Symphony Society has raised close to $450,000 to support our orchestra. Other successful events, including fashion shows, a Designer Showcase Home and musical soirees held in private homes, have become fund raisers in addition to the lucrative Holiday Tour of Homes and cocktail party. Members of the Society also usher at concerts, sell tickets to the Tour, assist in the annual subscription drive and perform other service activities.

From the 2009-2010 Tallahassee Symphony Society Yearbook
Submitted by: Mary J. Marchant, 2901 Springfield Drive, Tallahassee, FL 32309

Tallahassee Winds

Tallahassee Winds provides opportunities for advanced level wind and percussion players living in the Tallahassee area to play quality band literature in a concert setting. It brings together music educators, musicians from the community, university musicians, and outstanding high school musicians into a performance venue which is challenging, yet an enjoyable, format. Tallahassee Winds adds to the cultural opportunities available to Tallahassee and surrounding areas for musicians to perform quality band literature, and provides audiences a wide variety of band music enjoyable to hear.

Founded in 1997 by Dr. Bentley Shellahamer, the one hundred member Tallahassee Winds performs four formal concerts a season from September to May. The band rehearses on Tuesday evenings, plus a dress rehearsal for each formal concert. Guest conductors and soloists are frequently presented. Membership in the band is available by audition as seats become available. A commitment to participate an entire season is expected when an audition is arranged.

During its first thirteen seasons, Tallahassee Winds performed for FMEA/Southern Division MENC Convention in January of 1999; the National Convention of the Association of Concert Bands in March, 2001 and March, 2006; and completed a highly successful concert tour in Australia, which included a concert in the famed Sydney Opera House with conductor/composer Eric Whitacre.

Each season, with advertising help from the *Tallahassee Democrat,* half of all monies from ticket sales goes to a selected community service agency. Tallahassee Winds could not exist in its present form without the continued support of the College of Music at Florida State University, Don Gibson, Dean.
Submitted by: Ginny Densmore, 9173 Waters Meet Drive, Tallahassee, FL 32312

Tallahassee Youth Symphony Orchestra

The Tallahassee Youth Symphony Orchestra (TYSO), led by Dr. Alexander Jimenez, is the premier orchestral training program for the Big Bend area. The TYSO believes that one of the best ways to ensure that classical music is a thriving part of our community is to win over the hearts and minds of young people.

Our goal is to provide high quality music education programs that cultivate the next generation of musicians and patrons of the arts. The TYSO recognizes the power and importance of musical literacy and one that leads the state in its support of music education.

The TYSO offers five orchestras designed for various levels of playing ability, from beginning strings to an advanced symphony orchestra. Additionally the TYSO features four chamber ensembles (string quartet, woodwind quintet, brass quintet and percussion ensemble) and the Tallahassee Fiddlers which focuses on folk and ethnic music.

The TYSO employs some of the area's brightest music educators which includes several string teachers in the Leon County Public Schools and Dr. Alexander Jimenez, Head of Orchestras at Florida State University. The TYSO is also staffed by music majors from Florida State University's nationally renowned College of Music, each of whom exhibits a deep commitment to music pedagogy.

The TYSO offers partial scholarships for young students in need of financial help, made possible in part by funding from Capital City Bank Group, Publix Supermarket Charities, the Walmart Foundation and the Tallahassee Music Guild. The TYSO is also grateful for the assistance of its private donors and in-kind support from Beethoven & Company music store and the Florida State College of Music.
Submitted by: Mary J. Marchant, 2901 Springfield Dr., Tallahassee, FL 32309; Source: Internet: The Tallahassee Youth Symphony Orchestra

Theatre A La Carte

Theatre A La Carte is North Florida's award-winning musical theatre company, and has produced quality musical theatre in Tallahassee since 1990.

Founded by Eric Hurst with the backing of Elmer and Sara Horne, the first shows were *She Loves Me* (1990) and *Evita* (1991), performed in the Florida High School auditorium. In 1991-92, the season expanded to two shows, and the following season, productions were moved to the current venue at the Tallahassee Little Theatre. Notable productions include *Sweeney Todd (1993), Me and My Girl* (1994), *La Cage aux Folles* (1998), *Falsettos* (1999), *The Who's Tommy (2000), Jekyll & Hyde* (2003), *Ragtime* (2004), and *Nine* (2008), which won First Place in the Florida Community Theatre Festival and First Place in the Southeastern Theatre Conference Community Theatre Festival, and was presented at the bi-annual national festival sponsored by the American Association of Community Theatre in Tacoma, WA. Productions of *Peter Pan* (2001) and *Seussical* (2006), co-produced with Tallahassee Little Theatre, were the best-selling community theatre productions in Tallahassee to date.

Theatre A La Carte produces a unique assortment of Broadway hits and cult classics, and has received recognition for its commitment to producing the musicals of Stephen Sondheim, the musical theatre's foremost composer and lyricist, including two profiles in *The Sondheim Review,* the international publication dedicated to Sondheim's work.

Submitted by: Eric Hurst, 1516 Copperfield Circle, Tallahassee, FL ; Source: Theatre A La Carte website, www.theatrealcarte.org

LEON COUNTY BUSINESSES

Afro-American Life Insurance – Tallahassee District Office Connection

On a wintry evening, January 14, 1901, seven outstanding Negro citizens met in the parsonage of Bethel Baptist Institutional Church at the invitation of its progressive pastor, the Reverend J. Milton Waldron. After viewing the situation as presented to them, the public spirited citizens entered into fruitful discussion concerning the unhealthy conditions then surrounding the colored people, the presence of poverty in the midst, and the absence of adequate means of relief in times of distress. How to relieve these conditions was the topic chiefly considered among them. After much prayerful discussion among them, they finally decided to form an organization that would carry out their plan of co-operative service. One of the plans was to establish the Afro-American Industrial and Benefit Association of the United States of America. This noble venture rose to become one of the leading business enterprises in Florida, despite oppressive social, economic, and political conditions of the times.

Each founder paid or pledged $100 to purchase stock in what was to be chartered by the State of Florida in 1901 as the Afro-American Industrial and Benefit Association. The company had several among its executives: Abraham Lincoln (A.L.) Lewis, a founder, William H. Lee, James H. Lewis, James Leonard Lewis, and L.H. Burney II. The company was organized at a time when black enterprise was the exception, class poverty the rule. Its founders ascribed to the "principle of integrity and to the desire to help their fellow man".

Later known as The Afro-American Life Insurance Company, this oldest life insurance company in Florida celebrated its 75th anniversary in 1976. According to the program compiled for this observance, the company developed into one of the state's leading black enterprises, serving over $124 million of insurance in force. It had over 225 employees and operated 13 district offices in Florida, Georgia and Alabama from the home office in Jacksonville, Florida.

One of the district offices was located in Tallahassee, Florida. It was originally housed in Johnson Furniture Store, a white owned and operated business that was located at the corner of Tennessee and Macomb Street. When the owners asked the company to vacate the building, Mr. William H. Robinson, a teacher at the original Lincoln High School, had two buildings built on Carolina Street to accommodate the Afro, Central Life and Atlanta Life Insurance Companies. Each provided insurance during a period when other companies did not write insurance for black citizens. Afro was the most noted of these companies. Mr. W. A. Morris Jr. served as, and was the longest tenured, District Manager of the Tallahassee Office. Though still in perfectly good condition, the buildings were demolished in early 2,000 to make way for the Revitalization of Frenchtown. Many local families carried Afro insurance policies and there is evidence still in historical document formats of it being a thriving and contributing business for many years. District offices provided jobs for Tallahassee residents and others in other cities where offices were located.

When A.L. Lewis died in 1947, his loss was felt throughout the insurance world. He was the last remaining active founder. One of his daughters, Dr. Johnetta Cole, served as President of Spellman College in Atlanta, Georgia, continuing the legacy of outstanding contributions of the A.L. Lewis family. A.L. Lewis also established American Beach in Nassau County and helped develop three cemeteries, known as the Moncrief Road Cemeteries, in Jacksonville, Florida. The John G. Riley Center/Museum for African American History & Culture Inc., helped to document the history of the cemeteries in 1998-99 as well as research the history of the Afro Life Insurance Company.

Though the history began in Jacksonville, Tallahassee had a share through its District Office and the contribution of Mr. William H. Robinson who provided a home for the business. Descendents of the Robinson family, two sons and others, still reside in Tallahassee.

Submitted by: Florida Parker; Source: Riley Center Museum, Inc., Althemese Barnes (Director)

Alice's Beauty Center

Please let's not forget Alice's Beauty Center on North 6 Monroe Street in the Duval Hotel. Alice and Gladys Brown ran an excellent Hairstyling Salon. There were about twenty employees, who were always busy. I was lucky to become a member of her stylist family at the age of eighteen. At ten years old and upwards I had tagged along with my mother when she would go for her appointment at this beauty shop. I would stay behind a partition, watching the stylist do the curl permanent wave, and beehives, etc. They kept my mother so beautiful, but when the stylist would tell me to come on in I felt I should stay out of her way. During those many years, I became familiar with Alice. She took me aside when I was ready for my dream of a hairstyling education to begin. She and the Florida Hair fashion committee had picked me to receive their scholarship for school.

Alice had all the state's first place awards for hairstyling competitions. She won the National, which lead her to become the head of the Florida Hairstyling and Cosmetologist Association, then on to top the Nation H & C Association. The next accomplishment was the O.H.F.C. where she headed the Legislative involvements for the whole country. She taught me all she knew before she retired. This opened a lot of doors for me everywhere, even when I moved to California for ten years, where her reputation was praised at the very best salons there. Thanks to Dear Alice Brown-Melton for her belief in me.

Written and Submitted by: Bette Ann Barrett, 2870 Pharr Court South NW, Atlanta, GA 30305

Broadus's

My cousin Linda Bailes says Broadus's is what she remembers everyone calling the store our great uncles Henry and Broadus Wilkinson ran. It was a little store about 10 by 14 feet on the corner of the Wilkinson property on South Adams Street, next to where Eve's Beauty Shop is now, in the 1930's-50's. The store was right behind a big oak tree that still stands today. A concrete walkway ran from the store to the house.

The story is told that the sheriff came to arrest one of the uncles for selling moonshine out of the store and with both of them wheelchair users they brought a pick up truck and put the uncle and chair in back of the truck and took him to jail.

Broadus's Store/Licensed as Wilkinson Grocery

When the fair or circus would come to town they would send people by to get permission to put their posters on the side of the store and give us free tickets to the event.

Even though the store had been locked up for years, it looked like they had just locked it up to come back the next day for regular business.

Sometime in the early 1970s it was sold to Paul Beyers for his antique business and moved it down to Gaines Street where his business was. Soon after, Paul died and I don't know what happened to the store. If someone knows I would appreciate hearing from you.

Submitted by: Shawn Pearson, 421 Bloxham Cut Off Road, Crawfordville, Florida 32327

Businesses: 1950-1960

For being as small a town as it was in the 1950s and 1960s, there were quality, locally owned stores. There were a variety of businesses for the townspeople to use without having to go out of town. Parking was at a premium downtown, especially on Saturdays. It was common to park several blocks away from a destination.

Women's dress shops included May's, Lillian's, Turner's, Gibbs, PW Wilson, Linden's, Skagfield's, Mangel's, and The Vogue. Shops specializing in shoes were Mendelson's, Strickland's, Miller's, Vanity, Sears, and Penney's. Men had Alford Brothers, Nic's

Toggery, Brown's, Schwobilt's, National Shirt Shop, and Mendelson's. General merchandise stores included Sears, Penney's, Woolworth's and McCrory's.

People needing drugs and health items chose Burdine's, Hicks, Bennett's, Sullivan's, Fain's, and Rackley. Bennett's had a soda fountain. It was fun getting milk shakes, banana splits, etc. while waiting for prescriptions. Specialty shops included: Deeb's Hats; The Little Folks Store; Richard's Luggage; Tallahassee Camera; The Fairy Tale Shop and Gilberg's (sewing.) Eleanor Doyle and Artistic Flowers were two florists.

Furniture for the home could be found at Collin's, Grant's, Yates and Shaw's Furniture Stores and Sears Department Store. Jewelry and repair included Stafford's, Moon's, Benson's, Fite, and Putnam's.

Automobile repair shops were Perdue's 5 Point Service, Larry Strickland's and Manor's Garages, and dealerships of Proctor's, Ford and GM. Unglaub's and Johnson's, among others, supplied gasoline.

Travelers could stay at The Cherokee, The Floridan, and The Duval hotels. Motels were

North Florida Fair parade proceeding south Image courtesy of the Florida State Archives Photographic collection

beginning to become popular. The Tallahassee Motor Lodge at Lake Ella existed at that time. The Prince Murat Motel came later. Two bus companies, Greyhound and Trailways, served the city at one station.

Restaurants were the sites of much legislation being discussed and decided off the floor of the legislative halls. Two of them included Joe's Spaghetti House and the Silver Slipper. Other restaurants serving the people of Tallahassee included Seven Seas, Mutt and Jeff's Drive In, Cafeteria at West Adams, Angelo's, Talquin Inn, Stege's Cafeteria, M & N, The Floridan & Duval Hotels, Busy Bee and the F & T. Mutt and Jeff's was a popular hang out for teenagers, as well as young adults.

State Theater, Image courtesy of the Florida State Archives Photographic collection

"Entertainment was provided through movie theaters: The Florida, Kent, and State Theatres which showed films from the national studios. Several drive-in theaters came later. Black and white television sets were beginning to appear to provide entertainment in the home.

Community organizations formed to better the community were the Tallahassee Shrine Club, Masonic Lodge, Elks Club, Tallahassee Woman's Club, Junior League, Kiwanis and Rotary Clubs.

Nursing homes weren't available. Tallahassee Convalescent Home was perhaps the only one to my knowledge at this time.
Written and Submitted by: Mary J. Marchant, 2901 Springfield Drive, Tallahassee, FL 32309

Businesses Still Here After All This Time

In 1915, Gramling's seed and feed store opened between Blount and Adams Streets and the railroad track south of downtown. It is a trip down memory lane.

Pepsi Cola Bottling Plant was on Lafayette Street downhill from the Capitol Building and in front of Red Front Grocery, on the fringes of Smokey Hollow. Smokey Hollow spread from about South Gadsden Street to Lafayette Street to Franklin Boulevard, then to the railroad track and Myers Park Drive that crossed the tracks. The primarily black community is gone. J. Clyde Williams (son, Johnny) managed Pepsi. When moved to Jennings Street, the Father of Joe Hutto managed Pepsi.

On the south side of Smokey Hollow, facing Myers Park Drive was VanZant's Grocery, owned by Paul VanZant's Father. (Johnny, Joe, and Paul and the writer hereof were classmates - Leon High School Class of 1963.)

J.C. Penney's, formerly at Park Avenue and Monroe, is in Governor's Square Mall with Sears. The Sears building that housed Sears Roebuck 30 years at Monroe and Jefferson Streets, was a cigar factory until 1904 when Latin cigar makers left because Leon County became a "dry" county. Sears' X-ray machine showed feet inside the shoes it sold. Sears moved to the Parkway Shopping Center before the Governor's Square Mall.

Coca-Cola Bottling Plant left South Monroe at Oakland Avenue. Rose Printing Company moved to Jackson Bluff Road.

Remaining downtown since the 50s and 60s, Nic's Toggery moved from the 100 to the 200 block of South Monroe and Elinor Doyle Florist moved from Adams to College.

During the early 50s, a Firestone store was north of the Duval Hotel, the east side of north Monroe. Now they are all over Tallahassee.

Written and Submitted by Dorothy Lee (Dotty) McPherson, 24236 Lanier St., Tallahassee, FL 32310

Byrd's Grocery: "Everything Good to Eat"

In the early 1800's, Thomas Blake Byrd of Miccosukee entered the grocery business in Tallahassee. Partners over the years were William Denham, F.C. Coles, A.B. Blackburn and sons William and Bernard Byrd. William died in the killer flu epidemic of 1917-18. Bernard joined T.B. Byrd and Son post World War I.

Locations were on the west side of Monroe between College and Park, East Tennessee, and finally 1101 Thomasville Road. In later years, James Plant joined Bernard until the store closed in 1965.

Florida Governor LeRoy Collins wrote affectionately of his boyhood employment and friendship with T. B. Byrd. He described "fancy" groceries, the coffee roaster and peanut butter machine. He told of playing "hooky" from work to go fly fishing with Mr. Byrd. He credited his mentor for suggesting that he become a lawyer and grieved at his death in 1928.

Byrd's Grocery was known for phone number "One" in Tallahassee. At first, Mr. Byrd could only talk to the operator or "central". Later, "Number 1" became a business tool as ladies called in their grocery list, it was boxed and delivered. Doors were not locked, so Spurgeon Whidden may have deposited the groceries in the refrigerator if one was not home.

Byrd's Grocery interior

The best tribute to Bernard Byrd came from a stranger after his death. "When I was a little boy, our family had a hard time. My folks couldn't pay, but Mr. Byrd told us to keep coming as long as we needed food. I have never forgotten."

Submitted by: Martha Taylor Tilden (granddaughter of T.B. Byrd), 2512 Betton Woods Dr., Tallahassee, FL 32308

Capital City Bank Group

From humble beginnings, Capital City Bank has become one of the largest financial institutions headquartered in Florida. Capital City is Tallahassee's oldest bank and has survived depressions, natural disasters and two world wars. Built on a foundation of strong community ties, the company continues that tradition today, emphasizing a culture of community advocacy and volunteerism.

In the 1880s, dry goods store owner George Saxon made loans to farmers, which led to the approval of a state charter on March 20, 1895. Capital City opened its doors with one location, five directors and three associates, and by the end of June, reported $41,000 in total deposits and $84,000 in resources.

In 1917, Capital City Bank made a $10,000 loan to the City of Tallahassee, establishing itself as "the community's bank."

Though 18 banks failed, Capital City resources and liabilities surpassed $1 million in 1925, and assets continued to grow over the next decade despite the 1929 collapse of the national economy and subsequent Great Depression.

In 1940, Godfrey Smith became President of the newly formed Industrial Bank. When Godfrey was called to join the war effort 1941, the comptroller allowed the bank to pay off investors, liquidate assets, and temporarily close until hostilities ceased in 1946.

In 1963, a name change and second charter established Capital City First and Second National banks. Roughly a decade later in 1975, Godfrey Smith and DuBose Ausley, great-grandson of

Group portrait of Capital City First National Bank

George Saxon, founded Capital City Bank Group, Inc., uniting six local banks under a single body of directors.

After 50 years of service, Godfrey Smith retired in 1989 and was succeeded by his son, William G. Smith, Jr., who took the company public in 1995 and united the longstanding family of banks under the Capital City Bank name.

Today, Capital City Bank serves more than 40 communities in Florida, Georgia and Alabama.
Written and Submitted by: Julie Upchurch, Capital City Bank Group Employee, 217 North Monroe Street Tallahassee, FL 32301

Chez Pierre, from Café to Bistro

A four-time golden spoon award winning restaurant, Chez Pierre, has a golden spoon award hanging near its cash register. It identifies Chez Pierre as one of the finest restaurants in Florida, something most Tallahasseans have known for years. The restaurant has been a Tallahassee landmark in the capital city for over 30 years. From its roots on Adams Street when Favier and Cooley first purchased it from founders Pierre and Rainey Vivier, to its beautiful present day location on Thomasville road. Whose wide balconies and decks are shaded by sweeping oaks, and whose gardens were designed by Clara Jane Carroll-Smith.

In addition to offering live music and murder mystery dinners on site throughout the year, the restaurant supports Artists and Musicians though such organizations as, The Young Actor's Theater, The Tallahassee Little Theatre, The Brogan Museum, The Tallahassee Museum, The LeMoyne Museum, and The Challenger Center.

Chez Pierre is especially popular among State Legislators and FSU faculty, and has been one of Tallahassee's most unique restaurants in the chic midtown area of Tallahassee. The entire facility is conducive to socializing and lingering, with its outdoor band shell and dance floor. This new location has an intimate cocktail lounge, private dining rooms, an upstairs banquet facility that seats 25, all surrounded by an acre of property that is also used for festivals and special occasions. It is a 250 seat French bistro that also offers good old Southern hospitality. Chez Pierre has won a first class reputation from giving back to its community.
Submitted by: Karen Cooley and Chef, Eric Favier; Written by: Sharon Stewart

College Avenue and Other Downtown Businesses Gone

Gone from College Avenue between Monroe and Adams Streets are Strickland's Shoe Store, Annette's (women's fine garments), State Theatre (originally Daffin Theatre), and Sullivan Drugs.

Gridley's Music Store and A & P Grocery were in front of First Baptist Church between Adams and Duval Streets. The Dutch Kitchen was on the backside of the church where the Christian Life Center is located.

College Avenue between Monroe and Adams Streets, 1937

Shaw's faced Duval Street at the corner of College. Shaw's carried unique and high-end home furnishings and decor. The writer has an ornate trunk from Shaw's that has held her children's artwork and memorabilia since the 70s.

For 48 years, the "Democrat" was on the 100 block of South Adams Street across the street from the church. In 1951 its building was flanked on the north side by the police station, and by the fire station at the corner of Park Avenue. Carter's Sporting Goods was on the south side. The Democrat relocated to the corner of East Call and North Monroe Streets (1953-1968) before relocating to its site on North Magnolia Drive.

Hicks Drug Store was on Jefferson Street. Around the corner on Adams Street, the Goldsmith family owned a store. The Goldsmith's, including sons Leslie and Howard, lived on the corner of Flagler and South Gadsden Streets, across from this writer.

The taking of the whole 300 block between Monroe and Adams Streets for construction of the House Office Building and Capitol Complex, and the elimination of Jefferson Street between those streets, along with the sight of the Old and New Capitol Buildings side by side, are grim reminders that change comes with time and time runs out. Thank goodness for memories.

Written and Submitted by Dorothy Lee" Dotty" McPherson, 24236 Lanier Street, Tallahassee, FL 32310

The Dutch Kitchen

A restaurant where all races, creeds and classes mingled in downtown Tallahassee was called The Dutch Kitchen. Its doors opened in 1924, and remained successfully opened until 1956. This business was located at 102 S. Adams Street in the basement of the old Columns Mansion. The owner/operator was Mrs. Ada Summer-Clark, wife of Henry J. Clark, Chicago's Famous Coffee and Tea Salesman.

After the death of her husband in 1922, Mrs. Clark moved to Tallahassee where she immediately set up a Tea Room in one of Tallahassee's oldest buildings. Mrs. Clark leased the separate brick kitchen and moved into The Columns as a tenant of Mrs. Sarah Roberts. The Tea Room was such a success that by 1925 she turned it into The Dutch Kitchen Restaurant.

Mrs. Clark is pictured in this photograph with her staff, the people who made the Dutch Kitchen a success and a part of Tallahassee's rich heritage. The Dutch Kitchen maintained an impressive clientele including judges, politicians and royalty not only for the great food but because the prices were reasonable.

Mrs. Ada Summer-Clark and the staff of the Dutch Kitchen

The success of her restaurant allowed Mrs. Clark to obtain a mortgage for The Columns property in 1931, which she paid off by 1937. During this time Mrs. Clark's daughter, Ethel C. Stewart and family moved into the Mansion to help her manage the business property.

Mrs. Clark's descendants continue to live in Tallahassee and remember how great the Dutch Kitchen was and the wonderful times spent living in The Columns Mansion.
Submitted by: Carol D. Johnson; Written by: Carol D. Johnson/Nan Stewart, 2nd Great-Granddaughter of Ada Z. Summer-Clark

Envision Credit Union

On January 26, 1954 ten Leon County teachers, who raised $70 by pooling their resources, received approval from the State Comptroller to start the Leon County Teachers Credit Union. Those ten founding members were Edna Tait, Lora Lewis, Annelle Sterk, M. J. Longsdon, W. V. Ashmore, Lois H. Boggs, Mildred Wilfong, Tom K. Massey, Myrtle Rehwinkel and Helen Pope. During the first year of operation, it merged with the Leon County Teachers Federal Credit Union, which served black teachers.

In 1960, after growing too large for the Treasurer's bottom desk drawer at Leon High School, the Credit Union occupied offices on the second floor of a building across the street from our current Main Office, and Adelaide Owens became the first full-time manager. In March 1969, Ray E. Cromer, Jr., became manager of the Credit Union.

In 1979, our name was changed to North Florida Education Credit Union and a branch in Quincy opened after merger with the City of Quincy Employees Credit Union, which represented city and county employees.

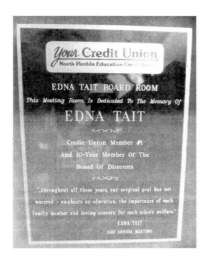

In 1980, the Big Bend Telco Credit Union, which served Centel employees, merged with us. Over the years, the field of membership was expanded to cover all school employees (and relatives) in Leon, Gadsden, Wakulla and Franklin Counties.

In 1984, the Credit Union chartered its subsidiary, United Solutions Company (formerly known as NFECU Services Corp and United Datatronics, Inc.), to establish an in-house computer service center for itself and other Credit Unions. During that same year, ATMs and Money Line were added to our growing list of services.

In 1987, it was obvious to the Facilities Committee that a new headquarters was needed. After extensive research, the Credit Union purchased the old Tallahassee Federal Savings and Loan Association building, a community landmark, and beautifully refurbished it before occupancy in the spring of 1990.

Envision Credit Union was the new name adopted as of January 2001. At the same time the Office of the Comptroller approved a new field of membership that includes anyone who lives or works in Leon, Gadsden, Jefferson, Wakulla or Franklin County. During all the years of growth and success, the goal of our founders has not changed: an emphasis on member education and service with concern for each one's financial welfare.

Mr. Cromer's becoming President/CEO of the Credit Union proved to be an outstanding positive decision. It was through his expertise, knowledge, wisdom, integrity and personal skills that Envision Credit Union has grown to a prominent standing in the community. Mr. Cromer retired in January 2010 and Mr. Darryl G. Worrell became President/CEO.

Submitted by: Mary J. Marchant, 2901 Springfield Drive Tallahassee, FL 32309; Written by Envision Credit Union Employees

Fain Drug Company

Llewellyn Donalson Fain, along with his brother, John Love Fain, established the Fain Drug Company in 1919 when they bought Hicks Drugs located on the northwest corner of Monroe Street and College Avenue. Here "Fain's" remained until after World War II when it was relocated across Monroe Street. The two brothers, L. D. trained in pharmacy and John in business, worked together until the store was sold in 1962.

Fain Drug Store on the NW corner of Monroe

Several have written in the *Tallahassee Democrat* of their memories of gatherings at Fain's. Malcolm B. Johnson, on December 27, 1967, wrote a column about the store saying: "It was not a glittering place. It was the kind of drug store-ice cream parlor that most small towns had. In good weather, the doors folded up for the full width on Monroe Street, and back for perhaps a dozen feet on College. So it was almost like a sidewalk cafe, with its bent wire tables and chairs."

The store was located in the center of the shops and offices along Monroe Street. Guyte P. McCord remembered the group of doctors, lawyers and business men, known as "Fain's Forum," who dropped in for coffee each day between 9:00 AM and 10:00 PM to discuss the affairs of the town, state and nation.

Looking along the west side of Monroe Street between College and Park, Tallahassee, FL

Mrs. Fain wrote: "The members of 'Fain's Forum' were not the only ones to use the corner drug store as a meeting place. Women would meet for a morning of leisurely shopping, then return for "a luscious malted milk, or a tall ice cream soda, or a sundae topped with gooey nuts and fruits, all made with ice cream from a hand cranked ice cream freezer."
Submitted by Rebecca Brooks Pinckney (Mrs. Fred), 5535 Errol Place, N W, Atlanta, GA 30327-4872

The Fairy Tale Shop
Thelma and Elmer McPherson's daughter and only child, Dorothy Lee "Dotty" McPherson, wore dresses from The Fairy Tale Shop. Thelma sold ladies fine clothing downtown. She and O'neill were good friends.

Ruby (Smith) Diehl with sons Theodore and Raymond

Thelma would buy Dotty five dresses at once; one for each school day, to Dotty's great joy. Dotty bought three of her daughters' clothes there. Her favorite style was smocked dresses by Polly Flinders. For gifts, Gordon Roberts, Dotty's husband, bought her outfits there, knowing he could not go wrong.

Dotty's first job was at the Fairy Tale Shop (1962). She was top salesperson many times, as it was easy to sell a product in which she believed.

While doing research, Dotty found Robert Dewitt Smith, a relative of the Diehls. He shared a picture of Raymond Diehl with his mother, Ruby Smith (Mrs. Henry) Diehl, in a horse drawn carriage on Monroe Street in about 1908. Ironically, the carriage is sitting across the street from what would become the location of The Fairy Tale Shop.

The Fairy Tale Shop was moved to the corner of Betton and Thomasville Roads, first on the south side of Betton, then on the north side into a vacated church. As O'neill approached retirement, June Diehl, her daughter-in-law, took over the store. The name was changed to O'neill's Fairy Tale Shop.

Whatever the name, the Fairy Tale Shop carried the best quality and cutest children's clothes in Tallahassee.
Written and Submitted by Dorothy Lee McPherson, 24236 Lanier Street, Tallahassee, FL 32310

Gibbs' French Shop
Gibbs' French Shop was a leader in fashion, design and style for several decades in Tallahassee. The owners, Lou and Nell Gibbs, were both members of mercantile families. Lou's family had a store in Live Oak. Nell's father and grandfather had stores in New York, and Ft. Lauderdale.

Lou handled the finances while Nell did the buying for the shop. She made four or five buying trips to New York annually. "I loved every minute of it," she says. Nell had a natural flair for style, design and color and 'what looks good,' as Dorothy Clifford, Woman's Editor, said in a *Tallahassee Democrat* article about her.

The depression was bad for the store and for all the family's stores, but they survived.

The Gibbs had stores in four locations: Early 1930's-Lou owned the French Shop (for shoes) on the corner of Monroe and Jefferson Streets; The 1940's- They stopped carrying shoes, moved to College Avenue and focused on women's and bridal wear; The1950's-They changed name to Gibb's French Shop and moved to the shopping hub on South Monroe Street where business flourished; and the fourth store was located in the Northwood Mall.

In addition to handling the finances of the shop, Lou had a passion for real estate. If he saved a dollar, he'd buy property, Nell said. Lou, being foresighted, built one of the first suburban shopping centers, Capital Plaza, on Thomasville Road. He is credited with beginning several shopping centers in the area that included Market Square on Timberlane Road.

Submitted by: Ginny High, 2428 Limerick Drive, Tallahassee, FL 32309 and Written by: Mary J. Marchant, 2901 Springfield Drive, Tallahassee, FL 32309-3274

Hood Insurance Agency

D.L. "Buck" Hood established Hood Insurance Agency in the late 1940s inside Hotel Park (*owned by brothers Ruby (Smith) Diehl with sons Theodore and Raymond Godfrey and Julian Smith*) which faced Ponce De Leon Park. He sold life insurance for Prudential; then added fire and casualty. Buck ran his business and managed the hotel in the vaulted lobby. Here Ruby Keller, Helga Griffin, and Elizabeth Brandon worked with him.

Helga Griffin and Elizabeth Brandon taken by Buck Hood, 1950's. Langston's Seafood Market 217 South Adams, Tallahassee, FL 1942

In the 1960s Hood, Griffin, and Brandon moved to North Adams and Carolina. There Buck also took over Yellow Cab Company. When the cab company turned around, sold at a profit, and duties decreased, Mrs. Brandon sought other employment. The agency sponsored a city Litwhiler baseball team and Buck coached. In the late 1960s, the agency moved to Williams Street. Mrs. Griffin retired and Buck employed his daughter Sandra. Buck mentored and provided space for men entering the insurance business: David Pichard, Tom Doxsee, and Rod Vaughn. He established a City of Tallahassee monthly employees' payroll deduction plan for automobile and homeowner's premiums. Buck gave his "young driver" talks to his insurers' children.

When Rod Vaughn Agency moved to Salem Court in the 1980s, Buck and Sandra moved with them. Later, when Buck was semi-retired, he moved his files to their historic "Hays-Hood" home at 906 East Park Avenue. Sandra worked part-time while pursuing a teaching career. As Buck aged, he referred his insurers to other agents but remained active and earned commissions until his death in 2002 at age 92.

Submitted by: Sandra Hood Walker, 401 Talaflo Street, Tallahassee, Florida 32308 850.222.5288; shwalker@fairpoint.net

Langston's Seafood Market

Flavey Langston began gill-netting mullet in the coastal waters of Wakulla County, traveling the surrounding counties even into South Georgia, selling fish from the back of his truck. Beginning in 1925, he had markets at different times in Tallahassee: on the corner of Duval & Pensacola, the corner of Adams & Pensacola, 104 West Jefferson and 407 North Macomb. When his adopted son, Maurice Council, graduated from Wakulla High School in 1937, he joined the markets.

Langston's Seafood Market 217 South Adams, Tallahassee, FL 1942

In 1942, the main market was moved to 217 South Adams after the building on the corner of Adams and Pensacola burned. After World War II, the Macomb Street location was closed.

Langston's sold fresh seafood to walk-in customers. People would call in for curbside service. Deliveries were made to sororities, fraternities, restaurants, and homes all over Tallahassee. Trips were made to the Florida coastal areas from Wakulla to Bay counties, and all the way to South Florida to procure the freshest seafood. The fish and other seafood were kept in iced-down glass cases which were cleaned out and re-iced every night. Everyone in Tallahassee knew if they wanted fresh seafood from a clean, nice smelling market, they could count on Langston's Seafood.

1975 Tallahassee Democrat ad for Langston's Seafood Markets

Working for Langston's from the beginning were Wakulla Countians Cephus Donaldson, brothers H.B. "Bee" and Fred Gavin, Charlie Johnson and So Donaldson. They were faithful workers and considered Flavey's family as their own. When Flavey died in 1971, someone asked Fred, "How many sons did Flavey have?" Fred replied, "Three: Maurice, Bee and me". Fred died in 1982 and Bee in 1998, but they would call Yvonne, Flavey's wife, to check on her welfare every week. If everyone could love each other the way these people loved each other, the world would be a better place by far. After Flavey's death, the markets, then located at 1443 South Adams St. and 2013 North Monroe Street were operated by Maurice until his death in 1972. They were then run by Maurice's wife, Inez, and their son-in-law, Jerry Pearson, until 1973, when they were sold to B. F. "Tommy" Thomas. Inez returned to Caroline Brevard where she continued teaching the fifth grade until her retirement in 1982. Jerry went to work for Capital City Bank and retired after 33 years.

Submitted by: Gloria C. Dowden and Marcia C. Pearson, 3227 Tanager Trail, Tallahassee, FL 32303; Sources: Family stories, Tallahassee City Directories, newspaper stories.

Lillian's Dress Shop

Mrs. Lillian Cox owned a boutique at 204 South Adams for 20 years in Tallahassee. Her husband was disabled, so she had to make a living for the family. She had no special training, but a flair for style and a distinct desire to serve people in the community.

She kept individual frocks in small numbers so that customers felt her merchandise was specifically for them. Originally, she had a partner in the business but decided later to buy the partner out.

Lillian Cox

She did the buying herself and transported it in the back of her car minus the seat to carry more merchandise. Her main source for buying was in Dallas, TX. When she first started, they told her to come back after hours to do her buying since she was out of their territory. It didn't take long for them to tell her to come any time because they knew she was a reliable buyer and had her customers in mind when she bought for the store.

Special family and friends also helped her. "Miss Lillian" is now 103, bright, sociable, meticulous, and her face radiates when she talks about her business. Anyone can see that she loved having a dress shop by the way she expresses herself.

She had on a dress (see picture) which was stunning and fashionable. When asked about the dress, she replied that she got the material from Hawaii before she closed the store, and that a friend of hers used a pattern that she liked.

Submitted by Ginny High and Mary J. Marchant, 2901 Springfield Drive Tallahassee, FL 32309-3274

Memories of Tallahassee Gas Stations

Gas stations don't go away, they just change their names and move around. Or so it seems.

Rainey Cawthon Distributor, Inc., was founded (1948) by partners, Rainey Cawthon, Charles Mayhew and Fred Pierson. Originally a Sinclair Oil distributor, it changed to Shell (1952). The North Monroe and Brevard Streets station became a Firestone tire distributor and sold televisions and appliances. Marvin Andrews, of an old Tallahassee family, later managed it.

Eli Roberts' Sinclair gas station, Tallahassee

Eli Roberts' Sinclair gas station, Tallahassee

Eli Roberts' Sinclair gas station, Tallahassee

The business survived the oil embargo, transition from leaded to unleaded gas, full serve to self-serve and more. In the late 80s, Mr. Cawthon sold the fuel oil segment to Edward Rooney, now operated by son, Charles.

Tallahassee's earliest station was Henry Palmer's located at the southeast corner of College and Adams, for Standard Oil Company.

Eli Roberts' Sinclair gas station, Tallahassee, FL

During the 50s, he had a station on the 500 block of South Monroe at East Palmer Avenue.

Graddy's Gulf Station, at 1458 South Monroe and corner of Jennings Street, was a block away from Henry Palmer's. Both their stations were popular as beer joints. Owner Kenneth Graddy moved his station across Monroe and north to the corner of Oakland Avenue. He stopped selling beer. It became a BP station.

In 1959, a Pure gas station sat diagonally across from the Floridan Hotel on North Monroe Street. A Standard Oil station was at McCord Point, where Thomasville Road begins at North Monroe Street during the 60s.

Other memorable gas stations were Blue Gables on East Lafayette, Steamboat William's on East Tennessee, Aubrey Barrow's on Thomasville Road, Tucker's at Four Points, and at Monroe and Tennessee Streets, Cecil Lett's Shell Station and Unglaub's BP.

Written and Submitted by Dorothy Lee "Dotty" McPherson, 24236 Lanier Street Tallahassee, FL 32310; Information obtained about Rainey Cawthon through website: www.raineycawthon.com/ index.php/about-us

Monroe Street Businesses Now Gone

Only memories and pictures of many Monroe Street businesses survive.

Moon Jewelry Company, corner of College and Adams (1937), relocated to North Monroe. From the northeast corner of Monroe at College (1950s) north were Grants, Jenkins Music Company and the Book Corner in the ground floor of the Gulf Life Insurance Company building.

Mendelson's 2-story department store

(preceded by Collins Furniture Company) was nearer Park Avenue. F & T Restaurant was next door.

Fain Drug Company, northwest corner of College and Monroe, was next to the Vogue. It moved across the street, north of the Book Corner, closer to Park Avenue. In 1957 it moved one door north of Gilberg's Fabrics, closer to College.

The west side of Monroe at College northward were Diana Shops, National Shirt Shops, Linden's, and Turner's, clothing stores in 1958. Also that side of the 100 block boasted Arnold's Men's Wear, Stafford's Jewelry, Lillian's, and the Ritz Theatre. Brown's Men's Wear (1952) was on the corner at Park Avenue. Past Park (1959) were the Florida Theatre, Woolworth's, J.C. Penney's, and the Floridan Hotel.

From College Avenue at Monroe going south were Bennett's Drug Store, Angelo's Restaurant, P.W. Wilson's Department Store, and others, and the Black Cat on the east side.

The western block of South Monroe from Jefferson to Pensacola was demolished to build the House Office Building. Weaver Pharmacy was on the south corner at East Jefferson and Butler's Shoes was on the north.

South of the railroad underpass were B & W Fruit Market, High Hat Restaurant, Shell Oyster Bar, the Oldsmobile place at Jennings and Monroe Streets, Florida Sheet Metal Works, Rocco's Plumbing Supply, Nic's Cafe, Thompson's Hamburgers, and the first major Winn Dixie to serve the South Side.

Written and Submitted by Dorothy Lee "Dotty" McPherson, 24236 Lanier Street Tallahassee, FL 32310; Sources: Memory, pictures from 100 Years The Tallahassee Democrat and Yesterday's Tallahassee, and friend's reminders.

Nic's Toggery

Nic's Toggery has been a leader of men's wear since 1950 in Tallahassee. Nic Gavalas opened the store on June 24, 1950. It was originally located on the corner next to the Old Capitol. Born in Augusta, GA, Nic came to Live Oak to visit relatives and wanted to see Tallahassee. After he visited, he realized that there were two universities with plenty of young people, and that it was a good place to open a business. He had learned to tailor from his father, George.

"You have to maintain the same work ethic as the person who came before you to maintain a strong business," Nic said.

Nic Gavalas (front) and his three sons

Nic said that back in the 1950s people dressed more appropriately, and more casually and that he prefers that style of dress. Lots of changes in dress have transpired over the years. Nic and his wife Janet, have three sons, Victor, Michael and George, all of which have joined the business. Each son is manager of a store.

The original store downtown grew through the years to expand to the Tallahassee Mall and the Governor's Square Mall. Mall locations were too costly, so separate locations were opened elsewhere. Each of the three stores has a Gavalas son operating it.

Victor started with his father in 1970. Michael joined the business in 1972 and George joined in 1979. All three graduated from Florida State University, and all three had worked in the store from very young ages, doing whatever they were asked to do every morning. His fondest memories of the business relate to family.

Submitted by: Ginny High and Mary J. Marchant, 2901 Springfield Drive, Tallahassee, FL 32309-3274; Source: "Gavalas sons learn father's business skills" Tallahassee Democrat, Sunday, June 20, 2010 by Elizabeth M. Mack

No Changes in Tallahassee?

When that Eastern Airlines plane landed in Tallahassee in September 1964, I knew that I was in for a change. Little did I realize the changes that were in store for me during the next few years.

Downtown Tallahassee was a shopper's paradise. From my job at the State Road Department, located in the Holland Building on South Monroe Street, I could walk to Morrison's Cafeteria or the bakery on South Adams Street. I could shop for an engagement ring at Vason Jewelers on Pensacola Street or enjoy Kentucky

Fried Chicken at Holland's Restaurant next door. I had a choice of several clothing stores – Nic's Toggery, P.W. Wilson's Department Store, Alford Brothers, Turner's fine fashions, and Mendelson's Department Store. The ladies could shop at Bertha Cooke's, Gibbs' French Shoppe, and the Vogue, and purchase shoes at Millers' Bootery or Rose Bootery.

Only a short walk away on West College Avenue was the little building housing Imports by Vardi, located across from Shaw's Furniture Company and the Colonial Grocery Store. Downtown movie theaters were the State Theater on West College, The Florida Theater on North Monroe, and the infamous Campus Art Theater on West Tennessee Street. One had to drive out of the city limits to attend the Perry Outdoor Theater or the Capitol Drive-In Theater.

Just north of Park Avenue was the block containing an Esso station, the Western Union office, the Leon County Public Library, and the Little Folks Store. Across the street was Woolworth's and, further north, the Floridan Hotel, on East Call Street, the *Tallahassee Democrat*.

Grocery Stores seemed to abound in Tallahassee. In addition to the Colonial Store on West College Avenue and the Parkway Shopping Center, we could walk to the IGA stores on East Tennessee Street or West Gaines Street. Jitney Jungles appeared all over the city. Winn Dixies were seen at Capitol Plaza, the Parkway Shopping Center, and University Plaza. A Setzer's Super Store sold groceries at Capitol Plaza.

One could eat and run at Tallahassee's only McDonald's on West Tennessee or at any of the three Chandler's Drive-Ins, located on South Adams Street, the corner of North Monroe and Brevard Streets, or the newly opened Chandler's on West Tennessee Street (where the special was 15-cent hot dogs!) I would be remiss if I failed to mention two of Tallahassee's fine eating establishments: Joe's Spaghetti House on Mahan Drive and the Silver Slipper on South Monroe Street.

Tallahasseans did not have to drive all over to shop for medicines either. Bennett's Drugs was centrally located on Monroe and College, Brown's Pharmacy was on North Monroe, and Burdine's had two locations – Thomasville Road and South Adams Street. Near Tallahassee Memorial hospital were Dalton's Drug Store and Medical Arts Pharmacy, both on Miccosukee Road.

You could walk to car dealerships downtown. Alfred Chevrolet was on North Adams Street near Capital Plymouth on West Tennessee Street. Proctor and Proctor sold Cadillacs, Pontiacs and Jeeps on North Monroe Street and Tennessee Motors featured Ford products on East Call Street at Calhoun. At the corner of North Monroe and Thomasville Road, you could find Mingledorff Motors, while further north on Monroe Street were Capitol Lincoln Mercury and Drake Motors. Palmer-Harrell Buick was located on Thomasville Road near Betton Road.

In 1964, J.M. Fields and its Pantry Pride grocery had just opened at the corner of North Monroe and Tharpe Street. Slightly further north was Velda Dairy and its fields, signifying the outskirts of Tallahassee.

These are among my memories of Tallahassee in 1964. Certainly, other people have memories of their favorite spots at that time.

Submitted by: Richard R. Sherwin, 616 Acorn Grove Court, Tallahassee, FL 32312 risher1@aol.com

Postmaster of Barrow Hill

Shadrack (Papa Shack) Gardner was the Postmaster of the Barrow Hill Community; his descendants have found pride and motivation in their heritage from a man who practically ran the whole Barrow Hill community in Leon County Florida. He was appointed Postmaster by the government not only because he was a leader in the community, but because Papa Shack was a businessman and land owner in Leon County who acquired a lot of wealth and respect after raising his children and putting money back into the community.

Papa Shack's store was located on Miles Johnson Rd. on an embankment across the road from James Austin's property. The address of the store was Route 1, Box 52, Lloyd, Florida. The original roll-top desk was located in the grocery store and had multiple purposes. One such purpose was a

Original mail desk of Papa Shack

postage service for the entire community where mail was received and posted. All incoming and outgoing mail, with the exception of the Proctor family, came to Papa Shack's roll-top desk. The desk also provided a safe haven for his business ledgers.

The ledgers from Papa Shack's merchant store with documented sales dating back to 1918 and 1920 and The roll-top antique desk with claw legs were inherited by granddaughter, Vivian Williams. This desk and a portrait of Papa Shack are now in the possession of his great-granddaughter, Dorothy Mitchell-Johnson, who still lives on the family's property.

Written and submitted by: Great-grand-daughter of "Papa" Shack Gardner, Dorothy L. Mitchell-Johnson, 2386 Chaires Crossroads, Tallahassee, Florida 32317

Proctor's Car Dealership

Proctor's Car Dealership has been in business for 100 years. Theo Proctor, Sr. started the business in 1910. When he went off to serve in World War I, brother Earl stepped in to keep the company running. "When the business started, Cadillac was the first line of cars, and in the early days, they probably did more business selling tires and fixing the cars than actually selling the cars because Tallahassee was such a small town, and it was something so new," said Martin Proctor, Earl's grandson.

Proctor's Car Dealership

"Three generations of Proctor's have sold and serviced the automobiles and trucks many thousands of area residents drive---a business venture that started when Tallahassee streets were largely unaccustomed to motorized travel." Theo Proctor, Jr. is still active in the business. Theo Proctor III and Martin are a third generation of Proctors in the business. Proctor's has a reputation for "exceeding customer service and expectations." The Proctors kept up with changes and they have "focused on customer relations" through the years.

Submitted by Mary J. Marchant, 2901 Springfield Drive Tallahassee, FL 32309-3274; Source: The Tallahassee Democrat, Friday, May 21, 2010.

The Shoebox of Tallahassee, Inc. aka The Shoe Box

In 1972, after many years working as a traveling shoe salesman, Earnest Weldon purchased Caraway's Shoe Store, a small retail operation of long standing, located in Quincy, Florida. Earnest and his wife, Marie, commuted daily between Quincy and Tallahassee, managing and growing their shoe business - adding their son, Billy, to the team.

The Shoe Box

With three retail years under their belt, the Weldon trio decided to open a store in Tallahassee. Thus, The Shoe Box of Tallahassee was established in the Southside Shopping Center @ 2525 S. Adams Street in February 1975. For the next three years, the family operated both The Shoe Box and Caraway's until closing Caraway's in 1978.

Surviving the tough economic times of the 70s, The Shoe Box relocated in 1984 to 2809 S. Monroe Street and welcomed Bill Day to The Shoe Box team in March 1990. When the store outgrew its space, Billy seized the opportunity to purchase property and relocate The Shoe Box in March 1998 to 2820 S. Monroe Street - its present location.

In January 2006, Billy's son, Geof Weldon, joined The Shoe Box team. Because it is rare for a family-owned business to survive beyond two generations, it is with pride that The Shoe Box continues to thrive through three generations. Geof has fulfilled requirements for designation as a certified pedorthist (CPed) to better service the needs of footwear customers.

Specializing in "fitting the hard to fit," The Shoe Box focuses on two major areas: quality products - shoes and clothing in a wide array of sizes and widths for the entire family – and customer service - placing emphasis on proper fit and service before and after the sale.

Written and Submitted by Debbie Weldon, dhweldon@embarqmail.com

Kristin Skagfield, Fashion Designer

Kristin Skagfield, an exceptionally talented fashion designer, has a BA degree in Home Economics and a Master's Degree in Fashion Design from Iceland, her native land.

Kristen Skagfield

She moved to this country from Iceland and settled in Tallahassee in 1950 with her husband, Hilmar, who studied at FSU. He was later Consular General of Iceland.

As her career expanded, she opened her studio in 1959 in the Randall House because she wanted home to be home, and business to be business. In 1962 she bought a home at 315 East Call Street for her studio.

Her advice to shoppers is be wise how you spend your money. Price is not always class. Beauty and quality of fabric are important in the design of a dress. She ordered materials from France and India; lace and embroidery from Switzerland and France; and wool from England.

Kristin's Fashion Shows were never done for personal business. Charitable organizations raised money for their projects through Kristin's unselfish efforts.

She has created gowns for wives of renowned political figures and local residents. Many of her exclusive creations appeared, in Miami, FL, St. Petersburg, FL, Charlotte, NC and Washington, DC newspapers. She created gowns for many years for several Mardi Gras; one had a 10- foot train of lace. She also created a wedding gown for the granddaughter of a prominent Tallahassean of heirloom lace from three families. She designed many gowns for Springtime Tallahassee and jackets for Andrew Jackson. Several of her creations are in the Florida Archives.

Many Tallahassee residents and individuals from other cities, states and countries visited her studio to find an elegant dress for special occasions.

Submitted by Ginny High and Mary J. Marchant, 2901 Springfield Drive, Tallahassee, FL 32309-3274

Remarkable Lady Barbara Townsend

Barbara Townsend was a remarkable lady who worked at Sears and Gayfers in the late 60s and 70s. Two store managers, Mr. Smith and Mr. Neicase, encouraged her to stage fashion shows using merchandise from departments within the stores. Her shows emphasized seasonal, community, and holiday events with children, teens and adult models participating.

Barbara started the Gayfer's Teen Board for high school girls in 1970. Each girl selected had to meet certain criteria, (including community involvement); they modeled and performed many tasks with fashion shows, while learning inside knowledge of what a model should or should not do. Her success with fashion shows was due to her attention to detail--fitting each model with coordinated outfits (hose, hat, shoes, belts, and other accessories). Most shows included music

Barbara Townsend wearing a gown by Kristen Skagfield
John G. Collins

and choreographed dancing, requiring rehearsals so everything ran smoothly,

In one notable show, Barbara performed "New York, New York" in costume.

Some assistants (whom she mentored conscientiously) went on to careers in fashion. They attribute their success to the attention to detail she taught them. Gayfer's fashion shows were greatly anticipated and attendance was typically standing room only.

She offered schools for "Young Charmers" and "White Gloves and Party Manners" at Sears and Gayfer's. These classes included, party manners, etiquette, and basics of ballroom dancing for girls and boys.

One significant contribution was Barbara's ability to work with blind students from FSU's Fashion Design and Merchandising Program in the late 60's. She taught them how to sew, how to place accessories on a model, and how to select accessories to use with different outfits.

Submitted by: June Townsend (Daughte-in-law of Barbara Townsend), 3301 Barrowhill Trail, Tallahassee, FL 32312; Written by: Ginny High, Karen (Kara) High and Mary J. Marchant

Tallahassee Democrat

The Tallahassee Democrat celebrated 100 years of publication in 2005. It has survived many changes in typesetting, editors, business managers, both private and corporate ownership, page layout, the great depression and recessions, readership and circulation, technology advances from manual typewriters to computers, five different locations, a half dozen names, weekly and daily publication, afternoon and morning delivery, but most of all, it has endured.

John G. Collins, Image courtesy of the Florida State Archives Photographic collection

John G. Collins started the one-man operation. Collins sold the ads, wrote the stories, composed the type and operated the press. He was passionate about politics and wrote extensively on the subject. The population of Leon County at that time was 19,597 people. *(Weekly Tallahassean, July 19, 1900).* Population for Tallahassee would be less than this figure. Tallahassee was considered "a newsy little capital."

John Collins, due to poor health, sold the paper to an Alabama newspaperman, Milton A. Smith. Smith had special interest in local commerce, the city's social life, litera ture and religion. In 1912-1913 the paper became the semiweekly *True Democrat* and was published twice a week. Smith published the paper daily during the 1915 legislative session as *The Daily Democrat* and continued as a daily afterwards. In 1924, Smith renamed it *The Tallahassee Daily Democrat.*

Tallahassee Democrat Building, Image courtesy of the Florida State Archives Photographic collection

In 1929 because of lack of funds, Smith sold the paper to Col. Lloyd Griscom, a wealthy New Yorker who owned Luna Plantation in Leon County. The paper under Griscom became more professional in appearance and content. He added comics, editorial cartoons, more photos, more national, international and state stories, a sports section and local news. Shortly after Griscom bought the paper in 1929, the name was switched back to *The Daily Democrat.*

Griscom was an absentee owner of the *Democrat.* Griscom left the operation of the *Democrat* to John "Jack" Tapers, who ran the paper for the next 41 years with the exception of three years service in WWII.

On Sunday, July 31, 1949 the name became *Tallahassee Democrat,* without any explanation or prior notice and has remained a daily paper since. Jack Tapers was at the helm when the change took place.

"The *Democrat* had been an afternoon paper since it had become a daily in 1915." A series of years saw both morning and afternoon papers, but in 1942, the morning paper ceased publication except for Sundays.

But other outside influences, such as television nightly broadcasts, prompted the newspaper industry to change to morning papers. The first morning daily *Tallahassee Democrat* was published January 3, 1978 and remains so. The switch signaled the unofficial end of the old Democrat.

Jack Tapers

The newspaper was privately owned for 60 years. In 1965 the *Democrat* was sold to Knight Newspapers which merged with Ridder publications in 1978. Knight built the paper's new home at 277 North Magnolia Publications. "The merger brought increased financing and further technological improvements.

Computers were introduced in the newsroom replacing typewriters and teletype machines. Additional space was added onto the North Magnolia building in 1978. The number of employees increased to 340 in the mid-1990s. Employees received broader benefits.

Many editors have had an indelible influence on the City of Tallahassee through the years. Early editors included John G. Collins and Milton A. Smith. John "Jack" Tapers became editor at age 25 in May, 1929 and continued to lead the newspaper for 41 years.

Jack Tapers came to the *Tallahassee Democrat* from Syracuse, NY. Although he first served as Circulation Manager, he soon became Editor and then Editor-Publisher. The *Democrat* was a small paper, and at one time or another, he filled almost every role, including photography. He retired in 1970.

Jack served three years in WWII as a Major, setting up governments in towns liberated from the Germans. After the war, he returned to the paper. He guided the *Democrat* through two relocations, which included a new building, changes in typesetting, and from a family owned to a corporate-owned newspaper.

Kit Tapers Wallingford, daughter of Jack Tapers, said that Jack was a perfectionist, very introverted, but loved the language. Kit said,

"When he was covering a Ku Klux Klan march on Tallahassee, and the hooded members demanded his film, he handed them a blank roll." Kit continued: "He was not an integrationist but he had a strong sense of responsibility. He was a tough old bird."

Vernelle Tucker (Democrat executive 1948-1980) relates: "Jack was a very hard person to get to know. He was not a warm person. But Jack and I got along great. I credit him with letting me rise. He paid a lot of attention to my ideas. But he was a difficult person to get close to."

Ernest Commander, circulation/pressroom, once said, "He just had a mind that was out there thinking about other things." In 1954 Tapers ceded editorial direction to the newly hired editor, Malcohn Johnson. Tapers then concentrated on business operations, guiding the newspaper through three major changes. "He (Tapers) was devoted to the *Democrat* and its employees and insisted on pension and other benefits for the employees." Malcolm Johnson described Tapers as a "complete newspaperman."

Reunion of Tallahassee Democrat Staff: 1st row 2nd from right isMalcolm Johnson and 3rd from right is Dorothy Clifford; 1st row, farleft is Bill McGrotha, Image courtesy of the Florida State Archives Photographic collection

Malcolm Johnson was the face and voice of the *Tallahassee Democrat* for three decades, serving as editor and wrote a daily front-page column titled 'I Declare.' He promoted Tallahassee enthusiastically, writing on politics, local history and nature. He started Funders, Inc. for underprivileged children attending summer camp; plant digs ahead of construction; and growth of the city's economy, state government and local universities. He influenced keeping the Capitol here in Tallahassee instead of moving it to Orlando before retiring in 1978.

A few other editors include: Gerald Ensley, Bob Gabordi, Mary Ann Lindley, and Mike

Beaudoin. Bill McGrotha, 1953-93, favorite sports writer, covered FSU football in the dynasty years. Dorothy Clifford covered the society events in Tallahassee and Martee Wills was an assistant women's page editor 1961-1975.

Dorothy Clifford, editor of the *Tallahassee Democrat's* Home section won a national award for excellence in home furnishings coverage. The Dallas Market Center chose Dorothy as one of four to receive its 22nd Annual Editorial Award. Her column was deemed best among American newspapers with a circulation of 500,000 or less. The Dallas Market Center paid Mrs. Clifford's expenses to Dallas to accept the award on July 12 of that year. She received a bronze sculpture by Texas sculptor Robert Parsons.

"The whole thrust of the awards is to find the best home furnishings coverage in the industry," said Delores Lehr, VP for public relations and advertising for the Dallas Market Center. "The judges look for material that's geared toward the consumer."

Mrs. Clifford tried to give people ideas about how to decorate with limited resources. Color photography is most important in showing people what furnishings look like. She said that people in Tallahassee make her job easier because a lot of people live graciously and have good taste.

Submitted by: Ginny High and Mary J. Marchant, 2901 Springfield Drive,Tallahassee, FL 32309-3274; Source: Tallahassee Democrat 100 years: by Gerald Ensley

LEON COUNTY COMMUNITIES

History of Bradfordville

A small crossroads community as recently as 1985, Bradfordville history has been tied to regional, state and national figures of renown since the 1820s. In March, 1822, the Territory of Florida was created, 18 months later Tallahassee was selected to be the territorial capital, and in Spring, 1825, the first settlers began to arrive. Among them was Colonel Robert White Williams who had accompanied General Andrew Jackson to the area as his Assistant Surveyor General. As the lawyer who represented Marquis de Lafayette and his heirs in years of litigation, and later son-in-law of Governor John Branch, Williams was particularly situated to realize the potential of this rich new land. He selected a large tract on the south shore of Lake Iamonia, extending into what would become Bradfordville.

In 1829, family records show that another Branch son-in-law, Dr. Edward Bradford, traveled to present-day Bradfordville and selected land for purchase. In 1831, he established Pine Hill Plantation. Later he added the horseshoe bend of Lake Iamonia which he named Horseshoe Plantation. Dr. Bradford's three brothers also settled near the community called Pine Hill. Richard Bradford developed Water Oak Plantation, just across the road and south a few hundred yards near Lake McBride. Henry Bradford lived a short distance further south on Thomasville Road, and Thomas Bradford established Walnut Hill in the same area. Dr. Bradford's nephew, Dr. William H. Bradford established nearby Edgewood Plantation. The ranch family, parents of Mrs. Martha Bradford and Mrs. Rebecca Williams, located more southerly on Waverly and Live Oak Plantations. Captain William Lester migrated from Georgia

Tombstone of Nicholas Ware Eppes

and bought land extending from east of Lake McBride almost to Lake Jackson naming his plantation Oaklawn. Another neighbor, Dr. G.W. Holland, came from Virginia and purchased large holdings on the northern shore of Lake Iamonia, constructing his house, Greenwood, at the crossroads of the growing community of Pine Hill, later to become Bradfordville.

Notables in Bradfordville history include not only John Branch, Senator, Secretary of the Navy under President Andrew Jackson and Florida's last territorial governor, but also includes Tallahassee's most revered and cultured local politician, Mayor Francis W. Eppes, grandson of Thomas Jefferson, who migrated from Virginia in 1827 and purchased land east of Pisgah Church. In November 1866, Susan Bradford married his son, Nicholas Ware Eppes, who became master of Pine Hill Plantation. Born into politics, Nicholas Ware Eppes ran for Leon County Commissioner of Public Instruction and was elected four times. He was well educated, by private tutor and West Florida Seminary, which his father Francis helped to establish. Florida State University remembers Francis Eppes' service with an Eppes statue, an Eppes building, and Eppes chair, and an Eppes trophy.

Soon after the War, wealthy northern industrialists discovered the healthy piney air of the Tallahassee-

Greene's store, now Veterinarian Clinic

Thomasville area and began to purchase huge tracts of land from local families for the establishment of superior quail hunting. The first was Howard S. Case of Pennsylvania, who purchased Live Oak Plantation in 1870 from the heirs of Governor John Branch. Later Captain Lester sold 6,604 acres in Bradfordville to

Clement A. Griscom for a newly defined Horseshoe Plantation.

Thomasville Road was rebuilt uphill on drier ground, its current location, with aid from Bradford neighbors Ralph Johnson, Sr. and Charlie Roberts. Soon Bannerman and Bradfordville Roads were built, the latter slicing through old Mt. Zion Methodist Cemetery. The crossroad community boasted two general stores, Dan Johnson's wooden grocery store on the northeast corner (later Joyner's, replaced by Rehberg's) and Greene Johnson's trading post across the road (currently veterinarian office). Public schools had replaced the Iamonia Ladies Academy. There was a small "snack" grocery near one schoolhouse, Tommy Carr ran a meat market on Saturday, and Judge Whitehead was Justice of the Peace. Sporting men from Tallahassee built a cockfighting barn and used an old tenant house as a poker club. Slowly these reminders have changed or vanished, or like Mt. Zion Methodist Cemetery, some graves removed with the remainder today covered by bamboo. The unrecognizable crossroad community has given way to commercial development, yet the history of Bradfordville, inscribed on stones in the National Register Bradford-Eppes Cemetery and remembered by descendants of first settlers, is vivid and instructive for its historical impact on the nation, the region and the state.

Submitted by: Sarah H. Lamb, 3998 Bradfordville Road, Tallahassee, FL 32309

The Legacy of Frenchtown

The history of Frenchtown area began in 1824 when General Marquis de Lafayette, a French military leader who fought in the American Revolution, was granted 36 square miles of land in the Leon County area near Bloxham and Meridian Streets. Lafayette arranged the transfer of several French immigrants to cultivate his newly acquired land. After the failure of the agricultural experience, the settlers left and migrated closer to town. The area they settled in and occupied for just a few years, in northwest Tallahassee was dubbed "Frenchtown." Years later at the end of the Civil War, former slaves moved from the rural plantations into the Frenchtown area. For many years, the area remained a stronghold of the African American community. Its original boundaries extended from Tennessee Street to Brevard Street, Martin Luther King Boulevard (previously named Boulevard Street), to Copeland Street.

Over the years, Frenchtown developed into a thriving middle-class African American community that included a network of schools, family residences, businesses, and churches. Out of both an inherent drive toward enterprise and the necessity created by segregation, many African American established businesses that were patronized by blacks throughout the city. The hub of Frenchtown was Macomb Street which housed numerous establishments, including restaurants, entertainment spots, grocery stores, schools, a funeral home, doctors' offices, and a hospital. The bustling activity made Frenchtown a regional attraction. During World War II, black soldiers training at nearby Camp Gordon Johnston and Dale Mabry Air Field frequented Frenchtown's bars and nightclubs.

Frenchtown entered a state of decline after the 1960s. The end of segregation gave African Americans the opportunity to live and spend their money elsewhere. Its educational stronghold, the Original Lincoln High School, was closed. Most businesses fell victim to the changing times. Only a few remained through the 1970s as the area became more occupied with drugs and crime, the displacing of middle class and other residents from the area for urban renewal, and many failed attempts to acquire public funds to support private initiatives. Only a few of the commercial buildings and homes, representative of the historic Frenchtown dating to a period immediately after slavery, remain as a testament of Frenchtown's legacy.

Those who remember the "golden" days of this important community will relate to black owned businesses, which, while no longer in existence, contributed to the character and legacy of the Frenchtown community. Among these were: Capital Theater-owned by Margaret Yellowhair. The Theatre served the black audience mistreated or unwelcomed by the segregated theaters in downtown Tallahassee. Open from the 1920s to the 1940s, it was located on Macomb Street, between Carolina and Virginia Streets. El Dorado Café was a restaurant and nightclub formerly located on Virginia Street between Macomb and Martin Luther King Boulevard on the southeast side of the street. It was owned and operated by Curtis Davis and family. Laura Bell Memorial Hospital and Campbell Clinic was located in the 300 block of

Virginia Street. Established in 1947 by Dr. Alpha Omega Campbell (1889-1977), this two-story, twenty bed facility remained open until the mid-1950s. The Red Bird Café, Tallahassee's Chittlin' Circuit, was a popular restaurant and nightclub in the district. Its last location and use was associated with the Knights of Pythias Hall. Located on the corner of Virginia and Macomb Streets, during its hey-day, the Red Bird hosted many famous entertainers including Cab Calloway, Ray Charles, Al Green, the Adderley Brothers, Lawyer Smith and more. Modern Cleaners was established in the 1940s in the 600 block of Macomb Street and was operated by Joseph Franklin. Franklin learned his trade while studying under Anatole Martin, an African American tailor whose business was uptown in the 100 block of East Jefferson Street. The Twine Cleaners and Laundry was at 600 West Brevard Street, and was operated by the Twine family. The family also owned the Twilight Inn and a boarding house on West Madison Street. St. Mary's Primitive Baptist Church, the oldest black primitive Baptist congregation in Tallahassee, built in 1873 on the northwest corner of Call Street, across from the Old City Cemetery, as well as St. Mary No. 2 were also part of the Frenchtown community.

The roll call goes on to include: Bethel A.M.E. Church, Bethel Baptist Church, Economy Drug Store, Tookes Hotel, Avery Photography Studio, Stevens and Williams Medical Clinics, Central. AfroAmerican and Atlanta Life Insurance Companies, Nims Grocery, Quick Service Taxi Stand, Sykes Shoe Shop, White's Barber Shop, Crumps Package Store, Artistic Beauty and Barber Shop, Yourway Barber Shop, Monroe Pool Hall, Star's Grocery, Speed Service Station, Howard Shoe Shop, Paradise Grill, Malone's Bar, Bessie Dixon's, Sullivan's Grocery, Sim's Barber Shop, Gilliam, Hadley's Grocery, Haywood Service Station, Grocery and Service Station, Bennett's Sandwich and Soda Shop, Sunshine Cleaners, later Super-X Food Store and many others as a testament to the significance of the area to the African American population.

During the turbulent times of staunch desegregation, "Jim Crow", and Black Codes, Frenchtown was a "Haven in Time of Storm"; an enclave that provided a place of protection as well as a sense of pride for many black families. Frenchtown, inhabited by African Americans, was an embodiment of industry, healthful family living, social, educational, and economic advancement. Its residents contributed in many ways to the city's development and history. Though not conclusive, this representation offers a general overview of the contributions of Frenchtown and its residents.

Submitted by: Florida Parker; Written by: Riley House Althamese Barnes (Director)

The Historic Village of Miccosukee

The rural community of Miccosukee, in east Leon County, has a history that reaches into the recesses of time. The first map showing the existence of "Mikasuki" was in 1767. Native Americans, American military leaders, antebellum planters, slaves, yeoman farmers, merchants, sharecroppers and wealthy Northerners all contributed to the history and development of this area on the western shore of Lake Miccosukee. *Community With A Rich Heritage* by Vivian Young, Historic Tallahassee Preservation Board.

The first to settle along the western shore of Lake Miccosukee were North Carolinians lead by Col. Richard Parish. They built plantation houses; many with magnificent views towards the lake. The days ahead promised wealth to these planters as Miccosukee of antebellum times became the heart of what was once one of Florida's richest agricultural regions. Read about the Parish, Blake, Byrd, Turnbull, Perkins and Yarbrough families and how Col. Parish's daughters connected these families in *Miccosukee - The Story of a Historic Village* compiled by Patricia Herold.

These early settlers first built their homes, organized churches; formed a volunteer militia and established a school for their children. A post office was established in 1831, and the polling place selected for the 1831 election was "Byrd and Parish Store" in Miccosukee.HTPB.

Miccosukee Academy-was established before 1838. These antebellum planters realized a need to educate their children and "old field" schools were established. (Dr. A. Rhodes, School Superintendent, 1937-1945, stated

Miccosukee Methodist Church, organized 1828

"...this was the oldest school in Leon County")

Churches-During the early 1820s, missionaries were sent into this new territory by the South Carolina Conference of the Methodist Episcopal Church to establish "societies". Circuit Rider, John Slade, later known as the "Father of Methodism in Florida" held services in this area during the organization of Miccosukee Methodist in 1828 and Pisgah Methodist Church in 1830.

Miccosukee Methodist Church-The first building was made of logs and stood in the woods about two miles south of the Miccosukee crossroads in an area known as Concord. As the church grew, a member, John Montford, donated nearby land for a new building. Years later, the church requested permission from the Methodist Episcopal Conference to relocate to the center of Miccosukee. Permission was also received to deed the old church building to the black congregation, Concord African Methodist Episcopal Church. Concord continues today as one of the oldest AME churches.

Indian Springs Baptist Church-In 1829, the Baptist were also organizing as they gathered in the home of Sarah and Arthur Burney. They would call their church Indian Springs because of its closeness to the springhead of Panther Creek. Before the War Between the States, Indian Springs would relocate south of Miccosukee on the old Newport Road (SR 59). The church house was built in 1854 with wooden pegs and is the oldest church structure in the area. In 1858, Indian Springs helped establish what was probably the first black Baptist church in Leon County known as Shiloh Baptist Church. Indian Springs is the oldest Baptist Church in Leon County and the fifth oldest in Florida.

Indian Springs Baptist Church organized 1829

Historic Indian Springs Church Cemeter-In 1997, graves dating back to 1831 were moved from the original church location to Indian Spring Church grounds south of Miccosukee. Sarah Burney had been the first to be buried and her husband, Arthur Burney, was buried in 1842. Six years later, their daughter, Mary Burney Byrd, wife of Benjamin Byrd, Florida's first state treasurer, was buried.

Pisgah Methodist Church, organized 1830

Pisgah United Methodist Church-Historic Pisgah is one of the oldest remaining church structures in Florida. Pisgah was organized in 1830 by Circuit Rider, John Slade, and the church building was dedicated in 1858. Pisgah and its historic cemetery are located in a grove of trees off Centerville Road 7 miles west of Miccosukee and have been in use since Territorial Days.

Native Trails Canopy Roads-The roads leading into Miccosukee are the trails of years ago. These historic byways are Miccosukee, Centerville, Moccasin Gap and Old Magnolia Roads which are deeply eroded into the red clay and lined with majestic live oaks draped in Spanish moss creating picturesque canopies.

During antebellum time, these roads were used by plantations to haul bales of cotton to ports on the St Marks River at Magnolia, St. Marks, and Newport - for shipment to the mills of New York, New Orleans and to London markets.

Scenic America has designated these and other canopy roads in Leon County as one of this nation's "Ten Most Important Scenic Byways".

Late 1870s into Turn of Century-After the War, it was a declining agricultural economy as the plantations

Miccosukee School in the 1950's, organized in 1870's

shifted to a sharecropping system. At the same time, many farmers were able to acquire their own land and this period became a heyday of the yeoman farmer. Miccosukee was on the rebound as an agricultural center and its story continues.
Submitted by: Patricia Perry Herold, Post Office. Box 91074, Miccosukee, Florida 32309

The Village of Miccosukee

The village of Miccosukee rebounds in the 1870s as an agricultural center and its prosperity continued into the 20th century. An important factor was the train. Florida Central Railroad served Miccosukee bringing new business and agricultural enterprises to the area.

An 1876 issue of *The Semi-Tropical* reported Miccosukee having two stores, a schoolhouse, a Methodist church, a Baptist church, a Masonic Lodge and two doctors.

In 1886, the *Florida Gazetteer* presented a new description: six general stores, a school, Methodist and Baptist churches, three justices of the peace, a teacher, postmaster and three truck farmers. The Florida Railway line runs out of Thomasville through Miccosukee.

During these years, the merchants advertising "Dry Goods, Groceries, Hardware, Hats, Boots, Shoes, Queenware, Bacon, Flour and General Merchandise" were John Henry and William Perkins. Leonidas Byrd, F. T. and Joseph Christie, J. A. Herring and J. W. Collins.

Woodfield Springs Plantation, Louise Ireland Humphrey

The first reference to a public school in Miccosukee was a notation found on June 1, 1878 when the Leon County Board of Public Instructions appropriated funds for the teacher at Miccosukee.

A two-story school house was built in 1920. By 1937, Miccosukee had outgrown this building and the Board applied to the Work Progress Administration (WPA) for assistance in building a new school house. By 1940, Miccosukee had a new brick school building. Miccosukee continued to have a school until 1985, when the Leon County School Board closed the Miccosukee School, transferring all area students to Tallahassee.

<u>Plantations-Hunting Estates</u> - Around the turn-of-the century, some Northerners were leasing land in the Miccosukee area for hunting rights while others began purchasing vast estates - the old cotton plantations. Wealthy Northerners arrived with their fortunes to finance the purchase of vast acres of land for their private winter hunting plantations. These hunting estates had a devastating impact on Miccosukee as they took thousands of acres of land out of agricultural production.

The plantations created around Miccosukee included: Ring Oak Plantation created on the western shore of Lake Miccosukee by Kate Hanna Ireland Harvey, daughter of coal baron H. Melville Hanna, as a duck-shooting lodge to accommodate day visits from her Pebble Hill Plantation in Thomasville. It is now a 5,515 acre plantation owned by the Ingalls family of Shaker Heights, Ohio; Loveridge Plantation was first a thousand acres on Lake Miccosukee purchased by George H. Love of Pittsburgh. Love enlarged his plantation by adding several thousand acres extending into Georgia; Norias Plantation located on the northern shore of Lake Miccosukee was jointly owned by Gov. Walter E. Edge of New Jersey and Walter C. Teague, chairman of the board of Standard Oil Company of New Jersey. At one time the acreage was 18,395 and was named for a rail stop in Texas where they used to hunt.; Sunny Hill Plantation - established by Colonel Lewis S. Thompson of New Jersey, whose family made its fortune through Standard Oil. His hunting estate eventually covering about 20,000 acres; Woodfield Springs Plantation was created on Moccasin Gap Road by George M.

Van Brunt House 1911

Humphrey. Humphrey was the former Secretary of Treasury and master of Milestone Plantation in Thomas County. He later gave Woodfield Springs to his son, Gilbert W. "Bud" and wife, Louise Ireland Humphrey.

After the turn of the century, the *Tallahassee True Democrat* in 1911 stated "The quiet village of an age ago is still a village but new houses are going up and it is taking on the proportions of a town. There are a number of pretty homes, with vine clad verandahs and front rose gardens, white bodies and green blinds."

The *Lands of Leon* described Miccosukee glowingly, "...The Florida Central Railroad provides quick transportation ... has become a shipping point of much importance…the village list five general stores, a grist mill, turpentine still, stock breeder, railroad agent, two physician and two justices of the peace."

Herring General Store in the 1920's, established 1850's

The period from 1890 to 1950 was the most critical to Miccosukee. Most of the historic buildings were constructed, the railroad provided transportation, there were thriving businesses at the crossroads, rural electrification occurred for homes and businesses, and Miccosukee flourished. Simultaneously, eventsl were taking place that led to Miccosukee's decline as a commercial center. The development of large hunting estates destroyed the agricultural base together with automobiles which provided convenient travel and drew business away from the rural crossroad community. Also, with easy transportation the children could be bused out of the community and residents could commute to jobs in the Tallahassee, Thomasville and surrounding area.

Miccosukee changed from crossroad to bedroom community. As it moved into the 21st century, Miccosukee grew as rapidly as all of Leon County. Despite all the changes, Miccosukee retains much of its early charm with its fine vernacular architecture, rural character and rich history.

Sources: Compiled from information relating to Miccosukee nomination to National Register of Historic Places. And manuscript to be published Miccosukee - The Story of a Historic Village by Patricia Herold Submitted by: Patricia Perry Herold, Post Office Box 91074, Miccosukee, Florida 32309-0074

The Chaires Community

The rural community of Chaires began with the arrival of three brothers whose family had

Verdura, Benjamin Chaires 16-room mansion, Verdura Burned in 1885 and only the columns remain

originated in Rouen, France, by the name of Jan De La Chaire; pronounced "ShaRay" and Americanized to "Chaires".

One of the brothers, Green Hill built his Evergreen Hills Plantation on land currently known as Chaires. His brothers, Benjamin and Thomas Peter, created thriving plantations (Vendura and Woodlawn) nearby and the Chaires brothers became influential Southern planters. Their legacies exist today in the area now known as Chaires.

In 1854, the Pensacola and Georgia Railroad began construction on land owned by Green HillChaires. At the completion of the railroad in 1858, the Chaires community was established and with the railroad providing transportation, the area became more settled. In 1891, land was received from members of the Chaires

Chaires Methodist Church, building dedicated in 1892

family to build a new Methodist church building. On January 1, 1892, the church organized as New Hope Methodist Episcopal Church and renamed, Chaires Methodist Episcopal Church moved into its new building with steeple and bell all ready for use. In 1992, at the 150th session of the Florida Annual Conference of The United Methodist Church, the 100th anniversary of the Chaires United Methodist Church was recognized.

Station 1 School, also known as Chaires School, is recorded in the Leon County School Board minutes as early as the 1870s.

Chaires School is one of the greatest historical gems of the Chaires Community. The one room schoolhouse was known as Station One and was recorded in the Leon County School Board minutes as early as the 1870s. By the 1920s, the area was outgrowing this small schoolhouse and on November 4, 1928, the Board of Public Instruction of Leon County received a petition from the people of Chaires for a new school. The community applied for the issuance of $50,000 worth of bonds to purchase land for the purpose of erecting a new school. The Board accepted the proposal and obtained six acres of land from Mr. David Green Chaires, a descendent of Green Hill Chaires. On June 23, 1929, the new school for Chaires District Number Three was completed and ready for occupancy. Mr. Virgil Townsend became the first principal with three teachers Mrs. Maggie Patterson, Miss May Bird Carmine and Mr. Thompson.

Lower right is Professor Woodbery, Foster G. Davis in the upper right wearing derby hat

Around the turn-of-the century, Mr. H. P. Woodbery was principal and high school teacher. He was known as one of the best teachers in Leon County. Students from Tallahassee would board with families in Chaires to attend high school under Professor Woodbery.

In a 1911 article in the *New Era Edition True Democrat*, Chaires is described as "one of the busiest places in the area". The community was just 12 miles east of Tallahassee on the Seaboard Airline Railroad and had an impressive gin house and cotton packing establishment "which shipped to the uttermost parts of the earth for the clothing of humanity".

The "dominant spirit in this pretty little village is Mr. Jno H. Patterson who conducts the largest mercantile establishment outside the City of Tallahassee". Chaires is a community of "culture and refinement" with a "Methodist and Baptist Church, a school and quite a number of cozy and attractive homes".

The Chaires Community Historic District was placed on the National Registry of Historic Places in 2000. The district runs along the Chaires Cross Road, the Road to the Lake and Hancock Street containing 300 acres and 15 buildings.

Submitted by: Dorothy Cooper Spence, 3982 Chaires Cross Road Tallahassee, Florida

Capitola: A Village of Days Gone By

Capitola is a turn-of-the century community located just two miles down the road from Chaires where the first settlers to move in were the DuPrees, Boyds and Upchurches. Originally known as Mays, it was later named for Capitola DuPree. A 1911 article in the *New Era Edition True Democrat* described Capitola as "growing rapidly with a considerable influx of good people".

H. T. Cotton, B. F. Boyd and J. P. Baum were enterprising merchants. J. C. Upchurch owned an extensive sawmill plant and C. T. Clarke's Clarke Lumber Company was a large stave mill which produced and exported hundreds of cars of stave and box material. The township was located at the junction of the Seaboard and Florida Central Railroads which provided necessary transportation for the thriving village. The Union Depot had a ticket office for both railroads and a telegraph office.

There was also splendid farming, cattle land and what seemed to be an unlimited supply of hardwood timber which all contributed to Capitola's prosperity. Two surrounding large landed estates of G. Noble Jones and Dannitte Mays also supported the growing community.

Capitola had convenient transportation, prosperous businesses, a schoolhouse, a church and many fine homes. Seven of these homes were pictured in the 1911 *True Democrat* article.

The Capitola of days gone by has disappeared and a remaining sign gives little evidence of its past. The historic villages of the Chaires-Capitola communities are being claimed by urban sprawl. The splendid farmland and forests are being divided and developed into communities which now serve Tallahassee.

The area has taken on a new life with the development of the Chaires-Capitola Community Park. The focal point for the park is the Community Center built next to the new Chaires School. Nearby, the Chaires-Capitola Volunteer Fire Department provides fire and rescue services for the citizens living in the area.

Submitted by: Dorothy C. Spence 3982 Chaires Cross Road Tallahassee, Florida 32317
Committee Note: The history of the Chaires and Capitola communities as submitted by community activist, Dorothy Spence, whose dedication to her community was recognized by the Board of County Commissioners of Leon County in the naming of the Chaires Community Center as the Dorothy Cooper Spence Community Center.

Woodville Portion of West Side Uptown 1910

Woodville was christened August 28, 1888. It is a picturesque village 10 miles from Tallahassee on the St. Marks branch of the Seaboard Air Line. H.G. Lewis was the first postmaster, and he named the town. He served as postmaster for 16 years, the first five of which paid a total monthly revenue of 75 cents. Since that time the income has increased considerably and T.L Page now holds that position. There is one mail a day each way. There are six general stores, chief among them being that of Rhodes, Russ & Bros, C.R. Langston, and S.C Williamson. The building occupied by the former firm is two storeys, with pressed brick front, and is one of the handsomest store houses in Florida. Woodville is surrounded by fertile farms and turpentine distilleries.

Woodville has a flourishing council of fraternal order of Woodmen. G.W. Rhodes is council commander; W.A. Register, clerk; T.A. Ferrell, banker; George Lawhon, advisor lieutenant; managers, P.D. Lewis, R.L. Rhodes and W.C. Robison.

Located midway between Tallahassee and the Gulf, Woodville is a delightful place to live. It is on the direct route of the Lakes to the Gulf highway. A good hard road thread the distance for several miles out of Tallahassee, and it is only a matter of time when the whole length of the road to St. Marks will be clayed.
Source: Reproduction of early newspaper article

Woodville Postmasters

The following are the names and dates that each person was appointed to be Postmaster of Woodville Post Office: H.G. Lewis-July 23, 1888; Thomas J. Isler-July 2, 1903; John D. Lewis-August 24, 1906; Troup L. Page-April 17, 1907; John B. Wilkinson-April 26, 1912; Thomas M. Hall; July 22, 1914; Charles W. Hannon (Acting)-May 28,1926; Mrs. Mildred I. Hamlin-November 22, 1926; Mrs. Lillian J. Hannon-November 2, 1929; Mrs. Estelle G. Gerrell-May 6, 1935; Mrs. Thetus Goff-February 16, 1943; Mrs. Ina R. Watson (Acting) September 30, 1957; Mrs. Anna L. Watkins-December 12, 1958; and Carolyn W. Harvey- February 10, 1990.
Submitted by: Carolyn Harvey

LEON COUNTY SCHOOLS AND UNIVERSITIES

Caroline Brevard Elementary School

The namesake of the school, Caroline Mays Brevard, was an exceptional woman of her time. (See Caroline Mays Brevard in another section of this book.)

The original downtown Caroline Brevard School at 727 South Calhoun Street was completed in 1925 and was the first elementary school in Tallahassee. The original building was a three-story, double-loaded corridor structure, located on a three-acre lot.

Caroline Brevard School

In the late 1940s family homes located near the school gave way to businesses and the Capitol Center. Thus, by 1958 the School building and lot were sold to the State of Florida and a new Caroline Brevard School was constructed at 2006 Jackson Bluff Road. The building was completed in February, 1959.

The lunchroom and auditorium were in the basement along with offices and storage. The playground was in the rear and to the side and had a minimum of playground equipment. The library was located on the Gaines Street side on the ground floor.

Principals of the school were the following: Mrs. Elizabeth Cobb, A. E. Shearer, Fred Gehan, Robert E. Bussard, W. V. Ashmore, Mabel Hamilton, Roy Napier, Sheldon Hilaman, Jo Glick, Dr. Gloria Poole, Nancy Byrd and Pam Hightower.

Caroline Brevard was always ranked high scholastically. It was listed as "State Accredited" for most of the years it was in existence. In 1962 SACS accredited Caroline Brevard and it has continued to be accredited through the years.

Many prominent people in Tallahassee, Leon County and beyond were educated at Caroline Brevard School.

As TCC, FSU, and FAMU grew, and since the location of the school at 2006 Jackson Bluff Road was close to these three campuses, and as the need for student housing increased, the area surrounding the school changed significantly from the neighborhood of 1959. The mobility of the population plus the decreasing number of elementary students in the area resulted in the closing of the school in 2007 to make way for SAIL High School. The building was renovated for a high school curriculum.

The State has now given the old Caroline Brevard School building back to the school system. Its future use hasn't been determined at this time.

The architecture of the school has been highlighted with paint to emphasize the building's fine architecture.

Submitted by Mary J. Marchant, 2901 Springfield Drive, Tallahassee, FL 32309

Florida A & M University

On October 3, 1887, the State Normal College for Colored Students began classes, and became a land grant university four years later when it received $7,500 under the Second Morrill Act, and its name was changed to State Normal and Industrial College for Colored Students. However, it was not an official institution of higher learning until the 1905 Buckman Act, which transferred control from the Department of Education to the Board of Control, creating what was the foundation for the modern Florida A&M University. This same act is responsible for the creation of the University of Florida and Florida State University from their previous institutions.

In 1909 the name of the college was again changed to Florida Agricultural and Mechanical College for Negroes; in 1953 the name was finally changed to Florida Agricultural and Mechanical University. Florida A&M is the only publicly funded historically black college or university in the state of Florida.

The September 2006 issue of *Black Enterprise Magazine*, named Florida A&M the number-one college for African Americans in the United States. This ranking is based on the graduation rate and the academic and social atmosphere. FAMU is a member school of the Thurgood Marshall Scholarship Fund. In 1997, FAMU was selected as the *Time Magazine Princeton Review* "College of the Year" and was cited in 1999 by *Black Issues in Higher Education* for awarding more baccalaureate degrees to African-Americans than any institution in the nation.

FAMU's main campus is in Tallahassee, FL with Schools of Law, Pharmacy and the Research and Development Center on extension campuses. FAMU is on the US National Register of Historic Places and US Historic District.

Submitted by: Mary J. Marchant, 2901 Springfield Drive, Tallahassee, FL 32309-3274

The Florida A & M Marching 100

The city of Tallahassee sports the largest and second largest college bands in the United States!

"The Marching 100", official name of the Florida A & M University Band, was begun in 1892 under Director P. A. Van Weller, with only 16 instruments, but now has grown to well over 440 members, and is the second largest band in the USA.

FAMU "Marching 100" band performs at halftime in 1985

"The Marching 100" has received accolades from national as well as international critics for its unique dance steps, its musicianship, and its pageantry. "The Most Imitated Marching Band in America" is credited with revolutionizing marching band techniques in high schools and colleges all over the United States. William P. Foster became Director of Bands in 1946 and created many of those techniques and published a book, *Band Pageantry*. Dr. Foster's career spanned more than 50 years with FAMU. Interestingly, Nat Adderly, famous professional jazz musician, was director from 1910-1918. The band is known for its intricate dance steps while playing instruments. The band has had many accomplishments in the past as well as present times. Some of these accomplishments include: First black band to appear in the Festival of States Parade in 1950; Has had featured articles in the following publications: *Ebony* (several times); *NewYork Times* Newspaper; *P. M. Magazine*; *Chronicle of Higher Learning*; *Black Perspective in Music*; *Sports Illustrated* and others.

"The Marching 100" has had numerous venues spotlighting their abilities and talents. They represented the United States in 1989 at the Bicentennial Celebration of the French Revolution and was recognized by the U.S. House of Representatives. They marched in Bill Clinton's two Inaugural Parades, and President Obama's 2008 Inaugural Parade. They have played for professional football and baseball games, and many other venues.

Written and Submitted by Mary J. Marchant, 2901 Springfield Drive Tallahassee, FL 3230-3274

Florida A&M University's Naval Reserve Officer Training Corps

The Florida A&M University (FAMU) Naval Reserve Officer Training Corps was commissioned on August 1, 1972 and was the fourth of six NROTC Units to be established on a historically black university campus. The FAMU NROTC Unit has also established cross-town enrollment programs for students from Florida State University and Tallahassee Community College. Commander Benjamin Hacker, the first Commanding Officer, went on to achieve the rank of Rear Admiral (Upper Half) before retiring in 1988. Significant first timers for the Unit includes: Ensign Robert Hill, the first commissioned officer, March 1975; Ensign Jeffrey Young, became the first enlisted commissioning program commissioned, June 1979; Ensign Harold Lomax, first selectee to the Nuclear Power Program in February 1976; Ensign Carol Skiber, the first female Aviator, December 1978; Sergeant, Robert Winchester, the Unit's first MECEP officer candidate in August 1989; and first MECEP commissioned in December 1991.

Since the Unit establishment, over 400 men and women have completed the NROTC Program at FAMU and have gone on to serve the country as officers of the United States Navy and Marine Corps.

FAMU'S NROTC Commanding Officers are: Cdr. Benjamin T. Hacker, USN, served from Aug 1972-June 1973; Capt Richard E. Williams, USN, served from Jul 1973- June 1976; Capt. Otis Brooks, USN, served from Jul 1976- Jul 1981; Capt. James L. Gilchrist, USN, served from Sep 1981-Nov 1984; Capt. Kenneth H. Johnson, USN, served from Nov 1984-May 1985; Cdr. Charles Roach, USN, served from May 1985-Feb 1986; Capt. Stanley J. Carter, USN, served from Feb 1986-Sep 1988; Capt. Royal H. Logan, USN, served from Sep 1988-Jul 1991; Capt. Audrey L. Smith, USN, served from Jul 1991-Jul 1994; Col. Melford M. Johnson, USMC, served from Jul 1994-Aug-1996; Capt. Donnie Cochran, USN, Jul 1996-Jul 1999; Capt. Robert L. Cunningham, Jr. USN, Jul 1999-Jul 2002; Capt. Thomas R. Daniel, Jr. USN, Jul 2002-Dec 2004; Capt. Anthony W. Jiles, USN, Dec 2004-Dec 2007; and Col. Elvis Blumenstock, USMC Dec 2007-Dec 2010

Written and Submitted by: James L. Gilchrist, 2103 Olivia Drive Tallahassee, Florida 32308

History of Florida State University

Florida State University had its beginnings as early as 1823 when the Territorial Legislature began to plan a higher education system.

On March 3, 1845, with an act supplemental to Florida becoming a State, two townships were granted to the State for the establishment of two seminaries, one east and one west of the Suwannee River, and with the act of the Legislature, January 24,1851, the purpose was "the instruction of persons, both male and female."

In 1854 the City of Tallahassee established a school for boys called the Florida Institute and in 1856, the Mayor of Tallahassee, Francis Eppes, grandson of Thomas Jefferson, proposed that the institution west of the Suwanee be located in Tallahassee. The Legislature passed the bill in 1857, for the West Florida Seminary. It was located on the hill where the Westcott Building now stands making it the site of an institution of higher education longer than any other site in Florida. This was only 12 years after Statehood.

After absorbing the Tallahassee Female Academy the school became co-educational in 1858.

The cadets from West Florida Seminary fought the Battle of Natural Bridge, keeping Tallahassee the only Confederate capital not captured during the Civil War.

Westcott Building, The Florida State University

Following the war, it continued to develop programs. In 1883 West Florida Seminary became the University of Florida by the Legislature, a fact which has never been repealed.

In 1901 it became Florida State College. In 1902 the student body numbered 252 men and women.

In 1905 after a reorganization of Florida's educational system by the legislature, six state institutions of higher learning were consolidated into two: the University of Florida in Gainesville east and Florida State College for Women, west of the Suwanee River. When the men went to the university of Florida in Gainesville, they took with them the fraternities and the College football team, which had been state champions in 1902, 1903, and 1905.

In 1946 the WWII veterans returning back home created a demand for the establishment of the Tallahassee Branch of the University of Florida. In May, 1947, the Governor signed an act of the Legislature returning Florida State College for Women to coeducational and naming it Florida State University. The student body of 4,056 students chose an Alma Mater and unanimously selected the Seminole as their mascot. The Flying High Circus was begun and football was started again. The first home game since 1905 was played in October.

In each succeeding decade, The Florida State University has added to its academic organization from the original four, which consisted of The College, the School for Teachers, the School for Music, and the College Academy. FSU presently is composed of 16 independent colleges. It has expanded from the original few acres and buildings to 542 buildings on 1550 acres. (Some acreage was formerly a farm which supplied food for FSCW.) The Seminole Reservation, the Marine Lab on the Gulf Coast, the FSU-FAMU College of Engineering, National High Magnetic Field Lab; and branches in Panama City, FL; international educational branches in London, Florence, Valencia and Panama are only a few additions that have enhanced educational opportunities for Florida State students.

After 159 years of its formation, the student population is now 40,000 and FSU is recognized as a major graduate research facility both nationally and abroad.

Paraphrased and Submitted by: Mary J. Marchant, 2901 Springfield Drive Tallahassee, FL 32309-3274; Source: Office of University Communication 2011

FSU Flying High Circus

The Flying High Circus at Florida State University is an extra-curricular activity under the Division of Student Affairs. All members of the FSU Circus are required to be a degree-seeking student registered at Florida State University.

The FSU Circus is primarily a three-ring aerial and stage presentation. Unlike professional circuses, "Flying High" has no animal acts. Student performers rig all of their own equipment, set up the circus's tent, sew costumes, and set lights and sound for performances.

Flying High Circus Big Top at the Jack Haskin Circus Complex

The Circus was founded in 1947 by Jack Haskin. The program was created to integrate men and women at the newly co-ed institution. The Florida State University Circus has been seen on "CBS Sports Spectacular," "ABC's Wide World of Sports," "On the Road" with Charles Kuralt, "NBC's "Real People," "PM Magazine," and ESPN. Individuals have been featured on "To Tell the Truth," "The Original Amateur Hour," and "I've Got A Secret.." In 1964, CBS took the Circus on a European tour. The Circus has visited Canada, the Bahamas and the Dominican Republic.

Through the School of Sports Management, Physical Education and Recreation, a one-semester, one credit hour "Introduction to Circus" course teaches students the basics of juggling, high wire, aerial ballet, and equipment rigging. Enrollment is encouraged but not mandatory for participation in the circus. The majority of student performers pursue a career in their chosen discipline. Only a small percentage of the performers seek a professional circus career.

The Circus generates its own revenue performing for sponsors throughout the Southeast and hosting Spring weekend shows on campus. Additionally the Circus conducts a summer program at Callaway Gardens and directs a children's camp on campus.

Submitted by: Mary J. Marchant, 2901 Springfield Drive, Tallahassee, FL 32309-3274

She Flies through the Air: Performing in the FSU Circus

My FSU student I.D. read Louise Wood, junior, in 1973. I searched extracurricular activities for something that would be fun and a good workout. Having participated in gymnastics in HS and Miami-Dade JC, the FSU circus looked interesting.

The "Flying High Circus" is an extra-

Louise Wood Collins on the "Sky Pole"

curricular activity whose only requirement for participation is that one must be a degree-seeking student registered at FSU. No previous training or skills were required.

With 18-22 circus acts taught, there is a place for everyone. I tried out for the Trapeze, Tight Rope, and Perch Pole, but I was chosen for the Spanish Web and Sky Pole.

Tryouts were simple. Coaches looked for grace (I had little), rhythm (not so much), coordination (had this), and a few acrobatics (some experience).

Spanish Web (aerial ballet) involves a vertical cloth covered rope with a loop attached near the top. A performer climbs and inserts her foot, wrist, or neck into the loop (I must have been really gullible to put my neck in that). A spinner at the bottom spins the rope, and centrifugal force holds the performer mostly horizontal as she performs a ballet routine. I knew I couldn't fall, but I had to overcome dizziness from the spin. This was the easier routine.

The Sky Pole (AKA the Russian Bar) combines gymnastics and trampoline skills on a 4 meter fiberglass balance pole. My partners, Thorn and BG, controlled the bar at each end, catapulting the "flyer" into the air to perform handstands, single and double flips. The weight requirement was 100 pounds. On Mondays when I stepped onto the pole, my partners accused me of eating too many ice-cream sundaes over the weekend!

After two years of "Flying High", I can brag to my grandchildren, "Did you know grandma was in the circus? No, I wasn't a clown".
Submitted by Louise Collins jiclouise@comcast.net

FSU's Marching Chiefs

An unnamed band had existed at the university since 1939 when the school was still the Florida State College for Women under the leadership of director Owen F. Sellers. With fewer than 20 students, the band made its first performance at the Odds and Evens intramural football game on Thanksgiving Day 1939.

The Marching Chiefs in formation during the 1955 homecoming game

A 1949 newspaper survey conducted by the FSU Student Government Association aided in selecting the title officially adopted by the university, "The Florida State Marching Chiefs." In 1971 FSU Alumnus and former Marching Chief Drum Major, Richard Mayo, took over as Director of the Marching Chiefs. That same year the band grew to over 200 members and was a finalist in the Best College Marching Band Contest on ABC-TV.

In 1974 the Marching Chiefs performed at the International Trade Fair in Damascus, Syria. While in the Middle East, the Chiefs traveled to Amman, Jordan for a command performance for King Hussein, thus the "world renowned" title that the Chiefs use today.

The Marching Chiefs in formation during the 1955 homecoming game

Several dates mark important growth for the band: 1982-the Chiefs were featured in a first time *Sports Illustrated* multi-page photo spread; 1988 the Chiefs grew to 400 members, making it the largest collegiate marching band in the world.; 2005 a million dollar donation provided a new practice field for the Chiefs; 2008 the Chiefs grew to 443 members; 2009 the Chiefs grew even bigger with 520 students auditioning for the band but only 460 making the cut; and the band has performed at all FSU Bowl games.

The Marching Chiefs remain the largest collegiate marching band in the world. FAMU's Marching 100 has 420 members, thus the two largest collegiate marching bands in the world are both from Tallahassee!

The Chiefs have several traditions established over the years. Charles Carter, a talented arranger, was brought here by Dr. Manley Whitcomb. Carter arranged unusual and interesting compositions for the field band and Whitcomb brought the Chiefs Step and the concept of marching 8 steps to 5 yards. The white

shoe covers and white gloves accent the sharp 90 degree arm swings and stiff foot salutes.
Written and Submitted by Mary J. Marchant, 2901 Springfield Drive Tallahassee, FL 32309-3274

Chief Osceola, FSU's Famous Mascot

Bill Durham, a Tallahassee businessman with Cherokee bloodlines takes the credit for introducing Bobby Bowden, Florida State's new head football coach in 1976, to the idea of the time-honored tradition of having a student dressed as Chief Osceola, on a Appaloosa horse named Renegade, riding from one end of the football field to the middle and thrusting a flaming spear into the ground. Durham claims to have thought up the idea when he was a student in 1962. The idea fell on deaf ears until Bowden, who liked the concept, made it a reality in a football game on September 16, 1978.

Chief Osceola and Renegade in 1985

The NCAA ruled that the 18 colleges which used Indian names as their Mascot would have to change to a non- Indian name. FSU appealed the ruling and won, the only institute of the 18 to do so, because the Seminole Tribe has long supported the use of the Seminole name as Florida State's mascot. The Seminole Tribe of Florida passed a unanimous resolution reinforcing its position of supporting Florida State's use of the Seminole name.
Submitted by Mary J. Marchant, 2901 Springfield Drive Tallahassee, FL 32309-3274; Source: Let's Talk Gymnastics.com written by Bruce Davis, Miami-Dade College, Used by Permission: Bruce Davis

Dick Gutting, Florida State's First Seminole Mascot

The student body had voted in the "Seminole" mascot name the same year that FSU became co-ed.

Dick Gutting, Florida State's tumbling and trampoline champion, became the first mascot in 1950, when football was started at FSU. Dick Gutting went to the then Coach Nugent with the idea of having himself dressed up as an Indian and tumbling in front of the football team as they came on to the field. Nugent liked the idea and Dick performed the tumbling for home games in exchange for a few meals in the football team dining hall.

Gutting was a poor non-scholarship athlete from Chicago and every little bit helped. Gutting had a special uniform made of long pants which were gold in the front and maroon on the back to show off his twisting movements and with bell bottoms so he could grab a tuck on his double backs

When Dick graduated in 1955, Chic Cicio succeeded him and became known as "Sammie Seminole," their new name at that time. Chic, a New Yorker and 1956 NAAU Floor Exercise Champion was also a non-scholarship athlete. He accompanied the football team to bowl games and performed at all the home football games.

Jack Ryder, the 1961 NCAA Tumbling Champion, became the second "Sammie Seminole." Joe Greene, a transfer student from Dade Junior College where Gutting was then head gymnastics coach, became the third "Sammie Seminole." Rick Miller, Bob Gramling and Barry Rowars followed, with Barry being the last "Sammie Seminole."

This led to the present mascot: Chief Osceola.
Submitted by: Mary J. Marchant, 2901 Springfield Drive, Tallahassee, FL 32309-3274; Source: Let's Talk Gymnastics. Com. Written by: Bruce Davis, Professor Emeritus Miami-Dade College

Florida State Football

Florida State Football began its 65th season the fall of 2011.

Before WWII, Florida had a female college called Florida State College for Women in Tallahassee. The male college was known as The University of Florida. After WWII was won, the soldiers were coming back to finish their education because the GI Bill of Rights, passed by Congress, paid college expenses for the returning soldiers.

A baseball game at Centennial Field where FSU played its first football game Image courtesy of the Florida State Archives Photographic collection

Thus FSCW became a co-ed school and efforts to form a football team for the renamed Florida State University in 1947 was begun by Doak Campbell, the President, and Coyle Moore, a professor at the school.

Ed Williamson, a PE coach, was named as the first head coach and Jack Haskin was an assistant coach. Jack later became the coach of the very successful Flying High Circus.

The team practiced and lived at the Old Dale Mabry Air Field, which later became known as "West Campus."

The first game was played at Centennial Field, a minor league baseball park. The first game was in October, 1947. The portable bleacher seating held only 6,000, but about 8,000 people showed up.

The team decided to call themselves "Seminoles" to honor the Native Americans who fought so hard to stay in Florida.

The record for 1947 was 0 wins five losses: Stetson won 14-6; Cumberland College won 6-0; TN Polytechnical Institute won 27-6; Troy State won 36-6, and Jacksonville State won 7-0.

It later took an act of the Legislature for FSU to play the University of Florida. "Bill Peterson, FSU's Coach from 1960-1970, put Seminole football on the national map with his high-scoring, pass-happy offense and reckless, risk-taking defense. His influence is indelibly stamped on Seminole football, as well as the university and Florida's Capital City."

Coach Bobby Bowden was an assistant coach under Bill Peterson from 1963-1965. Many of the assistant coaches under Coach Peterson went on to coach in the NFL. Coach Peterson left after the 1970 season, and an era ended. Several outstanding players were on the team with Coach Peterson: Gary Huff, Bill Cappelman, Ron Sellers, TK Wetherell, Kim Hammond, Philip Abraira, and Fred Biletnikof, among others. It was said that Coach Peterson's players would play far above their natural ability.

During the 1970s, FSU Football had a mixture of successes and failures. The year 1971 found Gary Huff as a Heisman Trophy Candidate and Barry Smith as an NFL first rounder. FSU played in the inaugural Fiesta Bowl in 1972.

From 1971-1975, several negative things happened: The Seminole Boosters disbanded but was called The National Seminole Club; the 1973 season was winless; and the next two seasons weren't encouraging. FSU was about to drop football, when in 1976, Coach Bobby Bowden was hired from West Virginia to jump-start the program.

In 1976 when Coach Bowden took over, everyone wanted to play FSU at their Homecoming, and car bumper stickers said, "Beat Anybody."

In 1977, FSU beat Florida for the first time. In 1979, FSU won 11 games. In 1980, and years

Judge Jim Joanos and family Image courtesy of the Florida State Archives Photographic collection

following, FSU beat #3 Nebraska and other football powerhouses.

From 1991-2000, FSU won two National Championships (1993 and 1999); played for three others: (1996,1998 and 2000); finished 14 seasons in Associated Press Top 5; had two Heisman Trophy winners, Charlie Ward and Chris Weinke. Christian Ponder, the 2010 quarterback, is projected as a candidate.

The 1999 national championship team was the first in college football history to go wire to wire as the AP #1 ranked team

Some of the many accomplishments for FSU: Only Division 1-A football team to compile 14 straight 10 win seasons (1987-2000); Two consensus National Championships: (1993 and 1999); NCAA record with 11 consecutive bowl victories (1985-1995) and 14 straight bowl trips without a loss; 31 bowl appearances in 34 seasons.; the highest percentage for winning bowl games; 28 straight bowl games-longest record in the county; and two Heisman Trophy winners: Charlie Ward and Chris Weinke.

Many FSU players play/played for the NFL; many received National Awards; many are coaches.

Submitted and written by: Mary J. Marchant 2901 Springfield Drive; Tallahassee, FL 32309-3274 ; Sources: The Tallahassee Democrat and Judge Jim Joanos' article in The Tallahassee Democrat, 8-9-09 entitled "How FSU Football Got Its Beginning"; Unconquered, Fall 2009 Seminole- Boosters.com; Bobby: Our Coverage of a Legend Presented by The Tallahassee Democrat

Florida State Football and Mickey Andrews

Mickey Andrews, Defensive Coordinator of 26 seasons with the FSU Football team, is a sports icon in his own right.

His awards and accomplishments are extraordinary. He coached top ranked defenses, had scores of All American and All ACC players, 18 first-round NFL draft selections, two National Titles and 12 Atlantic Coast Conference top teams. It was through the efforts of Coach Andrews that helped FSU earn two national titles.

Coach Andrews was hired on Feb. 10, 1984, and retired on the same date in 2009·

He was never one to seek the spotlight, deferring instead to credit others-to Coach Bowden, his assistant coaches and the players.

"Andrews, 68, was the architect of defenses that powered Florida State to 14 consecutive top-five finishes in the Associated Press poll (1987-2000), and head coach Bobby Bowden has said he deserves much credit for the Seminoles' national championships in 1993 and '99."

"Under Andrews, Florida State led the nation in pass defense in 1998 and the Seminoles were NO.1 against the run in 1996 and 1997."

His tenure at FSU produced 46 Associated Press All Americans and 17 Consensus All Americans. He has produced 73 NFL draft picks with 18 of those selected in the first round.

Five of his many awards include: Frank Broyles' Top Assistant Coach, 1996; National Assistant Coach,1991, 2000; National Defensive Coordinator, 1998; Top ranked total defense and passing defense, 1998; and won 5 national championships as player (3, Alabama) and coach (2, FSU).

Written and Submitted by: Mary J. Marchant, 2901 Springfield Drive, Tallahassee, FL 32309-3274; Source: Unconquered Magazine, Fall, 2009

Godby High School

Godby High School, located in the Northwestern part of Leon County and Tallahassee is a 9-12 comprehensive high school. The school had 1,265 students enrolled for the 2009- 2010 school year.

Godby HS began with the1966-67 school year, and opened as a Junior-Senior High School. The campus was shared with Tallahassee Junior College. O. D. Roberts was the first principal. The first graduating class was in 1969-70 after the building was completed.

The namesake for Godby HS was Mr. Amos P. Godby, a beloved teacher, coach, chairman of legislative committees, County Superintendent and President and Secretary of the Florida Superintendents Association. He launched an extensive building program for Leon County Schools while Superintendent. He worked tirelessly all over the state of Florida to improve education.

Godby High School's vision statement: "an engaging, safe and respectful learning environment that embraces change and produces high academic achievers who appreciate diversity and become conscientious contributors to our society."

Amos P. Godby

Godby HS is the ESOL Service Center in the county and is a Title I school.

Godby has excelled in Athletics. The Athletic Dept. holds 12 Team State Championships: 3 in football; 1 in weightlifting; 1 in girl's basketball; 1 in 5A boy's 4x100m; 4 in boys' track; 1 in baseball; and 1 in 2A girl's 4x400m. Godby's students also hold 18 Individual State Champions, 1 in wrestling and the rest in track.

Godby also has the following: National Art Honor Society; National Honor Society; National Spanish Honor Society; Anime; Drama; Gospel Choir; Invisible Children; KEY; SADD; SEA; SGA; SWAT; Brain Bowl; FBLA; History Fair and Science Fair.

Submitted by Mary J. Marchant 1717 West Tharpe Street, Tallahassee, FL 32303-4441; Source: Godby HS Web Site

Leon High School

Leon High School has celebrated 100 years of educating students in Leon County: 1827 to

Second Leon High School, built in 1911

2007. Leon High School's early beginnings started with the Leon Academy for Boys in 1827.

In 1903 Leon High School became the first public high school in Leon County. It was built on the corners of Duval, Tennessee, and Bronough. In 1911 the second Leon High School was built where the LeRoy Collins Leon County Public Library currently stands. And the third location is the present one, on East Tennessee Street. It is Florida's oldest continuously accredited high school.

The present building was constructed by the WPA. Much controversy arose over the size and cost of the building and being too far out of town.

Leon High is steeped in history, and the thousands of graduates have passed along Leon's traditions to their children and grandchildren.

Current Leon High School

This sense of community thrives as graduates return to the school as multigenerational students and teachers.

Some well known graduates are actresses Faye Dunaway (1958) and Cheryl Hines (1983); Legislator and Governor LeRoy Collins (1926) and Legislator Herbert Morgan (1961). Other elected officials include Willie Meggs (1961) and Sheriff Larry Campbell (1961). Carrie Englert Zimmerman (1975) is the first Olympian in gymnastics. Graduates include prominent citizens in many fields, including law, education, science, mathematics, and engineering locally and globally. A Grand Reunion was held in 1987.

A Grand Reunion 2 in 2007 was highlighted with a Broadway-style production with dance choreography, singing, drama, band, and chorus depicting each decade.

Leon HS continues to be an exemplary school academically, with volunteerism, social and character development and responses to current events influencing the lives of the student body.

Submitted by Mary J. Marchant; 2901 Springfield Drive Tallahassee, FL 32309-3274; Source: Tallahassee Magazine article, "The Grand Reunion 2," March, April 2007. By permission.

South City School, a/k/a Leonard Wesson School

South City School (desegregated), at Orange Avenue and South Meridian Street was for elementary students from Woodville and Crawfordville Highways, Springhill Road up to FSU stadium, and the Menlo Park neighborhood at Perkins, South Meridian, and South Monroe Streets.

Basic Reading, English, Math, Science, Social Studies, Music, and Physical Education were taught. With reading and English skills drummed into students, they could learn anything else. Using "ain't" for isn't or aren't was not tolerated. They could communicate, because everyone pronounced words the same, not however they felt sounded "cool".

Discipline was expected. Teachers could whack students' butts with a ruler and the only thing hurt was feelings. Troubled and troubling students were sent to the Principal's office for discipline, but they survived and became some of Tallahassee's most responsible workers, contributors to our economy, and soldiers in our military.

Children walked miles to and from school. Air conditioning was nonexistent, and when children returned from the playground, the classroom odor was awful.

Coaches Carter and McElwee, and a lady coach taught softball, kickball, loop tennis, tetherball, and dodge ball, amongst other sports and games. Earlier grades played Red Rover, Drop the Handkerchief, and Ring Around the Rosy.

Ruby Wilder and Dotty McPherson performing an "Adagio" Act at SouthCity School

Coaches organized a school circus -- Dotty McPherson and Ruby Wilder performed an "adagio" act with boy partners for the circus. The school had seasonal plays for which Kay Laing and Dotty played their ukuleles and sang.

In class, Mrs. McKenzie taught children to not smoke and Mrs. Guerry taught Spanish. After school, tumbling lessons were taught, and Girl and Boy Scouts and other school clubs met. It was a fabulous school.

Leonard Wesson is now closed and is used for the R.N. Gooden/Nancy Russell Center at Wesson for pre-school early childhood education
Submitted and Written by Dorothy Lee "Dotty" McPherson, 24236 Lanier Street Tallahassee, FL 32310

Strickland School: 1888-1950

Our great-great grandfather, Gillum Blount Strickland, moved with his family from North Carolina in the early 1800s. He married Mary Jane Hall of Thomas County, Georgia, and they settled in Leon County where they not only raised their family, but on May 22, 1888, deeded one acre of land to the Board of Public Instruction for a school to be built. This rural school would be known as the "Strickland School", School Number 15. Little did he know that not only his grandchildren and his great grandchildren would attend the school, but also his great-great-grandchildren. I was one of those along with my brother Ralph and four cousins, Tommy, Pleas, Mary Alice, and Edward.

Picnic on the last day of school, June 6, 1950

In 1906, Strickland School was one of two rural schools for white children in Leon County. The teacher earned $30.00 a month. In 1908, the school received a new roof, ceiling paint job, and two water closets (out houses), and in 1924, the school received a new cypress shingle roof. The Strickland School is still standing, but is now located on private property and unfortunately, without funds and proper documentation has not been repaired or recognized as an historical structure. In June 1950, the school was Leon County's last single room school to close. On that day, a picnic was held at the school honoring the many students who had attended the school. On June 6, 1950, the *Tallahassee Democrat* ran an article featuring Mrs. Louise Strickland with the last seven students standing on the steps of the school – it was and educational landmark ceasing to be after 62 years. Four of the pictured students were great grandchildren of Gillum Blount and Mary Jane Strickland.

Today's archives tell the story of a small one-room school house with a pot belly stove used to warm the room in winter, a pump that supplied water (after much pumping), outdoor sanitation facilities and a row of cedar trees planted with the help of our grandfather, T.P. Strickland, Jr., a student at the time. School Board Minutes reveal teacher names like J.A. Hendry, Mattie Billingly, M.H. Miller, Agnes Apthorp, C.J. Crutcher, Julia Brown, Belle Brown, Pauline Costa, Julia Lice, Audrey Maxwell, Ellen Coe and last, but not least, Louise Strickland, wife of Great Uncle Will. She began teaching at the school in February 1921 and continued until the close of school in 1950. At that time, she became a substitute teacher, then retired in 1951.

From early 1900 Teacher's Daily Registers, I found not only the name of my mother, Louise, but also her siblings, Blanche, Jean, Horace and Pleasant; also listed was our grandfather's nephew, Blount, Jr. After discovering the registers (class rolls), I contacted Aunt Blanche, our only living aunt with the news. As I read her the name of each student, she began telling me who was kin to whom. Who they married and who their children were. It was like reliving some of those school days years ago. Some of the family names listed on the registers were: Harrison, Sessions, Blair, Poppell, Coe, Hardwick, Houch, Davis, Greens, Hyatt, Rhodes, Griffin, Dickie, Bannerman, Wilder, Mitchell, Johnson, Collins, Lee, Carter, and of course Strickland. Many descendants from these families still call Leon County their home. Aunt Blanche remembers the days when the school was used for 4-H meetings, as well as a place to have fund raisers. One such fund raiser was for the local men's baseball team. The team played against teams from surrounding Florida and Georgia communities. Some of the games were played in my grandfather's pasture, just up the road fro the school. Sometimes due to rainy weather, church meetings would be held at the school. The clay road to the church was quite

Inside classroom – Edward Strickland, Ed Harrison, Herbie Carter, Pleas Strickland, Mrs. Strickland (teacher), Mary Alice Collins, Elvie Carter, and Tommy Collins.

hilly and could be very slippery after a hard rain. One might say the school building served many purposes for the rural community.

As a third grade student, I remember my cousins and I studying our lessons outside beneath one of the big oak trees while Aunt Weese taught some of the other students (she taught grades 1 through 6). George Washington's Birthday was always a special day. Aunt Weese would read the story about George Washington chopping down the cherry tree while we munched on her freshly baked hatchet shaped sugar cookies. Then there was the day I decided to file my nails during the class. Aunt Weese was quick to inform me that young ladies did not groom themselves in public. Once a year, the public health nurse would come out to give us our shots. One such day, one student decided to hide under the school, only to have a couple of the other boys pull him out just in time to get his shots. During recess we would play games and sometimes pass notes to each other (we were not allowed to do so during class). One, I vividly recall was passed to my cousin that said, "I love you better than a pig loves slop". We still laugh about that to this day. After all we did live in a rural community.

I now wonder if our great-great-grandparents ever realized the outstanding contribution they were making to the Leon County educational system by donating that one acre of land to the Board of Public Instruction for a school 120 years ago.

Submitted by: Mary Helen Fraser, 2981 Killearn Point Court, Tallahassee, FL 32312

LEON COUNTY LOCAL LANDMARKS

Centennial Field

Centennial Field hosted high school football games and semi-pro baseball games. East Bloxham and South Monroe Street and the railroad track bordered it. Folks parked in a huge lot with pecan trees west of South Monroe Street, entering from South Adams and East Bloxham Streets, then walked through a tunnel to the baseball stadium. The lot was always full for frequent ballgames – probably because there was no television.

Just east of Centennial Field was the city incinerator, a dog pound, three giant round gas storage tanks, and the Curb Market where fresh fruits and vegetables were sold Wednesdays and Saturdays. Such markets are all around Tallahassee now; but everything at Centennial Field is gone.

Elmer R. McPherson, an avid sports fan, took his only child Dotty to practically every semi-pro baseball game at Centennial Field. They would sit right behind the home base. If she was not eating peanuts and drinking Coca-Cola, she stood at the fence. It did not matter which team was playing. Whoever was pitching, she yelled for. She would yell, "Eh-eh-eh-eh-el, SWING!" and it worked lots of times.

Elmer also took Dotty to the Leon High School football games at Centennial Field. (He attended Leon when it was located where the Leon County Library now stands.) Dotty would follow Leon Women's Coach Eloise Batchelor and cheer with her cheerleaders. Elmer followed his friends handling the chains. They did the same at FSU football games, with Dotty chasing the cheerleaders at either side of the wooden benches on which the football players sat during their game. Those wooden benches are gone, too.

Written and Submitted by Dorothy Lee "Dotty" McPherson, 24236 Lanier Street Tallahassee, FL 32310

Centennial Field/Cascades Park

In 1824 a surveying company had camped at the foot of a thirty foot waterfall when they came to make the old fields of Tallahassee the new state capital, and the field was renamed "Cascades Park" to commemorate the waterfall. Eventually, proximity to human habitation degraded the sinkhole the waterfall fell into until it was finally filled in as the city dump in the 1930s. Centennial Field was built in the 1920s, surrounded by a limestone wall. My wife and I lived in the house her father had built in 1940 just over the hill, and I rode my bicycle down Gadsden through the park each day to the University and then to work. On the other side of Gadsden Street was the red brick building with the high arched windows and windows that opened like doors. Originally built to house the cities utilities, at this point in time it was used as a repository for state records.

Cascades Park

Some time during the elapsed years all of the structures had been removed from the field and the property lay vacant and overgrown, but still open. The state had accepted the land from the city in the late 1960s, the city being partially motivated to dispose of the property due to a dawning awareness of pollution and the costs a cleanup would incur. It has only been rumored that the state considered building a matching parking garage to the one they had built across Monroe Street, on the site of the segregated ball fields known as Ben Bradley Field, on top of Centennial Field to cap the pollution with concrete. It is known though that the grant deeding the land from the city to the state contains the condition that the land could only be used for green space. But experience has demonstrated that the strongest agreements have power behind them. The park had a powerful benefactor in Secretary of State George Firestone. With his support and guidance the state fulfilled the agreement and the land evolved again.

Albert Trull designed the master plan that called for restoring the natural streambed, lining it with limestone rocks, and lush plantings of natural vegetation throughout the park. Unfortunately, the plan became a victim of a common bureaucratic practice of diverting money from the designated project the taxpayers thought they were financing to other under-funded, or, more usually, over-budget projects. The "limestone lined streambed" became a concrete ditch with limestone boulders placed sparingly along the way. The "lush plantings of natural vegetation" were reduced to a few bushes and a single white oak on top of the mound of dirt piled to create a hill for the restored waterway to wind around.

Despite the deprivation of funds that denied the fulfillment of her designed beauty, she was a grand park. A delightful combination of flat open fields for soccer, football or catch, the hill for kite flying or learning to ride a bike or just watch the clouds, and the hidden places where you could lay in the shady seclusion for some serious contemplation. The waterfalls made much more exciting crossing than did the bridges, though the bridges were perfect for playing "Pooh sticks". The cracked granite and limestone of the railroad bed that has skirted the land since the 1840s made a pleasing splash when dropped into the water far below. On the other side of the tracks the water had cut into the hill side of the old city dump, exposing a rusted Model-T rear axle, layers of broken crockery and unidentifiable lumps of rusted metal. We would take our Boxer dog down to the park and stand on top of the hill as the dog ran wide circles around us, with our son taking a smaller inside track in a futile effort to catch him.

It was our park. One neighbor planted a banana tree that was still growing when the reclamation claimed it. Another neighbor proposed to his girlfriend by pouring rye grass seed on the hill side to spell out the words "Kelly Marry Me". For years after they had left the neighborhood the words were still discernable. Children learned to ride bicycles on the slope of the hill by taking advantage of gravity to build. It was our park and few days passed without a visit to it.

Submitted by Robert Olmstead, rolmstead@embarqmail.com

Jail Time

Much of my most significant work and many of my happiest memories are from my years spent in the old Leon County Jail. Two men were responsible for me being there: Senator Robert Williams and Explorer Ponce de Leon. During the 1960s and 70s, "Senator Bob" led a group of prominent Floridians working to solidify and educate the public on our role as the "oldest state". They received legislative funding and a place in the Department of State structure. At the University of Florida, the Florida State Museum was the official repository for the state's Natural Science collections and researches. In Leon County would be the Museum of Florida History and existing history related bureaus. They were to be housed in a building yet to be constructed. Now the Gray Building. Where to house this new enterprise until then? The old Leon County Jail would serve.

Leon County Jail ca. 1937, Image courtesy of the Florida State Archives Photographic Collection

Jim Macbeth was the first Director of the MFH. I was the first Curator. We had worked together at the Museum of Natural History of the Smithsonian Institution. Jim set about building a history team. I set about collecting specimens and artifacts to illustrate Florida's rich, long history. Bob Burke and Mark Driscoll came on to oversee the exhibition program. Kermit Brown and his artisans, who could build anything, produced the exhibits and visual aids. Lynn Rogers and John Locastro could render any concept into an attractive and useful graphic. So could Ed Jonas who could also sculpt like one of the old masters.

Similar "history" working teams crowded into the decaying structure. The archaeologists were the most visible. Especially the underwater crew. Spectacular treasure finds were being found down on the "treasure coast". Our divers ensured that our state would retain its share. A selection has always been exhibited in the museum. The teams surveying the state for historic houses and landmarks, the Bureau of Historic Preservation, joined us. Personally, I then had the rare opportunity to work with my archaeologist brother, Henry.

Every day we met a specialist from another discipline with a new idea. Ross Morell kept us all working together. What a rich environment. The time in jail for us was not just history. It was magic.

Written and submitted by: Thomas G. Baker

Leon County's First Airport

In 1928, the City of Tallahassee purchased 200 acres for its first municipal airport. Local officials named the airport Dale Mabry Field in honor of a Tallahassean, Captain Dale Mabry, son of former Florida Supreme Court Justice, Milton Mabry. The new airport was dedicated on November 11, 1929 and the first manager was Ivan Monroe who gave the first flying lessons on a Travelaire.

Dedication of first airport in Tallahassee, November 1929

The first commercial flight was with Atlantic Gulf Coast Airlines in 1930. By 1938, two more airlines used Dale Mabry Field: Eastern Airlines and National Airlines. Despite being closed to general aviation during WW2, Eastern & National continued to use the field.

In 1941, Mabry Field became an Army base where the Army's 3rd Air Force established a fighter pilot training school and developed 3 runways to serve their needs. African, Chinese, and French-Americans cadets also trained at Dale Mabry Field in 1942 through 1944. The original acres grew to 1,720 acres and 133 buildings during the course of the war. The base became a small town with its own housing, stores, schools, and churches which supported the more than 8,000 pilots trained at Mabry Field base.

Dale Mabry Field from the air in 1941

Mabry Field base was placed on inactive status in 1945, and eventually resumed its role as a civilian airport. When the airfield was transferred from the military to the city, Mabry Field's original hangar was dismantled and moved to St. Marks. Later it was moved to the new Tallahassee Municipal Airport in March of 1949.

Dale Mabry Field was abandoned by 1961 and the property eventually became the home of Tallahassee Community College, Lively Vocational Institute, and a variety of other public & private businesses and homes.

A commemorative plaque designating Dale Mabry Field was erected at the old site in October 2001. In 2003, a sculpture was placed at the New Regional Airport in honor of Dale Mabry Air Field and the pilots who served there. In 2004, a historical marker was placed at the northwest corner of the intersection of Pensacola Street & Appleyard Road. As of 2009 a portion of remaining runway of Mabry Field can be seen near the pavement which now serves as a parking lot for the James Messer Fields Sports Complex and Park.

Written and submitted by: Carol D. Johnson

The People of Dale Mabry Field

Alice Smith Ragsdale was the first base commander's secretary. Lt. Colonel Jacob Wuest, the base commander, hired her direct from secretarial school. Mrs. Ragsdale said, "Colonel Wuest was very protective of me, putting his desk in front of mine so the G.I.s would have to go through him first." She was advised by him to only date officers, not enlisted men. Some of the officers would rent horses to take her to the Silver Slipper, which then was located south of the Capital. Mrs. Ragsdale gave us a picture of Col. Wuest to donate to the Florida State Archives, and it is now on their website, Florida Photographic Collection.

My tapestry had developed nicely with Nick Fallier's help, and was displayed during Airfest 2005, 06, and 07. It received a lot of attention, and many people stopped to share personal stories about their WWII experiences. In the Fall of 2007, I donated it to Devoe Moore's Antique Car Museum along with a brief history of the field and Nick Fallier's article, "Reflections of Dale Mabry Air Field."

The experimental Airplane Association EAA445 group, wishing to honor those who served at Dale Mabry Field, during Airfest 2008 gave awards to Mrs. Ragsdale, Nick Fallier, and Mallory Horne. We took pictures and a video of this occasion.

While writing this article we learned that Mrs. Ragsdale passed away. She was a fine and gracious southern lady, and we enjoyed our many visits with her.

Submitted by: Lois Decoteau, ldecot@comcast.net

Reflections of Dale Mabry Field

During our many trips to and from our home, I could see remnants of cement steps leading to nowhere and cement foundations along the railroad tracks beside Roberts Avenue. I was always curious as to how the base was situated in comparison to today's street, homes and businesses.

Lake Bradford Sector Planning meetings then came about in which many questions arose as to what land might have been used by the military during the World War II years at Dale Mabry base. A friend, whom we shall call G.B., developed into our research assistant and found the Dale Mabry maps, and through phone calls made contacts with people who were instrumental. One of G.B.'s contacts was Mr. Nick Fallier, surveyor and engineer for renovations at Dale Mabry Field.

These maps enticed me into tracing them onto fabric in my effort to discover where the buildings were in reference to today's places. In our interviews with Nick Fallier, he described how the air field was camouflaged to deter any enemy flights from seeing the straight lines of the runways. We went for tours of the former Dale Mabry area, and he pointed out to us where the guard shack was. The guard shack possibly may have been the old building at the corner of Jackson Bluff and Mabry. He said while in the process of surveying for the runways, someone was test firing from a plane and almost hit his head. After he heard the ZOOM ZOOM, he turned around and looked for the spent shell casing that almost did him in. He has it in his military collection. He made mention of incidents of Chinese pilots crashing. Nick Fallier was a man of many titles: surveyor, pilot, game warden, scuba diver, treasure hunter, military collector.

Submitted by Richard Decoteau, ldecot@comcast.net

The Bomb in the Backyard

In March 1990, my husband and I, along with our two sons, purchased a house on Rankin Avenue. The weather that week was warm and the azaleas were in abundant bloom on our 2 acres of land. The fragrance from all these flowering trees and bushes added to the joy of our newly acquired home. It was quite invigorating to be outside in the clean air raking up leaves and pine straw.

My husband, Richard, and oldest son John started early in the day raking around the house. After about an hour, John spotted a black helmet under the bushes next to the house, and he called his father over to take a look. Peering under the bushes, Richard saw something else. About a foot from the helmet, and in very close proximity to the south side of the house, was what appeared to be the fins of an aerial bomb. Yes, a bomb!

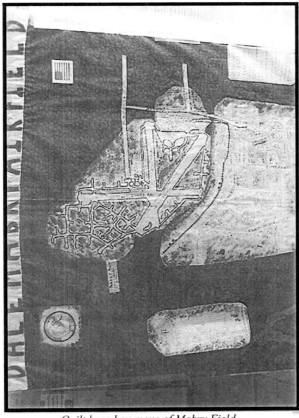

Quilt based on maps of Mabry Field

Richard's first thought was that the former owner's children may have been playing with a prank bomb and left it behind, so he called, expecting to hear "oh, that ol' thing, sorry about that." But this was not the case he knew nothing about it! Oh-oh. We had no choice but to call the police. When the officers arrived, Richard showed them the bomb.

Police examine a bomb found in the backyard of a home near Dale Mabry Field

The officer leaned down to look, then said he'd have to call his sergeant. The sergeant came, looked, and said he'd have to call his supervisor. The supervisor came, looked, then called the bomb squad. The bomb squad came with a special container, and the family had to evacuate the house while the experts removed the bomb. Curious, I asked where the bomb had come from, and an officer replied "Dale Mabry Field."
Submitted by Richard and Lois Decoteau,
ldecot@comcast.net

Remnants of Dale Mabry Airfield

A 2004 photo by Richard Travis shows the historical markers of Dale Mabry Airfield at the northwest corner of the intersection of Pensacola Street & Appleyard Road. Note that the text on the plaque has 2 fairly significant s: the plaque is located on the site of the north/south runway (not the northwest/southeast runway as stated, which is located some distance to the south), and the airfield opened in 1929, whereas the plaque seems to indicate that it was established in 1940. Another photo by Richard Travis shows a portion of remaining runway pavement, which now serves as a parking lot for the Jim Messer Sports Complex.

Some remnants of the runways are still in much evidence. In the northwest corner of the Appleyard Road / Pensacola Street intersection, on the TCC campus (at almost deadcenter of the frame), is a patch of aging pavement, sometimes used for overflow parking, which once was part of the north/south runway. In the 1999 USGS photo, the northsouth road running vertically through the center of the frame is now Appleyard Road, which runs in front of the TCC campus. My calculations indicate that Appleyard Road is virtually superimposed over the north/south runway of the old Dale Mabry Field. This area along Jackson Bluff Road contains a sports complex with numerous ball fields, the 2 circles forming a figure 8. Just to the east of these fields, on the south side of Jackson Bluff, is a fairly large parking area, with aging pavement similar to the TCC patch, commonly understood to be runway remnants, and my figures indicate it was once part of the northwest/southeast diagonal runway.

Craig Hiers reported to Richard; "I grew up on what was the old Dale Mabry Airport. The community we lived in was called Mabry Manor, and all the streets were named after military generals and admirals. The buildings of the elementary school I went to (Sable Palm Elementary) were part of the base.

The site of Mabry Field is located northwest of the intersection of West Pensacola Street & Appleyard Drive. Thanks to Lawrence Sharp (who once flew out of Mabry) for pointing out this airfield to me.
Written and Submitted by: Richard Travis: Photographer Tallahassee, Florida

The "Hump Bridge"

Back when I was in high school (the late Coach Cox was very big in those days so you know it was at least 100 years ago!), my father bought a car for my brother and I to share. It was a 1958 VW convertible and he paid $50.00 for it. Some of you may remember this car. It was in such bad shape we were embarrassed to take a date out in it and tried many times to damage it beyond repair without hurting ourselves or being too obvious.

I could go on and on with anecdotes centered around this vehicle but for the purposes of this story, I will concentrate on our efforts to make it fly. Surely you remember the Park 31 Avenue bridge over the tracks. That's right, "hump bridge". Many is the time we attempted to traverse the bridge at a speed fast enough to launch the VW, usually late at night and usually a little ... well we never did that! Anyway, if you were traveling east to west you could get the speed required but the bridge didn't "jump" right. You had to go west to east, uphill, and only when the moon and stars lined up could the VW make it. Then and only then would there be that half second of hope that when we landed, the wheels would fall off and the car would land with a splat that would finally render it useless forever

As you can guess, it never happened and I would bet that car is still on the road, unlike the "hump bridge", which is gone forever.

Submitted by: John L. Conlin, jconlin@netally.com

Gerrell Memories of Natural Bridge

The children of Walter and Jessie French Gerrell had the wonderful experience of growing up on a farm three miles west of Natural Bridge. With Gerrell grandparents, (George Allen and Minnie Wiggins Gerrell), on the west side, and French grandparents (James Roston and Mary Ann Hall French) on the east side of the St. Marks River, Marilee, Pete, Dale, and Lawson Gerrell knew the history of Natural Bridge very well. We knew that we often would go "over the river" to Granddaddy French's house. Our dad worked with Granddaddy French, who raised cattle, sheep, and hogs. Many long days were spent in the saddle by Granddaddy, Daddy, Pete, Dale, and Lawson, rounding up cattle. We lived with our Gerrell grandparents and Walter also worked with our Granddaddy Gerrell, who raised corn, peas, peanuts, watermelons, and other row crops. There was always good eating at both homes!

Each time we went "over the river", we passed through the Natural Bridge State Park and saw the tall Confederate monument commemorating the April 6, 1865 Battle of Natural Bridge. Being a family who remembered, reminisced, and wrote our family history (to borrow a phrase from our brother, Pete) we well knew our personal connection to this historical site.

Monument at Natural Bridge State Park

Great granddaddy George Edward Gerrell (1833-1878), Kilcrease Light Artillery, was at home ill when the Battle occurred. Getting up from his sickbed, he joined his unit to man his cannon. He was a cannoneer because he was so tall.

Great Granddaddy Lewis Franklin Hall (1844-1900) was in the Fifth Florida. He was home on the east side of the St. Marks River sick with malaria when Union forces came up the river and took him prisoner. They did not want a known Confederate soldier at their back. They returned him to his home when they returned defeated to their ship at the St. Marks Light House.

The Natural Bridge is a nature-formed bridge of limerock under which the St. Marks River flows to emerge on the south side into a series of rises and sinks, after which it rises into a large basin further south to continue onto the Gulf of Mexico.

The battlefield at Natural Bridge was given to Anna Jackson Chapter, UDC, Tallahassee, in March 1922, by our grandparents, James and Mary Ann French "for the purpose of establishing a park and erecting a monument and memorial at the scene of The Battle of Natural Bridge in Leon County, Florida, as contemplated by an act of the Legislature of Florida of 1921....."

The Battle of Natural Bridge was one of the last battles of the War Between the States. Because of the defense by the Confederate soldiers at this small bridge, Tallahassee would be the only Confederate capital not captured by Union forces.

Written by: Dale, Lawson, Terri Gerrell, and Marilee Gerrell Butler, PO Box 65, Calvary, GA 39829; Sources: Deed to Battlefield property, memories of Jessie French Gerrell, Frank French Blackburn, and Authors

Saving the Old Railroad Boarding House

There it towered in front of me - three stories tall, with over 4500 square feet of space!

The roof was a sieve, the porch was falling down and the foundation was askew—to mention a few of its obvious problems! As I stood aghast, I barely heard my son Mark giving all of its historical and architectural merits! "Mom, it is the oldest wooden structure in Tallahassee still on its original foundation. It has a mortise and tenon foundation that goes way back into the 1800s! Look! That is the separate kitchen that has been brought up to the house! The Historic Preservation Board would love to work with us on restoring it, and we could get it on the National Registry of Historic Places!"

Mark and Laura Jean in front of the old railroad boarding house

Well, what could a mother do!? I knew that he could do the work as we had restored our 1920s home in the Myers Park area, and he was planning to major in Historic Preservation. We bought the house from a very elderly couple, who had not been able to keep it up, and we started doing the research to make a plan for restoring the house and getting it on the National Registry.

These plans soon took a sharp detour, when a few months after we had bought the house, the City came out and served us with a condemnation notice! (Found out the house was condemned when we bought it!) We had to go before the Code Board to present a complete , detailed plan with timelines of how we were going to restore the house! Ouch! We hadn't counted on this! We were planning for Mark to live there, go to school, have some friends live with him to help pay for the house and repairs, and even exchange work on the house! Good plan, but not money intensive, like the City wanted!

Anyway, since the house was condemned, his friends couldn't live there, and we were up against a very tight timeline. To stay afloat, it took a lawsuit, and much working with the City. We spent over four of the hardest years of our lives getting the house on the Registry and bringing it up to code as a historic building!

We went to the Florida Archives, put on the little white gloves, and read back through some of the old handwritten ledgers from the Georgia-Pensacola Railroad. We found where Burfoot Williams, the freight agent, had petitioned the Railroad in 1860 to buy the property and dwelling. So the house was there back into the 1850s. They didn't sell it to him at that time, but he came back later and they sold it to him in 1863, during the Civil War. Of interest were notes on sending additional rails to Atlanta to replace the ones the Yankees were tearing up and bending!

With research on the actual house, my son found that it was one of the old "dogtrot" houses of four main rooms and an open hall. The mortise and tenon beams were pegged, no nails, and it was one solid beam from the front to the back of the house, part of the virgin forest of the area! The bricks in the house were made locally, out of a purplish clay, so the bricks had a dark purple hue. The method of baking the bricks was to stack them spirally, and cover and bake. The ones on the inside were baked at a higher temperature, so were stronger and used in the foundation piers and fireplace. The outside bricks were used in steps and paths. Later the hall was closed in, and a second story built on around 1900. This is when a Mrs. Allen bought it and turned it into a boarding house where people coming in on the train would stay. It was the Swan Hotel for awhile, and a third floor was built. It was used for troops coming in on the train during the Second World War, and, finally as boarding house and apartments, until the time that the old couple quit renting space.

My son did a mammoth job of research and work on the house. We may write a book one day! To sum up the story, the last six months before we got it on the Registry and up to code, I had to go in every month to the City Attorney's office with pictures and a process report. Our fines were up to $30,000! At the very end, when we went before the Code Board, we presented a complete picture history of the work, and that it was on the Registry! We had the State Preservation staff, the local Historic Board, FSU Historic Preservation faculty, and an attorney. We were granted compliance and the fines reduced to $200! What a gift after almost 5 years!

We sold the house to a group of architects interested in Historic Preservation and felt very lucky that we could take a deep breath again. So, it was saved! The Old Railroad Boarding House, given the Registry name of the Williams House, still sitting (rather, still towering) at 450 St. Francis Street!

Submitted by: Laura Jean (Kendrick) Huff, with Mark Kendrick, 814 Governors Drive, Tallahassee, FL 32301

Taking the Bus to Wakulla Springs

Two interstate bus lines operated out of Tallahassee: Greyhound and Trailways. Not everyone had one automobile, certainly not two. Relatives, from afar, road buses to Tallahassee and vice versa for extended visits. During the late 1940s-early 50s, Trailways provided day-trips to Wakulla Springs.

Besides crystal-clear, icy-cold water and virgin forests drawing folks, Wakulla Springs drew movie makers, including the first, and two more, Tarzan movies starring Olympic Gold-medalist-swimmer Johnny Weissmuller.

Scenic view at Edward Ball Wakulla Springs State Park in 2007

At the Springs, everyone swam, sunned on the platforms, jumped off the tower, and rode the glass bottom boat or the jungle cruise. A bulbous tank sat in the water off the side of the dock, whereby one climbed down the ladder to see underwater. A jukebox was in the outside part of the bathhouses, and everyone would dance barefoot on the cement in their bathing suits when they got tired of the water. A great old fashioned gift shop was in Ed Ball's hotel (1937), where they sold scoops of ice cream in cones.

The swimming area was not fenced off from the main water body, nor from the river. Alligators, abundant and huge and naturally afraid of humans, kept their distance. One time, however, a very large alligator swam within about 50 yards of the platforms. Lifeguards began blowing whistles and running swimmers out of the water. Another official jumped into a motorboat and ran off the seemingly fearless alligator. It was an exciting day at the springs that day.

Today, one must drive, ride bikes, or motorcycles, or hire a ride to get to Wakulla Springs.

Written and Submitted by Dorothy Lee (Dotty) McPherson, 24236 Lanier St., Tallahassee, FL 32310

Tallahassee's Water Works Wonders

During the period from 1880 through 1906, Tallahassee Water Works Plant was controlled by a private company. On August 13, 1907 voters approved a $25,000 bond issuance for the City to construct its own Water Works Plant, and the city council passed an ordinance declaring the City of Tallahassee create, construct and put into operation a Water Works Plant. By 1908 the city had constructed Tallahassee's first Water Works Plant. The 1919 legislature passed a new city charter for Tallahassee authorizing a Commission-Manager form of government for the Water Utility System, and by 1923 Tallahassee Water Utility added five new wells to the plant. In 1933 the first elevated tank was constructed at Lafayette Park and held 400,000 gallons of water. Presently, Well #2 is the oldest well still in operation since 1939. The Water Works Utility Plant has grown to its current status of 28 deep water wells pumps.

The Tram Road Reuse Facility (TRRF) provides recycled water for irrigation to conserve drinking water. The T.P. Smith Water Reclamation Facility reduces the nitrogen released into the environment. The Floridan Aquifer runs directly underneath the city and provides a pristine and dependable source of drinking water. The Tallahassee Water Works Utility goal has been to provide high quality water to its residents; they achieved this goal by following strict federal laws from the EPA and the FDA, who monitors water contaminants.

In celebration of their 100 years in operation, Tallahassee's Water Works won the 2008 American Water Association's "Best Drinking Water" for the State of Florida Award. In retrospect, Tallahassee's Water Works continues to work wonders

Written and submitted: Carol D. Johnson

LEON COUNTY ORGANIZATIONS

GFWC Woman's Club of Tallahassee

The Woman's Club of Tallahassee was formed in 1903 by six women who met at the Leon Hotel, today the site of the Federal Court House. They were Miss Anna S. Chaires, Mrs. T. M Shackleford, Mrs. George Davis, Mrs. Howard Gamble, Mrs. Charles Cay and Mrs. A. L. Randolph.

Community activists, the Club persuaded city officials to screen the city market, place sidewalks on Monroe Street, improve the railroad station, plant trees and keep the cemetery in order.

Education being a high priority, the Club successfully campaigned to raise taxes for construction of Leon High School. In 1910 Leon High School was built facing Park Ave between Bronough and Duval Streets.

In 1920, feeling the need for a Clubhouse and with the advent of the automobile, sites in the country were considered, and Los Robles, then known as "The Oaks" was chosen. Two developers, Lonnbladh and Thornton, gave the Woman's Club two of the lots on which the Clubhouse stands today. Architect E. D. Fletcher drew the plans and it was completed April 19, 1927. The Clubhouse has been used as a center of the community since. In 1987 it was listed on the National Register of Historical Places.

The Woman's Club organized the Junior Woman's Club, May, 1935, with 50 young women.

One notable project among many was the retrieval by members of old Florida documents stored in the old jail, some of which originated in the 1920s! During World War II the American Red Cross used the Clubhouse to roll surgical bandages, sew garments and whatever was needed. The Woman's Club of Tallahassee helped landscape the approach to the Capitol, working in cooperation with Malcolm Johnson, then editor of the *Tallahassee Democrat*, to obtain donated plants for the beautification of the then new Apalachee Parkway. The State Road Department provided a crew to assist in planting.

Many community projects too numerous to list were undertaken by the Woman's Club in decades that followed. Old documents, stored and forgotten by the State of Florida in the Old Jail, were retrieved by several Club members who sorted and identified each document. Some of the documents originated in the 1820s! Another project involved the Club's participation for restoration of the Union Bank Building in 1980-82.

In 1987, The Clubhouse was first listed on the National Register of Historical Places and remains there today: The Woman's Club provided free use of the Clubhouse and monetary donations for fund raising activities for the March of Dimes, Mother's March Walkathon and Leon Chapter of American Cancer Society.

The Club provides scholarships for women over 30 returning to school; gives a high school student a scholarship to attend Hugh O'Brian Youth Leadership Conference; supports Hacienda Girls' Ranch, Habitat for Humanity, and Boys Choir of Tallahassee.

The Clubhouse was restored with a $300,000 historical preservation grant. Intensive fundraising to match the grant was begun. The Club participated in the restoration of the historic gateway to Los Robles neighborhood.

The Club had fundraisers for Refuge House, PACE Center for Girls, Brehon House, Girl Scouts, Jazz Jams in schools, Big Bend Community Based Care, and literacy in schools.

Submitted by: Mary J. Marchant, 2901 Springfield Drive, Tallahassee, FL 32309-3274; Source: Woman's Club Yearbook, 2008-2009

Iota Chapter, Delta Kappa Gamma Society International

Iota Chapter was the ninth chapter of the Delta Kappa Gamma Society International to be organized in Florida. Plans to form a chapter were fostered by several members living in Tallahassee, by Dr. Norma Smith Bristow, and by Dr. Annie Webb Blanton, Society Founder. The chapter was organized in 1942 by Lois Morse, Mu State President, Boletha Frojen and Mary Woodberry, Mu State Founders, and Mrs. Edna Simmons Campbell, a Founder of Zeta State Mississippi.

The first formal meeting was held February 7, 1942 at the Cherokee Hotel in Tallahassee. The 13 charter members were: by transfer - Lois

Morse, Boletha Frojen, Mary Woodberry, Mrs. Edna Campbell, Joyce Pritchard, Eula Mae Snyder, Clarine Belcher; by initiation - Grace Fox, Sara Krentzman, Daisy Parker, Florence Tryon, Mrs. Maxine Putnam, and Dora Skipper. Later that year Anna Mae Sikes, Mrs. Evelyn Messer, and Martha Chapman were initiated.

Meetings were usually held at the homes of members, since all lived in Tallahassee. Initiations were held in the Faculty Lounge in the Longmire Building, Florida State College for Women.

An annual feature was the Christmas party. Honored guests included nurses from Dale Mabry Hospital, and, in 1944, 64 FSCW students who held legislative scholarships. From the beginning Iota Chapter "promoted liberal thinking in diversified programs involving all aspects of education, and the list of Iota members who have won recognition in their line is impressive."

Four other chapters have been formed from Iota: Alpha Kappa, Alpha Lambda, Beta Phi, and Gamma Eta. Iota chapter continues to support the purposes of the Delta Kappa Gamma Society International with enthusiasm, and honors the dedication of their founders.

Submitted by Dalene McGlocklin, President, Iota Chapter (mcglocd@fairpoint.net), and Donna Heald, Beta Phi Chapter, based on an article first published in the Florida Delta Kappa Gamma Bulletin, May, 1946

Jacques LeMoyne, Tallahassee Naturally

Since the time of the Indians, people skinny-dipped in the sinkholes and ponds south of Tallahassee. Jacques LeMoyne, namesake of the local art center, sketched a family wading to an island picnic over near Jacksonville as early as 1564, nearly 450 years of documented natural freedom in Florida. Swimsuits weren't even invented until the late 1860s.

College streaking and skinny-dipping grew into popular local activities in the 1970s. But when police began harassing swimmers, Tallahassee Naturally organized in 1986 (at first under the name Tallahassee Bare-Devils.) In 1990, the club rented a beautiful lake and woods near Monticello, open on weekends, where an estimated 4,000 people have experienced being at one with nature.

Tallahassee Naturally is a volunteer-run club that operates by consensus. As active citizens, group members evaluate political candidates, and have testified in many hearings before the state legislature. The club publishes the "Naturists: Upholders of Strong Family Values," distributed to state and local government officials across the country.

Year after year, the club has maintained about a 15% college student membership, the highest of any nudist organization in the nation. The annual College Greek Athletic Meet is the world's only authentic re-enactment of the ancient

A family crossing a river; a painting (after) Jacques LeMoyne probably by DeBry

pentathlon, and has become the oldest continuing nude college event in the U.S. Full-Moon Skinny-Dips during the warm months also attracts a younger crowd. The club maintains the high standards of both the American Association for Nude Recreation and The Naturist Society.

Written and Submitted by: Paul LeValley, paulevalley@peoplepc.com

Leon County's Search and Rescue Pilot

Jack Clayton Rosenau was born October 26, 1919 in Detroit Michigan. He served on active duty in the Marine Corps from 1940 to 1946. In 1964, he earned his private pilot license in Hawaii. Jack moved to Tallahassee, Florida in 1970 and brought with him his Cherokee 140 Aircraft. In 1974, he joined the U.S. Coast Guard Auxiliary (a volunteer organization), which supplies the manpower to the Coast Guard Search and Rescue squad.

Over a span of more than 30 years, Jack flew

Jack Clayton Rosenau in front of his aircraft in 2003

550 coastal patrols over the Gulf Islands and inland. This includes more than 100 marine environmental protection flights and 60 search and rescue missions in support of the Coast Guard Air Station, New Orleans. Jack was an invaluable resource to the Coast Guard and dedicated servant to the communities along the Gulf Coast, often responding to search and rescue cases hours before the Coast Guard aircraft could arrive on the scene.

Jack no longer pilots his plane, instead giving the plane to one of his five sons to continue in what has become a family tradition of fliers. Jack received an award from the U.S. Coast Guard for his many years of service to Leon County and other Florida counties.

Written and Submitted by: Jack Rosenau, 1177 Old Fort Drive, Tallahassee, FL 32301

Claude Sauls/Sauls-Bridges American Legion Post 13

The Claude Sauls American Legion Post 13, Tallahassee, was chartered by The American Legion June 9, 1919, granted on the recommendation of the State Organization. Captain R. A. Gray was first commander of Post 13.

It was initially designated the Claude Sauls American Legion Post after Tallahassee citizen Claude L. Sauls, the first Tallahassee resident to be killed in World War I.

Articles of Incorporation, signed by Judge E. C. Love on December 11, 1924, listed the then current members of Post 13, many of whom are familiar throughout Tallahassee's 20th Century history. Buildings, parks, and streets in Tallahassee and Leon County bear their names.

One explanation about how Post 13 became designated is that 13 was the Leon County numerical designation when automobile license plates were first issued in the State of Florida.

A more colorful tale relates that, as members from around the state were on the train to their first caucus in Bal Harbour (1919), they were claiming post numbers starting with Number 1. "Bidding" for designations was said to be fast and furious until "12" was taken. Into the ensuing silence Tallahassee Commander Bob Gray, who was then Secretary of State for Florida, reportedly commented, "Hell! Hardly anything ever goes right in Tallahassee. We'll take '13'!" And the rest, as they say, is history

Members met twice a month. One meeting they held at the county courthouse. Another meeting was at the Busy Bee Cafe. The proprietor said it was all very well and good for the group to meet in the cafe, but members must buy dinner whenever they met. It

American Legion Cannon Presentation, Tallahassee

was agreed and the dinner meeting started then and continues today on the fourth Thursday each month.

In 1922 the Claude L. Sauls American Legion Post 13 purchased a lot at Duval and Call Streets to erect a Post Home. Funds could not be raised for construction.

Members of American Legion Post 13 in 1945

While Post 13 accumulated funds to build in 1924, William Anderson laid the foundation for a dance pavilion, and later abandoning the project, William and wife Alice gave the Post the land with the dance pavilion foundation, deeding the property to the Post on June 28, 1930.

In 1923 Guy Winthrop, head of a committee consisting of K.J. Boyd, O.J. Nettles, Theo Proctor, Sam Wahnish, George Martin, William Galt, Bill Cates, Bill Wilson and Miller Walston, considered obtaining materials for the Post Home. Construction was possibly from 1925 to 1927.

Architect Al Moore designed a structure to fit the existing foundation which partially exists today.

The "acquisition committee" and other Legionnaires did all the work and the little money in the bank was used for necessities only.

After World War II the name was changed to Sauls-Bridges Post 13 honoring the first Tallahassee citizen, Ben H. Bridges, Jr., who died in a fighter plane on coastal patrol in California.

Syde Deeb and his wife Angie, active Legion and Auxiliary members, deeded land in the subdivision to the Post, with all property around the north shore of Lake Ella belonging to Post 13 and loaning the Post $7,500 for improvements.

In the 1950s, the Veterans Lounge, now Black Dog Cafe, a tenant business nestled in the southwest corner of the building, was added, providing a favorite gathering place for many Tallahassee citizens.

The Post Home is where many citizens recall attending sock hops, junior-senior proms, bingo, weddings, fireworks on the 4th of July and other special occasions on Lake Ella. The Tallahassee Board of Historic Preservation granted provisional approval of the site as an historic landmark in 2001.

Revitalization of Lake Ella and the surrounding park by the City of Tallahassee increased the walking traffic around the lake, enhancing local awareness of the Post Home.

Written by: Victor B. Hanna, U.S. Coast Guard, Historian, Post 13 from written records in the Post archives, records on file at Leon County and in the State Archives in the R. A. Gray Building; Condensed and Submitted by: Dorothy Lee "Dotty" McPherson (Relative of the Claude L. Sauls family) 24236 Lanier Street Tallahassee, FL 32310 and Mary J. Marchant

The Tallahassee Literary Club

Founded in 1899 by a group of friends, the Tallahassee Literary Club is the city's oldest, continuously meeting women's organization. This group of women, constitutionally limited to 25, has always existed in pursuit of knowledge of art, literature and science through books. In its earliest days members chose a topic of common interest and studied it through books and hour-long programs, each woman taking her turn in presenting information. Still meeting twice a month November through April, as the founders did, the club now hears two book reviews of works self-selected by members at each meeting, with occasional presentations by local authors or bibliophiles. Since 1899 more than 225 women have belonged to this club.

Initially, near neighbors in tiny Tallahassee members met in each other's homes. Given the changes in city size and life style of members it is now often more convenient to meet in one of several public venues. In all other ways, however, tradition is honored. Meetings are strictly limited to one afternoon hour with two twenty-minute book reviews and twenty minutes of club business. No food is served except at significant anniversary celebrations. The annual dues are still one dollar per member. Even in this small group parliamentary procedure is observed and members address or refer to each other formally. Over the years the Tallahassee Literary Club has donated books to local libraries and money to various charitable causes. It continues, however, to emphasize the sharing of knowledge among friends through books as its major activity. Complete Club archives are located in Special Collections, Strozier Library, Florida State University.

Submitted by: Mrs. Martha Jane Zachert, Club Archivist, 4436 Meandering Way, Apartment 108, Tallahassee, FL 32308

The Tallahassee Museum of Natural History

At the Tallahassee Museum, time slips, allowing visitors to step back two centuries to days when the piney woods and swamps of north Florida were inhabited by Florida panthers and the most important labor-saving device on the homestead was a mule.

The Tallahassee Museum, founded as the Tallahassee Junior Museum in October 1958, brings to life the cultural heritage and natural environment of the Red Hills region. It was begun in the late 1950s when a group of visionary educators and interested citizens saw

1958 Board Members Fran Fokes, Betty McCord, Mary Russell Cresap and Ruth Henderson, on the porch of the Museum's original downtown location, the McMillan house, 104 Madison Street

a need for children to enjoy hands-on experiences while learning about wildlife, nature, history, culture and other countries and customs. They worked tirelessly to meet this need and established the Tallahassee Junior Museum, chartered on July 24, 1957. Early supporting organizations included the Service League (now Junior League of Tallahassee), the Leon County School Board, the Association for Childhood Education, and the National Foundation for Junior Museums (now Natural Science for Youth Foundation).

Kay Nunez, Dan Branch and Jim Ballard review plans in 1960 for the Museum's present location, at 3945 Museum Drive, along Lake Bradford

Fifty years later, the Tallahassee Museum is thriving and growing, constantly finding new ways to present its timeless lessons to people of all ages, encouraging them to care for their natural world and value the role of history in their lives. Visitors can take leisurely walks through the 1880s working farmstead, which includes a farmhouse, a commissary, a blacksmith forge, a gristmill, live farm animals, a garden cultivated in the ways of yesteryear, and much more. This historical scene is brought to life by "living history" folk artists who dress in period clothing and demonstrate skills such as butter-making, spinning, sewing, hearth cooking, syrup making, and blacksmithing.

The Museum's other historical structures include 19th century Bellevue plantation house, former home of Princess Murat, which is on the National Register of Historic Places; the 1897 one-room Concord schoolhouse; the 1937 Bethlehem Missionary Baptist Church, built by a congregation founded in 1850; a 1924 Seaboard Air Line caboose; and a 1919 Model T that still runs like a top. Natural and cultural history are further displayed in the Museum's exhibit areas, including the Phipps Gallery for temporary and traveling exhibits, the Fleischmann Natural Science Building for temporary exhibits, and the Discovery Center, presenting hands-on science activities.

The Museum's "Wildlife Florida" exhibit provides breezy, elevated boardwalks from which visitors view indigenous animals living in natural habitats. These include endangered species such as Florida panthers and red wolves, as well as black bears, river otters, birds of prey, alligators, and various snakes, turtles and tortoises. Over the decades, the Museum has proudly contributed to endangered species recovery efforts, delighting staff and the community by having litters of panthers and wolves born to the rare animals in its care.

Submitted by Laura Cassels, Tallahassee Museum
www.tallahasseemuseum.org

Tallahassee Power Squadron Sextant

Power Squadron is an elite group of individuals who believe in safe boating through education, civic service, and having fun on the water. Power Squadron Recognition Levels are Awarded grades given to its members to indicate how far they have progressed in the continuing education program.

Anyone completing a grade level of at least Advanced Piloting (AP) and three Elective Courses receives the Educational Proficiency Award. It is an AP insignia with the Educational Proficiency bar below it. Anyone completing all Advanced Grade navigational courses that results in a grade of Navigator (N) and all Elective Courses receives the Educational Achievement Award. This award, also known as the Senior Navigator award, is the highest educational recognition awarded by USPS. Holders of this honor can be recognized in print by the "SN" following their name tag.

From 1973 thru 2007, Jean and Jack Rosenau were members of the Tallahassee Power Squadron. They recall a

Jean Rosenau Power Squadron Awards Ceremony.

memorable time when; on December 12, 1972, they were at Lake Jackson taking sextant sighting on the Moon for their work on the navigation course at the same time as Carmen and Schmidt from the Apollo 17 mission were walking on the Moon. They both gave service to this community through Projects that improved the waterways on Lake Jackson and Lake Munson. They obtained their training from 1970 through 1978 and achieved the "SN" title on their name tags signifying they were the best at what they did.
Submitted by: Jack C. Rosenau, 1177 Old Fort Dr. Tallahassee, Florida 32301; Written by: Carol D. Johnson

Tallahassee's Public Library Beginnings

In an article dated October, 1954, the *Tallahassee Democrat* noted that "Tallahassee Has Half A Million Books But No Modern, Free Public Library." This was the headline of the following article:

"There's no place a person can check out a book after 5 PM, read periodicals, look up a reference, or participate in activities that a public library service provides."

Where are all of these books located? Florida State University has about three fourths or 370,000 volumes. About 25 per cent is the type of material that might be found in a public library, but there are no children's books, and no current fiction. "The purchase of volumes is for research and for our students," said Norman Kilpatrick, FSU Librarian. Only FSU faculty and students can check out books and only occasionally a minister might be given the privilege for sermons.

Reference and reading rooms are open to the public, but public use isn't encouraged because space is limited for the 8,000 students enrolled.

The State Library in the basement of the Supreme Court Building has about 50,000 books, with 20,000 on hand for circulation in rural areas around the state. It's open to the public until 5 PM.

The David S. Walker Library on East Park Avenue is privately endowed and was established by a former governor. It's supported by member book rentals, membership dues of $.50 a month and by $500 a year by the county and $2,000 by the city. Interesting and valuable old papers, estimated to be about 15,000 volumes, are found there. On November 2nd, Leon County Freeholders will vote on whether to establish a free public library.
Submitted by: Mary J. Marchant, 2901 Springfield Drive, Tallahassee, FL 32309-3274; Source: Taken from an Article from the Tallahassee Democrat and the Florida Room of the State Archives, dated 10/54. Quotations show original sources; the rest is paraphrased.

Tallahassee Recreation Department in Old Tallahassee

The Tallahassee Recreation Department enabled children to play at parks all summer, providing sports equipment and board games, with supervisors leading field games and teaching sports skills. It provided arts and crafts lessons and a bowling alley at Lafayette Community Center.

Swimming pools were open all day. Because she was a latchkey child and became old enough to go alone, Dotty McPherson, daughter of Elmer and Thelma McPherson, walked from her home on Gadsden Street to Myers Pool where she swam all day with neighborhood friends. She taught herself to swim. She and her girlfriends would squeal with delight over the (older) lifeguards, Palmer Proctor and George Palmer. Sometimes, she rode the city bus to Levy Pool, where they adored lifeguard Burt Reynolds, before he was "somebody".

The Recreation Department created the Flying High Circus and trained performers. Dotty trained on the "web" and the triple trapeze. Many children were performers. The circus was held at Centennial Field

Once in Elizabeth Cobb Junior High and then Leon High, Dotty and her friends would hold parties at the community center. Each would donate $10 for the refreshments and their parents would chaperone. They played music on a record player and took intermission for mini-talent shows with skits or live musical performances. "Everybody" was invited, and so many attended, the parents had to mix Kool Aid and Ginger Ale in new, scrubbed, and sanitized garbage cans to meet refreshment needs.

Summer camps were held at Silver Lake out Highway 20. Whether it was the recreation department or school system that organized these camps, Tallahassee's children's lives were enriched with these opportunities.
Written and Submitted by: Dorothy Lee McPherson 24236 Lanier Street Tallahassee, FL 32310

RELIGIOUS COMMUNITIES/CEMETERIES

Tallahassee First Baptist Church

In 1849, the Tallahassee population had grown to almost 1800 men, women, children, black and white, slaves and free. From this diverse number, four men and five women organized the Baptist Church of Tallahassee.

The first church building was a frame structure situated on the south side of College Avenue on a lot purchased from Jackson Lodge No.1 F&AM and Leon Lodge No.5 100F for $500.

With missionary pastors sent from the Home Mission Board, the membership grew until the Civil War began. During the war the church building was used by both armies. After Federal occupation, it came back into Baptist control in dilapidated condition. With no pastor and only six members to be found, there was no record of ministry until 1880, when the Mission Board sent Rev. A. C. McCants to lead the church.

In September 1894 the name of the church was changed to First Baptist Church of Tallahassee. The Lord's Supper was first celebrated in February 1895. From meager purses the building was remodeled, refinished, and reoccupied on January 21, 1900.

The church purchased a lot on the northeast corner of Adams Street and College Avenue for $5,000, and the first pastorium was built in the center of the block. With the coming of Pastor-builder Rev. J. Dean Adcock, a new church seating 350, built to the proportional lines of the Parthenon of Greece, was dedicated in November 1915. Membership had reached 407.

This church served our needs during the 1920s and 1930s. In the 1940s World War II brought a great influx of military personnel. FSCW became coeducational (FSU), and students were filling every service. The time had come to build again.

God sent us another Pastor-builder. Dr. Harold G. Sanders, recently discharged from Navy Chaplain service in the Philippines, came to lead us through an eight-year building program which began with ground breaking for the Duval wing on May 29, 1949, and ended with the dedication of the Adams wing and sanctuary on September 29, 1957. Our Second Century Church was complete.

Still more churches were needed in Tallahassee. During the years we established six mission churches throughout the city.

Under the guidance of Pastor Dr. Robert M. McMillan, a Christian Life Center (recreation) was built in 1974, and the Chason Memorial Building (administrative offices and classrooms) was completed in 1987. In 1998 buildings at 201 West Park Avenue and 114 South Duval Street were purchased for further expansion.

The complete church history, *Window to the Past,* by Margaret Mash and Edith Sederquist, may be obtained in the church office.

Submitted by: Donna Heald, PO Box 1074, Tallahassee, FL 32302

Blessed Sacrament Catholic Church

In October, 1539, Hernando De Soto with 600 men and 12 priests arrived in Tallahassee to set up winter camp. Here is where the first Christmas Mass on the North American continent was celebrated. Almost 100 years later, Spanish Franciscan missionaries arrived in 1633 to establish Mission San Luis. The mission system ended in 1704 with the invasion of Colonel James Moore, from South Carolina with his English and Indian forces. Catholicism did not regain a foothold until 1845 when Bishop Michael Moore of Alabama purchased and deeded land on East Park Avenue to the Catholic Congregation for construction of Saint John the Evangelist Church. This Parish's first resident priest was Father Albin Degaultiers. Fire destroyed this church in 1847. In

Blessed Sacrament Catholic Church

1854 a second church, Mater Dolorosa, was built on the same site.

This church was administered by traveling priests until Father Joseph Leon Hugon was assigned in 1872, and under his direction Blessed Sacrament Parish Church was completed in 1898 at North Monroe and Carolina Streets. This church was condemned as a hazardous structure in the 1950s. Fortunately, the church had purchased additional land in the 1940s on Miccosukee Road, and Brevard Street, so a new church and school was built at this location. This building in time became a Parish Center, and a new church was completed in front of it in 1983. The church is still in use today, and Father John V. O'Sullivan has been the priest since 1979.

Written and Submitted by: Claude J. Kenneson, 1323 North Martin Luther King Blvd., Tallahassee, Florida 32303

Blessed Sacrament Catholic Church

Blessed Sacrament Catholic Church, today located on the corner of Miccosukee and Brevard Streets, had many incarnations during its 150 year history in Tallahassee. The first church, named St. John the Evangelist, was built of wood in a 14th century Gothic style in 1945. After only a year as the worship place for Catholics in Tallahassee, as well as in the surrounding communities of Lake City, St. Marks and Chattahoochee, the church burned down.

In 1854 the parishioners had a second church built on the same land, but with a new name – Church of St. Mary, Mater Dolorosa or Our Lady of Seven Sorrows. 1898 saw the construction of a new church for the growing Catholic population. This church, named Blessed Sacrament, was located on the corner of Monroe and Carolina streets. Blessed Sacrament served the Catholic population of Tallahassee from this location for 54 years.

One last move brought Blessed Sacrament to its present location on Miccosukee in 1952. The growing congregation had one more church built and dedicated in 1983 at this location and designated the original 1952 building as the present day parish hall. As the second oldest parish in the Pensacola-Tallahassee Diocese, Blessed Sacrament is comprised of over 1,200 families today, with Monsignor John V. O'Sullivan as its pastor. The oldest Catholic parish in Tallahassee, Blessed Sacrament continues to serve its parishioners and those attending Trinity Catholic School from Pre-K through 8th grade.

Submitted by: Amy Convery, 2721 Parsons Rest, Tallahassee, FL 32309. Compiled from the Blessed Sacrament website, www.bsc.ptdiocese.org and Blessed Sacrament: A Thriving Parish. by Amy M. Ferrara October 12, 2007.

Good Shepherd Catholic Church

Good Shepherd Catholic Church had very humble beginnings dating back to 1972. Bishop Paul F. Tanner, of the Diocese of St. Augustine, assigned Rev, Edward A. Kirby the mission of organizing a Catholic Church within the thirty mile wide area of Leon County north of the newly constructed Interstate-10. The first 34 families of Good Shepherd parish celebrated Holy Mass on January 28, 1973 in the Great Hall of Maclay School on North Meridian Road.

Within two years the families of Good Shepherd had tripled to over 100 and Pope Paul VI divided the Diocese of St. Augustine in two, by creating the Diocese of Pensacola- Tallahassee out of the western portion of north Florida. Plans for the first official church building were created by Bishop Rene H. Gracida, Rv. John V. O'Sullivan and the Good Shepherd Parish Council. Built in 1976 the church had a 425 seating capacity and served Good Shepherd's liturgical, recreational and social needs.

The third, and present day pastor, Rev. Michael Foley, had presided over an ever growing congregation since 1980, with more than 50 families a year joining Good Shepherd Parish. The consistent and burgeoning growth led to the construction of a separate church building in 1982 and a new parish center and church expansion in 1999. Growth and development in Tallahassee's northeast neighborhoods has inevitably made Good Shepherd Parish the largest parish in the Pensacola-Tallahassee Diocese, presently serving the needs of and faith formation of over 2,500 families.

Submitted by: Amy Convery, 2721 ParsonsRest, Tallahassee, FL 32309. Compiled from the history of Good Shepherd Parish, www.goodshepherdparish.org

Calvary United Methodist Church

On June 8, 1962 Reverend Orvis Steverson, a retired minister in the area, began canvassing the southwest neighborhood to see if it would be feasible to organize a new church. He and Travis Burdette and others worked tirelessly on the project. They found the need was great.

The first service was held in the cafeteria of Caroline Brevard School on Sept. 8, 1963. There were 183 people present. Many members came from Trinity and St. Paul's UMC but lived in the new neighborhood and close to the new church.

Calvary United Methodist Church

Those joining through December, 1963, would be considered Charter Members. Including children, 275 joined.

Construction of the church and Sunday school building began less than a year later in April, 1964 and was completed in November that same year. What a happy day that was when the first service was held in the new building! Rev. Steverson worked very hard to start the church and was the first that he had organized.

Having no pews, each family was asked to purchase a chair for each family member.

Rev. Steverson lived only a short time after the church was built.

A parsonage was purchased in 1971 which is rented to provide funds for many missionary projects of the church.

In the early 80s, Dr. Slosek, a well known physician, died and left the church a large sum of money which was used to purchase pews along with other church members. A fellowship hall was added in 1986, allowing the church to have a sanctuary which was dedicated in 1987 with pews installed.

Calvary has had 14 ministers of different races, ages and gender in its 46 years.
Submitted by: Wilma Bridges 1807 Atkamire Drive, Tallahassee, FL 32304

My memories of Pisgah United Method Church

On May 5, 1859, the current Pisgah United Methodist sanctuary opened its doors to the congregation for the first time; presently the church has 150 years of history, making it the oldest Methodist Church in Florida. I was born into two pioneer families from Leon County that were members of Pisgah Church.

I am a fourth generation on my father's side (Johnson), see Daniel Johnson family 1868. My grandparents were Daniel Robert Johnson, Sr. and Helen Sue Young Johnson. My Grandfather Johnson owned the largest general store in the Bradfordville Community. My Grandmother Johnson occasionally played the organ for church services. I am also a fourth generation on my mother's side (Roberts) see Theus-Roberts history 1829. My grandparents were William Roberts and Lillian Taylor Roberts. My Grandfather Roberts owned a large farm on Roberts Road that was established in 1829. My Grandmother Roberts was the first Home Demonstration Agent in Leon County. My parents are Daniel Robert Johnson, Jr., and Gladys Margaret Roberts Johnson. They were members of Pisgah Church, and were married there on June 30, 1925, and I was born eleven years later.

I have fond memories and a long association with Pisgah Church. I was told when I was 6 months old that I was sprinkled with water from a rose, and blessed by the church. As a child I attended Pisgah Church with my parents. At that time Pisgah Church held services once a month and I looked forward to going to church to sing my favorite hymn: "The Little Church in the Wildwood." Later as a teenager and college music major, I was still able to sing solos at Pisgah, which led to an ensemble ("Dayspring") at the First Baptist Church in Tallahassee. These opportunities are very special to me. The pews in the church are still divided into sections where men used to sit on one side and women on the other side of a partition. This tradition did not occur when I was a child, but this seating was always interesting to me.

An occasion I enjoyed so much was the Homecoming event, which still takes place the first Sunday in May since 1924. During World War II my Grandmother Roberts, who was one of the leaders of the Church, invited the soldiers from Camp Gordon Johnston to the church for homecoming services and dinner on the grounds. I remember a picture was taken of them on the steps of the church. I still attend Homecoming with my immediate family whenever possible. I am amazed at the beauty of the church and the historical nature in which it has been preserved. Except for lighting, heating and air conditioning, the church interior remains in its original form. My earliest recollection of the church is the beautiful lamps on the columns; they are now electric lights, but they still look like lanterns of the olden days.

Throughout the years most of my aunts, uncles and cousins of both the Roberts and Johnson families attended Pisgah Church, and served in various capacities. I shall always treasure the fond memories, worship experiences, and fellowship with families and friends at Pisgah United Methodist Church.

Written and Submitted by: Margaret Johnson-Allen, 2303 Armistead Road, Tallahassee, FL 32308

Pisgah United Methodist Church –Then & Now

I must confess that during Sunday sermons at Pisgah United Methodist Church, my mind sometimes wanders. As I sit on those historic old pews I can't help but think about the generation of worshippers that came before us. I know they gazed out the same windows, but it was an entirely different world they saw. Today we are faced with the stress of raising children, earning a living, paying off the mortgage and trying to adjust to a social environment that moves at an ever increasing pace. They on the other hand dealt with survival on a day to day basis. Just providing food, clothing and shelter consumed their time, not to mention the threat of having their scalps removed by Indians. Yes, it was a different world.

During the Seminole Wars from 1835 to 1842 the men of Pisgah kept their muskets at the ready during church service in constant fear of an Indian raid. One of the circuit riding ministers, Tillman D. Peurifoy, sent to serve the circuit in 1837, had his family attacked by Indians. They killed his children and mutilated his wife, scalping and shooting her but somehow she miraculously recovered. His Negro slaves were also massacred and scattered about the yard of his home. Other families in the area were also attacked and murdered. These wooded vistas weren't always so tranquil and quiet; our church ancestors did indeed have to sacrifice, all for the right to worship.

The Indian story was recounted in an earlier history of Pisgah by Norman Booth who was a former pastor at Pisgah.

Submitted by: Mike Conley, 9204 Old Chernonie Road, Tallahassee, FL 32309, sconley713@ernbarqrncil.com

Trinity United Methodist Church

As Tallahassee, Florida's new capital, was being settled in 1824, Methodist "Circuit Riders" came to preach and establish a Methodist society in the new community. The first church building in Tallahassee was erected the next year on the southwest corner of Park Avenue and Bronough Street. This was a small, unfinished wooden building with only shutters at the windows.

By 1837 the church had grown so that a larger place of worship was needed. Three lots were purchased at the corner of Park Avenue and Duval Street, and construction was begun on a new 40 by 60 building. It was similar to the Presbyterian Church next door.

Trinity Methodist Church and parsonage, ca. 1893

In 1892 the congregation again faced the need for more space, and so a new building was erected at the same site. With additions in 1910 and 1949 and the acquisition of more property, the complex served the congregation well until 1962 when it was deemed necessary to replace the old church. A structure containing a new sanctuary, chapel, fellowship hall, classrooms and offices was built.

Over the years Trinity has played a significant role in the history of other Methodist churches. The organizing conference of the Florida Annual Conference was held at Trinity in 1844. Trinity is the sponsoring church for several other United Methodist Churches in Tallahassee, and it has supported churches and missionaries overseas. Located in the heart of the city, Trinity has adopted the slogan, "The Church with a Heart for the City," pointing to its activity of service to those in need in Tallahassee.

Submitted by: Linda H. Yates, 1111 Wisteria Drive, Tallahassee, FL 32312

Reverend Dan

I moved to Tallahassee in 1941 from Greenville, Florida. We lived on the Perry Highway; now known as the Apalachee Parkway. Our farm was exactly five miles from the steps of the old capitol. The community was rather new. As the community began to grow some of the good people from downtown Tallahassee First Presbyterian Church decided to start a mission church in our community. I don't remember the names of all those dedicated individuals but two of them were Julian Alford and Walter DeMilly. Rev. Elmer Boyer, a Missionary home from Korea for rest and recuperation, was our first Pastor. Soon it was time to build a church building. Somehow land was acquired on what is now the northeast corner of Walmart's parking lot. Our adult members constructed the building. Herbert Mock, a local builder, was our contractor and members provided the labor. Some of us youngsters carried boards and other materials. We named our church the "Lafayette Presbyterian Church."

Some years later it was decided that we needed to hold a revival to increase our membership. We called Rev. Dan Graham from Danville, VA to be the Evangelist. Rev Dan was a rather fundamentalist preacher. Some would even describe him as a "Fire and Brimstone" preacher. On Friday night of the first week we had a rather large crowd. Rev. Dan got really excited and started condemning some practices currently becoming popular in the secular county. He preached rather loudly about the "Sins of Dancing, Playing Cards and Laying Half Naked on the Beach like lizards". Then he really got excited when he started in on the new Drive-In Theater under construction up the road at the corner of the Perry Highway (Apalachee Pkwy) and The Truck Route (Capital Circle). He loudly denounced "That Evil Passion Pit" and "Called down the Wrath of God on it and please totally destroy it". Two days later on Sunday night a large thunderstorm passed through town, it launched a massive bolt of lightning which totally leveled the massive concrete block movie screen. The next week we had a large crowd of converts and our membership grew substantially.

Lafayette Community was a wonderful place to grow up and I have many cherished memories of my childhood.

Submitted by: Rodney Letchworth, 4165 Diplomacy Circle, Tallahassee, FL 32308

Faith Presbyterian Church

Faith Presbyterian Church was colonized by the First Presbyterian Church. In the early 1950s, the physical facilities of the downtown church were inadequate to accommodate the growing congregation. Officers proposed colonization of a new church in the fast growing northeastern section of the city. A plaque in the narthex of the sanctuary names the charter members when Faith Presbyterian Church was organized November 7, 1954. For the first three and one half years, worship services and Sunday School classes were held at Kate Sullivan Elementary School on Miccosukee Road.

Church members learned of the current property at 2200 North Meridian Road, Tallahassee, FL during 1955-56 and the 9-acre tract was acquired. One of the favorite fellowship activities in the early days was a picnic supper on the grounds, followed by a volley ball game and impromptu hymn singing.

The Fellowship Hall was completed in May, 1958. The current Pre-School wing was added shortly thereafter.

The 750 seat sanctuary was built during the period between 1963 and 1966. The connecting wing to the Fellowship Hall was added shortly thereafter. The Sanctuary was dedicated on April 7, 1966.

The administrative wing was dedicated on November 11, 1990 and provided new offices for pastors and staff, greatly enlarged choir space, an elevator and additional Sunday School and other meeting rooms. In 2005, the Pre-School offices and drop-point were added to the north wing.

With a membership of approximately 1000 Christians, Faith continues as a vibrant center for Christian life and activity.

Submitted by: Linda Mabry Sources: Excerpts from the 1994 history prepared by Hendrix Chandler and Doug Smith with additions from conversations with various long-time members

Greenwood Cemetery Origins

Greenwood Cemetery is an all-black cemetery situated on Old Bainbridge Road between Tharpe and Volusia Streets, and is designated a historic landmark. It was formed when in the city's segregation policies were in place. Until the 1960s, Greenwood was one of the few cemeteries for blacks in Tallahassee.

In 1829, the Florida Territorial Council established an official burying ground on what was then the western boundary of Tallahassee. In 1937, the city ran out of grave spaces for "coloreds" and refused to bury more black citizens in the public cemeteries, so nine black citizens bought 16 acres and sold burial plots to black families, who agreed to maintain them. There is no official record of ownership of many of the graves and unused plots, and over time records were lost and owners moved away or grew too old to care for the property. The Greenwood Foundation was formed in 1985 to see the cemetery restored and regularly maintained.

Beginning in May, 1987, several clean up days were held, and a history of the cemetery, including a survey of grave markers, was researched and written under the guidance of the Historic Tallahassee Preservation Board. Greenwood Cemetery was rededicated on October 10, 1987, and acquired by the city. The John G. Riley House Museum and Center for African American History organized an anniversary celebration in 1997, and produced a commemorative booklet and self-guided walking tour. Greenwood was listed in the National Register of Historic Places in 2003.

Internments include Freddie Cohens, WWII, unmarked baby graves, and Willie L. Gallimore, FAMU three time All-American and Chicago Bears running back. There are over 100 names listed at findagrave.com.

Submitted by: Linda S. Mabry; Sources: Mitchell, S. Renee, "Greenwood Cemetery", Tallahassee Democrat, 8 Mar 1987, P1E; Findagrave.com

Greenwood Cemetery - Restored

Something great happened in Tallahassee in 1985 when a group of local citizens came together to establish the Greenwood Cemetery Foundation Inc. to support the documentation, restoration and preservation of Greenwood Cemetery on Old Bainbridge Road.

In 1937 the Greenwood Cemetery Company was founded "to acquire land so as to provide a burial place for the dead of the colored race near Tallahassee in Leon County." Founders were: J.R.D. Laster, William Mitchell, Erma Jenkins, Sam Hills, Maude Lomas, Rev. Robert L. Gordon, James H. Abner, M. Johnson, and T. J. McKinnis. Records show the company still in existence in 1954. In 1962, the President was Mr. T.H. McKinnis, and the Secretary was Dr. Gilbert Porter. Other members noted in minutes were: Mr. J.H. Abner, Mrs. Virginia Abner, and Mrs. Mamie Strong. Meetings were held at Strong and Jones Funeral Home and in the home of Mrs. Mamie Strong. The purpose was to sell grave spaces and provide for the maintenance of the cemetery.

In 1985, the Greenwood Cemetery Foundation was founded, purpose being to restore the cemetery "to a safe and respectable condition." Through the years, the original owners passed away and the cemetery was not being maintained. It was overgrown to the point that this 16 acres burial ground could no longer be identified from the road as a cemetery. Rev. James Vaughn was elected President of the Foundation. Other board members were: Linn Ann Griffin, Bartow Duhart, Rebecca Bryant, Nathaniel Adams, Mary Nasby, Sennie Baker Dewitt Small, Bettye Stevens, and Josette Dugan

As an extension of their work, a Greenwood Steering Committee was appointed by former Commissioner Dorothy Inman Johnson and approved by the Tallahassee City Commission to "develop a strategy to ensure perpetual care and maintenance of the cemetery". This committee included: Aquilina Howell, Althemese Barnes, Dr. Henry Lewis III, Kevin McGorty, Sharyn Thompson, Governor Leroy Collins, John Lawrence, Ben Harris, Mary Calhoun, Karen Cowger, Cornelius, Frank Williams, Judge George Reynolds III, Joe Musgray, Rev. James Austin, and Mr. Sam Hand.

On October 10, 1987, after many meetings negotiating a takeover by the city, several clean-up days by the community and a $50,000 successful fundraising campaign for initial major cleanup work, the Rededication of Greenwood Cemetery was held. The City of Tallahassee assumed ownership and responsibility for the perpetual care and maintenance of the cemetery. A kiosk was erected on October 10, 1997 and in 2007 a wrought iron fence with security gates were erected to protect this pastoral landscape.

Much of Tallahassee and Leon County's Black history rests in Greenwood and the site received the historic register designation in 2000 as a result of a partnership effort of the Riley Center/Museum and City of Tallahassee partnership. As a result of many community persons, user families, government and private organizations, the cemetery received protection and was aesthetically improved, demonstrating

how public and private entities can work together to accomplish important tasks.
Submitted by: Florida Parker; Source: Riley House, Althamese Barnes(Director)

The Plantation Cemetery at Betton Hills

Located on BettonRoad across from Winthrop Park, this State Designated Historical land in Florida Township #1 represents other forgotten sites. These are the graves of the unknown and the known who built our Capitol, our railroad, our income base, our finest homes and then served the owners well. It is a remnant of what the cemetery was. Homes are built upon the graves; in fact, gravestones were used in some home construction. Thus many stories lie here as well.

The land was included in the Lafayette Land Grant. By 1823, when the environs were chosen for the Seat of Government for the Territory of Florida, its first governor, Branch, apparently owned the site. General Lafayette, Governors Croom and Whitfield, Railroad President Call, Turbett Betton and the Winthrops followed in ownership. When you consider that the Winthrop line alone comes directly from the founder of the Puritans, and the roots of the other owners trace all of American history (and prehistory), this little plot in a residential neighborhood becomes more important.

By the end of the 1850s, Branch owned both Live Oak and Waverly, while Turbett Betton owned 1,200 acres between Centerville and Thomasville Roads called Betton Hill. In 1863, after Turbett Betton's death, Guy Winthrop purchased the land. The last Florida cotton plantation used this site, and it remained the Black Cemetery for Waverly, Live Oak and Betton Hill Plantations until 1945 when lot sales began for the Betton Hills development. Bryants, Edwards, Jones, Knights, Porters, Quartermans, Watsons, and Youngs are interred here, as well as unknowns from plantation time and before.

The Waverly, Live Oak and Betton Hill use is verified by descendant testimony and tombstone dates to January 11, 1904. Markers before 1904 were typically wooden or floral or simply absent. The 1904 site is within a fenced enclosure added long after burials began. Oral tradition is that the Winthrop family added the special enclosure to honor favorite servants. The many depressions without markers present indicate 50-100 graves within the remaining acre of land.

Gertrude Williams, whose father owned 80 acres along Centerville Road (Hill's Gate), a slave grant, walked in this site as a child and would jump the fences to get away from the cows. Her grandfather, Ned Johnson, lived to the age of 115 and told her a lot about the times before, including one story about how the ice room in the dairy was used as a morgue upon occasion and held public viewings.

Henrietta Smith, also known as Grandma Croom, owned 6,184 acres of NE Tallahassee and 149 slaves, according to the 1860 tax rolls. As the grandmother of Susan Evelyn Winthrop, wife of John, she was the link between Governor Croom and the Winthrop family. Henrietta chose to be buried in the Plantation Cemetery at Betton Hills with her family. It seems that family for her was the plantation life and all that kept it going. This family was black and white without hatred. The "hate" seems to have been added by others and mostly after the Civil War. Henrietta and her daughter were both buried here, only to be dug up and moved to the Winthrop plot at the "white" Episcopal Cemetery. Another name of note associated with this little plot of land is Henry Bryant. He was a body servant for Guy Winthrop's father and eventually became a landowner to include what is now Miracle Plaza. John Winthrop arranged to have the land sold to Bryant for a bargain price of $24 in 1904 out of concern that an outright gift might be questioned later in court. John and Henry were simply friends in addition to the complexities of black/white life of those times. Another property transaction with Henry Bryant reads "For and in good consideration of the kindly feeling and good will which they bear toward the said party of the second part ... etc. and $5 to the faithful servant of deceased Susan E. Winthrop."

The Plantation Cemetery at Betton Hills was given to the City of Tallahassee on a "please take care of it" verbal agreement between Guy Winthrop and the Mayor. It was never assigned to any formal city department for maintenance until it was designated a Florida Heritage Site in 1999, sponsored by the Betton Hills Neighborhood Association, the Riley House Heritage Museum and the Florida Department of State. To most people passing by, it was just a strangely vacant lot. To a few, like Athemese Barnes (Riley House Director), it will always be more. Some hydrangeas planted by Althemese's great aunt still grow there. To Imogene Hopkins, it was her backyard and as she said to me, "they have been very good neighbors here all my life."

Source: This article was adapted from an article by Dean Hansen that originally appeared in the Tallahassee Genealogist, vol XXI, n 3:p17-18.

LEON COUNTY SPECIAL EVENTS

Elections

When I was a child in the early 1930's, we had no radio station in Tallahassee. Local news was from newspapers. Without TV, campaign rallies with speeches by the principal candidates were important occasions for the voters. In those days the Democratic Party primaries were tantamount to election as there was very little Republican opposition.

For my mother these campaigns were of great interest, and she instilled this interest in her children. Most of her life had been spent literally living in the shadow of the capitol, having grown up on South Calhoun Street, and then later as an adult living on South Monroe Street. I had not realized until recently that women did not have the right to vote until after Mother was married.

Political rally at Old Capitol, Image courtesy of the Florida State Archives Photographic Collection

Having taken the right to vote for granted all of my life it did not occur to me that it was such a new experience for women. I wish I had asked her about the first time she voted. Since my father usually was working late, my mother took us to rallies at the courthouse and to election night parties downtown.

In those days the *Tallahassee Daily Democrat* office was on Adams Street between College and Park Avenues. People would gather on Adams Street, which had been blocked off, to hear the latest local and state returns broadcast from the newspaper's office. It was a time when people visited with friends and neighbors while they waited for the latest report. These returns were very important for many who were state workers because their livelihood depended upon the outcome of the election. Merit retention was not law at that time.

Submitted by: Rubie Butterworth, 4434 Meandering Way, Tallahassee, Fl 32308

Election Recount 2000

News media locally, state wide and nationally converged on Tallahassee to record the following events. "

The United States presidential election of 2000 was a contest between Republican candidate George W. Bush and Democratic candidate Al Gore. Bush narrowly won the November 7 election, with 271 electoral votes to Gore's 266. Gore came in second in electoral vote, but received 543,895 more popular votes than Bush."

Shirts sold across from the Old Capitol in Tallahassee, December 1, 2000

"The election was noteworthy for a controversy over the awarding of Florida's 25 electoral votes, the subsequent recount process in that state, and the unusual event of the winning candidate having received fewer popular votes than the runner-up." The closest election since 1876, it was only the fourth election that electoral vote didn't reflect popular vote.

Gore Political Rallt 2000. Image courtesy of the Florida State Archives Photographic Collection

On election night, news media reported nationally that Bush had won in Florida before all the polls had closed. Florida has two time zones. "However, as the night wore on, controversy arose with swing states, and it came down to Florida being the deciding vote. The final result in Florida was slim enough to require a mandatory recount (by machine) under state law."

Several lawsuits were filed between the two candidates' parties in the ensuing weeks including the Florida Supreme Court and the US Supreme Court. "

On December 12, the US Supreme Court ruled in a 5-4 vote that the Florida Supreme Court's ruling requiring a statewide recount of ballots was unconstitutional, and that the Florida recounts could not be completed before a December 12 deadline, and should therefore cease and the previously certified total should hold." So ultimately the US Supreme Court decided the election, which in itself caused controversy.

Written and submitted by: Mary J. Marchant 2901 Springfield Drive, Tallahassee, FL 32309-3274; Source: Wikipedia, United States presidential election, 2000

First Christmas in America

The First Christmas in North America was 470 years ago in Tallahassee. Archeologists knew for a century that Hernando de Soto spent a winter near Tallahassee in 1539-1540.

In April 1987 the late, legendary state archeologist Calvin Jones discovered the actual site on a hillside near downtown, east of the intersection of Lafayette Street and Myers Park Drive. Famous for 'reading the dirt,' Jones discovered the site as bulldozers cleared earth for an office complex. Among the most convincing pieces of evidence was the jawbone of a pig - because historians already knew De Soto had brought the first pigs to the New World.

Today a historical marker stands next to the office complex. The excavation is known as the 'Martin site,' because the adjoining home of former Gov. John Martin houses the Florida Bureau of Archeological Research.

There is no written account of Christmas being observed there, because chroniclers recorded only the riches and other things found for the King of Spain. No daily life in camps was recorded.

Michael Gannon, Florida historian, states that Christmas would have been observed because Christmas in the Catholic Church is a holy day of obligation and Christians much attend Mass.

December 15 would have been the day with the Gregorian calendar.

Holiday spirits would have been low because De Soto had taken an Apalachee Indian village, killing and enslaving many natives. The Apalachee responded in kind, killing half of De Soto's 600 men.

It was the last Christmas observed in the New World until 1565, when the nation's oldest city, St. Augustine, was founded. And Tallahassee has only lightly commemorated its place in Christmas history.

Submitted by: Mary J. Marchant, 2901 Springfield Drive, Tallahassee, FL 32309-3274; Source: Column originally was published Dec. 23, 2007 in the Tallahassee Democrat and edited slightly by Gerald Ensley for republication on Dec. 25, 2008.

Springtime Tallahassee Festival

In 1967 serious efforts were made in the Florida legislature to move the capital from Tallahassee to a more central location in the state. Determined to halt this attempt, a group of concerned citizens joined forces to thwart such a move. Inspired by Tallahassee's physical beauty and its cultural and historical heritage, a pamphlet was published describing the qualities of the city "Where Spring Begins." This slogan became a rallying cry and the motivating force for forming a citizen's festival. The first festival was held in March 1968 and by 1969 Springtime Tallahassee, Inc. was charted.

Springtime Tallahassee has grown from a small but dedicated organization to over 400 participants from all segments of the community.

State archeologist, Calvin Jones, excavating site of Hernando de Soto's 1539-40 winter encampment near present-day Tallahassee

Membership to Springtime is divided among "krewes" depicting the state's five historical periods: Spanish, American Territorial, Antebellum, War & Reconstruction and 20th Century. Period costumes are worn by members throughout the festival weekend.

Tallahassee Springtime Parade, 1968, "Where Spring Begins"

Each year the Springtime Tallahassee festival is held in late March or early April in downtown Tallahassee. The festival includes a parade, arts & crafts show, food court, children's park and over 3 entertainment stages.

While widely recognized for its entertainment value, the Springtime festival continues to enrich the quality of life in our community. Springtime Tallahassee provides a significant revenue source for local businesses, with the total economic impact estimated at over $5 million dollars.

While the festival continues to grow, Springtime holds true to the roots in which it was formed celebrating the natural, historical and cultural assets Tallahassee has to offer.
Submitted by: Springtime Tallahassee, 209 E. Park Ave., Tallahassee, FL 32301

Springtime Tallahassee Parade and Pageant

I arrived in Tallahassee with the coming of the year 1969, when my father retired from the Air Force and moved the family over the Christmas Holidays so we would not miss any school. My eldest sister got involved in the organization of the Springtime Tallahassee celebration to meet people, and, being the eldest, she took us all along with her.

It was the second year of the Springtime Tallahassee Parade and Pageant, the Parade portion of which continues to this day. It was initiated to highlight the beauty and the historic significance of Tallahassee at a time when the relocation of the State Capitol was being considered. When the Capitol building, built in 1845, became too small and cramped to be used any longer, there was a strong push from South Florida to move the state capital closer to the current population center of the state, which had shifted considerably south, to Orlando, where Disney World was scheduled to open in 1971.

Springtime Tallahassee was conceived as a means of promoting Tallahassee to the state legislators, who would make the decision. The North Florida region gets enough cold weather to make the explosion of flowers and new growth against the bare limbs noticeable, and in some years, remarkable.

My sister's involvement with the pageant part of Springtime Tallahassee was making beards and costumes and recruiting the rest of us to fill roles in the pageant depicting the founding of Tallahassee. I was volunteered to be a Spanish Friar, first seen preaching to the natives, and then reappearing with the flock to flee from the invading English soldiers. It was the first time I had ever seen Centennial Field and I was impressed immediately by the limestone wall surrounding the field and by the wooden bleachers with the open roof providing shade, which retained the look and the feel of the 1920s, the decade when they were built.

I joined the other pageant cast members in the bleachers, the only time I ever sat in those bleachers, and we received our instructions before moving out into the former ball field. It was a thrill for a wandering ex-military brat to imagine the history of that rickety old structure and to anticipate creating a connection to such an unusual place.
Submitted by: Robert Olmstead, South Meridian Street, Tallahassee, FL 32301

Tallahassee's Big Fire of the 1940s

I was living in Arcadia, Desoto County, Florida and came up to Tallahassee in August of 1942 to work for the Florida Industrial Commission during World War II. I found an apartment at 111 S. Duval Street, a half block past College Avenue. I was close enough to my work in the Knott Building, which was south of the Capitol, that I could walk to work everyday. In fact, I had not brought my old Model-A Ford with me because of the restrictions on having a car during Wartime. At that time state employees worked five and one half days a week, which included a half day on Saturday.

I remember one particular Saturday afternoon vividly. I had walked home for lunch but before it was time to start back to work, we were startled by the sound of many loud sirens going off down Duval and Adams Streets. We dashed out to see what all the commotion was about, and found the whole block west of the Capitol building was ablaze with flames. That block had been filled with unpainted wooden shops containing such wares as feed sacks, seeds, ropes, farm equipment, and such all kept in wooden containers. It looked like all the counters and furnishings were made from wood so the whole thing was bursting into flames as it spread from one shop to another.

Carolyn, Lillian and Mother, Ardelia, in front of 111 S. Duval Street

The fire trucks could not contain the flames, and eventually the whole block was consumed by smoke and fire. By that time it seemed that half the town's people were there to witness this spectacular event. Needless to say; nobody went back to work that Saturday afternoon. Though I can not pin down the exact date this fire occurred, it would have been between 1942 and 1949 when I moved from that Duval apartment to a further distance from the Capitol building.

After the fire the charred block was swept up and sat empty for quite a while, but I remember that the first enterprise to appear in the empty space was a temporary kind of kiosk store, which offered a new kind of milkshake to walkers passing down that street. They placed a large scoop of ice cream in a paper cup, followed by a dash of milk, and then an electric mixer was lowered into the cup to stir it up somewhat, but not thoroughly. It became popular with the public and soon this kind of milk shake was being offered all over town. I would still enjoy one of those old World War II milkshakes to this very day.

Submitted by: Carolyn Jane Gaines, 301 E. Carolina Street # 701, Tallahassee, Fl 32302

LEON COUNTY REMINISCENCES

1907 S. Adams Street or "The Wilkinson Mansion"

It is believed that my great granddad, John Lawrence Wilkinson, bought this house and property for his children to have. The property originally ran from Adams Street to part of what is now Capital City Country Club. Most of great granddad's descendants lived there at one time or another. My mother remembers the address while she grew up there in the 1930's and 1940's as Rt. 5 Box 8 and the first phone number was 901K. Recently I learned from my mom's first cousin Elizabeth Baird that she remembers people in the community calling it "The Wilkinson Mansion".

Wilkinson Mansion, 1907 S. Adams St. (Belair Road before being in the city

The house was 2 stories while the 2nd floor was never finished. The kitchen and dining room was out the back door with a covered porch going out to these rooms. My mother recalls the house used to sit closer to Adams Street before the 1950s. They were going to pave the street, so they moved the house back from the road. When they did, it put the kitchen and dining room over an old draw well. No one in the family recalls the well ever being used for water. While I was growing up it was full of debris and we added to it. My grandmother, Mary Rebecca Wilkinson Andrews, lived in the house until the mid 1970's. The house never had indoor plumbing in it and it was just a mile south of the Capitol Building.

Submitted by: Shawn Pearson, 4521 Bloxham Cut Off Road, Crawfordville, Florida 32327

Adventures on the South Side

Henry Palmer's Standard Oil Service Station originally was at the southeast corner of College Avenue and Adams Street. His later station at East Palmer Avenue and the 500 block of South Monroe Street had a bar Elmer visited.

One time, a black woman got shot in the face outside at the gas pumps. Elmer and Dotty, being ambulance chasers, arrived right after it happened. It was pretty gory and did not smell so good either. After Dotty saw the blood and thought she smelled ketchup, she stopped eating ketchup - and ketchup was a mainstay of her diet. She ate ketchup on her over-easy eggs and grits, and on her hot dogs, hamburgers, fish, and French fries.

Another time, Elmer and Dotty chased fire trucks all the way to St. Marks, the major port for oil. It had (and still has some) humongous oil tanks for storing oil. One of them caught fire. It was quite the sight to see all the firemen, fire trucks, and fire. The danger of it all must not have occurred to anyone, as the street was full of people watching.

Another beer joint that Elmer and Dotty frequented later on was Blue Gables on Lafayette Street. Dotty married Joseph Gordon Roberts, son of Hinton Gordon (who built the round Holiday Inn on Tennessee Street) and Mary Eunice (Morgan) Roberts. Gordon remembered playing in Blue Gables' parking lot with a little girl wearing a baseball cap. It could only be Dotty, as she wore a baseball cap everywhere and was always the only girl in the groups, unless she brought a girl friend from school.

After Elmer and Thelma divorced and Dotty lived with Elmer, they sometimes ate at restaurants along South Monroe Street. He was an excellent cook and had always cooked, even during his marriage. But Elmer and Dotty frequented Nic's Cafe. Nic catered to Dotty's every request and she loved him dearly for it. It is in the same location today.

Gone are Thompson's, home of the best and biggest hamburger in town, next to Nic's, and the Wagon Wheel, 1621 South Monroe Street - past

FRM Feed Store on the hilltop. The Freemans owned the Wagon Wheel and they, too, doted on Dotty.
Submitted-Dorothy Lee "Dotty" McPherson, 24236 Lanier St

Déjà vu for Bill and Pat Law

In the summer of 2002, my wife, Pat, and I knew we were coming home. Like so many others, we attended Florida State University and got our first "real" job in Tallahassee, and then followed a career path that took us far from North Florida. Yet, we continued to think of Tallahassee as our home-as the place we would return.

Our first Tallahassee adventure began in 1972 when we were graduate students, and continued until 1981 when we relocated to St. Petersburg so I could take my first position as a college administrator. In the intervening years, we began our family, Pat earned her MBA, and I worked for the Board of Regents as well as the new Commission on Higher Education, part of Speaker of the House, Hyatt Brown's vision of higher education reform. Those experiences gave me a clear sense of purpose-I wanted to be a community college president! So the move to St. Pete was a great opportunity at the right time.

While away from Tallahassee, memories of the time spent there were always on my mind. From that first time we stuffed freshly purchased camping gear into our tiny VW Karmann Ghia for an overnight experience in St. Joe State Park, our deep appreciation for the Big Bend's natural areas-not just the beaches, but also Wakulla Springs, the Ichetucknee River and other treasures of the region were deeply rooted.

I remember when we returned in 2002 to start the new challenge as president of Tallahassee Community College, we took a taxi from the "new" regional airport and Pat wondered aloud as we drove east on Pensacola Street-what the large structure was that we were passing. She was stunned when she discovered that the large, modern campus we were passing was TCC. As we approached FSU, I plunged into recollections of a time before the Seminoles became a national icon-when I could go out and hit a few golf balls right in sight of the stadium. Could this be the same town where I saw children collecting pecans from the trees downtown to sell at the market on South Monroe Street? This new Tallahassee stretched almost to the state line and had grafted an almost urban flavor to its relaxed southern charm.

We marveled at the way Tallahassee had evolved and yet retained the familiarity of home. We were delighted to return to the classic Springtime Tallahassee and Market Days events that we enjoyed so much-bigger and perhaps better than they were, but still Tallahassee originals.

Many of the people we met as young professionals were still here and had become civic leaders. Just before I took the helm at TCC, I attended an event in the Capitol. As TCC trustee, Bill Hebrock, prepared to introduce me to some of those in the "halls of power," we were both surprised as one person after another turned out to be a friend or acquaintance from that earlier era. For my family and for many others, Tallahassee is both a place of déjà vu and a place for new beginnings.
Written-Submitted by: Dr. William (Bill) Law, 2950 Giverny Circle, Tallahassee, FL 32309

Dixieland Remembered

There was controversy when plans were revealed for three new shopping centers out of the immediate area. Also, suburban communities rapidly began to sprout up all around the county. As these changes turned into reality, the undertone was fear of drawing the population away from this adorable, lovable, spirited town center. Look now at what you see as you might compare the past to the present.

Alligators—"they were last but not least a part of the community. We can't forget the wonderful Wakulla Springs, which once had a 35-foot-high deck to dive off. I just did that once, because alligators would swim along the side sometimes creeping towards the swimming area. They filmed "Creature from the Black Lagoon" in Wakulla Springs one year, while I watched, so scary! We could swim to a breathless depth in those springs, but when looking up the water was so clear it seemed like you were only two or three feet underwater.

Religions were only divided by one word: Race. There were churches interspersed around Tallahassee close enough for all to attend to their own discretion. Those religions were respectfully and quietly worshipped.

One should never forget the past, its effect on our present and the outcome of the future depends on our knowledge of it. Remember to frequent the Natural History Museums and help your young children to envision where we started

out from. Show them the arrow heads of the past. As I said, it wasn't unusual when I was a kid, to find Indian artifacts all around. It is a thrilling insight into the early history of Florida.
Written and Submitted by: Bette Ann Barrett, 2870 Pharr Court-South NW, Atlanta, GA 30305

Eats, After School, and Nighttime Cruising in Old Tallahassee

200 South Monroe Street at East College Avenue is the site of Lively's Corner (1875). During the 1880s, it was Leon Liquor Store, Bar & Pool Room.

It became Bennett's Drug Store where 50s and 60s teenagers hung out after school. We shopped, ate hot dogs and French fries, and chatted while waiting for parents to get off work. Next to the jewelry display with the latest in pierced earrings, some girls pierced their ears using a potato, pushing needles through their lobes. Why in Bennett's is unknown, unless they felt pharmacy staff would rescue them if something went wrong during the process.

Also on Monroe Street were McCrory's and another dime store. McCrory's had a hotdog bar at the Jefferson Street entrance. At the Monroe Street entrance was another food counter where we ate French fries and drank Coca-Cola or milkshakes. Both sides of that counter were always busy.

We spent a lot of time "cruising" the drive-ins: Mutt and Jeff's (The Blue Heaven during WWII) where we got the greatest slaw dog; the Corral, the Dixieland, and the Wagon Wheel on South Monroe Street; and Tucker's at Four Points where South Monroe and South Adams Streets converge.

When Tallahassee got McDonald's on West Tennessee Street, we loaded our cars as full as we could and rushed there from Leon High School, trying to return in time from our lunch break. Many ate at Garcia's Cuban Restaurant, a block west of Leon on East Tennessee Street. Vince made the best black bean soup and Cuban sandwiches ever!
Written and Submitted by: Dorothy Lee McPherson, 24236 Lanier Street, Tallahassee, FL 32310

Grandmother's Indian Stories

My name is Elizabeth Coldwell Frano and these stories were told to me by my grandmother, Mattie Black Hopkins when I was a little girl growing up in Tallahassee. My grandmother's backyard connected to my backyard, so for me her house was just an extension of my house. Grandma taught me how to quilt together all the bits and pieces of fabric she kept in her sideboard in the dining room. It was during these times together that she would sit and tell me her Indian stories. Some of the stories were told to her by her mother, Mary Ann Harvey Black, and some were stories she remembered herself from others.

The Harvey's and the Black's families built their houses in Gadsden County, Florida, amongst the pine forest, a half mile from the Ochlocknee River on the east bank of the Rocky Comfort Creek. The Indians were identified to me simply as the "Good Indians" and the "Bad Indians." "The Bad Indians" would come at night and go up under the house and out behind the trees surrounding the house and beat on plow shears and anything else metal that would make noise. They would keep this up for hours, in hopes that they could drive the Harveys out of their house, so they could get into the house to steal food. But, the Harveys, knowing what the Indians wanted, never left their house.

In late winter and early spring the Indians would come to the Harvey Plantation in Ft. Braden looking for food. The Harvey family knew if the Indians found the barns, house, and outbuildings locked they would burn down the locked building. So, all doors on the plantation were always left unlocked. When the Indians wanted food, they would come to the plantation and take cows, pigs, and chickens from the barns that were located out in the fields away from the house. The Indians never stole more food than they needed.

Another story grandma told was how "The Indians would come up to the 'big house' and just walk in the front door without knocking. When the Indians came in the house, the children and women would line up with their backs up against the walls of the living room, making sure to keep their hands behind their backs. The women and children were not afraid of the Indians. They knew if they did not make a sound and stood up against the wall, they would be unharmed." "

The Indians would come into the living room and go up to the fireplace mantel and take down the porcelain figurines. Then they would turn the figurines over and over looking at them. Then they would pass them on to the next Indian to look at. Next, they would take down the clock and put it to their ear and listen to it tick. Then they would burst out laughing. When the Indians had finished playing in the house they would just leave."

One Indian story my Grandma always used to tell me occurred when she was a young girl. Sometimes at night, when she would be getting undressed for bed, she would look over and see eyes staring at her through the knotholes that the Indians had punched out of the pine boards that made up the wall of the house. Her house had been built from virgin pine that her father had cut and milled. She would go over and stuff wads of cotton into the holes, so the Indians could not see inside her room. The Indians would simply punch the cotton wads back out of the holes onto the floor and continue watching. To get out of view of prying eyes, she would crawl under the bed where they could not see her and finish dressing for bed. My mother told this story of her great-uncle's encounter with Indians. "Uncle John and Uncle Mike were sent out to the barn, which was located out in the field, to get 6 or 8 ears of corn to be ground into meal for dinner. John, the oldest son, left his little brother as a look out for Indians outside the barn. Mike saw Indians out behind the trees, and not knowing if they where the 'good or bad Indians' froze where he stood, unable to even get a sound out to warn his brother. When John came out of the barn with his arms full of corn, he saw the Indians, dropped the corn, grabbed his little brother's hand, and then they ran back to the house as fast as they could run. There was a curve in the trail and just as they turned to go into the curve of the trail, an arrow flew by the boys' heads nicking Mike in the neck. Later, great grandpa went and pulled the arrow out of the tree where it had lodged, and took it back up to the house where it was hung over the mantel in a place of honor for many years."

Written and Submitted by: Elizabeth Coldwell Frano (Mrs. Christopher John Frano)

Kay Laing and Dotty McPherson Growing Up in South City

The John Laing family lived at the corner of South Monroe Street and Orange Avenue alongside a huge flood control ditch. Living at home at that time were his wife and children John, Jr., Evelyn, Kay, and Sammy.

John Laing, Sr., was the manager of Citizen's Oil. The plant was next door to their home. Citizen's became Bay Petroleum Corporation, and then Tenneco Oil Company. The plant is gone, but an automobile-related business occupies the remaining building.

Kay transferred from Demonstration School to South City School for the fourth grade. Dotty volunteered to give Kay an introductory tour of the school. They became best friends and, though their older lives took different paths, their friendship remains.

Kay and Dotty took tumbling lessons at South City School and later at FSU. Kay taught Dotty to play the ukulele. When their schools had seasonal plays, Kay and Dotty played their ukuleles and sang.

Dotty's Daddy, Elmer, arranged for them to sing at Grand Openings around town. Kay got them a gig at a radio station in the Duval Hotel. Kay had a beautiful voice, but she never left out Dotty.

Dotty, an only child, included Kay in everything Dotty did with her Daddy, exploring Tallahassee and Leon and Wakulla Counties. They were Brownies and Girl Scouts and went to 4-H and Silver Lake camps together.

Kay and Dotty played in that ditch, and behind Kay's home in a huge grassy field where they looked for four-leaf clovers. Closing the huge ditch and widening Orange Avenue took the Laing family home, but not the memories.

Written and Submitted by Dorothy Lee "Dotty" McPherson 24236 Lanier Street Tallahassee, FL 32310; Source: Information about Mr. Laing's business provided by Kay Laing.

Dotty McPherson- Growing Up with the Bass Family

Betty June Bass had several brothers. Two are Kirby and Gene. Dotty's Mother worked at Turner's (apparel on Monroe Street). The Bass family cared for Dotty when she was younger than four.

Gene was a mail carrier. Growing up, Dotty ran to greet him every time she saw him. Almost 60 years later Dotty learned why she was so attached to Gene. Gene was responsible for Dotty when she was at their house. He was the big brother she never had.

When Kirby returned from the war at Dale Mabry Field, the family took Dotty to meet him. Seeing Kirby, she broke into a run towards him, without regard for the whirling airplane propellers. They saved her from sure death.

One time when Dotty was sick, her Mother was about to give her some Milk of Magnesia.

Any time Dotty got puny, she was given Milk of Magnesia or Castor Oil, the cure-all for everything.

Their home was on a little dirt road that ran west off Monroe Street, a block north of Bass Street. Dotty burst out the door and ran straight to the Bass house. Her Mother chased with the spoon and bottle of Milk of Magnesia, yelling after her.

When Dotty got to the Bass house, Betty June was at the doorway. She formed a cross in the doorway using her arms and legs outstretched to the corners of the doorway. Dotty jumped left and through the hole under Betty June's outstretched right arm, and over her right leg. Mrs. Bass grabbed Dotty, whereupon her Mother caught up and dumped the spoonful of medicine into her mouth.

Written and Submitted by: Dorothy Lee "Dotty" McPherson, 24236 Lanier Street, Tallahassee, FL 32310

The Home Front During World War II

During WWII, all the available, healthy men were either drafted, or were signing up to fight after Pearl Harbor was bombed by the Japanese. With other alliances in play, we soon found that we were fighting all over the world.

Things were extremely tight during 1941-1945 and some time beyond.

Many changes were made in manufacturing plants: Cars weren't manufactured at all by any of the car makers. Those making machinery, and other appliances were switched over to make airplanes, tanks, guns, ships and other implements of wars.

Most women didn't work outside the home before WWII. With all the men gone to war, the women manned the factories making airplanes and other war machinery. This created a striking change in the way American women thought of themselves after this.

Most materials were scarce on the Home Front because some foods and other commodities were used to make war materials. As a result, families were put on Ration Stamps: a rationing of butter, oil, gas, metals, rubber, common foods, some types of clothing, and many other commodities which memory fails me. Families learned to exist on a lot less than what they were accustomed.

Food had to be made into instant C-Rations for the soldiers to carry as they moved towards their battle stations.

Butter and oil was hard to come by. It was used to make ammunition. Margarine was made with yellow powder and a butter-like material mixed together to appear as butter.

There was a War Ration Board in each town and city in the United States at that time. If there was to be any exception made to the allotment that people received, it had to go through the Rationing Board for approval. Gas had stamps with which to purchase gasoline. People weren't able to take trips in cars because they needed the little gas and tires they had to take care of daily needs, since there was little to replace them. Tires for cars were impossible to buy because the rubber had to be put on Jeeps, tanks, etc. for the war effort.

Young people were recruited as volunteers to wrap bandages for the Red Cross and to work in the War Rationing Board assisting the regular workers with the needs of the population and rationing.

Everyone bought War Bonds and there were extensive campaigns for purchasing them to help pay for the war effort.

Regular activities were pretty much put on hold until the war was won. Germany was defeated in Spring of 1945 and Japan in August of 1945. The war began Dec 7, 1941.

Written and Submitted by: Mary J. Marchant, 2901 Springfield Drive, Tallahassee, FL 32309-3274

Let's Zoom Through Dixieland's Past

As we zoomed through Dixieland we shouted from our cars for all to hear. I remember when we young sixteen years old and up, grouped in cars for the evening, circling passways and other great drive-in restaurants with curb hostesses. Gabbing and laughing we rode slowly down the streets looking for our friends, cute guys, or whatever. We stopped to order good old junk food as we carefully watched as each car passed, eyeing their content. We always shared the gas cost, which was a quarter apiece in those days.

Our teenager's dates were set in tradition. It started when the girls at fourteen years old could put on that red lip paint called "Lipstick"; mine was "Love that Pink." After that, the day was to come for us to put on our first high heels at age sixteen. It all fit right into our preference at the dress shops, to look at the chiffon gowns, and evening dresses before we checked out the casual wear. Dreaming of the time when we could look for high heels for our dates.

We had a community center on Jefferson and Adams. It was a pretty large building where the teenager mingled, but we always had chaperones. Many kids came in to play the juke box, shoot pool, or dance. Our town was a walking town; everything needed was within a three to four blocks square. At the end of the shops were the Capitol buildings. At the central corner of College Avenue and Monroe there was Bennett's Drugstore with its soda fountain. It was impossible not to stroll in automatically, to find some friends having a shake and hamburger. Outside you'd see motorcycles parked on the sidewalk.

We used to call the boys and men drivers; motorcycle cowboys or drugstore cowboys. I liked Martin's drugstore, just around the block. It also had an ice cream parlor, soda fountain booths and counter. Two of our movie theaters were always filled. During those times they had the news and a cartoon short, just before the movie. The State theatre was on College Ave and the Florida was two blocks around the corner from there. There was also the Ritz theatre, in the mid block of Monroe, where Old fashioned Cafes were spaced across and up the street from it.

Our dress shops were wonderful, because back then, there was always a dress code acknowledgement, which enabled our stylish and fashionable dress shops and men's wear stores to operate in a first class way. Women wore cute outfits with shoes and hats to match. Men wore flattops and crew haircuts. Their shoes were tied saddle oxfords, or neat looking loafers.

We kept the beauty salons and barber shops full from morning to closing time. Everyone was always trim and neat in those days. Jeans were call dungarees, and only worn on the farms. I spent lots of my time in Gibbs French shop. They knew to call me when they had a fabulous size nine outfit for me. There were shops similar to Gibbs lining the streets on all sides. There were also shoes, and furniture stores mixed in for good measures.

Written and Submitted by: Bette Ann Barrett, 2870 Pharr Court-South NW, Atlanta, GA 30305

Memories of Tallahassee, 1941-1944

In the summer of 1941 I had a second job in B. I. Gatlin's grocery, which was at the northeast corner of Monroe Street and 5th Avenue. It was an old frame building. Part of my job was to deliver groceries by bicycle to customers on Beard Street. During Fred Cone's administration, 1937-1941, Mr. Gatlin had the contract to furnish groceries to the Governor's Mansion. In the summer of 1942 I had a second job as a painter's assistant. The main task of the summer was to paint the woodwork around the windows of the Capitol. I stayed on the roof and moved the hooks that held up the scaffold on which the painters worked.

Leon High graduation was on Friday, June 2, 1944. There were 133 of us. Four days later, on June 6, the Allies invaded Normandy. Then I applied for enlistment in the Army Air Corps at age 17. On June 30 Jerry Carter's son, William, a World War II fighter pilot ace, the recruiting officer, swore me in. Sworn in with me were Carl Thompson, Jr., Glenn Turner, Sidney Hough, Ralph Cowart, and Rivers Buford, Jr., son of the Chief Justice of the Florida Supreme Court, who was present. Jerome Payne, Louis Rocco, Jr., and J.P. Love, Jr. enlisted on a different date. We entered a new era of our lives.

Submitted by: Sylvan Strickland, 3423 John Hancock Drive, Tallahassee, Fl 32312-1538

Memories of Tallahassee in the Mid 1950s

Tallahassee was a sleepy southern town in 1955.

Few apartments were available for 8,000 students enrolled at FSU and a smaller number at FAMU. No Junior College existed. Alumni Village housed married couples and dormitories provided for single men and women.

The population in 1950 was 27,237.

Bricked, uneven streets in the downtown shopping district supported approximately a 10 block rectangle of assorted businesses. There were no malls. With stores concentrated downtown, it was extremely difficult to find a parking space and was very frustrating.

Many residences adjacent to FSU were decades old and thus few parking places were available on campus.

Window units supplied what little air conditioning existed. Department stores first installed AC to draw customers. People opened their windows, used paper fans, and sat on the front porch.

The only high school at that time, Leon High, elected a May Queen and had a May Party under the May Oak on Park Avenue. All ages participated.

Tallahassee City Government has Commissioners and a Mayor form of government. The Commissioners rotated being mayor.

Centennial Field is a park located at Monroe and Apalachee Parkway across from the Capitol. A minor league baseball team played there. The first Springtime Tallahassee had its after-parade activities there.

R. A. Gray, Secretary of the Department of State, stated that Tallahassee is really three cities in one: The Capitol and State Government; The Universities with contributions in research, intellect, and culture; and Business, Professional Organizations who support growth.
Written and submitted by: Mary J. Marchant, 2901 Springfield Drive, Tallahassee, FL 32309-3274

Memories of Wilson Avenue

My mother, Judy Thompson Goodwin, shared these memories with me. On Sunday at high noon, March 30, 1941, she was born in a house on Cherry Street. Forsyth Hospital was located right around the corner on Gadsden Street, so her mother's doctor, Dr. Edward Annis, felt the hospital was close enough if there were problems.

Judy Thompson Goodwin & Romulus Thompson, Wilson Avenue, Tallahassee ca. 1945

Nine months later, Judy and her family including Romulus, Rachel and brother Carl moved a few blocks away to Wilson Terrace (the name was changed many years later to Wilson Avenue). The builder, Syde Deeb had built houses along the street located between Meridian and Miccosukee Road. The street was name after Mr. Bill Wilson who had a building supply business near Railroad Avenue in Tallahassee. The homes were modest but well built with hardwood floors, fireplaces and basements. Congressman Claude Pepper's mother and sister lived in a lovely two-story home at the west end of the street. My mother fondly remembers as a child when Mrs. Pepper would invite her to come down to help entertain young relatives who had come for visits.

Mr. and Mrs. Amos Godby lived two houses over. Mr. Godby and Romulus taught at Leon High School. Lafayette Park was just blocks away and holds many memories of swinging on swings, see-sawing, and skating on the concrete skating oval. There were a number of skinned knees from these activities.

My mother relayed that until she turned five years old, the family did not own an automobile. Her father walked the few blocks to Leon High School. There was a shopping strip on Monroe Street at Brevard with a grocery store, The Capital Pharmacy and the The Camellia Bakery. What fun to walk there for ice cream and magazines from the pharmacy or fresh donuts and cookies from the bakery. Oftentimes, the family would walk to the Florida Theater for movies and return by way of the pharmacy for treats. They would use the city bus system for trips further afield.

This is the story of a happy childhood that created many wonderful lasting memories of a Tallahassee past.
Submitted by: Jenna G. Eckland, 1104 Lochknoll Court, Tallahassee, FL 32308

Dotty McPherson - Mischief on Bass Street

Betty June Bass came down the street from her home on the corner of Bass Street and Monroe Street (Bass Street was 2 blocks from the Leon County Fairgrounds at the corner of Jim Lee Road and South Monroe Street.).

Dotty had a picture of herself with a haircut and permanent that Mrs.Bass gave her.Dotty's hair had been long, with a gentle curl. The perm burned her silky hair to a frizz. Her new hairdo made her look like the head of a Sphinx. She hated it and Thelma, her Mother, was livid.

Dotty's dislike of her hair or the unforgotten Milk of Magnesia incident could have brought the consequential

Betty June Bass and Dotty McPherson's "Sphinx" haircut

grudge that instigated Dotty and Ruby's trick on Betty June. It occurred years later when Dotty and her parents lived across the street and in front of the Wilders on Bass Street.

Ruby Wilder and Dotty told Betty June they were eating the peppers off the huge bush that Elmer had grown. They took the hot peppers and put them in their mouths and pretended to chew them up. They encouraged Betty June to follow suit, which she did - except, she really chewed the peppers.

She started screaming and screamed all the way to her home at the end of the block. Ruby and Dotty laughed heartily at their successful trick.

Dotty probably got a switchin' for that prank, as she got lots of switchin's by her Mother. Her Mother would get a limb off an azalea bush or a green bush that has yellow flowers on it that stung like the Devil when struck on bare legs.
Written and Submitted by: Dorothy Lee "Dotty" McPherson, 24236 Lanier Street, Tallahassee, FL 32310

Dotty McPherson—Mischief with Johnny Davis

Another time Dotty got worse than a switchin'. She and next door neighbor Johnny Davis went 2 doors past his house where the neighbor had the most gorgeous flowers all over her yard. They wanted to surprise the old lady by taking the flowers and decorating her whole front porch with them. They tore the flowers in tiny little pieces and sprinkled them everywhere.

The old lady came to the door and surprised them instead. She scolded them for destroying her flowers. She told them that, if they didn't go home and tell their mothers' what they did, she would.

Dotty was so horrified about being scolded, she took off her shirt and started sweeping the flowers off the porch, while crying and telling the old lady they were trying to make her a beautiful surprise. The old lady told her to stop and go home, which she and Johnny did.

Dotty forgot to tell her mother about that incident. The Wednesday afternoon following the incident, Dotty and Ruby and Delores Barnett (Dotty's future stepsister) were playing in a 5-gallon washtub and the water sprinkler. Thelma walked to the back porch and demanded that Dotty come inside, which she obeyed. Once inside, she saw the old lady. Dotty had to apologize to the old lady. Then she was taken to the bedroom where she was properly spanked.

After the spanking, she ran outside and jumped into the washtub so the cold water would cool her behind. Whether it did or not, she, Ruby, and Delores laughed so hard at what she was doing, she no longer felt the burn anyway.
Written and Submitted by: Dorothy Lee "Dotty" McPherson, 24236 Lanier Street, Tallahassee, FL 32310

My Memories of Tallahassee

I remember Tallahassee from the time of the Second World War. I was born in Quincy, Florida in 1936. My maiden name was Ruby Jean Livingston, a Southern family name.

Back in the early 40s, we would all get in our black, '39 Chevy and head to Tallahassee. We had to go by way of Havana. Highway 90 from Quincy to Tallahassee wasn't opened until after the War. It was a big happening! We would come in on Tennessee St. and head down Monroe. The old Floridan Hotel, with all of its lovely Art Deco architecture, was still across from St. John's Episcopal Church. We would park near the then post office on Park Avenue. As a child, I would gawk at the big, colorful murals there!

We would walk down one side of Monroe, looking and shopping, and stopping to have lunch at the counter in McCrory's five and dime. In back of the lunch counter were the most beautiful mirrors with art deco designs of cranes and reeds! The lunch counter went all the way to the back of the store! After lunch, we would continue our walk down Monroe to the Capitol Building, and then across the street to the big Sears store on the corner. Sometimes we would catch a movie. There were three movie theatres: The Florida, up by the post office, the Ritz on Monroe, between Park and College, and the State on College. When we saw Disney's Three Caballeros at the Ritz, I was not use to the color and motion, and it almost made me sick. And, just think about what we watch today! "Going to the big city" to look and shop was one of the highlights of my childhood.

In 1956, I transferred to FSU after attending a small women's college for two years. It was quite an adjustment, both the size and being co-ed, although there were only 6,000 students there at the time. I was a pre-med major taking science classes, and I remember in a Physics lab one day, the lab assistant said to the two of us girls, "I don't like girls in my labs." Talk about a shock! After being the science department's only assistant at my previous college, I felt like I had fallen through a hole in time.

I married in 1957, and we moved to Tallahassee to Mitchell's trailer park on West Call Street. It was very convenient; you could walk to campus! I finished my degree, and got a job in a Biochemistry lab on campus while my husband was still at FSU. My work was very interesting, in the Dept. of Oceanography with Dr. Sidney Fox. He was doing research on Synthetic Proteins that he had named "proteinoids", made by co-polymerizing amino acids. I had the privilege of making the first "microspheres", like cells, from these! My name was on several journal publications with Dr. Fox.

During this time, we had a daughter, Kaye Lynne, born in 1959, and twin daughters, Cynthia and Sandra, born in 1961. Life was quite busy, with three babies under three. I remember making the prophetic comment to my husband that life would be lots of things, but not boring!

In 1963, I went back to work teaching biology at Leon High School. The research that I had done with Dr. Fox was now in the new Biological Curriculum Studies! The rooms weren't air conditioned. We had big open windows and no screens. So, one day during a microscope lab, I looked up and saw one of my students staggering in the door, with leaves and dirt all over him. He said, "I fell out the window trying to catch a fly for the frog in the terrarium!"

After teaching for a year at Leon, I was offered a job back at FSU in the Food Science lab. This was very exciting, as it would give me a chance to work in research again, and finish my Master's!

Dr. Betty Watts was my major professor. I was given the job of lab supervisor to see that all the equipment and inventory was maintained, the lab kept in order, grad students informed on the use of the lab, plus working on USDA grants. I finished my Master's in 1967, and worked on my Doctorate as a teaching assistant for another year. I published my Master's thesis with Dr. Watts; my doctoral work gave a breakthrough on a research question that went back to the late forties.

In 1969, our son was born. I finished my teaching career by working for the Dept. of Education the last 20 years, retiring in 1999. There is no place like home-this beautiful, springtime fairyland city! Thank you for my memories, Tallahassee!

Written and Submitted by: Laura Jean Kendrick Huff, 814 Governors Drive, Tallahassee, FL 32301

Patricia B. Ryerson

As many of us have found, the places I've lived in Tallahassee reflect its history. For example, when my family moved here from Gainesville in 1941, we rented a brick house on Lake Ella across from the American Legion Home on the lake and from Mr. Chandler's motel on North Monroe. When I was a responsible age, I walked across Monroe to visit Mr. Chandler, and when I was school age, I walked around the lake and up the hill to Sealey Memorial, now the Police Station. We moved across town to Palm Court when I was going into the 4th grade and I met my best friends for life, Carmean Tribble Johnston, Ginger Graham Tillman, and Sandra Calhoun Touchton. We formed our "Gang," controlling the dead end street and checking every car that entered, just as my dog Tuffy controlled the entrance stairs to the top floor of an old house where we lived. Then we built my father's dream house on Betton Road on one of the first lots sold by Mr. Winthrop, who lived in what I thought was a haunted house on North Monroe where a city utilities drive through is now. I lived off and on in this house until my mother died, after which I moved "across town and the tracks" into the Myers Park Historical District to a house built in 1935. I love the land, a tract given to General Lafayette, the beautiful old houses, and my neighbors who share a love for one of the few designated historical neighborhoods in Tallahassee.

Written and submitted by: Patricia B. Ryerson, ryerson6869@yahoo.com

Pearson Home, 112 Polk Drive

This is the address to the house I grew up in during the 60s and 70s. My mom still owns the house. The John L. Sullivans lived next door to us. The Tadlocks lived on the other side. Across the street was Tenneco Gas Company truck terminal and garage. GMC trucks had a dealership there for awhile. The city bus service moved in that location after being down on Gaines Street across from the old city jail. This is when the Carter family owned the bus service before they sold it to the City of Tallahassee. Polk Drive is just a block north of Orange Ave. It has three sections to it: A section that runs between Monroe and Adams. This is the section we lived on. Another section runs between Monroe and Meridian. The other section runs from Meridian and used to curve back into Orange Ave. This end

was recently reconstructed and I am not sure where Polk ends now. Back in the 1960s the street signs were concrete posts painted white with black letters with the block numbers painted above the street name. Behind our house at 112 was and still is a ditch with a natural creek running in it. Our dad, Lawrence Pearson did not want us playing in it for fear of cave in. Needless to say we got a whooping every time he caught us playing in it. From our house we could hear the FAMU Band practicing.
Submitted by: Shawn Pearson, 4521 Bloxham Cut Off Road, Crawfordville, Fl 32427

Places of Old Tallahassee, Elmer McPherson Family

Buildings and landscapes and old fishing holes help us make and remind us of some great memories. The good thing is, they usually remain longer than people. Sometimes, however, people like "newer, prettier, and finer," and take the "good ole" away from us. Hopefully, memories will outlast them all. This is just the beginning of memories of many of the Places of Old Tallahassee.

In the fifties, when Tallahassee still had moonshiners who produced hard liquor and sold it from the trunks of their cars and clandestine locations, Tallahassee had lots of beer joints. After work, men from all stations in life frequented them.

Elmer McPherson, a man of many talents and interests, with a tremendous work ethic, was mostly and truly a "family man". Because Thelma, his wife, worked until 6 PM 4.5 days a week, and Saturdays, Elmer cared for their daughter, Dorothy Lee "Dotty" McPherson. Dotty went with him everywhere, except to the hunting camps where he and his cousins and uncles hunted every year - and "she" went to Church every Sunday with Andy and Louise Wilder and their daughters, Mary, Ruby, Sadie, and Katie.

Thelma worked for Turners on Monroe Street (later for Annette's on College Avenue and Lillian's on Monroe Street - all fine dress shops). Lillian Cox, owner of Lillian's, a member of the GFWC Woman's Club of Tallahassee, is living at age 104 today. When Dotty had her tonsils out at Briley's Hospital at McDaniel and North Gadsden Streets, the Turners visited her and gave her the Raggedy Ann and Andy rag doll set. One of Dotty's daughters has those dolls today.

A master of his trade, Elmer worked nearly his whole life for Florida Sheet Metal Works at Jennings and Monroe Streets, owned by the Nettles family.

Leo Nettles, son of O.J. Nettles, Florida Metal Works

Leo and Elmer were friends as well as co-workers and later boss and worker. They frequently visited each other's homes with Dotty in tow. She even attended their union meetings.

If Elmer had to work while Dotty was not in school, Dotty was at the shop fronting 115 Jennings Street. She was well behaved and never in the way. All the workers catered to her, but mostly Leo. She knew all the equipment in the shop and what it did to metals - bending, cutting, welding. Today, inside the shop door is a picture of a woman's profile Elmer drew for her.

Dotty saw Elmer make a Bowie Knife at the shop. He cut and filed down a blade from thick metal. Then he melted metal in a rectangular pot and poured it into a mold he made for the handle. The blade was carefully placed in the molten steel. Dotty gifted the knife to her grandson, Sawyer Williamson. She packed it in a tackle box Elmer crafted out of sheet metal. It originally was a sewing box for Thelma. He also built a sheet metal casket for his favorite dog, Spike, a Feist. He crafted a funnel to strain particles out of gasoline, which Dotty has.
Written and Submitted by: Dorothy Lee "Dotty" McPherson, 24236 Lanier Street, Tallahassee, FL 32310

Ruby Hopkins Coldwell Remembered Tales

Ruby Hopkins Coldwell remembered her grandmother Mary Ann Harvey Black, telling her about an uninvited visit by Indians to the Harvey Plantation in Ft. Braden. "One day the women were working out in the kitchen when they heard noises coming from the house. One of the sisters went into the house to see what the cause of all the commotion was. She discovered that Indians had entered the house and were rolling around the floor under the beds. They were laughing and having a good time tickling their noses on the tassels attached to the edges of the bedspreads. She ran out of the house and over to the kitchen and told her sisters that the house was full of

Indians. Since they did not know if they were 'Good or Bad Indians', one of them ran to get the men who were working out in the fields. The Indians always came when the men were working in the fields. The men, hearing that Indians were in the house, took up their hoes and axes they had on hand as weapons and ran back to the house. The men found the Indians still rolling around on the floor laughing, never having seen anything like fringe before. The men realized they had the 'good Indians' in the house, and let the Indians stay until they grew tired of the game. The Indians left on their own a couple of hours later".
Written by: Elizabeth Coldwell Frano; Submitted by: Ruby HopkinsColdwell

South Monroe Street Early Times

Across Jennings Street from Florida Sheet Metal shop was Graddy's Gulf Station, 1458 South Monroe Street. Kenneth Graddy had a bar inside. It was a hangout for loyal beer drinkers.

Elmer and his friends were always there after work with all their children. Dotty and they played in the side yard of the station; drank Coca Cola; and ate peanuts, chocolate candy bars, and hand-dipped ice cream. The Dads never got drunk and were not boisterous, and the children were satiated with all those good treats.

Back in those days, hand-dipped ice cream was in about every store they frequented, and Dotty got the double cone with double dips in each side. That and chocolate milk is how Elmer got her calcium intake, as she would not drink "white" milk. When they went fishing, they stopped at stores on Crawfordville Highway and Woodville Highway for ice cream - going and coming.

After Mr. Graddy moved his station to the block at the railroad underpass, across the street from the High Hat restaurant, shaped like a black top hat, and B & W Fruit Market, he became religious and stopped serving beer.

Although they still visited Kenneth Graddy, Elmer found new bars to meet his friends. One place was a house that stands right next to the sidewalk, owned by an elderly German couple. They sold groceries and served beer. The house remains today at 1614 South Monroe Street.
Written and Submitted by: Dorothy Lee "Dotty" McPherson, 24236 Lanier Street, Tallahassee, FL 32310

Tallahassee Memories of Charles Blankenship

My father, George W. Blankenship, migrated to Florida in 1934 from Jackson, Tennessee during the Depression as a Civilian Conservation Corps worker. A WWI veteran, he lived in Blountstown, White Springs, Hilliard, Perry, and Lake City (1940 & 1942).

The second time he came to Lake City he brought his family, but then Pearl Harbor changed everything. The CCC was dissolved, and the men and organization were put under the authority of the War Department. The entire Motor Repair Shop at Lake City was ordered to move to Tallahassee, Florida on 26 October 1942. The shop was to take all the equipment, tools and vehicles. Per Diem for the move was $6. Travel by personal automobile was reimbursed at .03.5 cents per mile, and the ration board issued ration tickets for extra gasoline. The Ordnance Service Command Shop was located at 528 West Madison Street (now the parking lot for the Civic Center) to support Dale Mabry Field where American and foreign pilots were trained. Within a year the shop was transferred to Camp Gordon Johnston 53 miles south of Tallahassee to prepare troops for amphibious landings in Europe.

I do not recall the date of my first arrival in Tallahassee (one of my favorite cities), but I do recall where we lived - 329 Roosevelt Drive in Mabry Heights, which still exists on the western-most part of the FSU campus. The back yard was wide open all the way to the main buildings. In 1943 we moved to Carrabelle and Camp Gordon Johnston. In 1947 we moved to Carrabelle Beach. There is little evidence of the wartime effort still in existence today.
Source: Taken from an article by Charles Blankenship in the Tallahassee Genealogist, vol 12 #3, Spring 1993.

Tallahassee Sixties

My final years in Tallahassee ended in the sixties, which brought to our little town a "Counter Culture" seen most evidently by 1965. We had Beatniks at first, then a change in psychology of some in our nation. That Counter Culture changed more than some might recall. I saw the dress code of neatly styled ladies and gentlemen, boys and girls, become wash and wear, bedraggled, and unkempt. A look these young activists used to defy the establishment.

The music of Dean Martin, Perry Como, Doris Day, and the like, allowed us to use a ballroom that was for the Waltz, Foxtrot, two-steps or East Coast Swing be switched almost instantaneously into non-touch dancing called the Jerk, the Twist, and the Pony. The young of that time got lost in an unsophisticated "Age of Aquarius".

Make-up and hair-styles were gone. During this period in the 1965, we experienced a riot that began on South Monroe Street and spread to the North and West side of town. The burning and rioting of people scared us all as we learned of a fine family grocery store that was set on fire, where the twenty-year-old junior in college was suffocated and burned to death, whose brother had become a University Professor. Those arrested included bused in activists from the North, which we heard were spurring similar Southern riots that we could never have dreamed of. Things had changed now as youths experimented in new and destructive styles of behavior. My private life with my family was still loving and close knit, but Tallahassee began to lose the identity I saw in my youth.

Written and Submitted by: Bette Ann Barrett, 2870 Pharr Court-South NW, Atlanta, GA 30305

Kamal Youssef - Self-proclaimed "King Love"

Every city seems to have a resident character or two – perhaps Tallahassee has had more than its share, but none of them could compete with King Love for high visibility. Kamal Youssef crowned himself King Love and no one disputed his right to the title. He was instantly recognizable and could usually be seen waving to traffic from a busy street corner. He delighted in making people laugh – and think. He was an unabashed promoter of tolerance and the right to be different.

Kamal Youssef – aka – King Love stands on a Tallahassee street corner

My first encounter with King Love happened within days of my arrival in 1994. I was checking out the produce at a local grocery store when I felt a light tap on my shoulder. I turned around and was greeted with a cheery, "You've been loved." It was the King himself, dressed in some sort of crimson-red cape that was trimmed with fake ermine. A crown, fashioned from plastic materials of questionable origin, sat crookedly on his head and it framed a face with the most infectious smile I'd ever seen. The King had a full white beard that gave him more of a Santa Claus look than a person of royal bearing. He was wearing glasses in the latest wire-frame style.

The tap had been delivered with a wand. Well, actually, it was a wooden dowel with some stars glued on the end of it. He was traveling around the store in one of those electric carts, but there were no goods in his basket and – as I would learn later – there was no physical reason for his riding the scooter. As he motored away, he admonished me to "Spread some love today!" I saw him many times after that and never failed to return his enthusiastic wave or accept a tap with his magic wand. If he temporarily disappeared from his favorite corner at Tennessee and Monroe, I felt disappointed. At various times, his sign would let people know he was in the market for a new wife or was lobbying on behalf of a righteous cause. He ran an unofficial campaign for Governor in 1998 and used an over-sized, plastic soda bottle to collect financial contributions.

King Love passed away in 1999 at age 66 and some claim, if the Florida sunshine hit just the right angle and intensity, you can still see him around town, waving one hand in the air and carrying a protest sign in the other.

Submitted by: Julianne Hare

Old Orchards and the Bee Hive

Mother remembered, "There was a tall old apple tree on the north side of the house that reached up to the balcony of the second floor." Orchards had been planted from saplings that the Harvey's had brought down from North Carolina. They had figs, pears, apples, peaches, and scuppernong muscadine grapes. One year blights infected the fruit trees killing them. The orchards were replanted several times, but the saplings would only become spindly and die. The fruit from these trees was dried for year round.

The Harveys used the honey for their sweets. They also grew sugar cane, which they boiled down into syrup to pour over their biscuits. The spring Steven and his brother Mark Harvey had found on the side of the hill was used for fresh cool drinking water, and it is where they stored the glass jars of milk and cottage cheese.

The kitchen, which was located on the east side of the house, was detached from the house for safety reasons since kitchens had a history of catching on fire. Another reason for having their kitchen detached from the main house was to help keep the house from heating up in the summer. The kitchen was a large building that was used by the women as their workroom. It had a front and back door and tall windows for ventilation. On the east wall of the kitchen was the immense brick fireplace that had cast iron cooking hooks built into its sides. The cooking hooks would swing out from the fireplace so the women could hang the cast iron cooking pots on them.

Using the hooks to push the pots over or away from the coals was the way they were able to control the temperature for cooking. Built on the right side of the fireplace were brick ovens used for baking bread. The kitchen held the walking spinning wheel and the loom they had brought from North Carolina. There were a couple of long worktables in the room, used for everything from a place to knead bread dough to carding the cotton. The wash was done in the kitchen and hung up to dry outside. To move from the kitchen to the main house, they walked under a grape arbor that offered them some protection from the sun and rain, as they carried the prepared foods through the side door of the house leading into the dining room.

The barn was located east of the kitchen. It wasn't too far from the house. We had to climb over a high fence when we wanted to go out to the barn. "The smokehouse was built a distance from the house, so in case of a fire the house would not burn. In the fall, after the pigs had been fattened up on all the acorns they had eaten, they where butchered and cured. The sausage was cooked and then placed in a wooden barrel, alternating a layer of lard and then a layer of sausage until the barrel was full. The lard was used as a preservative. Then as the year went by, they would dig down into the lard and take out the sausage they wanted and heat it up for their meal. When the supply of smoked meats was running low, the men and boys would take their guns and go out to hunt for wild turkey and deer.

In the winter, they grew their own greens in the garden, so they would always have a fresh supply of vegetables. The mustard greens were grown from the seed they had saved from the previous year. One of the first years the Harveys were in Florida was "the year there was no summer" as it became known. Due to an unseasonable heavy frost in May, everyone lost their crops. To save the family and the families on neighboring plantations from starving, the Harvey men rode on horseback to North Carolina and brought back seed for new crops. The Harveys were always considered heroes by their neighbors.

As a mosquito repellent for the house, they would place a cow dung on the windowsill then stick wood splinters into it. They would light the splinters and as the wood burned down into the dung, it would cause a heavy smoke and odor to fill the rooms repelling the mosquitoes.

During the Civil War, to do their part for the war effort, "ole man Harvey", would go to meet the trains as they came carrying the dead from battle fields all over. The dead soldiers had been laid out on the open flat bed cars with nothing covering them but maybe an old piece of cloth or a palm frond. 'Ole' man Harvey' would ride to the train stop in his wagon that was pulled by his mule, and if there were any dead from Leon County he would take the time at the train stop to build each man a coffin. They would then load the coffins into the back of his wagon. Then he began his sad journey down the sand rutted roads of Leon County, going from home to home, returning the dead to their families.

"Ole man Harvey" may have been referring to James Raford Harvey who put in a pension request for his work taking wounded and dead soldiers to their home from the trains, or it may have been his brother Mark Harvey. Both men were too old to have gone off to fight in the war. Stories remembered by: Ruby Hopkins Coldwell (Mrs. Walter Amze Coldwell)

Written by: Elizabeth Coldwell Frano (Mrs. Christopher John Frano); Submitted by Elizabeth Coldwell Frano's grandson: Christopher Theodore Frano

LEON COUNTY FAMILIES

Dr. James H. Ammons, President, Florida A&M University

Born December 23, 1952, Dr. James Henry Ammons, Jr. is the younger of two children of James and Agnes Ammons of Winter Haven, Florida. Ammons grew up in the heart of Florida's citrus belt and received support from his church, Hurst Chapel A.M.E. Church, and the community at-large. In 1970, he graduated from Winter Haven High School. He went on to attend Florida A&M University where he graduated cum laude with a B.S. degree in political science in 1974. He earned the M.S. in public administration in 1975, and the Ph.D. in government in 1977 from Florida State University. He began his teaching career in public policy and administration in 1977 as an assistant professor at the University of Central Florida.

Dr. James H. Ammons, 2008

He returned to FAMU in 1983 as an associate professor of political science, and in 1984, he was promoted to the position of Assistant Vice President for Academic Affairs. In 1989, he was promoted to Associate Vice President for Academic Affairs and also served as Director of Title III Programs. He was promoted to Provost and Vice President for Academic Affairs in 1995. During his tenure at Florida A&M University, he developed more than 22 bachelor's, master's and Ph.D. degree programs, and he worked to reestablish the FAMU College of Law. In 2001, he was appointed chancellor of North Carolina Central University. At NCCU, enrollment reached an all-time high during his tenure, climbing from 5,476 in 2000- 2001 to 8,675 in 2006-2007 - a 58.4 percent increase. NCCU became the fastest growing institution in the University of North Carolina System. NCCU had many successes in fundraising under Ammons' leadership. From 2001 through 2006, NCCU received more than $40 million in private gifts to support the establishment of the Biotechnology Research Institute and Technology Enterprise, construction of facilities, scholarships, faculty development and outreach programs.

On July 2, 2007, he became the tenth president of Florida A&M University. Since Dr. Ammons' arrival at FAMU, he has built a top-notch, strong leadership team. In addition, he secured accreditation from the Accreditation Council for Pharmacy Education in which the board voted to reaffirm the College's accreditation status through June 30, 2010. During his first year, the University received its first unqualified audit in three years from the Auditor General's Office, and admitted students to a new doctorate program in physical therapy.

In 2008, he was selected as the 2008 recipient of the "Leader of the Year Award" from Leadership Tallahassee for his effort in restoring the public's trust in FAMU. During his tenure, FAMU has received many accolades including being selected by Business Week as one of the nation's "Most Innovative Colleges" in the area of technology transfer. He is a member of Bethel A.M.E. Church in Tallahassee and is married to Judy Ammons (Ruffin) and they have one son, James, III.

Dr. Ammons continues to promote higher education standards for the country and supports community involvement for his students and residents of Leon County, Florida.

Written and submitted by: Dr. James H. Ammons; Sharon P. Saunders, Executive Assistant to the President, Florida A & M University, 103 Lee Hall, Tallahassee, FL. 32307

Steven Andrews, A Lawyer Paints

Steven R. Andrews was born in Houston, Texas, March 5, 1954. He married while studying at FSU; they have four children. After high school graduation, Steve attended Florida State University where he was the recipient of the Walter Mann Outstanding Student Award, and at Stetson was Editor of the Stetson Law Review. He was admitted to the Florida Bar in 1978, the U.S. District Court, and all Districts Courts of Florida. His education includes: Florida State University

(B.S., 1975); Stetson University (J.D., with honors, 1977); New York University (LL.M. in Taxation, 1979). Steve is a member of The Florida Bar's Academy of Florida Trial Lawyers, and The American Board of Trial Advocacy.

Steve Andrews continues to live in Tallahassee, Florida, where he has raised his children and found an additional talent for being a professional painter for more than ten years. He is largely self-taught, subscribing to the proposition that to get better you must paint, paint, paint. He is represented in corporate and private collections and his work can be seen in Tallahassee, Jacksonville, and Destin, Florida. Steve says "You could call this "A Lawyer Paints" or more accurately "A Painter who's also a Lawyer". The marketing gurus would say: "Keep these things separated; your legal clients don't want to know about your artistic ability and the collector only wants to deal with a true professional who is struggling with his life and art." Well, this is me, and if art paid like being a lawyer does, I would certainly give up the legal part (except those clients that are a pleasure to help). But the reality is that's not going to happen soon, so I have decided to embrace my circumstances. I am an artist who can afford to do whatever he wants to do artistically. I paint what I want to paint because it inspires me and I want to try to communicate that inspiration. My name is Steve, and I am a lawyer.

Steve Andrews, Attorney and Artist

My favorite music to listen to when painting is Dave Matthews Band live albums. I like the live albums because I think I can appreciate the creative energy in them. It's a lot like good painting should be. Just do it and live with what you get. Kind of like a John Singer Sargent painting: lyrical and quick, but perfect of course. The longer I paint, the more I realize that good painting sometime involves many retakes. You put something down and think it could be better and you wipe it off and try again. The fact is this is what Sargent did; the trick of making it looks lyrical and quick, but perfect every time, which takes practice and discipline.

Written and submitted by: Steve R. Andrews, Atty, 1296 Timberlane Road, Tallahassee, Florida 32312, sandrews@andrewslawoffice.com

Apthorp, A Long Trek to Tallahassee

The Apthorps have lived in Tallahassee for six generations. The first was William Lee Apthorp and his wife Charlotte Child Apthorp. The path that led Apthorp to Tallahassee is pure chance, because he was assigned here following the Civil War. For the next few years he was a part of the reconstruction government. He was convinced there was opportunity in Tallahassee so he stayed on following the war.

William Lee in Civil War Uniform-1864

William Lee Apthorp was born in Lee County, Iowa on August 31, 1837. His father William P. Apthorp was a frontier preacher and missionary for the Congregational Church. He had a number of relatives in the Boston and New York City areas. His father sent him back east to college at Amherst. He was a member of the class of 1859. Following graduation Apthorp taught music in Georgia and New York before volunteering for service in the Union Army. His military career began in 1861 as a private in the 90th Regiment of New York Volunteers. While a member of that unit he achieved the rank of sergeant. In 1863 he was promoted to Captain (2nd South Carolina) 34th Regiment U.S. Colored Troops.

During 1863 through 1864 Apthorp and several other officers were sent to South Carolina to recruit freed slaves for service in the Union Army. They signed up several companies of troops and trained them at Hilton Head Island.

Captain Apthorp was promoted to Lt. Colonel in 1864. He was deployed with two companies of troops to Jacksonville, Florida. They found little resistance and occupied Jacksonville until the unit made several sorties up the St. Johns River and to other nearby locations. They encountered little fighting. The rest of the war was spent in and out of Jacksonville. He was mustered out of military duty in February, 1866 in Jacksonville, Florida.

Many officers were assigned jobs in the reconstruction government. Apthorp was first assigned to the Freedman's Bureau. He traveled around the north Florida area checking on the condition of the former slaves. He next helped form the federal government for Florida. He served as Secretary of the Senate and was sent to Tampa to be president of the Board of Registration. Voter registration was important because the federal authorities wanted to elect as many Republicans as possible in the election of 1870. While in Tampa, Apthorp also was appointed County Judge. His wife, Charlotte, was appointed Assistant Postmistress.

Following his service in Tampa he returned to Tallahassee where he was joined by his brother John P. Apthorp. Together they started a dairy on the north shore of Bull Pond (now Lake Ella). William Lee also served as Chief Clerk for the US Land Office in Tallahassee. In 1877 and 1878 he published Apthorp's Map of Florida. The brothers became contract surveyors for the Land Office. They conducted many of the original government surveys in central and southwest Florida. In Highlands County there is a lake called Lake Apthorp. We can assume the brothers named it for themselves or it was named by a friendly fellow surveyor

During this active period of their lives the brothers were much involved in their community. In the 1870s William, Lee also served on the board of the Seminary West of the Suwannee. This school became "Florida State College", then "Florida State College for Women", and finally "Florida State University". He was appointed to the board in 1873. In 1874 he became president of the board where he served until he resigned in 1877.

John P. Apthorp had three daughters. All graduated from Florida State College: Mary Apthorp 1896, Alice B. Apthorp 1903, Agnes K. Apthorp 1905. William Lee Apthorp's great-grandchildren graduated from Florida State University: James William Apthorp in 1961, and George East Apthorp in 1965. In 1877 William Lee Apthorp contracted malaria, likely a result of the months he spent in the swampy bug infested areas of south Florida. Because of his illness he left Florida and died in New Jersey in January 1879. His wife Charlotte died the following year. They left four young children under the age of eight. The children were returned to Tallahassee in the care of William Lee's brother, John P. Apthorp.

William Lee and Brother John Apthorp Dairy Truck-1942

The dairy business was continued by William Lee's oldest son, George Henry. The location at Bull Pond would not accommodate the dairy's growth. George Henry swapped the Bull Pond property for 160 acres four miles out Old St. Augustine Road. His herd grew to 60 head of Jersey milk cows. Winifred, his wife, ran an egg business that complemented the milk production. The Apthorp delivery truck made home delivery of milk and eggs all over Tallahassee. George Henry and Winifred had two boys, James William and George Henry Jr. who continued the farm until it was sold in the 1950s.

Written and submitted by: James W. and Cheri Apthorp, 813 Greenbriar Lane, Tallahassee, Florida 32308

Terry Arthur

Terry has lived in Tallahassee, Florida for over 30 years with his wife Susan. He started turning in November of 1996, and has never attended any classes on wood turning, which makes him completely self-taught. Originally inspired by the wood works of Don Duden, former Assistant Executive Director of the Florida Department of Natural Resources, and the works of Melvin Lindquist, author of many wood turning books, Terry has shifted towards nonfunctional wood turning. Terry has made art from native woods in Southern Georgia and Northern Florida. In later years he has shown influence from the art works of Mark Lindquist.

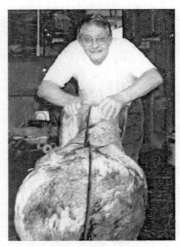
Terry Arthur with a piece of one of his favorite woods

Terry is drawn to working with burl wood the most, but starting with burls or wood blanks that have strong spalting presents both artistic and mechanical challenges. Burls may fly apart under the centrifugal force of the lathe. The chance of keeping all the bark in a continuous edge is just one in four. As he surmounts the challenges of wood physics, Arthur listens to the wood, shaping simply in consonance with the native structure. Even after he starts on a piece of wood he lets the wood talk to him as to what shape it will take. Terry states: "The beauty of the wood is more important then the shape." He also uses inlays such as turquoise, copper and pink coral in many of his pieces. Many patrons comment on the fact that the inlays looks like they grew in the wood naturally.

Terry has turned many custom wood jobs: bowls, platters, vases, ash urns for loved ones, designer pens, pen and pencil sets and all kinds of desk sets. Since starting his career Terry Arthur has done at least ten fine arts shows per year in the southeast alone, showing his work is in high demand. His works are in the permanent collections of the Mobile Museum of Art and the Annette Howell Turner Center for the Arts in Valdosta, GA, as well as many private and corporate collections throughout the United States, Europe and the Mideast. You will see many of his custom pieces in the office of the Attorney of the Americas, in the Old Executive Office Building in Washington, D.C. during 2001 and 2002.Terry has also shown at Axminster, the largest and most prestigious woodturning show in Europe.

Written and submitted by: Terry Arthur, 3338 Barrow Hill Trail, Tallahassee, FL 32312 thur.s.terry@gmail.com

Barrett, The Good Ol' Days

I was three years old in 1944, so I can remember the grand experiences available right around our house. There were my two older sisters, Anita and Helen and our parents which, I believe, were the best of the best. Kids in Tallahassee then were taught manners and discipline, necessary in building character, in our fine little town of about 35,000.

We had plenty of space to play and explore where we lived on North Jackson Street. Only three blocks down the street was Byrd's Woods where Ruediger Elementary and Raa Middle Schools are now. We walked and rode our bikes through the woods, exploring the whole area. Sometimes we'd have wiener roasts there, our father, an avid outdoorsman always in charge. So many kids lived in that area called Sunniland. Jackson Street was unpaved until about 1946. To us, that meant playing in the streets, softball, football, and hopscotch, while bicycling around waiting for the ice cream truck to jingle up for us to get ice cream. There was also the ice truck that came regularly and we watched the ice man use the tongs to grab blocks of ice for the "ice box", no electric refrigerator then!

The Jewel Tea Company truck came by selling coffee and tea and other things like bread, sugar, flour and candy! Occasionally, a farmer would pass our house on a muledriven wagon selling nick-knacks. There was a small grocery store on Eighth Avenue which treated the neighborhood to a movie in the evening in the tiny parking lot in front. We would sit on the ground and watch whatever movie they showed.

Levy Park between Eleventh Avenue and Tharpe Street was adjacent to Byrd's Woods. We played there a lot. Covered picnic tables were clean and nice. We played pingpong in the brick storage building, swings, tetherball, basketball, skating on the tennis court. When the pool opened in the early 1950s they had high and low diving boards. Mama knew she could really have some free time now! I was about ten years old then, when we kids spent many, many hours swimming there. My father was a swim instructor and lifeguard in his earlier years. He taught us to swim like fish at three years of age.

We were members of the Tallahassee Tumbling Tots, and then associated with FSU Gymkana, that gave us the added skills to flip and fly off the high-dive. All I liked to do was fly off those boards. Most all of the kids swam like fish. Our father Claude Barrett had a Junior Rifle Club which he started in 1946, affiliated with the NRA. It was in the basement of the Armory, now the Senior Center on Monroe and Seventh Avenue.

He organized it because he was alarmed at reports of firearms accidents by unskilled rifle and pistol users. We kids were his assistants carrying the rifles the six blocks for the meetings, as we did not have a car, but those were the "Good Ol' Days!"

Written and submitted by: Bette Ann Barrett, 2870 Pharr Court South #207 The Concorde, Atlanta, Georgia 30305

Cal Belton

Semper Fidelis, or Semper Fi...it's a greeting one marine gives another when they meet. Semper Fidelis, "Always Faithful" surely describes Cal Belton. A more passionate Christian you will never find.

What gives Cal the strength and drive that he shows us? Was it growing up in a poor little North Carolina mill town? Was it his year in the cotton mill after he graduated high school? Maybe it was his tour with the Marine Corps during World War II? A seventeen year old boy can take on a pretty sharp edge of steel with that elite service. Perhaps it was his 18 months in a motorcycle platoon with the U.S. Army occupation force in Augsburg, Germany.

Coming back from the war, Cal did what a lot of ex-GI's did, he started his college education, first at Brevard College in North Carolina, then the Indiana Institute of Technology in Fort Wayne where he earned his degree in engineering. After graduation Cal worked a series of jobs, starting with the Virginia Bridge Company, then Peden Steel Company in Raleigh, and finally Brenner Iron and Metal in Winston-Salem.

Cal was "sorta Methodist" then, living on borrowed faith. That is until 1953...and Beth. They met on the boarding house steps. Cal already lived there and Beth was moving in. A pair of shoes fell out of the box Beth was carrying, Cal retrieved them, and he's been carrying her shoes ever since. Her faith in God inspired Cal to really become a Christian, and lit the fire of fervor that has fueled his study for Bible truths ever since.

No one ever said life was easy, but the Bible does say God never gives you more than you can handle. It's a pretty good thing that He doesn't because, in 1958, bad news came from the bosses at Brenner. Cal had lost his job. He was out of work with a wife and four children for close to two years.

Friends told Cal about a possible opening at the Florida DOT. It seemed like a long shot. Cal went to his pastor in Winston-Salem. They talked and prayed together. His pastor said "Just have faith in God". So he hopped on a bus, leaving Beth and the four children at home and came to an unfamiliar city, to an interview with a man he'd never met, for a job he wasn't even sure he could get. Faith in God brought him here, and he firmly believes that faith in God got him the job.

So, in 1960 Cal, Beth and four little ones moved to Tallahassee and to the Florida Department of Transportation, where he served until his retirement in 1987. They settled into Parkway Baptist Church where Cal took on the duties of a Sunday School Teacher. When Faith Baptist Church was starting up Cal and Beth played an important role. Cal continued his teaching there, while training the new Church's Sunday School Director.

In 1978 Leo Hebert called Beth with news about a job opening at FBC, and she became the Church Receptionist. Cal once again switched his teaching skills, this time to First Baptist, and he has been a valuable part of the teaching program here ever since.

What is the worst thing that an old Marine and staunch believer sees in today's generation? Cal thinks it is the downward spiral of spiritual and ethical values that is damaging so many of the young people. There is right and there is wrong, and Cal can quote you chapter and verse to prove it.

Submitted by: Cal Belton; Written by Carol Ann and Bill Boydston ©, 1639 Twin Lakes Circle, Tallahassee, FL 32311

Bernard, Blake, Bradford and Byrd

"The Four Bs and the Family Bible" is the story of the Bernard, Blake, Bradford and Byrd families who came to Leon County, Florida in the early 1800s. Their lives became linked through marriage. None of the surnames survive, but are carried by descendants as first or middle names.

Records of births, marriages and deaths were once recorded in thick, heavy family Bibles. Bible and census records may convey the only evidence of a person's life. An ancestor becomes "real" if letters and diaries are preserved. Our family is fortunate to have Bibles for three of the Bs — Bernard, Bradford and Byrd. Letters and diaries are held by family members, libraries and archives. The following is taken from these and other sources.

Jesse Talbot (J.T.) Bernard (b. 8/20/1829, Portsmouth, VA; d. 10/29/1909, Tallahassee, FL), the second child of Overton and Martha Thomas

Jesse and Mary Bradford Bernard with grandchildren (Florida Archives), 1888

Bernard, came to northern Leon County in 1849, and taught at a plantation school from 1851-53. He married Mary Elizabeth Bradford (b.10/20/1827, Talladega, AL; d. 3/8/1900, Tallahassee, FL) of Walnut Plantation in 1850. Mary was the daughter of Thomas and Elizabeth Eelbeck Bradford. Thomas was one of four brothers who came to Leon County in 1832 from North Carolina. Thomas' plantation was Walnut Hill; Edward's Pine Hill; Richard's, Water Oak and Henry's was not listed in From Cotton to Quail.

J. T. and Mary moved to Newnansville, Alachua County, Florida where their four children (Thomas, Martha, Overton and Rebecca) were born. J.T. received a law degree from East Florida Seminary and practiced until he entered the Army of Northern Virginia in 1861. The family moved to Walnut Hill during the war. Their fourth child, Rebecca "Rubie" Bradford Bernard (b.1 0/3/1859, Newnansville, FL; d. 6/14/1934, Tallahassee, FL), was a toddler at the time. More about Miss Bernard later...

Meanwhile in Miccosukee, Blakes and Byrds were migrating to Leon County. Flavius Augustus (F. A.) Byrd's (b.4/16/1822, Fayetteville, NC; d.12/26/1874, Miccosukee, FL) parents were Nathan and Sarah Eliza Parish Byrd. The Byrds and Parishes came to Leon County in territorial days (1826) from Lenoir County, North Carolina. Nathan served in the legislative council and had been reelected when he died in 1834. Young Flavius was educated at the University of Alabama and Jefferson Medical College, returning to Miccosukee to practice medicine. His first wife was Catherine D. Lloyd who died in 1854.

Flavius then married Catharine "Kate" Sarah Blake (b.3/30/1832, Fayetteville, NC; d.1/13/1878, Miccosukee, FL). They were married in Greensboro, NC, November 19, 1856 and produced seven offspring (William, Thomas, Flavius, Jr., Eliza, Fannie, Caroline and Flavius Gibbs). Kate was the daughter of Thomas Clifton and Eliza Caroline Smith Blake. Kate's parents never lived in Leon County, but her uncle, Miles Blake, came to Miccosukee in territorial days.

Robert and Martha Tilden with daughters Beth and Becky, 1986

Second son of F.A. and Kate Byrd, Thomas Blake Byrd (b.10/14/1859, Miccosukee, FL; d. 9/7/1928, Tallahassee, FL), married Miss "Rubie" Bernard from the Bernard/Bradford union, thus joining the four "B's" It was written in their 1884 wedding announcement, "May she always be to him a Ruby above price, and may he be a Byrd that will sing at home without caging."

The Bernard/Byrd marriage resulted in eight children (William, T. Bradford, L. Clifton, A. Bernard, Rubie, Janet, Kate and Elizabeth). The T. B. Byrd and Son Grocery supported the large family (separate article). The youngest, Elizabeth (b.9/20/1903, Tallahassee, FL;

d.2/12/1985, Tallahassee, FL), was my mother. She told us many stories of growing up on Calhoun Street, going to Lanark beach on the train, attending Leon High School on Park Avenue and getting her college degree at F. S. C. W. Her first job was in the public health laboratory with Dr. L. L. Dozier as "boss".

Elizabeth, also called "Doc" and "Nantie", married Robert Alphus Taylor (b. 8/28/1893, Minneapolis, MN; d.11/24/1970, Tallahassee, FL) in 1930. Their daughter Martha Elizabeth was born in 1940, and son Robert Byrd arrived in 1943. Both children attended Leon High School, but Martha graduated from the University of Florida and her brother, Florida State University. This has created a Gator/Seminole rivalry!

Martha married Robert Luther Tilden (b. 1940) in 1971. Their two daughters are Evelyn Elizabeth "Beth" (b. 1972) and Alice Rebecca "Becky"(b. 1974). Both daughters graduated from Leon High and Florida State. Beth obtained a master's from Ohio University.

Becky married Greg McCarthy (b. 1970) in 1996 and has presented us with two fine grandsons, Joseph Tilden (b.2000) and Quinn Patrick (b. 2004). Beth married Brant Beck (b. 1970) in 1998 and they have also given us two wonderful grandsons, Jay Tilden (b. 2001) and John Reagan (b.2004).

The Leon County Four "B" saga began in 1826 and continues in 2008. Because family members have saved old Bibles, letters and photographs over the years, we can know our forebears as personalities. They came here in wagons, lived through the War Between the States, married, had babies, grieved over lost babies, worked as teachers, housewives, doctors, lawyers, farmers and more. When they played, they often went to St. Teresa or Lanark on the Gulf of Mexico.

A letter from Dr. F. A. Byrd dated November 16, 1874, described building a home at St. Teresa. Many Leon Countians formed a happy, carefree, vacation society there. The delightful letter inspired our family to compose a book, *Tides That Bind*, describing St. Teresa adventures and memories. Here are a few lines from the introduction.

"Spending happy, family times at the coast somehow contributes to the kind of people that we are. It is an elusive quality, difficult to describe .... Collecting family history and stories can serve many purposes. It connects us with our larger family, both past and present, and is one way for parents to teach their children values ... William Raspberry (Tallahassee Democrat, July 31, 1990) writes, If we want our children to grow up strong, secure and upright, if we want to show them paths out of moral chaos, we should scour our family histories and tell them stories of the heroes we find there."

This is the story of my heroes.

Submitted by: Martha Taylor Tilden, 2512 Betton Woods Drive, Tallahassee, FL 32308

Mary Black, 100 Years, So Far

Tallahassee is proud to claim Mary Elisabeth Lowe, who celebrates her one hundredth birthday on May 30, 2008. She's been honored by a number of organizations already and a family picnic is scheduled for the big day. Her neighbors in Los Robles have held a party in the park and dedicated a 100 year-old-tree in her honor. Asked for the secret to her vigorous longevity, she cites good genes, assisted by avoidance of tobacco and alcohol and following her mama's good advice - eating right, sleeping, staying active, and having friends.

Mary Elisabeth's ancestors have been "over here" longer than most.

Mary Black on her 100th Birthday.

A founding member of the Tallahassee Genealogical Society, she also claims membership in Colonial Dames, Daughters of the American Revolution and Daughters of the Confederacy Societies. A friend piqued her interest in family research and she never turned back. One immigrant ancestor entered Charleston, South Carolina in 1692 and is buried in Christ Church there. Mary Elisabeth's documentation has been of assistance to many researchers who have contacted her for guidance. Fortunately, she has passed her interest on to some family members who are organizing her information on a computer, and the Colonial Dames have saved some of her memories on DVD. Her roots are English, Scots-Irish and French. Some of her family names include Bellah/Bellagh, Abernathy,

Hancock, Frost, Bray and Farr in addition to Lowe and Craig.

Born Mary Elisabeth Lowe in Miami, she was the oldest daughter of Bessie Craig of Tennessee and Lewis D. Lowe, a Methodist minister, born in Georgia and son of a Methodist minister. Both grandfathers were Methodist ministers, and an earlier ancestor traveled with Methodist leader Francis Asbury. One of Mary Elisabeth three brothers and one of her two sisters are living. Mary Elisabeth says: (with a smile) she always had to set a good example for others as the oldest child of a minister.

At one time, her father was the Presiding Elder at Trinity Methodist Church in Tallahassee, and the family lived on Adams Street across from the current bus station. Adams Street was paved with brick while she lived there, the only paved street outside of the central downtown area. The ministry moved the family around a lot to live in several towns in Florida.

Mary Elisabeth married first Wylie Poag, with whom she had a daughter and three sons. She was a teacher of high school English, Spanish and Latin but was unable to find employment when they moved back to Tallahassee during World War II. After taking a business education course, she was hired by the Federal Corrections Institution to translate the letters of Puerto Rican citizens incarcerated for refusal to serve in the military. Male staff was in short supply because of the war. Later, she worked for the Department of Education, issuing teaching certificates until she retired after Wylie Poag died in 1964.

When her last child left the nest, Mary Elisabeth married Francis J. Black, a retired Eastern Airlines pilot in 1977. Mary now has six grandchildren and four great-grandchildren.

They have been a mainstay in the Los Robles neighborhood ever since then. This is where everyone knows them. I guess we could say after one hundred years she is still setting a good example for the rest of us.

Submitted and written by: Mary Black, 1555 Cristobal Drive, Tallahassee, FL 32303

The Scottish Black Family from Jura Isle, Scotland to Leon County, Florida

The first known record of the Black family in Gadsden County, Florida is found in the list of voters in the February 3, 1834 election held in Quincy, Florida. Because of this record, we know that Archibald Black and his wife Margaret migrated to Gadsden County, Florida before February 1834, in a family caravan of at least five wagons, with four of their grown children and their families. The wagons contained everything they needed to start a new life in the Florida Territory. They built houses on their land close to each other between Rocky Comfort Creek and Bear Creek in Gadsden County, Florida.

During the 1836 First Seminole Indian War, brothers Alexander, James, and Neill Black fought together as Privates. It is presumed that Alexander was killed that spring during the fighting because his wife and children, afraid of continued Indian raids, moved that summer to Walker County, Alabama.

In the 1840 Florida census, James, Neill, and Catherine Black and her husband John McDougald are seen living in houses next to each other. Their widowed mother, Margaret, lived with her son Neill Black and his family.

The best description of the Black family living in Gadsden County, Florida comes from the paper written in 1914 by Rev. William Black. Rev. Wm. Black's paper was written after a trip he made to Liberty County, Florida in 1913 to meet his cousins for the purpose of recording their families' genealogy.

The following is an excerpt from his paper: "Neill Black, and James Black, as has been said, returning to their former residence in Florida, bought large tracts of this land and settled permanently, between Rocky Comfort and Bear Creeks on part of the Forbes purchase where they cleared large tracts of lands, opened up new roads and in every way helped to build up the then almost entirely unsettled section in which they located. Their selection of lands for healthy good spring water, productiveness and in other respects was most admirable and there is not to be found in Florida today a more beautiful section. Here it is quite hilly, the soil slightly red with clay subsoil well adapted to the growth of almost any crop, especially of Cigar tobacco. On the banks of the creek, Rocky Comfort, near their residence, which banks are quite steep, there are numerous springs of the finest freestone water.

These two brothers built homes within a half-mile of each other and for that day and time were fine homes, commodious and well built and painted, presented a good appearance. Here they lived till their death. In this section of Florida, now in 1914, it is currently believed that Duncan Black (should read Archibald Black) was dead at the time these sons went to Florida, and that their widowed mother accompanied them, lived there until all under cultivation."

Hugh Black, son of James Black and Elizabeth Thomas, met his future wife, Mary Ann Harvey, at a ball that her parents, Stephen and Agatha Callicott Harvey, had given on their plantation located on the Ochlocknee River near Fort Braden, Leon County, Florida. At that time families from the surrounding area would travel by boat up and down the rivers to attend gala balls given on neighboring plantations. Hugh and Mary Ann Black were married in Ft. Braden on July 13, 1860.

In 1866, after Stephen Harvey died, Hugh and Mary Ann Harvey Black moved from Liberty County, Florida to Leon County near Fort Braden, Florida on the Ochlocknee River. They built their home on land Mary Ann had inherited from her father. Hugh made his living cutting timber and running his saw mill. In 1868 Hugh was elected as the Clerk to the Legislature. Later, on July 10, 1883, he became the Post Master of Bloxham, Florida. The Florida State Gazetteer and Business Directory 1883-84 listed Hugh Black as a farmer in Bloxham, Florida. In 1889, 1891, and 1893, he, along with his close friend, Julius Diamond, served as County Commissioners for Leon County. Hugh was also a schoolteacher. On December 14, 1906, Florida Governor Napoleon B. Broward appointed Hugh Black as the Honorary Chickamauga Park Monument Commissioner for Leon County.

Hugh Black enlisted to fight in the Third Seminole Indian War in Tallahassee, July 29, 1857 for six months. He served in and around Fort Myers and Okeechobee, Florida. He furnished his own gun, powder and horse.

Hugh's "Name first on the list" when he was appointed 2nd Lt. Co., A 6 Regt, Fla. Hugh was wounded in the Battle of Chickamauga, September 19, 1863, in Chattanooga, Georgia. His younger brother Neill Jr. was wounded and his youngest brother Calvin Waterberry Black was killed in the same battle.

Submitted by: Sarah Elizabeth Frano (Elizabeth's daughter), 8500 Indian School Rd., Scottsdale, AZ 85251; Written by: Elizabeth Coldwell Frano

The Move to the Harvey's "Big House" in Leon County

Sometime after Michael Harvey, Jr. died in 1832 "when the Ochlocknee River was at its lowest," Stephen and his brother, Mark Harvey, waded across into Leon County in search of the best location to settle permanently. They found this creek. It had the biggest body of water coming out of the land. The land they chose to build on had a spring coming out of a hill.

The Harvey men cut the timber and made the lumber for a two-story plantation house. The shingles were handmade for the roof and all the furniture for the house was made from the wood from their land. The Harvey's house looked exactly like the Gregory's house that stood at Ochlocknee Landing from 1831 until 1936, when it was moved across the river to Torreya State Park, Florida.

Looking at the front of the house, which faced south, on either side of the front porch were planted hedges of hydrangeas, blue on one side of the steps and pink on the other side. They achieved the pink color by spreading chicken manure around the base of the hydrangeas, and got the blue color by fertilizing with horse manure.

The house was built five feet off the ground on brick pilings as a protection from high water and animals. As was the style, the exterior features were balanced with a large door in the center and two tall windows framing each side. The front and back doors on both floors had sidelights with four panes of glass each. Above the doors were five panes of glass, since glass was very dear.

I remember there being five steps leading up to the front porch, because that was the step Grandma Black always sat on. Grandma Black would sit up on the porch chewing her tobacco and spitting off the side of the porch, as she would tell her stories to us. She used a flat tobacco leaf that she would tear pieces from and then chew.

The house porches, both front and back, were just wide enough for the chairs that the family would sit on to relax in the late afternoon, and to catch the cool breezes after a long day of working. The second floor porches had railings that ran between the columns to keep the children from falling off.

When we went in the front door, we would be in a wide hall which ran the length of the house, with a back door equal in size to the front door. Opening these doors gave the house excellent cool air circulation in the hot Florida summers.

On the right side of the hall were the stairs that curved up to the second floor. Located immediately to the right of the front door was the dining room with its long table and chairs, big enough to sit the whole Harvey family. On the east wall of the dining room was the side door that led outside to the kitchen. On the left side of the hall were two bedrooms. The front bedroom was the master bedroom used by Uncle Hugh Harvey and Aunt Lila Carraway Black. The back bedroom was used by Grandma Harvey Black. Upstairs, leading off the hallway, were four bedrooms identical in size and location as the first floor rooms. In one of the rooms were four beds where the boys slept. Each bedroom had a tester bed with a crocheted canopy over the top and a crocheted bedspread with tassels along their edges. The tassels were so long that they hung down to the floor.

The four Harvey sisters had crocheted the bedspreads. The beds were built high off the floor, so high that steps were needed to climb up into the beds. On each bed were "warm" feather mattresses that the women had made from the fine chest down of the geese. The rooms on the left side of the house had their own shallow wood-burning fireplaces to take the chill off the rooms in winter. The four fireplaces backed up onto the hall, with their chimneys running up through the center of the house, forming one large chimney on the roof. The bricks were made on site from the rich red clay. The house was never painted. Paint was unheard of in Florida in those days.

I used to sit outside on the top step going up to the front porch of the "big house". I would listen to my Grandma tell the stories of the Harveys leaving North Carolina and coming as pioneers to Florida. Grandma would tell her stories and then she would take my sister Corrine and me up to the attic on the third floor. There, locked away for safekeeping, were two tall gold pier mirrors, a beautiful big book, camel back trunks, and a seven-foot long chest.

Grandma Black would open the chest and let us see all the beautiful bustled silk and water taffeta ball gowns that they had worn before the Civil War. Corrine and I would stand there, looking at all the beautiful ball gowns, with eyes as big as saucers. There were men's frock coats with tails, and men's suits, and tall beaver hats. We found the envelopes that held the formal invitations to balls that had been held on other plantations in Leon County that Grandma and her sisters and brothers attended. Grandma would tell us how they would go by boat, up river, to neighboring plantations to attend the balls.

The Harveys hosted grand balls of their own during this time. It was at one of these balls that Mary Ann Harvey, Stephen Harvey's youngest daughter, met her future husband, Hugh Black. She would be the only daughter to marry.

What Grandma valued the most were the trunks which contained stamped letters from the Civil War and before. She even gave Corrine and me each a letter. About that time, we could hear Uncle Hugh coming up the stairs. Tramp! Tramp! Tramp! "Now Ma, that's enough." And that would be the end of looking at all Grandma's treasures for that day.

Submitted by: Christopher Walter Frano (Marie's Son); Written by: Elizabeth Coldwell Frano (Mrs. Christopher John Frano)

Charles C. Blankenship & Tisha A. Kelley

From 1985 until 1988, Tisha and I lived on Egret Lane in Tallahassee, Florida. Tisha was employed at J. C. Penney at the Governor's Mall and I worked at the Tallahassee FAA Flight Service Station at the Tallahassee Municipal Airport. We previously had lived in Mobile, Alabama and just began to have an "empty nest." Our children, Christine, Jackie, Steve and Charles (IV) were strung out along I - 10 in Jacksonville, Mobile and New Orleans. This made it possible to visit with them for short periods of time and return home within a few days.

In 1987, they began giving us grandchildren, so we did make many trips to visit them. The oldest, Drew West visited us in 1988 and I took him to the Old State Capitol for a visit. When I stood him up on an old desk and told the lady volunteer that "this boy's ancestor served in the Florida House of Representatives," she replied, "so did mine." Her ancestor was Charles Bannerman and my grandson and mine was James Rinaldo Nicks who actually served in the house with Bannerman. They were

1988 Old Capitol, Tisha Blankenship with daughter, Jackie and grandson, Drew West.

neighbors who lived north of Tallahassee. J. R. Nicks lived on the north and east side of Lake Iamonia and Bannerman lived on the western side of what is now called the "Strickland Arm" and close to WCTV and Tall Timbers.

Actually, 1985 wasn't the first time I had lived in Leon County as my family first moved from Lake City to Tallahassee in 1942. We moved into Dale Mabry Heights on the outskirts of what is now known as FSU. Then our back yard on Roosevelt Drive was quite a ways off from the campus. We remained there while my father, George W. Blankenship worked over on Madison Street before being transferred down to Camp Gordon Johnston in 1943. We lived in the Pickett apartments (now known as Lanark Village) from 1943 until 1947. From there we returned to Tallahassee many times, often staying out on the Bannerman Road with Ralph W. Scott. His home had no electricity and drew water from a well.

Tisha and Charles Blankenship, 2008

My father, a Virginian and WWI veteran had migrated to Florida in 1934 in search of a better job during the Depression. When FDR started the WPA and CCC's, he entered the CCC's at Blountstown, transferred to White Springs and Hilliard, Florida. There, while working under Victor M. Clark, he was introduced to his daughter, Frances Fair Clark in 1936. She was named after the wife of James R. Nicks whose maiden name was Frances Fair. They were married in Callahan and transferred to Perry, Florida where I was born. A month later, they moved to Lake City until 1940, before moving to Jackson, Tennessee only to return to Lake City in 1942 and then to Tallahassee. So when people say "you can't go back," I usually tell them about Lake City, Tallahassee and Jackson, TN where I returned in 1990 after 50 years.

Written and submitted by: Charles C. Blankenship 55 Country Club Cove, Jackson, TN 38305-3909

George W. Blankenship

G. W. Blankenship (1890-1968) first came to Florida during the Depression Era of the 1930s. He was working in St. Petersburg, Florida, when FDR's administration allowed WWI veterans to join the CCCs. In July 1934 he enlisted in the CCCs at Blountstown, FL. where he served as a Leader with P-70 camp. After one year he transferred to White Springs P-73 camp, before moving in October 1935 to Hilliard P-74 camp, serving first under Dolph Walker and later his future father-in-law, Victor Clark. During this time, he met Victor's daughter, Frances Fair Clark, a seventh generation Floridian. She was living and enrolled in a beauty school in Jacksonville, Florida. In September of 1936 they married in Callahan, Florida and moved to Perry, FL to serve with the Motor Repair Shop. His first-born son, Charles was born there and they moved once more to Lake City where his daughter, Sandra was born.

In November 1940, the family again moved to Jackson, TN where his second son, George was born. They all remained in Jackson, TN until just after Pearl Harbor and returned to Lake City in early 1942. During that year, the War Department took over all the CCC Motor Repair Shops and the U. S. Army moved the entire personnel and equipment to Tallahassee, Leon County, FL. The location of their offices was on Madison Street (now the parking lot to the Civic Auditorium in downtown Tallahassee).

George W. Blankenship, with; Charles, Sandra, George Jr. in Tallahassee-1943

Several CCC families moved into Dale Mabry Heights on Roosevelt Drive. Those houses' backyards were a small distance from what is now FSU's campus. During 1943, the open field had only cattle grazing and some old oak trees. During this time in Tallahassee, George's father, Charles C. Blankenship visited the family from Norton, VA. He and his grandson Charles enjoyed many walks near the State Capitol. In less than a year, the entire contingent of personnel transferred to Camp Belle in

Carrabelle, Florida and later to Camp Gordon Johnston for the remainder of WWII.

From 1943 to 1948, G. W. Blankenship would remain at Camp Gordon Johnston. By the time World War II ended, he became a Surplus Administrator in charge of selling off much of the equipment at the camp. That required many trips to Tallahassee with overnight stays. In the spring of 1948, G. W. Blankenship left Florida for New Mexico and returned to Florida before moving north and finding a Civil Service job in Kingsport, Tennessee. After retirement in 1960, he spent most of his time visiting his three "CCC brats" and their children in New Port Richey, Eglin and Tyndall Air Force Bases in Florida. He also visited his old CCC friends along the Florida Panhandle. He spent weeks on end in Lake City and Jacksonville, and finally in 1968, he called his son, George to come pick him up in Jacksonville and take him to Biloxi, Mississippi. There he entered the VA Hospital and died. He is buried in the VA Cemetery alongside other veterans dating back to the Civil War and every other war thereafter.

Written by: Charles Blankenship, Submitted by: Sandra Blankenship- Werner, 4932 Marlin Dr., Jackson, TN 38305

Coach Bobby and Ann Bowden

Bobby Bowden was born November 8, 1929 in Birmingham, AL. He was educated in Birmingham City Schools, and graduated from Woodlawn High School.

He played football as a freshman quarterback for his mentor and idol, "Bear" Bryant at the University of Alabama. He graduated from Howard College, (now Samford) and played football there from his sophomore through senior years as a quarterback. He earned his graduate degree from Peabody College.

He is married to Ann Estock, his high school sweetheart, and they have six children: Robyn, Steve, Tommy, Terry, Ginger and Jeff. Coaching seems to be a family tradition. Tommy, Terry and Jeff have coached Div. I-A college football, and Tommy coached against his father while at Clemson, the first father-son duo to do so. Terry, (head coach) and Jeff (receiver's coach) are coaching at University of North Alabama.

"From 1954-1962, he was an assistant football and track coach at Howard; head football coach at South Georgia Junior College; head football coach at Howard." Coach Bill Peterson, head coach at FSU, hired him as a receiver's coach from 1963-1965. In 1966, he became Offensive Coordinator at West Virginia and from 1970-1975 was the head coach. In 1976 he became head coach at Florida State University until 2009.

His career at Florida State is unprecedented for accomplishments: 1. Second place wins nationally in major college football with 389. On October 25, 2003, he was ranked first and stayed in this position for quite a while. 2. "Only coach in history of Division I-A to compile 14 straight 10 win seasons (1987-2000)."

Paraphrased and Submitted by: Mary J. Marchant, 2901 Springfield Drive, Tallahassee, FL 32309-3274; Source: Bobby: Our Coverage of a Legend Presented by The Tallahassee Democrat by permission from Editor Gabordi Quotation marks denote direct quotes from the book.

Congressman Allen Boyd

A fifth generation farmer, Boyd graduated from Florida State University in 1969 and served his country in the Vietnam War. To this day, he continues to oversee the family farm operations on land that has been in his family for five generations. He and his wife, Cissy, reside on their farm in Monticello, Florida. They have three grown children and one granddaughter.

Allen Boyd was sworn into office on January 7, 1997, as a Democratic member of the 105th Congress representing Florida's 2nd Congressional District. The district spans 16 counties, from South Walton County through Leon County, almost reaching Jacksonville, making up the largest geographic congressional district in the state. This area of North Florida is distinctly rural, yet surprisingly diverse. The regional economy is as reliant on small fishing villages and rural farming operations as it is the higher education and state government communities of Tallahassee.

For the past 12 years, Congressman Boyd has been a leader of Congress' Blue Dog Coalition, a group of 51 Democratic members of the U.S. House of Representatives who advocate fiscal responsibility in the federal budgeting process. The Blue Dogs are centrist legislators working to forge middle of the road, bipartisan answers to the current challenges facing the country. Over the years, the Blue Dog Coalition has been called upon to lead the House to a comprehensive fiscal policy anchored in federal debt reduction for America and tax relief for all citizens. Boyd was instrumental in the successful efforts by Congress to reach the historic 1997 balanced budget agreement, and as the Blue Dog

Co-Chair for Administration in the 110th Congress; Boyd led the Blue Dog charge for the return to pay-as-you-go (PAYGO) rules in the House. In the 111th Congress, Boyd was appointed Chairman of the newly established Blue Dog Budget and Financial Services Task Force. This 15-member group will work to promote policies and strategies that reflect Blue Dog priorities through sustainable and responsible fiscal reform.

A leading voice on fiscal responsibility in the House of Representatives, Congressman Boyd was named to the House Budget Committee in the 110th Congress. As a member of the Budget Committee, Boyd is actively involved in every aspect of the nation's fiscal policy and works to implement budget enforcement tools that are necessary to restore our country's fiscal house.

In the 106th Congress, Boyd was appointed by his peers to the highly-coveted Appropriations Committee where he works to ensure fairness in funding to North Florida's priorities. Throughout his tenure in Congress, Boyd has worked to protect Florida's military community and bring much-needed aid to the agriculture industry. In the 110th Congress, Boyd's understanding of our national defense and strong commitment to our military were recognized by his appointment to the powerful Subcommittee on Defense of the House Appropriations Committee. Boyd's work on this subcommittee allows him to improve and strengthen North Florida's military bases and promote defense-related economic development projects in the district. Boyd also serves as Co-Chair of the Congressional Mine Warfare Caucus. This bipartisan group promotes initiatives relating to mine warfare that maintain the security of our domestic waters and advance America's international sea power.

Congressman Allen Boyd

In the 111th Congress, Boyd joined the Financial Services Subcommittee of the House Appropriations Committee. In this new role, Congressman Boyd will oversee the budgets of multiple agencies, including the Treasury Department, the Internal Revenue Service (IRS), the Federal Deposit Insurance Corporation (FDIC), and the Judicial branch. In addition to the Subcommittees on Defense and Financial Services, Boyd continues to serve on the Agriculture, Rural Development, Food and Drug Administration, and Related Agencies Subcommittee of the House Appropriations Committee where he works to provide funding for a safe food supply and a healthy agricultural economy in Florida and throughout the nation.

As a farmer and business owner, Congressman Boyd is conscious of the issues facing small businesses and workers in today's economy. He knows that in order to grow the economy and achieve long-term stability, government must act as a catalyst, not an obstacle, for empowering companies to grow and thrive in a changing world market. He believes that government should provide an economic model for businesses to follow in order to stimulate growth. That central belief has earned him endorsements over the years from the United States Chamber of Commerce and the fiscal watchdog group, the Concord Coalition.

From 1989 until his election to Congress, Boyd served in the Florida House of Representatives. Throughout his career in public service, Boyd has led the charge for government reform and fiscal responsibility. He is also known as an articulate voice for consensus building and reasonable compromise. As Chairman of the Florida House Democratic Conservative Caucus, Boyd helped build bridges between diverse interests on such difficult issues as public education, healthcare, and welfare reform, issues he continues to work on in Congress.

Written and submitted by: Allen Boyd, 1650 Summit Lake Drive Suit 103, Tallahassee, FL 32301

Judge Joseph A. (Joe) Boyd and Ann Boyd
Joe Boyd was born in Hoschton, GA in 1916. He was educated in Jackson County, GA schools. Ann was born in Bonaire, GA in 1917 and was educated in Perry, GA, and in Dade County, FL schools. After completing his first year of Law School at Mercer University, Joe moved to Miami in 1939 where Ann had lived since 1925. To pay their college expenses at Piedmont College in GA, Joe sold Bibles in the summer time and Ann worked in the college President's office. This was during the depression,

so no scholarships were available. Ann and Joe met at Piedmont College. Piedmont College at that time had a rule that women couldn't get married while in college, but if they did, they would lose any credits earned after the marriage took place. Ann and Joe eloped and kept the marriage a secret until Ann could receive her college credits. Other rules for girls included no smoking on campus, and they could not wear short pants. Boys could smoke on campus, however.

Joe Boyd and Ann Boyd in Tallahassee, FL

Joe went into the Marines during World War II and after three years in the Pacific, he came back home and was admitted to the University of Miami Law School. To be admitted to Law School, he had to register the day after he arrived home. After being admitted to the FL Bar, Joe practiced law for 21 years and Ann became a secretary for the Mayor of Hialeah, Florida. Eventually Ann resigned as secretary to the Mayor of Hialeah and worked as Joe's bookkeeper and as a realtor. They had five children: Jo Ann (deceased), Betty Jean, Joseph R, James D. and Jane Boyd. Joe was always interested in politics. He was city attorney for Hialeah, and then resigned to run successfully for Dade County Commissioner, Vice-Chairman, Chairman and Vice- Mayor.

Joe Boyd and Ann Boyd in Miami, Florida

While serving in these offices for 10 years, he met many famous people including Presidents Truman, Kennedy, Carter, and Clinton. In 1969 he became a Justice for the Florida Supreme Court, and served as the Justice during part of his tenure. His mandatory retirement came in 1986 when he reached his 70th birthday.

With all the honors bestowed upon Joe and Ann, they are typical citizens who volunteer their time and knowledge to make our community a better place to live Ann served as President of the Tallahassee Women's Club and has served in other offices; she is an active member of the Garden Club, the Killearn Ladies Club and acts as auctioneer for the Civic Clubs. She is known for her unusual installation of officers. Joe died of heart failure at the age of 89 in Tallahassee and is buried at Culley's Meadow Wood Memorial Park. Ann continues to be her vibrant, happy, enthusiastic, joke- telling self.

Submitted and written by: Ann Boyd, 2210 Monaghan Drive, Tallahassee, FL 32309-3125

Bill Boydston

Would you believe he is the only clown in this room? Bill has been in radio, television and advertising all of his adult life. Most memorable are his "Bozo the World's Most Famous Clown" years at Channel 12 in Jacksonville. Prior to that he was Barnaby the Sailor, a clown and Sir Laffalot, a clown.

Could he top that? This quiet, shy man was the singing, dancing spokesman on TV for the Winn Dixie Corporation for seven years. His striped jacket and straw hat was well known throughout the Southeast. Bill was also responsible for writing and producing each week thirty or more new Winn Dixie TV ads seen throughout the Southeast

Bill was born in Chattanooga, Tennessee. He was four years old when his mother died and, following that sad event, his family moved around a bit. You see, his corporate lawyer father retired at 36 years old. They lived in Pinehurst and Hamlet, North Carolina; Cocoa Beach and Winter Park Florida; and Santa Cruz and San Jose, California, before settling here in Tallahassee.

Bill says the most wonderful thing that ever happened to him was meeting his wife, Carol Ann. They met in a speech contest in their senior year at Leon High School. Later, they went to Florida State University together. Bill majored in Art and Advertising.

In 1959 they married in this very Chapel and moved to Jacksonville, eventually perpetuating the Boydston name with two sons and two daughters. In Jacksonville, Bill worked for Radio Station WJAX, earning the Freedom Bell Award. He became a licensed broadcast engineer, holding a Federal Communications Commission First Class Radio/Television Broadcast Engineers license for over twenty-five years. Later he made his way into advertising and television, earning various advertising awards for Winn Dixie, Sears and First Union Banks.

He has lived most of his life in Tallahassee. Moving back from Jacksonville in 1974, Bill worked at WCTV-TV (Channel 6) as an on-air announcer and co-host with Anna Johnson and Frank Pepper on "The Good Morning Show". When his wife opened Boydston Advertising and Creative Services, he left television to make commercials in his own agency, winning 144 awards for creative excellence. He is a Past President of the Tallahassee Advertising Federation and an American Advertising Federation Silver Medal Award winner.

In 1992 Bill joined the Florida State Park Service, served 16 years and he has just retired. He received five State of Florida Employee Awards and wrote many, many brochures highlighting Florida's beautiful state parks.

Bill was baptized and became a member of the First Baptist Church in 1957. He has come back to FBC because he wants to help others and this church has the programs in place to do that.

His favorite Bible verse is: "Be careful for nothing; but in everything by prayer and supplication with thanksgiving... let your requests be known unto God. And the peace of God, which passeth all understanding, shall keep your hearts and minds through Jesus Christ".

The worst thing that has ever happened to Bill was the death of his 21-year-old son, Christopher. The best thing to ever happen to him is his wife, Carol Ann. Tallahassee is his home and that is why he is still here.

Bill thinks we have lost our way in America and that the decline of our morals, spiritual values and happiness is weighing this great country down. He is most concerned about the spiritual decay of our nation.

Submitted by: Bill Boydston; Written by Carol Ann and Bill Boydston ©, 1639 Twin Lakes Circle, Tallahassee, FL 32311

Carol Ann Boydston

It was not quite twilight on a warm summers evening in 1952. Two young people, a twelve-year-old girl and her fourteen-year-old brother set out on foot for the long walk from the 990 block of East Park Avenue to the Doak S. Campbell Stadium, on the far side of FSU. The Billy Graham Crusade was in town, and they both were compelled to make that long trek to hear, be moved and dedicate their lives to Christ. The young girl was Carol Ann Colwell. That night changed her life forever. She put her faith into action.

Carol Ann was born near Detroit, Michigan, but moved to Tampa. Her mother died in Tampa when she was just seven years old. Her family of three brothers and an older sister came apart. The two oldest siblings stayed in Tampa, one brother joined the Navy and Carol Ann, her dad and the youngest brother moved to Williston. A few years later her father got a State job in Tallahassee and the three moved again. In her teen years Carol Ann was at First Baptist Church even when the doors weren't open. She volunteered in the office, worked in the nursery Sunday mornings, started and produced a Church weekly Youth Newspaper, a copy of which is included with the historic documents in the cornerstone of our sanctuary. When she started dating Bill he had to come to the church just to pick her up for a date. They had met in a speech contest at Leon High School. Carol Ann honed her communication skills in High School. She was elected Graduation Speaker of the Leon High Class of 1957. She also won the Journalism Award as "The Best Writer of The Year" and the "I Speak For Democracy" contest for all of Leon County.

Carol Ann and Bill attended FSU together. Carol Ann majored in Journalism and minored in Speech. When Bill began his career in broadcasting, they married right here in the First Baptist Church Chapel and moved to set up their home in Jacksonville. Four children in ten years sure got her started in life and Carol Ann took up the obligations of raising the children, sharing time for PTA, studies at Jacksonville Community College, a little acting in documentary films and managing the Alhambra Dinner Theater. But Tallahassee always had a siren call for Carol Ann, and in 1974, the Boydston's returned to Tallahassee to raise the children in a true family city.

In 1977 Carol Ann opened her own advertising agency, Boydston Advertising and Creative Services, Inc. As she says, when she could afford him, Carol Ann hired Bill away from

WCTV and they began a thirty-year odyssey in local advertising, winning 144 awards for advertising excellence. She is a Past President of the Tallahassee Advertising Federation, a former Governor of the American Advertising Federation, 4th District Florida/Caribbean. She is the proud recipient of a Silver Medal Award for Outstanding Work in Advertising from the American Advertising Federation.

Carol Ann was also President of the Tallahassee Association of Female Executives, Vice President of SCORE Credit Union, and held offices in the Tallahassee Sales and Marketing Association and the Jacksonville Advertising Federation. She is retired now and enjoys her Sunday School classmates, helping with the feeding of the homeless, singing in First Joy Choir, having her family around her, and seeing her two granddaughters in First Baptist.

Family always brings joy and sadness, too. Carol Ann's worst memory is the death of her 21-year-old son, Christopher. The best thing to happen to her is her husband, Bill. She says there is no one who even compares to him, but then, it ain't over 'til it's over. What does she see as the biggest change in America during her lifetime? She sees a society that refuses to accept responsibility for its actions, a generation that lacks personal morals and ethics. There has never been a better time for a spiritual rebirth in our nation.

Written and submitted by: Carol Ann and Bill Boydston, 1639 Twin Lakes Circle, Tallahassee, FL 32311

The Bradfords of Bradfordville

They came in family groups traveling in large caravans of people and livestock, camping out or staying with relatives or in inns along the way. It was a bit of chance, coupled with a bit of knowledge that brought them to the frontier land of middle Florida. They were searching for fertile land to replace their worn out fields in Halifax County, North Carolina. It was the early 1830s and they were the Bradford bothers – Henry Boen, Thomas Anderson, Dr. Edward, and Richard Henry. Their decision to move to Florida would make a lasting impact, not only on their families, but also on Leon County.

The sons of the Reverend Henry and Sarah Crowell Bradford, they came from a successful farming family. Francis Asbury of the early Methodist church married their parents and their father was active in the growth of Methodism in North Carolina. Their grandfather, John Bradford, was involved in North Carolina politics and was a delegate to the assembly that established the Halifax Resolves, a precursor to the Declaration of Independence. Both John and Henry fought the British in the Revolutionary War.

Richard Henry Bradford (1800-1883)

Two older brothers had already left the family community of Enfield to try their luck in Tennessee and Georgia. The four remaining brothers considered following them, but in the end were influenced to move to Florida by their cousin, John Branch, former North Carolina governor and later territorial governor of Florida. He was convinced that the lands of middle Florida were perfect for growing cotton, the crop that was quickly becoming the staple of the South. Henry was the first to move to Florida, because the 1830 US census shows him in Leon County. The others were established in their new home soon after the death of their father in 1833. Their widowed mother Sarah along with their sister and brother-in-law, Mary Crowell "Polly" Bradford Whitaker and Eli Benton Whitaker, also became residents of

House of Bradford Family on Water Oak Plantation (ca. 1876

Leon County later.

The decision of what land to buy was driven by the need for fertile fields and a water supply. They purchased large tracts north of Tallahassee near Lakes Iamonia and McBride (between present day Meridian and Thomasville Roads and east of Thomasville Road) and set about clearing the lands for planting. Among their plantations were Pine Hill, Horseshoe, Water Oak, and Walnut Hill. In her book, Florida Breezes, Ellen Call Long describes the area north of Tallahassee and the people who live there. She states, and "further beyond, on the road we have left, is a large settlement, all 'Bradford's,' - North Carolinians, too; they make a good population for any country especially a new one; economical, industrious; in short, they mind strictly their own business."

They were not completely alone in this new land, for many extended family members also settled near them, including the Branch family. Life on the frontier was not easy. Disease, Indians and weather caused problems. Many women of the time died in childbirth. Yellow fever was rampant in the 1830s and 1840s. The Henry Boen Bradford family lost three of their little children in 1841 - most likely from yellow fever. During the 1840s and 1850s the families grew and their farms prospered. Trouble was ahead, though, for the years of the Civil War brought pain and heartbreak to the entire nation, but especially to the South. The Bradford family was no exception. Their sons were quick to enlist in the Confederate Army, and unfortunately, one was quick to die. Richard Henry Bradford, Jr. was the first Confederate officer killed in Florida, for he died in October 1861 in the Battle of Santa Rosa Island. A few months later by Legislative order Bradford County was named for him.

Three of Richard Bradford's other sons, John, Edward and Robert Fort, fought in the war. Another son, Dr. William Henry Bradford, remained in Leon County to help take care of the medical needs of the families that were left behind. John R. Bradford, son of Henry Boen, and William Mumford, Henry, and Thomas, sons of Thomas A. Bradford, also served in the Confederate Army. Henry was captured and imprisoned at Johnson's Island.

The years after the war brought many changes. The Bradford brothers were now three, for Henry Boen had died. The remaining brothers and their sons continued to farm. They diversified and began growing new crops. Richard is credited with bringing the first Jersey dairy cows to the county. The dairy farm he began was continued by his son, Robert F. Bradford, and in turn by his grandson, Robert F. Bradford, Jr. Another son, Colonel John Bradford, a surveyor and civil engineer, started the first businesses in Bradfordville. Along with a friend he established the general store "Bradford and Ross", a gristmill, sawmill and cotton gin.

The Bradford lands were eventually sold to wealthy northern families who enjoyed them as hunting preserves. Robert F., Jr. was the only one still farming by the 1930s when he sold his land to the Griscom family. He then relocated his dairy to Ausley Road in Tallahassee where he continued to farm until the 1950s. His son, Richard Henry Bradford, great-grandson of the original Leon County resident, Richard Bradford, moved his dairy to Jefferson County and farmed there until 1999.

Over the years the Bradfords and their descendants served as farmers, merchants, teachers, and government and church leaders and, as such, made numerous contributions to Leon County and North Florida. Many remain in the area. On the Edward Bradford side they include Preston DeMilly and members of the Eppes family. The Neal Bradford family members are descended from Henry Boen Bradford. Among the descendants of Thomas Anderson Bradford are Rubie Butterworth, Martha Tilden, and Clifton Van Brunt Lewis. Descendants of Richard Henry Bradford include Mary Alma Roberts Lang, Nora Parker McDaniel, Paul Parker, Susanne Bradford Mahaffey, Katie Bradford Linch, and their families.

Written and submitted by: Susanne Bradford Mahaffey, P.O. Box 1648 Quincy, Florida 32353 oaknolia@tds.net; Sources: Family records, Census records, Books/papers on Middle Florida

Bill and Nolia Brandt

William (Bill) and Nolia Parrish-Brandt were married in 1972 in Tallahassee, Florida. They have been an influential couple in Tallahassee's business sector since the early 1980s. They have sponsored and donated much of their time and money to charities for over thirty years. The Brandts have served on many community service boards; Nolia works with non-profit organizations and associations dedicated to education and economic development, and Bill works on delivery of services to individuals and communities, making them a truly dynamic duo.

Bill Brandt is a 60-year-old information technology consultant, property manager and past co-owner of Brandt Information Services. He has lived at 1412 N. Randolph Circle for over 17 years. Though his tax bill has increased 54 percent over the past 12 years he still remains concerned for his tenants. Taxes on an apartment complex he owns have risen from $1,979 in 1999 to $3,889 last year. That's a 97 percent increase in eight years. Bill doesn't think property taxes are unfair, but he's worried that the tax burden is making it harder for first-time buyers. "Since they fixed the insurance problem, two of my insurance carriers have pulled out of the market, but if property taxes go down significantly, I think landlords will be able to give a break in costs to their tenants," he said.

Dr. Nolia Brandt is an Associate Director of the Jim Moran Institute for Global Entrepreneurship (JMI) at Florida State University's College of Business, and she was also President and Co-owner of Brandt Information Services, a successful, award-winning information technology company. Dr. Brandt has over thirty years of highly recognized leadership in business, information technology, and social services. She specializes in organizational, human resource, and leadership development. Dr. Nolia Brandt holds a Ph.D. in Education and two Master's degrees from Florida State University. Dr. Nolia Brandt also provides business consulting services to entrepreneurs and small businesses, mainly in Florida and South Georgia. She runs the JMI Mentor-Mentee Program, and develops other small business programs. Dr. Brandt's very successful publications address business and entrepreneurial issues.

Bill and Nolia Brandt: Business Award ceremony- 2003

When they owned Brandt Information Services, Inc., they grew revenue by 465% in a three-year period, putting the company on the "Inc Magazine's" list of 500 America's fastest growing private companies. Other awards that the company obtained under the Brandts' leadership include winning the Multiple Diversity Business awards in 2003, 2004, and 2005 as a Top Diversity-Owned Business in outstanding leadership, entrepreneurship, and for outstanding community service. Another award was from the Software Magazine's list of the top 500 software for three years, and the company was honored by the Tallahassee Chamber of Commerce with the "Technology Business of the Year" Award in 2003.

Written and submitted by: Bill and Nolia Brandt, 1412 Randolph Circle, Tallahassee, FL 32308

Caroline Mays Brevard

The namesake for Caroline Brevard Elementary School, Caroline Mays Brevard, was born Aug 10, 1860. She was the oldest daughter of Colonel Theodore W. Brevard (1835-1905) of Alabama and Mary Call (1840-1920). She was the sister of Doctor Ephraim M. Brevard, Richard C. Brevard, Jane K. Brevard-Darby, and Alice H. Brevard. Her maternal grandfather was Governor Richard Keith Call, who was Governor of Florida when it was just a territory.

Caroline Mays Brevard

Caroline was educated in a private grade school and a State High School and graduated with Honors from Columbia University for her writings.

She taught history and English at Leon High School and for five years prior to her death, she was a teacher at the Florida State College for Women. Caroline was regarded as a Pioneering Woman after she established better studies for females during the Women Suffrage campaigns.

As one of Florida's most eminent women and a descendant of several of Leon County's prominent families, Caroline was a distinguished educator, historian and author. She was the author of "History of Florida" that was used in public schools and wrote at least three other books before her death on March 27, 1920. Presently there is a book in the McClay School library called History of the Government in Florida which Miss Caroline Brevard wrote, and which was donated by Mr. and Mrs. Malcolm Johnson.

During her lifetime she was an inspiration to many who chose to become teachers. She never married but instead spent her entire life raising the children of Leon County.

Written and submitted by: Mary J. Marchant (retired music teacher of Caroline Brevard Elementary School), Springfield Drive, Tallahassee, FL 32309-3274; Sources: Florida State Archives Florida Room; Library

Brokaw (Brogaw) Family

Leaving France because of religious persecution, the Brogaw family settled first in Germany and then emigrated to America, probably in the 18th century. They settled near Brooklyn, NY with some members later moving into the neighboring colony of New Jersey. Among these pioneers was Abraham Brokaw, who purchased land for a small farm outside Bound Brook, NJ. He married Eliza Bonney, and in 1814 welcomed their first child, Peres Bonney Brokaw.

Peres left home as a young man and settled in Alabama, supposedly a planter, during the 1830s. Perhaps falling on hard times, he moved south to Tallahassee in 1840 and took a partner, Jacob A. Miller. In 1842, they opened a livery stable and retail carriage sale business and began to acquire real estate as they prospered. Town lots were purchased in the 1840s, and by 1853 they owned eleven parcels around the city.

Carriages ranging from the simple two-wheeled sulky to the elegant Rockaway barouche were displayed at the "carriage repository" located on Calhoun Street. They offered carriages, buggies and harnesses for sale to Tallahasseans and Middle Florida residents. By 1853 the firm's stock-in trade totaled $8,107.

In 1850, the partners purchased a quarter section of the Lafayette grant for $960 at a sheriff's sale and began to farm, producing 3,500 bushels of corn, 320 pounds of rice, 100 bushels of peas and 100 bushels of sweet potatoes in the fall of that year.

Farm hands and unskilled laborers for the city business were regularly bought at local auction. Skilled laborers were purchased when necessary. Brokaw bought "George", a black smithy, and twelve other slaves for $8300 after Miller's death in April, 1853. The remaining eight slaves were either sold or distributed among Miller's heirs.

Peres met Cornelia O. Tatum, the seventeen-year-old daughter of John Tatum of Jackson County, and married her on April 10, 1850. Reverend George W. Pratt, pastor of the Trinity Methodist Church, performed the ceremony. A son, Abram, was born in 1857 and Phebe was born in 1859.

As commonly occurred in Tallahassee, a fire destroyed Brokaw and Miller's livery stable in 1853. It was rebuilt on the corner of Pensacola and Calhoun. An attached blacksmith shop was opened in 1854. H. B. Fitts, a master blacksmith, was brought into the shop in 1856, although the partnership did not last.

About 1856, Brokaw began the construction of a two-story frame dwelling on a portion of his farm property. Completed around 1860, it included a landscaped yard enclosed by a perimeter fence and cost nearly $6000.

John H. Rhodes, the local sheriff and later Confederate official, was another business partner, operating a turpentine distillery and general store in Wakulla County. From New York, Brokaw purchased a "Broadway Omnibus", which he used to transport visitors from the railroad depot to the city hotels.

Brokaw became active in the community. In 1856, he won a seat on the city council and served until 1860. During his service, the council appropriated funds leading to the construction of the first building associated with Florida State University. Brokaw was elected to the Florida House of Representatives in 1856. In 1860, he was elected to the Florida Senate and given the chairmanship of a standing committee. Everyone soon became embroiled in the secession debate and all agreed to adjourn.

Brokaw did not attend the secession convention held in Tallahassee in December, 1860. The decisive vote may have been difficult for a New Jersey native who still had relatives living there at the outbreak of the war. Yet Brokaw participated in the formation of the Tallahassee Guards even though he was not subject to conscription because of his age. Composed of local citizens, the company was organized in February, 1862. Brokaw was selected to be the commanding captain, a position he held until his resignation in May, 1862. A man of means, he was probably requested to furnish horses, tack and wagons for the various military operations. He did not, however, invest in Confederate bonds. The Union equipment depleted his merchandise, but he continued to take loans, do business, and purchase land and slaves.

Cornelia died in the fall of 1863, leaving Peres to rear three small children. Eliza, the youngest child, was born in 1861. He was married again on December 20 to Elizabeth Amanda Keen, his former sister-in-law and business associate, by Rev. John E. DuBose, pastor of First Presbyterian Church.

Following the War, Brokaw retained only a nominal interest in his business, concentrating instead on cash crop cultivation. In 1869, he brokered agreements with several newly emancipated slaves in which he furnished land, a team, farm implements, and food in return for three-fifths of all crops produced on his land. Brokaw and other planters organized the Leon County Agricultural Society. At the first meeting on September 8, 1868, he was elected director. He was also appointed master of the Tallahassee chapter of the Grange in March 1874.

In order to maintain his business and farming Peres' expenditures constantly exceeded his income, and he borrowed money and mortgaged his home. Elizabeth tried to assist him by taking in boarders at $10 a week or $40 a month. Paying guests occupied the main part of the house, forcing the Brokaw sisters to stay in a "little room at the end of the hall and separated from it by a board partition which did not reach the ceiling", while Abram "occupied a comfortable room in the cottage" and Mrs. Brokaw slept in "a room cut off of the back piazza."

Brokaw's death in 1875 prompted his creditors to seek satisfaction of their loan. Richard A. Shine was employed to liquidate the assets of the livery business. His farm animals, tools and 1875 crop were sold under court order, and the city foreclosed on the city property and sold it at auction. Elizabeth was forced to file bankruptcy.

Submitted by: Linda Mabry, 2404 Oakdale Street, Tallahassee, FL 32308 mabryrj@comcast.net

Michele's Candle of Essence Peaceful Glorious Habitation

Michele Bess Brown is an individual who has conscientiously started and maintained her own retail business in Tallahassee, Florida. 2009 is the second year of her business, MICHELE BESS BROWN, and she has successfully achieved a productive, persistence, and patience strategy that will help her business achieve a profitable income to accommodate her goals in life: to be a valuable asset to her community networking as a unique and extraordinary writer.

Michele Bess Brown was born in Elizabeth, New Jersey to Robert Louis Bess and Martha Annette Bess. Robert was born in Vernon, Florida in 1937 and Martha was born in Crescent City, Florida in 1942. Michele's grandparents are Lola Mae Haynes and Frank William Haynes, Senior. Lola Mae Haynes was born in Vernon, Florida in 1912. Frank William Haynes, Senior was born in Madison, Florida in 1908. Michele's educational history includes Vernon High School, Crescent City High School, Tallahassee Community College (TCC), Chipola Junior College, International Career Institute, Lively Vocational Technical Institute, Washington Vocational Tech, and Denmark Technical College. Presently, Michele attends Strayer University online. She has worked as a nursing assistant with many medical health facilities in Tallahassee, and she is a retired custodial worker from the Apalachee Center. She is a devoted Christian and a member of the NAACP, Big Bend Mental Health Coalition (BBMHC), NAMI, Easy Profit Strategies Club, Freelance Writers, and Lulu Poetry Club.

Carl and Michele Brown, children; Carshell, Careale, Carl, and Zechariah

She was happily married to Carl Wendell Brown, Senior and has five beautiful, healthy, intelligent, and Christian like children from their God-fearing union. Carshell Wenashia Brown is the first-born and the innocuous and inquisitive child. She was born in Palatka, Florida. Carshell is a Leon High graduate of 2004. She is a model, TCC student, and is employed by Checker Corporation. Careale Rendell Brown is the second-born and is a radiant child; that is, a raisonneur. He was born in Tallahassee, Florida and graduated from Leon High in 2008. He is enrolled at TCC as an Engineering Major and is employed by Bill's Bookstore and Quizno. Carlyle Wendon Brown is the thirdborn and is the diplomatic and scientific child. He was born in Tallahassee, and will be a Leon High School graduate in 2010.

He will pursue a meteorologist career at TCC and is now employed by Subway. Carl Wendell Brown Junior is the fourth-born and the systematic and logical child. He will be a Leon High School graduate in 2011. He will pursue a Law Degree at FAMU. Zechariah Cornelius Brown is the fifthborn and the courageous and emphatic child. He will be a Leon High School graduate in the year 2012. He will pursue a Law Degree at FSU. All Michele's children are volunteers with BBMHC.

Michele is a dedicated mom and inspirational divorcee, in recovery with a mental disability from her marriage with Carl Wendell Brown, Senior. Carl works on his anger-management skills daily as a local minister. Michele and Carl Senior have a life-long friendship, showing God's love in action. She is the former President of the BBMHC, and a vital member of the Governor's Commission on Disabilities.

Written and submitted by: Michele Bess Brown, P.O. Box 13902, Tallahassee, Florida 32317 bmichele33@yahoo.com

Brown and Griffing-Ships that pass in the night

In 1860 Tallahassee, a young man on a journey of self-discovery and an old politician writing a memoir enjoyed a brief friendship. Almost 150 years later the young man's diary was transcribed and published on the Internet by a descendant who discovered it in Florida.

"Ships that pass in the night, and speak each other in passing; Only a signal shown and a distant voice in the darkness; So, on the ocean of life we pass and speak to one another, Only a look and a voice; then darkness again and silence."
Henry Wadsworth Longfellow

Ralph Goodrich's descendant, Bill Griffing, writes that the young man, just twenty-three years of age in 1860, was born into a farming family near Oswego, New York. He graduated from Hobart College in 1858 where he "witnessed first-hand the dramatic sectional differences in culture and politics expressed by the students from the North and the South on the eve of the Civil War. For some inexplicable reason, Goodrich seemed to favor the Southern lifestyle. He didn't object to slavery. His Southern friends had convinced him that the abolitionists were only stirring up trouble, misrepresenting the institution and slandering their fathers. To Goodrich, life in the South held a certain charm and he longed to visit or possibly live there one day. He read for the New York bar, but failing that, he went south to become a teacher, first in Camden, South Carolina and then in Bel Air, Florida.

The old man was former governor of Florida (1849-1853), Thomas Brown, who in 1860 was seventy-five years of age, living in Bel Air, outside of Tallahassee. He was a widower who lived with his unmarried daughter Margaret (Mag), a widowed daughter Mary Archer, another daughter, Frances (Lizzie) Douglass and her children, plus some Key West residents, who often spent the summers with them. Captain Brown was writing a memoir, and his mind was probably much in the past. He was raised on plantations in Westmoreland County, Virginia and moved to Leon County in 1827. His only son, Alexander, died in 1836.

Florida 7th State Governor, Thomas Brown

Young Ralph called on the former governor soon after arriving and found him to be "a fine old Virginia man," but the inexperienced teacher was not happy with his situation. "I feel lonely and homesick. Mr. George Ward is a kind man, but fear I shall have to work hard here. Some of them can scarcely read decently. I hope and trust that I shall succeed." He later wrote, "I think I am treated coldly and neglected since I came."

Three of Mr. Brown's grandchildren, Susan and Tom (Tod) Archer and Betty Douglass, were enrolled in the school, as well as four Ward children, three Chaires', four Maxwell's, etc. "Gov. Brown's grandchildren had gone home and told things about me that made the family angry.

In the evening I went over and settled it with the Governor. He seems reasonable enough but the mothers of the girls Sue M. Archer and Betty Douglas were quite enraged. He said he would send them back to school in the morning."

It seems that the Brown's residence became a refuge for Ralph. Over time his visits became more frequent and longer lasting. On July 4 "about eleven went over to Governor Thomas Brown's house and stayed to dinner, till nearly 5 o'clock. He treated me to good whiskey and talked about everything. He has been to England. Told some of his exploits, and about the courts in England. He was in the War of 1812. There is but one good gentleman here and that is Governor Brown. Miss Mag Brown is the only lady. The rest of the females are wayward and foolish."

On one occasion Ralph went "over to Governor Brown's to tell Mag about the polar star. She and I went into the Governor's office and staid until nearly eleven. The Governor told stories and what had befallen him and what he had known to have taken place. Our conversation was about ghosts, apparitions, and was in fact very ghostly." Ralph's emotions and opinions rode a roller coaster, and in one diary entry he wrote "I was not designed for a school teacher, that is evident and I will never succeed. Oh God, help me, counsel me what to do in this life. Guide me into that pursuit for which I am fitted and in which I may be able to do good."

On another day after tea "I went over to Governor Thomas Brown's house. Told Governor all my troubles and told him I was going to leave town. The conditions on which I came to retain this position have not been met. He seems to agree with me and said I acted the part of an honorable person in offering to resign as I did. He is a clever man. I like him. I hope he thinks well of me."

Mag Brown (a spinster of twenty-eight, thought by Ralph to be "refined and intelligent") also befriended the young teacher, and they had long talks, walking on the railroad tracks or "sitting on the porch admiring the clouds." Ralph began to look for another position on August 27th "My 24th birthday. I let them have another holiday from school. Went over to Governor Thomas Brown's place and got his recommendation Had a long talk with him and got almost tipsy on toddy and Staid nearly all day."

According to the *National Cyclopedia of America Biography*, Goodrich moved on to Arkansas and at the out-break of The Civil War "enlisted as a private in the Confederate service, but toward the close of the war was offered the commission of captain of engineers in the Federal army.

In 1866 he accepted a deputy clerkship in the U. S. Courts at Little Rock AR and in 1873 was appointed clerk of both the U. S. circuit and district courts. Goodrich became conversant with many languages and a noted Sanskrit scholar and author. Like Governor Brown he collected a large library and became a high level Mason. Governor Brown lived through the deprivation of the war. Though extremely frail, he made a last visit to Virginia to speak to the Florida regiments there in 1872.

Written and submitted by: Lucinda Brown 4580 Trails Drive Sarasota, Florida, Cindybrown4580@verizon.net; Source: http://www.griffingweb. com/, Goodrich diaries May – October, 1860

Jacqueline Bryan Perrin

My name is Jacqueline Bryan Perrin and I was born in Cordele, Georgia. My father was a salesman at Robins Department Store. He was promoted to manager of a new store in Tifton, Georgia when I was six months old. My mother was Alice Tison Bryan (1905-1958) of Sylvester, Georgia and father was Warren Candler Bryan of Worth County, Georgia (1906-1999). Growing up in a small town of Georgia guided by Christian parents was a great way to begin life, even though the country was coming out of the Depression. My family was poor but we did not know we were poor, because everyone we knew was in the same situation. Mother's parents were William Woodruff Tison (b. 1863- 1938 in Georgia) and Sarah Van Houston (b. 1879- 1962 in Georgia). Candler's (as my dad was known) parents were John Falton Bryan of Lee County GA (1875-1963) and Leola Smoak, GA (1879-1962).

I went through grade school in Tifton and finished at Tifton High School. After finishing two years at Valdosta State College, I went to the University of Georgia in Athens, Georgia and graduated with a BA degree. My first work opportunity was as a secretary to the Baptist Student Director for Georgia Baptist Convention in Atlanta. I met my husband, Tom Perrin, through an employee at work. When she got married, I was introduced to her first cousin, who was a graduate of Georgia Tech, as a civil engineer working in Perry, Florida at the Buckeye Paper Mill. We married at my home church in Tifton, and had three children, Tommy, Kimberly and David, while living in Perry.

Tom and two of the top management of the engineering company decided to form their own company and we all moved to Tallahassee, Florida in 1965. The Watkin Engineers and Constructors Incorporated was based in Tallahassee and did industrial work throughout the Southeast and was sold to Dillingham Holdings in 1984. Tom retired as president in 1987.

I have always been a stay-at-home mom, Community volunteer, Sunday school teacher, and sewing teacher. Tallahassee has been a super place to raise our children, and has given us wonderful friends, who were a support system for our children. Our church was First Baptist Church and we were very involved in its functions, as were our children. They all live here with their families today, and have made wonderful citizens. We give credit to the training and raising them all from the values we learned from this church.

We remember the moving of the Column's (Chamber of Commerce building) and the Union Bank from the property where the church built the Christian Life Center. This gave us many opportunities and missions to help many other people, who were not so fortunate. I especially enjoyed working with English as a Second Language for International people, and am doing that now at the Bradfordville First Baptist Church, where our son-in-law, Mark Wilbanks is pastor. Tom and I have had some great trips overseas, but we are always happy to return to Tallahassee, Florida.

Written and submitted by: Jacqueline Bryan Perrin, 551 High Oaks Court, Tallahassee, Florida .Jacquebp@aol.com

Joshua Byrd

(The following is a copy of an article that appeared on the front page of the Florida Record on Thursday, August 22, 1918.)
TALLAHASSEE NINETY-TWO YEARS AGO
Interesting Letter, Dated Jan. 21, 1826, Written By An Early Settler
JOSHUA A. BYRD OF KINSTON, N. C.
Made Journey to This State By Carts and Mules and Bought Vast Property.

All Tallahasseeans will read with interest the following letter, written from Tallahassee ninety-two years ago. One of the early settlers of Tallahassee was Joshua H. Byrd, who came here from Kinston, Lenoir County, N. C., early in January, 1826. As the letter points out, he made the long trip over the country, by carts and mules, accompanied by a number of his faithful slaves. It was an exploration journey, and while in this section Joshua Byrd bought vast tracts of land at the remarkable price of $1.25 per acre. The conditions of North Florida at that time, as pointed out in this interesting document, are somewhat of a contrast with present day conditions.

Miss Evelyn Blake has kindly consented to the publication of this letter in the Record. It was written by her grandfather to her grandmother, and the original letter is a worn bit of paper, almost faded and obliterated. No envelopes were used in those days. The letter was merely folded, and the edges confined by sealing wax. Instead of postage, the letter was marked "25c" in the upper right hand corner, designating the fact that the fee to that amount had been paid. The letter is as follows:

"Tallahassee, Fla , Jan. 21, 1826
Dear Wife:

On the 18th inst. We arrived at a little town in Florida, called, Quincy, about 25 miles from this place, and the next day we went out in the woods to look at the land, and continued our route to this place, where we arrived last night, and have been looking over the lands in this neighborhood all day, and find the land much better than I expected, and the cotton stalks much higher than I had ever heard of. This country produces corn very well, but not as well as it does cotton and sugar cane. They make the best sugar and molasses here that I have ever seen. It so happened that all the land we have seen since we have been in Florida is good. This is the highest country I have ever seen; we have not seen any low lands.

We have heard various reports since we left home about this country. One was that corn would not grow here; another that the country was sickly. But to the contrary, I find the land produces the most corn I have ever seen any land produce; and there has not been but one death in this town in twelve months, and that was a man who came here sick, and only lived a few days. General Croom left his carts and negroes in Quincy, but I directed mine to come on here, where they arrived today about noon in company with Mr. Barrows, and in the morning I shall send them on to Miccosukee Lake, about 20 miles from here, where Col Parrish settled. Mr. Jackson, Gen.

Croom, Bryan and myself will start out early in the morning and expect to reach Mr. Parrish's tomorrow night. We have seen plenty of good land to be taken up at $1.25 per acre, but want to see the lands on the Lake before we settle, as it is said the lands on the Lake are better than any I have seen.

I know nothing to the contrary, but that I shall be home the time I set before I left, as I expect to start back about the 10th of next month.

We are all well, as I very much hope to find you, my dear wife, and our dear children. The weather is quite cold here, but does not seem to hurt vegetation. Collard plants are large enough here to set out, and garden peas are half-leg high, notwithstanding, we are too cold with our great coats on. Jacob say he would hardly be back to North Carolina for his freedom, and told me to write you that he could support you better here than ten negroes could in North Carolina, If 66 I cared to hire my hands out I could get $150 a piece for them. In fact, Jacob could make $50.00 a month here riving boards, as he could get $3.00 per hundred, but I think it best to set them to clearing land, as soon as I find out the best place. Corn does not do well planted after March, and as I shall not get much planted before that time, I expect to go principally on rice, as any of the high land will bring from 50 to 75 bushels per acre.

I have nothing more, my dear wife, at present, but remain,
Your most affectionate husband, forever,
　　JOSHUA H. BYRD
　P. S. -I shall come to this place again before I start home, with the hope of receiving a letter from you, my dearest of all.
　　Please send word to Genl. Croom's and Mr. Jackson's family that they are both well and will go home with me. We have a large frost this morning. J. H. B."
Submitted by: Rubie P. Butterworth, 4434 Meandering Way #309, Tallahassee, FL 32308

The T. B. Byrd Family, A Union of Pioneer Families

When my grandparents, Rebecca (Ruble) Bradford Bernard and Thomas Blake Byrd, were married at the Methodist Church in Tallahassee on March 5, 1884, four pioneer Leon County families were joined. Their very names were those of families who came as early as 1826, only two years after Tallahassee became the capital of the new territory of Florida.

Tom Byrd, the son of Catharine Sarah Blake and Dr. Flavius Augustus Byrd, grew up in Miccosukee in eastern Leon County where his grandparents, Nathan and Eliza Parish Byrd, had settled after moving from Lenoir County, NC. Her father, Col. Richard Parish, Nathan, his brother, Joshua Byrd, and Miles Blake, also married to one of Parish's daughters, moved their families to the Miccosukee community in the late 1820s. Here Nathan became a member of the territorial legislative council. Tom's father died early, leaving Tom to help support the family. By the time he was 21, Tom had moved into Tallahassee to open a grocery business that served the community until 1965 when his son, Bernard, closed the store.

Rubie's father, Jesse Talbot Bernard of

Byrd family home

Portsmouth, VA, was the "late comer," having arrived in 1849 to teach children on the Bradfordville plantations. There he met Mary Elizabeth Bradford, daughter of Thomas Anderson and Elizabeth Eelbeck Bradford, whom he married on November 28, 1850. Bradford was one of four brothers of Halifax County, NC, who settled in northern Leon County in the 1830s. Jesse and Mary Bernard moved their family to a home on North Calhoun Street in Tallahassee following his service in the War Between the States. Here he twice became mayor of Tallahassee and a county judge.

After their marriage, Tom and Rubie Byrd moved into a home on South Calhoun Street, living there until 1924 when Caroline Brevard Elementary School was built on that property. Their home during their last years was on the northeast corner of Monroe and Gaines Streets.

Together the Byrd's had eight children:

William Parish Thomas Bradford, Lina Clifton (Mrs. William E. Van Brunt), Augustus Bernard, Rubie (Mrs. C. L. Hardwick), Janet Laurie (Mrs. James D. Plant), Kate (Mrs. W. Leroy MacGowan), and Elizabeth (Mrs. Robert A. Taylor), most of whom continued to live in Tallahassee. A niece also made her home with them following the death of her parents.

Higher education was important to this family. Tom had to forego college; Rubie graduated from Longwood College in Virginia. Her father was secretary of the Board of Education for the West Florida Seminary, a forerunner of Florida State College. It was important for the children, including the niece, to have the opportunity for college educations. The sons each graduated from a different college; all of the girls were alumnae of Florida State College for Women. During their college years the Byrd home served as the "home away from home" for many young people who were separated from

Byrd family portrait on the steps of their home

their own families for the first time.

For all of their lives, the Methodist Church was central. Long members of the church now known as Trinity United Methodist Church, they both served as officers, teachers and examples. Their children were leaders in the Sunday school and youth groups, and as adults they continued to be leaders, teachers and examples for their own children.

On the Byrd's wedding day the newspaper observed, "May she always be to him a Ruby above price, and may he be a Byrd that will sing at home without caging." From all accounts of the life of this couple this wish for them was fulfilled. Accolades at the time of their deaths attested to the esteem in which they were held. When Tom died in 1928 an article in the Tallahassee Daily Democrat observed: "Tallahassee today mourns the passing of a beloved citizen, a pioneer who has helped to build the city we now enjoy, but above all a man of integrity, character and faith."

When Rubie died in 1934 one tribute stated, "As one who has partaken of the beautiful hospitality of Mrs. Byrd's home, the news came to me as a painful shock. I can appreciate to the fullest extent just what the death of this gracious lady means to her children and other relatives… Her life was a benediction and a greater heritage to her children than all the gold in all the banks in the world."

My mother was daughter, Janet. For a few years after her marriage in 1921 to James Daniel Plant of Madison, FL, they made their home in Georgia. My sister, Laurie, and I were born in Albany. Our family returned to Tallahassee where Laurie and I grew up attending Caroline Brevard, Leon High, and Florida State. After my grandparents' deaths, we lived in the house at 725 South Monroe Street surrounded by loving aunts, uncles and cousins. This was "down home" for all. The memory of holiday gatherings spent there and later in various family homes in Tallahassee is precious to me.

Just as my parents did, I, too, spent some years away from Tallahassee, beginning our family in Brevard, North Carolina after my marriage to Charles A. Butterworth, Jr. As has been the case with others in the family, we were drawn back to Tallahassee. While our older son, Charles, III, spent only a short time here, our younger children, Jim and Beth, grew up in Tallahassee. They became part of the third generation of the Byrd family to attend Leon High School. Beth also joined many who have graduated from Florida State, while our sons pursued their education and careers elsewhere. Our children, as well as some of their cousins, no longer make their homes in Tallahassee; however, this place pulls them back often.

Going back to the Parish family, nine generations have lived in this county. At present, members of the last four still live here, and the bond of love that Tom and Rubie Byrd created within their family has carried over to us. No longer is there a house on South Monroe Street; it was long ago removed to make way for a capitol center building, but we will forever be "down home" when we all get together.

Submitted by Rubie Plant Butterworth, 4434 Meandering Way, Apartment 309, Tallahassee, FL, 32308

Mrs. Susie (Mama Susie) Wilson Cain

The women of an African American family in Leon County Florida: stories my great-grandmother told us.

My sister and I grew up in a household of four generations of proud, cherished, mostly widowed women. Likewise, my mother grew up with four generations, as did my grandmothers before. This narrative recounts only a few of the many, many conversations and stories about Mrs. Susie Lillian Wilson Cain (Mama Susie), our great grandmother, who lived, married, and raised her children in Tallahassee, Florida from about 1887 until 1914, after her beloved husband, Mr. Arthur J. Cain died. Throughout her life, she favored God and family. Her heart, joy, friendships, and memories of exciting times, stemmed from her days there... Thus, our deep connections and roots in the Tallahassee clay soil.

Minerva Bythwood Prince Wilson (Big Mama) (1855-1941)

Susie Lillian Wilson Cain (Mama Susie) wearing widow's weeds. (1871- 1965)

As children, Mama Susie would tell story after story reminiscent of family life in Tallahassee; working at the depot, church affiliation, property ownership, community and social events, gardening, holidays and happy times, (as well as word of a lynching). She would describe those times as "horse and buggy days". The vignettes that follow are my recollection of "Stories My Great Grandmother Told Us".

Number I, her voice:

It must have rained every day that week. I was scheduled to do the most important performance of my life. The streets of Tallahassee were wet and muddy; you would have to be very thoughtful about how to navigate one of the highest hills in the city. That was the only way to get up to the new college. It was a blessing when our horse, named Charlie, mustered up strength and pulled the buggy up the slippery hill that led to the campus of the State Normal and Industrial College for Colored Students (now Florida A&M University) . Charlie pulled the buggy and I walked beside him, to lighten the load. I, a soprano, was on program to sing at a Sunday Vespers Service. From the stage, they announced me as the featured soloist. After singing, "I come to the garden alone..." I bowed to the applause and took my seat.

Number II, her voice:

It was sometimes during the summer of 'nineteen aught two' when my youngest sister Frances, taught my daughter Matilda to ride a wheel (bicycle). Their long skirts would just get in the way, so they tied their skirts tight around their knees with shoelaces. They needed to have their legs and feet freed up to push the pedals and keep themselves from falling. It took those two girls a full day of falling and weaving and bobbing before they rode together, teaching and learning how to balance each other so they could peddle with all their might. My husband and I would

laugh so hard about their antics and the falls they endured while learning to ride. Even the dogs got tired of chasing after them. But, they were still at it, taking turns and trying hard. It commenced to getting dusk dark, so I made them come in the house. They would not give up... Determined!
Number III, Her voice:

The ways to make a living and provide for your family in the old days were to trust in the Lord with all your heart. A garden was a necessity, so we always had a big one. We could grow lots of things in the Tallahassee red clay, if done right. Vegetables and fruit could be preserved in jars using the boiling method. Pears were free and could be 'put up' (preserved) easily. Pear trees were abundant and pears made good preserves. We made enough to keep, sell, give away, or swap with people in the neighborhood. Bake your own bread every week. Pump your own water if you had to.

Matilda Lottie Cain Wise (Mama Tillie) (1891 - 1986)

Somebody had to have a smoke house to preserve the meat. The Nixons, our friends who lived on the Thomasville Road, usually smoked our meat along with theirs. Most people had chickens. We churned butter and ate clabber. Most times we had extra money coming in because we rented a little house to a family at the church. People needed a place to stay, so they will rent your property if it is nice and clean. We always had good renters. Mama's little house was for railroad workers who needed to stay in town a night or two.
Number IV, Her voice:

We worked hard at the Tallahassee Depot. Mama, me, Lena Mae, and Mack (three siblings) worked on the freight and passenger sides. The railroad became our livelihood and this 'occupation' carried over to others in our family. Occupation means your job keeps you occupied. Ha-ha-ha. G r a n d m a Hannah (lived mostly in Monticello). Mama and me were also seamstresses. Little Matilda was our helper. We sewed all our clothes and curtains and saved much of what we earned. After supper, all of us, four generations, would sit on the porch until evening tide doing all kind of "fancy work"; crocheting, tatting, quilting, embroidering; ribbon/lace, and cut-work. Our specialties were wedding trousseaus and christening gowns. The son of one family for which they worked later became the Sheriff of Leon County.
Number V, Her voice:

I was one of the organ players at Bethel African Methodist Episcopal Church where my family attended. Our son (Robert) would pump the organ bellows to keep the organ sound going while I played. Our daughter Matilda learned to play the piano and became a music lover and music teacher during her adult life. Bethel Church is near the City Cemetery where my husband is buried along with family members, and a small child whose family had no place to" lay her." I called my husband Mr. Cain. He was a popular bartender in the city, although he never touched a drink of liquor for himself. He was anxious and happy for the college to take root. Mr. Cain always talked about how the college would progress our people and benefit the community.mPeople will come from all over to go to college. Our church welcomed them.
Number VI, Her voice:

The holidays were the most special time of the year for our family. Our friends, the Garretts and Nixons, would always stop by the house and we would exchange gifts. Most of the time, we ate Thanksgiving dinner at home with family, in Monticello, or at the church. Christmas was always celebrated at home and we usually had company from Tallahassee and our family from Monticello to join us. Mr. Cain, Grandma Hannah, Mama, my brother, Mack and my three sisters, Lena, Frances, Lula and our children with handmade decorations and wax candles. Once everybody was there, the candles were lit only for a few minutes, because we did not want to cause a house fire. We always kept a bucket of water near the tree in case of an emergency. The house was decorated with big bunches of magnolia leaves on the mantles and over the doors. Wet pinecones and orange peels would be burning on top of the logs in the fireplaces and the house smelled so nice. We also roasted chestnuts in the hot ashes. Everybody would get one or two gifts and maybe a surprise. Most gifts were made; not bought.

The women would cook all night using both kitchens inside and outside our house, so the food would be fresh and hot for the next day. There would be plenty of good cooking, and Mr. Cain would make a big turkey with sage cornbread stuffing. Everybody would help. I would cook the vegetables and rice and cakes, greens, beans, yams, purlieu, jelly cake, lemon-cheese cake, floatin' island. Mama would make her special dark fruitcakes weeks ahead of time, soak them in juice or wine, and make the bread. There would be 20 different things on the buffett to choose from including ham, pickle relish, cranberries, and ambrosia. We would set the table with the good dishes and linens and the children's table. Sweet water and eggnog would be part of the menu and grape scuppernong wine, too. We would end the day with coffee, tea and dessert. However, the meal would not begin until Big Mama said grace and somebody got happy.

Number VII, Her voice:

One day we received word of a lynching somewhere to the East. Somebody did a disgraceful thing to that boy. He didn't do nothing! Somebody saw him walking down road "drylong- so" slang for fste or dullness). A few days later, he was found hanging from a tree. I just don't know. That was the saddest news since I lost my husband.

Number VIII, her voice:

Yvonne, Beverly, Karen, and Rodney the family pecking order goes like this. Remember, you are the great, great, great grandchildren of Hannah Prince (called Grandma Hannah, born during slavery time). You are the great, great grandchildren of Minerva Prince Blythewood Wilson (called Big Mama, born during slavery time). You are the great grandchildren of, Susie Lillian Wilson Cain, (me, Mama Susie). You are the grandchildren of Matilda Lottie Cain Wise, (Mama Tillie) and we all once lived in Tallahassee, Florida. Now, who are Mama Tillie's children? In our family, each new generation of children was named after old family members - Minerva, Matilda, Lottie, Lena Mae, Pete, Frances, Mack. All written down in the bible.

There are fifty more stories that I could write about our great grand-mother's memories of family and life in Tallahassee. Their multigenerational family (three to four generations) maintained strong ties, work ethics, and abiding spirituality that was passed on to us. Through them, we witnessed the dynamics of strength, struggle, faith, and endurance of African American women during the old days (particularly after their husbands died). Shortly after Mama Susie's husband's death in 1914, she reluctantly left the comfort of her Tallahassee community and friends and moved to Jacksonville. She was "following the railroad" and the promise of expanded opportunities, to provide for her family. In the first wave of family members were her children and her Mother. Then, one by one, her siblings moved and she helped them get jobs at the Jacksonville Terminal. At one time, there were three generations of family working in various capacities at the train station. The family arrived in Jacksonville on the train, and their belongings were brought "through the country" on a horse and wagon. In Jacksonville, the Wilson family and children again became property owners, members of the Mount Zion African Methodist Episcopal Church. They married, joined the Masonic Order and Eastern Stars, and participated fully in the local community with social movements, groups and organizations.

Mrs. Susie Lillian Wilson Cain (Mama Susie), our great grandmother, passed away in

Wise Children, named after ancestors; Minerva, Evelyn Pete, Dorothy Lena Mae

Dorothy Lena Mae Wise Hicks-Bazzell (Age 90) and daughter, Dr. Frances Yvonne Hicks

1965. She was buried in Tallahassee, next to her beloved husband, Mr. Cain. Three matriarchs of our four – generation household, lived ninety years or longer including my Mother, Dorothy Lena Mae Wise Hicks-Bazzell, in 2009. Each generation showed an endearing reverence for the ancestors and each other. Not a day passed without mentioning Mama (or Papa, or Big Mama). Something like: "Mama used to put honey on her strawberries", or "Big Mama liked to rinse her sheets in bluing". Today, in our family, we do the same things. Throughout my childhood and my adult years, I vividly remember that several times a year, we would load up the car with a bucket, broom, rake, garden hoe, a plant, and our lunch. At first light, we would be on our way to the Old Cemetery in Tallahassee. We would pray, clean, paint and plant flowers at the gravesite marked "CAINE" (name misspelled).

1st row; Bobby, Arthur, Sallie, Margaret, 2nd row; Mary, Hazel, Martha and Hettie, 3rd row; Joe, Karia, and Spurgeon Camp

Afterwards, we would visit longtime friends (the Nixons) who lived on the Old Thomasville Road. Although the highway had changed, Mama Tillie, our grandmother, would point out where to turn off the main road. Sometimes we would return to Jacksonville with pears... hard, green pears from similar old trees on the same land that Mama Susie spoke of over the years. We would put up pear preserves and I would eat green pears until I was sick as could be! Sometimes we would return with a trunk load of clay soil and once we returned with a "six sisters" rose bush from the old land... As not to let go of the loving past.

Submitted by: Frances Yvonne Hicks, Ed. D., 1973 Ribault Scenic Drive, Jacksonville, Florida 32208, fyvonnehicks@aol.com

Camp Family

This is about the large Camp family, who came to Tallahassee in the '40's. It is a tribute to the oldest child who returned home from Atlanta after losing her husband, and completed her college work at FSU. There she met and married Charles Barrier. She taught in several schools including Woodville Elementary (fourth grade) in Leon County.

Some of the other children began college work as far back as the depression years. Name explanations are: Mayor is Mary Nell, Raye is Martha, and Madgie Padgie is Margaret. Lines written on Karia's graduation from FSU June 6, 1959.

It started back in '43 When FSU was FSC And
Hettie wrangled the first degree
In the cap 'n gown parade.
At Stetson, then, in '46
Hazel pulled the great big "fix"
And came up with a bag of tricks
To join the promenade.
Then Joe, another Stetson Hatter,
Scaled the academic ladder
With Doris to boot on a silver platter
And finally made the grade.
And then if it hadn't been for Paul
Mayor mightn't have made it at all....
The trek through Gainesville's hallowed halls
In the charge of the Gator brigade.
Then Spurgeon tried in measures drastic
To sell Ann on him and the public on plastic
Before he tripped the light fantastic
To pomp and circumstance.
When Raye descended on FS Y'all
With the big green eyes and the southern drawl,
She snowed the profs and deans and all
And took off on the road to romance.
From Madgie Padgie came the cry,
"If the others can do it, why not I?"
At least I guess it's worth a try—
And then there were just two more.
Then here comes Bobby crashing thru
The ivied walls of FSU,
With Mary's help and the motley crew
He evened up the score.
And now our final candidate
Defies all reason, rhyme and fate
And sails thru education's gate
With a list of "A's" that just won't wait
And on top of that a wonderful mate.
We think it's time to celebrate
Karia, here's to you!
For an epilogue we'll be quite brief.
Mother and Daddy breathed a sigh of relief!
Written by Karia's siblings.

Submitted by Margaret Camp, 4434 Meandering Way, Apartment 306, Tallahassee, FL 32308

Marjorie E. Campbell

Marjorie Evelyn Van Duzer was born September 26, 1926 in Sugar Loaf, New York. She is the second of three sisters (Dorothy and Willard) born to Gertrude Mary Jacqmein (1898-1968) and Willard Stevens Van Duzer (1898-1968) of New York. Marjorie's summers, during her youth, were spent with her maternal grandparents, Emma and Adam Jacqmein, at their "camp" on the Neversink River in Sullivan County, New York.

Her maternal grandparents are Emma Grandy Barnes (1867-1944) NY and Adam Jacqmein (1870-1951) NY. Her maternal great-grandparents are Susanna Dorr (1839- 1916) GER and Ludwig Daniel Jacqmein (1839-1913) GER, and Sarah Jane Rumsey (1835- 1902) NY and Isaac Barnes (1825-1905) NY. Her paternal grandparents are Nora Wood Stevens (1871-1936) NY and George Lewis Van Duzer (1857-1921) IE.

Nurse Marjorie E. Campbell. 1945

Her paternal great- grand parents are Sarah Elizabeth Schreeder (1828-1882) NY and Lewis Van Duzer (1830-1895) NY and Agnes Wood (1847-1931) NY and Mills Davis Stevens (1841-1921) NY.

Marjorie attended Chester Elementary School (1940) NY, Chester High School (1944) NY, Alfred University (Nursing Diploma 1948) NY, Tallahassee Community College (AA 1976) FL, Florida State University (BSN 1982) FL. She was Service Director for Upjohn Healthcare Services in Tallahassee (1976-1983), Staff Nurse and Nurse Educator at Tallahassee Community Hospital (1983- 1994), and Staff Nurse and on the Medical Records Staff at Tallahassee Outpatient Surgery Center (1994-2008). She retired in 2008 with a nursing career spanning sixty years, including the time she was in the Cadet Nurse Corps at Alfred University during WWII. She was a resident of Florida since 1965 and of Tallahassee since 1976.

Marjorie married Joseph John Campbell (1923-2001) in 1948 in Goshen, New York, and they divorced in 1976. She has one daughter Kathy Stinson; three grandchildren: Rebecca Kutz, David Stinson, and Michael Stinson; and two great-grandchildren: Sophia and Jack Kutz. Her passion for some forty years has been genealogy, especially her own family history and ancestry. She is a member of the Daughters of the American Revolution, Colonial Dames of the XVII Century, United States Daughters of 1812, Daughters of the American Colonists, Women Descendants of the Ancient and Honorable Artillery Company, Society of the Descendants of the Colonial Clergy, National Huguenot Society, Flagon and Trencher, the Orange County, New York Genealogical Society, and the Tallahassee Genealogical Society. Marjorie has traveled extensively throughout the United States, Mexico, Canada, and Europe. On one of several trips to Europe, she spent the better part of a week in the small Rhineland vineyard village of Godramstein, Germany where her maternal great-grandparents, Susanna and Ludwig Jacqmein, emigrated from in 1867.

This village was in Bavaria when they lived there, the country of Germany was yet to be formed. All the village people who assisted her in her quest were pleasant, helpful, and gracious hosts. Marjorie contributes her research success to the Catholic priest, the Lutheran minister and his daughter, the Civil Registration Office staff, and a retired Lutheran minister, who was a genealogist who assisted her at the Archives in Speyer on the Rhine. On July 26, 2009 Marjorie E. Campbell made her final journey to be with her ancestors, and will be missed by her family, friends, and all whom knew her.

Submitted by: Kathy Stinson, 3987 Forsythe Park Court, Tallahassee, FL 32309; Written by: Marjorie E. Campbell

James Baker Carlisle

James Baker Carlisle was born in Maryland in 1809. His wife, Mariah McCoy Alexander, was born in Virginia in 1816. They arrived in Florida by 1840, living in Tallahassee. They then moved to Magnolia where he was a merchant, moving again to Port Leon. When Port Leon was destroyed by a hurricane, the family moved to Newport. In September of 1846 he was the publisher of the *Newport Gazette*.

James and Mariah Carlisle were married in Washington, D. C., April 26, 1834. Two of their four children were born in Maryland and Virginia. The other two children were born in Florida. Mariah Carlisle's brothers were Amos Mark, Robert and Albert Alexander, born in Virginia. Robert and Albert Alexander were newspapermen also, having established the *Commercial Gazette* in Port Leon in 1843.

From 1849 to 1858, James Baker Carlisle was publishing the *Wakulla Times* (dates not inclusive). In 1850, Charles E. Dykes sold him half-interest in the *Floridian*, a paper being published in Tallahassee. Carlisle and his family moved to Tallahassee where he retained his half-interest until his death in Tallahassee of congestion of the lungs, November10, 1863. He is buried in an unmarked grave in the St. John's Episcopal Cemetery in Tallahassee.

Written and Submitted by: Gloria Dowden, 3227 Tanager Trail, Tallahassee, Florida 32303; Sources: Washington D. C. Marriage Records, Florida Census Records, Leon County Tax Records, and St. John's Episcopal Church Records

Dorothy Lane and John Carswell

Dorothy Lane Carswell is the daughter of Elsie and Fields Lane. She attended Caroline Brevard Elementary School with her siblings and later graduated from Leon High School. She attended TCC and met her future husband, John Lamar Carswell, in Marjorie Nam's Anthropology class. They were married on the Autumnal Equinox in 1971. The ceremony was performed by a dear family friend, Dr. Edwin Hartz, under the graceful canopy of an ancient, Spanish moss adorned with live oak, majestically rooted in the woodland of Dorothy's childhood playground of Myers Park.

After their marriage, their mentor and teacher, Marjorie Nam, called them to her office after class and presented them with a Pawleys Island rope hammock. They bought 40 acres in Wakulla County and built a cottage completely by hand, including the furniture. They continued to live in their little two story cottage on Mill Creek for 5 years before moving to Gainesville, Florida, where John attended grad school and Dorothy taught Montessori school.

Dorothy and John, along with their sons, Matthew Lamar Carswell, born 1974 and Benjamin Lane Carswell, born 1980 moved to Maryland after John's graduation from the University of Florida with a Masters Degree in Computer Science. While living there, John was Director of Health Policy for Paralyzed Veterans of America and worked in their national office for 15 years. Their sons graduated from Woodberry Forest School in Virginia. John was born in Jacksonville, Matt in Tallahassee, and Ben in Gainesville, Florida, while Dorothy was born in Tuscaloosa, Alabama, but moved to Tallahassee as a young child and lived there until her marriage to John.

Dorothy served as a volunteer on the Board of the Women's Committee for the National Symphony Orchestra at the Kennedy Center. She chaired a major new fundraiser for the orchestra and named it "Conduct the NSO." It was a raffle with the prize of conducting the NSO in one selection on stage at the Kennedy Center. It was chosen as one of the best new fundraisers for that year. After this event, she represented the Women's Committee/NSO at the American Symphony Orchestra League's conference in Portland, Oregon.

When John retired, they moved to Jekyll Island Georgia where Dorothy became the writer and editor of a cookbook created to benefit the Georgia Sea Turtle Center. The cookbook was chosen as one of the top 10 cookbooks in 2005 by Morris Press, the largest publisher of cookbooks in the nation.One hundred percent of the profit went to the Georgia Sea Turtle Center. Dorothy's mother, Elsie Lane, moved to Jekyll Island in 2009 and resides with them. Many of Elsie's family recipes are included in this cookbook!

John and Dorothy Lane Carswell in 2007

Submitted by: Dorothy Lane Carswell, 649 Old Plantation Rd., Jekyll Island, GA 31527. Written by: Mary Marchant

Dean A. Carvalho - Memories of 1005 Hays Street F

During my early childhood in Tallahassee, I had the unique experience of having a close relationship with two of my great grandparents. Myrtle and Leroy Strickland, or Gaga and Gramps as I knew them, were amazing and I truly feel lucky to have known them so well. Some of my fondest memories are the days I spent with Gaga and Gramps.

One of my first conscious memories was when I was probably about four or five years old. From the moment I walked into their house I would wait, with anticipation, not unlike a child feels on Christmas morning, for Gramps to get up from his big cushy leather recliner. As soon as he was on his feet I would run over to the chair, dismantle the cushions and begin my treasure hunt. Without fail I would always come away with a handful of shiny coins. I always thought I was so clever finding the change that fell out of Cramp's pockets. Not until I was in my twenties did I come to find out that he would intentionally put coins there for me to find. Clearly he was more clever than I gave him credit for, granted I was only four years old! This would not be the last time that I was fooled by my seemingly senile great grandparents. Gramps would then give me a crisp dollar bill every time I would leave. To leave every visit with a dollar and some change made me feel like a millionaire.

Home of Leroy Strickland Sr. 1005 W. Hays Street

Gaga, equally as witty as Gramps, also use to play jokes on me. One afternoon she was babysitting me and for whatever reason I decided to hide from her. I crawled under the coffee table in the living room and waited. For probably an hour I sat with my hands over my mouth trying to hold back laughter as Gaga slowly walked around the house searching. Finally, thinking I had won the game, I jumped out triumphantly declaring where I had been hiding. Again, not until I was much older did I come to find out that she had known where I was camped out the whole time. Looking back on it, the joke was definitely on me as it was probably the only time in my childhood that I had sat quietly without moving for an hour.

Dean A Carvalho in 2000

When I wasn't trying (unsuccessfully) to outwit Gramps and Gaga, I entertained myself with the abundance of old fashioned treasures found throughout the house. One of my favorites was Cramps' antique typewriter that rested on an even older desk in the back office. Even before I could read and write, I would sit up on my knees so I could reach the desk, and pretend I was an old-time private eye typing away trying to solve an important crime. The click-clack of the type and the resulting ding at the end of the line was music to my ears. The resulting page would be a jumbled mess of consonants and explanation points, but to me it was always a masterpiece.

When I got bored rummaging through the house, I would head outside to the giant pecan tree that sat in their front yard. While there were plenty of perfectly ripe pecans on the ground ready to be cracked open and enjoyed, the best nuts always seemed to be hanging on the branches that were just out of reach. I remember spending hours trying to climb the huge trunk. I was a very athletic child and a good treeclimber, but I never seemed to make it up that tree. After accepting defeat, I would head back into the house to prepare for one of my favorite childhood activities.

Gaga used to keep a large array of magnifying glasses on the table next to her recliner. I remember looking over each one, examining them like a gladiator picking out a sword before battle. I would put one in each pocket like a cowboy puts six-shooters in their holsters and head back outside. From there I would spend hours magnifying the sun's rays and taking out my wrath on unsuspecting colonies of ants and piles of dried leaves.

These are just a few of my fondest memories of the days I spent with Cramps and Gaga. Looking back on these years I have come to realize how lucky I was to have known not just one but two of my Great-grandparents. I also know how lucky they must have felt to have spent so many years with their great-grandchild and I hope I have the same privilege in my life.

Written and submitted by: Dean A. Carvalho (Grand-son of Roy Strickland), Tallahassee, Florida 32304

Jewell Cassels

Close your eyes and try to imagine a Central Florida of old, just a few years after "The War to End All Wars." Picture in your mind narrow, dusty, dirt lanes winding their way between fence rows and farmers fields to the sleepy little town of Plant City. Everybody knew everybody there. No one ever locked their doors at night, there was no need to. Into this quiet, peaceful world is born Jewell Cassels. Of course her last name wasn't Cassels then. She was a sweet, gentle young girl, expecting to spend her life right there in Plant City. But time and life had a different plan for Jewell.

Jewell was eleven years old when she found her way to Christ. The strength of her favorite Bible verse, John 3:16, carried her through her teens in her quiet little town. While at Plant City High, she found another strength and soul mate in Carl, her high school sweetheart. Jewell and Carl began dating before she turned sixteen. She was just eighteen when they were married in 1937 in the pastor's home in Hopewell, a little community south of Plant City.

Tallahassee called out to the Cassells family in 1955. Jewell, Carl and their precious family of two growing boys followed the call of work to the Capital city. Jewell made a good home for her family. She filled her spare time working twelve years at home as a dressmaker. Then she found time to take on the chores of mending ripped seams and replacing missing buttons for a local dry cleaner. Before retiring, Jewell also worked for twenty-one years in the State Treasurer's Office, in the Division of Financial Responsibility.

But for all of her life Jewell's true passion has been her family, caring for and loving two fine sons, then her five grandchildren and six great-grandchildren.

The strength and joy of being a Christian has always been a wonderful blessing to Jewell. Even though rheumatoid and osteoarthritis have humbled her body, her joy in Jesus Christ has kept her spiritually strong and always here each Sunday at First Baptist. This is the church she found when she came to Tallahassee and it is here that she has made her Christian home.

If there are any gifts she could pass on to the young people of today, Jewell says it would be her strong faith in God and the high moral standards that she learned as a young girl in the sleepy little town of Plant City. She has carried these virtues with her all through her life.

Submitted by Jewell Cassels; Written by: Carol Ann and Bill Boydston, 1639 Twin Lakes Circle, Tallahassee, FL 32311

Cavanaugh/Russell

In the 1800s, my great aunt Mary Cooper and her husband William Cooper moved to Leon County from Scotland. They acquired over 300 acres on both sides of what is now Old Bainbridge Road, North and South of I-10. With the death of

Cavanaugh Home-1917, the Sears House, 2701 N. Old Bainbridge Road

William in 1899, Mary needed help to run the farm. She asked her brother, John J. Cavanaugh (my grandfather) and her sister, Josie Cavanaugh-White to come from Ireland to help, which they did. Upon Mary's death in 1915, she left the property to John and Josie Cavanaugh. Since Mary had no children of her own, her siblings divided the land and each raised their families on the property.

My Aunt Josie had one daughter, Mildred, who married into the Harts-field family. Some of that property is now Harts-

John J. Cavanaugh and Annie Mae (Russell) Cavanaugh

field Plantation. My grandfather John married Annie Mae Russell, who had family history in both Wakulla and Leon County. Annie's father was Eli Webster Russell, a circuit riding Baptist

preacher. My grandmother Annie rode with him many times on a wagon during his circuit. A lot of her relatives grew up in Wakulla County on Springhill Road and on Hwy 20 in Leon County, with marriages into the Stoutamire, Harvey, Wilkes and Brown families. My mother is Margaret Mae (Cavanaugh) Callahan. She is 95 years old (b. 1914) and the oldest of four children. My father was Roy Callahan who came to Leon County when he was young from Georgia. I am one of six children. I was born in 1935 at the old Sears house constructed by my grandfather on Old Bainbridge Road, which has been demolished to build The Oasis Apartment complex.
Written and Submitted by: Carolyn (Callahan) Losey, 3379 Lakeview Drive, Tallahassee, Florida 32310-6312

Margaret Mae (Cavanaugh) Callahan - A Brush with Movie Stars

John J. Cavanaugh bought one of the first cars in Leon County. He had only one condition from the salesman to purchase the car from his dealership, which was that they teach his then 16 year old daughter, Margaret Cavanaugh, how to drive the car. After Margaret learned how to drive, she drove around Leon County alone, which was unheard of in those days. One day she was driving along North Monroe and got a flat tire. Not knowing how to change a flat tire, she waited for assistance from another driver on the road. By chance two young men stopped to assist her and were very caring and gentlemen-like to Margaret.

After fixing the flat, and as they were leaving, Margaret thanked them and asked what their names were. The gentlemen replied: My name is Errol Flynn and this is Eddie Cantor, my friend. We are on our way to Miami to make a movie. With that they waved goodbye to Margaret and she never saw them again. When she returned home and told her family what had happened to her, they found it hard to believe that a movie star would change a

Margaret Mae Cavanaugh in her High School Band uniform around 1930

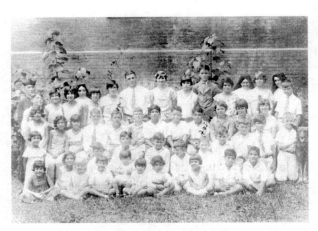

Margaret-14, Hansel-12, and John-7 at Blessed Sacraments Catholic Church in 1928.

tire for a lady who is stranded by the side of the road. Even with their disbelief, Margaret was motivated to take acting lessons at school and she found small parts in bit plays in Leon County. After she married Roy Callahan and had children, Margaret forgot about acting and focused her attention on her children and husband. But she always remembered the kindness of the two actors she met by the side of the road.
Submitted by: Margaret Mae (Cavanaugh) Callahan, 3377LakeviewDr, Tallahassee, FL. 32310 glosey@nettally.com; Written by: Carolyn Losey

Private Daniel Chaires

PFC Daniel B. Chaires of Tallahassee, Florida was born May 26, 1986 and was the son of retired Leon County Sheriffs Capt. Harry Chaires and his wife, Nan Cuchens, who taught at Florida State College of Nursing. Harry Chaires, who retired in 2005, is a descendant of one of Leon County's pioneer families. He spent more than 30 years with the Sheriffs Office and for many years directed special operations, including security at Florida State football games. Nan Cuchens, a registered nurse, was director of the emergency room at Tallahassee Memorial Hospital before joining FSU and is a volunteer at the Red Hills Horse Trials. Daniel promised his father that after he finished his term in the Marines, he wanted to come back and join the Sheriffs Department. A park near Chaires Elementary, on land once owned by Daniel's great-grandfather Benjamin Chaires, has been dedicated in his memory, and is called the Daniel B. Chaires Community Park.

Private Daniel Chaires

The park has baseball fields, tennis courts, a basketball court and a community center located throughout its scenic landscape. His Mother recalls how he used to ride horses when he was barely able to walk, and how he would race through those fields when he was a boy and before the park was built. He loved to play basketball and tennis in the park when he was home on leave.

Daniel became a fine Marine because he ran through the parks frequently to get in shape before joining the Marines. He was a marine officer's ideal cadet while in basic training. After basic training Daniel was stationed with the 2nd Battalion, Third Marine Expeditionary Force in Kaneohe Bay, Hawaii.

Following his assignment, he was transferred to Al Anbar, Iraq where he was wounded and never recovered. Daniel died on Oct. 25, 2006 and is buried in the Chaires family cemetery located on property owned by his great-great grandfather, Benjamin Chaires of Tallahassee, Florida. He is remembered by all the residents in the Leon County community for his selfless act of courage.

Written and submitted by: Caroline Bowman and Todd Chaires, Brother of Daniel, 4801 Chaires Crossroads, Tallahassee, FL. 32317

Chandler - Still loving Tallahassee

When I was a child my mom, dad, and I rode a train from New York. to this area to visit my mom's family. Her parents D. W. and Reba Davis Shealey raised twelve children, my mom Elizabeth Chandler was their third child.

Florida was beautiful, everyone was nice, and the weather was great. My mother's family made us feel so welcome, I knew right then I wanted to be with my grandmother, aunts and uncles. My Grandmother was a true Proverbs 31 lady all the days of her life.

To my mom's and my delight, when I was ten years old my dad transferred from Bridgeport, Connecticut, to Tallahassee as the manager of the Federal Bakery at 310 S. Monroe St. It was a block from the Capital, across from the Court House, and Sears, and two doors down from the Black Cat News Stand. Bennett's Drug Store and two movie theaters, the State and the Floridian were within walking distance. They did their banking at Lewis State Bank, and we ate some late night meals at Nick's Restaurant. My dad drove our new 1950 black Dodge convertible in a parade that we watched from the top of the building.

I attended Caroline Brevard School on Calhoun Street. It was sold to the State in 1959. I also attended then First Baptist Church, which is stronger than ever.

My dad left for work before 4 a.m., six days a week. He did most of the baking and ran the back. My mom decorated the cakes, ran the front, made sure everything was clean, and ready for inspection at all times. They worked long after we closed and everyone had gone but us. At the end of each day the Salvation Army came to pick up baked goods; fresh one's were made daily. Only God and we know how many times my dad felt there wasn't enough, so he baked more or added other items. We never left until they came even if they were late. I liked that because then we would eat out.

Elizabeth and daughter, Reba Chandler in 1949 at the bakery

As an only child, I spent hours with them at the bakery, the older I get the more grateful I am to them for the life I've lived. Over the years they donated to all my school activities, and to many others places. I am sure the blessings our family has received over the years came from their abundance of good deeds.

After my dad died, my mom worked for TMH, FSU, and Publix. She purchased this house in 1962. Mission Road was not paved and was in the county. Now it has three lanes, and is lined with beautiful Crape Myrtle.

Our girls, Sherry and Jody, were born at TMH. Our son Danny was born in Monticello. My first husband and I moved here when Sherry was five, Jody was three, and Danny was 3 months old. It was March of 1965. They attended Belleview and Godby Schools. Jody has worked for Comcast for over 20 years. We had a painting and cleaning business from 1970- 1990. We worked with awesome builders that built some of the first houses in Killearn, Killearn Lakes, Golden Eagle, apartments all over, and many other houses in and around Tallahassee.

We have great neighbors that have been here for years, the main reason I chose not to move. We've seen many changes, mostly for the better. My mom lived to be over 90 years old. Both she and my first husband died in this house. I was their care giver, and honored to be with both of them when they went to be with the Lord. I'm grateful for the blessings of the family, and wonderful people who have been in our lives, Billy Hudson, The Lighthouse, and everyone associated with it, the Joy Sunday School Class from the First Baptist Church, neighbors, and many friends.

I have a new life now here with my wonderful husband; we hope to live here the rest of our lives. I still feel the same way about this area as I did that first time I stepped off that train almost 65 years ago.

Submitted by: Reba E. Williams, 2927 Rexwood Dr., Tallahassee, Fl 32304 Reba Williams@comcast.net

Dorothy Clifford: The Person
Born Dorothy Ring in Kingsport, TN, she is an Alumna of Agnes Scott College in Decatur, GA and the University of TN where she was an English major. Her newspaper career began in her hometown with the *Kingsport Times- News*, as women's editor and covering courts and police. Her next career stop was Savannah, GA, where she was a city and school reporter for the *Evening Press*. Later, she became women's editor for both the *Evening Press* and the Morning *News*. She married Gordon H. Clifford, Jr. in 1957 and they have three children: Wiley, Elizabeth and Mary Gordon.

She was hired at the *Democrat* in 1959 as assistant women's editor, and became women's editor in 1961. In 1962, she was awarded the prestigious Penney-Missouri Award for best women's section in the nation, in small-daily newspaper category. She received editorial awards from the Florida Press Association.

The Clifford children in 1969; Wiley Clifford (7 yrs.), Elizabeth (5 years), Mary Gordon (2 years) - (Richard Parks Collection)

Taken from Florida Photographic Collection

She left the *Democrat* in 1962 and returned 10 years later. Shortly afterwards she was named assistant city editor in charge of the women's section for the newly named "People" section on March 11, 1974.

"All I've ever done is journalism." she once said.

In 1982, along with being editor of the Home section, she wrote a weekly social column, "Capital Scene" and was fashion editor. In 1981, a special supplement on fall fashions won first place award from the Tallahassee Advertising Federation. She covered fall fashion collections of American designers in New York City.

Her community contributions included being President of the Junior League and Florida Press Club's VP. She's listed in *Who's Who Among American Women* and *Who's Who of Florida*.

Submitted by: Ginny High; Source: "Democrat's Home editor wins award" by John Habich; Tallahassee Democrat May 30, 1982, Written by: Mary J. Marchant 2901 Springfield Drive Tallahassee, FL 32309.- 3274

Coe – Stanley, Childhood Memories
I was never bored. Looking back, I had an idyllic childhood growing up in Tallahassee. When I started attending FSU, the students, especially the girls, were always complaining there was nothing to do in this town. I was astounded that they could ever think such a thing.

I was born December 27, 1930, on the site

Chief Pinkney (Pink) Coe and daughter

of Kleman Plaza, exactly on the grassy spot at 308 South Duval Street. My parents were Thomas Pinkney Coe and Maude Atkinson Coe. My brother Ridgway was eight and a half years old and my sister Lucile was four and a half. We rented a house from Mrs. Burns who was later my first grade teacher at the old Caroline Brevard Elementary School on Calhoun Street. The school building is still there and is even more beautiful now.

Mother was born in Leon County and my dad was born at Coe's Mill, which is now Hosford. Daddy moved to Tallahassee in 1883 at age two. My granddaddy Coe bought many acres of land and built a log house at the corner of what is now State Road 20 and Coe's Landing Road. His land stretched from Coe's Landing Road to the river where Lake Talquin Dam is now. He farmed and even had rice patties on part of the land.

Daddy started with the fire department in 1906 and was one of three firemen. They had one horse-drawn fire wagon with two white horses whose names were Tom and Jerry. They later had five horses, two fire wagons, and one equipment wagon. In 1912, Daddy became Fire Chief. He had no days off but could come home for lunch. The fire station was a block away on Adams Street across from the present City Hall. If the fire bell rang, he would run up the hill and be there when the fire truck pulled out. He was usually accompanied by our dog, Tige, who would jump on the truck's running board and ride to the fire.

My family was close then and we still are. We had so many good times. One summer we stayed in Dick Long's cottage on the water at Rock's Landing in Panacea. I remember three things: Daddy taught me to swim, Mother made delicious deviled crabs stuffed in their shells, and a crab bit Daddy's toe. We also rented a cottage at old Newport Springs. My aunts; Bessie Levy, Rosa Eubanks, Gasoline Reeves, Mattie Hatton, and their families also rented cottages. That was really fun to have all our cousins there. I always thought those springs were colder than Wakulla Springs!

Every Easter after church, our families would meet at the Turtle Pond on Springhill Road for lunch. The food was so delicious and Aunt Rosa's many-layered yellow cake with cooked chocolate icing was always a big hit. The cake would fall in the middle and the icing would run down the sides. After lunch we would have a glorious time hunting Easter eggs. We always had a lot of relatives there.

There were plenty of children in our neighborhood. The four Grimsley children lived next door, the Malloys around the corner on Pensacola Street, and the Yunis family around the other corner on Jefferson Street. My aunt Bessie Levy lived down the street.

The backs of the Grimsley's house and our house were built high off the ground. We set up a play office and school under the Grimsley's house. The Industrial Commission Building was one block down Duval Street and they discarded

Fay Left to right: Malcolm McCoy, Joel Coe, Chief Pinkney (Pink) Coe.

hundreds of IBM cards. We loved filing them, even though we didn't know how! One afternoon, we were going to a movie and walked past the alley behind Moon's Jewelry Company. It is now part of Gallie Alley. Mr. Moon had had a window display with a replica of a diamond. It was huge, about eighteen inches high and covered with silver glitter. To our absolute delight, he had thrown it in the trash. That also went under the house and fascinated us for a long time. We also found a big block of chocolate with nuts behind Christo's 5 & 10 Cents Store. The Grimsley kids took it home, broke it up and sold it to the neighborhood children. I suppose it was outdated, but it was so good!

Very few streets in town were paved. Duval Street wasn't paved until I was a little older. I used to watch the farmers and people from the country coming into town in their wagons every

Saturday. Nichols' Grocery Store was half a block up Jefferson Street and Gramling's Feed Store was on the corner of Adams and Jefferson. On the other side of the Martin Building (where Andrew's Restaurant is now) was Van Brunt and Yon Hardware Store. Everything was close to us and we were only two blocks from Monroe Street. The Martin Building, now City Hall, housed state offices and also the State of Florida Museum. Children were allowed to go many places alone in those days, and the museum was right inside the back door, probably only 180 feet from our home. When I was around eight years old, I'd go and see the mastodon from Wakulla Springs and other exhibits.

Almost every Saturday, Daddy took me to the double feature cowboy movies at the Ritz Theater. He especially liked Hopalong Cassidy. There was always a short such as Flash Gordon. Who knew someday we would actually fly in space and even land on the moon? We would stop by Christo's Dime Store before the movie and get ten cents worth of Hershey's chocolate candy. It came in a big block. The salesgirl would take a big, heavy butcher knife, put the point on the candy and cut it into small chunks. It tasted better than a Hershey bar!

These are just a few happy memories of growing up in my beloved Tallahassee. I will be here until I am buried in the family plot Daddy bought at Oakland Cemetery many years ago. I continue to watch the city grow, but wish I could see it as it was in the 1930s.

Submitted by Fay Coe Stanley 2086 Greenwood Drive Tallahassee, Florida 32303 Email: ellisstanley@aol.com

Coe – Stanley, More Memories of My Mother

I've lived the life of early Tallahassee through the recollections of my Mother, Fay Coe Stanley. Her story in this book ended when she was about nine years old. I'd like to continue her story.

Mother's Aunt Mattie ran a boarding house, the Tully House, next door to them. She was getting married again and talked my grandmother into taking it over. They lived there several years. My uncle Ridgway and Aunt Lucile were attending Leon High School and Mother was at the old Caroline Brevard School. They always had a lot of friends and relatives coming by. Ridgway was dating Dorothy (Dot) Griffin. Mother thought her sister Lucile, Dot, and Alice Summitt Englert were the three prettiest girls she knew. Years later, she would teach Alice's daughter and grandson in third grade at Kate Sullivan School. Mother was the only teacher there who had Miss Kate Sullivan for her sixth grade teacher at Caroline Brevard and then interned and taught at Kate Sullivan School. Uncle Ridgway had grown to be a handsome fellow who was co-captain of the football team at Leon. He was inducted into the Leon High Football Hall of Fame a few years ago.

Mother's family next moved to 306 North Adams Street where the Greyhound Bus Station now stands. The house, known as the Johnson House, looked very much like the old Governor's Mansion. It was beautiful inside, with a lovely oak staircase in two sections with a big landing in between. Most of the rooms had hand-carved mantles over the fireplaces. The grounds stretched from Adams to Duval Street and covered almost the whole block. Soldiers from Camp Gordon Johnson were always looking for rooms on the weekends. Grandmother put single beds in a huge, almost ball-room sized sun room. The previous owners had held dances there. They could put six to eight tables on each side. There was a huge fireplace in the middle. Grandmother charged $1.00 a night for a bed. She had to turn soldiers away. She also rented a room to the senior Mr. Culley of Culley's Funeral Home. He was a fine gentleman and a good friend. When Granddaddy told Mother the city was condemning the Johnson House to build a bus station, she was broken-hearted. Grandmother had to get rid of all those single beds!

Mother, Grandmother, and Granddaddy then moved to the Van Brunt House on the corner of Duval and St. Augustine Streets. It is now part of the new Capitol grounds. One morning Grandmother had been sitting at the sewing machine. She went to the kitchen and they heard a really loud noise - bap-bap-bap-bap-bap! When they examined the house, they found bullet holes exactly where Grandmother's head would have been! Several Army officers came and determined the bullets had been accidentally discharged from an Army fighter plane sitting on the runway at Dale Mabry Field. The bullets went through their house and into the Industrial Commission Building across the street. That was an exciting time!

Grandmother decided they would finally move into their own house at 921 South Duval Street. It was a Craftsman type house made out of heart of pine. Granddaddy had it built some years before. Granddaddy and Uncle Ridgway built a nice brick retaining wall on the south side which is still there. The State bought the property in the late 1960s. The property is undeveloped and still has a pear tree and pecan trees.

Granddaddy retired from the Fire Department in 1940 and then worked as City Fire Inspector. He died in 1948 when Mother was a senior in high school. In 1954, Grandmother married John B. (J. B.) Harvey, Jr., another fine man. J. B. always loved horses and dogs and I still remember the horse rides he gave me. Both he and Uncle Ridgway retired as Assistant City Fire Chiefs.

Mother and Daddy married in 1952. They lived in Fayetteville, N.C. for three months while Daddy was in training for the first Special Forces Unit at Fort Bragg. That was enough time away from Tallahassee for Mother! We've lived here since Daddy came back from Korea when I was five months old. We love it and will never leave!

Submitted by Susan Faye Stanley, 2086 Greenwood Drive, Tallahassee, Florida 32303 Email;ellisstanley@aol.com

The Collins Family: FSU Seminole Tribe

Dan Collins and Louise Wood attended Miami-Dade Junior College and upon graduation we moved to FSU to complete our degrees in 1975. We both lived in apartments on Pensacola Street, My roommates and I lived across the street from the famous\Jim and Milts BBQ place. Dan lived two blocks down toward the stadium at Pensacola apartments. Walking to football and baseball games was convenient and we listened to the concerts in the stadium from Dan's apartment which saved us money.

Dan and I didn't rush into any fraternity or sorority groups because of the costs. We both paid for our own college expenses. Dan was involved in ROTC and intramural sport, while I was in Angel Flight (sister organization to ROTC), the Flying High Circus, and Kappa Delta Gamma (a professional women's educator organization). Dan was commissioned as a Second Lieutenant in the United States Air Force with his private pilot license after graduation. He majored in business administration, while I majored in education, achieving the Dean's List my senior year.

Some memorable moments for Dan in ROTC: dropping flour bags from the Air Force ROTC contract Cessna training plane on the Army ROTC during their training. The flyboys hadn't learned about centrifugal force, leaving small dents in the Army jeeps. Oops!!! In another esprit de corps prank, the Air Force cadets filled the Army commander's office with all the army students' desks that could possibly fit intermingled with balloons filled with beer.

Our children, Danielle and Paul Collins, also attended FSU after completing junior colleges. To promote brother and sisterly love, Danielle's senior year and Paul's freshman year, they shared an apartment. Paul describes it as "The best experience he never wants to do again."

Danielle studied in the school of Human Resources majoring in Fashion Merchandizing, graduating December 2001. Making the Dean's List four times and she was awarded the Richs/Lazarus/Goldsmith: Academic and Professional Excellence Scholarship.

She had an internship in Atlanta at the headquarters of Rich's Lazarus and Goldsmith department stores. After graduation in December 2001, Danielle accepted a position as a Retail Sales Manager with Richs/Lazarus/Goldsmiths at their Flagship Store in Lenox Mall.

Paul completed his criminology degree in 2005 and did course work to prepare him for passing his C.P.A. interestingly, both children lived on Pensacola Street as Dan and I had. While Danielle lived at MonSel Apartments, I lived in the next apartment complex, Park Point Place. Paul lived on Edwards Street before the stadium, about two blocks from where Dan lived at Pensacola Apartments. In other words, we all lived with-in three-tenths of a mile in proximity.

After seventeen moves and twenty-one years in the military, Dan and Louise Collins retired in Tallahassee. Eventually Danielle moved back in 2008 and Paul works in the accounting department for FSU. I guess that now makes us an FSU Seminole tribe all living in the place where we attended the university.

Submitted by: Louise Wood Collins, 1808 Morning Star Lane, Tallahassee, FL 32312, jiclouise@gmail.com

Collins Surprise 25th Wedding Anniversary

My parents' 25th anniversary was a surprise, not only to my mom, but all the guests as well, because my dad, former fighter pilot and Southwest Airline pilot, planned the entire event.

Of course, his behind-the-scenes planning had a military flavor. My dad, Dan Collins, used the military cliché, "If you tell, I'll have to kill you", meaning not to slip and tell Mom. I asked if he'd hired a wedding planner to organize caterer, flowers, appetizers, the reception place, plus order a cake.

"No," he replied proudly, "I'm doing it all myself, unassisted!" "But Dad, how do you know what to do? You don't want this to be a tacky affair." He replied, "I purchased a wedding planner magazine. It informs you what to do month by month. It's just like a flight manual. No problem."

I watched in amazement as he designed the invitations on the computer, putting their wedding picture on the front. Inside the invitation were the typical details, but at the bottom of the invitation was another military warning, "This is top secret, don't tell Louise. I asked, "But how will we get the invitations addressed with Mom in the house?" Dad replied, "We'll go over to Bill and Lynn James' house (their friends from high school and college) and work. I've also arranged to take Mom over there early because the caterers need extra time at the house to prepare for the reception." Dad had me try on a dress he wanted her to wear to make sure it still fit Mom (we're the same size). He assigned Paul to wear his ROTC uniform as Best Man. As the Maid of Honor, I picked my dress while Dad wore the military uniform he wore for their wedding August 14, 1976.

Dad is such a detailed guy. He asked Mom's favorite choir member to sing *Through the Years* by Kenny Rogers and the song from their wedding, John Denver's song *Follow Me*. I laughed at the appropriateness of this song since Mom followed him, moving seventeen times in a twenty-nine year Air Force career.

Mom thought Dad was taking her to dinner. Instead, he entered the Bradfordville Baptist Church parking lot and stopped at the entrance.

Dan and Louise Collins with Paul and Danielle on Dan and Louise's 25th Wedding

The photographer, Uncle Warren, opened the door and took a picture as Mom's jaw dropped in surprise. "We're renewing our vows," Dad said. Mom laughed and cried through the whole ceremony, but she still didn't know about the reception at our house. A guest asked if she was in a hurry to get home to greet the guests. "What guests, what reception?" Mom inquired.

Paul and his friends shuttled the guests to the house in golf carts. The front and back porch were lined with little round tables for the guests. The best part was, the caterers served the food and cleaned up, so I was off the hook. Dad used Mom's Teacher of the Year gift from her school "One Night at the Governor's Inn" for their honeymoon getaway in Tallahassee. I hugged Dad and complimented him "Mission Accomplished"! I hope he'll be my wedding planner!

Written and Submitted by: Danielle Collins, 1808 Morning Star Lane, Tallahassee, FL. 32312

Governor LeRoy Collins

Tallahassee, at the time that LeRoy Collins was growing up, was very different from the present day Tallahassee. He was born over 100 years ago in March of 1909. Florida was still an agricultural state and had less population than any other state in the South.

Tallahassee had no hospital, and only two or three paved streets. The Capitol was fenced to keep cows off the grass. Malaria was prevalent, much like our flu today. Whites still fought "The Lost Cause," that of the Civil War in emotions if not in actuality. Blacks couldn't vote, and lynchings took place. All whites didn't condone racial violence, but few spoke out defending non-violence of race relationships.

When LeRoy Collins ran for Governor in 1954, he pledged to maintain segregation as "a part of Florida's custom and law." Two years later, he did not consider it one of the important issues. Important issues to him were honest, open and efficient government, fair apportionment of the Legislature, a junior college system, better roads, prison reform, and a modern constitution.

However, ten years after his election, when he served as the first director of the federal Community Relations-*Anniversary* Service, Collins declared that civil rights was to be "the most important moral issue of our time."

Governor LeRoy Collins

He spoke out against segregation on buses and at lunch counters, the first Deep South Governor to do so. In a March, 1960 statewide speech on television, he stated that while segregation of facilities was still legal, it was inconsistent with "moral, simple justice," and that white people shouldn't expect black people to "just stay in their place." He and his wife, Mary Call Collins, were ostracized in much of Tallahassee society at that point.

Collins was pictured with Martin Luther King, Jr. in Selma, AL where his mediation prevented a second bloody showdown between the civil rights marchers and state police.

He was defeated in his last political campaign for the US Senate in 1968, and adding to his anguish, lost Leon County in the election.

Even though many people disagreed with him at that point in time, his stand for "moral, simple justice" led to his being named by the Florida House of Representatives as "Floridian of the Century," at his death in 1991.

He demonstrated fundamental courage to change deeply held beliefs once his conscience, experience and faith persuaded him that he had been wrong, much to his own personal detriment, but for the good of the State of Florida and for the nation as a whole.

Submitted by: Mary J. Marchant, 2901 Springfield Drive, Tallahassee, FL 32309-3274; Source: Tallahassee Democrat, March 8, 2009 and "A courageous governor" by Martin Dyckman taken from his book, "Floridian of the Century: The Courage of LeRoy Collins."

The Convery and Guercia Branches Intertwine at FSU

Before meeting and marrying in Tallahassee, Florida, Kevin and Amy (Guercia) Convery's family stories both began in New York.

Kevin Convery was born in Kenmore, New York in 1963 and lived in Lewiston, a stone's throw from Niagara Falls, most of his young life. He and his younger brother Mike enjoyed the small town life along the Niagara River near Lake Ontario, as well as their occasional trips across the bridge to Canada. Kevin has family ties in Canada, since both his grandfathers, Leslie Elson Ross and Reginald Convery were born in Canada. Kevin's ancestors originally emigrated from Scotland and Ireland. His grandmothers, Annie Haley and Evelyn Golden, were born in Scotland and the United States respectively. Kevin's parents, George Convery and Janet Ross, raised their sons and niece Karolyn (Wendy) Clark in Lewiston until George's retirement from the New York State Police in 1977. During that summer, they moved the family south to Spring Miff, Florida.

The summer of 1977 saw Amy Guercia's family also leaving New York for Florida. The third of Charles and Eileen (Kelly) Guercia's five children, Amy was born in Staten Inland, New York in 1966. Amy's Italian and Irish ancestors both settled in New York City. Amy's maternal grandfather, Harry Peter Kelly, worked as a New York City policeman while married to Catherine Farrell and raising four children. Amy's father, Charles Guercia Jr., like his father before him, was in construction, and became a licensed plumber. Due to the ups and downs of the economy, as well as a growing dislike for the cold northern winters, Charles and Eileen decided to move their family from New Jersey to Florida, settling in Seminole, located across the bay from Tampa, in Pinellas County.

In 1981, after graduating from Springstead High School, Kevin left Spring Hill to attend Florida State University. Three years later, Amy graduated from Seminole High School and also went to Tallahassee to attend Florida State. So, after both moving to Florida in August of 1977, Kevin and Amy meet in Tallahassee in August of 1984. They continued to date for the next six years, while both earning their degrees. Kevin graduated with his bachelor's in Interdisciplinary Physics with Computer Science (1986) and Amy completed her bachelor's (1988) and Master's (1990) in Criminology. In May of 1990, Kevin and Amy married in Seminole, Florida at Blessed Sacrament Catholic Church. Upon returning to Tallahassee, Amy worked for the Florida Senate Committee on Reapportionment and later for Florida Department of Law Enforcement, while

Kevin continued in his position as a scientific programmer for FSL. They recently celebrated their 19th wedding anniversary. Presently, Kevin is working for the State of Florida's State Resource Center as a Program Administrator. They are also both kept busy by their three children; Nicholas, Katharine and Gabrielle and enjoying family life in Tallahassee 25 years after these New York natives' paths first crossed on a college campus in Florida.

Submitted by: Amy Convery, 2721 Parsons Rest, Tallahassee, FL 32309

"Miss Lillian" Cox

Lillian Todd Cox was born Feb. 22, 1907 in Quincy, Florida, the second daughter of Robert Todd and Jennie Ola Parramore Todd. She remembers riding the train with her sister Melba from Quincy to Tallahassee to visit the O. C. Parker family on College Avenue in the 1920s. The two girls wore dresses made by their mother, with matching hats and gloves. Miss Lillian also recalls traveling in a horsedrawn buggy to attend inaugural ceremonies of Florida governors in Tallahassee in the teens and twenties. She graduated from Gadsden County High School and attended Florida State College for Women.

On Nov. 4, 1925, Lillian Todd married Thomas Henry Cox, a carpenter and builder. They moved to a small house on three lots situated on the corner of Gunter and East Georgia streets in Tallahassee in 1939. Tom added rooms to the house over the years. He also expertly grafted hundreds of camellias in the large yard, planted azaleas, hydrangeas and other flowering shrubs and trees which Lillian tended to for the 70 years she lived there.

As she rides around Tallahassee today, Lillian Cox sees evidence of her late husband's construction skills throughout the older residential sections of the city and enjoys pointing out numerous houses that Tom Cox helped build. When Tom was no longer able to work because of his health, Lillian Cox began her career in retail and for over 30 years she sold women's clothing in downtown Tallahassee. She began as co-owner of Nelly's Shop on College Avenue for 10 years. Then in 1957 Miss Lillian owned and operated a dress shop called "Lillian's" on South Adams Street at the current location of the Governor's Club. In 1973, the local American Business Women's Association honored Lillian Cox as the "Woman of the Year."

Her personalized service made "Lillian's" a premier women's apparel store in Tallahassee until she retired and sold the store in 1976, just a few months after Tom, her husband of more than 50 years, died. Soon there were numerous gentleman callers from Florida to Texas to court "Miss Lillian" during her widowhood, and she turned down several offers of marriage. She "didn't want to marry anyone" Lillian declared, but she mentions that she does enjoy the company of generous male friends, some of whom gifted her with jewels and other presents.

*Dancing at the Denim **and** Diamond Ball.*

Since Miss Lillian turned a Centenarian, there are still suitors for her attention. Miss Lillian is recognized always by the silvery upswept hairdo that is her trademark coiffure, originally designed by her longtime hairdresser Richard Merryman. Because of their life long friendship, Richard was buried next to Lillian and Tom Cox's cemetery plot.

After surviving three bouts of cancer. Miss Lillian designed a loose style of the "A-line" dress, and had many of them made from different Hawaiian fabrics. She had her seamstress, Jean Southall, create openings with zippers and ribbon ties on these garments so she could easily step in and out of them without mussing her hairstyle. Today, this garment style allows her to maintain her independence when dressing herself. Mrs. Lillian has traveled extensively to numerous countries and uses a lot of the styles of foreign countries in her garment designs. Her traveling days, however, were over when she reached her 90s.

Miss Lillian is a member of the Daffodil Garden Club, the Camellia Society, the Old Town Neighborhood Association, the Pilot Club and several other organizations. She was a charter member of the White Shrine and the America Business Women's Association and a Life Member of the Tallahassee Women's Club. She enjoys attending the First Baptist Church's home decorating, gardening, and flower arrangement projects. Her active lifestyle allows her to visit with family and friends, and she frequently is invited by friends to attend dinner at church, especially the Woodville Baptist Church and their annual fish-fry honoring Emergency Medical Service workers.

In February of 2007; more than 350 friends and relatives celebrated Lillian Cox's 100th birthday at the Women's Club in Tallahassee. The centenarian wore a striking aqua dress that she designed more than 30 years ago in her dress shop. Her daughter and son-in-law, Carolyn and Richard Partch, came from Texas to host the gala event, along with Lillian's grandchildren and great-grandchildren. After traveling from Houston for the celebration, Carolyn Partch-Cox, Lillian and Tom's only child, remained in Tallahassee because of her poor health. She needed 24-hour daily care, which was provided by her mother over the next year at her home on Gunter Street. Lillian's daughter Carolyn Cox Partch died in Tallahassee Memorial Hospital on March 7, 2008, at the age of 80, and her mother never quite recovered from the loss of her only child. Carolyn's ashes were buried between the grave of her father Tom, and the future resting place of Lillian Cox in Roselawn Cemetery.

Mrs. Lillian Cox on 100th Birthday

In November 2008, Lillian Cox was chosen as the "Honorary Survivor" for the American Cancer Society's local fundraising event, Cattle Baron's Denim & Diamond Ball. After reminding the audience that she was a three-time cancer survivor, Mrs. Cox joined the dancers on the dance floor, wearing her rhinestone-studded denim outfit.

In September 2007, television producers flew Mrs. Cox to New York City, where Barbara Walter interviewed her for Ms. Walters' April 2008 television special, *Live to be 150*. In addition, the syndicated TV show Inside Edition featured Miss. Cox as one of the oldest drivers in the country and showed scenes of her driving her 1984 white Cadillac around Tallahassee. Local radio and television stations and other broadcast reporters across the country interviewed her by telephone in hopes of discovering the secret to her longevity. Lillian's advice to others is always; "keep active and drink plenty of water." She takes special pride in the fact that she only drinks water straight out of the tap with no ice first thing in the morning and with her meals. Miss Lillian finally gave up driving because of failing eyesight when she reached her 102nd birthday in 2009, and she also put her home on the market and moved into the Cherry Laurel Retirement Residence, where she became acquainted with many new friends and eased the minds of her greatgrandchildren about her safety. Miss Lillian remains active in her disposition and hopeful on her outlook on future opportunities in life.

Submitted by: Lillian Cox; Written by: Annette Hannon-Lee, 2450 Laurelwood Couit, Tallahassee, FL 32308

Governor Charlie Crist

Since his inauguration as Florida's 44th Governor on January 2, 2007, Charlie Crist has worked to lower the cost of doing business and living in Florida, increase people's access to government, strengthen Florida's economy and ensure the safety and worldclass education of Florida's children. Upon taking his oath as Governor, Governor Crist immediately established the Office of Open Government by Executive Order, in order to make government more accessible to the people it serves. Governor Crist also continues to address high property taxes and property insurance costs and works with both Democrats and Republicans.

Governor Charlie Crist was born in 1956 in Altoona, Pennsylvania, but his family soon settled in St. Petersburg. As a public school student, Governor Crist quickly learned the value of

Governor Charlie Crist

participation, leading him to serve as class president at St. Petersburg High School and, later, as student body vice-president at Florida State University. In high school, Governor Crist was the starting quarterback for his football team. He later played football at Wake Forest University before transferring and receiving his undergraduate degree from Florida State in 1978. Governor Crist then earned his law degree from the Cumberland School of Law in Birmingham, Alabama.

Governor Crist received invaluable experience in Florida's criminal justice system while interning in the State Attorney's Office before accepting a position as general counsel for the minor league division of the Baseball Commissioner's Office. Governor Crist began his government service as state director for former U.S. Senator Connie Mack before later returning to the private practice of law with the Tampa firm of Wood and Crist.

In 1992, Governor Crist won a seat in the Florida Senate. For six years, Governor Crist served as Chairman of the Senate Ethics and Elections Committee and as Chairman of the Appropriations Criminal Justice Subcommittee. A strong voice for public safety, he sponsored, among other legislation, the Stop Turning Out Prisoners (STOP) bill requiring prisoners to serve at least 85 percent of their prison sentences. This earned him numerous honors, including appointment as an Honorary Sheriff by the Florida Sheriffs Association - only the third person to receive the honor in the organization's long history.

After Governor Crist completed his Senate service, Governor Jeb Bush appointed him as Deputy Secretary of the Florida Department of Business and Professional Regulation. In 2000, Governor Crist won a special election and became Florida's last elected Commissioner of Education. Governor Crist's path of public service next led him to seek election as Attorney General in 2002. He carried the general election by more than one-third of a million votes to become Florida's first elected Republican Attorney General. On November 7, 2006, Charlie Crist was elected to serve as Florida's Governor. Governor Crist is a lifelong member of the St. Petersburg Chapter of the NAACP. Governor Crist and his wife Carole have been married since December 12, 2008. They were married in his hometown of St. Petersburg, Florida.

Written and submitted by: Governor Charlie Crist

Edward and Juanita Cruce

Edward "Ed" Mirel Cruce settled in Tallahassee in 1953 with his wife, Juanita, upon the end of his Navy commission. Ed, the oldest son of Marion and Lorena Cruce, was born in Miami on September 20, 1928. He grew up in Perry and lived there until he left home in 1945 at age 17 to join the U.S. Navy.

Ed and Juanita (Baxley) met while he was on leave in Tallahassee visiting his parents. They met through a childhood neighbor of Juanita's, a shipmate of Ed's. Their first date was at Jim and Milts at Seventh Avenue and Meridian Road. After a year of dating and letter writing, they married in Dothan, Alabama on August 22, 1952. Upon the end of Ed's commission in 1953, they rented their first home on Jefferson Street, moved to Bronough Street in 1954, and later to North Boulevard. In 1957, they built their first house on West Tharpe Street where they raised their two children. Their daughter, Paula Renee, was born on May 31, 1955 and son, Edwin Michael, on September 7, 1959. In 1974, they built and moved into their second house on Reece Park Lane, where Juanita currently resides.

After the Navy, Ed started a business, Cruce Floor Sanding, with his father. He owned and operated the business until he developed health problems in 1966, requiring a lengthy hospital stay. After recuperating, Ed managed and owned several local businesses including Varsity Texaco on W. Tennessee Street, Parkway Shell, and Thomasville Road Shell. He sold the businesses and retired in 1981 at age 52. In 1982, he purchased a coin laundry business with several locations including W. Tennessee Street, Pensacola Street, and Lake Bradford Road. Ed had many talents including being a beekeeper, pilot, carpenter, and mechanic. Ed suffered a debilitating stroke in 1991 and died June 24, 2001 at

Michael, Juanita, Ed Cruce and Renee Starrett, January 1999

age 72. He is buried at Memory Gardens along with his youngest brother, Leon.

Juanita, the eldest daughter of William and Nena Baxley, was born on December 5, 1928 and grew up on a farm in Geneva County, Alabama. Juanita graduated from Holmes County High School, Bonifay, Florida in 1947 and moved to Tallahassee in 1949. Her first job in Tallahassee was at S. E. Telephone Company at Calhoun Street and Park Avenue. Except for a short separation after her marriage, she worked there until the birth of her first child in 1955. After that, she worked at Florida State University from 1957 until the birth of her second child 1959, and later from 1987-1991. In 1960, she began her long career at Sears and Roebuck Company working various full-time and part-time positions until 2003, except for several separations to help her husband in his business and attend Lively VoTech. Juanita has been a member at First Baptist Church of Tallahassee since 1949, where she is very active and sings in the First Joy Choir. She was also a member at Lakeview Baptist Church on Seventh Avenue from 1956-1974.

Submitted by: Juanita Cruce, Tallahassee, FL 32301

Marion and Lorena Cruce

Marion Hiram Cruce and Mattie Lorena Woodard were very simple folks who originally came from Perry, Florida, but spent their later years in Tallahassee beginning when they moved here in 1949. They married on October 21, 1926 and had nine children: Vertie Marie, Edward Mirel, Evelyn Pauline, Samuel Bridges, Sarah Beatrice, Frances Lorena, Franklin Marion, Lloyd Marion, and Clayton Leon. Three of their sons died tragic and unexpected deaths. The second son, Samuel, died as an infant; the youngest son, Leon, died at the age of 20 on June 21, 1965 because of injuries received while serving in the Marine Corps in Vietnam; and the third son, Franklin, died of a suicide in 1973. Ed, the oldest son, died at the age of 72 after a long illness from the effects of a stroke. Of the living children, Lloyd and Frances are the only two who remain in Tallahassee.

Marion held many jobs in Tallahassee throughout the course of his life, including floor finishing for Bishop Floor Finishing and Henderson Floor Finishing, and night watchman for Elberta Crate Mill. He did floor finishing work for his son Ed's business where he provided knife

Lorena and Marion surrounded by their children in the 1970s

and saw sharpening services, which started out as a hobby for Ed.

Lorena was a homemaker while her children were young, but took in sewing to help with household expenses. Once her children were grown, she spent time working at a local day care center. She also kept many of her grandchildren, who called her Big Mama. This name was given to her by her daughter-in-law, Juanita. It seems that her baby girl, Renee, started called Lorena mama. To distinguish between the two, Juanita told Renee that Lorena wasn't Mama, she was Big Mama, and the name stuck. Lorena never appreciated the name, especially when her grandchildren screamed it in public places.

The Cruce's were very spiritual folks who loved to attend church. However, while they were able, they continued to drive to their hometown of Perry to attend. Their passion was gardening. Marion loved to piddle in his vegetable garden and Lorena loved her flowers, especially her roses and potted double impatiens. Lorena was proud to make beautiful arrangements of her roses for her youngest son's grave at Memory Gardens,

Marion died on June 14, 1985 at the age of 85 and almost 19 years later, Lorena died at the age of 95 on February 18, 2004. Both died in Tallahassee, Florida, but they were buried in their hometown of Perry, Florida. They left behind many grandchildren and great grandchildren with happy memories of them.

Written by: Juanita Cruce, Tallahassee, FL; Submitted by: Renee Cruce-Starrett, 2029 Ermine Drive, Tallahassee, FL 32308

Vi (Violet) and Dan Cupp

Violet and Dan Cupp came to Tallahassee from Ft. Lauderdale in 2001. They had become disenchanted with congested South Florida and wanted a more peaceful environment. Since they had family in this area, and are avid Seminole fans, they decided to move to Tallahassee. Vi's nephew, Charlie Hill and his wife, Linda, live next door.

Vi was born and raised in Marianna, FL. Her parents were Felix and Maggie Goodwin Ingram. She graduated from Marianna High School and after graduation, she moved to Ft. Lauderdale.

Dan's parents, Daniel and Molly Gordy Cupp, were a ministerial family with the Church of God, so Dan moved around quite a bit as a youngster. His father was from W VA and VA and his mother from GA. Dan has two siblings: a sister, Justine Cupp and a brother, Edmond Cupp. Neither married. Dan graduated from Lake Placid High School in 1951 and attended Lee University in Cleveland, TN, a church affiliated school.

Dan and Vi Cupp

Dan worked for his uncle before entering the Army in 1953. The 25th Infantry Division took him to Korea for a year, and then to Honolulu, Hawaii and Japan. In 1955, he returned from the service to work for Florida Power and Light in Ft. Lauderdale and met the love of his life in church.

Vi and Dan were married and settled in Ft. Lauderdale. They have two girls: Vicki, born in 1959 and Dana, born in 1963. Dana lives in Atlanta and has two children: a boy, Daniel Cowan and a girl, Kelci Cowan. Vicki lives in Tallahassee and graduated from and works for FSU in Athletic Academic Support as Office Manager.

Dan retired in 1993 and Vi retired in 1997. Vi worked for Sun Trust Bank for 37 years and retired as a VP/Manager. She continued her education and training through The American Institute of Banking, Broward Community College and the University of South Florida.

Vi works part time with the Tallahassee Area Convention and Visitor's Bureau as a Customer Service Representative. Dan volunteers in community activities. His hobby is working in the yard. His yard is much like gardens seen in *Southern Living Magazine*.

Written by: Mary J. Merchant, 2901 Springfield Drive, Tallahassee, FL 32309-3274;
Submitted with permission from: Vi and Dan Cupp, 2904 Springfield Drive Tallahassee, FL 32309

The DeMillys

The DeMillys, a pioneer family of the Tallahassee area, were not unusual people, but they were good citizens; they were good people. They happened to come to this part of the country during some very interesting historical times. Their lives touched directly, or indirectly, on international, national, territory, state, and county and city matters in this area. My sources are by word of mouth, by the research done by a DeMilly grandchild, Mary Lamar Davis, by the memoirs of Mrs. John Louis DeMilly, and by a personal visit I had to Count Jacques de Milly in France.

It all started back in about 1767. John Charles DeMilly was born in Paris. He was a soldier of one of Napoleon's outfits and later came to the West Indies, to San Domingo. Another family there who later came to Tallahassee was the Cay family. They probably knew each other, maybe in France, but probably in San Domingo. In 1793 there was a revolution in San Domingo and both families left; the Cays eventually settled in the Savannah area; the DeMilly family went to one of the Carolinas. John Charles DeMilly, unsatisfied with the education possibilities in Carolina, took his two sons, John Louis and Charles Leonard, back to France. After a few years, they all returned to North Carolina and then to Tallahassee. John Louis' home was on the northwest corner of Adams and College, and his brother chose some lots on North Gadsden Street. The census of 1828 lists the DeMillys as Tallahassee residents.

Charles Leonard, who later called himself Leonard Charles, was a tax collector. His son, Walter A. DeMilly, my grandfather, also became a tax collector, as did my father, Charles Leonard DeMilly. While in office, Walter DeMilly started an insurance business known as W. A. DeMilly Insurance Agency. When my dad became of age, it became W. A. DeMilly and Son. Later, in the 1930's, it became DeMilly and Yaeger when

Henry Yaeger became a partner. Still later, the firm merged with Mr. Landrum.

My grandfather, Walter DeMilly, married Martha Branch Taylor, the daughter of Sarah Bradford and Junious Littlepage Taylor. She was the granddaughter of Dr. Edward Bradford and his wife, Martha Branch, the daughter of Governor John Branch, the last territorial governor of Florida. He had also served as governor of North Carolina, U. S. Senator from North Carolina and the Secretary of the Navy of the United States in Andrew Jackson's cabinet. Martha and Walter DeMilly had three children, Martha Branch, Margaret, and Charles Leonard. When his wife Martha died, Walter married Lila Cay, whose family had moved to Tallahassee from Savannah. Their children were Georgia who married Lauren Merriam and lived in Panama City, FL, and Augusta, married to Morton Turnley. After Lila died, Walter married her sister, Winnie. They had one daughter, Winifred, who was married to Frederick Clifton Moor.

My mother, Ethel Waite, was the granddaughter of a Presbyterian minister who came to Georgia near Savannah and married into an old Georgia family. Her mother was a Winn. Her great aunt, Georgia Winn, married John David Cay and lived in Tallahassee. This is the same family whose earlier members had been in France and San Domingo, as were the DeMillys. On a visit with the Cays, my mother met my father. Their three children were Walter Augustine, Elizabeth and Preston Waite. Walter married Sanna Jane Taylor. They lived in Tallahassee and were the parents of Sanna Kay and Walter A. DeMilly, III. Elizabeth married John Patrick McIntee and they were the parents of four children; Ann, John Charles, Ellen and Becky. Their home was in Louisville, KY. I have never married and am the last male with the name DeMilly now living in Tallahassee.

Now, getting back to the other side of the DeMilly family— John Louis, my great grandfather's brother. He later had a house on East Jefferson Street, right next to what is now the campus of FSU. He married a lady named Marie Louise Morris, who for some reason was also called Eliza. Eliza has a very fascinating history, the subject of another story. Her parents brought their seven children to Tallahassee, but died soon after, leaving the children to be cared for by other families. John Louis and Marie Louise DeMilly were the parents of fifteen children, seven of whom lived to adulthood. John was the first treasurer of the city of Tallahassee and held that office for fifty-two years. His wife apparently did much work besides having children; she helped run hotels. There were at least two different hotels that they ran and boarding houses, too. They ran the old Dixie Hotel across the street from the Capitol. Of all those DeMillys, there are some descendents here in Tallahassee, but no male DeMilly.

These people, really, not any one of them—including my own self, my own brother, my own father, grandfather, great grandfather—no one of us was really a stellar person or person of any real significance. We didn't do anything, but we prospered, we persevered, we made it, we made a place. I am proud of those early DeMillys who had the courage to come to a brand new territory and settle in the little community that became Tallahassee. It was a rough, tough little town. They settled and they made a way. And for that reason I am proud of them and have to write about them.

Submitted by: Preston Waite DeMilly (note: deceased, 2/15/2011)

Miss Ruby Diamond

From Beyond the Grave:
A Word by Miss Ruby Diamond.
September 1, 1886 - March 8, 1982
Interlocutor - Rabbi Stanley J. Garfein
Tallahassee, Florida Fall 2009.

Well, I see they couldn't build the new Aloft Hotel without mentioning that I used to live in the old Floridan Hotel, which was on the site of the present Aloft. Yes, I suppose I was considered the phantom of the Floridan. After our parents died, my brother, Sydney, and I sold the Diamond family home. We moved into separate domiciles. I chose to live in the Floridan, because it offered a modicum of security, which in those days was important to a woman living alone. I rented some of its tiny rooms for entertaining, dining, basics of living, and storage of the furniture, furnishings, and other memorabilia that I, in my nostalgia, did not want to leave behind. The city had to condemn the Floridan to push me out and make me seek other arrangements. I ended up living at the hotel at Adams and Park, which has had a number of names.

At the Floridan, several of my windows looked out at historic St. John's Episcopal Church. Bell ringers were wont to hold their practice on Saturday afternoons, but the loud ringing interrupted my nap. Instead of suffering in silence, I phoned the rector, The Rev. Lee Graham, to ask if bell practice could be held at a different time. Mr. Graham graciously acquiesced in my request. Years later, I gave Rabbi Stanley Garfein a beautifully illustrated pulpit-sized King James version of the Old and New Testaments. It had never been used; I could not even lift it. Rabbi Garfein, in appreciation of St. John's neighborliness, gave this museum quality Bible to the church.

Miss Ruby May Diamond at age 25

My mother and father were of the same family. They were first cousins once removed. We used to chuckle about that, because such a close relationship is said to make the offspring "cuckoo." Before arriving at the American shores, the family had lived in Wreschen, a town in Prussian-occupied Poland. They spoke German, as testified by correspondence that I placed in the Strozier Library in my family files. I wrote a note there stating that the correspondence was of no consequence. This was certain to arouse the curiosity of future historians. Perhaps the most famous person to have come from Wreschen was Ludwig Lewandowski, who had moved to Berlin and composed liturgical music for organ and choir for Reform Jewish worship around the world.

Evidently, the Diamond family was in the coal business in Wreschen, and they continued in that business after moving to Pittsburgh, before some of them sank roots in Tallahassee. My maternal grandfather, whose name was anglicized to "Robert Williams" (original surname Wolf), was a "forty-niner." He left Central Europe around the time of the failure of the liberal revolutions in 1849 and participated as a merchant in the California Gold Rush. He married Helena Dzialinski, ("z" unpronounced), whose family became active in the early development of Jacksonville. From what I understand, the Williams' spent the years of the War Between the States in Savannah. After Sherman's March to the Sea, Yankee officers were billeted in the Williams' home. As the story goes, one evening some drunken Yankee soldiers staggered into the house and headed for the kitchen, looking for something to eat.

There was a freshly baked goose in the oven. The Williams' domineering cook defended her turf, saying, "Y'all can have all the goose you want, but don't you dare touch Miz Williams' schmaltz!" (Schmaltz is the fat rendered from a goose, chicken, or any other fowl. It was used for cooking or flavoring certain food, such as chopped liver. It is usually eschewed by the modern dieter.) Robert and Helena Williams had five daughters: Rachelle, Eumena, Sippi (nickname for Zipporah), Henrietta, and Ida. Legend has it that Rachelle was born in a little cart pulled by a horse, with a pet deer walking alongside, as the family was moving south. She was thought to be the first Jewish girl born in Florida, until it was later discovered that another Jewish girl was born before her in Pensacola. Having settled in Tallahassee, my grandfather, Robert Williams, purchased a retail store from the Goodman and Wertheimer families, who then moved to New York City. I was betrothed to the Goodman son, (or grandson?) but he was killed during World War I.

Our family was known and respected for its civic mindedness. Grandfather inaugurated street lighting by having lanterns placed on top of wooden poles. He and my father served many terms on the city and/or county commission; my uncle, Jacob Raphael Cohen, was a leader of the Masonic Lodge and also the city commission. He also arranged for the first Jewish burial ground in the old city municipal cemetery. My parents were Henrietta Williams and Julius Diamond. On March 19, 1879, they were married in Tallahassee by Reform Rabbi, Isaac Pereira Mendes, who was brought in from Savannah. My full name was Ruby May Diamond, as is proven by my childhood autograph book, which is somewhere in the Temple Israel, Tallahassee archives.

My name was not Ruby Pearl, a moniker which was someone's idea of a joke based on the character who was featured on Grand Ole Opry. We were frequently made fun of because we had money and because we didn't throw it around or flaunt it wastefully. Some thought us "cheap" because we did not entertain lavishly or spend unnecessarily on ourselves. I especially was out to teach a lesson that even pocket change could add up, if one didn't throw it away on silly things. I did spend money on what was thought to have intrinsic value, like my jade (onyx?) snuffbox collection, which I intended eventually to give to my alma mater, (which is now) Florida State University. That offer, however, when it was extended, was not accepted by FSU.

After Brother died, I had no one to lean on emotionally, nor give me financial advice. My driver and agent, Smiley Bruce, helped me collect payments on rental property, which included Monroe Street stores. Rents enabled me to pay my bills and maintain myself in my latter years. By the way, the play, *Driving Miss Daisy*, was not based on the relationship between Smiley and me, as some have claimed. It was rather just an example of a widespread phenomenon at a time when women were considered too weak to go out and perform certain tasks. I would like to have become a lawyer like my brother, but when I was young, women could not enter such a profession.   My family took great pride in our Jewish heritage. However, my brother and I were among the very few Jewish children to grow up in Tallahassee. We did not have a Sunday school; whatever we learned about Judaism came from our family. Brother and I became founders of Temple Israel in 1937. Many of the ritual artifacts at Temple Israel came from my family. To name several of them: 1) The original Torah scroll, which is the tallest in the Ark; 2) The pair of tall, silver candlesticks on the bema (dais)—candlesticks that are used for the lighting of candles to welcome the Sabbath; 3) The silver filigree spice box for inhaling the sweetness of the Sabbath as it departs on Saturday night; 4) The Mizrach, used for determining the direction of prayer - the Mizrach is covered by antique blown glass and placed in a magnificent mahogany and gold frame.

I donated land appraised at $100,000.00 to FSU. It is where the Fine Arts building's parking garage is now located. When the newspaper publicly announced my donation, it listed every civic organization in which I had been involved, except for Temple Israel. I was appalled at this oversight or slight. I wanted the general community to know that I had given that land as a proud Jew, not as a closet Jew. I contacted the publicity office at FSU, and the next day the announcement was reprinted with Temple Israel included in the list of my affiliations. In return for my gift of real estate, the auditorium in the Westcott Building was named after me. I sought to extend myself to others without limiting friendship to those who bore a particular label. However, I was cautious of those whom I suspected of feigning friendship, because they wanted something from me. When I sensed that I was dying, I hosted a series of dinners for my true friends.

I died when I was almost 96, being the oldest native Tallahassee Jew ever to reach such an age. I had arranged for my estate to purchase the cheapest casket for my burial. Why? Because I wanted my money to stay above ground. In Tallahassee and Leon County I wasn't the wealthiest person, nor had I given the most to charity. But I did contribute a goodly amount for the well-being of others, while stinting on myself. I have been a better "pay-er" than "pray-er." I have no regrets. I had a good life. My will, which was patterned after Cousin Morton Robert Hirschberg's will, favors primarily Jewish causes, both here and abroad, especially Temple Israel of Tallahassee.

Rabbi Garfein officiated at my funeral, which was held in the sanctuary of Temple Israel. Tallahassee. After the funeral, I was taken in my casket in the Culley's hearse for burial in the family plot in the temple cemetery in Jacksonville.

Miss Diamond's Synagogue, Temple Israel on Mahan Drive. (l-r) David Hirsch, President; Albert Beryl Block; Rabbi Stanley J. Garfein; U. S. Senator Richard "Dick" Stone placing cornerstone, Oct. 1972

That family plot is a story in itself, because every time my grandmother, Helena Dzialinski Williams, moved from Jacksonville to Tallahassee, or vice-versa, she would disinter my grandfather, Robert Williams' remains. Finally, Grandmother's last residence was in Jacksonville, so that is where the family burial plot ended up. In the hearse Rabbi Garfein sat in the front seat on the passenger's side, with Joe Culley in the driver's seat. I was in the back of the hearse in my casket. My caretakers, SmileyBruce and his wife Minnie Whitaker were to follow in my powder blue Cadillac, which I'd willed to Smiley. Before departing Tallahassee, Walter Culley, Sr., who was but a few years younger than I, walked over to where Rabbi Garfein was seated and whispered in his ear. "Rabbi, watch out for my son, Joe Culley, while he's driving, he's had several heart attacks." Fortunately, both the trip over to Jacksonville and the trip back were without incident.

Written and submitted by Rabbi Stanley J. Garfein, 1110 Lasswade Drive, Tallahassee, FL 32312

Llewellyn Donalson and Louise Clark Fain

John Louis DeMilly settled in Tallahassee soon after it became Florida's capital. He married Mary Louise Morris and had a long career in public service. Their daughter, Ellen Hawkins DeMilly married Asa Bushnell Clark, an agent for the Seaboard Railroad. Louise Stayner Clark, their third child, was born on September 5, 1893 at the home of her maternal grandmother, Mary Morris at 423 West College Avenue.

When Louise was less than two years old her father died, and when she was five her grandmother died, so she was raised by her mother and her mother's brother, John DeMilly, who lived with them. Louise's mother supported the family by taking in boarders, and her Uncle John furnished the groceries from his grocery store in town.

The original house on College Avenue was a large antebellum home which burned in 1891, but was rebuilt and enlarged after the fire. On the eastern half of the block where Louise's mother lived was the home of Louise's Uncle Harry and Aunt Kate DeMilly with their children, Kathleen and Harry Jr. Between the two houses was a vacant lot with a barn where Uncle John kept his grocery wagon and horse. On the other side of the house was the large kitchen of the original building, which had been renovated into a home

Llewellyn Donalson and Louise (Clark) Fain-1970s

for Louise's Uncle George and Aunt Lena Davis with their children, Mary, Nelle, George MacKay, and Elsie.

Surrounded as she was by aunts, uncles and cousins, Louise did not suffer from the fact that her two brothers were five and ten years older than she was. At Christmas time the family would drape Simlax vines around the house, and on Christmas Eve all the cousins would hang their stockings by the fireplace at the big house. Christmas morning they arrived at daylight saying "Christmas Gift! Christmas Gift!" and the whole family would have Christmas together.

Louise's family attended Trinity Methodist Church. She attended the children's Sunday school called the Sunbeams. In the *Tallahassee Democrat* newspaper, Louise reminisced about the Methodist Sunday School picnics: "As soon as school was out, the church would charter a whole GF&A train to carry, not only the Methodists, but all the people in town who wanted to go spend one glorious day of swimming, sunning, and picnicking at Lanark on the Gulf. Louise's Uncle, Harry DeMilly, was the County Superintendent of Schools and the principal of Leon Academy, which Louise attended. The Academy was a two story building with separate classes for each grade. One of the teachers she especially remembered was Miss Kate Sullivan. Louise played basketball in high school and took piano. However, she didn't graduate, but went to Florida State College for Women after her eleventh grade. At that time, the college had a sub-freshman class which she entered in 1909.

Following her year as a sub-freshman, Louise went on into college. At Florida State she joined Kappa Delta sorority and majored in languages. She graduated from Florida State

College for Women in 1914. After graduation, Louise accepted a teaching position at Osceola High School in Kissimmee, Florida where she taught Latin, Spanish, and Botany for three years.

In the summer of 1915, Louise and Llewellyn Fain met. He had come to Tallahassee in 1912 to work at Holmes Drug Company after working for a short time in Cairo and Pelham, Georgia. Llewllyn Donaldson Fain was born in a shanty on a dirt road in Faceville, Georgia on August 10, 1888. He was the second child of James Love Fain and Llewellyn Donalson Fain. He was namesaked from his mother. When L. D. was still a child, his family moved to Fowlstown where they bought a house owned by his maternal grandparents, the Donalsons. He rode a mule to school and back, and the family attended the Presbyterian Church.

L. D. didn't learn much about farming, but remembered driving a wagon load of potatoes to market in Bainbridge and Quincy. After the crops were in, Mr. and Mrs. Fain would take the younger children by buggy and the men and boys by covered wagon to Lake Jackson near Tallahassee. When L. D. entered his teens, his father sent him to school in Climax, Georgia because there were good teachers there. His father then sent him to the University of Georgia for a two-year pharmacy course. He graduated on June 15, 1910 and was licensed by the State of Georgia as a pharmacist.

In 1917, L. D. enlisted in the Army and was stationed in Macon, Georgia with a medical division. On the 21st of December he telephoned Louise and asked her to marry him. L.D. Fain and Louise Clark were married on December 24, 1917 at the home of her mother. On Christmas afternoon, the newlyweds took the train to Macon. Louise came home by New Years to teach school, and then went back to Macon to spend the summer. Just after the Armistice was signed, L. D. sailed to France where he worked in the Medical Corps until May 1919, and their first child was born while he was overseas.

In October of 1919, he and his brother, John Love Fain bought Hicks Drug Store in Tallahassee and established Fain Drug Company on Monroe Street until 1962. In 1922 L. D. was appointed with five other Florida pharmacists to a committee to establish a School of Pharmacy at the University of Florida. He was a member and one-time state convention chairman of the Leon County Pharmacy Association.

L. D. and Louise Fain had seven children: Nelle DeMilly, Llewellyn Donalson, Jr., James Love, Martha Louise, Asa Clark, Bill Gray, and John Donalson. The family attended Trinity Methodist Church. Both were active in civic affairs. L. D. was a charter member of the Tallahassee Kiwanis Club, the American Legion Post #13, the Elks and Masons. He also served as President of the Tallahassee Chamber of Commerce and the board of directors for Tallahassee Federal Savings and Loan. Louise was active in P.T.A., Boy and Girl Scouts, Garden Club and the Women's Club. She was also a charter member of the Tallahassee Hospital Auxilary, president of the Florida Pharmaceutical Auxiliary, and active in several genealogical societies.

When L. D. Fain died in 1984, and Louise Clark Fain in 1990, they left behind a legacy of leadership and service to Tallahassee that began with her ancestors who pioneered the development of the fledgling community of Tallahassee.

Submitted and written by: Martha (Fain) Brooks, 4417 St. Teresa Avenue, Sopchoppy, FL 32358

The Legacy of Samuel Lewis Douglas
Samuel Lewis Douglas was born March 31, 1908 in Lake Jackson Leon County, Florida to Mr. Riley (1869-1933) and Essie Douglas (1869-1946) who was also born and raised in Lake Jackson, Leon County, Florida. Samuel (Deke) was the tenth of thirteen children. He excelled in his studies and became very interested in building things at an early age.

Deke's father, Riley Douglas was the only son of Frederick (1843-1902) and Lucinda Douglas (1855-1885). He did not want his children to grow up alone and enjoyed having a house filled with laughter. But with such a large number of children in his family, Riley knew it would be difficult to educate them all. He finally thought of a good way to make it work. Since the price was $2.00 per month per child to send his children to school in Leon County, Riley Douglas started sending his children to clean up the local churches in the area after they finished their work at home on the farm.

In return for the children's labor in and around the church buildings, they were taught to read, write and learn some arithmetic by the deacons and sisters of these churches. It is believed that this is where Deke found his calling

Deke at his 100th Birthday Celebration

in the construction trade because he recalls how much he enjoyed reading about building things when he was a boy.

Deke finished his education at the area schools and went on to be educated at the Leon County High School in Tallahassee. After graduating from high school in 1928, Deke took college courses at Florida A & M University while working full-time and living with one of his sisters in the town of Tallahassee. This was due to the fact that the walk home was so far from school he would not been able to study and do all he needed to do with his 10 mile walk everyday. He graduated from Florida Agriculture and Mechanical University in 1934 with a Bachelor of Science in Engineering. During this time there was a shortage of competent engineers in Tallahassee so Deke was in high demand, but decided to become a subcontractor before he retired.

There have been Four generations in Samuel Douglas' family who have laid their life on the line to serve and protect Leon County, Florida when they joined the Military. The first known soldier was Grandfather Frederick Douglas who was a Private in the Civil War from 1863-1867. The second generation to serve was the father, Riley Douglas, who was a Private in World War I from 1919-1922. The third member of this brave family legacy was the son, Samuel Douglas, who was drafted in as a Private in World War II from 1941-1944; and the last known military soldier is Riley's Son Douglas Jr. a Private in the Vietnam War from 1972-1975. All returned from the wartime and made a prosperous living for their family.

In 1938, during the start of World War II, Deke met and married Emma Jane Walker from Gadsden County. Deke and Emma had four children from this union. They are; Riley II, Christopher, Rosa D. Germany, and Jane Douglas.

Deke joined the Greater St. Marks Primitive Baptist Church in 1955 and to this day is a dedicated deacon. Deke grew up with a lot of love from his parents and siblings. He proved this by sharing with everyone he met. His neighbors never forgot the kindness he showed when they needed help, and would often come by his house to return the favor to Deke or just to sit and listen to his wisdom. Deke would reply: "the lord's giveth to those who give", and offer them some home made ice cream which he loved to churn on Sundays after church services.

Deke served the Mount Olive Lodge #5 for over 60 years and was honored by them and many others for his devotion and dedication to the community.

Deke celebrated his 100th birthday in March of 2008. He has ten grandchildren and twenty great-grand children. Family and friends were present at his birthday celebration held at the Tallahassee Community College Banquet Facility. Several presentations were given to catalog Deke's life so far. Deke was quoted as saying he's looking for a wife. Samuel (Deke) Douglas departed this life in his sleep on November 14, 2008 and will be surely missed by all who knew him.

Submitted by: Cathereine Douglas; Written by: Carol D. Johnson

Drake, A Pre-Statehood Family of Tallahassee

This narrative shows how life was lived before Florida became a State. Spelling and phrasing are left as they were originally written.

Dan Drake, a descendent of Exum Drake, b. about 1785, has copies of original letters written by Exum Drake from Territory of Florida, Leon County, dated Dec. 13, 1838. It is addressed to Francis Drake and Richard Drake family, Washington County, Georgia.

Here are some of the excerpts from that letter:

"Dear Brother, be sure to move if you can and fetch Francis and his family. I am now making a waggon (sic). This is a great place for your trade. Be shore (sic) to come when I rite to you there is peace"{with the Indians).

"Felithia and Cerena give their loving compliments to you all. Your Ant (sic) Elizabeth gives her loving compliments to you all. Nothing more at present but remain your loving Uncle until Death."

Signed Exum Drake December 13, 1838

Another letter:

"Der Cosen and Uncle, I once more take my pen in hand to inform you that I am well at present. Hopping these few lines may find you all in good health. I must inform you of my bad misfortune the 23 day of September I lost my oldest child called Isabel Jane; the 2 of October I lost my Der (sic) wife and I regret to write this to you. My Last Child is well. I call her Dorcas Fremon. don't know what I shall do another year. I have many opportunitys of good bisness at present. I would be glad you would all move to this Country. I no you would do better ..... Give my love to Winfred and all my inquiring friends. Right to me when you can. James is gone up the country."

Signed "John F. Williams, his love to all"

Anna Lee Drake & Alex Drake standing; seated: Dan Drake and Kathy Drake from Trinity UMC Membership album

Another letter: Exum Drake letter dated December 13, 1838 Territory of Florida Leon County

"Dear Nephew and Brother, I received your letter the 10th of December with pleasure to hear from you and your family and Brother gives me great satisfaction. Dear Nephew, this is to let you know that we are all well at present. ...we have had bad times with the Indians here, hopping the God of heaven will send us peace once more. This country is great if our enemies were subdued, but I can't tell when, but as quick as you hear we have peace be shore (sic) to move to me as quick as you can when I Rite to you and fetch your father with you, for this is great Country for him and you, and your wife and children ...come to my family thirteen miles this side of Tallahassee.

Crops of corn is good, Cotton is sorry. This Country is great for corn, Cotton, peas, potatoes and Everything.

My daughter Nancy is dead. Died looking to the Lord the Savior of the World to save her, gives me great faith in the God of heaven. Your Ant (sic) and I and Fillithia are in the Baptist Church …will make your calling and election shore (sic). Rite to me every month till you move to this country.

Your Ant has had Eight Children ? all Dead to Filiithia, Jenkins James Drake and Cerena, one son and two daughters.

Dear Brother and Nephew, this is to let you know we have taken out land at last - you can take out land at $1.25 per acre."

Line of descendency as given by these letters:
1. Exum Drake b. about 1785; 2. Jenkins James b. Dec. 18, 1823; 3. William Henry Drake, b. Mar 4, 1846; and 4.Taylor A. Drake b. July 21, 1876

Submitted by Dan Drake 2309 Glenshire Ct Tallahassee, FL 32309- 3015

Reverend Walter Homer Duggar

Homer Duggar was born on February 18, 1904. His parents were Katie Roberts and Walter A. Duggar. His mother's parents were Lewis Abraham Roberts and Catherine E. Barineau. Lewis A. Roberts was a Baptist minister and founded Leon Ebenezer Baptist Church in 1880.

When Homer's mother married the second time to William Zolezzi, Homer didn't get along with his new family, so he went to live with his Grandfather Roberts. He admired his Grandfather Roberts and would imitate him by standing on a stump and preaching to the cows in the pasture.

On June 7, 1924, he married Lizzie Harriet Smith in Thomasville, GA. They had eight children. The eldest child is my mother, Virginia Lucille, who married Bob Johnston and lives in Woodville, FL. The other children are as follows: Melvyne Elizabeth, who is married to Dr. Edgar Cooper and lives in Jacksonville, FL.; Ernest Homer and wife Eula, both deceased; Patricia Ann of Tallahassee whose husband, Rev. Elbert Barineau, is deceased; Mary Helen who lives with her husband, Bill Battles, in Oldsmar, FL.; Betty Josephine, who lives with her husband, Rev. Glen Lawhon, in Lake City, FL.; Marilyn Jeanette Webster of High Point, NC.; and Sandra Elaine, who lives with her husband, Rev. Don Crane, in Scotch Plains, NJ. There are many grandchildren and great grandchildren, etc.

Homer learned typesetting and worked for several printing houses in Tallahassee as a pressman. He worked for Buckley Newman Commercial Printers on Pensacola St., Florida Print House and Rose Printing Co. When there was no work in Tallahassee, he moved the family to St. Augustine for work. The first time was in 1933 for one year and again from 1936 until 1939. He worked at the *St. Augustine Record*. While in St. Augustine the second time, they were members of Ancient City Baptist Church and he preached at a mission across the river.

Before their third child Ernest was born in 1930, Homer built a small 2 room house, with the help of his step father, on a parcel of land on the west side of Capital Circle SE across from where part of Southwood Development is now. He later added more rooms and when they went to St. Augustine, he would rent it out. He was ordained as a Baptist Minister on April 26, 1942, and was a founding member of Immanuel Baptist Church on Boulevard St. He sold the house in 1944 when he moved the family to Bogalusa, LA near New Orleans to attend seminary. Before he moved to Bogalusa, he was pastor at Sopchoppy First Baptist Church and lived in the pastorium.

Reverend, Walter Homer Duggar

When he returned from Louisiana, he pastored at First Baptist Church Crawfordville and lived in the pastorium. In 1947 he became pastor of First Baptist Church Woodville. In 1948 the, church facing west on Old Woodville Highway, burned. He helped rebuild the church facing north on Natural Bridge Road and was pastor there until 1950. He performed my wedding ceremony there in 1966 when I married Harold Lee Lewis.

He was full time or interim pastor at many churches in Leon County and beyond, including, but not limited to; First Baptist Church in Sopchoppy, Leon Ebenezer Baptist Church (1956-57), Fellowship Baptist Church, Concordia Baptist Church, Southside Baptist Church, churches in Floral City, Inverness, Cantonment and Calvary, GA. Even after he retired due to heart problems, he continued to serve as interim pastor and preached almost every Sunday until he died of a heart attack on August 10, 1978, while visiting family in Raleigh, NC. He is buried in Roselawn Cemetery in Tallahassee with his wife Lizzie Duggar, who died on June 14, 1999. He was always teasing and joking with his children and others. He was a happy man who loved his family, gardening and sharing the gospel.

Written and submitted by: Virginia E. Johnston Lewis, 1913 Family Lane Woodville, FL 32305

Don Dughi

Photographer Don Dughi was born on July 9, 1932 inHampton Beach, New Hampshire, and grew up in St.Petersburg, Florida. He attended St. Petersburg Junior College and the University of Florida. By his third year he had won a scholarship in photography, which provided him the opportunity to attend and graduate from Florida State University in 1962. In addition to his academic career, he served three years in the Marines, 16 months of which were spent as a rifleman in Korea.

From 1963 to 1970, he served WCTV behind the camera and spent much of his time shooting scenes from the Florida State Capitol for the station's coverage of the legislature. In 1970, Dughi joined the United Photographer International (UPI) as the photographer for its Tallahassee bureau.

Don Dughi with Muhammad Ali at Civic Center, 1970s

Don continued to cover important events for Florida all over the world. He was one of the photographers, chosen by Michael Jackson to cover his concert in Tampa. Florida. Jackson viewed Dughi's work as one of the best photographers he had ever seen. With his career and professional reputation continuing to grow, Don worked for UPI until 1991, When he was

Don Dughi on Fishing trip with Governor Chiles, 1999

given an opportunity to work for the Associated Press. One year after he changed jobs, the UPI ended its operations in Tallahassee, Florida.

In 1992, Dughi took a position with the Florida House of Representatives as its photographer. He worked for the House for nine years until his retirement in 2001. Don Dughi, married Susan Hartsfield, native Tallahassean, and they have two children and two grandchildren. Don was involved in a fishing accident and never fully recovered. He died on April 6, 2005.

Written and submitted by: Carol D. Johnson, 214 N. Columbia Drive, Tallahassee, Florida 32304

Ansel Elliott - Pursuit of Happiness

My maternal Grandmother, Bertha Johana Moran, was born near Utica, New York on March 20, 1886. Upon graduating from highschool, she left for New York City to train as a nurse at "The Polytechnic School". After graduation she accompanied a new M.D. to Jacksonville, Florida, as his Private Duty Nurse. She rarely nursed in town; usually her patients were out on the farms.

William Ansel Elliott was born March 9, 1886 in Nashville, Tennessee. After high school, he worked at the *Nashville Banner,* then left Nashville to work at another two newspapers and then to Tampa, Florida. In 1907, at age 21 he was recruited by the *Times-Union* in Jacksonville, Florida.

These two working singles did not meet at church, for my Irish (Yankee) grandmother arrived in Jacksonville as a practicing Catholic, and Ansel was not Catholic. They were friends for about four years and at the age 25, Bertha felt that Ansel was not serious enough for marriage so, she accepted a marriage arranged by her family in Utica, New York. Before arriving in New York Bertha said yes to a family friend a man 20 years her senior, and recently retired from the military.

Back in Jacksonville, in October of 1911, unsuspecting Ansel went to Bertha's lodgings inquiring if she had telephoned to say how much longer she would be working out of town. The landlady replied, "She is no longer nursing here, yesterday she phoned to say she will no longer live in Jacksonville and tomorrow she will go with her Mother and sister to shop for a trousseau. I think she will marry soon!"

Distraught, Ansel went pell-mell to the *Times Union* office. He passed the hat amongst his peers but did not say a word to his boss about his emergency trip; he then went to his bank, then to his room at the boarding house to pack his suitcase. He took the next train to New York City, leaving his coworkers worried about the possible futility of his trip.

Some-how, Ansel found Bertha in New York, and she broke her engagement and accepted Ansel's proposal. They were married at the Rectory of St. Patrick's Cathedral on Oct. 12. 1911. They returned to Jacksonville immediately, because Ansel had not given proper notice to his boss. Upon his return, Ansel found that management was seriously considering his termination. But, luckily for Ansel, his young coworkers had kept the telegraph line open between Jacksonville and New York, and his boss was happy to hear that Ansel had found his true love.

L.to R.: Bertha Johanna Moran (Ansel's love), William Ansel Elliott, and MiriamElliott, Ansel's sister

Ansel Elliott's April 9, 1933 obituary is on file at the State Library; a cardiac death at age 47, and as Managing Editor of the *Times Union* newspaper. He was married for 21.5 years: Bertha outlived him by 40 years as of Oct. 8, 1973.

Bertha and Ansel's daughters, Catherine and Suzanne, kept Ansel's memory alive. He has been the friendly ghost who is much a part of our family. My sister, Cathy, b. 1950, my brother, Howard, b. 1951, and I, Suzanne, b. 1948 think we knew him from all the stories that were passed down to us.

In 1937, Governor Fred P. Cone, appointed Mrs. Bertha Elliott to the Florida Milk Board Commission, and she served for 17 years. The Florida State Archives holds the minutes to these meetings where her signature occurs regularly amongst the papers. Her daughter, Catherine, was the assistant typist for this Commission during this time.

The photographs, the obituary of these minutes of the Milk Commission with my grandmother's signature, some of these minutes were typed by my Aunt, Suzanne Elliot. These are some of my associations with Leon County.
Written and submitted by: Suzanne McCloud Rosenblum, Ansel's granddaughter

Ansel and Bertha Elliot; Bertha's Wedding Rings

When Bertha said: "Yes, I will marry you rather than the man I traveled to NYC to marry," Ansel promptly purchased a thin gold band, and Bertha proudly wore this ring a few years after the wedding. One day she took it off while housekeeping and never found it again. As a "woman ahead of her time" this did not bother her, but Ansel wanted her to wear a wedding ring.

At this juncture of their lives, Ansel had more than enough money to buy another wedding ring for Bertha. So, the replacement ring he purchased was a wide gold band with ever so many diamond chips in it. The chips were arranged into the shape of three flowers. It sounds gaudy to me; but Mother claimed that it was lovely.

Bertha wore this ring for years after he put it on her finger. Then in 1925 they, made the then arduous trip from Jacksonville to Sanibel Island by automobile, because they liked Sanibel despite the fact that you needed to load water into the car while in Fort Myers, for after the ferry brought you to Sanibel Island there was no fresh water to drink. Years late, when they complained about the mosquitoes on Sanibel with fond memories, my memories of the visits was that we did think that they were the size of Chihuahua puppies or flying puppies.

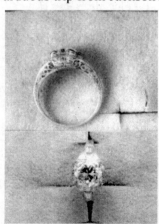
Ansel Elliott third wedding ring to his bride, Bertha Elliott

They did have one serious mishap on Sanibel Island. While collecting shells in shallow water, without Bertha realizing it, her replacement ring slipped off her finger! Everyone on the beach that day began to look for that ring, but to no avail. Once again, if Bertha and Ansel were at some function together and when someone said to Ansel, "That woman in the doorway, the lady wearing the blue dress, is she your wife?", Ansel would crane his neck and look, then reply "She's not wearing a ring, she must not be married."

Since Ansel was on salary during the Great Depression (Managing Editor for *the Florida Times-Union*), the Elliott's weathered the economy better than most. Eventually Ansel received another ring from a friend who owned a jewelry store. The friend said, "Ansel, before it is known that I will be in receivership of some fine rings in a couple of days, come to the store and see if you want to purchase anything." After his visit to the jeweler, Ansel gave Bertha the third ring in the picture. It is a 1.3 carat mine cut, flanked by baguettes, set in platinum wedding ring. Bertha wore this ring for the rest of Ansel's life.

After Ansel died and I grew up this was my wedding ring. To this day, I think of it as "Ansel's ring" for that it how Bertha referred to it as I was growing up and it always reminded me of how proud he was of her as his wife and how much he loved my grandmother, Bertha.
Written by: Suzanne Rosenblum; Submitted by: Catherine Elliott

Fair - First Cousins from Leon County in the Civil War

Three Fair sisters and one brother from Charleston, South Carolina who settled in Leon County in the early 1830s, had sons who grew up on the north shore of Lake Iamonia and later served as Confederates in the Civil War. The sisters by their married names were Elizabeth Jane Van Brunt, Mary Ann Greene and Frances Nicks. The brother, Joseph Fair married J. R. Greene's sister, Martha Mariah Greene.

The 1840 Census lists the Fair girls' family households, including J. R. Nicks, J. R. Greene and Richard Van Brunt. Joseph Fair was married and lived in Leon County too. After marrying Mariah, his first-born son, Richard McKeen Fair was born in Leon County before he and J. R. Greene moved north, finally settling in Opelika, Alabama. Both Greene and Fair households were enumerated on the 1850 and 1860 U. S. Census rolls in Opelika.

The 1850 Census for Leon County included Richard C. Williams Van Brunt, named after his father and maternal grandfather, at the age of 25 living with his parents. He had been born in South Carolina, but grew up and lived the rest of his life in Leon County, Florida. Many of his descendants still live in the vicinity.

In the J. R. Nicks' household, three sons were listed, including William R., age 17; Francis R., age 13; and Benjamin R., age 11. Even though the census enumerator, Hutchins listed the son's birth state as Florida, a later Civil War Pension file for William R. Nicks stated that he was born in Thomasville, Thomas County, Georgia.

The Nicks family moved from Leon County to Hernando County around 1853. The 1860 Census for Hernando County is missing, but tax records indicate the three sons had begun homesteading on their own. After the boys enlisted and left the county, their taxes had to be returned. Their Mother's Day Book had a poem written in it that foretold the impending war. It opens:

"Go gallant youth at honors call
The glorious path to fame pursue...
and ends "...
On falling on the unburied heads
Which ruthless war denies a grave."

Mary Ann and James R. Greene's first born son, Rinaldo McKeen Greene was born in Leon County. He is listed in his parents' household in Opelika, Russell County, Alabama in 1850 and by 1860; he was married to Martha Bullard and in his own household at the age of 22. Rinaldo MeKeen Greene would survive the Civil War and live his lifetime in Alabama.

The first cousins and their Civil War outfits: William Richard Nicks,Co. C, 9th FL Inf. Regt and FL Cowmen; Francis R. Nicks, Co. C, 3rd FL Inf. Regt.; Benjamin R. Nicks. Co. C, 3rd FL Inf. Regt.; Rinaldo McKeen Greene Co. H, 6th AL Inf. Regt; Richard Van Brunt, Co. , GA CAV; Richard McKeen Fair Co. B, 45th AL Regt.

Other brothers and cousins also served, but the six above were either born or lived in Leon County for a brief period before moving on.

Francis and Benjamin died before and after 1870 from illnesses contracted during the war. They did not get to enjoy life as their other cousins.

William R. Nicks lived in Hernando County and grew oranges. He died in 1905 and is buried in the Townsend House Cemetery in Pasco County, Florida. William's youngest brother, Robert Henry R. Nicks, born 1852 in Leon County was too young for the Civil War, but may have served with the so called "old men and young boys" who tried to repel the Union Army's Brooksville Raid in July 1864. Robert was pictured with other Confederate Civil War Soldiers from the area. R. M. Greene served as a Captain in the Civil War. Afterwards, he lived a good life having organized and served as president of the Bank of East Alabama. Richard Van Brunt of Leon County married his first cousin Frances Elizabeth Greene and had six children. Richard McKeen Fair married his first cousin, Anna Burr whose mother, Sophia Fair was another Fair sibling. They had two children and after the Civil War moved with Richard's parents to Hope, Arkansas. The Joseph Fair children all migrated to the same area and today live in Texas, Arkansas and Oklahoma.

Written by: Charles C. Blankenship; Submitted by: Frances Katherine Werner-Watkins, 7210 Tanglewood Dr., New Port Richey, FL

Descendants of Elizabeth Jane Fair

Elizabeth Jane Fair, aka Elizabeth Jane Van Brunt was born c. 1808 in Charleston, SC. Her parents were Richard Fair and his wife, Elizabeth Harrison originally, from Cavan County, Ireland. (See sketches for Fair - Nicks' siblings) Elizabeth and her siblings grew up over the boot and shoe shop owned and operated by her father on King Street in downtown Charleston.

Sometime in 1824, Elizabeth married Richard Van Brunt, bookbinder in Charleston. At one time, they lived on Bay Street. After the death of her father in 1817, her mother remarried a teacher, Joseph DeWitt Nicks. At some point, Elizabeth and her husband became the guardian for her youngest brother, Joseph Harrison Fair. Several deeds filed in Charleston courts reveal some costs involved with seeing to Joseph's education and care. Those same deeds named all the children of the late Richard Fair.

When her sister, Frances Fair married James Rinaldo Nicks during 1832, they moved first to Thomasville, GA and in 1833 settled at

Lake Iamonia in north Leon County. Mary Ann Fair married James Russell Greene in June of 1832 and settled at Lake Iamonia. Around 1836, Elizabeth and Richard purchased land very-close to today's Tall Timbers Research Station and relocated from Charleston to Leon County, Florida.

Soon, the entire sibling group also settled around the J. R. Nicks family on the north side and west of the Strickland Arm of Lake Iamonia near Section 13, Township 3N and Range IE. The 1840 U. S. Census listed the families of Nicks, Greene and Van Brunt. Another family, that of Celete (Greene) Sauls (sister of J. R. Greene) was also close to the other families. Celete's son James D. was to marry Sarah Ann Nicks (half-sister to Fair siblings) and Celete and J. R. Greene's other sister, Martha Mariah was to marry Joseph Harrison Fair.

Elizabeth's husband, Richard, had given Frances Fair a small day book signed by him and her sister, Mary Ann that is dated June 14, 1831 when she was still known as "Miss Frances Fair." Inside that book are notations that EJVB borrowed several scoops of sugar. Apparently, the young married sisters were keeping an account of their households. Later on, one of Elizabeth's descendants ran a country store and kept journals for his accounting purposes.

That story, titled "Van Brunt's Store, Iamonia, Florida, 1902-1911," by Clifton L. Paisley covers the early 20th century Van Brunts. It also gives the location and some history of the Lake Iamonia community. The article is available in Florida Historical Quarterlies that are now online.

Between 1840 and 1850, the Fair - Nicks siblings began a northward migration, first to Columbus, GA and next 87 across the river to Girard, AL. They finally settled in Opelika, Russell (now Lee) Co., AL. Only the Richard Van Brunt and J. R. Nicks families remained in Leon Co. The 1850 Census enumeration, revealed (for the first time) the names of others in two respective households.

The children included Richard J. (25), James E. (20), Francis S. (18) and Sophia (14), all born in SC. The children born in Florida included Ann E. (12), Sarah Jane (9), Elizabeth (6), Albert (4) and Martin C. (4/12). The household, number 99, was three houses away from Elizabeth's sister, Frances Fair Nicks and her family.

Frances and J, R. Nicks moved in 1853 to Hernando County, but returned to serve in the Florida General Assembly as State Representative from Hernando. Certainly, the families got together and it is possible the two sisters went to Opelika, AL to visit their other siblings. Nicks family legend has it that Frances and James came to Hernando in 1859. The source of that family lore was the obituary of Frances' youngest son (1852-1928). He probably remembered coming back from an Opelika visit in 1859, not knowing he was born in Leon County in 1852 and moving to Hernando in 1852.

Richard Van Brunt and Elizabeth do not appear on the 1860 Census. Their eldest son, Richard's household is listed with wife Frances and their three children, Mary E., Edwin and Laura. He also had his siblings, Frank, Sarah, Elizabeth and Martin. Very little else is known of the parents' fate. The Van Brunt Cemetery leaves no clues.

Because the Hernando County 1860 Census is missing, their family members are unknown too. An 1867 Chancery Court suit for the portioning of their estate did give the dates of death for James as c. 1861 and Frances as c. 1864. Their final resting place is also unknown.

Richard Van Brunt, son of Richard and Elizabeth Jane, named his son Rinaldo Francis after his uncle J. R. Nicks. He appears on the 1870 census. R. F. Van Brunt is the person who ran the Van Brunt Lake Iamonia Store. Rinaldo's son, Rinaldo Francis Van Brunt became a U. S. Army Major General. He served during WWII and the Korean Wars.

Richard C. Williams Van Brunt (1825-1876) married his first cousin, Frances Elizabeth Greene (daughter of Mary Anna Fair and James Russell Greene). She was born in 1833 in GA and died in 1900; Her burial is in the Van Brunt Cemetery in Lake Iamonia. Frances and Richard were married in 1853 in Opclika. Once again, this would indicate a possible sibling gathering in Alabama.

The children of the Greene-Van Brunt marriage and descendants thereafter are listed in Frank Hawthorne's book, "Kissin Kin & Lost Cousins." Copies are in the Opelika City Library and the Alabama State Archives in Montgomery. Several Mesne Conveyances and a Marriage Settlement written for the 1818 marriage of Mrs. Elizabeth Fair, widow of Richard Fair and Joseph DeWitt Nicks list the children of Richard and

Elizabeth. One son, Richard Robert or vice versa, died in Charleston before reaching his majority.

Descendants of Elizabeth Jane Fair and Richard Van Brunt still live in Leon County and throughout Florida. Their history spans Florida's Territorial era and now well into the 21st Century.

Written by: Charles Blankenship for Susan Eckstein, 8735 Old Post Rd., Port Richey, FL 34668

Descendants of Frances Fair

Frances Fair, aka Frances Nicks and Mrs. Rinaldo Nicks, was born in Charleston, SC c. 1815. Her parents (Richard Fair and Elizabeth Harrison) were from Cavan County, Ireland. They had immigrated to Charleston, SC before 1800. Both married in 1804 and moved to King Street in downtown Charleston about 1813. Frances and her siblings; Mary Ann, Elizabeth Jane, Sophia, Richard Robert and Joseph Fair lived above their father's boot and shoe shop.

Frances' mother believed in education and had a tutor for her children. After the death of Richard Fair in October 1817, the tutor, Joseph DeWitt Nicks became their stepfather in December 1818. Their children included Sarah Ann, Martha and James.

Frances received a 5 x 6 day book from her older sister, Elizabeth Jane and her bookbinder brother-in-law, Richard Van Brunt who had married her sister. The book, dated June 16, 1831, was inscribed "Miss Frances Fair." Inside the book, Frances listed her female classmates. She also wrote poetry and many years later in July 1864, her son, Francis R. Nicks wrote a Civil War letter to his Captain, Walter Terry Saxon. His description indicated his mother was "very low," and she died after the date in Brooksville, Hernando County.

After the marriage of Elizabeth Jane to Van Brunt, the family started an outward migration through Georgia. Her sister, Mary Ann, married Isaac McKeen James Russell Greene in Thomasville, Thomas County, GA in June 1832. Frances also married that same year, but the location is unknown.

Frances married James Rinaldo Nicks, who may have been a half-brother of Joseph DeWitt Nicks. J. R. Nicks' mother, Eleanor (?) Greene Nicks had settled in downtown Thomasville around the county courthouse. Eleanor had purchased almost 200 acres in north Leon County on the west side of the Strickland Arm of Lake Iamonia.

In March 1832, Eleanor deeded the same property, which included Lots 4 and 5 of Section 13, Township 3N and Range 1E to Frances and her children. The same land was in trust to Eleanor's son by Benjamin Greene and was not Frances' property until around 1853.

Frances Fair Nicks and J. R. Nicks moved into the Lake Iamonia property around 1833. They would remain there until 1853, before moving south to Hernando County. Both the 1840 and 1850 census reports included the J. R. Nicks household. The latter indicated the members of their household, including William Richard, Frances R., Benjamin R., Susan A. and James R. Nicks (Jr.). Another son, Robert Henry R. Nicks was born there in November 1852. Indenture records for Leon County reveal that J. R. Nicks farmed and raised cotton. Judging by the Tax Rolls for Leon County, the family did well and purchased a carriage at some point.

J. R. Nicks was involved in early Florida Territory politics. He became a Notary Public for Leon County. He also was an inspector for the 1845 Statehood Vote and attended at least one Democratic Convention. After their move to Hernando, he would return to Leon County and the General Assembly for years 1856-58-59 as a State Representative from Hernando County.

Frances' siblings (with the exception of Elizabeth Jane Van Brunt) moved away from Florida, first to Columbus, GA; across the river to Girard, AL and finally to Opelika, AL. It is almost certain that Frances and her family visited the siblings in Opelika because family legend from the 1928 obituary of her son, H. R. Nicks stated the family came to Brooksville from Opelika in 1859.

H. R. Nicks did not realize the family's 1852 or 1853 move from Leon Co. to Hernando Co. as he was age five or six when they returned from Opelika to Brooksville. Three of Frances' sons enlisted and served in the Civil War from 1861 to 1865. The eldest, William Richard, served in Co. C., 3rd Florida Infantry and later as Florida Cow Company moving cattle to north Florida to provide meat for the Confederates. Both Francis R. and Benjamin R. served in Co. C, 3rd Florida Infantry Regiment known as the Hernando Wildcats.

Francis and Benjamin were among the sick and wounded which eventually took their lives. Francis died before the 1870 Census and Benjamin died shortly after the same census.

Their father, J. R. Nicks, died sometime in 1861 and their mother after July 1864. There is no known cemetery resting place for them. Two CSA markers, one in the Brooksville City Cemetery and another at the Spring Lake Cemetery indicate F. R. or Frank Nix/Nicks. One is most likely Benjamin's final resting place.

Because of a missing 1860 census report for Hernando County, the fate of Susan A. and James R. Nicks, Jr. is unknown. Just recently, five unused or empty spaces in the Brooksville City Cemetery next to the CSA gravestone for Francis R. Nicks were disclosed as H. R. Nicks' property. It is possible the other members of the family are interred there too.

Only two of Frances' children (William and H. R.) had children. William R. Nicks married Sophronia Mitchell in Hernando County. His children and Frances' grandchildren are enumerated on the 1870-1900 census reports. William secondly married Jane Mizell and their only child was Joshua Lamar Nicks.

In June 1873, Robert Henry R. Nicks married Alatha Frances Jane Hope, daughter of Henry Hope and Alatha Frances Garrison. Their children appear on census reports for 1880 and 1885. His wife died in 1894 and H. R. Nicks raised the children who appear on the 1900-1920 census reports.

Two of Frances' grandchildren, Sheldon S. Nicks and William O'Berry, lost their lives acting as law enforcement officers. Both are among the listed "Fallen Heroes" on Pasco County monuments in Dade City, FL. They died in the line of duty.

With the exception of William Richard, all of Frances and J. R. Nicks' children were born at Lake Iamonia, Leon, County, Florida. They spent two decades in north Florida., Frances Fair Nicks' descendants still live in Hernando and, Pasco County.

Written by Charles Blankenship for Frances Fair Clark Mallett, 8735 Old Post Rd., Port Richey, FL 34668

Jim Fair, Politics

Every town has at least one Jim Fair counted for ten. This decorated World War II hero returned to Tampa after the war to start Tampa's premier discount "Get It For You Wholesale" Center on South Franklin Street, just north of where the Cross town Expressway would eventually pass by. That was long before skyscrapers made their appearance downtown.

Jim was Tampa's beloved eccentric and political gadfly, a political sleuth, who started the Salvation Navy at the three story brick building on the east side of Franklin Street. There, Fair sold novelties and useful items to people who didn't have much money and he gave street people a place to hang out for the night. He was friendly, always had a smile on his face, but was quick to file lawsuits about almost anything that did not seem fair. He often said he "never met a lawsuit he didn't like."

Fair was often jailed for contempt of court for mouthing off at judges and witnesses in open court. If he had something to say he'd say it no matter what the rules were or who was present and he was always willing to accept the consequences and sue to have them changed. He ran dozens of advertisements in every issue of The Tampa Tribune with his famous phone number, 2-2222 which later changed to 229-2222. He had to sue the phone company to get that particular number. Each advertisement he placed boasted that FAIR could "Get It 4 U Wholesale," whatever it was you wanted.

Jim Fair, 1972

Ironically, he filed many lawsuits against the newspaper for not getting its facts straight and his love-hate relationship with reporters was legendary. If there was a slow news day, and there often was in the fifties and sixties, Fair could always be counted on for an exciting turn of events that would entertain readers. Jim Fair was part of the local and well-respected Farrior family of lawyers and doctors but changed his name in the fifties as a symbol of his non conformity to the system. He despised anything "government" but ran for Public office dozens of times; like the mayor to county commissioner to state senator believing, if you want something done right, do it yourself.

When he ran for each office, he always sued to have the filing fees declared unconstitutional. Failing at that, he found other ways to get his name on the ballot. After multiple failures at elected office seeking, the citizens finally voted him into the Supervisor of Election's Office in 1964. By 1966, he had screwed the operations of the rather obscure office up so bad that then Governor Claude Kirk had to remove him and appoint a successor. But he did put this division on the map.

Fair spent nearly a decade of his post-political years in Tampa filing lawsuits, many directed at the Florida Public Service Commission and local utilities alleging corruption and lack of public interest. In the mid-seventies, Hillsborough County took Fair's Salvation Navy property by condemnation to make way for entrances to the soon-tobe built Cross town Expressway. He sued to keep his property, but lost. In protest, he never picked up the check for nearly $300,000 in payment that remained for him with the Clerk of the Circuit Court. He once directed WFLA-TV reporter Tony Zappone to go pick up the check and then called the clerk not to release it to him as a joke.

In 1976, as part of an agreement with a local court, which held him in contempt for numerous violations of conduct, he left Hillsborough County for Florida's State Capitol. He wasn't in Tallahassee five minutes when he became the same center of media attention he had been in Tampa. He made speeches everywhere people would listen and sometimes, he even made sense. In 1980, he ran unsuccessfully against State Senator Dernpsey Barren (D-Panama City), again protesting the qualifying fee.

Fair remained in Tallahassee, fighting the utility companies and big business in local and state courts. He lived modestly in an apartment until his death in the early 1990s. He seldom made sense, he was eccentric, but he was loved. Most of the people in the state of Florida felt his passing left a big gap in the collective souls of Tampa and Tallahassee when he was around no more.

Written by: Tony Zappone, www.teddweb.com; Submitted by: Carol D. Johnson, 214 N. Columbia Drive, Tallahassee, FL 32304

Descendants of Mary Ann Fair

Mary Anna Fair aka Mary Ann Fair and Mary Ann Greene was the eldest child of Elizabeth Harrison and Richard Fair of Cavan County, Ireland. She was born in downtown Charleston, SC on October 4, 1805. (See sketches for Fair - Nicks siblings) As the oldest, Mary Anna did not marry until she was 27 years old.

Most likely, she helped her mother raise the younger children, especially the three from her second marriage.

In June 1832, Mary Ann married James Russell Greene (aka Isaac McKeen James Russell Greene) in Thomasville, Thomas County, GA. For a short while, she and J. R. Greene lived in Hebron, Washington Co., GA. Their first two children were born in GA. By 1836, J. R. Greene purchased land on the north shore of Lake Iamonia, Leon Co., FL. Their oldest child, Rinaldo McKeen Greene (1837-1907) was born in Leon Co., Florida. He was named for his uncle, James Rinaldo Nicks and paternal grandfather.

J. R. Greene was the son of McKeen Greene and Frances DuBose. McKeen and his brothers, Benjamin and John were Rev. War Veterans. He was also active in the Florida Patriot War of 1814. He and two of his sons-in-laws (Daniel Sauls and Michael Henderson) signed the Elotchaway Petition at Ft. Mitchell, Florida on January 25, 1814. McKeen was also the brother-in-law to his brother Benjamin's wife, Eleanor (?). After his death, Eleanor married William Nicks and their son, James Rinaldo Nicks became a brother-in-law with his marriage to his wife's sister, Frances Fair.

Some time in 1836, Mary Anna and J. R. Greene moved to Lake Iamonia and purchased land from his cousin, Benjamin Greene, single man of Screven Co., GA. The 40 acres was described as Lot. No. 3, Section 13 within Township 3N and Range IE. The same area was very close to that of J. R. Nicks, Richard Van Brunt and his sister, Celete Sauls, wife of Daniel Sauls and just east of Tall Timbers.

They were joined by Mary Anna's siblings and her mother. All are enumerated on the 1840 Census within the Nicks, Van Brunt, Sauls and Greene families. His other sister, Martha Mariah Greene married Mary Anna's brother, Joseph Harrison Fair in Leon Co.

According to a Rinaldo McKeene Greene bio in a "Lee County and her Forebears," book, the family moved to Opelika (then Russell Co.), AL in 1847. Another source states that the Greene family first moved to Columbus, GA then settled in Opelika. When the 1850 U. S. Census was taken, the J. R. Greene family was enumerated in Opelika.

Mary Anna and J. R. Greene had nine children, including Frances Elizabeth, Anna Mariah Harrison, Rinaldo McKeen, James Harris,

Amanda Harris, Benjamin Howell and Laura McKeen Greene. Twin Infants, born and died in 1847.

Their eldest daughter, Frances Elizabeth Greene married her first cousin, Richard C. Williams Van Brunt in Opelika in 1853. They returned to Lake Iamonia, Leon Co., FL and raised six children. (A more detailed family lineage can be obtained from Frank Hawthorne's book, *Kissin Kin & Lost Cousins*)

James R. and Mary Anna continued to live in Opelika until their deaths in the 1880s. Both were lifelong Methodists. A June 27, 1885 diary entry by James acknowledged their 53rd Wedding Anniversary. James died in 1885 followed by Mary Anna in 1886. Both are buried in the Greene Lot; Block No. 58 of the Rosemere Cemetery in Opelika, Alabama. Many of their descendants are buried there too.

Mary Anna's sister, Sophia (Fair) Burr and three of her daughters also rest there. Sophia died three years prior to Mary Anna. Mary Anna was the last of the Fair daughters to die and only her brother, Joseph H. Fair died later. Her mother, Elizabeth (Harrison Fair) Nicks had died in Girard, AL the same year that Florida became a State. The Fair siblings (Mary Anna, Elizabeth Jane, Sophia, Frances and Joseph) lived in the Territory of Florida. Their half-sisters (Sarah Ann and Martha) along with their mother, Elizabeth Harrison (Fair Nicks) were also residents of Leon County, Florida. Only Frances and Elizabeth Jane continued to live in Florida when it was admitted to the Union in 1845.

Descendants of all live throughout the south and southwest. Thanks to those who kept records, especially Frank Howard Hawthorne, John Howard Greene, Paul T. Greene, Charles E. Fair and Jacqueline H. Wright, their past is often revisited. Jacqueline's research and subsequent book helped to bring three of the "...Lost Cousins," back together.

Because of the distance separating the families and the effects of the Civil War, the families of Frances Fair Nicks, Sarah Ann Nicks Sauls and Martha Nicks Durr were forgotten. Perhaps these Leon County early resident sketches will honor all the siblings.

Written by: Charles Blankenship in honor of those other researchers mentioned; Submitted by: Charles Blankenship, 55 Country Club Cove, Jackson, TN 38305

Descendants of Sophia A. Fair

Sophia Fair, aka Sophia Burr, daughter of Richard Fair and Elizabeth Harrison of Charleston, South Carolina was born November 29, 1813. She and her siblings: Mary Ann, Elizabeth Jane, Frances, Robert and Joseph Fair, lived in downtown Charleston where their father was a boot and shoemaker at their residence and business at 337 (now 170) King Street.

Their father died in October 1817. In December 1818, Mrs. Elizabeth Fair remarried Joseph DeWitt Nicks and continued to live on King Street beyond 1820. Elizabeth and Joseph Nicks had three more children: Sarah Ann, Martha and James W. Nicks. Elizabeth Jane married bookbinder, Richard Van Brunt and around 1832, two sisters (Frances and Mary Ann) married and moved into Georgia.

Frances settled first in Thomasville and second in Leon Co., FL near Lake Iamonia.

Mary Ann settled first in Hebron, Washington Co., GA and then followed her sister into Leon Co. as did Elizabeth Jane Van Brunt and their mother, Elizabeth Nicks with her two Nicks children (James W. had died) and Sophia Fair.

The 1840 U. S. Census for Leon County enumerated an extended family in the household of Mary Anna's husband, J. R. Greene. Frances Fair was in J. R. Nicks' household and Elizabeth Jane was in Richard Van Brunt's. Sophia, Martha, Sarah Ann and Mrs. Elizabeth Nicks were the extended members.

Sophia was still single when she witnessed a Deed (DBK G, p183) by her mother to Richard Van Brunt and wife on April 24, 1841. On June 13, 1842, Sophia married Allen Burr (1805-1853) from CT. Allen had been living in Jefferson Co., FL. Sophia and Allen followed several of Sophia's siblings and mother towards Columbus, GA across the river to Girard, AL and finally to Opelika, AL.

Allen Burr became a partner with John Mizell (husband of Martha Nicks) as merchants in Girard, AL. He later served as an Executor of the Mizell estate and his sister-in-law, Martha Nicks Mizell received estate settlement and moved to Opelika. In June 1844, Sophia's mother, Elizabeth Nicks, widow, formerly of Leon County, Territory of Florida, now of Russell County, Alabama conveyed property and farm equipment to Allen

Burr. The deed is recorded in DBK I/J, Leon County, Florida.

Sophia's family appears on Census reports in Opelika until 1910. Sophia and Allen were enumerated on the 1850 U. S. Census in Opelika with their children, Anna, A. E., A., Amanda, Almyra and Alice Fair. After Allen's death around 1853, she was the head of the household on the 1860-1870-1880 Census. In 1870, her neighbor was her sister, Mary Ann Fair and James R. Greene. Sophia's occupation was described as Sewing on the 1880 report and her twin daughters, Amanda and Almyra were seamstresses in 1900 and 1910.

Sophia died in July 1883 and is interred in the J. R. Greene plot in the Rosewood Cemetery, Opelika, Alabama. Her gravesite is located in the J. R. Greene plot alongside her daughter, Alice Burr (1852-1899). Anna Burr married her first cousin, Richard McKeen Fair in Opelika on August 30, 1865 and moved to Texas and Oklahoma. They had two children: Ella Fair and Joseph Allen Fair.

Ella had six children and her brother, Joseph Allen had five. Sophia Fair and Allen Burr's known grandchildren and descendants are listed on the two Charles E. Fair books (see sketch on Joseph Harrison Fair) written by him in the early 1950s.

Written by: Charles Blankenship, 55 Country Club Cove, Jackson, TN 38305

Chef Eric Gaston Favier

I had the good fortune of meeting Eric at one of the Faviers' Famous employee parties. My late husband, Michael Johnson worked for Karen and Eric Favier at Chez Pierre, so I am a living witness to Chef Eric's ability to perfect any entrée, and his charming personality when dealing with his employees. Chez Pierre is a great place to eat and work. For many years it has provided a unique place for patrons and employees alike in Tallahassee.

Eric Favier was born in the province of France in November of 1956. He moved to the United States in 1971 with just one suitcase in tow and a desire to enhance the life of all who came in contact with him. He found work at Disney World in California as a pastry chef and soon built a strong reputation for mastery of his cooking craft. After a short time he moved to Tampa Florida, where he worked at a small cafe. Things were going great for Chef Eric, but they were about to get better. In 1985 he met Karen Parker Cooley, a dynamic businesswoman and native Floridian, and they soon discovered that they both had a fondness for cooking, and went into business together with a small cafe in Tampa.

After relocating to Tallahassee, Eric and Karen purchased another small cafe on Call Street and Adams in 1992, where the new Federal Courthouse is now. They decided to keep the name of the cafe, which was called "Chez Pierre." In the later half of 1999, Chez Pierre was relocated to its present day location on Thomasville Road. This new location fueled the fire for Chef Eric's creativity in providing delicious pastry and mouth watering meals. Since meeting Karen and Eric, I can truly say that they go out of their way to find the best people to work for them. Pastry chef, cooks and even bus boys can't imagine working anywhere else. They all feel working at Chez Pierre is like working for family, not only because of the great employee parties, but also for the concern they show for their employees' personal lives. They all feel that Karen and Eric are owners who really care about their employees and this makes for better customer service practices.

Chef Eric Favier and Bride, Karen Parker Cooley

Chef Eric knows that making his customers happy is also the key to success. The ambience of the restaurant decor, the excellent customer service, and the wonderful delectables of all descriptions from the kitchen certainly makes for satisfied patrons. This spells success in the restaurant business for Chef Eric and Manager Karen, who are considered to be one of Florida's top 20 restaurant owners. For Chef Eric, this is a dream come true, and after 18 years of providing great food and customer service in Leon County it is a well deserved reward. In 2007, Chef Eric sold his business interest in Chez Pierre, but he continues to provide quality food and excellent service to his patrons. Bon Appétit!

Written by Carol D. Johnson. Submitted by: Eric Jean Gaston Favier, 2960 Lake Bradford Road, Tallahassee, Florida 32311

Fisher-Parker

June 27, 1959 was the day that changed my life forever. That day an overflow crowd of more than the 1250 seating capacity of the church witnessed the exchange of wedding vows between Army Captain Herbert Gerald Parker and me, Florida Lucylle Fisher. The wedding was at White Rock Baptist Church at White Rock Square in Durham, North Carolina, with my father, Rev. Dr. Miles Mark Fisher, officiating. In the one hundred three degree heat, rice thrown landed inside my gown and had cooked by the time I changed clothes.

Married life led to many new horizons. The first was genealogical pursuits, particularly my husband's side of the family. Having learned that his mother's maiden name was Fisher, as was mine, and that she had a brother named Miles Fisher, as did I, along with my father, great grandfather and great uncle having that same name piqued my curiosity. My enthusiasm for genealogical finds led to my becoming a charter member of the Tallahassee Genealogical Society and memberships in several national and state societies. Additionally, I presented at society meetings/conventions. Being more knowledgeable about the Parker and Fisher families led to my being a source of interest to many.

Wedding Day of Florida Fisher and Herbert Parker in 1959

A military wife, I was exposed to many cultures of the world through travel here and abroad. The Far East was home for three years, providing great exposure to many world cultures and the military's other branches. Teaching at the Taipei (TAIWAN) American School 1962-1965 brought a greater appreciation for the Orient. As organist and pianist at the naval base chapel there and at several stateside posts. I honed my music skills. Playing the piano at the American ambassador's residence for American holidays and military events led to interfacing with many in the diplomatic corps on the island. My level of awareness regarding protocol was raised greatly because of the military situations in which I was engaged.

As a commander's wife, I headed the ladies of the many units in which my husband was involved. I was part of wives clubs wherever we were stationed, often singing in chorales there. Community participation has always been an integral part of my life. Focusing more on children after my marriage both Girl and Boy Scouts claimed my time, serving as Field Representative, Troop Leader, and Cookie Sale Chairman for my hometown.

Boards of Directorships included Greensboro, North Carolina YWCA, on which I was the first person of color to serve, LeMoyne Art Foundation and Leon County Library's Friends in Tallahassee. Being a successful fund raiser thrust me into that venture wherever we lived. Faculty wives clubs at North Carolina A&T State University and Florida A&M University provided great introductions to the faculty community. Singing groups claimed my time whether in church or the community.

Motherhood was a new adventure. Two daughters were born to our union. Daughter Christie Lynne Parker Smith has a son, Matthew Warren Smith. Daughter Patricia Ann Parker died in infancy. Some of Christie's friends and young neighbors have also become my children. Teaching experiences ranged from elementary through high school and the college freshmen years.

June 27, 2009 marked our 50th wedding anniversary. This was a wonderful time to reflect on our lives and surroundings. Although Colonel Parker is in an assisted living facility for health reasons, we are still together to cherish the life enriching experiences we've had through the years.

Written by: Mrs. Florida Parker; Submitted by: Christie Parker Smith(Daughter), 3510 Tullamore Lane, Tallahassee, FL 32309-3127

John B. Fletcher and the Battle of Natural Bridge

I was told about the Battle of Natural Bridge that took place south of Tallahassee. Then I learned that my great grand uncle, John B. Fletcher, had not only fought in the battle, but had been instrumental in getting a monument placed there. When I learned that I could join United Daughters of the Confederacy through John, I was overjoyed. I found out about our connection from a family book I have entitled; History of the Joseph "Little Joe" Fletcher Family by Isabelle Suber and Hentz Fletcher.

John Bunyan Fletcher, born Jan. 7, 1843 - died April 7, 1926, was the 5lh son of Joseph "Little Joe" Fletcher and his wife, Ann Tomberlin Fletcher. John was born in Georgia but moved to Gadsden County, Florida with "Little Joe" and his family in 1851-1852. John married Elizabeth Ann Shepard on January 7, 1875. John and "Lizzie", as Elizabeth was called, lived in the Flat Creek Community in Gadsden County, Florida and are buried in the Flat Creek Baptist Church Cemetery.

When John Bunyan Fletcher was 17 years old, he became a Confederate soldier in the Civil War. He stayed in Florida to fight, not far from home. He enlisted in the Home Guard in January 1865 in Company L, First Florida Reserves at Chattahoochee, Florida, under Captain S. C. Gilchrist, and served until the close of the war. He was stationed at Newport and Natural Bridge, about 15 miles southeast of Tallahassee.

On March 6, 1865, the Colonel J. J. Daniels Regiment of the Florida Reserves, of which John was a member, and with Colonel George W. Scott's 5th Florida Battalion of Cavalry, fought and won the battle that kept the United States Army and Navy Operation from taking St. Marks. The next objective of the Federals was Tallahassee, but they were defeated by the Confederate soldiers at Natural Bridge. John B. Fletcher was very proud of their victory and was most anxious to erect a monument for this important event. With persistence and help from his loved ones, his wish came true.

The first monument was built at the site with the help of John's friends and family. They rode from Tallahassee to the Natural Bridge in a Model T. Those involved included a brick mason, and Norton Fletcher, a nephew from Greensboro, and others. The monument of brick and stucco was erected in 1919. Various marble slabs set-ins were inserted that honored individuals and units.

The Florida Board of Parks and Historic Monuments tore down the original marker built by "Uncle Johnny's" loved ones and built the one standing today. The marble slabs from the original have been incorporated into the present one and "Uncle Johnny" was recognized for his efforts. Two of these inserts read, respectively:

This stone is presented by J.B. Fletcher and comrades in memory of Col. J. J. Daniels Regiment of 1st Fla. Reserves and Col. Geo. W. Scott 5th Fla. Battalion of X Cavalry, who was in this battle. Mar. 6, 1865 J.B. Fletcher And This monument erected by J.B. Fletcher of River Junction, Fla. Sept. 9, 1918 in memory of the Battle of Natural Bridge, March 6, 1865, Gen. Wm. Miller in Command,

I have been to the monument several times and have been impressed with the present monument and the additional set-ins that have been added, including one from our own Anna Jackson Chapter, U.D.C., of Tallahassee, Florida: "Anna Jackson Chapter, U,D.C. places this tablet in grateful memory of Col. George W. Scott and his gallant men"

Written by: Sandra Fletcher Genetin, Anna Jackson Chapter, U.D.C. Submitted by: Helene Genetin-Falkinburg (daughter), 869 Stone Road, Bradenton Florida

Lois Fletcher, Our Eternal Sweetheart

My mother, Lois Maxine Lyman Fletcher, was born 8 May 1911 at "The Columns" in Jacksonville, Florida where her parents. Louis Atwater Lyman and Pearl LaVerne Mitchell were living. Mother's family moved to Melbourne, Florida in 1917 where Lois grew up. She also had two sisters, both younger. Mother would rather be outside or playing basketball than doing the "ladylike" things such as cooking, entertaining, things like that. Pearl was however, able to instill in Mother the social graces that stood her in good stead later in her life. Mother (Lois) became a great cook, enjoyed entertaining and keeping a spotless home.

Mother graduated from Florida Slate College for Women in Tallahassee Florida in 1933 with a degree in Sociology (Social Work). She was in one of the first classes that had an internship program for Social Workers. She said that a number of her cases were in the "Smokey Hollow" area of Tallahassee. After an article in the Tallahassee Democrat told what was left of that area, I took her to sec it. It is much smaller than it was when she visited clients. Mother

Ward Thomas Fletcher in 1936

would be glad to know that it is now on the National Register of Historic Places.

When Mother was a senior in 1932 her father died and she earned scholarship money as a "dining room girl" to be able to stay in school her last year. Each server had two tables, ten people to a table, and they were served in a very formal manner. She said, "The trays were huge!" While at FSCW she met Ward T. Fletcher, a Leon High School teacher, on a blind date. They were married 30 March 1934 in Melbourne Florida. Mother had to return to Jacksonville Florida to work as a Social Worker for Duval County for the rest of the year before they could " set up housekeeping" in Tallahassee. While living in Tallahassee two girls, Maxine and I and one boy, Lyman, were born.

Since my father graduated from the University of Florida and had received his

Lois Maxine Lyman in 1933

Master's in education from Duke University, he was called into the army in 1942. We spent five years at West Point, USMA, where he taught the "goats", who were plebes (first year cadets) who needed extra help with math. Those were very enjoyable years. While at West Point, my youngest brother, David, was born.

After returning to Tallahassee in 1947, my father taught math and was the assistant principal at the FSU University School, then called the "Demonstration School." During the summers of 1948 and 1949 and the school year of 1949/1950, my father worked on his Doctors Degree at Columbia University, Teachers' College in New York City.

Lois typed the first draft of my father's Master's thesis and his Doctoral dissertation. She typed his dissertation the year of 1949/1950 at Columbia while also taking care of her four children ranging from fifteen years old to four. Maxine and I helped her take care of Lyman and a very active David. After returning to Tallahassee, Daddy taught students in the Education Department at Florida State University, as well as working in the department's Test Service Bureau. On 10 August 1952 Daddy died of coronary thrombosis, and Mother never remarried. Lois worked as a Social Worker in Leon County and the surrounding counties for the first year after Ward's death. Because of the age of my two brothers she decided that she needed a different job with shorter hours.

With the help of some of my parents' friends from FSU she got a job in what evolved into the Financial Aid Office of FSU. She worked there for over twenty three years and was assistant director when she retired 6 July 1977. While in this position she helped a lot of students with loans, getting jobs, budgets, and even sometimes giving money out of her own pocket. She also let some of them live at our house after Maxine and I left home. A number of these were Sigma Chi "brothers" of Lyman, and David. Our home was lovingly referred to as "The Fletcher Hotel."

This brings us to why she was the Eternal Sweetheart of Sigma Chi. Both of my brothers, Lyman and David, were Sigma Chis. In 1966, David's senior year their housemother had to leave, and Mother was asked to fill in for her. Mother had ridden on the instrument bus for the Leon High School Band when both of my brothers were in high school, so she was no stranger to chaperoning. At that time fraternities had to have housemothers and Mother agreed to do it. Mother, or "Mom" Fletcher, as the brothers called her, stayed for about twenty five years. In 1981 she was awarded the National Housemother of the Year. They called her "Our Eternal Sweetheart" and The Little Sisters (who acted as hostesses for the brother) called her "The Sweetest of all Sweethearts." One of the several plaques they gave her is a good example of how every Sigma Chi whose life she touched felt about her.

"Our Eternal Sweetheart"
With open hands and warm heart, she stands Our Mom Fletcher
Forever grateful, we proclaim this day to be hers with all our love
Epsilon Zeta Chapter of Sigma Chi Spring, 1977

There were several stories Mother used to tell us, with laughter, about her years as a housemother. One of them was about one of the breakfasts she was to prepare for the pledges the week before their initiation ceremony. Someone was supposed to leave the door to the kitchen unlocked but didn't. The pledges were waiting fur their breakfasts to be served and saw Mother crawling along the roof to a window to get into the kitchen. With surprise, they helped her in and soon had their breakfasts. She also prepared a dinner for them at her home the Sunday before "silent week" before their initiation. There were frequently twenty men present.

In 1998 the Sigma Chi's who were in school during her years endowed a scholarship for the needy Sigma Chi's in her name. That same year She was also awarded the FSCW Emeritus Commitment to Excellence Award. Mother was active in her church, the Trinity United Methodist Church, as a communion steward and a member of the United Methodist Women division; she was also a member of the Woman's Club, the Garden Club, the Social Work Association, and an organization dear to her heart, the Daughters of the American Revolution. She joined the DAR in Melbourne, Florida in 1949. She transferred to the Caroline Brevard chapter in Tallahassee, and was one of the founding members of the Fort San Luis Chapter in Tallahassee, where she served as Regent twice. She was very proud that three generations of her family were members of our chapter: Lois, Sandra (me) and my daughter, Helene Genetin Falkinburg.

Mother had always wanted to live until 2000, and she got her wish. She passed away 3 April 2000. In keeping with their feelings for Mother, twenty Sigma Chi's sang "The Sweetheart of Sigma Chi" to her at her funeral on 7 April 2000. She was a wonderful person and met every challenge life threw at her and conquered each one. She loved doing things for people, especially those in need.

Written and submitted by: Sandra Fletcher-Genetin, 2027 Shady Oaks Drive, Tallahassee, Florida 32303

Ward Thomas Fletcher

My father, Ward Thomas Fletcher, was born in Greensboro, Gadsden County, Florida July 1, 1907 to Roy Daniel Fletcher and Ettie Gertrude Van Landingham. They actually lived in Juniper, a nearby community. Roy was a farmer and Ettie was a homemaker as well as the postmistress of the Juniper post office.

Ward went to school at Greensboro Elementary and graduated from Greensboro High School in 1925. He received his BS from the University of Florida, Gainesville, Florida in 1929 and his Masters in Education from Duke University, Durham, North Carolina, on June 6, 1939. He received his Ed.D from Columbia University School of Education, New York City, New York in 1950.

After graduating from the University of Florida Ward taught at Leon High School, Tallahassee, Leon County, Florida, I believe from 1929 until the early 1930s and then transferred to Florida High which was part of the Florida State College for Women Demonstration School (where teachers learned how to teach). Florida High is also located in Tallahassee, Florida. I believe that he taught Math and Science at both Leon High School and Florida High.

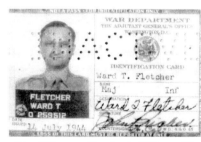
Ward Thomas Fletcher's Military-ID, 1941 at West Point, USMA. New York

Ward met Lois Maxine Lyman, a senior at Florida State College for Women, on a blind date and they were married March 31, 1933. They had four children, Carol Maxine (called Maxine) was born December 6, 1934; Sandra Mitchell was born February 18, 1937; Lyman Thomas was born May 17, 1941 and David Roy was born June 7, 1944. All but David were born in Tallahassee, Florida and David was born at West Point (United States Military Academy), New York.

Ward had taken ROTC while at the University of Florida and therefore was a 1st Lieutenant in the Inactive Reserves in 1939. When World War II was declared, he was commissioned as a 1st Lieutenant, Infantry May 5, 1941.

Ward spent his first year of enlistment at FORT McPherson, Georgia (near Atlanta). Then he was sent to West Point, the military academy, to teach math to the "Goats", the plebes or 1st year cadets that were behind in math. His enlistment lasted from 1942 to 1946.

He was asked to stay in the Army and continue to teach at West Point but he and my mother wished to return to Tallahassee, Florida. My father also wanted to finish his doctorate in education at Columbia University in New York City. From 1946 to 1949 he taught math and was the assistant principal at the University School (1st grade to 12th grades) at FSCW, which became Florida State University during that time.

During the summers of 1947 and 1948 he attended school at Columbia (attending short courses at a college at Plymouth, New Hampshire one summer and Michigan State at Lansing, Michigan the next). The summer of 1949 through the summer of 1950 he stayed in New York City for his residency at Columbia University. He was awarded his Education Doctorate the summer of 1950 and successfully defended it in 1951.

After receiving his Ed.D Ward started teaching at FSU in the School of Education, teaching teachers how to teach math and science. He also worked in the Test Service Bureau at this time. They used punch cards and a large mainframe computer to grade FSU student tests.

Ward had had a coronary thrombosis (heart attack) during maneuvers (military activities in the field) one summer while at West Point and a second August 10, 1952 which was fatal. He was 45 years old and had only used his Ed.D for two years. His death left a hole. My mother was left with four children ages 6 to 17 years old. He was a faithful husband and father and a good teacher. He belonged to the Theta Chi Fraternity, was active in the Tallahassee Kiwanis Club and his church, Trinity United Methodist.

Written and submitted by: Sandra Fletcher Genetin, 2027 Shady Oaks Drive, Tallahassee, FL 32303
sfgenetin@embarqmail.com

Fletcher Travel Memories

These were trips I took with my family as a child. They occurred mostly during WWII between 1943 and 1946 or 1947. The first trips I remember were trips we took on trains from New York City to Florida, mostly to Melbourne. My father, Ward Thomas Fletcher, was stationed at West Point, the U.S. Military Academy, as a

Fletchers 1940s (l-r) Sandra, Lyman, Lois, David, Ward, and Maxine

teacher and was unable to go with us. Most of the trips were with my mother, Lois Lyman, my older sister, Carol Maxine and my two younger brothers, Lyman Thomas and David Roy Fletcher.

While in Melbourne we took trips to the beach on the Atlantic Ocean. I remember air force guys coming to that beach from Patrick Army Air Base to go surfing. They used large pillow cases or duffel bags that they closed and filled with air. They used these to ride the waves into the shore.

One summer we went by train from Melbourne to Miami to visit one of Mother's college roommates. The train was a coal burning train and the coal cinders would fly inside the open windows since there was no air conditioning. We all got very dirty from the cinders. This was during WW II and there were a number of soldiers going to Miami by train. The train was crowded and my youngest brother, probably a baby, rode on the lap of one of the soldiers.

We took one trip with both of our parents that we spent the night at a motor court along the shore of Lake Erie. The water along the shore was very smelly because of rotting vegetation. Actually, it was terrible. The rooms didn't have inside bathrooms so we had to go outside along a wood path to take showers, etc. I think that was the worst place we ever stayed. Most were nice.

One night we stayed in a Bed and Breakfast when we were going by car from West Point to Florida. The Bed and Breakfast was on the top of a hill and the rooms were on the second floor. Breakfast was served family style on the main floor. Sometimes it was hard to find a place to stay because there were six of us, my parents and four children, but this Bed and Breakfast was large enough for all of us.

The one trip I remember fondly is when we left New York City after my father had completed his Ed.D from Columbia University Teacher's Collage. It was July or Aug, 1951, and the car was parked going up the hill on 121st Street between Broadway and Amsterdam Avenue. The car was a 1941 or 1942 Chevrolet two door and they filled the trunk and the floor boards in front of the back seat. There was also a car top carrier that held some other suitcases.

We, my older sister, I and my second grade brother sat in the back with our legs resting over the things on the floor. My youngest brother sat in the front seat between our parents. All of our neighbors from the apartment building were wondering if the car would be able to make it up the hill. It did make it up the hill and all the way back to Tallahassee.

We had comic books and coloring books to keep us busy. These trips were the only times we could buy comic books. We also passed the time counting cows, horses and houses that only had the chimneys standing. We sang songs too. Before, during and after these trips, our "home base" was Tallahassee, Florida. During the early years in Tallahassee, FL three children were born to Lois Lyman and Ward Thomas Fletcher. My youngest brother was born while we were at West Point, USMA, NY.

Fletchers' Christmas 1972 (l-r) Lyman, Sandra, Maxine, Lois, and David

My mother gradu-ated from FSCW in 1933 and my father taught at Leon High School and the University School or Florida High, both in Tallahassee. He taught students how to teach in the Education Department at FSU after receiving his Education Doctorate. My mother also worked in the Financial Aid Office at FSU and was the "house mother" for the Sigma Chi fraternity of FSU.

Written and submitted by: Sandra Fletcher-Genetin, 2027 Shady Oaks Drive, Tallahassee, Florida 32303
sjfgenetin@embarqmaij.com

Dr. William P. Foster

Dr. William Patrick Foster was born August 25. 1919 in Kansas City, Kansas. He is the son of Dr. Foster and began his music career by learning to play the clarinet at age 12. While in high school his talent was recognized by appointment as a student director of his high school orchestra in Kansas City, Kansas and in 1936 he became the director of an all city band. He received his BA from the University of Kansas in 1941, his MA from Wayne State University in 1950, a Doctor of Education Degree at Columbia University in 1955, and the Honorary Doctor of Human Letters Degree in 1998 from Florida A&M University. Dr. Foster is also known as the "Maestro" who created the noted Florida A&M University "Marching 100". He served as the band's director from 1956 to his retirement in 1998. His innovations revolutionized marching band techniques and the perceptions of the collegiate band.

Dr. Foster is the first recipient of the United States Achievement Academy Hall of Fame Award and the Outstanding Educator Award presented by the School of Education Society of the University of Kansas Alumni Association.

Dr. William P. Foster

In 2003 Dr. William Patrick Foster, was inducted into the Hall of Fame and recognized as one of the world's most renowned band directors. From 1955 thru 2001 he was the creator and band director of the internationally acclaimed Florida A&M University (FAMU) "Marching 100" Band for over 40 years. His innovative approach to marching band entertainment resulted in his own unique style of band pageantry, which dazzled thousands and brought great recognition to the State of Florida. As an artist and an educator, Dr. Foster truly revolutionized marching band techniques and reshaped the perception of the art form.

Dr. Foster's FAMU "Marching 100" Band has entertained audiences from all over the world. In 1989, the band was the official representative of the United States at the French Bastille Day Parade in Paris. The band has also appeared in films, commercials, presidential inaugurations, magazine and newspaper articles, and has been featured in over thirty nationally televised programs. In 1985, the band received the prestigious John Philip Sousa Foundation's Sudler Trophy. Dr. Foster has written 18 articles for professional journals, 4 published marching band shows, and the textbook, Band Pageantry, considered "The Bible" for the marching bands in America. He is the composer of Marche Brillante, National Honors March, March Continental, and Centennial Celebration.

Others have recognized Dr. Foster's accomplishments in band direction and education. He is a member of the Hall of Fame for several organizations including the National Association for Distinguished Band Conductors, the Florida Music Educators Association and the Afro-American Hall of Fame, to name just a few. In 1994, he was elected president of the American Bandmasters Association and in 1996, the United States Congress approved Dr. Foster's appointment by President Bill Clinton to serve on the National Council of the Arts. Since his retirement in 2001, Dr. Foster devotes most of his time to the William P. Foster Foundation and recently authored a new book, The Man behind the Baton.

Written and submitted by: Dr Foster's grandson, Anthony Foster, 1003 Tanner Drive, Tallahassee, FL. 32305

Carole Franco-Crist

First Lady Carole Crist grew up in Roslyn, New York, a suburb of New York City, as the youngest of five children. After graduating from Roslyn High School with honors in 1987, Carole attended Georgetown University in Washington, D.C., where she majored in accounting. In 1991 she earned a bachelor's degree in business administration, along with the high academic honor of magna cum laude. As a result of her education in accounting, coupled with a strong interest in the financial markets, Carole was recruited to work as an auditor in New York City's financial district. She later obtained her real estate brokerage license in New York and joined The Corcoran Group, one of the city's top firms.

First Lady Carole Franco-Crist with Gov. Charlie Crist and his official portrait

Carole later joined Franco American Novelty Company LLC, a wholesale distributor specializing in designing and manufacturing Halloween costumes and accessories. Founded by her grandfather Sam Oumano in 1910, Franco is the oldest American Halloween company and distributes products all over the world. After her grandfather's death in 1977, her father Bob Franco became the company's president. Upon his retirement, he recognized Carole's strong business acumen and integrity, Bob decided to entrust Carole with the management of the day-to-day operations of the Franco Empire.

Carole's drive and determination resulted in record sales and profits for the company, and she went on to become president of the company in 2000 after her father's death. Though Michele Oumano, Carole's sister and vice-president, has taken over the management of Franco, Carole continues to work as a consultant for the company. First Lady Crist's community service includes support for charities that enrich the lives of children. She supports the March of Dimes, which is dedicated to ensuring the health of babies by preventing birth defects, premature birth and infant mortality. Another organization she has assisted is the Make-A-Wish Foundation, which enriches the lives of children with life-threatening medical conditions through its wish-granting work. The First Lady also supports "ARTrageous," an art auction which benefits foster children in New York City through the Edwin Gould Services for Children and Families

In 2006, Carole moved to Florida with her two daughters. She became First Lady of Florida on December 12, 2008, when she married Florida Governor Charlie Crist in his hometown of St. Petersburg, Florida. As Florida's First Lady, Carole will focus on the state's most critical issues, as well as continuing her philanthropic work.

Written and submitted by: Carole Franco-Crist, Governor's Mansion, 400 N. Adams, Tallahassee, Florida 32302

Betty-Jane Tappan Free

In late September of 1949, my parents and I drove into Tallahassee where I was enrolled at FSU, planning a major in Medical Technology. That began several years of memories - dorms with House Mothers who kept track of us, sometimes more strictly than our own parents might have. "Sign out" cards were regularly checked to make sure that all of "their girls" were abiding by the rules that were drilled into us during freshman orientation.

Many of us made contacts with local churches and I chose the First Christian Church on the corner of W. Park Ave and Bronough (now the site of a US Post Office). Our college-age group activities included "dine-a-mite," held every Sunday evening. Aside from a good fellowship, many of us learned how to cook for a group, a good experience for me up to the present. One of the ladies in the church also invited us into her home a couple of times a year and I remember that we all were enthralled to be in a "real home" with thick carpets and beautiful decor. The dorm "parlors" were nice but our rooms were rather bleak!

My future husband, DeWayne, came to FSU as a Junior September 1951. We were introduced by a mutual friend during the Spring semester of 1952. When DeWayne came to call for me for our first date, he had one arm in a sling and had sprained both wrists - a result of a trapeze accident with FSU's Flying High Circus. Actually he was one of the riggers and had gone on the trapeze on a dare!! Although we dated that spring, we both left FSU that June. He graduated and I went to Atlanta for my senior year to intern, coming back in August 1953 to graduate.

Eventually, DeWayne and I started dating again and married in March 1956, five years after our first date at FSU! The first five years of our marriage took us to several other towns around Florida but in the fall of 1960 we eventually got the opportunity to return to Tallahassee and we were happy to be back! Although DeWayne died in the fall of 1987 as a result of an accident on the "Shrine Train," I have lived in the same house that we bought in 1960. Our neighborhood was in Leon County, then was "taken in" by Tallahassee and has seen a whole generation of children grow up and many of them are moving back and bringing up their children in the same neighborhood. Grandchildren come back also.

Many changes have taken place in Tallahassee in the past 48 years, and it is "fun" to talk with others and remembering many of the old landmarks. Do you remember when Penney's was where the "new" Federal Courthouse now stands? - when the Floridian Hotel was across Monroe Street from St. John's Episcopal? - the first football game in Doak Campbell Stadium? Think back and see what you can remember about a VERY special town.

Submitted by Betty-Jane Tappan Free (April 2009), 113 Tryon Drive, Tallahassee, FL. 32312

Kathleen (Kitty) W. and Walter (Walt) C. Funderburk, Jr.

Kitty was born in 1926 to Carl and Wilma Wagner in Miami, FL. She was educated at Redland School, which was, at that time, the largest consolidated Grade 1-12 public school in the nation.

Kitty and Walter Funderburk

She graduated with a BS Degree in Home Economics and Music/Band/Orchestra from Florida State University after attending the University of Miami for one year. Her MS Degree was in Home Economics from FSU.

Walter was born in 1921 in McIntyre, FL, the "suburbs" of Carrabelle, Florida, to Walter and Betty Funderburk. Walt's father was involved in businesses concerning rail traffic, commercial and recreational fishing, planing and sawmilling. His mother was Postmistress for McIntyre. Walter and his family moved to Tallahassee in 1934. He went to grammar school in Carrabelle and graduated from Leon High School in 1939.

Kitty came to Tallahassee in 1945 to get her BS degree. Walt and Kitty met in front of Westcott at FSU in 1946. He was a Navy Lieutenant JG in his dress whites. He dropped Kitty and a friend off at Trinity Methodist Church. They began dating and were married in 1948.

In 1946, men were enrolled at FSCW. In 1947 it became FSCW-FSU. In 1948 it officially became Florida State University.

Kitty was in the first graduating class of FSU in 1948 and played in the Marching Chiefs, which had just been organized since football was just beginning, too.

One interesting thing about Kitty's graduation/wedding day: She had graduation practice in the morning; married at Trinity Methodist Church that afternoon; graduation ceremony that night and went to a job interview in Jacksonville, FL the next day! Whew!!

Walt graduated from Emory University in 1943 and worked as a chemist for Owen Illinois Glass Company in Jacksonville, FL and for Florida Agriculture and Consumer Services in Tallahassee. He is also an Alumnus of FSU.

Kitty worked for 10 years as a Home Economics and Science teacher in Jacksonville, FL.

The Funderburks have 3 children all born at Riverside Hospital in Jacksonville, FL: Paul Edward, Carol Jane, and Nancy Gail.

After moving back to Tallahassee in 1966, Kitty worked 26 years as Director of Curriculum for Home Economics for the State of Florida in the Department of Education. She developed curriculum for the nation through Congress to require Home Economics in schools. Kitty was instrumental in establishing the Family Institute at Florida State University. She worked in developing a Life Management Skills course and co-authored "Teen Guide to Homemaking" which was a best selling textbook.

Kitty has a large number of educators in her family. Her father was principal of Redland School, Miami Beach Senior High School, and director of Curriculum and Research for Dade County Schools. There are about 10-12 members of her family that are teachers, in several counties and over a span of at least three generations, which includes two daughters.

Written by: Mary J. Marchant, 2901 Springfield Drive, Tallahassee, FL 32309-3274; Submitted by: Walter and Kitty Funderburk, 4314 Jacksonview Drive, Tallahassee, FL 32303

Shadrack Gardner Legacy

During the mid 1800s Leon County began showing a marked decrease in successful farming due to African-Americans' move to the north for better job opportunities and the introduction of the industrial revolution. The drift away from farming plantations became more and more plentiful until all who remained in farming did so only on a parttime basis or as a hobby. The departure of an estimated 2500 Blacks from Leon County during the years 1890 through 1892 led the local newspaper, the Tallahassee Weekly Floridian, to call it "An alarming decrease in the only real farming population of the county." The Blacks who remained in Agriculture owned their own land and Shadrack Gardner was one of those people.

Shadrack Gardner (-1890)

Shadrack Gardner's parents were Christine (1825-1877) and Allen Gardner (1817-1887) and they were both born in Virginia. It is not known if Allen was born free or obtained his freedom by purchasing it, but he taught his sons the fine art of running a successful business. One of their sons, Shadrack is originally believed to be from Metcalf, Georgia. During the late 1800s, Shadrack (Shack) Gardner (1853-1925) and his bride, Rose Ferrell (1861-1941) migrated to Tallahassee to seek their fortune and rear their family. Shack and Rose Gardner reared six (6) children: Betty Elizabeth Gardner-Meeks, Rosetta Gardner-Crump, Garfield, Cornelius, James and Ellis Gardner. Rosa and Shack lived the rest of their life off Highway 90 East, which is now known as Miles Johnson Road.

Brothers Mack and Shack Gardner became farmers and both operated their own store. Shack Gardner's store was located off Jacksonville Highway, and it was a profitable enterprise in a time when supplies were

Rosa Ferrell (-1890)

furnished on credit. Papa Shack's store was a prominent two level building, the upstairs level sold weaved baskets, horse collars, tubs, buckets and outdoor equipment, while the downstairs level sold dry goods, meats, bolts of fabrics, shoes, thread, and tobacco products; for safety reasons kerosene was sold outside. The store was located exactly off Chaires Crossroad and Highway 90 (Jacksonville Highway) with electricity powered by a power house pump. Papa Shack was one of the few residents to have electricity, so a large part of the community would hang around the store to socialize and hear the news from his electric radio.

Shack Gardner made his first recorded land purchase in 1896, paying seven hundred dollars for one hundred acres at the intersection of Jacksonville Highway and Chaires Crossroad. Later he added eighty acres of the old Barrow Hill Plantation to his holdings in 1901 by paying eight hundred dollars to the owner, John S. Winthrop. In 1904 he purchased another eighty acres from Mr. Winthrop for one thousand dollars. Shack Gardner extended his holdings north and south of his acreage in subsequent years, by paying two thousand dollars for eighty acres, formerly owned by the Chaires family. The Gardner's family holdings were later divided among his surviving children following his death after World War One.

In addition to being proprietor of his own grocery store, and owning a large tract of farmland, Papa Shack remained involved in community affairs during his entire life. He contributed labor and funds toward the construction and maintenance of (community churches, schools and houses. Papa Shack owned Black Dodge truck that he used for deliveries; the truck was also used to transport children to and from school on rainy days. He sometimes used the truck to transport people to State functions throughout the county and community. The truck was equipped with two rows of seats in the back and one high back seat in the front.

Papa Shack continued to farm with the assistance of sharecroppers who produced cotton, corn, fruit trees, and pecan groves. Some of the crops were sold or exchanged in the store or with other farmers. Papa Shack passed away in 1925, and in the spring of 1941, Mama Rose passed away.

Papa Shack and his lifelong mate Rose Ferrell Gardner's resting place after death was on Hwy 90-East, parallel to the road leading to the Union Brand Church off Wadesboro Front Rd. The construction of homes at that site forced the family to move the cemetery to Chaires Crossroad and it became known as Barrow Hill Cemetery, which is located behind Shady Grove Church. It is kept up by church members. Presently many of the Gardner's descendants are buried there, and constants remembrances are evident by the frequent display of plants and flowers on the graves. After their deaths their land holdings and other possessions from their home and store were passed down to their descendants. A Winchester rifle once belonging to Papa Shack was passed on to his son, Cornelius Gardner, Senior. Mama Betty Meeks inherited Mama Shack's dining room suite, love seat and Papa Shack's roll-top desk. Other items originally belonging to his daughter, Mama Betty were passed down to her daughter, Betty Meeks-Roberts. The ledgers from Papa Shack's merchant store with documented sales dating back to 1918 and 1920 and the antique roll-top desk with claw legs was inherited by his granddaughter, Vivian Williams. The antique desk and a portrait of Papa Shack are now in the possession of his great granddaughter, Dorothy Mitchell-Johnson, who still lives on the family's property.

Some of Papa Shack's land holdings as of 1993 remain in the ownership of the Gardner descendants, which includes small tracts of farming land located on both sides of Chaires Crossroad and Mahan Drive (Highway 90 East). This is evident by the yearly growth of corn, okra, greens, and fruit trees. Cattle grazing is still present under the watchful eye of Cornelius Gardner Junior. Houses of descendants of Papa Shack continue to sprout up on the land. Hopefully, our family ties will increase with the influx of new family members back to their ancestral homestead area of Barrow Hill.

Special thanks goes out to Aunt Ruth Meeks, Aunt Lee Etta Meeks, cousin Vivian Williams, and cousin Olivia Meeks and to my mother, Everlene Meeks-Mitchell, who taught me that when life gives me what appears to be an impossible task, remind myself of my great grandfather, Papa Shack, and the fact that the same blood flows through my veins.

Sources: (Pioneer Family) - Federal Census, 1880- Leon County- Gardner; Written and submitted by: Great-granddaughter of "Papa" Shack Gardner, Dorothy L. Mitchell-Johnson, 2386 Chaires Crossroads, Tallahassee, Florida 32317

Tallahassee History of The Gatlins
The Gatlin family is a very large family, as well as a pioneer family of Gadsden County and Leon County.

Richard R. Gatlin, Sr., (1812, North Carolina-1898) joined the 42nd Regiment, 11th Brigade, Alabama Volunteers at Ervington (Eufaula), Alabama, and was discharged under the command of Captain McInnis as a 2nd Lieutenant (1836) after fighting in the Creek Indian War.

He married Motildia (sic) Hicks and lived in Alabama where they begat Thomas (1843-1863), William B. (1844- c.1903), and Richard R., Jr., (1845-1869), after which Motildia (sic) died. Richard then married Rachel Delila Rudd (1826, South Carolina), daughter of Elias David Rudd.

Richard and Rachel had numerous children: Elizabeth m. "Lizzie" (1846, Alabama-1930) – married William R. Hagood; Francis M. "Fannie" (1847, Georgia-1928) – married Thomas Joshua Drake. Their son, Thomas Walter Drake (1888-1977), married Cora A. Stoutamire and lived in Leon County; Elias T. (1849, Gadsden County – 1925) – married Julia I. Drake; Zelphia A. (c.1850) – married A.C. Pickett; Luguinney (c. 1851); Wright T. (1854-1930) – married Lucinda "Lou" Hopkins (1869-1944), daughter of Green Berry Hopkins (1869-1944); Marrell (1855 - married Annie Sykes; Manor Andrew (1858-1906) - married Mary Margaret Houck. Their son is Ira Lee Gatlin. Jackey M. (1863-1949) - married William H. Hopkins, son of Green Berry Hopkins and brother of Lou Hopkins Gatlin; and Joshua J. (1864-1945) married Emma Owens, parents of Cecil Gatlin.

Wright T. and Lou Hopkins also had numerous children: Berta Estelle (1888-1974) – married Allie Stoutamire; Barney Oliver (1890-1956) – married Florence Eliza Allen; Daisy Ethel (1892-1983) – married Daniel "Stout" Stoutamire; Berry Ira (1894-1963) – married Elsie Stoutamire; Fredy Wright (August 9, 1896 - October 2, 1896); Pearl Leona (1898-1973); Myrtle Elsie (1900-1985) – married William Jenning Revells; William Lamar (1902- 1992) – married Nettie Murl Ogbourn; Alma Eunice (1904- 1979) – married Talmadge Lee Sellers; and Thelma Eva :Dolly" (1906) married Omar L. Allen.

Berry Ira Gatlin (1894-1963) is the son of Wright T. and Lou Hopkins Gatlin. He married Elsie Stoutamire (1905) March 3, 1925, at the home of the Frank Stoutamires on South Bronough Street where the R.A. Gray Building stands.

Berry and Elsie lived in town and opened a gas station and grocery store on the northeast corner of Monroe Street and 5th Avenue. They lived near the Eppes, Moodys, Cores, and Drakes. The road was dirt and Bronough Street ended at 4h Avenue. Between their home and Havana, and their home and 4h Avenue, was solid woodlands.

Their second son Berry Kenneth (1934) attended Sealey School, which had been built on 7th Avenue (where the police station now stands). He has a brother, Willard Earl Gatlin (10/8/1936) who first married Margie Anna Langston and then Lisa Nolte McAlister. His first brother Berry Ellis (June 19, 1932) died at one day old. Kenneth is retired and living in Bloxham with his wife, Joan Hawley Halford.

When the wife of Charles A. McPherson, Sr., became ill, he depended on the Gatlins to raise his and Annah Leone Sauls McPherson's children, Elmer Renaldo, Charles A. Jr., and Mildred Lorraine. They grew up with the Gatlins at Bloxham.

The Gatlins were farmers, hunters and fishermen, truly living off the land at Bloxham and Lake Talquin. Some of them were teachers, particularly during early times. They had a strong sense of family, were tenacious workers with the best of work ethics, and kept their faith and sense of humor even in the worst of times.

Elmer and Charles lived in Tallahassee their whole adult lives. Mildred moved away. What they learned from the Gatlin family is priceless.

Sources: 20 Faces and Places, A History of the People of Highway 20 and the Ochlockonee River Area, tells the family history and stories about the families of the area; Written and submitted by: Dorothy Lee(Dotty) McPherson 24236 Lanaier St.Tallahassee, FL 32310

George Edward Gerrell
George Edward Gerrell, born 1833, and his wife, Margaret Morris, born 1834, came to Wakulla County, Florida in late 1850 or early 1851 from the Lumberton, North Carolina area. There are a lot of Gerrells now living in the Whitesville and Tabor City areas. Traveling with George Edward and Margaret were her parents, John O. Morris and his wife Sarah, and their family. Wilmer Gerrell, a descendant, said that they traveled by ox-cart to their new home.

George and Margaret settled first on the west side of the St. Marks River, a few miles north of the town of Magnolia. Pete Gerrell remembers this as being called "The Old Gerrell Place." George Edward was a cooper (barrel maker) by trade. Needing a good supply of white oak from which to make barrels, he bought land on which there were many white oak trees. George Edward would have farmed to provide food for his family and to barter for other necessities. Since his home was so close to the St. Marks River, they would have had fish for dinner often. Might this be the reason that so many Gerrells are now so avid about fishing? Maybe it is in the blood.

The young couple had seven children, Alice, Ellen, Walter, William Oliver, Martha, John, and George Allen

In the Spring of 1861, the War Between The States began. George Edward, already a family man with several children, enlisted April 21, 1862, in Cap't Gamble's Company, Leon Light Artillery, Florida Volunteers, for the duration of the War. He enlisted at Camp Leon, south of Tallahassee. Military records describe George Edward as having dark hair and complexion, with blue eyes. Great-great grandson, Allen R. Gerrell, Jr., states that George Edward would have been a front gunner on the cannon because of his height.

Margaret Morris Gerrell 1833-1878

In 1863, Gamble's Artillery was divided and the Kilcrease Artillery was formed. George Edward was assigned to Kilcrease, which went on to fight in Florida, Georgia, and South Carolina. By 1864, the troops were not well-supplied with clothing. Many had no shoes and had to march barefoot. However, they must have been eating well enough. A report said "No complaint is made against rations."

In the spring of 1864, George Edward was "sick in hospital at Tallahassee, Florida." He had received a wound to his left breast and about that time had contracted tuberculosis.

The story has been handed down in the Gerrell family about how he was ill at his home near Natural Bridge. Arising from his sick bed, he joined the Kilcrease Artillery at New Port and marched seven miles north to fight in the Battle of Natural Bridge. Because of that battle, Tallahassee was the only Confederate capitol not captured by Union Troops. George Edward's name appeared on a List of POWs surrendered 10 May 1865 and he was paroled at Tallahassee along with many of his comrades.

George Edward Gerrell 1834-1878

After the War, the Gerrell family moved north into Leon County on the Old Plank Road.

In 1878, George Edward died, Margaret following him in death on Chrismas Eve, 1897. They were buried in the Morris/Gerrell Cemetery on their own land. The cemetery has been well-maintained over the years by Gerrell family members.

One of the sons, George Allen Gerrell, and his wife, Minnie Lee Wiggins, homesteaded three miles west of Natural Bridge in 1900. This couple had seven children, Ira, Everitt, James Castello, Walter, Maggie, Allie, and Isabelle. Walter and Jessie French Gerrell's children were raised on the homestead. They are Marilee Gerrell Butler (Ermon Butler), Allen Roston Sr. "Pete" (Terri Hamer), Walter Dale (Devota McCranie), and James Lawson (Jadon Grantham).

There are many Gerrell descendants from the emigrant couple, George Edward and Margaret Gerrell. An annual Gerrell/Wiggins Reunion is held at Natural Bridge in October.

Sources: Research by Pete Gerrell and Marilee Gerrell Butler; Memories of Marilee, Pete, Dale, and Lawson Gerrell; Statement by Wilmer Gerrell; Military Records; Grave Stones; and Census Records; Written and submitted by: Marilee Gerrell Butler, P O Box 95, Calvary, GA 39829

Nell Lehrman and Louis Gibbs

Nell Lehrman was born in Homestead, FL in 1914, the oldest of four children, to Max and Rose Lehrman. After migrating from Russia, Nell's grandfather moved to Ft. Lauderdale in 1916, where her father opened a department store.

When Nell was 12 years old, Ft. Lauderdale School awarded her a "Roll of Honor" Award for high academics and attendance. On the back was a note wishing her well and signed by a school officer.

In 1928 a hurricane wiped out her father's business. "There was no welfare. People helped each other," Nell said. She took business courses to help support her parents. She continued to send them money during the depression.

She was born into a family of merchants: grandfather, father, cousins, and husband. Lou's family owned a store in Live Oak. Lou was already in business when she met him.

Having had only three dates, Louis (Lou) and Nell got married in October, 1936 and moved to Tallahassee.

There were no apartments in Tallahassee in 1936. The "Wilsonian" was originally built as a grammar and high school in 1886. Mr. Wilson's son turned the building into 6 apartments, where they began their married life.

They had three sons: Harold, born 1940; Arnold, born 1942 and Benji, born 1948. Harold is in real estate and construction; Arnold is an environmental company executive in Orlando. Benji is deceased (1973). Their first child, a daughter, died in 1938.

The Gibbs' had stores in four locations:

Harold, Nell, Louis, Arnold Benji Gibbs

Early 30s; Lou owned The French Shop (for shoes) on the corner of Monroe and Jefferson Street. The 40s; stopped carrying shoes, moved to College Avenue, and focused on women's and bridal wear. The 50s; changed name to Gibbs French Shop and moved to the shopping hub on South Monroe Street. The fourth store was located in the Northwood Mall.

One reason for the success of the shop was the fact that Nell had a natural talent for design and color and "what looks good." Nell did the buying while Lou handled the finances.

Lou had a passion for real estate. He built one of the first suburban shopping centers - Capital Plaza. He built or owned other shopping centers in the area including Market Square on Timberlane Road.

After Nell retired as a retailer in 1976, she taught herself to do floral arrangements in watercolors. She transferred her zeal for design to LeMoyne where she ran a gift shop known as "Nell's Nook." LeMoyne threw a party for her 85th birthday in 1999 after devoting 35 years of service. She and Lou began traveling after their 25th wedding anniversary, first to California, then Canada, Japan, Europe, the Caribbean, Mexico and Israel. She travels with her sons and grandchildren to Santa Fe.

Nell's community contributions included: Twice President of Killearn Ladies Club and Killearn Antiques Club; Tallahassee Little Theatre; founding member-Temple Israel; Sunday School teacher for years.

Submitted by: Ginny High; Written by: Mary J. Marchant, 2901 Springfield Drive, Tallahassee, FL 32309-3274

Mack Gilchrist

Think about your early years, growing up, going to school, and about all of the school teachers and principals that touched your life in elementary, Junior High and High School, I know you remember a very special principal at your school, one who shaped and molded your ideas and attitudes, a person so special that you will always remember his or her name. We know a man like that, who is so special that Tallahassee named a school in his honor.

Mack Gilchrist was born in 1916 in Crenshaw County, Alabama, not far from where his wife Quinnie was born. They didn't meet for years, not until Mack came home on furlough from the Navy and went on a blind date with a friend and coworker of his sister in Andalusia. They were married in Longbeach, California in 1943. Mack recalls exactly how long he was in the Navy, four years, two months and twenty days. That was pretty much "for the duration" of World War Two. He saw heavy action in the South Pacific while attached to the First Marine Division, including four months in the thick of it on Guadalcanal.

At the end of the war he was ready to get out of the Navy and get on with his life. Quinnie had come back home to Alabama when Mack went overseas. Together once again, they moved to Tallahassee, where Mack worked for a while at the Sweet Shop, just off-campus near FSU. He then picked up his studies and enrolled at Florida State, earning BS and MS Degrees in Education.

That's when he discovered the joy of teaching, a love that would take him on a twenty-seven year odyssey through the Leon County School System, as a teacher and as a Principal. His assignments included Kate Sullivan, Cobb, Chaires and Timberlane schools. A career so distinguished that upon his retirement from Principal at his last assignment, Timberlane Elementary the school was renamed in his honor Gilchrist Elementary School.

Although he and Quinnie had no children of their own, Mack considers the thousands of students he taught, nurtured and mentored as his family. He was an extraordinary teacher!

He counts among his many blessings finding Quinnie, his wife of sixty-five years, the joy and serenity of being a Christian, and the comforting fellowship that he found at the church God led him to, First Baptist Church.

His darkest days came in the 1960's, with the mid-term upheaval and teacher walkout. He struggled to keep his school going and educational standards high with temporary teachers, unfamiliar with the simplest school procedures and routines.

From his perspective of ninety-three years of living, Mack looks back on the war years of 1941-1945 as a time of coming together of all Americans. Millions of young men and women were fighting for their country and their way of life all over the globe. More millions of people at home sacrificed to supply the tools and food to keep the war effort alive. This oneness of purpose and resolve brought victory to America, at home and abroad. There has not been such a coming together in unity of purpose before or since.

Written by: Carol Ann and Bill Boydston ©, 1639 TwinLakes Circle, Tallahassee, FL 32311; Submitted by: Mack Gilchrist

Quinnie Gilchrist

Big families were important in South Alabama in the early 1900s, that's how you kept a small farm running. That's how Quinnie Gilchrist came to be one of eleven children growing up in Brantley, Alabama.

Quinnie came to know Christ at an old time CampMeeting Revival. She was in her teens then. She attended several churches in the area, growing in her faith. While she was living and working in Andalusia, Quinnie put her belief in God into action and helped start a new church there.

It was on that small farm in Crenshaw County that Quinnie learned how to get along; you had to with ten brothers and sisters. She learned the strengths of life that helped her form a strong, sixty-five year marriage with her loving husband Mack.

Quinnie and Mack had grown up in the same county, attended the same schools, but never met. Quinnie had graduated from high school and gone to work in a sewing factory in Andalusia. Mack joined the Navy at the start of World War Two.

Mack came home to Alabama on furlough. He met and dated a friend of his sister. They fell in love and were married in 1943 in Longbeach, California. While Mack worked at the Navy Base Quinnie took a job with the Baskin Robbins Ice Cream Shop just across the street from where they lived.

When Mack was transferred to duty in the South Pacific Quinnie returned to Alabama and did what all Navy wives do, she waited for her man to come home. And he did.

But where would they go? Where would they live? They chose Tallahassee to start their life together again. Mack took up his studies at FSU and Quinnie took a business course at Lively and went to work in the Registrars Office with another fine Baptist, Charles Walker. She worked at FSU for seventeen years.

Quinnie counts her accomplishments as her joys; becoming a Christian, meeting and marrying Mack and sharing life with him for sixty-five years. Her deepest sorrows were the loss of her parents and her twin brother. Of the eleven children in her family three remain, she and her two sisters.

Why have they stayed all these years in Tallahassee? Quinnie says it's because they stayed "until it was too late to leave". They have sold their home of many years and are now comfortable in their new surroundings at Westminster Oaks.

Many viewed the Depression as a dark time in America, but Quinnie saw the changes that came during those days On a little farm in South Alabama she saw her first radio and her first electric light Sure her momma cooked on a wood burning stove, and the farm chores were demanding of a young girl. But she learned to give and take, to share in the warmth of a close-knit family. She saw that the Depression brought about a whole new life, where things got better and better.

Quinnie and Mack have been a part of First Baptist Church just about from the minute they set foot in Tallahassee in 1946. Words cannot express what this church has meant to her. She counts as her personal blessing all that this church and its loving congregation has done for her. Today, First Baptist has, as she says to all who will hear, the "best pastoral staff since she joined the church".

Written by Carol Ann and Bill Boydston ©, 1639 Twin Lakes Circle, Tallahassee, FL32311; Submitted by: Quinnie Gilchrist

Charles Goodwin - From Science Camp to the Courtroom

One afternoon in April of 1958 near the end of my junior year at Robert E. Lee High School in Jacksonville, I was leaving chemistry class when our teacher, nicknamed by some students as Dot, told me to stay briefly and asked if I would join a group of her selected students to attend two weeks of summer Science Camp at Florida State University in Tallahassee. Growing up in the "Gator fan" dominant environment of Jacksonville in the 1950s, I was not aware of FSU and many of us approaching our senior year talked about applying to the University of Florida or some university in North Carolina or Virginia.

My two weeks at FSU were interesting, with lectures and labs in various sciences and no studying or tests. We had free time to explore the campus, the Capitol complex and downtown Tallahassee where almost all retail stores, barber shops, movies, and many restaurants were located, as there were not any shopping malls here in 1958.

Finishing my senior year at Lee High included part-time jobs at Jacksonville radio stations WPDQ and WIVY and I considered majoring in broadcasting, which was offered at FSU. Many of my classmates also planned to attend FSU, and in September of 1959 on my 18th birthday, my father drove me to FSU in rainy weather and I got settled in at Magnolia Hall dormitory (since demolished) on the western perimeter of Landis Green. The rain continued for about 40 days.

A few weeks later in a large amphitheater style world history classroom I recognized Roberta, a young lady a few years my senior that I had known in Jacksonville through piano lessons, and she introduced me to a red haired girl wearing a white sorority pledge dress seated directly behind me who was a native of Tallahassee and lived at home. In 1959 freshmen

Warren Goodwin and the Austin Healy Sprite, Lake Jackson 1960

were required to live in supervised dormitories and were prohibited from having automobiles at FSU. However, freshmen from Tallahassee living at home were allowed to drive and all students with autos were encouraged to give rides to other students to town from the gates in front of Westcott or back to FSU. A few weeks later that first semester I got a haircut downtown at the Sanitary Barbershop and was walking along College Avenue at Duval Street hoping for a ride when that red haired girl drove up in her red Austin Healy Sprite convertible with the top down and gave me a ride back to campus.

In January of 1961 we were married at Trinity Methodist Church on Park Avenue at Duval Street and thirteen months later our son Darrell was born at Tallahassee Memorial Hospital when fathers were not allowed beyond the public waiting room by the front doors. While at FSU majoring in radio/TV broadcasting including courses in marketing, speech, and writing, I worked part time at WFSU-FM. WFSLI-TV, and then at WTNT radio owned by Frank Hazelton and Hurley Rudd, who later became Mayor of Tallahassee and then a state legislator for this area. My wife Judith also helped put me through FSU by working at Gibbs French Shop and at Tallahassee Federal Savings & Loan.

Upon graduation April of 1963 we moved to Jacksonville where I briefly sold radio advertising for WPDQ, and in October I was hired by Ford Motor Company in their management training program in the Jacksonville district office. Our daughter Jenna was born at St. Vincent's Hospital in April of 1964. 1 remained with Ford for seven years in various departments as a customer relations service representative assisting dealers in 46 counties across south Georgia, and then as a field zone sales manager in the Miami branch office of Ford responsible for sales to assigned dealerships from Vero Beach to Key West, through the Everglades, around Lake Okeechobee, and over to Fort Myers and Naples. Several years of up to four nights weekly away from home on the road helped me to decide to change careers, and I was accepted into the College of Law which had been established at Florida State University in 1968.

In September of 1970 we moved from the Fort Lauderdale area back to Tallahassee, where we have remained ever since. Upon graduation from law school in April of 1973, I was appointed by State Attorney Harry Morrison as an assistant state attorney prosecuting criminal cases in this six county circuit. Our major case during this period was Theodore Robert Bundy, a nationwide serial killer who in 1978 murdered two young women in the FSU Chi Omega sorority house and seriously injured several others. About eleven years later Ted Bundy was executed in the electric chair at Florida State Prison in Raiford.

After the 1980 election and the untimely heart attack death of Mr. Morrison in December of that year, Don Modesitt became the State Attorney for this circuit and I continued as a senior assistant during his four year term. In January of 1985 William "Willie" Meggs became the elected State Attorney and I remained as a chief assistant state attorney prosecuting criminal cases, serving as legal advisor to grand juries, assisting law enforcement officers in obtaining arrest or search warrants, and other assigned prosecutorial courtroom and office duties.

After four years at FSU for a Bachelor of Arts degree, seven years with Ford Motor Company, three years back at FSU for a Juris doctor degree, and thirty-two years as a State of Florida prosecutor for the second judicial circuit courts including Leon. Jefferson, Wakulla, Franklin, Gadsden, and Liberty counties, I retired in May of 2005.

My name is Charles Warren Goodwin and it was a life changing event when "Big Dot" had me wait after class and asked me to attend Science Camp at Florida State University in the summer of 1958.

Written and submitted by: Darrell Goodwin 5660 Bradfordville Road, Tallahassee FL 32309

Daniel Robert (Bob) Graham

Graham is the son of Ernest (Cap) Graham, a Florida State Senator, mining engineer and dairy cattleman, and Hilda Simmons, a school teacher. He is the youngest of four children; William, Philip, and Mary Graham-Crow. Bob Graham was born on November 9, 1936 in Dade County, Florida, where he grew up on his family's dairy and beef cattle farm. He attended public schools in Dade County, the University of Florida, where he graduated with honors in 1959, and Harvard Law School, receiving his LLB in 1962. Bob Graham married Adele Khoury Graham of Miami Shores in 1959 and is the father of four daughters; Gwen Graham-Logan, Cissy Graham-McCullough, Suzanne Graham-Gibson, and Kendall Graham-Elias. Currently Bob is the grandfather of 12 children as of 2007.

While working in the family business, which expanded to include the development of the New Town of Miami Lakes, Graham served 12 years in the Florida Legislature. In 1978 he was elected Governor of Florida and served two terms. In 1986 he was elected to the United Slates Senate, and he was re-elected in 1992 and 1998. As Governor, Graham served as chair of the Education Commission of the States and the Southern Regional Education Board. In 1985 he was recognized for his leadership in education by the Chief State School Officers. While in the Senate, he served on the Select Senate Committee of Intelligence from 1993 to 2003 and as its chairman in 2001 and 2002.

Bob Graham, ex-Governor, Senator, House Representative for Florida

Since 1974 Graham has taken "Workdays" in various occupations and profession, beginning as a high school civics teacher. In December 2004, he completed his 408th Workday. He credits his three decades of experiences laboring side-by-side with average Americans for his insights into the need for better education about the role of government. He will draw extensively from those experiences throughout the book.

Since 1977, Graham has carried a pocket-sized spiral notebook with him wherever he goes. In these notebooks, he records the details of daily life; a log of activities (distinctly not a diary): notes of telephone conversations; persons met and a summary of the discussion; notes on meetings attended and Workdays worked; and a list of things to do that day. Information from these will also be utilized as a primary source and for the refreshment of memory.

Graham has written two previous books, one about his Workdays (published in 1978) and Intelligence Matters (Random House. 2004), about his role investigating the tist attacks of September 1I. 2001. Bob chose to retire from public office in early 2005 and now concentrates his efforts on the newly established Bob Graham Center for Public Service at his undergraduate alma mater, The University of Florida. He has been a lifelong advocate of public education and preservation of the environment. After teaching at Harvard University for the 2005- 2006 academic year, Graham is now focused on founding two centers to train future political leaders at The University of Florida and The University of Miami. In 2006 Graham received an honorary doctorate in Public Service from the University of Florida. Currently Graham spends most of his time with his family and friends.

Written and submitted by: Robert Graham, 6843 Main Street, Miami Lakes, Florida 33152

Florida DuBignon Turner Granberry

It was the fall of 1964, my first year in college at Emory University, when I first met my wife-to-be Miriam Bryan Gillespie and her family. Miriam's mother, Charlotte Granberry Gillespie knew that I was born and raised in the north Florida town of Chattahoochee. This brought to the conversation at our original meeting Charlotte's statement "oh, my very dear grandmother Florida DuBignon was born in Tallahassee. Florida's parents were members of the Kindon family who settled in Tallahassee in the mid-1800's". At that time, and at subsequent mentions of this fact, it had little impact on my association with Tallahassee. Only after our moving to Tallahassee in July, 1978 and immersing ourselves in the Tallahassee community, was there a bonding of our lives with the birth place of my mother- in-law's grandmother Florida DuBignon. What brought Florida's grandparents, an immigrant family from Wales, to Tallahassee in the 1830's (see related article on Kindon)? The availability and the accessibility of local records stimulated the quest for more answers, and started my interest in genealogical research.

Florida's mother, Charlotte Maria Kindon was born December 28, 1848 inTallahassee, the daughter of William H. and Eliza Ann Kindon. Florida's father, William Turner DuBignon was born May 21, 1843 in Brunswick, Georgia, the son of Sarah Aust and Henri Charles DuBignon, heir of Jekyll Island. Research has not revealed the date of William's initial assignment to Tallahassee, but his military record stated that Sergeant DuBignon. a member of the 4th Regiment of the Georgia Cavalry, was paroled in Tallahassee on May 12, 1865. After being paroled, William returned to his native town of Brunswick Georgia, and Glynn County records state that he was elected as the county coroner in January 1866.

Emily, Rebecca and Margret McLarty, Westview Cemetery, Atlanta, 1993

Prior to the ending of the Civil War, it is unclear how much time William's regiment was in the Tallahassee vicinity so as to afford him the opportunity to establish a relationship with a local young lady. Leon County court records exhibit the April 5, 1866 certificate of marriage for Charlotte Maria Kindon and William Turner DuBignon. As taken from the Wm.T. DuBignon family Bible (in possession of the submitter), two children were born in Tallahassee. A son was born in1867, but died a year and a half later. The second child, a daughter, was born July 14. 1868 and given the name Florida. Records at Trinity United Methodist Church find William's sister Rosalia Elizabeth DuBignon a member from June 1867 to late July 1868. It is surmised that Rosa came from her finishing school studies in Jacksonville to assist her sister-in-law Charlotte through the births of the two Tallahassee children. Soon after Rosa's departure from Tallahassee, she was married in Jacksonville to Duncan Cameron Cook in November 1868.

The 1870, Georgia census (Glynn County) finds Florida's family of three away from Tallahassee and in Brunswick, Georgia. The family continued to live in William's native Glynn County, and the 1880 Georgia census gives elevenyear- old Florida with three younger siblings; but now the family name is Turner. Though it is not apparent why this took place, but through the Superior Court of Glynn County in the fall of 1875, Florida's father William Turner DuBignon changed his name to just William Turner. Subsequently, court records of the family, as well as entries into the family Bible, were of the last name Turner. Florida was born a DuBignon, but married under her acquired name

Florida DuBignon Turner Granberry and Robert Lee Granberry, Atlanta, GA c.1922. Granchild in arms-Shorter R. Granberry; foreground, Robert Monroe Bush, Jr; l-r Edwin R. Granberry, James R. Granberry and Charlotte H. Granberry.

Turner. Her marriage to Robert Lee Granberry (b. August 20. 1867) was in Brunswick at the McKendree Methodist Church on June 10. 1891. This was one of the first marriages performed in this newly organized church. His occupation at that time was with Hilton and Dodge Lumber Company of St. Simon's Mills, Georgia. Between January 1893 and August 1902 there were four children, three boys and one girl, born in Brunswick to Florida and Robert Lee Granberry. The family moved to Atlanta and can be first found in the 1907 City directory, listing Robert I., as a clerk for Southern Railroad. Their home was just southwest of the downtown area at 42 Windsor Street. The eldest child was my mother-in-law's father William Raymond Granberry who married Clara Edna Lynes of Atlanta, September 17. 1913, her twentieth birthday. At the time of her wedding to Raymond she was living with her parents at 240 Bass Street, only two blocks from the Granberry residence. In possession of the writer is a beautifully written letter dated August 17, 1913, from Raymond to his beloved father and mother (Florida) which tells of his love to them: but at the same time, sets the stage for the forthcoming giving of himself to his new wife Clara.

Charlotte Hazeltine Granberry Gillespie, now age 95, has always spoken fondly about her grandmother, Florida, whom she called "Mama", a dear, sweet person. Mama was a petite lady: a kind, genteel, educated, and loving grandmother.

Charlotte's memories of her grandmother began in childhood in the 1920s. Beginning in sixth grade, Charlotte attended North Avenue Presbyterian School (NAPS) on Ponce de Leon Avenue in Atlanta and her grandmother and grandfather lived in an apartment on Durant Street, just across Ponce de Leon. Charlotte spent many afternoons after school with her grandmother and grandfather as their children were grown and out of the home.

Charlotte could not say enough nice things about Mama. "She was a honey. She and I got along great! We would laugh and have the best time together talking about something. We would talk and talk and talk. It wasn't like we were grandmother and granddaughter; we were two people together enjoying each other's company. It is a special memory and it tells you that people don't have to be certain sizes or certain ability, as long as they are just together

Florida DuBignon Turner Granberry 1890, Brunswick, GA

and enjoy each other. It was very special to me and I think to my grandmother, too. I loved her dearly, and she knew it too." Her grandfather. Papa, was kind, yet quiet with little to say.

Although unable to remember about Mama's child-hood, Charlotte said Mama was "well trained to be a nice lady", could carry on a decent conversation, and used proper English. She was very particular in taking care of herself. She would get all dressed up, put on her hat and have something nice on her dress, such as a pin or flower. They looked different in their clothes than we look, because they were in a different period of wear. Mama was known to be petite. As a comparison of size, Charlotte commented that when she was in sixth or seventh grade, "Mama was about the same size that I was, but she looked different than I looked, because I was a child and she was a grandmother."

She could crochet easily. After World War II, Florida was living in Tampa with her son Robert Lee Granberry and his wife Martha. Florida crocheted a "slumber robe" in three shades of purple in a zigzag pattern. Her work was so beautiful that Martha encour-aged her to enter it into the 1947 Florida State Fair. She won the blue ribbon! The blanket and its blue ribbon are now in the possession of Florida's great-granddaughter. Jan Gillespie DeLong in Atlanta. GA.

Jan tells a story of when she was about four years old about 1950, "I can remember sitting in the dining room with Mama and her offering me a cup of hot tea. She was telling me that when my mother was a little girl that many days that is what they did after school. It was real important when you made tea that you pour the hot water over the leaves and you serve it in a very thin china cup. I remember her holding the cup up where you could almost see through it. She held it up before the tea was in it. She was trying to teach me that when you had tea, you drank it from a thin, china cup. I remember her being very frail, and she seemed tiny to me in her stature, but she had a real sweet smile. And that's what I remember."

Florida died Christmas Eve 1951, having suffered a massive aneurysm at the Atlanta home of her daughter Ruth Granberry Bush. Florida and Robert Lee (d. 12-14-1940) are buried at Westview Cemetery, Atlanta. There has been no mention in the family history of Florida ever returning to her native city of Tallahassee. Because of Florida's lineage here in Tallahassee, Florida Pioneer Certificates from the Florida Genealogical Society were awarded in November, 1993 to my mother-in-law Charlotte, my wife Miriam, and my three daughters Emily, Rebecca, and Margaret. The three daughters were the first of this ancestry to be born in Tallahassee in a hundred and fifteen years.

Written and submitted by: E. Lynn McLarty, 2102 Olivia Drive, Tallahassee, Florida 32308

The Grant Family

John "Jackie" and Rachel Grant moved to North Florida around 1840 along with several other families who had been members of the Bethel Baptist Church near Olanta, SC. These included the Revells, Roberts, Hodges and Langstons, many of whom were related to each other by marriage. John voted in the first statewide election held in Florida on May 26, 1845. The Grant family settled in Smith Creek, Wakulla Co., and were members of the Mt. Elon Baptist Church. John Grant had 510 acres and farmed 60 of these. Jackie and Rachel's son Pleasant G. Grant married Mary Elizabeth Revell in 1853. Their son John Pleasant "Pleas" was born in 1859. In about 1890, Pleas married Almyra "Myra" Roberts. Pleas and Myra had nine children. They were Andrew, Alcona, Roscoe, Grace, Alfonso "Fonse", Bill. Winnie, Marcia, and Paul. Andrew and Paul spent most of their lives in Tallahassee, as did many of their nieces, nephews, and cousins.

John Andrew Grant (1891-1967)

Andrew came to Tallahassee in 1911 at about age twenty. He worked for Cox Furniture Co. and fought in France during World War I. He began by carrying stretchers on the front lines. His abilities were spotted, and he was transferred to a clerk's job away from the worst danger. In the 1920's, Andrew established his own store, Grant Furniture Co., at the main intersection of town, College Avenue and Monroe Street. The address was 125 S. Monroe and the telephone number was 100. Tallahassee had dirt streets then and his cousin, racer Fireball Roberts, is said to have driven through town at 100 mph. The store stayed in that location for several decades until the lease was up, then moved to 213 S. Adams until Andrew's death in 1967. During the Great Depression, Andrew Grant hired several of his siblings, partnered with his brother Fonse in business, and sent money to his parents in Sopchoppy to help support the younger children and grandchildren.

Andrew invested in and was a director of the Tallahassee Bank and Trust (later Bank of America), president of both the Shriner organization, and the Florida Furniture Dealers, and was a faithful member of at least ten other organizations. Across the street from his store, Herschel Johnson managed Steyerman's Dress Shop for about ten years. She had attended FSCW for a year but quit when her father died. Herschel and Andrew were engaged for much of the 1930's and married in 1940. Their only child, Andrew, Jr., was born January 2, 1941. He worked in the furniture store from an early age. He graduated from Leon High School ('59), Harvard ('62) and Duke Medical School ('66). He married his high school sweetheart, Eleanor Cunkle, whose father, economist Dr. Arthur Lee Cunkle worked in the Legislative Reference Bureau. Andy and Eleanor settled in Galveston. TX

Herschel Johnson Grant (1905- 1989)

The youngest of Andrew's eight siblings, Paul Grant, came to Tallahassee in 1943. During the war, he ran the coal yard at the military camp west of town, and then owned a series of Grant's Grocery, the first being on W. Tennessee, others on Macomb and Gaines. He and wife Audrey had 2 children, Paul Jr. and Dot (Melton). Paul Jr., born in 1932, had a chiropractic clinic for decades. His wife, the former Nan Grubaugh, and their only child, Kathy Morris, worked with him. Paul is a star volunteer with the Florida Highway Patrol Auxiliary club. Their grandchildren are Kelli and Kyle Morris. Still living in Tallahassee are Fonse's daughter, Hilda Winterle, Marcia's son Pleasant Vause, a retired preacher, Dot Grant Melton, and Paul, Jr.

Written and submitted by: Eleanor Cunkle Grant, 1025 Bamar Ln., Galveston, TX 77554

Gray-Golden Days in Tallahassee

My parents, Elizabeth Carroll-Gray and Silas Emanuel Gray, moved to Hardaway near Havana in 1927, when I was just six months old. My grandparents, Eliza Moody- Gray and Edward Gray had a farm west of town, just south of Highway 20 in Leon County. That land is now Roberts Sand Pit. My grandparents, Martha VanZant-Carroll and Ephriam Carroll lived west of Tallahassee also. We eventually moved to Tallahassee to be closer to our family, because from the age of six, my six siblings and I were raised by my Dad. We had a lot of hard times and moved around a lot, but no matter where home was we had a lot of love. I remember living on Lafayette Street and playing in the red clay hills of Tallahassee.

In 1932 the only streets paved with red brick were Monroe, Adams, College, and Gaines. Every Saturday the farmers brought their produce by horse and wagon to the curb market on the corner of Boulevard and Madison Streets to sell, and on this day there were more horses and wagons on the street than cars. In 1932 I started school at Caroline Brevard on Calhoun Street; it is a State building now. During this same year we moved to the Woodville community, where I attended the Red Oak School, a little one-room school house, which served first through eighth grade. Part of our school day included cutting wood for the wood heater, and pumping water from the well for drinking. In those days there were no day care centers, so at six years old I had my first babysitting job by taking my four year-old sister,

L-R; Silas Emanuel Gray, Aunt-VanDelia Gray-Fountain, and Uncle VanBuren Gray L-R;

Deloise to school with me every day. I later attended Woodville Elementary School where my first grade teacher was Miss Rhodes. In 1935 we moved to Silver Lake off of Highway 20. Since jobs were hard to find during the depression, we lived off our garden, rabbits, squirrels, chickens, and fish. Once my Dad built a room onto a man's house and the man couldn't pay him so my Dad bartered him out of two milk cows. He tied a rope around their necks and walked them over ten miles to our house. These same cows gave us milk for over ten years.

While living at Silver Lake we caught a school bus to Sealey Elementary, which was on Seventh Avenue where the City Police Department is now. I had a really good teacher named Miss Thorton, so this was the year I really began to like school. In the afternoon the bus would drop us off at Aenon Church Road and we would walk another four miles home to Silver Lake. We loved living at Silver Lake, where I learned to swim out of necessity when I slipped off a log into the lake. We moved again when the house and property we rented from Miss Jones was sold to the government.

We moved to an 80-acre farm owned by Mr. Luther Hartsfield on Barineau Road. There were a lot of chores to be done because the chickens and cows moved with us, and it wasn't long before Dad had a garden. Some of these chores had to be done before we went to school and again after school. My chores were getting up and milking those bartered cows every morning, carrying water from the spring and chopped wood to the house. I loved the farm life though. It's interesting how hard work will make your brain work better. I got creative and built a homemade wagon to make my chores a little easier by carrying three times as much wood in one trip, hauling 5 buckets of water instead of one bucket full. In those days, 55 gallon drums caught rain water for bathing, and we carried our clothes to the spring every Saturday to wash them.

In 1940 we moved in with my Aunt VanDelia Gray-Fountain after her husband passed away. She didn't want to live alone and thought she could help my Dad with seven children. She lived on Jackson Bluff road and a man named a street VanDelia after my aunt. It was great living with her, but some adjustments had to be made in our way of thinking and acting, because Aunt Delia was like our Mother, very strict in her straight-laced way. She had that yes look and that no look and it didn't take us kids long to learn them.

In 1941, I attended Leon High School and remembered when the classes assembled in the auditorium to hear President Roosevelt declare war on Japan for the attack on Pearl Harbor. Leon High was a wonderful school, where I enjoyed a lot of sports by placing first in the 100 yard dash, second in the chin-ups, and third in high jumps. The best part of the day though was coming home to find Aunt Delia had set out a basket of sweet potatoes for us kids to have as a snack. After the Navy in 1944-1946 needed a vehicle to drive, so I took an old Model-A frame and put a rebuilt engine in it. My Dad built a truck body on this frame and I now had my first vehicle. I have done construction work all my adult life, except for one year when I worked for the Tallahassee Fire Department. I was real happy when Mr. Jesse Turner, a contractor hired me.

The Gray Brothers; James, Silas, Simon, and Fred Gray

In 1948 I formed a company with my brother Simon called "Gray Brothers Quality Builders". I first married Louise Allen, who had two children from a previous marriage, Karen and Gary and our two, Patti and Andy Gray makes four very happy and healthy children who were raised in Tallahassee and who have made me very proud. I am now married to Christi Ward-Gray, and we enjoy life in Tallahassee. The farming days still come out in me every once in a while. We have a garden and several fruit trees. I added a tin roof over our back deck so I could hear the rain fall on it. I love sitting on the porch swing thinking back over my life during the "Golden Days" in Tallahassee. I still work in construction about six days a week.

Written and submitted by: James Andrew, Sr. and Christi Ward-Gray 2145 Longview Dr., Tallahassee, Florida 32303

Daniel R. and Betty O. Green and Family

Dan Green and his wife, Betty Jo, came from Crawfordville to live and teach in Tallahassee in late 1959. They chose to live on the south side of Tallahassee near Lake Munson as they wanted to be near their beloved Wakulla County where they grew up and their families remained. They both had graduated from FSU and he began his teaching career at Lively Technical School, (on Park Ave.) in 1958. She had taught in Sopchoppy and then in Crawfordville prior to moving to Tallahassee. In the Fall of 1960, she began teaching at Leonard Wesson School and Dan took the industrial arts teaching position at Elizabeth Cobb Junior High where he remained until his retirement in 1986.

While still living in Crawfordville, their first child, Daniel Dale, was born in Tallahassee on President Eisenhower's 65th birthday in 1955. When the family moved to Tallahassee, Dale began first grade at Wesson where he remained throughout elementary school. His sister, Joni, was born in February of 1960 and her grandmother Green from Crawfordville came to Tallahassee every day to care for her. Joni went to kindergarten in the first class of Tallahassee Christian School and then she attended Wesson where her mother was teaching. The years 1960-1968 were busy years with both parents enjoying their schools and the children involved.

Sgt. Dale Green, Tallahassee Police Department, 1998

Dan and Betty Green with children, Dale and Joni, 1973

Dale was proud to be on the school patrol in the 4 and 5th grades and in 5th he began his musical training under the direction of Mr. Patterson. He went on to play in all the bands at Rickards, serving as drum major in his junior and senior years. His director, Mr. Shellahammer, went on to direct FSU bands.

February of 1968 began a trying time for Florida's schools and all associated with them. The so-called "Teacher Walkout" took place at that time as an effort to call attention to the overcrowded and under-funded classrooms throughout the state. Dan and his wife felt they had to make a stand and they went out at great cost to themselves but they and the children weathered the remaining school year, although Betty stayed out until September when she began teaching at Augusta Raa Junior High. She retired from there eighteen years later.

Dale graduated from Rickards and pursued an FSU degree to become a band director, but in his last semester, he decided he did not want to battle with, or for, band financing. At that time he had been working as manager of McDonald's and his income was more than a teacher with considerable year's experience. In later years, Dale was a gunsmith at a sporting goods store where he met many of the local police. Following the death of one of those policemen, who was shot to death in 1988, Dale chose to join the force, where he truly felt his calling. Little did anyone suspect Dale would be the next Tallahassee Police fatality. Sgt. Dale Green was shot to death on November 13, 2002. His daughter, Kristen Green Collier, lives with her husband, Ronnie, and daughter, Cameron, in Tallahassee where she teaches in the public school system. His son, Ryan, lives with his mother, Deborah, in Crawfordville and attends FSU.

Joni completed school in Tallahassee and now lives with her husband of thirty years in Knoxville, Tennessee. Dan and Betty returned to Wakulla County in retirement where she lives today. Dan died July 27, 2003, eight months after his son, and is buried in the Arran Cemetery near Crawfordville.

Written and submitted by: Betty Green, P. O. Box 969, Crawfordville, FL 32326 1973

Descendants of Eleanor (?) Greene Nicks

Eleanor Nicks was first married to Revolutionary War veteran Benjamin Greene. Benjamin and his brothers, John and McKeen Greene were from Beech Island (Aiken), SC. All three served in the Revolutionary War. DAR and Pension Record applications exist for McKeen and spell out his war experiences. Benjamin died before receiving a pension, but a DAR record does exist from a descendant of his marriage to Eleanor. It appears that he died about 1803 and left several children, including John Bryant, Susan, Benjamin, William and Elizabeth. The records do not reveal the maiden name of Eleanor.

Around 1805, Eleanor and William Nicks of Savannah, GA filed a marriage settlement similar to a prenuptial agreement today before marrying and living on the Benjamin Greene land in Screven Co., GA. The land lied along the Savannah River and north of Briers Creek. Eleanor and William had one son named James Rinaldo Nicks born c.1808. He too grew up on the Screven Co. land. During the Georgia Land Lottery years from 1825 to 1832, he registered for and received land draws. His mother and Benjamin purchased land in Leon Co., Florida during that same time.

The land was located on the north side of Lake Iamonia just west of land named the Strickland Arm. Around the same time Eleanor purchased land located around the Court House in Thomasville, Thomas Co., GA. She moved there and about the same time made a friendship with Elizabeth Harrison Fair Nicks. Elizabeth's daughter, Mary Ann Fair married Eleanor's nephew, James Russell Greene (son of McKeen) in Thomasville in June of 1832. Her son, J. R. Nicks married Mary Ann's sister, Frances Fair during the same year. During 1833, Eleanor made a Deed of Gift in Trust to her son, Benjamin, bachelor of Screven Co., GA to Frances Nicks and her children for the 200 acres at Lake Iamonia.

Her son and daughter-in-law settled on that land and their son, William Richard Nicks was born in March of 1833. Eleanor lived with her son, J. R. Nicks, but she traveled back into Georgia where she witnessed the Revolutionary War application for her brother-in-law, McKeen Greene in 1834. Some time in 1834, Eleanor died and records of her Probate exist in Thomas Co. By then, others began to relocate to the vicinity of Lake Iamonia (see Greene, Sauls and Van Brunt sketches). The families were enumerated in the above families on the 1840 U S. Census. Eleanor's son, Benjamin sold his Lake Iamonia land to J. R. Greene. Richard Van Brunt purchased land part of which today is part of the Tall Timbers Research Station.

Richard Van Brunt and James R. Nicks continued to live at Lake Iamonia after the other siblings moved to Columbus, GA, Girard, AL and finally to Opelika, Russell (now Lee) Co., AL. The two men and their families were yeoman farmers, but also early participants in the politics of their times. Both became Notary of Publics and J. R. Greene became an Election Inspector for the Florida Statehood election of 1845. J. R. Nicks also attended a Democratic Convention during the 1850s. He and his family sued in Chancery Court around 1852 to have the 200 acres revert to Frances Fair and her children (William R., Francis R., Benjamin R., Susan and James R. Nicks, Jr.) His half-brother, Benjamin had died about the same time. The land was transferred and J. R. Nicks sold much if not all to Griffin W. Holland and moved to what was then Pierceville, but now Brooksville, Hernando Co., FL.

By 1856, J. R. Nicks returned to Tallahassee to represent Hernando Co. in the Florida House of Representatives. He would do the same for 1858 and part of 1859. At the same time, his family must have visited with the Van Brunts and also the other Greene, Sauls and Fair siblings in Opelika, as an obituary for Frances and J. R. Nicks' youngest son, Robert Henry R. Nicks (1852-1928) reported the family first came to Brooksville from Opelika in 1859. At the time, H. R. Nicks was only 7 years old and did not know his parents came down in 1853.

Eleanor was the catalyst for all those families who ventured from Charleston, SC and Screven Co. and other counties in GA into Leon Co., FL. Her purchase of land located in Township 3 North and Range 1 East was later joined by all those who came and left. Her land in Screven Co., GA was partitioned to her children by Benjamin Greene around 1816. The deed was filed in Granville Co., SC. It lists the children and what they received. They continued to live there and a graveyard on the property (now called Brannon Plantation), with broken tombstones, show where most were buried. Only Eleanor's burial spot is unknown and could be in either Leon Co., FL, Thomas Co., GA or old Washington Co., GA where her brother-in-law, McKeen Green was living in 1834. Eleanor's descendants still live in Florida. Her great grandson, Sheldon S. Nicks was recently honored as a Florida law enforcement officer killed in the line of duty in 1909. That honor, including his name etched on the honor stone monument between the Old and New Capitol buildings was finally accomplished 100 years after he was killed. He joined another cousin and great-great grandson, William Henry Nix O'Berry who was honored for his loss of life in the line of duty in 1926.

Both of her sons (William R. and H. R. Nicks) were the only two Nicks children to have children. Three grandsons (William, Francis and Benjamin) served in the Civil War, but both Francis and Benjamin died before and after 1870 from illness and or injuries contracted during the war. Descendants of the two surviving grandsons live throughout the South and especially in Florida and amount to over 10 generations of Floridians since 1832.

Written by Charles Blankenship for: Christine Blankenship Orrell, 5304 Miramar Lane, Colleyville, TX 76034

Ancestors and Descendants of Martha Mariah Greene

Martha Maria Greene (aka Martha Mariah Greene or Martha Mariah Fair) was the daughter of McKeen Greene and his second wife, Frances Dubose. Martha was born February 18, 1814. During that period, her father was involved with the Florida Patriot War and was one of the signers of a petition at Fort Mitchell in East Florida on January 25, 1814 and two of his son-in-laws (Daniel Sauls and Michael Henderson) also were signers, who married his daughters by his first marriage to Eleanor McCall. At this time, the Greene's were living in Tattnall County, GA.

Martha's father, McKeen Greene, was the son of Susannah Harris and Thomas Greene of Beech Island, SC. They had at least three sons, Benjamin, John and McKeen. All three served in the Revolutionary War and afterwards lived in Georgia. Martha's mother, Frances, was the daughter of Isaac Dubose and his wife and first cousin, Sarah Dubose. Their heritage goes back to Normandy, France.

About the time her father, a Revolutionary War Veteran, died in 1838, Martha moved to Leon County, FL along with her brother, James R. Greene, who had married Mary Anna Fair of Charleston, SC in Thomas County, GA in 1832. On Dec. 4, 1839, Martha married Mary's brother, Joseph Harrison Fair, also of Charleston in Tallahassee, Leon County, Florida. The two were enumerated on the 1840 U. S. Census in Leon County, Florida. By November 7, 1840 heir first son, Richard McKeen Fair, was born in Leon County. Throughout his lifetime; Richard always gave Florida as his birth state on census reports.

Sometime between 1840 and 1843, Joseph and Martha moved and eventually settled in Opelika, AL where their second son Joseph Greene was born in April of 1843. The family continued to live in Alabama and other children, Robert James, Mary Louisa and William Harrison were born between 1848 and 1853. Both Richard McKeen and Joseph Greene participated in the Civil War, serving in the 45th Alabama Infantry. After the Civil War, the family continued to live in Opelika until around 1869 when they began to move toward Jefferson, TX and finally to Hope, AR. Robert joined them in 1872. Richard had married his first cousin, Anna Burr, daughter of Allen Burr and his father's sister, Sophia Burr who had married in Florida before moving to Opelika, AL.

Richard McKeen Fair and Anna Burr had two children, Ella and Joseph Allen Fair. After the death of Anna Burr Fair, Richard married Mollie Hayes and had three more children, Mary Anna, James Augustus and Charles Fair. Martha's husband, Joseph Harrison Fair died in 1896 in Jefferson, TX. He is buried in the Smith Family Cemetery. Martha lived until December 2, 1902 and died in Cove, AR. She is buried in the Pleasant Grove Cemetery. An obituary was published in the Arkansas Methodist on June 10, 1903. It acknowledged that she had lived a good Christian life in the M. E. Church South. She had converted at the early age of eight. Her last years were spent visiting all her children and afterwards returning to Joseph Greene Fair's house. Martha and Joseph's children and descendants continue to live throughout TX, AR and OK. To this day, many descendants are schoolteachers living in all three states.

Sources: #1 - FAIR descendants were researched by the son of Joseph Greene Fair and his wife, Alice Elenora Hayes. #2 - The son, Charles E. Fair researched and wrote two small books about his Fair-Dubose lines. #3 - A third book, Kissin Kin & Lost Cousins by Frank Howard Hawthorne, published in 1989 continued the Charles E. Fair tradition in even more detail. #4 - Appropriately, both authors lost some Fair cousins probably due to the Civil War and early death of some siblings. #5 - See Fair-Nicks sketches for Frances Fair, Sarah Ann Nicks and Martha Nicks to complete the siblings. #6 - The books, A Biographical Sketch of John Fair and Descendants in 1953 and Greene-Dubose, a Supplement to John Fair and His Descendants in 1954 gives a very detailed description of the Joseph H. Fair and Martha Mariah Greene line. Written by: Charles Blankenship; Submitted by: Abner Irwin "Buddy" Fair, 8928 W. Warren St., Wichita, KS 67212

Dot Grimsley

The gently rolling hills and spreading oaks of Miller County, Georgia frame a quiet place to be born and to grow up. Colquitt, the county seat, is not the most exciting town in Georgia, even on a Saturday night, but it was Dot Grimsley's home for a long time. Living on the family's cattle farm, attending Miller County schools, finding your friends where you could, it was a quiet life, filled with simple pleasures and a simple lifestyle. Dot learned of the saving grace of Jesus when she was 14, accepting Him as her savior and being baptized in her family church, protected in the knowledge and belief that Jesus Saves!

She was a pretty young girl; elected Miss Freshman at Miller County High School That is where she met Garland, her future husband. Their families knew each other. At first Garland and Dot were just classmates, then friends, and when their friendship grew to become much more they were married in Miller County in 1944.

When you are young in the 1930s and 1940s you dream about bigger and better things for your life, but even Dot couldn't imagine where life would take her. Their first home was far away from her comfortable roots in rural Georgia, way off in Mountain Home, Idaho, where Garland was stationed with the U. S. Air Force. After a few months there it was off on the proverbial serviceman's merry-go-round of different military bases in different cities and different states.

As their family grew, the call to return home to quiet Southern ways of living grew louder. Tallahassee was a good place to put down roots, close enough to familiar surroundings of South Georgia and a fine town in which to raise her two daughters. The Grimsley's joined the good, Christian family at Forest Heights Baptist Church in 1969.

But duty called Garland to Jacksonville, and the family made the move to Florida's "Bold New City of the South" in 1970. By that time Dot had become a full time chauffer for an active teenage daughter. One of her regular stops was at First Baptist Church of Jacksonville, where the Grimsley family had set up their religious household.

After a few years Dot and family returned to Tallahassee, and they settled into the warm, friendly congregation of First Baptist Church, and have been with us ever since. Dot was able to put her knowledge of farming to good use, working for the U.S. Government in the Federal Farm Loan Office. After that she was a secretary at the Florida Education Association, and later became a valuable asset in the office of Florida State Attorney Willie Meggs. One of her fondest recollections is of her retirement party from the State Attorney's office, the wonderful people she worked with there and the lovely going away gift they gave her.

The loss of her husband Garland to a heart problem and a fall was an unexpected and deep tragedy for Dot and her daughters. Her faith in the message of John 3:16, that "whosoever believeth...shall not perish but have everlasting life" has sustained her. She now shares the good memories of life in Tallahassee with her oldest daughter who lives here.

When she thinks of the changes that she has seen in her lifetime, Dot thinks that the decline in personal and national values and morality are the most disturbing. There is no better time than right now for America to return to the values taught in the Bible and the simple guidelines of the Golden Rule.

Written by: Carol Ann and Bill Boydston, 1639 Twin Lakes Circle, Tallahassee, FL 32311; Submitted by: Dot Grimsley

William J. Gunn - Buggy Driver to Healer

William J. Gunn was born into slavery in September of 1857. Local historians believe William spent his early years on a plantation owned by W. J. and Harriet Gunn in Gadsden County, Florida.

Emancipated slaves were first identified by name on the 1870 Federal Census. That year William was attending school and living in the Quincy home of

Dr. William J. Gunn (9/1/1857-2/22/1954) Image courtesy of the Florida State Archives Photographic Collection

Perry and Patsy Washington. Perry was a teamster — skilled in driving wagons and buggies. He trained young William to do the same sort of work. Around, 1875, Gunn moved to Tallahassee and secured employment as a buggy driver for the well known and beloved physician, George Betton.

Gunn had an insatiable appetite for learning and was fascinated with the healing arts. Betton recognized William's talents and often allowed Gunn to assist with minor medical procedures. Betton provided the resources for Gunn to attend the then new Meharry Medical School in Nashville that had been established to train doctors of color. Gunn graduated in 1882 and returned to Tallahassee.

Dr. Gunn opened an office on Duval Street between College and Jefferson Streets. Census records indicate his home was nearby. Within four years, he married Nannie Anderson. Nannie's mother, Fanny, resided with them as well as a woman named Helen Spaight and a young girl named Maude Demilla. Though Gunn had a thriving practice of his own, he continued to work in association with Dr. Betton until Betton's death in November 1896.

There is no record of the Gunns' having any children. Nannie passed away before her 60th birthday and the doctor never remarried. William had patients of all colors and continued to work until his death in 1954. At that time, it was common practice for new doctors to work under the tutelage of an established physician. When the young Dr. Alpha Omega Campbell came to town, William took him under his wing for a short period of time.

Dr. Gunn died at age 97 in 1954. His will contained the following provision:

"I do hereby give and bequeath to my esteemed friend Mrs. Margaret McLeod Betton, widow of my friend Dr. Geo. W. Betton, deceased, the sum of $500.00 in cash, to belong to her absolutely and forever; and my executor is hereby directed to pay said amount to her in full immediately after my death, and if there shall be insufficient money on hand with which to pay this sum promptly then my executor is hereby directed and authorized to make immediate sale of my property not specifically devised herein…"

Gunn was an excellent fiscal manager and there was no problem paying the widow Betton the sum he wanted her to have. He also left money to Meharry College and the Colored Episcopal Church of Tallahassee. He did not mention his protégé A. O. Campbell, nor did he leave instructions regarding disposition of his medical equipment and books.

Submitted by: Julianne Hare 850-385-6440

Gutsch — Heidi's Bakery

In April 1951 Wilhelm and Helene Gutsch, together with their children; Lucy age 20 and Willi age 15, arrived in Tallahassee by way of the old train station with all their worldly-possessions in a wicker basket and a suitcase and speaking no English. They were from the city of Lodz, Poland, population several hundred thousand. Their first impression of their new home was what kind of god-forsaken place had they come to?

They had a dream of one day having a bakery of their own again. Wilhelm had a bakery in Lodz, but it was destroyed when the Russians occupied Poland. Since they were German nationality, after WWII they sought their future elsewhere. The Lutheran church sponsored them here and Wilhelm and Willi immediately began working for Camellia Bakery on North Monroe Street.

In 1959, Willi married a Tallahassee girl who was from pioneer families in Waiton County by the name of Willie Lou Bell. Soon we had daughters Heidi and Julie.

In January 1964 Wilhelm, Willi and I put all our money together and opened Heidi's Bakery at 1018 N. Monroe Street. We were also the three employees in the beginning. The shop was an immediate success and slowly we increased our staff. Our son Andrew was born while at this location.

Business was rapidly increasing, so in January 1969 we ventured out again and built our own building at 1449 Thomasville Road. By then we had gained quite reputation for our birthday cakes often making 150-200 a week. Our wedding cakes were also a big hit and we did as many at 10-15 on a weekend. Many times over the years our brownies, centerfilled cookies, pastries and other fondly remembered delights were mailed to family members away at school, in the armed forces or to loved ones that had moved to other parts of the country.

Wilhelm died in 1971. He was a tremendous loss to our family and the bakery. I fondly remember hearing many conversations in German between Willi and his father as they worked long days together in the baking area which was not air conditioned.

In 1976 Thomasville Road was widened and we decided that our future would be better served in the Capital Plaza Shopping Center. By then Heidi was old enough to serve customers and Andrew was just tall enough to stand on a box and help his dad in the back with the mixing and baking. Julie was somewhere in between and I was busy decorating cakes and keeping the office. Our total staff was between 10 and 15 and they were becoming like an extension of our family.

Wedding Cake from Heidi's Bakery

Our busiest time of the year started with football season building up to a crescendo on Christmas Eve. By then the shop was filled with the wonderful smells of gingerbread boys, fresh breads, fruit cakes, cookies, pies, our famous parker house rolls and all the many things that made the season so wonderful. I remember the smiles on little children's faces as they peeked through the windows of the cases looking at all the yummy goodies. By Christmas Eve night all the employees were filled with the joy of the season and looking forward to a much deserved break until after New Year's.

In 2000 we sold the shop and at the same time Willi suddenly died. Our whole family has been sustained by the wonderful memories shared by the many customers we encounter wherever we go. Over the years I have come to appreciate what the bakery has meant to the people of Tallahassee. A dream, hard work, great employees and loyal customers made it all possible.

Submitted by: Lou Gutsch, 6731 Roberts Road, Tallahassee, Fl 32309 gquilts@embarqmail.com

David Walker Gwynn Family

One of the older pioneer families of Leon County is the Gwynn family. As noted in Florida history, the Gwynn family is of Welsh origin and originally came to the Chesapeake Bay area in the early 1600s. From Maryland and Virginia, the Gwynns of Leon County moved to Kentucky. David Walker Gwynn (1822-1892) and his brother, Walter Gwynn (1828-1897) came to Tallahassee from Logan County, Kentucky when Florida had just become a state, about 1845. David Walker Gwynn now resides in the Old City Cemetery below an obelisk monument.

Young D.W. Gwynn practiced law in Louisville, KY, when he received encouragement to come to Tallahassee from his uncle and Kentucky native, David Shelby Walker (1815-1891) and cousin, Richard Keith Call (1792-1862). Both Call and Walker served as Florida governors. David Walker Gwynn settled on acreage that is now the campus of Florida A.& M. University, formerly Florida Agricultural and Mechanical College. Hon. David W. Gwynn named his plantation The Oaks. There are streets near the campus named after family members Barbour, Throckmorton, Call. Gwynn built a working plantation and became part of the Florida planter's society. He is known for his development of the finest thoroughbred horse stock and tobacco in Florida. Gwynn's sons, Clifton B. Gwynn and George H. Gwynn, formed Gwynn Tobacco Company and grew shade tobacco into the 1900's. Gwynn and his sons also grew LeConte pears. The boom in LeConte pears was in progress

David Walker Gwynn, 1822-1892

through 1891. David W. Gwynn is listed on the Leon County census in 1850 as a lawyer. He had a working plantation, with slaves and a law practice. By 1851, he served as county judge while operating The Oaks Plantation. During the 1800's, some families had working farms even if the head of household held a professional job, such as lawyer or physician.

David Walker Gwynn also served as postmaster, director of the first railroad from Tallahassee to St. Marks, Trustee of West Florida Seminary and other positions of public trust. He also fought in the War Between the States as Captain of Company C. Gwynn then played an important roll in reconstruction in Florida. D.W Gwynn's two sons, Clifton Blake Gwynn, Chief Clerk of the Florida State Land Department, and Dr. George Humphrey Gwynn, physician, continued to serve their communities into the twentieth century. C.B. Gwynn married Mary Wellford Wilson. His brother George Humphrey Gwynn married Alice Brevard who was part of the Call family. After Alice Brevard's death, he married Jennie Perkins.

The Gwynn, Walker, Call, Wilson, Brevard and Perkins families were involved in early Florida politics serving in numerous capacities.

The D. W. Gwynn descendents who currently reside in Leon County Florida are great grandchildren of Gwynn and his second wife, "Una", Caroline Anne Blake Gwynn (1833-1866). Their children are Clifton Blake Gwynn Sr. (1860-1933) and Dr. George Humphrey Gwynn Sr. (1862-1931). Although Blake relatives lived in Micosukee, Lina's parents never lived in Tallahassee. Three of their daughters married Leon county men. The marriage of Lina and David Walker Gwynn linked them with other pioneer families. Lina's sister, "Kate", Catharine Sarah Blake married Dr. Flavius Byrd of Leon County. From this lineage, the Gwynn, Blake, Byrd, Van Brunt and Lewis families are linked. The third Blake sister, Eliza Smith Blake married John C. Smith. Their daughter, Eliza Blake Smith married Dr. William Louis Moor. The three Blake sisters link generations of prominent Leon county physicians; Dr. F.A. Byrd (1822-1874). Dr. William Louis Moor (1852-1927), Dr. Frederick Clifton Moor (1879-1941), Dr. George Humphrey Gwynn Sr. (1862-1931), Dr. George Humphrey Gwynn Jr. (1892-1956) and Dr. Humphrey Wilson Gwynn (1891-1972) of Leon County. All are important to our medical community from the 1840s.

My interest in David Walker Gwynn grew when my father's aunt, Alice Brevard Gwynn (1893-1981), told us my father, Judge James Clifton Gwynn (1913-1974), always wanted to be a judge like his great grandfather. D. W. Gwynn. Judge J. C. Gwynn's grandfather, C. B. Gwynn Sr. (1860-1933) fostered community values in his grandson. My father's father, Clifton Blake Gwynn Jr. (1890-1928) died young. Judge James Clifton Gwynn married Annie Pauline Shelley Gwynn (Vereen) (1916-2002) in 1936. They had three children, Dr. James Clifton Gwynn Jr. (1937-1992). William Shelley Gwynn (1942) and me, Anne Blake Gwynn (1952). I married Clifton M. Culberson (1951) and have a son, Clifton Blake Culberson (1990).

The descendents of these pioneer families still shape our community. Currently, the great grandson of David Walker Gwynn owns The Cypress Restaurant. He and his wife Elizabeth Lee Gwynn are blocks from the site of the old Gwynn homestead on Calhoun Street, now owned by Capital City Bank Group. Like his great grandfather. David Walker Gwynn, and father. John Gwynn, George Humphrey Gwynn works as an attorney in Tallahassee. William Shelley Gwynn is a contractor in Tallahassee. Other Blake and Gwynn descendents still live in our community and beyond. They respect and love Leon County and its environs.

Submitted by: Mrs. Anne Blake Culberson, 978 Winall Down Rd. NE, Atlanta, GA 30319

Bert Hadley - Historian and Philosopher

Bert Hadley, Sr., was born to Robert and Josephine Hadley on the Hayward Hall Plantation on October 16, 1911. His grandparents, Josh Hadley and Nancy Ford, lived on this plantation and his great-grandmother, Josephine Ford had been a slave on the same plantation. The area is now known as The Bradfordville Community. Bert was the eldest and last living of four children. His siblings were Arthur Hadley, Robert Hadley and a sister named Josephine Hadley. At the young age of twelve, Bert began plowing with a horse named Moe for his uncle, Willie Carr. Bert thought that if the boy Jesus could begin working at twelve then, so could he. Bert went on to work as a hired hand for three years at Rose Hill Plantation and for twelve years at Phipps Plantation.

In 1928, Bert was converted by Revivalist G.T. Moore's sermon and admonition to him: "First seek ye the kingdom of heaven and His righteousness." He then joined the Bethlehem Primitive Baptist Church for a while and shortly after this time he joined the Elizabeth Popular Spring Primitive Baptist Church where he was a continuously faithful member for over seventy-five years. In 1956 Bert was ordained as a deacon and served on the church's Deacon Board under the leadership of five previous pastors Simultaneously, he also led the church school for over twenty years as the superintendent.

With his beloved wife of sixty-three years, the late Mother Eva Hadley, Deacon Hadley reared his family of eight children Andrew (deceased), Louise (deceased), Bert, Jr., Gloria, Rebecca, Fred, Wilmon and, Samuel in the church while continuously serving the both his church and the Blocker community in other capacities.

Bert Hadley, Sr.

In 1938 Bert was the first employee hired by Mr. Eugene Ellis, founder of the now Tallahassee Nurseries, Inc. and was a loyal employee until his final retirement in 1990. In 1991 the nursery hosted a gala celebration entitled "Three Sheets from the Wind of Slavery" on the Nurseries' grounds under the giant live oaks, which Bert had planted himself decades earlier. This gala was in recognition of Hadley's ninetieth birthday. Amongst the beautifully landscaped scenery and amidst the attendance of his entire family, nursery employees and other admiring friends, Hadley received gifts and the honorable title of "Resident Historian and Philosopher of Tallahassee Nursery." Some of his most often quoted words of wisdom: "If a man beats you thinking, he'll beat you living" and "Two things won't betray you: God and a dollar." The highlight of the evening was a plaque donated by owner, Eugene Ellis, and presented by the late Professor James N. Eaton, founder of the Florida A&M University Black Archives. This fitting tribute is displayed on the "Wall of Distinction" in honor of Bert and Eva Hadley at the Black Archives on Florida A&M University Campus.

On October 27, 2007, a Recognition Banquet was sponsored by the C. H. Henry Lodge # 543, FA&M, PHA at the Rock Hill Missionary Baptist Church where Worshipful Master Timothy A. Williams presented Bert Hadley with two plaques. The first plaque was for fifty years of continuous membership and the second plaque was for his dedicated service to the lodge as its chaplain. In this office, Deacon Hadley often used his favorite spiritual tools: Scripture, John 3:16; hymn, "Amazing Grace" and song, "A Charge to Keep I Have."

At the age of ninety-six years old, Hadley voluntarily resigned from active leadership of the largest ward of Elizabeth Popular Spring Primitive Baptist Church, under the current pastor ship of Elder Connell Leonard, Sr. But as a deacon emeritus at ninety-seven he still served the Lord, rarely missing Wednesday night Bible study or Sunday morning worship. Bert Hadley Sr. maintained his involvement in overseeing the welfare and spiritual growth of his church family, always dispensing wisdom to ministers and laity alike. His encouraging words to them were: "Faith and Grace will help you run this Christian race." Deacon Bert Hadley's advice for all Christians was simple: "Love ye one another because Christ first loved us." On the morning of March 13, 2009, he slept quietly away and went to be forever with Jesus Christ, his beloved Lord and Saviour. He left most of his children still residing on Hadley Road in Northeast Tallahassee. The street was named for him in the 1970s. Bert Hadley, Sr., was a vigorous paragon of exemplary Christian maturity for Leon County's entire community. Finally, Deacon Bert Hadley exemplified the words of Proverbs 13:22: "A good man leaveth an inheritance to his children's children."

Written and submitted by: Klara Shannon Hadley, Wife of FredHadley, 2500 Elliott Street, Tallahassee, Florida 32304

Muriel Hanes

Have you ever noticed that all the really good love stories have an incredible twist that brings the young man and woman together? Muriel Hanes' love story has just such an unusual event.

In Muriel's case, the Second World War was over and the boys were coming home. And many of the young soldiers returning were just that, boys. Thousands had quit high school to join the armed forces and go to war. Marshall Hanes was one of these youngsters, returning to his home and family, picking up his education where he had left off.

The government made it possible for these young GIs to enroll in High School, complete their studies and graduate. And here's where that remarkable twist comes into play. It just so happens that Muriel (the future Mrs. Hanes) and Marshall were in the same senior class. They met, graduated together in 1947, and married one year later.

But let's start at the beginning of Muriel's life. She was born and raised in Altha, Florida. Muriel says she has always been a Baptist, from when she welcomed Christ into her life at fifteen. She was quite accomplished in her years in Altha. Besides being Valedictorian of her graduating high school class she had won many awards and recognitions during her school years. One such honor was from the Daughters of the American Revolution for outstanding citizenship.

Of all her accomplishments in her young life, Muriel is most proud of her time spent teaching young children as a Sunday School Teacher in the Altha Baptist Church.

Now, let's get back to our love story. Muriel and Marshall settled into a happy married life. They were blessed with one lovely daughter. Muriel and Marshall were together for fifty-two wonderful years. She counts their time together, and the loving memories she holds as the most wonderful times of her life.

Although she had been trained as a nurse in a private nursing school in Dothan when the family found its way to Tallahassee Muriel joined the staff at Capital City Bank. She retired from the bank following twenty-nine years of service.

After thirty-four years in Tallahassee, the Hanes returned to Altha for a time to care for her aging mother and father. Muriel's mother passed away in 1989 and her father died in 1991. They moved back to Tallahassee in 1995. Inez Locke invited them to come make their Christian home at First Baptist Church, and she has been happy here ever since.

Tallahassee has been Muriel's town for a long time. She has seen it grow and change over the years. Her daughter is here as was a grandson she loved and lost last year at just thirty-six years old. She has seen the town mature and grow from a small college and government town to a city of diverse culture.

She wishes that the moral and spiritual strength that she found in Tallahassee those many years ago would come to the forefront again. Perhaps if the youth of today could find the love of Christ in themselves and their fellow man, that strength of purpose could thrive, again.

Written by Carol Ann and Bill Boydston ©, 1639 Twin Lakes Circle, Tallahassee, FL 32311

A.G. and Leila Hardee

Leila Frances Richbourg, daughter of (Caswell) Joseph Tobin Richbourg and Elizabeth "Bettie" Johnson Richbourg, was born May 26, 1888 in Castleberry, Conecuh County, Alabama. In the 1890s, her family moved to Woodville, Florida.

On August 13, 1905 at Woodville, Leila married Alagora "A.G." (Shady) Hardee, son of John A. Hardee and Niza Wright (daughter of James Calvin Wright and Elizabeth J. Harrelson Wright). John and Niza Hardee married April 2, 1868 in Columbus County, North Carolina. A.G. was born March 8, 1877 in Iron Hill, North Carolina. By 1900, he moved to Florida and was working turpentine in Marion County.

In 1910, the young Hardee family was enum-erated in Leon County. Sometime thereafter they moved to Hosford in Liberty County and remained for their lifetimes. A.G. Hardee died June 24, 1941, and Leila Frances Richbourg Hardee died September 1, 1958. Both are buried in Hosford Cemetery.

Leila Richbourg Hardee

Nine children were born to Leila and A.G. Hardee.

#1 - Nizie Mae Hardee was born November 23, 1906 and died September 15, 1987. On June 16, 1928, she married Nollie Sykes. Nollie was born

March 12, 1907 and died March 10, 1979. Both are buried at Hosford Cemetery. Children: Ruby Ivaleen Sykes and James Morris Sykes.

#2 - Noel Wright Hardee was born December 18, 1909 and died August 30, 1946. On October 9, 1932, he married (1) Bernice Mercer (October 9, 1914-December 28, 1988). Children: Lowell Hardee (born and died June 22, 1933) and Marion Olivia Hardee. Noel married (2) Pauline Stanley. He is buried at Hosford Cemetery.

#3 - Ernest Lee Hardee was born March 18, 1913. On July 10, 1935, he married Ora Chason (August 20, 1915-April 29, 2006). Daughter: Annette Hardee.

#4 - David Leondas Hardee was born April 18, 1916 and died November 10, 1947 near Camp LeJeune, North Carolina. He is buried at Hosford Cemetery. David Hardee was a Staff Sergeant in the USMC and served in the Pacific during World War II.

#5 - Joseph "Joe" Tobern Hardee was born August 3, 1920 and died March 4, 2006. On April 1, 1941, he married Doris Todd (April 21, 1923-September 10, 1975). Both are buried at Hosford Cemetery. Joe, a U.S. Marine, served in the Pacific during World War II. Daughter: Sandra Hardee.

#6 - Alia Gora "Nig" Hardee was born September 5, 1923 and died October 19, 2003 in Gulfport, Mississippi. Nig is buried at Hosford Cemetery. A career U.S. Marine, he saw combat during World War II and the Korean War. His former wife, Violeta, daughter Myra, and granddaughter Nicole live in the Philippines.

#7 - William "Bill" Cleveland Hardee was born January 4, 1926 and died February 10, 1998. In 1943, he married Clearcy Mae Moore, born August 21, 1927. Children: Jimmy, Greg, Allene, Judy, Wanda.

#8 - Bettie Lurline Hardee, known as Myrlene, was born May 5, 1928. On February 8, 1952, she married Amos Ira Chason (October 16, 1917-June 25, 2004). Children: David, Denice, Gayle, Carla, and Diane.

#9 - A child, born and died February 5, 1931, is buried at Hosford Cemetery.

Written by Judith Richbourg Jolly, 11541 Arlhuna Way, Dade City, Florida 33525; Submitted by Marion Olivia Hardee Mercer, P.O. Box 75, Hosford, Florida 32334

Descendants of Joseph Harrison Fair

The sole surviving male son of Richard Fair and Elizabeth Harrison, Joseph Fair assumed Harrison as his middle name after the death of his older brother, Richard Robert Harrison Fair. Born in downtown Charleston, SC c. 1816, Joseph was the youngest of siblings: Mary Ann, Elizabeth Jane, Sophia, Frances and Richard Robert Fair.

Joseph's father died in October 1817, leaving his mother a widow with six children. Elizabeth's household above her late husband's boot and shoe shop on King Street included over 200 books. She also had a tutor for her children's education. In fact in late December 1818, Elizabeth Harrison Fair filed a Marriage Settlement, protecting her children's inheritance and married Joseph DeWitt Nicks, teacher.

They continued to live on King Street past 1820, but sometime during the next decade, moved in with Elizabeth Jane's husband, Richard Van Brunt. To Elizabeth and Joseph Nicks three children were born, including James W., Sarah Ann and Martha Nicks. Joseph Fair's older sister, Elizabeth Jane had married Richard Van Brunt and both operated a bookbinding business in Charleston. Elizabeth Jane and Richard Van Brunt took custody of Joseph and saw to his education. Several lawsuits reveal the costs and possible family angst regarding young Joseph Fair. In the early 1830s, Richard Robert had died from lockjaw and Joseph Harrison Fair would be the onty male Fair to continue the family surname.

The Fair-Nicks children began their migration out of Charleston to Hebron, Washington Co., GA and by the late 1830s joined Frances Fair and her husband, James Rinaldo Nicks in north Leon County, Florida. Mary Ann married James Russell Greene and purchased land in Leon Co. as did Elizabeth Jane and Richard Van Brunt. Joseph's mother and J. R. Nicks' mother, Eleanor Nicks became mutual friends. Eleanor was formerly married to Benjamin Greene. Benjamin was a brother to McKeen Greene, father of Celete,

Richard McKeen Fair, born in Leon County 1840

Martha and James R. Greene. Both were Rev. War Veterans.

McKeen Greene's daughters, Celete Greene Sauls and Martha Mariah Greene would join the Fair-Nicks siblings in Leon Co. Between the families would later become some marriages, especially Martha Mariah Greene who would become the wife of Joseph Harrison Fair. In fact, in December 1839, Joseph and Martha married in Leon Co., FL.

The 1840 U. S. Census recorded the four families of Sauls, Nicks, Van Brunt and Greene that includes the widow Nicks and her unmarried daughters within the families of other siblings and their spouses. Joseph is also listed on the 1840 census with a female (Martha) and no young children.

Joseph and Martha's first-born son, Richard McKeen Fair was born in Leon Co., FL on November 7, 1840. Their other children: Joseph Greene, Robert James, Mary Louisa and William Harrison Fair were born in Alabama. Richard and Joseph served in Co. B, 45th AL Infantry Regiment during the Civil War.

Martha and Joseph had moved to Opelika, Russell Co., AL after 1842. In 1845, Joseph purchased almost 40 acres land from the General Land Office at Montgomery located in Russell County, Alabama. They lived in Russell County (now Lee County) until around 1869, moving first to Jefferson, Texas. Afterward, they moved north up the Red River to Hope, AR. All the Fair children joined them and lived in the three states: AR, TX and OK throughout their lifetime.

The eldest son, Richard McKeen Fair who had been born in Leon Co., married his first cousin, Anna Burr, daughter of Joseph Harrison Fair's sister, Sophia Fair who had married Allen Burr of Jefferson Co., FL They too had joined Joseph, Mary Ann and the two Nicks' girls: Martha and Sarah Nicks in Opelika.

Joseph and Martha's grandson, Charles E. Fair, son of Joseph Greene Fair and Alice Elenora Hayes, has written much of the family's migration history and genealogy. His two books, *A Biographical Sketch of John Fair* and *Descendants and Greene-Dubose, a Supplement to John Fair and Descendants* written in 1953 and 1954 truly document descendants of Joseph and Martha Fair.

Frank Hawthorne (descendant of Mary Ann Fair and J. R. Greene) wrote another compilation of the Greene-Fair-Burr and Van Brunt families in 1989. Frank's book, *Kissin Kin & Lost Cousins* continued Charles E. Fair's work, but missed the actual parents of the Fair siblings.

Ancient Charleston, SC Mesne Conveyances and Marriage Settlements written in the early 1830s and 1818, actually document the parents, Elizabeth Harrison and Richard Fair whose marriage in 1804 appeared in the local Charleston newspaper. An 1818 Marriage Settlement between Joseph DeWitt Nicks and the widow, Mrs. Elizabeth Fair noted Richard Fair's death date the previous year. Later, the suits between Mrs. Elizabeth Nicks and Elizabeth Jane and Richard Van Brunt named all the Fair siblings. (See Eleanor Nicks, Elizabeth Harrison and Fair and Nicks' children sketches.)

Written by Charles Blankenship for Rebecca Fair, 3124 Herrick Place, Pueblo, CO 81003

Descendants of Elizabeth Harrison (Fair Nicks)

Abstracted death notices by Brent Holcomb from the Charleston, SC based Methodist newspaper: Southern Christian Advocate dated 26 December 1845 relates the death of Elizabeth Nicks as 8 October 1845. Although sketchy, the notice is accurate in that she lived in Charleston, SC and Florida before moving to Girard, Russell Co., Alabama. Who was she and who were her descendants?

Elizabeth's birth surname was Harrison. Charleston Orphanage records listed her parents as John and Ann Harrison. At the age of 7, her widowed mother placed her and her brother, James, age 4, in the Orphanage in December 1794. In July of 1795, her youngest brother, Joseph, age 3, was placed there too. Ann married Robert Gilbreath/Galbreath in 1797 and the three children were indentured to his household.

In 1804, Elizabeth married a young boot and shoemaker named Richard Fair. According to records in Charleston, both immigrated from Cavan County, Ireland. Charleston City Directory publications and deeds, list their residence and workplace as King Street in downtown. Over the years, it was numbered 337 and later as 170 King Street.

Early in 1817, Elizabeth's mother died followed in October by her first husband, Richard. A little over a year later, Elizabeth signed a Marriage Settlement to protect her children before marrying Joseph DeWitt Nicks. The Settlement named her children by Richard Fair, including Mary Ann, Elizabeth Jane, Sophia, Frances,

Richard, Robert and Joseph Fair. The two married on 31 December 1818.

They continued to live at 170 King Street for a short time and Elizabeth had three more children. A young son died in infancy, but two daughters, Martha and Sarah Ann Nicks, later moved with their mother until their marriage in GA and AL. It is not known when Joseph D. Nicks died, but census reports for 1820 and 1830 can be studied to determine their residency. On the latter year, they may have resided with Elizabeth's brother, Joseph Harrison.

Their outward migration began in the early 1830's and several Mesne Conveyances filed in Charleston renamed the same Fair children and this time their spouses. Elizabeth Jane was married to Richard Van Brunt, Mary Ann to James R. Greene and Frances to James R. Nicks. Some evidence exists that Mary Ann Greene may have lived a short time in Hebron, Washington Co., GA. Frances Nicks had moved to Thomasville, GA and later down to Lake Iamonia, Leon Co., FL. Her mother-in-law, Mrs. Eleanor Nicks made a Deed of Gift of about 200 acres of land just inside the GA/FL state line to Frances Nicks and her children. The date of the Deed was witnessed by Elizabeth Nicks on 28 August 1833.

During the next few years, the Fair-Nicks family was joined by Frances' siblings, their spouses and children. Elizabeth Nicks also moved to the area. The 1840 U. S. Census for Leon Co., FL lists four families, and one can analyze the households of James R. Nicks, James R. Greene, Richard Van Brunt and Celete Sauls where it appears that Elizabeth and her daughters are in the household of her daughter, Elizabeth Jane Van Brunt

After 1840, several Leon Co. Indentures can be studied too, up to the time several of the extended families moved northwest, first to Columbus, GA, across the river into Russell Co., AL. One indenture, dated 8 June 1844, stated "I, Elizabeth Nicks (widow)...formerly of the county of Leon, Florida, but now of Russell County Alabama." is proof she had moved from Florida to Alabama.

Before 1835, Elizabeth's sons Robert and Richard were deceased, but Joseph Harrison Fair married J. R. Greene's sister, Martha Mariah. Her daughter, Sophia, married Allen Burr of Jefferson Co., FL. Daughters, Sarah Ann Nicks married Celete's son, James Daniel Sauls, and Martha Nicks married first a Mizell and second, James P. Durr.

The 1850 Census shows the Burr, Sauls, Fair and Greene families living in Opelika (then Russell Co.), AL. Only two Fair sisters, Elizabeth Jane and Frances, remained in Leon Co. This, the 7th U. S. Census named household members and it is the first time that Elizabeth Harrison Fair Nicks' grandchildren were listed. (Descendants should carefully study the names of children and compare them to all genealogy sheets at all migration points for this family.) Subsequent Census records show that the families continued to break up, especially after the Civil War.

Frances Fair Nicks' family by 1853, moved to Hernando Co., FL. That county's 1860-census report is missing and only tax reports exist to prove their existence near Brooksville, Florida. One son, Henry Robert R. Nicks was born in November 1852, just before the family moved south. His obituary in 1928 stated the family had moved to Hernando from Opelika in 1859, but that must have been his memory from a visit to the aunts, uncles and cousins and return to Brooksville.

After the Civil War, Joseph Harrison Fair's family moved west settling in Arkansas and Texas. Sophia and Mary Ann lived out their lives in Opelika and are buried in the Rosemere Cemetery. There is a Van Brunt cemetery at Lake Iamonia. Martha Durr moved to Jefferson, Texas and Sarah Ann Sauis lived in Opelika with her family returning to Quincy, FL by the next census without her. J. R. Nicks died in Brooksville in 1861 and Frances Fair Nicks in 1864, but their resting place is unknown.

After more than 160 years, Elizabeth Harrison Fair Nicks has not been forgotten by her descendants. Her life's path began in Ireland and ended in Girard, Russell County, AL. In he daughter, Frances Fair's little daybook titled "Miss Frances Fair's Book, and first dated 14 June 1831, there is a poem titled "The Mother's Grave," The poem begins:

"They stood beside the grave of her who watched their Infant years"... and ends with...

"To fit us for a brighter Sphere to be with her in Heaven."

There are 12 lines to Frances' poem. It's rededicated to both Elizabeth Nicks and Eleanor Nicks.

Source: Charleston, SC Mesne Conveyances, Leon Co., FL Deed Records, Charleston Orphanage Records, Southern Christian Advocate Death Notices, Charleston Marriage Settlements and Marriage Notices, Frances Fair's 1831 Day Book. Submitted by: Charles C. Blankenship, 55 Country Club Cove, Jackson, TN 38305-3909

Michael Harvey, Jr. and Martha Cole Harvey

In 1821, Mary Ann Harvey Black's grandfather, Michael Harvey, Jr. and his wife, Martha Cole Harvey, came to the Florida Territory to help establish the first Florida government. Michael Harvey, Jr. had been a prominent resident of Randolph County, North Carolina. He had served as a State Representative for North Carolina for the years 1798, 1800-1803, and again in 1805. In 1809-1810 he served as a State Senator for North Carolina. Michael Harvey, Jr. was born in Randolph County, North Carolina in 1767. His father, Michael Harvey, Sr., was born about 1727, and his father, also known as Michael Harvey, Sr. was the "English man."

Michael Harvey, Sr. was a founding member of the Back Creek Friends or Quakers. Back Creek was the oldest Monthly Meeting in the Southern Quarter. On the "12th of the 11th month, 1792 Back Creek was granted a meetinghouse" located in Randolph County, North Carolina. Michael Harvey, Jr., in the company of his wife and their sons and daughters and their families, formed a caravan in Randolph County, North Carolina and started overland for Florida. After a long and tiresome journey of almost two months, the little party arrived in Gadsden County in 1821. The Harveys came south from North Carolina traveling in covered wagons pulled by oxen. The brothers and sisters walked next to the wagons all the way. At night the women would sleep inside the wagons while the men would sleep under the wagons. "When they got to Gadsden County, they settled on Rocky Comfort Creek, just west of Little River. They built a one-room log cabin as temporary lodging. The cabin was located by a spring that gave them fresh water for themselves and their stock.

The log cabin they built had a 'huge' fireplace where they did all their cooking. They had brought with them a big walking spinning wheel to spin the cotton they grew and a loom for weaving the spun cotton. The whole family use the cabin as their place to sleep and eat. They built a tremendous barn for the horses, oxen, cattle, pigs, chickens, peacocks, guinea hens, and wagons which they had brought with them from North Carolina. They also brought their dogs for protection and for hunting.

Wayne Grissett remembers his Granddaddy, Calvin Grissett, telling him of going across the Ochlocknee River from Leon County into Gadsden County and seeing the old Harvey house: "There was a two story log cabin with shutters on the windows. The shutters had holes cut out of them to give the Harvey men a place to put their guns to defend against Indians. In the event of the Indians coming close to the house at night, the Harvey men made piles of trash out between the house and the surrounding woods. When the Indians came, the Harvey's went out and set the piles of trash on fire so they would have light to watch the Indians running from tree to tree. "The roof of the house was made of big wide boards with wood shingles. After many years of standing vacant, the house rotted down because no one was there to fix the leaky roof."

"After the family had settled in the log cabin, the men traveled back to North Carolina to get the mill stones they would use when they built their grist mill for the processing of the grains they raised. The mill was also used as a lumber mill for the timber they cut. In Leon County, Florida their grist and lumber mill was located on Harvey Creek where it was run by water power." Calvin Grissett told his grandson Wayne Grissett that the way the corn grinding worked was: "...ground on a toll a share - a pound for a pound." The last time the level of Lake Talquin went down the old mill pond site could still be seen.

In 1823 Michael Harvey, Jr. was appointed the first "Justice of the Peace" for Gadsden County, Florida. His son, Mark Harvey, was appointed to the "grand jury," and his son, Elijah Harvey, was appointed a "petit juror." On the Little River survey map, drawn in 1824, the locations of only five plantations are shown on the map; one of these five is the house of Michael "M. Harvey", Jr.

On April 11, 1824, Michael Harvey, Jr. along with Judge Jonathon Robinson, and Sherrod McCall worked their wagons "up the gentle slope of the hill that commanded the surrounding Apalachee County...On a ridge to near a waterfall that cascaded twenty or thirty feet into a pool 200-feet wide." Joining John McIver and his family, the "judge's slaves felled the trees for a clearing at the top of the hill. They then began constructing

three log buildings in the stump-filled clearing, in preparation for the third Legislative Council for the Territory of Florida, which was expected to meet in this wilderness the following month...During the fall and winter of 1824 the Legislative Council moved into the temporary two-story log cabin. On December 11, the Council officially christened the village "Tallahassee..."
Ante-Bellum Tallahassee
Written by: Elizabeth Coldwell Frano (Mrs. Christopher John Frano) Submitted by Ruby E. Hopkins Coldwell (Mrs. Walter Amze Coldwell)

Tawanna Meadows Hay and William L. Hay

Born in Panama City, Florida on August 14, 1938 moving to Tallahassee when she was five, Tawanna is a full fledged Tallahassee girl. She attended Caroline Brevard and Sealey Elementary schools and graduated from Leon High School in 1956 after having attended seventh through twelfth grades. Upon graduation she was hired by Sam Lastinger, Dean of Students at FSU, working at the University for six years for Mode Stone, Stanley Marshall, Herman Frick, J. R. Skretting, Dwigh Burton, Malvin Trussell and others.

In 1957 Tawanna met the man who was to be her husband of almost 52 years. William L. "Pete" Hay was rooming in the house next door to her while attending FSU.

They were married April 19, 1958 and had three children, Karl, Sheryl, and Keith. Karl and Sheryl attended Tallahassee Community College and Keith graduated from FSU. God blessed them with nine wonderful grandchildren, at this writing ranging in age from four to twenty-eight.

Pete was employed with the Department of Highway Safety and Motor Vehicle for 33 years retiring in 1995. In 1962 he was transferred to Miami, Florida where the family remained until 1972, then returning to Tallahassee. At this point Tawanna was hired by Parkway National Bank on a part-time basis and worked her way up through two mergers becoming an Assistant Vice President and Consumer Compliance Officer. After retiring from the banking industry, she went to work part-time as Office Manager for Marks & Associates, owned by wife of our Tallahassee Mayor, John R. Marks.

In 1978 Pete's father and Tawanna's mother were married, both having been widowed a number of years earlier. They shared 32 years together, making Pete and Tawanna half brother/half sister and proving much fun and many laughs over the years.

A highlight of their life together was serving at First Baptist Church, Tallahassee. They were both in the Sanctuary Choir for years and later in the Senior First Joy Choir. Tawanna also taught Sunday school for many of those years. This church family became Tawanna's lifeline, along with her children and grandchildren, when God too her beloved husband home on January 10, 2010.

Tallahassee is special to Tawanna and she has many memories of it being a small town, with McCrory's Dime Store, Rose Printing Company, Mutt and Jeffs', May Day in the park, only three movie theaters, and eventually one Drive-In. It was a great place to grow up and still is a wonderful place to live.
Written and submitted by: Tawanna Hay, 3305 Lemoyne Ct., Tallahassee FL 32312

C.E. "Sonny" Hay, Jr.

Clifford Eugene "Sonny" Hay, Jr. came to Tallahassee in 1943 in response to the City of Tallahassee's search for a golf professional for the city-owned Tallahassee Country Club. Born and raised in nearby Thomasville, Sonny Hay descended from pre-statehood Jefferson County, Florida, pioneer John J. Edwards, whose daughter Sarah Ann Elizabeth married Thomas County Sheriff Daniel F. Luke. Sonny Hay was son of Solicitor General of the Southern Circuit of Georgia, C. E. Hay Sr., and Attorney Sarah Eva Luke Hay, the first woman lawyer in the Circuit, admitted to the Bar in 1923. Sonny was assistant golf pro to Leland Crews at Glen Arven Country Club in Thomasville and golf pro in Brunswick, Georgia, before accepting the position of City of Tallahassee

Sonny Hay in 1951

Country Club golf professional.

Sonny Hay's relocation to Tallahassee in 1943 was followed by months of fruitless searches for housing in the chaotic World War II population boom. Sonny's wife Louise and small daughters finally joined him in residence in the Dixie Hotel opposite the Capitol on Monroe Street. For youngsters this was a delightful arrangement: crossing the quiet street to play in the echo chambers of the Capitol, sliding down the old banisters, pretending cannons on the Capitol steps were horses, entertaining visitors in the Dixie Hotel lobby; and all this with Caroline Brevard School an easy walk across a red clay playground filled with school children on weekdays and military vehicles from Camp Gordon Johnston on weekends. At the Tallahassee Country Club in the forties and early fifties, Sonny Hay enjoyed being golf pro, teacher, club manager and greens keeper of the impressive golf course located in Country Club Estates. In 1946, Sonny Hay hosted the first annual Tallahassee Junior Golf Tournament, and soon after he initiated the Jim Lee Open and the Shamrock Ladies Tournaments, bringing to Tallahassee many golfing greats. In addition to

1949 Tallahassee Country Club

private individual lessons and countless golf clinics, Sonny Hay taught golf classes at both Florida State and Florida A&M Universities, and he was architect and designer of the Jake Gaither Golf Course.

Representing the City of Tallahassee, Sonny Hay competed successfully in invitational golf tournaments nationally and in Canada, entertained government officials daily and visitors during Legislative sessions, and he introduced many Tallahassee people to golfing. He was active in the National Professional Golfers Association and the Florida PGA and was very proud of his several students who joined the pro tour. He remained at the Tallahassee Country Club until the facility was leased to a private organization. Sonny and Lou raised their children in Tallahassee, and grandchildren and great-grandchildren continue to reside in this community.

Submitted by: Sarah Hay Lamb, 3998 Bradfordville Road, Tallahassee, FL 32309

Henderson Family

My family moved to Tallahassee from Atlanta in August 1943. Rental property was at a premium due to military bases, Dale Mabry Pilot Training and Camp Gordon Johnston Training Base at, and near Tallahassee. My mother was able to find an apartment in Los Robles; however, it would not be available until September. So, our residence for one month was Clark's Motor Lodge on Highway 27 North, on property now known as Bradford Road (across from the now Northwood Mall). We had one room, and an efficiency one bedroom for my parents, a second room equipped with a small kitchen, table and chairs (by moving the table, a cot for me was placed by a window), which looked out over a cow pasture. The other room was a bedroom used by my two brothers.

Saturday, the day after we arrived, my mother needed to go to Byrd's Grocery on the corner of Monroe and Tennessee Streets. My father drove her to "town", parking near Pensacola Street. She was dressed as she always did in Atlanta: hat, gloves, heels, and hose! No one had told us that CampGordon Johnston furnished buses to drive the soldiers to "town", and Dale Mabry gave all their pilots and other personnel leave, Tallahassee was teaming with military. In order to become better acquainted with Tallahassee, Mother walked north on Monroe, and was duly shocked to find an open front of a large billiard parlor between Park and College. What really gave her the "vapors" was how many times "Men" wanting to know if she was "free" approached her! She scurried back toward where she was to meet my Father. When she did, she informed him that she would not "raise" their daughter in this type of town, and we were not staying! Dad took her to Bennett's Drug Store, so she could have a cold Coca Cola and calm down.

While sitting at one of the tables, in walked a former neighbor of Dad's from Brooksville, Florida, where he had grown up. Mrs. Lucy

Burwell had come to have a prescription filled and immediately recognized "Bertie". She learned we were moving to Tallahassee and immediately invited us to Sunday dinner after church at her home on Calhoun Street. She sat with Mother, and explained it was not safe for any lady to be on Monroe Street on a Saturday, certainly unescorted by her husband. "Aunt Lucy", as she became known to us, pointed out some of the downtown churches. She and her daughters attended Father Alfriend's St. John's church, but knowing we were Presbyterians, walked Mother to the corner of Monroe and Park, pointing out Brother Caldwell's church on Adams Street.

As I look back upon this episode my Mother was a very beautiful, 43 year old lady, and can now understand, how young service men would have misunderstand her status! As time passed, she loved to relate this incident, but always concluded, she had been terribly shocked!
Submitted and Written by: Elizabeth (Betty) M. Henderson, 2364 Carefree Cove, Tallahassee, FL 32308

Joseph (Joe) Victor and Pauline Haynes Herold

Joe's parents, Rudolph Rentsch and America Herold, had settled in Miccosukee, where he was born in 1897. Pauline Haynes was from Pensacola and had secured her first teaching job in the Miccosukee Community. Joseph and Pauline married at her parents' home at Ferry Pass in Pensacola on September 1, 1920. Joe continued working with his father and their first home was on the family farm, which extended down to Lake Miccosukee, which is today's entrance to Loveridge Plantation on Old Magnolia Road, while Pauline (Polly) continued teaching at the Miccosukee School.

In 1929, Joe and Polly bought Dr. Strickland's house, where they raised their five sons, Joseph Victor Jr., Haynes, Earl, Fred and Don. Joe was very active in several businesses including a grist mill and a cotton mill, in addition to being a farmer and

Polly and Joe Herold-1930s

Strickland-Herold House, built-1908 in Miccosukee, Florida

lumberman. Joe Herold was one of the organizers and original members of the Board of Directors for Talquin Electric Co-operative Inc. It is rumored that Joe thought of the name "Talquin", since the power plant would be located between Quincy and Tallahassee. He served on the regulating committee for the Farm and Home Administration, which established loans to assist needy farmers after the Great Depression. He also served as Justice of the Peace and Constable for the Miccosukee Community.

Joe and Polly spent their entire life involved in their church and community functions. Their home was always open to family, friends, and strangers. While growing up in Miccosukee, Joe was an avid sportsman and an expert marksman. The Herold family had a pond on their farm, where they would gather for fishing and picnics; often the catch of the day was cooked on a grill down by one of the ponds. Hunting season was an exciting time for the Herold house and Joe and his sons never missed opening day of duck season on Lake Miccosukee. This tradition continues today with Joseph's grandsons and great-grandsons.
Submitted by: Kerry L. Herold, Donald Lee Herold's Granddaughter; Written by: Donald "Lee" Herold, II, Great-Grandson of Rudolph Herold, 9402 Herold Hill Road, Tallahassee, Florida 32309-0074

Rudolph and America Herold

Rudolph Rentsch Herold arrived in the Miccosukee area of Leon County in 1896. A native of Switzerland, his family settled in Iowa, when he was 11 years old. Rudolph and his wife, America Herold, settled on 60 acres of land, where he built a home for his family. They had

Seated-in-car; Rudolph, Joseph, Adelien, America, Emma with son-Emmett, Rudolph, Jr. and Elwin-standing

two children, Adelien and Joseph Victor. Rudolph continued increasing his real-estate holdings until his farm included over 400 acres. Within a few years, he had half interest in 600 additional acres which joined Lake Miccosukee. His wife, America had attended music school back in her home state of Illinois. She was an accomplished pianist and during her short life, there was always music in the house. America died during childbirth and Rudolph was left with two young children, ages 10 and 9 years old.

In 1907, Rudolph married Emma Sophia Amelia Popp of St Louis, Missouri. Rudolph continued to do well and the *New Era Edition True Democrat* tells that "Rudolph Herold of Miccosukee has prospered as few planters living in Florida have, with growing anything but cotton for money, so today he is well off." Herold wrote an article for the *Southern Ruralist* entitled "Real Hay Making" which tells of his success with hay and forage crops. Rudolph built a beautiful 2-story home and a newspaper article states

"The outlook from the Herold windows is one of entrancing beauty." He purchased a Model T Ford and was the 2nd person in Leon County to own an automobile as well as new farm machinery

America and Rudolph Herold - 1890

that few others owned, including a Thresher and a Moline tractor. His willingness to experiment with modern agricultural methods and technology contributed greatly to his achievements.

Rudolph and Emma Herold had thirteen children, who together with his two oldest children, Adelien and Joe, grew up on a hilltop home in Miccosukee overlooking the family farm known as "The Herold Place". With a house full of children, there was always time for family, friends, and fun.

Written and submitted by: Donald "Lee" Herold II, Great-Grandson of Rudolph Herold, 9402 Herold Hill Road, Tallahassee, Florida 32309

Charlie and Linda Hill Family

Charlie Hill and Linda Jane Wardman were married in Tallahassee, Florida in 1982. Charlie was born in Marianna, FL in 1946. His parents were J. C. Hill and Emily Jean Ingram. Charlie had 2 siblings: Gwendolyn Hill Folsom and Shirlene Hill Barrentine.

Charlie graduated from Marianna High School and went to work in the retail business. He has been the Florida Agency Manager for Cotton States Insurance Company for over 25 years. Charlie has several hobbies: playing golf, drawing pictures, writing short stories, and working in his yard, when time permits.

Linda Jane Wardman was born in PA in 1949 to Joseph J. Wardman and Elizabeth J. Ayres. She graduated from New Castle High School in 1967 and attended Slippery Rock College in PA. She has 2 siblings, they are: Joseph W. Wardman and Sandra S. Wardman-Wilson.

Linda likes to decorate her home and helps decorate friend's homes when the opportunity arises. She also loves to shop, and travel. Their travels together include Amsterdam, Holland; Acapulco, Mexico; St. Thomas, and St. Croix, Virgin Islands; Maui, Hawaii; CA, PA, TX, NY including many other states in the USA. Since coming to Tallahassee in 1984, Linda has worked in the financial world.

Charlie and Linda are members of Immanuel Baptist Church. They have one son together, Adam Hill, who is married to Teri Jackson. Linda has a son, Gary A. Caruthers, Jr. from a previous marriage. Gary has a son, Landon T. Caruthers from a previous marriage. Landon is married to Deborah McCormick, who has two sons, Josh and Zachary McCormick from a previous marriage.

Linda and Charlie enjoy visiting with their grandchildren and relatives. They also find time to enjoy community functions in Tallahassee while enjoying their retirement.

Written by: Mary J. Marchant, 2901 Springfield Drive, Tallahassee, FL 32309-3274; Submitted by: Linda Hill, 3601 Garden View Way, Tallahassee, Florida 32309

Michael and Renee Hoch

As we drove into Tallahassee in March 2002, we were awed by the verdant hills, the magnificent oaks eerily draped with Spanish moss, the dogwoods, the shady canopy roads, the old historical buildings and the myriad parks and lakes. Within days we had found the ideal apartment for one year on Blairstone Road, compact with two bedrooms, two bathrooms, dining area, lounge, patio, ample storage space, and a view of the pool. Then, we furnished it from garage sales, thrift shops, and the Goodwood stores.

We bought a second hand Toyota Corolla; after all, we were only going to be here for a year. We were particularly impressed by the helpfulness and friendliness of the locals. Mike's one colleague astonished us by arriving on our doorstep with a dining room suite and others were also very generous. We had heard and read much about the charm of the Southerners and we were now experiencing it first hand. The atmosphere of Tallahassee, a blend of politics. education and religion, reminded us of Pietermaritzburg, also a state capital with one university, a community college, and many churches, so we felt immediately at home.

Above all, Tallahassee houses the largest magnet in the world at the National Magnetic High Field Laboratory and it is here that my husband Mike works as a visiting scientist. To his joy, the yearly contract continues to be renewed and we continue to enjoy all that Tallahassee has to offer. My life is comprised of exercise classes and lectures at the senior center, lunching with various friends, playing dominos and walking with the mall walkers. New experiences have included tubing, canoeing, hiking and camping with the senior adventure club. Culture abounds in the form of art galleries, ballet, theater and music of all varieties. We also enjoy trying the various restaurants with their different cuisines. There are several beaches and St. Marks Wildlife refuge just a short drive away.

Over the years we have watched with sadness the character of downtown Tallahassee alter as high rise condominiums have sprung up and old businesses and restaurants, such as the Silver Slipper have closed their doors, the results of the current recession. Our furniture looks weary and our car even wearier, but after seven years, it is difficult not to think of Tallahassee as home, although we are still officially only on HI visas. Tallahassee appears to attract with an irresistible magnetic force, which does not weaken with time, and had our family been able to join us here my happiness would be complete.

Submitted and Written by: Renee and Michael Hoch, 501 S. BlairstoneRoad, Tallahassee, FL. 32301

The D. L. "Buck" and Rebecca Hood Family

Buck and Rebecca Hood came to Tallahassee in 1940. They had married in Milton, FL on October 21, 1939. Buck's hometown was Pensacola, where he was born Darrell Leslie on August 20, 1909, son of Robert Repard Hood and Frances Thomas. He grew up in Pensacola, then "went to sea" and traveled the world as a teenager. He came back to Pensacola to finish high school, where he was outstanding in all sports.

Buck and Rebecca with Diana. 1940

Rebecca was born on September 15, 1914, in Chipley, FL, daughter of William Oscar Johnson and Belle Mullins. She grew up on a farm there, went to business school in Jacksonville, and also studied pre-school education.

In Tallahassee, Buck

Diana and Robin in Gypsy costumes for Halloween, 1944

operated a cafe on the edge of Lake Ella. Their daughter Diana Rebecca was born on November 8, 1940 when the couple lived at 723 N. Monroe St. As a toddler, she enjoyed going to the café and talking to the customers. The family moved first to Green St., then to 906 Hillcrest. Their second daughter Robin was born on July 7, 1942.

In early 1943, Buck joined the Seabees in WW II. He was stationed on the island of New Caledonia, serving as Chief Commissary Steward. Rebecca worked in the office at Dale Mabry Field during the War. She often made "motherdaughter" dresses for Diana, Robin and herself.

After the War, the family lived in Pensacola for two years, where Buck and Rebecca managed Hood's Cottages and Cafe. Their third daughter Sandra was born there on Sept. 7, 1947. In late 1947, the family moved back to Tallahassee, living at 519 Talaflo. In 1949, Rebecca realized a dream when she and Buck bought and remodeled the Queen Anne house at 906 E. Park Ave., that was built in 1910 by Jesse Hays and is in the Magnolia Heights Historical District. Diana and Robin attended Caroline Brevard School. Buck worked for a time selling trucks, then found his calling in the insurance business. He initially had his general insurance agency adjacent to Hotel Park, which he also managed. A son Donald Leslie was born on March 14, 1953. Rosalie Gaines then worked for the family, helping as the children grew up.

Buck with Diana, Robin, and Sandra, 1948

Hood family under camphor tree

Rebecca always had interesting crafts and activities to do with the children; when they were not climbing in the camphor tree or riding bicycles around the neighborhood. She was active in the Tallahassee Garden Club, becoming a flower show judge, and was a Sunday School Superintendent in the Primary Department at Trinity Methodist Church. She was appointed by a County Commissioner to the Advisory Board to establish the LeRoy Collins Leon County Public Library, and was trained as an early Hospice

Historic Hayes-Hood House, 906 E. Park Avenue, built 1910

volunteer. Rebecca's elderly parents lived for a number of years with Buck and Rebecca, where she cared for them until they died. Then Rebecca went to FSU, earning a Master's degree in Social Work.

The children, and any friends they could snare, often participated in Buck's "yard parties", where they raked and cleaned around the house. He took the family on a trip out West; another time they traveled up the East Coast. In addition to his insurance agency, Buck operated a taxi company for some years and was active in local political issues, running for City Commissioner.

Buck, Rebecca, Diana, Robin, Sandra and Don, 1960

He also coached youth baseball teams. He loved to play golf and was on the Greens Committee of Capital City Country Club.

The children attended Leon High School. Diana went to FSU Nursing School and married Michel Gendron in Canada. She taught nursing in Toronto for 28 years and now lives in Severn Bridge, Ontario. Robin went to college in GA, married Thomas Davidson, taught school in the Atlanta area and raised sons Tommy and Buck. Sandra Hood Walker worked for Buck in his insurance office for many years, raised her sons Judd, Travis, Chad and Eric West, then studied special education at FSU and taught in Leon County schools. Don was a taxidermist; now a longtime firefighter in Tallahassee. He and his wife Veronica enjoy their blended family, Brian and Katie Hood and Brittany, Carly, and B.J. Layne. Buck died on May 11, 2002. Rebecca sold the Hays-Hood House in 2005 to the Florida Trust for Historic Preservation and was pleased to see its restoration. She enjoyed living at George Belle Apartments and died February 8, 2009.

Submitted by: Diana Gendron, 1279 Graham Rd., Severn Bridge, Ontario, Canada, POE 1NO

Papa John Hopkins' Sawmill

You wouldn't believe it, papa had his own sawmill! When Papa was seventeen his father died. I don't remember how many brothers and sisters there were, but the court ordered that the oldest brother was to take care of his brothers and sisters. Uncle Bill Hopkins decided Papa was going to work for him. Papa didn't like going to work for his brother. So, he went to work at the post office. After that, he went into the lumber business for himself.

Papa cut virgin timber off of Grandpa Black's land in Leon County and bought the timber rights on other lands. He purchased land for 50 cents an acre, up and down the Ochlockonee River, for his timber company. He owned several oxen, teams and load wagons that were used to haul the timber from the woods down to the riverbank. He said it was real important to keep his oxen and horses in good condition.

For lunch he would make a soup called "Hoppin' John" for his hired hands. His recipe for "Hoppin' John" made a rich and spicy soup that called for Papa to fill a pot with water, and then slow cook overnight the black-eyed peas, to make them nice and tender. In the morning, he would add rice and sausage to the black-eyed peas, but no salt was added. Then the peas and rice would all swell up. This filled the men up for the day, giving them the energy they needed to work.

The trees were cut and trimmed up, then sawed up into all kinds of sizes and thickness. Big chains were used to lift the logs up onto the load wagons. The wagons had extra big wheels at least 6 feet tall on them to get the heavy loads down sand trails to the riverbank. Load after load of wagon pulled by oxen went down the trails. Once the wagons reached their destination, the trees were carefully unloaded and rolled down into the river. Papa knew the time of the year when the rains came, to make the river wide enough and deep enough, to float those big timbers down to Carrabelle.

In the fall, when a year worth of trees had been cut, Papa and his hired hands would nail the logs together forming large log floats. It would take several men to get a log out of a cove and move it this away and that way, to get it into position with the float, so it could be nailed to the float. They made float after float until they were ready to go down river. It would take four or five men to maneuver each float. The men would sleep in tents and eat on the floats the whole length of the trip. Depending on the weather, the trip would take a week or so. The men would have to poke this way and that way, to keep the floats from getting hung up on fallen tree stumps or sandbars. Sometimes a flash flood would come along and wash the logs away.

They would navigate the floats down the Ochlockonee River to the Ochlockonee Bay, where they were tied up along the banks of the river with other timber companies' logs that were waiting to be sold. Lumber agents would go from float to float counting the logs, and then putting their little ditty marks where they stopped. When the agents had added up the amount of trees in a float, they would go from owner to owner to negotiate for the best price to buy the timber. The timber was then pulled out of the river and loaded onto load wagons. Long oxen trains were formed, and the wood was hauled to the big sawmill in Carrabelle, Florida, to be cut into lumber. The finished lumber was then shipped out of Carrabelle on big ships.

Before they were married, Papa had finished a successful year of cutting and had his floats tied up in the Ochlockonee Bay, along with the other thousands of logs waiting to be sold, when a hurricane hit Carrabelle. In a matter of hours, a year's worth of profit for all the lumber companies that had their lumber ready to sell in the bay was lost, being swept out into the Gulf. The Gulf was full of lost timber. Papa lost a year's income. It was a struggle for Papa and Mama to get through that first year till the next sell of timber.

Papa thought a good education was the most important thing he could give his children. While Papa was away at work, he wanted Mama to be able to take care of the children and the house, so he built a school about 50 feet from the house from the lumber from his land. Then he dug a well. There was a law that said you had to have so many children to have a school, and each school had to have its own well. So Papa waited till he and my aunts and uncles and our neighbors had the right number of children to open the school. Then he went into Tallahassee, to Florida State College for Women, to select a teacher for all grades up to 8th. Papa hired Miss Agusta Raa and brought her home in his buggy. Miss Raa lived with us while she taught school. Families that lived on the other highway had to walk over to our school.

The last day of school was always a day to celebrate. Papa would hire someone to play the fiddle and someone to play the guitar so we would have lots of music. Papa was a great one to have pictures taken. He would bring in a photographer on the last day of school, and we would all stand out in front of the house with our teacher, the fiddler, and the man with the guitar, and then we would have our picture taken.

Written by: Elizabeth Coldwell-Frano (Mrs. Christopher John Frano); Submitted by: George Amze Frano (Liz grandson), 422 Fladers Drive, Indialantic, Florida 32903

Franklin Delano Howard PhD

Frank was born in Blountstown, FL on the seventh of November 1932 and was named after the newly-elected President Franklin D. Roosevelt. He was the first child born to Joel Amos Howard Sr. (5/12/1909 -7/29/2000) and Florence Josephine Davis Howard (5/12/1915 - 7/19/2002). He was known to some as Frank, to others as Delano and also had a nickname of "Sonny." His grandfather, Joseph Irvin Davis (6/15/1887 - 12/9/1981) was a carpenter and taught him to work with wood using hand tools at a young age. He excelled in academics; played clarinet in the high school band and graduated in 1950.

During the Korean War he served as Airman First Class in the US Air Force from 1951 to 1955. Frank married Mary Frances Halley in 1952. While stationed at Travis Air Force Base, California, their first two daughters, Regina and Diane, were born. In 1956 he and his family moved to Tallahassee, FL, where he attended Florida State University and graduated with a Bachelor of Science degree in 1960 - becoming the first in his family to graduate from college. Their third daughter, Susan, was born soon after.

Cartoon by Franklin Howard

Frank began his teaching career at Augusta Raa Jr. High in 1960 and inspired many students in the fields of Earth Science and Math. In addition to teaching he sponsored the Photography Club, State Science Fair and served as a Student Council Advisor. To this day, many of his students remember his distinctive, long fingernails and the red necktie he always wore on test days. Between 1961 and 1979 he also instructed adult students in high school math at Lively Vocational School. Raa's ninth grade class named him "'Best

Franklin Delano Howard

Teacher of the Year" in 1967. In 1969 he accepted the position of Assistant Principal at Raa. As an Assistant Principal he assisted in the desegregation initiative by transferring to Nims Middle School in 1970 and returning to Raa in 1972. He left Raa in 1987, the same year he received a Master of Science degree from Nova University. During his years as an administrator, he served on many committees for county wide school curriculum development, gifted programs, district testing and alternative education. He served from 1988 - 1991 at Griffin Middle School as an Assistant Principal before retiring.

He was involved in the community as a member of the Florida Association of School Administrators, United States Power Squadron, Charter member of Apalachee Archaeological Society, Apalachee Bay Yacht Club, Florida League of Middle Schools, Leon High Crew and was a Lifetime member of the Gulf Coast Community College Foundation. Frank was a gifted artist and cartoonist and made a cartoon for just about every occasion. He is fondly remembered by his colleagues for his ability to doodle the perfect tension-breaking cartoon during long meetings.

Frank and Mary Frances were married 45 years. She supported him in all areas, including volunteering at Raa when all the student records and class schedules were first transferred to a computer system. She proofed many lists to help ensure he and the staff had a smooth transition into the new school year. He deeply appreciated her continued support and assistance in all his projects and interests.

He had a passion for sailing and owned a few sailboats, some of which he built. The Tallahassee Democrat featured him in a 1967 article while he was building one of his sailboats. On the weekends you couldn't find him at home because he spent most of his time at the beach. Frank was a collector and builder of antique guns. He would start with a block of wood, parts of metal and after many countless hours, he would carve and shape into a one of a kind working fire arm. On occasion he would practice shooting these guns.

During his retirement he wrote and published local historical interest articles that are now reprinted on the Internet. On occasions, when he would guest lecture at schools, he would bring a collection of Indian artifacts and some replicas he had made himself. He, himself was of Native American descent. Before his death on January 8, 1998, he had become skilled in the art of violin making and had made a few. He spent as much time as possible with his grandchildren, teaching...always teaching! He was truly a man of many talents!

Submitted by: Susan H Sapronetti, Diane H Hamilton & Regina H. Blackstock, 2918 Pearl Dr., Tallahassee, FL 32312

Warren (Price) Huff's Three M's

My husband Peter and I have lived in Tallahassee, Florida for 33 years. It has been the home of our daughter Moya since her first birthday. When Moya was in her twenties she met Price Huff through a mutual friend. They were together for three years before they were married in the gazebo near the pond at our home in 2006. Moya and Price had our granddaughter in 2007. Her name is Mia and she is joined by Maja, her step-sister who is 10 years old now. She is Price's daughter from his first marriage. Even Price sometimes makes a slip up with the 3M's: Moya, Mia, and Maja.

(R-L) Price, Moya, Donalee, holding Mia, Maja, and Peter

Warren Price Huff was born in Tallahassee, Florida at Tallahassee Memorial Hospital (TMH) to Linda and William Huff. Price's father is deceased now, but his mother lives near and enjoys seeing her grandchildren. After attending both Lincoln High School and North Florida Christian Academy, Price worked in the construction trade for a while, but found construction work was not a stable job for raising a family. Since he was raised around caring people in the medical field, Price decided to attend Lively Vocational Institute's Licensed Practical Nurse Program. He was motivated to succeed by his mother and aunt who are nurses as well.

After practicing his skills at TMH, he joined the practice of Dr. Kepper and has won recognition as a valued member of the medical staff. Patients are drawn to him because of his patience with them in their time of need, for giving good advice, and for his comforting ways when you need someone to hold on to. Many people have brought him gifts of appreciation for his caring personality.

Price has been very helpful to us in many ways and has become a special part of our family. We are proud to think of him as the son we never had. His hobbies include fishing, movies, and riding his motorcycle. He also loves to cook; even through he can't boil an egg. His plans for the future are to raise his family and someday buy them a house of their own. He is now making plans to further his career with more education.

Written by: Donalee Pond-Koenig; Submitted by: Moya Price, 7605 Broadview Farm Lane, Tallahassee, FL. 32309

Laura Huff Memories of Tallahassee

I remember Tallahassee from the time of the Second World War. I was born in Quincy, Florida in 1936. My maiden name was Ruby Jean Livingston (a Southern, family name.)

Back in the early 40s, we would all get in our black, '39 Chevy and head to Tallahassee. We had to go by way of Havana. Highway 90 from Quincy to Tallahassee wasn't opened until after the War. It was a big happening! We would come in on Tennessee St. and head down Monroe. The old Floridan Hotel, with all of its lovely Art Deco architecture, was still across from St. John's Episcopal Church. We would park near the then post office on Park Avenue. As a child, I would gawk at the big, colorful murals there!

We would walk down one side of Monroe looking and shopping, and stopped to have lunch at the counter in McCrory's five and dime. In back of the lunch counter were the most beautiful mirrors with art deco designs of cranes and reeds! The lunch counter went all the way to the back of the store! After lunch, we would continue our walk down Monroe to the Capitol Building, and then across the street to the big Sears store on the corner. Sometimes we would catch a movie. There were three movie theatres: The Florida, up by the post office, the Ritz on Monroe, between Park and College, and the State on College Ave. When we saw Disney's Three Caballeros at the Ritz, I was not used to the color and motion, and it almost made me sick. And, just think about what we watch today! "Going to the big city" to look and shop was one of the highlights of my childhood.

In 1956, I transferred to FSU after attending a small women's college for two years. It was quite an adjustment, both the size and being co-ed, although there were only 6,000 students there at the time. I was a pre-med major taking science classes, and I remember in a physics lab one day, the lab assistant said to two of us girls, "I don't like girls in my labs." Talk about a shock! After being the science department's only lab assistant at my previous college, I felt like I had fallen through a hole in time!

I married in 1957, and we moved to Tallahassee to Mitchell's trailer park on West Call Street. It was very convenient; you could walk to campus! I finished my degree, and got a job in a biochemistry lab on campus while my husband was still at FSU. My work was very interesting, in the Dept. of Oceanography with Dr. Sidney Fox. He was doing research on synthetic proteins that he had named "proteinoids", made by co-polymerizing amino acids. I had the privilege of making the first "microspheres" like cells, from these! My name was on several journal publications with Dr. Fox.

During this time, we had a daughter, Kaye Lynne, born in 1959, and twin daughters, Cynthia and Sandra, born in 1961. Life was quite busy, with three babies under three. I remember making the prophetic comment to my husband that life would be lots of things, but not boring! In 1963, I went back to work teaching biology at Leon High School. The research that I had done with Dr. Fox was now in the new Biological Curriculum Studies! The rooms weren't air conditioned. We had big open windows and no screens. So, one day during a microscope lab, I looked up and saw one of my students staggering in the door, with leaves and dirt all over him. He said, "I fell out the window trying to catch a fly for the frog in the terrarium!"

After teaching for a year at Leon, I was offered a job back at FSU in the Food Science lab. This was very exciting, as it would give me a chance to work in research again, and finish my Master's! Dr. Betty Watts was my major professor. I was given the job of lab supervisor to see that all the equipment and inventory was maintained, the lab kept in order, grad students informed on the use of the lab, plus working on USDA grants. I finished my Master's in 1967, and worked on my Doctorate as a teaching assistant for another year. I published my Master's thesis with Dr. Watts; my doctoral work gave a breakthrough on a research question that went back to the late forties.

In 1969, our son was born. I finished my teaching career working for the Dept. of Education and retiring in 1999. My son and I bought and restored the oldest wooden-structured house in Tallahassee still on its original site. It was called the Old Railroad Boarding House at 450 St. Francis Street. When we bought the house, the City was in the process of condemning it, which was not revealed to us at the time of the sale. The outcome of this was a law suit and several years of intense work with the City to get it up to code and off the condemned list! It was the greatest battle of my life!

While we were working on getting the house restored physically, we were also working on getting it on the National Registry of Historic Places. The local Historic Preservation Board went to bat for us. And the Dept of State and FSU helped us through the complicated application process of submitting a proposal to the National Registry! We did our own archival searches, going to the Florida Archives, putting on white gloves and looking through the old handwritten ledgers. We found that a Burfoot Williams, who worked as the freight agent, had petitioned the Pensacola-Georgia Railroad to buy the property and structures in 1860. So, the house dated back to the 1850s. It was truly interesting to discover all the history and special architectural features of the house. My son did extensive research and seemed to have a knack for working with restoring old buildings. We had previously restored our own home in the Myers Park area, which was built about 1928. After over 4 years of working on our house, with the City, Federal and State governments, we were awarded both a certificate for the Williams House as it was named, and a waiver of the code violations and most of the fines! There is no place like Tallahassee's beautiful fairyland city! Thanks for my memories!

Written-Submitted: Laura Jean Huff, 814 Governors Drive, Tallahassee, FL 32301 richardhuff814@comcast.net

Linda Harvey-Husbands

Tallahassee was a small town in the 1950s and 60s. Most of the stores were downtown and as children, we walked or rode our bikes everywhere. We lived on West Georgia Street not far from the Governor's mansion. I grew up with three sisters and lots of neighborhood kids.

There was a vacant lot nearby and we spent many hours playing kickball, dodge ball, flag football, softball or whatever we could dream up. There were no parents and we made our own rules. There was less bickering as we all understood what was expected if we wanted to play.

I remember walking to school and downtown to the library on Park Avenue. As early as seven years old, we were allowed to cross Tennessee St. or Monroe St. We usually went in groups but our parents didn't worry about traffic or predators. It was a very safe and friendly town to grow up in.

On Saturday morning, they had free cartoons at the local theatres. We often smuggled in our own drinks and I remember having a glass coke bottle that I kicked over and it rolled all the way down to the front of the theatre. Of course I didn't admit it was mine. The cost of a movie was 14 cents for children and 25 cents for adults. We usually picked up coke bottles and turned them in to the stores for 2 cents each to earn money for the movies.

We went skating at the old armory which is now the Sr. Center. It cost 25 cents to rent skates or 15 cents if you had your own skates. We went swimming at Levy Park and attended activities at Lafayette Park, often walking or riding bikes. On weekends, our parents would take us to the drive-in movies and Mom would make popcorn to take with us. We went picnicking and swimming at Silver Lake, Dog Lake and Lake Hall. There always seemed to be lots to do.

I remember trick or treating at the Governor's mansion while LeRoy Collins was Governor. There was no fence or security gate and the Governor and his wife met all the children at the door and handed out candy. We thought it was neat but also very normal.

During the summer, we had to help Mom shell peas, butter beans and shuck corn. Of course this was all done on the front porch and we usually had lots of neighbor kids to help. I might add that we didn't have air conditioning either, only fans. My parents had a window unit in their bedroom in the early 60s but never in the rest of the house. Our car was not air-conditioned either. I guess you don't miss what you never had. We grew up very independent and also knew the value

of saving and working. Tallahassee was a great place to grow up.
Submitted and written by: Linda Harvey-Husbands, 196 Main Street Monticello, Florida

Opal Hyatt

If you are looking for a rock-strong down-to-earth Christian who can take whatever God sends her way and make it into a ten-layer chocolate cake, you are looking for Opal Hyatt. This lovely woman takes to heart Paul's admonition in Philippians 4:13, "I can do everything through Jesus Christ who gives me strength." Born in Chipley, Opal has spent most of her life in North Florida. She grew up in a part of our state that did not prosper and flourish in those days. Coping with those hard times gave her the grit and tenacity that is the backbone of her strength and spirit today.

She found her faith at thirteen. Her love and belief in Jesus Christ has been her bedrock foundation in good times and bad. It supported her during the joy that a first child brings, and buoyed her up with the untimely death of another child. Opal married, in 1950, the son of a woman with whom she worked while a high school student. She raised a family of six children, three boys and three girls, all of whom live here in Tallahassee.

While she worked at the State of Florida Department of Revenue in Tallahassee, it was probably her time spent with the public school lunch program in Panama City that got her rubbing shoulders with the greats. Opal learned how to cook for big crowds of people, a skill that has earned her the respect and appreciation of the Bobby Bowden brood. When they plan a family get-together, Opal is who they call on to come and "fix the grits!"

Opal believes that her Christian faith is one of the most wonderful things that has happened to her. She lives her faith, helping out wherever and whenever she can, visiting and talking to those who need extra concern, cooking for families in crisis, always ready with a ride, or a shoulder to cry on when needed.

A lot has changed in our nation during her lifetime. When asked what she thought was the biggest change she saw, Opal felt that the lower moral standard of today was the biggest change. Not jet airplanes, not interstate highways, not even color TV, but the crumbling of our country's moral fiber and disrespect for one another is our greatest change. And you know that Opal has an answer to that problem!
Written by: Carol Ann and Bill Boydston, 1639 Twin Lakes Circle, Tallahassee, Florida 32311; Submitted by: Opal Hyatt

Frieda and Paul Ireland Co-op

Frieda and Paul Ireland were members of the Tallahassee's New Leaf Market co-op for a number of years. They were married in Leon County on November 9, 1987, and spent the rest of their life together in support of this coop.

Paul Richard Ireland was born January 10, 1914 in Illinois to Kate and Joseph Ireland. He has one sister, Bernice Watt and one brother, Joseph Ireland. Paul served in the Military during WWII until he was honorably discharge in 1945 from Fort Blanding. He moved to Tallahassee in 1950 to raise his family until his wife died in 1980 and he moved to be near his children.

Frieda K. Ireland was born in New York and moved to Florida in 1982. She was a long standing owner of New Leaf Market. Confronted with an unwanted diagnosis in her fifties, Frieda turned to food to address her health. She embraced the vegan and raw foods movements and never turned back. Her involvement included legislating for better food laws and writing her own book.

Over the years she has supported the Co-op in many ways. From volunteering to teaching seminars she shared her knowledge of nutritious food. Frieda could often be found sharing her passion for food with employees and customers alike while she shopped the aisles. She lived what she taught and enjoyed a remarkable life, free of chronic disease well into her eighties. Frieda was a beloved customer, owner and friend to many at the co-op.

In honor of Frieda's dedication to the New Leaf Market Co-op, "The Frieda Ireland Memorial Assistance Program" was established The Irelands lived in support of the co-op until

their death, Frieda in 2007 and Paul in 2004. They both shall be missed by all who knew them.
Written and Submitted by: Frieda Ireland, 3874 Imaginary Rd, Tallahassee, Florida 32312

D.M. and Posthuma Johnson

Davis Montgomery Johnson, known as D.M. Johnson, was born July 16, 1868 in Covington County, Alabama. He was the son of Noah Johnson and Matilda Dixon Johnson an the grandson of Nicholas Johnson and Nancy Rachels Johnson. His maternal grandparents were Wiley B. Dixon and Elsie Helen May Dixon, daughter of James David May. Great-grandparents were Jeremiah Dixon, a Revolutionary War veteran who purchased land on the Conecuh River in 1823, and Elizabeth Goff Dixon.

The 1900 Leon County, Florida census recorded Davis Montgomery Johnson, age 31, in the home of Noah and Matilda Johnson in the Woodville community. Both men were farming. D.M. Johnson, a boarder, was also recorded in the 1900 Wakulla County. Florida census as a woods rider.

On April 25, 1901 in Wakulla County, Rev. Thomas J. Isler conducted the marriage of Davis Montgomery Johnson and Posthuma Dorothea Rodgers.

Posthuma, daughter of Aaron T. and Sarah A. Rodgers, was born August 12, 1877 in Williamsburg County, South Carolina. D.M. and Posthuma Johnson lived in Leon County, Florida for several years during the early 1900s. He was a farmer and owned eleven acres of land west of the St. Mark's Railroad.

In addition to his parents, two sisters, Elizabeth "Bertie" Johnson Richbourg (wife of Caswell) Joseph Tobin Richbourg) and Leila Johnson Lowery (wife of James Hill Lowery), also lived in the Woodville community. The 1930 Leon County, Florida census recorded Davis and Posthuma Johnson with their niece, Clyde Lowery, then age seven, living south of the St. Augustine Road on the Shepard Plantation. Clyde was adopted by D.M. and Posthuma Johnson after the death of her mother.

By about 1913, D.M. Johnson moved his family to Hosford, Liberty County, Florida, where he owned several pieces of property and worked in a turpentine still. He sold his Liberty County property in the early 1920s and moved to Nicholls, Coffee County, Georgia. The 1930 census recorded D.M. there as a woodsman in the naval stores business. He was also a cotton and tobacco farmer. His nephew, Wilson Emmet Richbourg, worked with him one summer, and D.M. gave young Wilson a gold pocket watch when the summer came to an end and Wilson returned home to Clearwater, Pinellas County, Florida.

Davis Montgomery Johnson died February 9, 1940. Posthuma Dorothea Rodgers Johnson died June 6, 1968. They were buried in the Hall Cemetery (Dry Creek Church) south of Nicholls.
Written by Judith Richbourg Jolly, 11541 Arlhuna Way, Dade City, Florida 33525; Submitted by Patricia Richbourg Stephens, 4423 E. Brandon Drive, Marietta, Georgia

I Remember Michael Johnson

Michael Johnson (1955-2005) was born in a small factory town in Germany. His mother died in childbirth, so Michael was sent to America to be raised by his military father, Raphael Johnson, who was reassigned stateside just before Michael was born. It nearly a year for him to arrive in this country as an orphan so his father could adopt him. Michael's life was pretty much routine while he was growing up. He got into the usual fights and bad notes to his parent like most children, but he had more opportunities because his adopted parents were college professors. This provided Michael with a better grasp of reality, an extra keen sense of humility, and an ability to learn from some of the best minds in this nation.

I believe this is what attracted me to him. I could see the brilliance of his fire, blazing like a glorious candle to light my

Carol and Michael Johnson Wedding Reception -1998

way. I did not know this when I first met him, because Michael was so unruly and selfish. He enjoyed dumpster diving, sleeping in parks, and taking vacations in jail. Not once did he show any remorse for losing his temper when not warranted.

My attitude changed when I saw him stand up for someone who was being bullied and picked on. I was immediately attracted to his personality after this. I swore I could change his other bad habits, but instead he ended up changing me for the better. He possessed a pleasing personality and could charm the sox off anyone, man or woman. I also found that he had a unique gift of gab and could make people feel like he understood them.

They trusted Michael so on April 20, 1998, Michael and I, Carol D. Phillips were married at the First Baptist Church in Downtown Tallahassee, Florida. Not long after the honeymoon, I found his spirit was restless and he wanted to return to the North. He met my relatives and they liked him immediately. Another distraction I tried was to gather and mingle with all sorts of people. Michael enjoyed entertaining, cooking, and playing cards; he had a great sense of fashions and would advise me on the latest women's wear, since I only dressed for comfort. It was a pleasure to see him dress up.

In 2003 Michael returned to Washington DC, where his adopted mother lived. For me it was as if he was there only when I needed someone and then when he felt I could stand on my own two feet, he was gone as quickly as he arrived. I do not know what drove him, but while he lived here I was happy and glad to bask in the glory of my marriage with him. On October 1, 2005 Michael Johnson died in the hospital in DC, I felt a great lost of his presence on earth. I shall always remember this man for what he has shown meand for the spirit he left behind for so many others like me,that carries me on.

Written by: Carol D. Johnson (Michael's Ex-wife); Submitted by: Mrs.Ruth Perry (Michael's Adopted Mother), 1004 Hamilton Street NE, Washington, DC 20011

Malcolm B. Johnson

Malcolm B. Johnson was the Executive Editor of the *Tallahassee Democrat* from 1954-1978, writing a daily column called "I Declare" and editorials. He was born in Wardner, Idaho. His family homesteaded in Alberta, Canada and later moved to Jacksonville, FL where Johnson attended public schools. He received a degree in Journalism from the University of Florida in 1936. He worked for the *Jacksonville Journal* and the *Daytona Beach Sun-Record* before moving to Tallahassee in 1937. As an Associated Press reporter, he covered the announcement of the opening of Disney World.

In Tallahassee, Johnson covered home-front stories during WWII. He married Dorothy Burt of Jacksonville and they had one daughter.

As Executive Editor of the *Tallahassee Democrat*, Johnson, part of the power elite of Tallahassee, took the opportunity to gather city leaders in his office to deterimine policy. Johnson wanted Tallahassee to grow in size and wealth. As a community leader, Johnson made many lasting contributions to improve living conditions in the city. Some of his contributions include: transportation and the development of roads; Innovation Park; The Donald Tucker Leon County Civic Center; the 1961 and 1986 airports; improvements to Tallahassee Memorial Hospital; Interstate 10; encouragement of industrial growth in Tallahassee; improving public services in the community and economic development.

Malcolm B. Johnson

"Typical of southern political leaders before the Civil Rights Movement, Johnson had a distaste for the movement to integrate white and black society. As a result, the *Tallahassee Democrat* earned the unpleasant moniker of *Tallahassee Dixiecrat*. The 1956 Bus Boycott had several "I Declare" columns, some conciliatory, some not so."

His influence has had a lasting effect on Tallahassee.

Source: State Archives of Florida Online Catalog: Article on Malcolm B. Johnson: Record Group Number: 900000 M82-77; Submitted by: Mary J. Marchant, 2901 Springfield Drive, Tallahassee, FL 32309-3274

Noel and Matilda Johnson

Noel Johnson, known as Noah Johnson in pre-1900 census and other records, was born August 30, 1836 in Hancock County, Georgia. His parents, Nicholas Johnson and Nancy Rachels John parents son, married October 9, 1834 in Warren County, Georgia and arrived in west Florida, possibly Jefferson County, by May 20, 1844. A court case involving Nicholas Johnson was moved from Jefferson County to Leon County in 1850. The 1850 census of Conecuh County, Alabama included Noah Johnson, age 15, with his parents. By 1855, Nicholas and Nancy Rachels Johnson were established in Covington County, Alabama, where Nicholas was granted a homestead certificate for 159 acres in the Conecuh River community. He and Nancy Rachels Johnson died sometime after the enumeration of the 1870 Covington County census. The surname in that census was recorded as Jhonson.

Noel Johnson enlisted in Company H (New) First Florida Infantry, CSA on May 13, 1862. Military records described him as 5' 6" tall, with dark hair and skin, and hazel eyes. He was wounded in the left side at Missionary Ridge, Tennessee and was captured, hospitalized at Nashville, later imprisoned at Louisville, Kentucky, and eventually sent to Fort Delaware, where he remained until the end of the war. Following the war he returned home to Covington County.

On August 20, 1867, in Conecuh County, Alabama, Noah Johnson married Matilda Dixon, daughter of Captain Rufus Wiley Beauregard Dixon and Elsie Helen May Dixon, daughter of David May. Matilda Dixon was born April 22, 1840, and grew up with her 13 brothers and sisters on the family home place deep in the Conecuh Forest.

Noel Johnson's CSA Record

The small cemetery behind the home is the resting place for many family members. The site today, known as the Solon Dixon Forestry Education Center, is owned and maintained by Auburn University. Matilda's great-grandfather, Jeremiah Dixon, who served in the Tenth Regiment of the North Carolina Continental Line during the American Revolution, bought land in Covington County in 1823. He died July 26, 1835, during his pension application process and was buried, per family tradition, in the Teel Cemetery. His wife, Elizabeth Goff Dixon, died June 15, 1840.

Noel and Matilda Dixon Johnson, with their children and grandchildren, moved to Woodville, Leon County, Florida during the 1890s. Noel Johnson farmed the land where he and his family lived. He died August 7, 1912 and was buried in the White Primitive Baptist Church Cemetery in Woodville. A large, upright granite marker identifies him as Noel Johnson. However, a CSA military marker placed many years later identifies him incorrectly as Noel Wright Johnson. A greatgrandson, Noel Wright Hardee, son of Leila Frances Richbourg and Alia Gora Hardee, was named for Leila's maternal grandfather, Noel Johnson, and the family of Alia Gora's mother, Niza Wright. During the 1950s, it was assumed by subsequent generations that Wright was part of Noel Johnson's name, and Wright was recorded in UDC and other published records (Hartman's *Biographical Rosters of Florida's Confederate Soldiers 1861-1865*). Wright family research has since revealed the and clarified the name.

During the last years of her life, Matilda Dixon Johnson lived with her son, Davis Montgomery Johnson, who moved from Woodville to nearby Hosford, Liberty County, Florida. Matilda died September 8, 1919 and was laid to rest beside her husband in Woodville. Noel and Matilda Dixon Johnson were parents of three known children. Census records indicate that four children were born to them.

#1 - Davis Montgomery (D.M.) Johnson (listed as Noah in the 1880 census) was born July 16, 1868. He married Posthuma Rogers.

#2 - Leila Johnson was born September 24, 1869. On July 13, 1887 in Conecuh County, Alabama, she married James A. Hill Lowery. Leila died following the birth of their daughter Clyde. It is assumption that Leila Johnson Lowery is buried in the White Primitive Baptist Church Cemetery. Clyde was adopted by her uncle and aunt, D.M. and Posthuma Johnson.

#3 - Elizabeth "Bettie" Johnson was born August 16, 1871. On July 13, 1887 in Conecuh County, Alabama, she married (Caswell) Joseph Tobin Richbourg.

#4 - The 1900 Leon County census listed four children born to Noah and Matilda Johnson but only three were living that year. The identity of the fourth child remains unknown to family history researchers.

Sources: Census, military, family, and cemetery records; Submitted by Judith Richbourg Jolly, 11541 Arlhuna Way, Dade City, Florida 33525

Bradfordville, From Crossroads to Suburbs

Recently I have been reflecting over the past 75 years of my life and some not so obvious facts have come to mind. First, I am a fourth generation Leon Countian on my Daddy's side (Johnson) and a sixth generation on my Mother's side (Strickland). My father's father, Daniel Robert Johnson, Sr. was born near Dawkin's Pond on the south side of Lake Iamonia on October 29, 1868. He married Susan Helen Young from Metcalf, GA and later moved his family to Bradfordville. Bradfordville is where I spent a good part of my youth.

Bradfordville consisted of a few families and several stores. Since people could only travel by mule or horse about 10 miles round trip in a day to get groceries, etc. there was a store or community about every 10 or so miles. Bradfordville was one of those communities.

I was born in my maternal grandparent's home on County Road 12, but I spent the first 4 or 5 years of my life on a 140- acre farm (south of Chiles HS) across the road from the entrance to the Eppes Family cemetery in Bradfordville. My mother was a homemaker and my father was an inspector for screwworms, and boll weevil. He also farmed and was a constable. My paternal grandfather Dan R. Johnson, Sr. ran one of the 3 general stores in Bradfordville. It was a two story building put together with wooden pegs instead of nails. The upstairs was rented as a Lodge. Cousin Green Johnson ran one of the other general stores and Judge Whitehead (Justice of the Peace) ran the third which is said he used for court.

Grandpa Johnson (Papa to the grandchildren; Mr. Johnson to grandma) and Grandma raised two girls (Julia and Helen) and three boys (Dan, Ralph, and Jessie) in Bradfordville. They attended Bradfordville School. The oldest daughter, Julia, taught at the school in 1919 & 1920 for $30 a month. As their children became older and moved to town, Papa would tell his children that they didn't need to go to town because Tallahassee was coming to Bradfordville. How could he have predicted that more that 70 years ago?

Mrs. Julia Virginia Johnson, Wife of Papa, D. R. Johnson

In 1938, my parents moved closer to Tallahassee. The house was located about a half-mile north of where I-10 now crosses Thomasville Highway. Daddy had a job in town making $16.00 per week and Mama stayed home. The year I entered Sealy Elementary School as a first grader, I took a knife out of the kitchen and started whittling on a stick. The knife slipped and stuck into my left eye. I immediately removed the knife. My parents drove me to Dr. Brown's office then to Johnston's Sanitarian for treatment. Dr. Brown was not able to completely save my sight in that eye.

Shortly after my accident, Papa had a stroke and fell off the running board of a car. He could no longer run the "big" store, so we moved back to Bradfordville. The upstairs "Lodge" was converted into living quarters for my family. Mama and Daddy took over the store. They ran a grist mill behind the store. I guess our moving back was a boon for Bradfordville because that increased the population to 18 in the community. Thirteen of those were from Pioneer families. There were the 2 Johnson Families, and the Roberts family.

There was only one telephone in Bradfordville and that was on the wall in Daddy and Mama's store. To get an operator you turned a crank on the side of the phone. When the operator answered, you gave her the number or name of the person you were calling and she would connect your call.

Papa, D.R. Johnson at his Bradfordville store with Pete-the-Dog.

During WWII there were aircraft observation stations to track the movement of aircraft (radar was not good in those days). The store was a station and Mama was the "Chief Observer". She scheduled the volunteers and if they didn't show up I got the job. I could identify the number, the size and the direction of travel just by the sound of the engines. This information was reported to the Army at Dale Mabry Field. Later the Army installed better phones and even built an observation building on the corner of Bannerman and Thomasville Roads so we could move the observation post from the porch of the store. I liked it better on the porch; it was closer to the candy counter.

While living at the store, I experienced my first lesson in business. One day a horse trader came by the store. He had a nice little horse on his truck. I had a bicycle but I wanted that horse in the worst way. The man agreed to take my bicycle and $40.00 in "Buffalo Nickels" that I had saved (I wish I had them today) for the horse. We traded and he left. As soon as he wa out of sight I wanted by bicycle back. Daddy said "no," I had made a deal and I had to stick to it. I have remembered that lesson all my life and have lived by it. Only God can take away a person's word, but everything else can be taken away by man.

There are only two of the original buildings still standing in Bradfordville. One is the "Bradfordville School House" which has been relocated on what used to be the Lauder's property and the other one, the "Green Johnson House" which has been remodeled and it now a vet clinic.

As I look at Bradfordville today I see the growth that Papa predicted many years ago. It's no longer a small tight community, but a larger community with many opportunities and people who are proud to be residing in Bradfordville. I often wonder if Papa is sitting in his rocking chair up in Heaven watching the many cars go by saying "I told them so!"

Submitted by: Ralph E Johnson, Jr., 2860 Minuet Lane, Tallahassee,FL 32303

Trellis Johnson-Smith

In 1952 Trellis Johnson-Smith was born in Chicago, Illinois to Willie Mae Johnson (1929-2002), but was raised by her step-father, Albert Flowers (1900-1978). Trellis has eight siblings, of which she is the oldest female of three- Arnold, Zebra and Elaine Johnson, and the youngest of five step-brothers; Donald, Andrew, Albert Jr., Oscar, and Ronnie Flowers. Trellis' maternal grandparents are Elnora Johnson (1911-1932) and James Ivory (1897-1935)

Trellis graduated from Shakespeare Elementary School, and attended Forestville High School in Chicago, Illinois, which provided a stepping stone for her to excel in English literature. Upon completing her studies Trellis met and married Dennis McDaniel in 1978. Trellis has been a dutiful mother to five daughters for over 40 years and they have made her the proud grandmother of seven grandchildren; Samantha and Roy Person (Diandra and Alex), Becky and Maureen Branden, Danielle and Darryl Dickson (Damien), Donnieka and David Cross (Princedavid and Domenick), Tiyashica Urea and Darryl Wilson (Romeo and Brianna). plus one great-granddaughter by Diandra named (QuinLavette Coons). Trellis met Derrick Smith in Miami in the late 1980s, and they have been together for over 20 years. They have shown their love and respect by renewing their wedding vows in 2004.

Trellis states;"I was a pioneer in changing the laws that allowed pregnant teens to continue their education in Illinois. I have since seen favorable results from this change, when my daughter became a teen mother, and was allowed to continue her education and graduated with honors. Since moving to Tallahassee my daughter has continued to benefit from this law by graduating from FSU with a BA in Business Administration. I also helped petition the state for more childcare money in my community."

In 1994 Trellis and Derrick Smith moved to

Trellis Johnson-Smith and Daughters-(L-R) Samantha, Mother-Trellis, Becky, (back row)Tiyshica, Danielle, Donnieka

Tallahassee where they have lived and worked and continue to enjoy the beauty of this great city. Trellis has held a variety of jobs in the past, and they were usually a position within one of her family's many businesses. She enjoys cooking and children, she now keeps her grandchildren and is considered the Mother of the neighborhood to all the children in her community. Trellis has found Christ and studies her Bible faithfully. She has been a member of the New Hope Missionary Baptist Church for many years and continues to practice her faith. Her hobbies include reading, writing, puzzles, studying religious theology and attending community functions. Trellis is a member of the "Women on the Move in Tally", a community group that supports women who want to start their own business, and also motivates young women in maintaining their health and fitness through exercise and fundraising functions. Since retirement Trellis enjoys more time with her family and friends at social gatherings.

Written and submitted by: Trellis Johnson-Smith, 759 Basin Street, Tallahassee, Florida 32304

Mozelle Kates

Not everyone has the good grace to be born in the state of Florida, but a few have the good sense to move here as quickly as possible. Mozelle Kates was one of those most wise persons. At the age of six she dragged her family from Oklahoma City to Orlando and spent many, many years in "The City of a Thousand Lakes". Life in Orlando then was laid back and easy. Surrounded by citrus groves and all that water and warmed by the central Florida sun, it was a lovely place to grow up.

Mozelle was sixteen when she was baptized, growing slowly and steadily in the Christian faith that she found reflected in her favorite verse from the Bible, Isaiah 41:10,

"So do not fear, for 1 am with you; do not be dismayed, for I am your God. I will strengthen you and help you; I will uphold you with my righteous right hand".

Things were kind of rough in Florida in the late 1930s, with the depression and all. So, to insure a steady supply of milk, cheese and dairy products, Mozelle married the milkman! Her husband John actually owned a dairy in the Orlando area and was the milkman on the route where Mozelle lived. Mother Kates, John's momma, was Mozelle's Sunday School teacher.

John and Mozelle were married in 1938, in Orlando and began a family that grew into two boys and two girls.

"Sugar and spice and everything nice", that's what makes first born baby girls a delight. Mozelle counts her first born daughter a special joy to her.

Gainesville called to the Kates family to move just up the road, and most of her life was spent there. The time she spent in Business College prepared Mozelle for her career as a bookkeeper, but she also dedicated herself to helping others. She was awarded special recognition for her twenty-one years of volunteer service. She also served the women of The First Baptist Church of Gainesville as President of the WMU.

What do you see as the biggest change in our country during your lifetime? Mozelte sees it as the change in communication. Back in the forties and nineteen-fifties it would be days or weeks before we learned about what was happening halfway around the world. Hurricanes would be upon us almost before we knew they were coming. Now, sometimes, we seem to know too much, too soon. The world has grown from the little two lane roads that Governor Fuller Warren built as his "Sign of Progress", to super highways that take us to more places than we want to go.

One of the best changes we have seen in Tallahassee and First Baptist lately is the addition of Mozelle Kates to our church and our Sunday School class. We are certainly happy that her daughter Joyce came to us as Pastor Dorch's secretary, and we are happy to welcome Mozelle to our church family.

Written by: Carol Ann and Bill Boydston ©, 1639 Twin Lakes Circle, Tallahassee, FL 32311; Submitted by: Mozelle Kates

Claude J. Kenneson

Claude Kenneson was born in Breaux Bridge, Louisiana in 1944, but by the age of one had moved to Carencro, Louisiana, where he obtained a high school education from Carencro High School in 1962 and a Bachelor of Arts in History from Saint Joseph Seminary College in Saint Benedict, Louisiana (near Covington) by 1970. Claude has been a resident of Tallahassee, Florida since 1989, when he came here to manage the Good News Outreach Soup Kitchen in Frenchtown, a position he still holds today.

Claude James Kenneson

After a stroll through Old City Cemetery in downtown Tallahassee in the year of his arrival, Claude was inspired to start a research project centering on burials of Tallahasseans, which was eventually published in 1992 by the Historic Tallahassee Preservation Board, and later in 2001 it was posted on the website of the City of Tallahassee. This project gave rise to extensive research on Tallahassee and Leon County people and events; the topics are numerous and give full details of historical events that have occurred in Leon County for the past years. The State Library of Florida was gracious enough to catalog and shelve some of these compilations, for research purposes only. They are unique, one of a kind, not published, nor for sale works.

Claude Kenneson has done assistant research work at the State Library for the people of Tallahassee for over 10 years. He has assisted numerous people to locate information for research papers, articles, and genealogical projects. A considerable amount of materials have not yet been catalogued and are stored in a large filing cabinet at the State Library. The Tallahasseans and Leon County subjects include: Genealogy, Black and White Communities (With and Without Post Offices), Suburbs and Subdivisions, Black and White Schools and Colleges, Apalachee Country, Civil War Veterans (Brief Biographies), Plantations (With and Without Post Offices), Bodies of Water, Spanish Missions, Roads and Streets, Parks, Vineyards, Forts, Cemetery Records, the Lafayette Land Grant, and much more.

Claude enjoys researching Leon County History and if anyone is looking for information on Tallahassee or Leon County, Florida, they are welcome to contact Claude J. Kenneson some afternoon at the State Library. He will gladly allow you the use of his files and will even help you with your search.

Sources: For a complete list of Old City Cemetery Gravesites; http://www.talgov.com/pm/kenneson.cfm For a complete list of Articles;
http://ibistro.dos.state.fl.us/uhtbin/cgisirsi/x/x/0/49; Written and Submitted by: Claude J Kenneson, 1323 North Martin Luther King Blvd, Tallahassee, Florida
claudejkenneson@;yahoo.com

Dot Kidd

These days, families don't seem to mean as much in our society, not like they used to when Dot Kidd was coming up. Then, family was everything. Dot was born in Coleman, a little town in Southwest Georgia. She grew up there, answered the call to Jesus at eleven, and lived with her grandmother for a time, all the while dreaming as young girls do, of a family of her own. Little did she know when she met her future husband, Roy at a community dance, that they would have a wonderful family of five children.

Dot and Roy were married on January 1, 1939. They lived in Southwest Georgia for fourteen years, nurturing a family that would grow to include three boys and two girls. In 1953, the Kidd crew of then three boys and one daughter moved from Albany to Tallahassee. They eventually settled into a comfortable home on Lafayette Circle, a quiet little street just off Sixth Avenue. Dot and her family attended Forest Heights Baptist Church for a time but her teenage boys had friends at First Baptist, so the family moved their worship to FBC, and she has been here ever since.

With five children, and the second daughter being born here in Tallahassee, the opportunity for involvement in young people's activities was very strong. Dot took advantage of every chance to be a part of her children's lives. She was a leader in Girl Scouts and Boy Scouts. She was a Gray Lady at her children's elementary school. Gray Ladies helped in the classrooms when needed, giving the teachers a much-needed hand in the classes. To be a Gray Lady in those days you had to pass a Red Cross course, so you would know how to handle the everyday bumps and bruises the kids would get, and be ready to assist in any real health emergency that might arise.

As her baby girl turned fourteen Dot could see that her days as a stay-at-home mom were about to come to an end. Anyone who has raised five children knows that an empty nest that has housed five fledglings can be deafening in its silence. Dot found a new career at Mendelson's Department Store. She was with them for fifteen years, finally retiring from their Northwood Mall store in 1983.

Dot counts her life as a success, filled with many blessings; when she became a Christian, her marriage to Roy and her family of five wonderful children. She has been guided through life by her favorite Bible verse, Micah 6:8, "He has showed you, O man what is good, and what does the Lord require of you? To act justly, and to love mercy and to walk humbly with your God."

Two deaths in her life hit her very hard; the passing of her life-mate Roy, and the death of her oldest son, Wayne at sixty-four. But today she is surrounded by loving family. Her four remaining children, twelve grandchildren and eleven great-grandchildren all live in Tallahassee. Dot Kidd has fulfilled those dreams of a young girl from Coleman, Georgia, her dreams of a healthy, happy family of her own. She is living her dream.

Written by: Carol Ann and Bill Boydston, 1639 Twin Lakes Circle, Tallahassee, Florida-32311; Submitted-by: Dot Kidd

Charles Kimber, Keeper of Humanity

CharlesMack Kimber was born December 15, 1942 to Johnnie Mae Lawson and Theo Kimber in Franklin, Tennessee. He married Frances Lavinia Robertson July 30, 1964 in Nashville, Tennessee, daughter of Richard Robertson and Marguerite Mears. She was born May 18, 1940 in Charleston (Charleston County), South Carolina. Charles and Frances produced three children, Chinene (Jean Bidlot), Chawne and Carlos Kimber.

Charles lived with his family in Wedowee in Randolph County, Alabama where Charles attended school and graduated in May 1959. He then enrolled in Tennessee State University, Nashville, Tennessee where he served as Editor-in-Chief of the campus newspaper. After graduating in June 1963 with a BA degree in Romance Languages, Charles enrolled in the graduate level Psychology program at this same University while being employed at Meharry Medical College in the Public Relations office as the Assistant Director.

After graduating in June 1964 with a MA Degree in General Psychology, Charles served two positions under the Tennessee State Department of Mental Health. The first job was in October of 1965 as a Staff Psychologist at the Greene Valley Hospital and School. Then, in June of 1967, he transferred to Cloverbottom Hospital and School where he served as their Staff Psychologist.

In August 1967 Charles accepted the position of Director of the Foster Grandparents Program at the Kentucky State Department of Mental Health. His work was so outstanding he was promoted in April 1969 to Superintendent and Program Director of the Frankfort State Hospital and School under the Kentucky Department of Mental Health. In March 1970 he was appointed the Facility Director of a new $14 million dollar facility in Somerset, Kentucky.

News of Charles Kimber's outstanding reputation for improvements reached Tallahassee, Florida, and by March of 1973 Charles was asked and accepted the appointment of Superintendent at the Tallahassee Sunland Center under the Florida Division of Mental Health. The next year in July 1974, he was promoted to Florida Regional Director (regionII-b) for Mental Health. He was forever striving for improvement in the field of Psychology so that by 1976, Charles was appointed Deputy District Administrator for Health and Rehabilitative Services with administrative and programmatic responsibility for Florida's fourteen county areas.

From March 1977 until June 1984 Charles served as the Program Staff Director for Developmental Services in the Florida Department of Health and Rehabilitative Services (HRS). He remained in this position until he was promoted to Deputy Division Director for Mental Health for the State of Georgia. But, in 1993 Charles transferred back to Tallahassee to accept the position of Assistant Secretary for Developmental Services at HRS now known as Department of Children and Family Services (DCFS).

In 2000, Charles

Charles Kimber, 2000

transferred to the Facilities section of the Alcohol. Drug Abuse and Mental Health Office within DCFS where he remained until his death in August of 2008. Charles is remembered for his devotion and contributions in the field of Psychology to humanity in their weakest hours. His wife has moved to South Carolina but his son continues to serve Leon County in the Hospitality Sector.

Written by: Francis Robertson-Kimber; Submitted by: Fran Kimber

Kindon

...Sold,...thus marking the ending of a continuous fortyplus- year participation of the Kindon family in the life of Tallahassee history. On September 5, 1881 on the steps of the Leon County Courthouse, Lot Number 168 (as described in the original plan of the City of Tallahassee), was sold to the highest bidder ($650.00) William P. Slusser due to a lien against the estate of Emma Kindon. recently deceased of Jacksonville, Florida. Presently, this property, located at the southeastern corner of Adams and Jefferson Street, is part of the Capitol complex parking garage. For many years this corner was the site of K.B. Perkin's pharmacy, a City Market,

Castelnau's sketch of Jefferson St. looking east - 1839. Right corner, Kindon home. First left building, Kindon Bakery

and the Tallahassee Fire Department. Across Jefferson Street the family owned the eastern 30 feet of lot number 169, and it was here that Kindon's Bakery and Confectionery was located. These two corners in the business district of old Tallahassee were sketched by Castelnau during his visit to Tallahassee in 1837-38. It was at the time of sketches that the Kindons were property owners and probably both structures are represented in this sketching. In the mid 1830s, a bakery and confectionery was established by the immigrant patriarch of the family George Kindon and fellow worker Mr. Davis. Soon after, The Florida Sentinel began advertising the Bakery and Confectionery, but it was now operated by W. (William) and H. (Henry) Kindon, both sons of George. The Bakery was included in the leveling of many city blocks by the fire of 1843.

The first entry of our Kindon family into the United States was by the patriarch George Kindon. He came into New York from London on May 7. 1834. aboard the ship Ontario. He was 53 years old and gave his occupation a carpenter. Immigration documents have a George Kindon, age 55 and listed as a cabinetmaker, arriving again in New York July 16.1938, on board the ship Westminster. This entry into the United States has his being accompanied by 53 year old wife Charlotte, his 30 year old son William Kindon (occupation confectioner) with his wife Eliza and their two children. It is assumed that George came to the US and established himself, then went back to England to bring his family. Many other Kindons followed the trail of George and came to Tallahassee.

The Kindon family came to Territorial Florida prior to 1840 and settled in Tallahassee, bringing with them their skills as confectioners. In Bertram H. Greene's book Ante-Bellum Tallahassee, the writer was surprised to find that ice was brought to Tallahassee as early as 1835, and was packed and stored in sawdust at Kindon's candy factory. Not only was Kindon Bakery on Jefferson Street wellknown for their pies, cakes, and loaf bread, but they exhibited a wide assortment of exotic-flavored candies. Advertised in Tallahassee's Florida Sentinel on July 16, 1841 was the following:

"Ice Creams! Ice Creams!! W. and H. Kindon respectfully inform the public that they will have constantly on hand, during the ensuing season, a plentiful supply of this choice delicacy, which they will serve up in first rate style at their Confectionery."

Other crafts brought to Tallahassee by the Kindons were cabinet making and tinning, and a keen sense of business. Minutes of the Leon County commission on January 15, 1870, authorized payment of $2.50 to G .A. Kindon for repairs to the lighthouse. As documented on the immigration manifest George was a tinner by trade, so it was possibly a repair to the roof of the St. Marks Lighthouse.

In the Territorial Papers of the United States, there is a petition to Congress by the

Jefferson Street, 1885 - #30, lot 168, Previous Kindon home. #33, eastern 30 feet of lot 169-previous Kindon Bakery Beck and Pauli lithographers

Citizens of the Territory, dated January 26, 1839, which has the signature of two Kindons, namely H. (Henry) and George T. Lindon (Kindon?).

In December 1842 a case was brought to the Superior Court for Leon County, Territory of Florida, against William H. Kindon, Sr. He was judged by his peers to be guilty of the indictment for "retailing spirituous liquors without a license". He was given a fine of twenty-five dollars and given imprisonment in the County jail for one hour. This brings a conjecture regarding the one hour confinement. From historical accounts of early Tallahassee it was common practice for an individual to be placed in a pillory in the town's busy market. This punishment to William would have been short, but open to public scorn, and may have satisfied the court's one hour imprisonment verdict.

An interesting Leon Court Deed record of 1849 finds William H. Kindon (1810-1878) indenturing his seventeen year old son George Kindon to Elijah B. Clark "to learn and acquire the craft and mystery of carriage making...until he shall reach the age of twenty- one." It further states that George will be schooled with the plain English education by providing for him regular instruction for three months of each year during his apprenticeship. Also during George's indenture, Mr. Clark will provide board and seasonal clothing. At the expiration of his apprenticeship, George will be given fifty dollars in cash and a new suit of clothes.

A deed record in Leon County from January 1863, finds Emma Kindon selling to P.B. Brokaw the house and lot (number 13 in the new plat) on the southwest corner of Virginia and Meridian, directly across the street from the present day Brokaw-McDougal House.

In the 1930s William George Dodd compiled a listing of the early Postmasters of Tallahassee. In the listing in post- Civil War times are found members of the Kindon family involved in the collection and local delivery of the mail. Appointed September 21, 1865, was 60 year old Donald Cameron (wife Matilda Kindon). Donald's 20 year old daughter Louisa Cameron received the appointment on May 3, 1866. She married William H. Avery in Tallahassee on June 18, 1868, and William was appointed the Postmaster as a Special Agent on August 1, 1868. Soon to follow (April 16, 1869) as Postmaster in Tallahassee was Simon L. Tibbitts (wife Ada Minor Kindon). He served until March 1873. Of interest is the state of birth for Avery (New York) and Tibbitts (Maine). Whether their recent allegiance to the Union was the basis for their

Jefferson Street, early 1900s Right corner-Market; left corner-Munro Opera House

appointment can only be speculated, but Federal troops did occupy Tallahassee for several years after the Civil War. Tibbitts was complimented with a May 24, 1870, letter in the Floridian for his untiring efforts to serve the people of Tallahassee—"...though a Republican in politics, his way of doing business is decidedly

Democratic, and of course all who are acquainted with him soon become warm personal friends."

Names of Kindon and related family members are found in the archives of Trinity Methodist and St. John's Episcopal churches. Records from these churches reveal also the burials of many Kindon members in the City Cemetery.

Toward the end of the 1860s and early 1870s the Kindon family began to disperse to surrounding areas. Subsequent local records and federal census reports find the Kindon name in the Georgia counties of Thomas, Muscogee, and Jefferson; in Duval county Florida; and. in Limestone and Freestone counties, Texas.

In 1978, after a hundred year hiatus of the Kindon family living in Tallahassee, a direct descendant moved here. My wife Miriam is a direct descendant of this Kindon family, and subsequently are our three daughters. Due to the Kindon family being in Tallahassee prior to the statehood of Florida and our being able to show direct lineage to this family, my mother-in-law Charlotte Cranberry Gillespie, my wife Miriam Gillespie McLarty, and my three daughters, Emily, Rebecca, and Margaret were appropriately recognized with Florida Pioneer Certificates in November 1993.

Written and submitted by: E. Lynn McLarty, 2102 Olivia Drive, Tallahassee, FL 32308

Lieutenant Governor Jeff Kottkamp

Jeffrey D. Kottkamp took the oath of office as Florida's 17th Lieutenant Governor on January 2, 2007. Kottkamp was born on November 12, 1960, in Martinsville, Indiana. He moved to Cape Coral in Southwest Florida in 1977. Kottkamp graduated from North Fort Myers High School in 1979. Jeff Kottkamp was first introduced to the state Capitol while representing his high school as a delegate to The Boys' State Club. Jeff started his college career at Edison College in Southwest Florida, where he served as Editor of the student government newspaper. He received an Associate of Arts degree in 1982, and then attended Florida State University, where he was also active in student government and a member of the Phi Alpha Theta National Honor Society. He received his Bachelor of Science degree in Political Science from FSU in 1984. In 2007, the Florida State University Alumni Association named Kottkamp to their "Circle of Gold." He attended the University of Florida College of Law and received his Juris Doctor degree in 1987. He is an Honorary Member of Florida Blue Key Society.

Before becoming an elected official, Jeff Kottkamp served as a law clerk for U.S. District Court Judge Joe Eaton, who served in the Florida Senate from 1957-1959, and U.S. District Court Judge Sidney Aronovitz. He then returned home to Southwest Florida to practice law. Jeff Kottkamp first ran for public office in 2000, when he was elected to the Florida House of Representatives, and he was subsequently re-elected in 2002 and 2004. While in the Florida Legislature, Representative Kottkamp served in numerous leadership positions including Chairman of the Judiciary Committee (2002-2004), Chairman of the Governmental Operations Committee (2005), Chairman of the Judiciary Appropriations Committee (2006) and Vice-Chairman of the Rules and Calendar Council (2004-2006) and the Select Committee to Protect Private Property Rights. He also served as Deputy Majority Whip. In addition, Representative Kottkamp served on the American Legislative Exchange Council's Task Force on Civil Justice, and on the National Council of State Legislators Law & Criminal Justice Committee.

Jeffrey D. Kottkamp, Lieutenant-Governor. 2008

One of the most important pieces of legislation Representative Kottkamp sponsored during his term was the Marvin Davies Civil Rights Act of 2003. The bill provided the Attorney General's office with the authority to take action when a 'pattern or practice' of discrimination occurred. He also sponsored numerous pieces of legislation to reduce and eliminate taxes, including the repeal of the Intangibles Tax, and served as Co-Chair of the Taxpayer- Protection Caucus.

During his service as a member of the House of Representatives, Jeff Kottkamp received many honors and awards including the "Legislator of the Year Award" from numerous organizations, the "Champion of Business" Award from Associated Industries, the Florida Catholic Conference "Defender of Life" Award, the "Faith and Family" Award from the Christian Coalition of Florida and the Florida Academy of Trial Lawyers "Outstanding Representative Award", the Florida Prosecuting Attorneys Association Leadership Award, and the Florida Chamber of Commerce "A" Honor Roll for five consecutive years.

Lt. Governor Kottkamp's wife Cyndie is a fourth generation Floridian. Kottkamp and his wife were married in 1995. They have one son, Jeffrey Jackson Kottkamp.

Written and submitted by: Jeffrey D. and Cyndie Kottkamp, 3311 Dartmoor Dr., Tallahassee, Florida 32312

Wallace Carlyn "Carl" Lamb

Wallace Carlyn "Carl" Lamb was born in Columbia County, Florida January 23, 1884, son of Samuel William Lamb and Minnie Hickson, grandson of pioneers John Josiah Lamb and Maria Graham. Carl moved to Jacksonville where he met Floride Marion Mullryne. Her father, Dr. Thomas Alexander Mullryne, had recently drowned near Savannah and her mother, Floride Marion Robert (Mullryne), had moved to Nassau County near her sisters. Floride Mullryne was born in Savannah December 5, 1890 and she and Carl Lamb were married in Fernandina in January 1908. Carl and Floride relocated to Tallahassee when Fred Cone was elected Governor. Floride Mullryne Lamb died in 1948. Carl died in 1964. They are interred in Oaklawn Cemetery in Tallahassee. Carl and Floride had four children: William Carl Lamb, Marion Dupont Lamb, Catherine Floride Lamb (Tharpe) and Richard Pringle Lamb, D.D.S. Descendants continue to live in Tallahassee.

Submitted by: William Tharpe, 2004 Ellicott Drive, Tallahassee, FL 32308

Elsie Hardin and Fields Hampton Lane

Elsie Hardin Lane was born in Stafford, AL in 1918 and Fields Hampton Lane was born May 1, 1910, in Ramseur, Randolph County, NC. Several generations of the Lane family have been named Hampton.

After Fields and Elsie were married they had five children, all born in Tuscaloosa, AL. They are Bobby, born 1941; Dorothy, born 1947; Randy, born 1950; Billy, born 1952 and Susy, born 1954. The family moved to Tallahassee from Tuscaloosa. All the children attended Caroline Brevard School, except Bobby. Four of them graduated from Leon High School.

Mrs. Elsie Hardin Lane son, Billy and daughter, Dorothy

Fields began his career in the tile business as a ceramic tile setter. Shortly after the children were born, he became the manager of Lane Tile and Marble Company with offices in Tuscaloosa and Birmingham. The family moved to Tallahassee after Fields took the managing position at Cambridge Tile Manufacturing Company, which later became Duval Tile and Supply Company. Elsie worked for the State of Florida: Licensing and Registration, Marine Patrol, and Natural Resources. She retired in 1985.

Elsie was an active charter member of Calvary United Methodist Church. She was the first Volunteer Coordinator for the Country Store at the Junior Museum representing Caroline Brevard School PTA.

Fields was noted for his Sunday Brunches which he enjoyed preparing. Because so many friends heard about this famous Sunday feast, the children took turns inviting a friend.

Susy, who died in 1965, and Fields, who died in 1992, are buried in Roselawn Cemetery, Tallahassee. Billy died in 2008 and is buried in CulleyMeadow Wood Memorial Park, Tallahassee.

Elsie now resides with her daughter, Dorothy, on Jekyll Island.

Submitted by Dorothy Lane Carswell, 649 Old Plantation Road, Jekyll Island, GA 31527

Lang Family in Leon County

The first members of the Lang family to come to Florida were Richard Lang and his younger brother, Isaac (my g.g.g. grandfather).

Colonel, David Lang-1861; 8th Florida Infantry

They arrived from South Carolina in 1785, after the Revolutionary War. Both were given Spanish Land Grants on the St. Mary's River near Kings Ferry, Florida. Isaac married Catherine (Kate) Wilds in 1789. Kate was the daughter of Nathaniel and Pricilla Turner Wilds who had emigrated to Florida from Wales, England.

Richard Lang became involved in an attempted "French Revolution" against the Spanish, and as a suspect, was arrested in 1794 and placed in solitary confinement in the old fort in St. Augustine for a year. His treatment was far from pleasant and it resulted in him spending two months at the Spanish hospital after his release - at his own expense. At that point, both he and Isaac and their families moved to Jeffersonton (later shortened to "Jefferson"), on the Satilla River, in Camden County, Georgia. Richard didn't forget his treatment by the Spanish and led a number of French sympathizers in raids against them in the Cowford (now Jacksonville) and Amelia Island area, including capturing Fort San Nicolas, on the St. John's River at Cowford.

Isaac's son, Robert, married Margaret Atkinson, daughter of Burwell and Ann Felder Atkinson of Camden County. In the 1850s they moved to Houston, Florida, in newly established Suwannee County. Robert operated his 880 acre farm on land that is the present site of the Episcopal Church's "Camp Weed". Their son, David, my great grandfather, graduated from Georgia Military Institute in Marietta, Georgia, and returned home to be elected County Surveyor. He continued that profession until the outbreak of the Civil War when he enlisted with the Gainesville Minutemen and fought at the Battle of Santa Rosa Island, Florida. Later he returned to Suwannee County to form Company "C" of the 8th Florida Infantry Regiment, and was elected their captain. The company was sent to Richmond to serve in the Florida Brigade of the Army of Northern Virginia.

David was elevated to the rank of colonel and became commander of the 8th Florida Regiment following the Battle of Fredericksburg. On a number of occasions, including Gettysburg, he commanded the Florida Brigade in the absence of its commander, General Edward A. Perry. He participated in many major battles, including Second Manasaas (Second Bull Run), Fredericksburg, Sharpsburg (Antietam), Gettysburg, Chancellorsville, The Wilderness, Spottsylvania Court House, Cold Harbor, and the Siege of Petersburg. He was badly wounded on several occasions, but successfully recovered. David was in command of the Florida Brigade at its surrender with the Army of Northern Virginia at Appomattox Court House. (His wartime letters, of which I have 20, are priceless in detail and information).

While serving in Virginia, David met and became engaged to Mary Quarles ("Molly") Campbell, daughter of Dr. Joseph D. and Sara Atkins Campbell, of Louisa County. At the war's end in 1865, David returned to Suwannee County to begin a new life, in February 1866, he returned to Virginia to marry Molly and bring her back to Florida.

Their first child, Robert Campbell Lang (my grandfather), was born in Houston on Christmas Day, 1866. David continued his surveying career in several Florida counties until 1885, when his old brigade commander, Edward A. Perry was elected governor of Florida. He appointed David as Florida's first Adjutant General and he and Molly moved to Tallahassee. As commander

Major General, David Lang; Adjutant General of Florida

of Florida troops he formed the units into a cohesive military force and instituted training and annual encamp-ments. As such, he became the father of Florida's present day Army National Guard.

Following eight years as Adjutant General and Major General of Florida troops, he then served as Private Secretary to Governors Mitchell and Bloxham during their terms of office. He and Molly raised a family of four children: Robert Campbell Lang (my grandfather), Joseph Atkins Lang, Paul Virginius Lang, and Helen Augusta ("Nellie") Lang. David and Molly lived the remainder of their lives in Tallahassee, Mollie dying at age 41 in 1889 and David died in 1917. Both are buried in the Old City Cemetery.

Campbell Lang, the oldest child, became the Florida representative of a large Savannah, Georgia grocery company. During his travels, he either met or renewed his acquaintance with Margaret McCarty of Old Town, daughter of Joseph McCarty and Lucy Cottrell McCarty. They married and raised a family of six children on the banks of the Suwannee River, (Campbell, Jr., Joseph, David, William, Lucy and Eugene). Campbell helped found the first bank in Trenton and later became its president. His employment meant that he had to live in Trenton during the week and commute to Old Town by train and boat on weekends. This ended @ 1915 when the river home burned and he moved the family to Trenton.

Joseph Adkins Lang, the second son, became a pharmacist and moved to Richmond, Virginia, where he opened a pharmacy, raising a family and living there until his death. Paul Virginius Lang, the third son, lived his entire life in Tallahassee and became Clerk of the Circuit Court in 1917, continuing in office until his death in December of 1942. Paul was married to a widow, Frances Pringle, who had two daughters, Mary and Frances Pringle. Many people remembered Uncle Paul for his habit of whistling a tune while out walking, however, I remember him because he always gave me a shiny silver half-dollar whenever we met. That was big money in those days! Helen Augusta ("Nellie"') Lang, David and Molly's daughter, married Burwell Boykin McCaa. They lived in Tallahassee and for several years in Norfolk, Virginia. Nellie died at age 39 and of the three children born to them, none survived childhood. All are buried in the Old City Cemetery.

David Lang, my father, married Liska Collins of Evinston, Florida in 1925. Liska was the daughter of Clarence M. and Isadora Sikes Collins of Evinston. When David and Liska met, she was a young widow with a young daughter, Fentonette. I was born in 1932 and in 1937, during the tough days of the Great Depression, our family moved to Tallahassee from Trenton, Florida. My father was good friends with a campaign manager of newly elected Governor Fred P. Cone, who told Dad to meet Governor Cone at the train station in Jacksonville on a certain date. In a brief visit, Governor Cone told Dad to "Report to work in Tallahassee on Monday morning". David became one of the first employees of the old Florida Industrial Commission (later to become the Department of Commerce, etc.), where he retired as Fiscal Officer. Their first office was on the second floor, across the street from the State Theater on College Avenue. They soon moved to the old Leon High School building on W. Park Avenue (now the location of the Leon County Library), then the "City Administration Building" adjacent to the capitol, and later to the Caldwell Building. In addition to his love of deer and turkey hunting and fishing, his favorite activity was raising prize-winning camellias. Both of my parents lived an active life until their death. My father died just before his 97th birthday in 1998 and my mother died at age 100, a year later.

In the late 1940s my father's sister, Lucy Lang, a home economics teacher in Trenton, moved to Tallahassee, where she was employed as a Home Economics Supervisor with the Department of Education. She retired from that position and continued to live in Tallahassee until her death in 2000. Lucy never married, but was very outgoing and was the life of any party.

I attended Leon County public schools and graduated from Florida State University in 1954, entering the Army as a lieutenant that Fall and serving with the 2d Armored Division in Germany. I met my wife, Mary Alma Roberts, daughter of Charles C. ("Charlie") and Martha Bradford Roberts in the summer of 1957, and in 1958 I began employment with the then Florida Division of Corrections at the State Prison in Raiford. We were married that same year and returned to Tallahassee in 1959, where I began employment with the Clerk of Circuit Court and Mary Alma became organist for Holy Comforter Episcopal Church and Temple Israel. Later she became a classroom teacher at Hartsfield, Gilchrist and Springwood schools. I served in various positions in the Clerk's Office and in other court offices until 1992, when I was elected Clerk of the Circuit Court. We are both retired - Mary Alma in 2000 and I in 2001. I left office with a "bang" due to the 2000 presidential election recount and the court actions that took place in the Leon County courts. As you remember, it was nothing short of a circus. We built our home on Mary Alma's family farm on Roberts Road in 1985, and we now enjoy a slower pace of life. Our son, Chuck and his wife, Patty Burkman Lang (children Charlie, Jonathan and Collin), reside in Tallahassee. Our daughters, Susan Lang and Sandra Lang DeAngelis and her husband. Dax (sons Dain and David) reside in Tampa and Jacksonville Beach, respectively.

The last member of our family to move to Tallahassee was a cousin. Melinda Lang Hilsenbeck, daughter of Robert Campbell Lang, Jr. and Rebecca Jean Atwood Lang of St. Augustine, Florida. Melinda and her husband, Richard moved to Tallahassee in 1991. Richard is an Associate Director for the Nature Conservancy and Melinda is a teacher in the public schools and also a realtor.

Written and submitted by: David Lang. Jr., 6025 Roberts Road, Tallahassee, FL 32309

Dr. William D. Law, Jr.

Dr. Law received a Bachelor of Arts degree in English from LeMoyne College and both a Master Degree and his Ph.D. in Design and Management of Postsecondary Education from Florida State University. Dr Law is married to Patricia C. Law, and they have two sons. Now in his twentieth year as a community college president, Dr. Bill Law can be described as a passionate advocate for education with a strategic vision for success. After serving previously at Montgomery College in suburban Houston and Lincoln Land Community College in Springfield, 111., he became president of TCC on March 25, 2002. Since then, he has dedicated himself to issues such as workforce development, student success and retention, community outreach and the first-ever capital campaign.

Dr. Law's leadership has been instrumental in bridging the academic and business communities. His successes include: TCC 250, a program that works to increase enrollment in academic healthcare programs to meet community employer needs; an emphasis on the arts that culminated in the opening of the Hurst Gallery; and his leadership role on behalf of the Council on Community College Presidents for his work with the Florida Legislature. He also serves on numerous local boards including the Economic Development Council, and Mary Brogan Museum. His drive, vision and passion make him a true asset to Tallahassee, the business community and the state education system.

TCC has experienced both record enrollments and record levels for degrees and certificates awarded in the past year. TCC President Bill Law says he's fought hard to keep faculty pay where TCC is the second highest paying two-year college in Florida, with its average full time faculty member making more than $70,000. 41% of 180 faculty members made $80,000 or more last year, which is compared to 12% of 140 faculties making that much in 2003. The top ranking college is Indian River Community College in Fort Pierce, Florida. Law says the college's focus has always been students first, but he says the best way to do that is with top notch professors.

William D. Law, President of Tallahassee Community College

Dr. Bill Law was evaluated on 34 separate items covering areas related to resource management, organizational strategy, community college advocacy, communication, collaboration and professionalism. The review was reported at the May 18, 2009, meeting of the Board. Of particular merit, the Board noted the strong financial leadership provided by Dr. Law during the ongoing budget crisis in the state. The Board noted Law's leadership in moving forward with the financing and construction of the Ghazvini Center for Health Care Education, as well as the recent opening of The Learning Commons, an academic support facility for students.

Written and submitted by: William D. Law, 2950 Giverny Circle, Tallahassee, Fl 32309

Alfred (Al) Lawson Jr.

Alfred "Al" Lawson Jr. is a Democratic member of the Florida Senate representing the 6th District since 2001. Previously he was a member of the Florida House of Representatives from 1983 through 2000. Born September 21, 1948 in Tallahassee, Florida to Alfred J. Lawson Sr. (1921-1994) and Hattie Brown (1925-1997), grandson of Solomon Lawson (1900-1988) and Hattie Gatlin (1902-1954). He married Delores J. Brooks of Tallahassee in 1956 and two children were born to this union: Alfred James III and Shani A. Grandchildren are Kobe and Henry.

Lawson received his Bachelor's degree from Florida A&M University (B.S.-1970). His undergraduate activities included Student Government, basketball and track. During his postgraduate, he served as a Administrative Assistance to the State Legislature, which lead to his Masters Degree in Public Administration from Florida State University (M.S.P.A.-1973),

Senator Alfred "Al" Lawson, Jr.'s Legislative service started in 1982 and has grown to include the Senate in 2000, where he was reelected subsequently to Democratic Leader, 2008-2010. Lawson has served many important Committee Memberships such as the General Government Appropriations, Vice Chair Policy and Steering Committee, Governmental Operations Policy Committee, Steering Committee on Ways and Means, The Banking and Insurance Governmental Oversight and Accountability Committee, Health Regulation Committee, Reapportionment Rules Committee, Joint Select Committee on Collective Bargaining, and The Joint Legislative Budget Commission

Lawson's occupation for the past twenty years has been Insurance Agent, first for Northwestern Mutual Life Insurance Co. 1976-Present, and then President for Lawson and Associates Inc. (Marketing Firm), 1984-Present. Religious affiliation is Episcopal and some of his hobbies include basketball, reading, and gardening

Submitted and written by: Alfred Lawson, 2610 Gunn Street, Tallahassee, Florida Alfred (Al) Lawson, Jr.

Alfred (Al) Lawson, Jr.

Judge Joseph E. Lee

Joseph Edward Lee was born April 15, 1848 to Josephine Lee in Philadelphia, Pennsylvania. His mother died during childbirth while he was very young. His brother, William Henry Lee and he were raised by devout Irish-Catholics. So, Joseph learned how to be a true Humanitarian. Joseph's foster father was a political figure in Pennsylvania, where the Nation's Capital was located during this time in history, and this is where Joseph studied to be a lawyer. Many of his friends referred to him as "Joe the terrier" because once he made up his mind to do something he would follow through to the end no matter what.

Joseph moved to Tallahassee in the late 1870s where he met the love of his life, Rosa Bell Taggart (1856-1929). They remained married for over fifty years and had six children: Robert, Martha, Caroline, Joseph Jr., and two who died in infancy. This veteran attorney must have shaken with delight when, on October 13, 1890 he opened Florida's first College of Law Department in Jacksonville, Florida. Joseph had seen the seasons change for over forty-one years and stood before-the bar exam for nearly two decades before his admittance, but by then it would have taken something truly remarkable to stir him from his pursuit. As a lawyer Joseph E. Lee had seen wonders of life and bitter disappointments in his chosen career, but by now as the century drew to a close; he sensed great expectations on the horizon while living in Florida.

Joseph's story began in Philadelphia, having enjoyed

Painting of Judge Lee in office -1915

an upbringing that stressed education as a continuing process of life. In the state's capital of Philadelphia, he had inhaled the excitement of formulating times, where future promises seemed unbound and prosperity appeared to wait around every corner. After graduating in 1869 as class valedictorian and before pursuing the dream of a legal education he was allowed to enter one of this city's most prestigious educational institutes one year after the Civil War ended in Washington D. C. As if to confirm the promise of freedom, the District of Columbia Courts welcomed him to practice law as soon as he completed his studies in 1873.

While in Washington D.C. the direction of this young attorney's life was changed dramatically by inspiring words from a well respected mentor and Congressman from Florida, who invited him to Leon County to practice law after receiving his law degree. At this time Florida was a developing state that urgently needed the skills of a man of education with an acute legal mind. When Joseph stood before the state's Supreme Court in Tallahassee on April of 1873, he found that no less than the Attorney General, William Archer Cocke himself, was prepared to approve his bar admission that very day. All were in accord that he was the best man for a political career in Florida. Once his family was started, Joseph decided he was need more in another part of the state, so he moved to Jacksonville to establish his new practice. Joseph's law practice got off to an excellent start due to his keen intellect and broad grasp of legal principles. His clients remember him as a man with stern integrity, a native shrewdness and good common sense. He conveyed all his capacity for truth and his self worth in every case he represented. Some say he was the master of his domain.

Joseph knew he could not limit his activities to his profession alone because the times demanded men willing to serve the public during reconstruction, and Joseph was willing to oblige. His public service career spanned five decades, which included serving in the House of Representative from 1875-1879 for Duval County. He sat as State Senator in 1881-1888, though in the later part of 1888 he was elected Police Judge for Duval County. In 1889 he was elected County Clerk for Duval County. In 1890 he received a Federal appointment as Custom Collection for Port Saint John in Jacksonville, which he held for four years. In 1897 he became Superintendent for the state's Internal Revenue Service, which lasted until 1913. This required him to spend most of his time in Leon County on the land he had purchased for his brother's family. Senator Lee serviced two different county seats at once, which was not heard of in those days.

In the late 1880s Joseph sought ordination from his denomination as a Minster. For him it seemed to be just another stepping stone to his true calling, "Public Servant of Florida". Once ordained he used the power of the church as an educational outreach tool to initiate the building of a high school in Jacksonville, and soon after the institution was built he spearheaded its transformation into a college. Once the college was up and running he convinced its trustees to train lawyers as well as preachers and teachers. One of his deputies is quoted as saying; "Judge Lee was favorable and well known to all classes of citizen in Florida as well as in Washington DC." In his later years Judge Lee became president and founder of the Florida Progressive Baptist Association, Trustee of the Edward Waters College and a life time member of the African Methodist Episcopal Church.

Joseph E. Lee remained active in community concerns until his death on March 25, 1920. He is buried in the Old City Cemetery in Downtown Jacksonville. His tombstone holds the names of his entire family, and is shaped like the arch to a church steeple. He is gone but not forgotten by all whom he influenced in Florida. Judge Lee's descendants still live in Leon County on land purchased by him in many of the Tallahassee communities.

Written and submitted by: Carol D. Johnson, 214 N. Columbia Drive, Tallahassee, Florida 32304 Carold913@yahoo.com

Perry Muriel Lewis

Perry Muriel Lewis was born on March 4th 1914 in Woodville, FL to William Bloxham and Thehna Ray (Nims) Lewis. He was the oldest and only boy of four children from that marriage. His sisters were Eliza, Opal, and Thelma. His mother died at an early age, but he later had three more brothers, Bernard, James, and Lynn and one sister, Olga, when his dad married Jimmy McDonald.

His early years were spent in Woodville. They first lived in a house near Page and Old Woodville roads. He said he could remember the train stopping near by for water and his grandmother, Victoria, selling lightered wood that

Perry and Juanita Lewis

was used to help keep the fire in the engine going.

After his daddy went to work for the State Department of Agriculture, the family moved down in Levy County to Bronson. During this time he met Juanita, his wife to be for over 67 years.

Perry and Juanita married, moved to Woodville, and raised their family of twelve children-Eugene, Dorman, Dorothy, Ray, Carolyn, Elizabeth, Mary Ellen, Donald, John Allen, Brenda, Keith and Jerry.

Things were hard back in the WPA days, but he worked there four or five years then at the college until war broke out and Dale Mabry airfield was built. He worked there until the war was over and the base was broke down.

From there he went on to farming and that was a great part of his life. He said he enjoyed so much being able to make things grow. Although most of his land was in planted pines, he also raised cattle and hogs and had a corn crop. The family always grew enough vegetables to put in the freezer. In 1966, they were selected the outstanding farm for Leon county. He ended up working for the Department of Agriculture as a livestock inspector for Leon, Wakulla and Liberty counties.

Two of his greatest loves were deer and fox hunting. He loved to hear the dogs run. He said, if you don't believe it, just ask Juanita. He also enjoyed the years that he helped with the Wakulla swine show by doing a b-b-q, and was always willing to help whenever a need arose.

After years of butchering and hanging meat in the old magnolia tree in their yard, he finally built a real meat house where he butchered, cut and wrapped deer, hogs, and cows. He even made and smoked his own much sought after sausage. He said that was some great days not to mention hard work. He was especially proud of butchering a 4-H cow (with help, I might add) on his 80th Birthday!

He suffered a stroke on May 20th, 1995 that changed his life from being that of hard working and independent to one being dependent on others. He died December 10, 2005, at the age of 91.

Submitted by: Julia R. Lewis, 5831 Natural Bridge Rd., Woodville, FL 32305

Captain Dale Mabry

Dale Mabry was an American World War I aviator. He was born in Tallahassee. FL, the son of former Florida Supreme Court Justice Milton H. Mabry and Ella Dale Bramlett.

He went on to become an airship pilot and captain in the United States Army.

Captain Mabry died piloting the Army airship Roma, a dirigible he was testing, when it crashed in Norfolk, Virginia on February 21, 1922. The event marked the greatest disaster in American aeronautics up to that time, resulting in 34 deaths. He was survived by a brother, G. E. Mabry of Tampa, Florida.

See Florida Photographic Collection online and at the Florida Archives for the following: Dale Mabry's tombstone at Arlington National Cemetery, Arlington, VA; Picture of Roma, the airship he was testing; He is pictured with Walter Reed in one of the pictures. Would this be Walter Reed for whom the Army Hospital is named?

Dale Mabry Highway in Tampa, Florida is named for him. Dale Mabry Municipal Airport in Tallahassee, Florida, the city's first airport, was named for him Nov. 11, 1929. The original Tallahassee Airport location was on Dale Mabry Field, A WWII Army Air Corps flight training facility. In 1945, Dale Mabry Airfield was placed on the inactive status and eventually resumed its

Captain Dale Mabry

role as a civilian airport after WWII.

Dale Mabry Field is home now to Tallahassee Community College, the Highway Patrol Training Academy, Messer Baseball complex, some private homes and a few businesses.

Sources: #1 - "Dale Mabry—What?" From Killearn Cloverleaf Monthly Newsletter, July 2009: by Allen Nobles, Killearn, Homeowners Board Member #2 - Wikipedia, The Free Encyclopedia: Internet
http://en.wikipedia.org/wiki/Dale_Mabry
Submitted by: Mary J. Marchant, 2901 Springfield Drive, Tallahassee, FL 32309-3274

The Madden Family of Pioneer Florida

Two children from Florida's pioneer days have looked upon members of my family for several generations. Their austere expressions and stylized poses are frozen in time, in separate oil portraits. The paintings depict James M. Madden (1839-1906) and his sister Catherine Ann (1836-1857).

Catherine Ann Madden was born June 18, 1836 in New Brunswick, New Jersey. Eight days later, her father Levi A. Madden purchased for $350 a lot and dwelling-house in St. Marks, Florida. (At that time, the thriving port of St. Marks was in Leon County.) Madden's name appears often on deeds and on lawsuits filed in Tallahassee between 1838 and 1841. He owned a general store in St. Marks, and had to use the courts to settle debts. Merchandise sold in Madden's store included homespun fabric, screws, Brogan shoes, linen, horse collars, tin buckets, coffee pots, oil, rope, hair combs, sugar, cigars, nails, knives, silk handkerchiefs, coffee, bridles, oats, potatoes, fur hats, pants, vests, pumps, coats, and calico. He also sold spirits. The price per gallon was 50-cents for rum, $1.50 for gin, and $2.00 for brandy. Madden must have prospered in his business. On March 7, 1840 he bought a new house, including annexed buildings and a 'Bale Alley,' from Gustavus O. West for $2,000.

In 1841 Madden saw an opportunity he couldn't resist. The newly-built Tallahassee-St. Marks railroad, which connected the plantations to the ships that transported cotton, tobacco and hides to Northern factories, was extending its tracks across the river to a new town, Port Leon, about 3 miles south of St. Marks. Madden purchased several lots, and moved his family to Port Leon. His partner in land speculation was Ezekiel Madden. Census records reveal the Ezekiel was two years younger than L. A., and both were born in Massachusetts. They were most likely the sons of Levi Madden and Sarah (Sally) Rockwood of Milford, Mass. The Maddens had at least 10 children, including sons named Asia, Africa, America Levi, and Michael Europe! America was born in 1812 and his brother Ezekiel in 1814. In Florida the older brother switched the order of his given names, using 'Levi A.' Madden.

Ezekiel was elected the sheriff of Wakulla County after it became a separate county in March 1843, with Port Leon as the county seat. Port Leon had a questionable reputation, however. There was no church and no jail in this town of 200-300 residents, and public drunkenness and swearing were commonplace. L. A. Madden owned the building in Port Leon that housed a dry goods store, and he had at least one warehouse near the docks.

In 1842 he mortgaged his Port Leon house, including all household furniture and a 'negro girl named Polly, about 10 years of age, of yellow complexion, to John W. Argyle of Tallahassee for $2,500. The following year another mortgage for $8,000 was granted by Amos Madden of Brooklyn, New York, for nine other Port Leon lots and attached buildings, plus ten cattle and two carts. Exactly how L. A. Madden intended to use those loans is unknown, because life was about to change — suddenly and completely — for everyone in Port Leon.

On Sept. 13, 1843, a violent hurricane battered Port Leon for almost 15 hours, bringing a storm surge of 10 feet, and near total destruction of the town. In a letter published Sept. 29 in the *New York Herald*, an eyewitness gave 'Particulars of the Storm in Florida,'

Catherine Ann Madden (1836- 1857)

including this statement: "I saw Brodie's warehouse fall, and Madden's go off in the stream." Fourteen people died at St. Marks lighthouse, one family in Magnolia lost its mother and children, and there was considerable damage in St. Marks. A committee of Port Leon town folk decided to build on higher land upriver, about two miles south of Magnolia. Their new town would be called New Port.

L.A. and Mary Madden then took their family to New York, where the two child portraits were probably painted. Mrs. Madden likely visited her family in New Jersey, because in 1847 her sister Johanna Martin of Piscataway married Gustavus O. West, the sea captain/pilot who formerly lived in St. Marks. By 1850 both families settled in Newport, Florida. The newly widowed Mrs. Madden was landlady at the Wakulla Hotel initially, but after 1853 she ran the Washington Hotel, renting it from Daniel Ladd for $100 per quarter. Her daughter Catherine Ann Madden (the girl in the painting) married the town druggist, James Skipper, but she died in 1857, after giving birth to two children who also died, Skipper the married Mrs. Madden's younger daughter, Mercy Eliza Madden. He died in 1858, and is buried with his first wife and their two babies at Magnolia Cemetery.

James Madden (1839-1906)

James M. Madden, subject of the other painting, graduated from Tulane Medical School in New Orleans, and became an assistant surgeon during the Civil War. He was stationed first at a CSA hospital in Staunton, Va., later with the Virginia 61 Infantry, and finally returned 'home' to Fort Ward at St. Marks, Florida. Upon his surrender in Tallahassee in May 1865, he was described as 5 ft., 10 in. tall with brown hair, gray eyes and light complexion. Later he moved to Brunswick, Georgia, and married Maria Morris of Waynesboro and Richmond Bath, widow of Thomas Spalding McIntosh, who died at the Battle of Antietam (Sharpsburg). Newport lost its importance for shipping after the railroad between Tallahassee and Jacksonville was built, and caused Mrs. Madden to move to Monticello about 1862. She purchased the Monticello Hotel adjacent to the courthouse square and renamed it the Madden House. This afforded her a comfortable living until her death about 1883. Her son James rose to prominence in Brunswick, after changing his profession from medicine to banking. He had three children, whose descendants now live chiefly in Columbus, Georgia and Jacksonville, Florida.

This is what we know about the Madden parents and two of their children, whose portraits have survived from territorial Florida and early statehood to the present day.

Written and submitted by: Alva Theresa Stone, 5478 Pedrick Crossing Dr., Tallahassee, FL atstone@law.fsu.edu

The Mallett Twins

Lester and Chester Mallett were born in Carrabelle, Florida, on June 9, 1932. After attending school in Carrabelle, where they graduated from high school in 1949, they enrolled in college at Florida State University (FSU) in Tallahassee. For one year the twins commuted on the weekends back to their home town in Carrabelle to work. Before entering FSU, Lester and Chester tried to convince their widowed mother, Susie, to move to Tallahassee, while they were attending college. Their mother, Susie Clara Chason Mallett, was reluctant to leave her home in Carrabelle, Florida. When Lester fell ill and required treatment in the University's infirmary, it convinced Mrs. Mallett that a move to Tallahassee was necessary to better care for her twin sons.

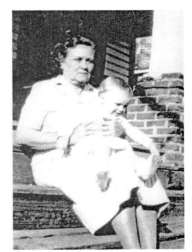

Walter J. Mallett with grandma, Susie Mallett's Tallahassee home

In late 1949, Lester, Chester, and their mother Susie moved into an upstairs apartment on West Lafayette Street. Mrs. Mallett didn't like living in an apartment, so soon the three Malletts moved into a house. One day the twins' older brother, Leonard, and his family visited from Carrabelle. Their nephew was just learning to talk and had never seen both twins together at once. When Lester and Chester walked into the house or lunch, the astonished nephew looked at Lester and said; "There's Tet-ta," then pointed to Chester, and said; "there's more Tet-ta."

Susan F. Mallett with grandma, Susie Mallett's Tallahassee home

During the summer of 1950, Lester stayed with his brother Leonard in Carrabelle to work, while Chester worked in Tallahassee. They both worked for the State of Florida Road Department, but one of Lester's special jobs was to take a state car into the shop to be reupholstered. This car was assigned to Governor Fuller Warren's sister, who served as "Florida's First Lady, until Governor Warren married.

The twins attended FSU from 1949 through 1951, and they left FSU in 1952; Lester enlisted in the U.S. Army, while Chester continued to live with his mother and work in Tallahassee. By 1953, Chester bought a newer home for their mother with the help of his family at 618 West 10th Avenue in Tallahassee. A short time after this, the Mallett twins switched places; Chester was drafted into the Army after Lester served two years, then Lester returned to Tallahassee to take Chester's job.

Chester Mallett- 1950s

Lester Mallet with the Florida First Lady's Car

While Chester served in the army, Lester continued to work and live in Tallahassee for a time. He married a woman he met while attending FSU. The couple lived in the city with their young son Victor Alan and their daughter Vivian, who was born at Tallahassee Memorial Hospital.

The twins' mother, Susie C. Mallett, came to love living in Tallahassee after she became acquainted with the city. The city's bus system afforded her a new found freedom. She could catch a city bus to ride anywhere she wanted to go. For the first time in her life, she enjoyed the freedom of going to church, shopping, or visiting friends on her own time schedule. Susie C. Mallett lived in her 10th Avenue home in Tallahassee until her death in 1960.

Lester Mallett-1950s

Written by: Susan and Frances Mallett;
Submitted by: Lester Mallett, 7704 James Clark Street, Port-Richey, Florida 34668

Jackie Marchant

Jackie Marchant was born April 13, 1932 in Bainbridge, GA to Shellie Williams and John Franklin Marchant (Jack) of Sneads. FL.

An unusual event happened in Sneads every 30 years – the school burned three times. Jackie was in second grade when it burned once. Jack (his father) helped supply a building for the second graders. Jack and Shellie were always staunch supporters of the school system.

Jackie graduated in 1950, third in his class. He enjoyed sports and tried out for the basketball team his senior year. Although he wasn't a talented player, nevertheless his love of sports continued throughout his life. He was a devoted Seminole fan of Florida State University football and basketball. He, along with his family and friends, attended many out of town regular season football games and several Bowl games. Nothing stopped Jackie from watching FSU football on TV. He attended all home games and was a season ticket holder for over 40 years until his death in 1999.

Jackie took piano from Mrs. Carpenter in Sneads, FL and became quite proficient playing jazz, ragtime, boogie woogie, popular Broadway tunes, and other forms of easy listening music. He also sang well. He shared his talents with several civic organizations.

Jackie Marchant Family; Seated: Carol Ann Marchant and Ray Edward Marchant, Standing: Jackie Marchant and Mary J. Marchant. By permission: Richards Photography, July 4, 1991

After graduating from FSU in 1957, he went to work at the University Laundry, then later for the State of Florida in Personnel with the Depart-ment of Admini-stration which assisted all state agencies. He retired in 1988; he began working at the Department of Transportation in 1989 for ten years.

He and his wife, Mary J. Marchant, were active charter members of Calvary United Methodist Church which began in 1963. They continued their membership until 1992 at which time they returned to Trinity United Methodist Church. They had been members at Trinity from 1955 to 1963.

Jackie died December 14, 1999 and is buried in Pope Cemetery in Sneads, FL.

Submitted by Ray Marchant, 1633 Via Roberto Miguel, Palm Springs, CA 92262

Mary J. Marchant

Mary Magdalene Jones (Maggie) was born in Birmingham, Alabama to George W, Sr. and Ada Jones in 1931. The name Mary Magdalene has been passed down through five maternal generations. Her siblings are George W. Jones, Jr., and Clayborne Jones.

It seems Mary's family preferred to use nicknames instead of given names: for instance; George Jr. "Bubba"; Mary "Tissy" and later "Sis;" brother, Clayborne "Cabey"; grandmother "Dottoo" and aunts "Doodle and "Idee."

In 1953 Mary met Jackie Marchant and they were married in Killeen, Texas while he was in the Army. After Jackie's military service, they moved to Tallahassee for him to finish college and where the children, Mary Magdalene Marchant (deceased), Carol Marchant and Ray Marchant were born., Jackie Marchant died Dec. 14, 1999 and is buried in Pope Cemetery in Sneads, FL.

Mary's father was born in Tullahoma, Tennessee on September 15, 1887 to Katie Hide and J. W. Jones. George worked on Southern Railway as a brakeman until he reached age seventy. His friends called him "Tango" because he liked to dance in his youth. He died August 15, 1970 and is buried at Oakwood Cemetery in Tuscumbia, Alabama.

Mary's mother, Ada Magdalene Schmidt, the youngest of seven children, was born in Tuscumbia on March 24, 1893, to Lena Waeckel and Henry Schmidt. Ada graduated from a one-room school house with 11 grades and was a

Mary J. Marchant

housewife. She died August 3, 1974 and is buried at Oakwood Cemetery

Mary's maternal grandparents were Lena Waeckel and Henry Schmidt. Lena was born September 22, 1852 in Alsace/Germany/France. She migrated with her family to America twice, in 1853 and 1864, settling both times in Sandusky, Ohio and later moving to Tuscumbia, AL where she married Henry Schmidt in September, 1877. Henry Schmidt was born around 1853 and migrated from Baden, Germany to America around 1870 at age eighteen. The Waeckel's ship experiences were very interesting and life threatening.

Mary attended public schools in Tuscumbia and graduated from Deshler High School in 1949 ranking third in a class of 85. Her Tuscumbia friends called her "Maggie." She obtained her BS Degree from Florence State Teachers College, Florence, Alabama (University of North Alabama) in 1953 majoring in Business Ed and Music. Mary received the "Turris Fidelis" Award at FSTC for service to the college at graduation. In 1985 Mary obtained her MS Degree from Florida State University. Mary taught music Pre-K through 12, retiring after 34 years in 1990 from Caroline Brevard School where they named the new music room for her.

Since retirement Mary enjoys volunteering, having held offices in several civic clubs and churches and traveling worldwide with Jackie and friends. A life-long Methodist, she's a member of Trinity UMC in Tallahassee

Sources: Ohio and AL Federal Census Records; Family Oral History, Mormon FHC, Tallahassee, Salt Lake City Mormon Library; Sandusky, OH Courthouse, Tuscumbia, AL Courthouse, Germans to America Book Series; Strasbourg, France/Germany Civil and other records.
Submitted by: Ray Marchant, 1633 Via Roberto Miguel, Palm Springs, CA 92262

Ray Edward Marchant

Born to Jackie and Mary Marchant in 1962, and the brother of Carol, Ray Marchant grew up in Tallahassee. He attended Caroline Brevard Elementary School, Belle Vue Middle School and Godby High School, where he graduated in the top percent-tile of his class. At Godby, he was involved in the French Club, Band, and Theatre, lettered in swimming and studied in Europe one summer.

While attending FSU, he was involved with the Seminole Boosters and Pi Kappa Alpha, where he received the highest award given by his Fraternity. He minored in Theater and received his Bachelors and Masters Degrees in Mass Communication.

Ray Marchant in Paris, France on Assignment -2002

After college, he worked for Disney/MGM Studios in TV production working on popular TV shows and large press events. Later, he was part of the TV team opening Euro-Disney out from Paris, France, and where he helped produced a show that aired in Germany.

Living in Dallas, he produced a feature film called "No Turning Back," which won a Dove Award. In 1996, he took over as Director of "The Promise" - an epic musical theatrical production with 165 actors at the 3200-seat Texas Amphitheatre. Under his direction, the show reached sold out performances for the first time in its history.

In 2005, he moved to Los Angeles to get back into television where he was the top Production Executive and CFO of the Emmy winning company, iCandyTV, a Television Development and Production Company.

Ray is an avid weightlifter, cyclist, and enjoys the outdoors, international travel and cuisines.
Submitted by: Ray Marchant, 1633 Via Roberto Miguel, Palm Springs, CA 92262

John R. Marks III

A graduate of Class XX of Leadership Florida, he is a life member of the NAACP, and was formerly a political analyst/ co-host on the local television show "The Usual Suspects". Marks received his B.S. degree in 1969 from the Florida State University School of Business and

John R. Marks III, Mayor of Tallahassee

his Juris Doctor degree in 1972 from the FSU College of Law, after which he served four years in the U.S. Air Force as a Judge Advocate. He is married to Jane Awkard Marks, a psychotherapist, and has one son, John, IV, a professor at FSU and a daughter-in-law Cristina, an attorney/clerk with the Second Judicial Circuit.

John Marks, Mayor of the City of Tallahassee, is also the Managing Partner of the Tallahassee Office of Adorno & Yoss, LLP. Prior to his association with Adomo & Yoss he was a shareholder and lead utility regulatory attorney from 1987 onward in the law firm of Katz, Kutter, et al., P.A. and thereafter from 1997 onward with Knowles, Marks & Randolph, P.A. Appointed by Governor Bob Graham in 1979, he served eight years on the Florida Public Service Commission (FPSC); the last two as its Chairman. Before serving on the FPSC, he was an Administrative Law Judge with the FPSC. He has been an adjunct professor at the Florida State University College of Law teaching utility regulatory law and a faculty member of the National Association of Regulatory Utility Commissioners' utility rate school.

A member of the American, National, Florida and Tallahassee Bar and the Tallahassee Barristers Associations, Marks is also a member of the American Law Institute, the ABA's Public Utilities Law Section and the Florida Bar's Local Government and Administrative Law Sections. He is past chairman of the Florida Bar's Public Utilities Law and the Equal Opportunities in the Profession Committees. Florida Super Lawyer Magazine named him Super Lawyer in the area of Utility Regulatory Law.

Apart from his professional affiliations, Mr. Marks was elected Mayor of Tallahassee in 2003 and re-elected in 2006. He serves on the Board of Advisors of the U.S. Conference of Mayors and was recently appointed to the position of Vice-Chair of the Transportation and Communications Committee.

He also serves on the Community and Economic Development Committee for the National League of Cities. In addition, Mayor Marks served as the charter President of the Florida League of Mayors (2005-2007) and was recently elected 1st Vice President of the Florida League of Cities, therefore President-designate for the 2009-2010 terms. His Board affiliations include Fringe Benefits Management Company, a privately held financial services company, the Tallahassee Economic Development Council, the Alliance for Digital Equality, the Tallahassee/Leon County Civic Center Authority, the Sunshine State Governmental Financing Commission, the Collins Center for Public Policy and the Economic Club of Florida.

Written and submitted by: Mayor John R. Marks III, 3713 Bobbin Brook East, Tallahassee, Florida, 32302

Glynn Marsh Alam, Writer

Glynn Marsh Alam is a native Floridian, born to Ulys Bowdoin Marsh of Alabama and Clara Strickland of Florida. She has one sister, Dianne Marsh. While growing up in Tallahassee Glynn was known for her curiosity about nature. She enjoyed her family outings at Wakulla Springs swampy area, while growing up in Leon County which may be due to the fact that she had the influence of four paternal uncles. Also since Glynn lived in the country she usually found herself in the company of her sister Dianne while exploring the swamp land of Leon County.

Glynn graduated from Leon High School in Tallahassee where she excelled in English literature. After graduating from Florida State University, she worked as a decoder/translator for the

Glynn Marsh Alam, Writer

National Security Agency in Washington, D.C., and then moved to Los Angeles where she taught writing and literature, while earning her MA in linguistics. After many years of traveling from California to Florida twice a year, she now lives in Tallahassee permanently, and writes full time.

Glynn's novels are thoroughly enjoyable. They offer, in addition to a good read, a fascinating look at the swamp land of northern Florida and the world of diving in mysterious rivers and bottomless caves. Glynn is familiar with the live oak forests and cypress swamps of the area. She also knows the sink holes and reptilians that are abound there. She often swims in the cold, clear springs above the openings to fathomless caves. These are the settings for her Luanne Fogarty mystery series and for her literary novel, River Whispers. Glynn belongs to some impressive organizations that support and inspire her writings Mystery Writers of America, Sisters in Crime, Tallahassee Writers Association, National Speleological Society, and Leon County Sheriffs Department Citizen Academy.

Submitted and written by: Glynn Marsh-Alam, glynnauth@comcast.net

Franklin P. Marsh, Pioneer Dairyman

Franklin Porter Marsh (1890-1959) was one of three children born to Melissa Ezell (1856-1918) and Noah Albert Marsh (1854-1893) in Coffee County, Alabama. Porter spent most of his youth delivering milk to his neighbors. With no formal education, Porter learned the dairy business and knew the market for milk delivery was needed most in the rural county areas. In 1909 after starting his own Dairy business, Porter met and married Pearl Edna Bowdoin (1895-1957) in Coffee County. They had six children:

Franklin Porter Marsh w/son, Rudolph, Noah, and grandbaby, Wesley Marsh.

Edna Ruth (1910-1911), Albert Franklin (1912-1930), Lloyd Edmond (1913-1991), James Woodrow (1916-1998), Rudolph Noah (1922-2004), and Ulys Bowdoin (1919- Present).

In 1923 the Marsh family moved to Leon County, Florida, where Porter started another dairy business by renting farmland, complete with a house and barn from Mrs. Baker for $10.00 a month. He delivered his dairy products in his old Ford Model-T truck to the Northern and Eastern parts of Leon County, and on Saturdays he sold his products at the Market Square in downtown Tallahassee. By charging 10 cents a quart for milk and 6 cents a dozen for eggs Porter was able to make a good living for his family of eight.

Many people have heard of the heroes of the great Wars in Leon County, but few have heard of the Hero of the Dairy. The battle to supply fresh milk to children in the rural areas of Leon County was high from 1929 to 1949. Many dairy farmers charged outrageous prices for their dairy products, but not Porter. He went out of his way to make sure children received fresh milk. After The Great Depression and World War Two, no one forgot Marsh's Dairy's kindness at a time when the economy was at its worst in Florida.

His humanitarian efforts to deliver milk during the price wars contributed to saving the lives of a lot of children. Porter became a hero for delivering fresh raw milk to Chaires and Capitola communities without regards. Some say that he did it because he remembered the death of his oldest child due to the lack of fresh milk in the community, and swore he would never allow this to happen to another child.

During WWII Porter stepped up to the plate again. At a time when the nation was at its weakest, he lowered his milk prices to win a government contract for free milk to the communities in Leon County. This free milk project was the forerunner for today's WIC program, where the government provides fresh dairy products to children and pregnant women in need. By 1940 Porter was blessed to move his family into their own home near the Chaires community. Porter Marsh continued to sell Marsh's Dairy products until 1954 when he retired and sold the business to Borden's Milk distributors. When you drive down Highway 27 East in Leon County remember to stop by Marsh Road and take a look around at a community where one man's dream of supplying a generation of babies with milk has grown into a healthy town.

Written and submitted by: Ulys B. Marsh, 4919 Lester Rd., Tallahassee, FL 32317

Ulys Bowdoin Marsh's "Gift of Gab"

Ulys Bowdoin Marsh was the fourth of five sons born to Edna Pearl Bowdoin (1895-1957) and Franklin Porter Marsh (1890-1959) in Coffee County, Alabama. When Ulys was a young boy, he was considered as having "The Gift of Gab" and was able to talk his way out of many chores, often tricking one his brothers into finishing his tasks for him. Ulys and his brothers loved to fish in the creeks. But Ulys was so good at it that they said he could talk the fish into jumping on the hook. Even after a long day of working on his father's dairy farm Ulys found time to sneak to the creek and surprise his mother with a large catch of fish for dinner.

In 1923 Ulys' family moved to Leon County Florida, where he continued to practice his "Gift of Gab" by telling tall tales in the community of Bradfordville while delivering milk. During the later part of the 1930s and into the Great Depression, Ulys studies at school came easy as he excelled in reading and writing. But due to his family's limited funds, Ulys had to quit school and help with the family's dairy business full-time. Still, many knew he would go far with his "Gift of Gab" and by 1941 he graduated from Leon High School.

In the later part of 1943, Ulys B. Marsh met and married Clara Strickland, a sales clerk for a family store in downtown Tallahassee where Ulys hung out frequently. Ulys did not want to lose the love of his life so, using his "Gift of Gab" he talked her family into allowing them to marry without waiting the engagement period of Leon County. Shortly after they were married, Ulys signed up for the Navy during World War II. After basic training Ulys was stationed aboard the Navy's taskforce ship called "Auburn", as a Communication Specialist which patrolled Guantanamo Bay. While in the military service, Ulys welcomed the birth of his first daughter, Glynn Marsh, and after his Honorable Discharge two years later his second daughter Diane March was born.

Now a family man Ulys obtained employment with the Railways Express Company as a Transportation Specialist, and after 34 years of service he retired in 1978 and was able to collect his pension from the United States Railway Retirement Board, But after only two years Ulys' mind grew restless, so in 1980 he decided to learn a new career as a security guard and, thanks to his "Gift of Gab" skills, Ulys found employment with the Capital Security Police Service as a Guard. Four short years later he was forced to retire due to his health.

Since 1984 Ulys has enjoyed his retirement and can recall more interesting times in Leon County, like his friend Bill Hodges, owner of Goodwood Plantation; "I remember when Bill and I use to hunt in the rural part of Leon County on the land where TMH is today. Those are the things I miss most about living in Leon County." As of 2009, Ulys and his wife, Clara, have the same birthday, and they both look forward to their sixty-sixth wedding Anniversary on their 90th birthday.

Written by: Carol D. Johnson; Submitted by: Glynn Marsh

William and Sarah Massey of Woodville

Bill and Sarah Massey spent their honeymoon at one of the wooden cabins in Tallahassee alongside Lake Ella in 1956. They loved the area so much that when the opportunity arose to relocate to Tallahassee from Jackson, MS, they moved. Both arrived in Leon Co. in 1975 and moved to Woodville where they remained for almost 30 years.

Bill and Carol Massey (left front), 1943

As if their honeymoon cabin was following them from Lake Ella, it became a library near the Woodville School.

Bill was born in Columbus, Muscogee Co., GA in 1926. His parents were Sidney Calhoun Massey and Linnie Merle Sims. Sarah parents were Samuel Greer and Merle Boles. She was born in Red Level, Conecuh Co., AL.

After their marriage, Bill entered the FAA, working first in the Atlanta ARTCC in Hampton, GA. His next assignment was at LaGrange, GA before moving on to Savannah, GA and later Jackson, MS. A fellow co-worker in Savannah, Robert Hayden would become his Air Traffic

Bill and Carol Massey with Tisha Blankenship

manager in Tallahassee. While at LaGrange, he met Charles and Mamie Avery who became lifelong friends.

In 1975, Bob Hayden selected Bill to be his first line supervisor at the Tallahassee Flight Service Station at the Municipal Airport. Bill reported to work in 1975. Their children included Merry, Marion and Jerry Massey. Their home was along Highway 363 in Woodville.

Bill was always a history buff and especially interested in the Civil War. At Woodville, he learned of the Battle of Woodville or the Natural Bridge and of the ancient railroad from Tallahassee leading to St. Marks. One of his ancestors was at Pensacola just before the beginning of the Civil War.

He also studied the Rev. War as one of his Breed ancestors had a hill named after him and a battle became known as Bunker Hill. The Civil War was his primary interest and from 1985 to 1988, he and his fellow supervisor, Charles Blankenship began to sit in on Civil War classes at the FSU Conference Center. Their professors were under FSU history professors, Jim Jones and William Warren Rogers.

Both attended a Civil War reenactment at Woodville and swapped many yarns regarding the two major battles in Florida before the end of the war in 1865. The professors likened us to relics from that time era.

In 1988, Bill became Air Traffic Manager at the Tallahassee FAA FSS and retired in 1989. After Blankenship left for Knoxville, TN in 1988, both kept up with each other meeting in Atlanta for FAA Chiefs conferences. When Blankenship moved across the State to Jackson, TN, Bill told him to look up his old friend, Charlie Avery. He did and Charlie took over from Bill regarding Civil War research.

Bill and Sarah lived at Woodville until the 2004 before moving to Baton Rouge, LA to be near their daughter, Merry. Their son, Jerry had died, followed by Marion in 2004 and Sarah in 2005. Bill is now introducing his grandson to the Civil War.

Written by Charles Blankenship for William Massey, 664 East Majestices, Baton Rouge, LA 70810

Ira Curtis 'I.C.' & Minnie Lee Mayfield

Ira Curtis 'I.C.' Mayfield was born about 1912 around Missouri, he married Minnie Lee Spence in 1933. Minnie Lee Spence was born 1915 in Reno, Georgia. Children born to them were: William Curtis Mayfield, Richard Carroll Mayfield, Raymond Lee Mayfield, Ralph Eugene Mayfield, Gloria Geraldine Mayfield, Merlene Mayfield, Margaret Mayfield, and Loretta Mayfield.

Ira Curtis 'I.C,' and Minnie Mayfield taken about 1955 down at the sand pit, are standing beside their green Buick

Ira Curtis 'I.C.' Mayfield had his own sand business in Leon County, Florida in the late 1940s till 1956. The name of the sand company was "Mayfield & Son Sand Company."

In those days the sand was pure white. He pumped the sand from different places, but the one I remember most is the Ochlocknee River in Leon County, Florida, right off Highway 27. We lived at one time in a big house on the Old Bainbridge Road in Tallahassee, Florida, where the J. Lee Vause Park is now - right up from Lake Jackson. The house had a high back porch with about 12 steps on it.

At one time Geraldine (our sister) was making biscuits for supper and our little pet pig walked up the back steps and stuck his nose right in that bucket of flour, Geraldine was just a yelling and hitting that little pig with a home made broom.

Then later we moved to our new block house on highway 27 where our dad passed away

3 Mayfield sisters, Loretta, Merlene, Margaret.

in 1956, and the sand business was sold. Minnie Lee (Spence) Mayfield later married Jack Sheffield. Minnie Lee (Spence) Mayfield Sheffield passed away in 1994.
Submitted by: Loretta M. I. Hannah, P.O. Box 233 Wattsville, AL 35182

My Father - Aviation Leader Hugh L. Mays

My father was Hugh L. Mays. He was my inspiration for being around airports since about 1929 when the old airport was dedicated. Ivan Monroe's daughter, Teresa, and I were five and six years old. We were there with little aprons on giving out some kind of tickets and watching people take rides in an open cockpit plane.

Hugh Mays was an early aviation leader. He had been appointed State Aviation Inspector by Governor John W. Martin in 1925. Mays was the only military-trained flyer in the capital of Tallahassee. He was a flying cadet toward the end of WWI and graduated from Kelly Field, Texas in 1922. Back then, it was called the Army Air Service. He returned to live in Tallahassee and owned Mays Electric Company.

A site for the first Tallahassee airport was recommended by my father, Douglas Henderson and Theo Proctor Sr. about 1926 or 1927. The Chamber of Commerce Aviation Committee then selected 200 acres lying about three miles west of Tallahassee. They paid $7,000 for what was mostly a cornfield. It was the beginning of the Dale Mabry Field and it was dedicated in 1929. There were no runways; aircraft took off and landed on grass turf.

Hugh L. Mays was also commander of Company M 124th Infantry of the Florida National Guard. The armory that housed the National Guard on North Monroe Street was made possible through his efforts and the citizens of Leon County who held Mays in high regard.
Submitted by: Julia Frances Mays-Wood

Frances Mays-Wood — Local Girl Gets Her Solo Wings

On September 1, 1939, after ten hours of instruction by airport manager Ivan Monroe, Julia Frances Mays - age 16 and a Leon High School student - soloed in a Taylor Craft airplane.

Ivan Monroe was known as the father of aviation in Tallahassee. He said Julia was by far the youngest girl student to solo. Julia weighed about 90 pounds - so light, the aircraft would have lifted off too fast without Ivan in the cockpit. He used sandbags to replace his weight.

Julia was the daughter of Frances Woodward and Hugh L. Mays. Julia's mother died

Julia Frances Mays: Solo Flight Sept., 1, 1939

in May 1939 when Julia was 15 and her sister Ella was eight. Julia's father asked his friend Ivan to give Julia flying lessons. He hoped it would help her overcome some of the sadness of losing her mother.

After Miss Mays' solo flight, she continued to fly on weekends. She maintained a record of her hours in her log book, practiced maneuvers toward qualifying for a private license and did odd jobs around the airport. When she graduated high school in 1941, she entered the Florida State College for Women. With a busy college life and the outbreak of WWII, Julia took a break from flying, but in 1945 she graduated FSCW and returned to the airport. She trained as a meteorology aid to weatherman Jesse W. Smith. She drew weather maps, learned weather terminology, provided pilots with up to date weather information and maintained shift records.

After WWII ended, Julia married her high school sweetheart, Charles S. Wood.

Written and submitted by Frances Mays-Wood 7148 Anglewood Lane Tallahassee, FL 32309

John McDougall

In the early 1840s, John McDougall, a thirty-year-old Scottish immigrant, arrived in Tallahassee and opened a bookstore with Alfred E. Hobby. They offered a varied selection of literary works-including Shakespeare, Dante, and Dickens. By 1860, their stock-in-trade totaled $5,000.

When the state chartered a local bank in 1860, Peres Brokaw and John McDougall were selected for the interim board of directors. The Bank of Tallahassee apparently never went into operation. In 1862, they were involved in the organization of the Gulf State Insurance Company. Company officials included Brokaw, McDougall, B. C. Lewis, and Daniel Ladd of Wakulla County.

John McDougall prospered with well-constructed financial deals. In 1870, the fifty-nine-year-old bachelor was joined by his nephew, John McDougall, a twenty-five-yearold native of Scotland. Upon his arrival, he entered his uncle's employ as a clerk in the bookstore, joined the Republican Party, and became politically active. The elder John died in May, 1876 and his other nephew, Alexander, arrived to claim his share of the estate, which totaled $73,581.19.

The McDougall brothers jointly managed the family business and maintained their uncle's investment in the Tallahassee Manufacturing Company, a local cotton ginning enterprise. After the war, small plantation gins were supplanted by commercial facilities designed for high volume. Tallahassee Manufacturing Company competed with other companies for raw cotton and built a three story frame "cotton factory'" in 1875. It was destroyed by fire in May, 1876. The factory was rebuilt and resumed business in the fall of 1877, but a second fire in 1878 doomed the company. Cotton ginning was abandoned and John developed a cotton mill, producing finished cotton products. Additional income was obtained from a steam powered grist mill on a branch of the St. Augustine River,

In 1878, Alexander purchased one of the largest brick buildings in Tallahassee, with the intention of opening a cotton warehouse. He and Phoebe Brokaw were married by the Reverend N. P. Quarterman, pastor of the Quincy Presbyterian Church, on August 15, 1878. *The Weekly Floridian* called the wedding a "brilliant affair" and described it in great detail. The couple took the evening train to New York, where they honeymooned for several weeks.

Two daughters, Eliza and Mary, were born within the next four years. In 1883, a son, John, was born. Phoebe did not recover from the difficult childbirth and died on January 29 in her home in Tallahassee. Alexander then married Phoebe's sister, Eliza Brokaw on December 2, 1884 at First Presbyterian Church in a simple ceremony by the Reverend Theodore Smith.

Following a New Orleans honeymoon, the couple moved into the Brokaw mansion, which Alexander had recently acquired for $2,000. John McDougall, Jr. was appointed to a four year term as assistant postmaster for Tallahassee in 1884. In 1888 he was selected as a clerk in the local federal court. Four years later, he was appointed postmaster and served until his death on April 24, 1912. Funeral services were held two days later at the First Presbyterian Church, with the Reverend W. H. Zeigler officiating.

His brother, Alexander, assistant postmaster at the time, was appointed to replace him and served a four year term. After a lengthy illness, he died in a Thomasville, Georgia hospital on April 1, 1936. His two-story house was left to his son, Peres Brokaw McDougall. In 1914, Peres married Emma Trammell, the young sister of then Governor, Park Trammell. The Reverend T. J. Nixon, Pastor of the Trinity Methodist Church, performed the ceremony at the governor's mansion. The couple moved into the house in 1936, sharing the premises with Eliza until her death in 1942. Peres continued to live in the house until his death in January, 1960. Emma remained there until the property was acquired by the State of Florida in 1973.

Written and submitted by: Linda S. Mabry, 2404 Oakdale Street, Tallahassee, Florida 32308

Edward Wilk McElvy, a Great Uncle

Edward Wilk McElvy was born on Mar 30, 1895 and died on June 26, 1969. Edward was the brother of my maternal grandmother, who was born in Concord, Florida. He spent some of his young adult life near Beachton in Grady County Georgia, where his parents had bought property and moved after 1910. My first memory of Uncle Wilk was around 1935, when I was about three years old. He was running a fishing camp on Lake Talquin, west of Tallahassee. Daddy, Bert Watson took us there on a picnic and fishing trip. What I remember most clearly about the trip was that a big Collie dog attacked me and Daddy came to my rescue.

A short time later Daddy and Mama arranged for Uncle Wilk to live with us on the Revell's farm just, west of Woodville. He arrived just in time to get everything ready to pull the crops for the year; mainly corn, velvet beans, peanuts and watermelons. I remember also that Uncle Wilk came with Mama and Daddy to see me in Umatilla, Florida in 1938, when I was there for two years with polio at the age of six.

Uncle Wilk would go away after the crops were laid by, to visit other relatives or to work somewhere. After we move into Woodville in the fall of 1939, Uncle Wilk continued to live with us for several years and did the farming. But when WWII broke out in the early 1940s, he went to

1942 Uncle Wilk (far-right), in front of suspended tank lighter.

work at Newport Ships in Newport Florida, where tank lighters (L.C.M Model-3) were being manufactured. He stayed at the Outz Boarding House in Newport while working there.

Some of my fondest and most vivid memories of Uncle Wilk are of the fishing and camping trips my brother, Don and I shared with him. On some trips we camped out for several days at a time. Having never learned to drive an automobile, he used a wagon pulled by a mule to take us on some of these camping trips.

On one trip in the early 1940s he loaded the camping gear and some fresh corn into the wagon, hitched up our mule, Pett and tied his hound dog, Rommy behind the wagon and off to the Eight Mile Sink Hole we went. The place was several miles west of Woodville, Florida. We stayed there for three days and nights, setting trot lines and having a great time. Uncle Wilk dug a small hole in the ground, filled it with burning oak wood to make some hot coals, covered them with a thin layer of dirt, put the fresh unshucked corn on top of the dirt and cooked it beautifully.

Another memorable fishing/camping trip was to the Basin just below Natural Bridge on the St Marks River. Uncle Wilk rented a small house trailer from Frank and Nina Rakestraw who ran the fish camp. We also rented a boat and went fishing every day. On the last day Frank Rakestraw took me fishing in his boat. I did the paddling and he fished, but he did catch several nice Large Mouth Bass for us to take home. Since it was about 10 miles from home, Daddy fetched us there and back in his truck

In 1949 when I was seventeen years old, Uncle Wilk and I ventured off to Tampa in an old 1942 Ford, that we Watson boys had bought for transportation to and from Leon High School. He wanted to visit his Niece, Holly McElvy-Billingsley and her family. Holly's mother had died, when Holly was a very young child and she had then lived with Uncle Wilk's father and mother in Concord, Florida. Figure 2 is a photo made of us and Holly.

In the late 1940s, Uncle Wilk bought some land in Leon County just south of the present Oak Ridge Road and about one mile east of the Eight Mile Sink, Daddy helped him build a little house there. I was impressed with Uncle Wilk's ingenuity at making or driving a shallow Water Well. He rigged up a pole tripod affair and used a rope and pulley to raise and drop a heavy oak block on the pipe to drive it into the ground. In 1950 I had started attending FSU and neglected visiting Uncle Wilk very often.

A couple years later he had a light stroke that left him, a confused and bitter man. After

1949 Tom Watson in middle, Uncle Wilk, and Holly McElvy-Billingsley

graduating from FSU in 1954, I moved to Bay County to work at the United States Navy Mine Defense Laboratory and visited him even less often. He fell out with my parents, blaming them for most of his real and imagined woes. Holly Billingsley heard of his plight, and came up in the mid 1960s and carried him to Tampa. He lived with The Billingsleys' until his death on June 26, 1969.

Written by: Thomas C. Watson, 540 Sunflower Road, Tallahassee, FL. 32305; Submitted by: Maurice Watson, 540 Sunflower Road, Tallahassee, FL. 32305

Benjamin Earnest Mclin

Benjamin Earnest McLin moved with his family from Tennessee to central Florida in 1885. Politics brought the family to Tallahassee soon thereafter when B. E. McLin was elected to the Florida Senate in 1894. He was reelected and served until he was elected Commissioner of Agriculture. He served in the Cabinet from January 1, 1901, until his death on January 31, 1912, during a speaking engagement in Orlando. His remains were returned to Tallahassee to lie in state in the rotunda of the Capitol, followed by interment in the Old City Cemetery.

B. E. McLin's first wife, Malinda Peak Smith, died soon after their move to Florida. Their sons, Eugene Earnest and Walter Smith McLin, were raised in Tallahassee by B. E.'s second wife, Sarah Josephin Glidewell, with halfsiblings Linnie Pearl, Rubie Bearden and John Blair McLin V. Josephine "Granny" Glidewell died in Tallahassee January 19, 1945, and is interred in the Old City Cemetery beside B. E. McLin.

Walter Smith McLin (b. 25 May 1884 d. 24 Aug. 1965, buried Oakland Cemetery) married Eleanor Mae Bell on 11 April 1906 in the Tallahassee home of her parents, Mary McDonald Blunt and Francis "Frank" Burnley Bell. Mary was the daughter of Dr. Angus Fraser Blunt and Caroline Wilson Hunter of Marianna; Frank was the son of John Murrell Bell and Frances Burnley Taylor. The couple lived in Iola and Wewahitchka before moving to Tallahassee.

Walter S. McLin began working for the State of Florida Department of Agriculture in 1906. He was elected Leon County Representative to the Florida House of Representatives in 1929, he served as State Motor Vehicle Commissioner under Governor Doyle Carlton, and thereafter he served under five State Comptrollers. In 1949, planning to retire after 43 years of State service, he was drafted to serve as Sergeant-at-Arms in the House of Representatives.

Known as "Buddy" by most and "Pop" by the countless Leon High School ball players he coached, Walter McLin had played football for the University of Tennessee and was part of the legendary Florida State University football team that played, and defeated, the University of Florida in Lake City in 1903. Walter's brother Eugene Earnest McLin officiated at some early games as well. Walter played baseball with the Tallahassee Capitals also, but coaching was his life-long passion. Walter and Eleanor's children, W. S. "Buddy" McLin, Jr. and Mary Louise McLin Lamb, raised families in Tallahassee. Sixth generation descendants continue to reside in this community.

Submitted by: B. E. McLin, 7008 Alhambra Drive, Tallahassee, FL 1906 wedding in Tallahassee

George Aubrey McMullen

A native of Clearwater, Florida, George Aubrey McMullen was born 2 February 1944, the older son of Bethel Lee McMullen (1898 to 1948, born and died Pinellas County, FL) and second wife Nannie Lee Layfield (1909, Pinellas County, FL, to 1991, Leon County, FL). Paternal grandparents were Birton Lee McMullen (1866 to 1950, born and died Pinellas County, FL), and Virginia May Mitchell (born 1869 in Bartow, Polk County, FL, died 1940, Pinellas County, FL). Maternal grandparents were Henry Albert Layfield (born 1883, Columbia County, FL, died 1940, Pinellas County, FL), and Catherine "Katie" Olivia Dukes (born 1883, Union County, FL, died 1969, Pinellas County, FL).

George McMullen was proud that his great grandparents were early settlers of Pinellas

1906 wedding in Tallahassee

County, when the area was part of Hillsborough. James Parramore McMullen, born in Quitman, GA, in 1823, was sent south by his family in 1841 to recover from "consumption." After spending time in the Tampa Bay area, he married Margaret Elizabeth Campbell in Brooksville, Hernando County, FL, in 1844. The couple moved to the Tampa Bay area, building what is the oldest existing log cabin residence in Pinellas County by 1852. James recruited his six other brothers, John Fain, David, Malcolm, William, Thomas Fain, and Daniel, to settle in Florida.

George grew up in Dunedin, north of Clearwater, and attended Dunedin High School. He joined the Marines in 1962, earning his GED and beginning college courses while in the service. After his honorable discharge in 1966, George began working with the Pinellas County Sheriff's Department, and attended the University of South Florida, receiving his bachelor's degree in 1975. About 1976, George moved to Tallahassee, Leon County, FL, to work with the Florida Department of Law Enforcement, first with the Division of Criminal Justice Standards and Training, later as a special agent with the Division of Local Law Enforcement Assistance, concentrating on domestic marijuana eradication.

For many years, George enjoyed learning how to use and to build muzzle-loading, black powder rifles. He was a marksman who enjoyed competition with the old-style guns. He made rifles from wooden blanks, carefully designing, carving and smoothing the stocks by hand, "browning" the barrels, and carefully finishing them. Bullets for the rifles were made from lead melted in a smelter. In the last few years of his life, he began creating wooden furniture, using colonial-era techniques, including hand-cut dovetails. In addition, George was a devoted supporter of the Florida State University's Seminole football team, and he loved fishing on north Florida lakes and rivers.

George was married first to Nancy Hart, of Pinellas County, Florida; they had two sons, David Lee and Bethel Lee McMullen. George then married Mary Anne Johnson, originally from Birmingham, Jefferson County, Alabama; they had no children. On 28 October 1989, George died in Leon County of lung cancer, and was buried in the McMullen Cemetery on Old Coachman Road in Pinellas County, established by his great grandfather.

Written and submitted by: Mary Anne Johnson Price, gmaprice12@comcast.net

McPherson

The descendants of Archibald McPherson were as follows. December 19, 1842, Archibald McPherson (born in Chapel Hill, NC; a carpenter, slave overseer, and soldier) married Kity Ann Tew (Katherine Teugh). They migrated from Barbour County, Alabama, to Jackson County, Florida.

Kity bore their 6 children: James (1845), Alexander (1847), Benjamin Franklin (1848), John Tewy (1851), and twins, Nancy Jane and Missouri (1852). Kity died after the twins' birth.

Archibald married Deborah Ann Edenfield in 1859 at Marianna, Florida.

Archibald, James, and Alexander are listed on the Muster Roll, 6th Florida Company A (Reprinted from Robertson's "Soldiers of Florida" the 6th Florida "Florida Guards" – listing Archibald's death of pneumonia at Knoxville May 10, 1863; and Alexander a Musician [A second source lists Alexander and James as Drummers.]. James enlisted in the Confederate army at Chattahoochee, Florida, in Captain R.H.M. Davidson's Company "A" 6th Florida Infantry, April 1862.

Deborah died April 13, 1919 in Grand Ridge, Jackson County, Florida.

James McPherson's descendants were as follows. The Edwards family in Gadsden County were true pioneers, poor, uneducated, and looking for free or cheap land. Cullen Edwards, Sr., progenitor of the Edwards family, had a son, William (1802 - 1866) who held a land patent recorded in 1827 and signed by John Adams, President. He married Honor Darby (No connection verified, but Hon. Leroy Collins and Mrs. Collins had a daughter named "Darby" - Mrs. Collins was a Darby.) William and Honor had 8 children, the fifth being Ellen.

Ellen first married John Browning, enlisted in 1862 and killed in Fredericksburg, Virginia, July 4, 1863 while a private in the Confederate Fifth Florida Infantry. They begat two daughters, Ida Mary and Louisa Susan, who married John Tewy McPherson, James' younger brother.

On September 23, 1866, Ellen married James McPherson. Their home was near Gretna, Florida, on the acreage she inherited. She bore their six children: Charles A. (1867), Archie, Anne Elizabeth, Alexander or "Sandy", William or "Bill", Henry Lee or "Lee". Charles A. McPherson, Sr., who migrated to Tallahassee, is the Grandfather of Tallahassee native, Dorothy Lee "Dotty" McPherson, and Charles and Glenn Barnard. They never met their Grandfather.

Descendants of Charles A. McPherson and Annah Leone "Annie" Sauls were as follows. Charles A. McPherson, Sr. and Annah Leone "Annie" Sauls had 3 children: Charles A., Jr. (1907 or 1908), Elmer Renaldo (January 13, 1909 - January 27, 1987), and Mildred Lorraine.

Thelma Lee McPherson

Charles A. McPherson, Jr., owned a plumbing business in Tallahassee. He was a Mason and Shriner. He and wife, Willie Dell Jerrigan [sic - Jernigan?], Pensacola, lived on College Avenue, east and uphill of Franklin Boulevard. He built a 2-story brick home on a very large lot. Preparing for retirement, he built duplexes in front of and behind their home. All remain today. After their deaths, the property was sold, and another apartment house was built in front of the main house.

Charles had a garage that would easily keep 4 cars, but he kept much of his plumbing supplies stored in it. He did park their immaculate Packard car in it. On the back side of the garage was his office. From the back of the home, a dirt drive went downhill to the area that has the former Florida Bar Building that faced Franklin Boulevard and Apalachee Parkway.

At Charles and Willie's home during the fifties, Charles and brother Elmer built a brick barbeque grill. It had a chimney and was equipped to move the grilling racks up and down for meat to be closer to or farther from the fire. Elmer, being the master sheet metal worker, constructed a metal cover so they could "smoke" their meats. A pulley enabled them to raise and lower the front of the cover so they could turn the meats. The barbeque area behind their house became a gathering place for their family and friends.

One time the Newman's, Willie's friends, who were in the printing or publishing business in Tallahassee, featured a McPherson barbeque in a local magazine. Charles, Willie and Elmer served up the best of barbeques that evening. The article showed the whole family around the tables eating.

Elmer's wife, Thelma, got caught with a headscarf tied around her head and with a mouthful of food. She worked for Turner's (a fashionable, high-end clothing store on Monroe Street), so was very particular about her appearance, especially her hair. Her entire life, even when she was dying with cancer, she got her hair done at the beauty parlor EVERY week. Bershe Kelly was her hairdresser until she no longer did hair dressing.

The article also included a picture of Rusty, Charles and Willie's hound dog. His hair was white with a hint of gray splotches everywhere and large black spots, including around his eyes. He was well-trained, and had to be, as Willie was an immaculate housekeeper. She would not tolerate him messing up her house. The byline for the picture was "Rusty enjoys his share, too."

Wherever Charles went, Rusty went. He and Willie had no children. Elmer's daughter, Dorothy Lee "Dotty" McPherson, was the closest they had to a child, as they spent many a weekend fishing with Elmer and Dotty or with Elmer and Dotty visiting their home. Back then, there were no 2-seater pickup trucks, but Charles, Willie, Elmer and Dotty fit into Charles' just fine.

Although Charles and Elmer lived their adult lives in Tallahassee, they spent much time hunting and fishing in Leon County and the surrounding counties.

Charles and Willie had a cottage at McIntyre, an old community south of the Ochlockonee River in the National Forest. Next door was a cottage owned by Tallahasseean Gerald Gandy, who trapped black bears down there (possibly with the help of Charles). The cottages were situated over a mile off Highway 316 and back in the pine forest, a good way south of the river.

Charles died in the mid-fifties. En route from the cottage, he felt sick and stopped at a drug store in Crawfordville. It was closed, although people were still inside. They would not go to the door and he got in his truck and died of a heart attack. Willie lived to her 80s in Tallahassee, but her sisters took her back to Pensacola when her eyesight failed, and there she died. Willie was a long-time employee of Rose Printing Company that was first situated on Monroe Street.

After Charles' death and Elmer and Thelma's divorce, it was Elmer and Dotty who carried on the tradition of fishing and hunting — another story.

Written and Submitted by Dorothy Lee (Dotty) McPherson
24236 Lanier St., Tallahassee, FL 32310

Charles A. McPherson and Annah Leone "Annie" Sauls Family

Not much is known about Charles A McPherson, Sr. He married Annah Leone "Annie" Sauls January 3, 1906. Annah and Charles begat three children, Elmer Renaldo (1909-1983), Charles A. Jr. (1907-1955), and Mildred Lorraine.

Charles Jr. and his wife, Willie Dell Jernigan were childless. Elmer and wife, Thelma Lee Tillman of Moultrie, adopted Dorothy Lee "Dotty" McPherson, at three days (1945). Mildred married Arthur Barnard. Their children, Glenn and Charles, are younger than Dotty.

Charles, Sr., worked for the railroad in Tallahassee and in Dunnellon where he took Annie, Elmer and Charles; but Annie and the boys returned to Tallahassee. He later took the children to the Gatlin family in the Bloxham/Lake Talquin community out Highway 20 West after their Mother was institutionalized at Chattahoochee. As part of the Gatlin family they learned to be avid hunters and fishermen, and learned to live off the land.

Elmer and Charles moved into town as adults and remained in Tallahassee the rest of their lives. They taught Dotty to fish. Elmer taught her to hunt, and they spent much time with the Sauls family, also a hunting and fishing family.

With Grandmother Annah not in her life, Dotty thought Mamie Sauls was her Grandmother. Mamie's husband, James Martin Sauls, was Annah's first cousin.

Mamie's house at South Calhoun and East Lafayette Streets was always filled with family, including Elmer and Dotty. Being a block from Monroe Street and the Capital Building, Mamie and her sons had many visitors on her huge wraparound porch of chairs. The State bought that home and the whole block, and built the Carlton Building thereon.

Dotty knew most all the Sauls; they all were very masculine men, who hunted and fished all the time. Dotty recently read a Journal kept by Martin Sauls, Mamie's husband, and found a side of the Sauls family she never knew. This is not to say that they did not have a gentle side. They treated her like a little princess and were truly family-oriented.

When Dotty was very small, Mamie's youngest son, Carl ("Cooter") visited Elmer, Thelma, and Dotty often. He would sit patiently and allow Dotty to twist his long, black curly hair into spit curls and pin them with wire bobby pins. He was Dotty's favorite of Mamie's sons.

Her cousins, Marvin, Margie, and Carl, lived around the corner from Mamie on Madison Street, across from the old Caroline Brevard School, and next door to their grandparents, Florence and Pap. The four played together regularly. The older Marvin teased them a lot. The girls avoided baby Carl.

Marvin and Carl Sauls by the cannon at the Old Capitol

Sometimes, they ventured to the Old Capitol Building (the ONLY capitol building) and played on the cannons on the front portico, now gone after the last major restoration.

One time, they were so bold as to climb the stairs/ladder to the dome - unsafe looking and full of pigeon droppings. They did not feel comfortable enough to go to the top, so missed getting a bird's eye view of what is now Apalachee Parkway.

Beside Mamie's house was a very steep hill that ran from Calhoun Street down to Gadsden Street. When Marvin was young, he would jump in his wagon and roll down that dirt street, which was part of the longer Lafayette Street. At the bottom of the hill was a lot of sand. He could steer the wagon into the sand so that it stopped his descent. Today, that part of Lafayette Street enables one to avoid the Parkway, just before the right-hand merge lane onto Apalachee Parkway.

Walking to town was a great pastime. They never ventured away from town across Gadsden Street towards Smoky Hollow, where Franklin Boulevard and the DOT Building sit. That was practically out of town. They avoided an old structure, that surely hid monsters and kept away nosy children, situated on the corner of Gaines and Gadsden Streets - the old waterworks building and a half underground water tank, used 1924 to 1958. These buildings remain on the site of Tallahassee's original water service of 1889.

Mamie had a sewing machine that required peddling for the machine to sew. When Dotty was very young, she would sit on Mamie's footstool and peddle while making car engine noises.

One time, Dotty found a large rattrap in the pantry on the back side of the kitchen. She picked it up and asked Mamie what it was. Mamie warned her that it would "bite" and that she should return it. Dotty, being a stubborn child, decided to see what the wires would do — and, YEP, it bit her. She, of course, was screaming at the top of her lungs while Mamie got the rattrap disconnected from Dotty's tiny fingers - a lesson hard-learned, but learned well.

One Christmas, James Jefferson "Jeff' Sauls (1925-1993) appeared at Mamie's house as Santa Claus. He performed his "Ho Ho's", then bent over to take presents out of his sack on the floor. When he bent over, his britches split open. He had on red and white undershorts. Mamie took him away and stitched up his pants. All of this was to Dotty's great delight.

Jeff is the son of H.R. Sauls and Mattie "Mattie G" Gilbourne [sic-Gilbert(?)} (Gadsden County). H.R. owned a plumbing company in Tallahassee. Pat Sauls is Jeff's stepbrother.

Jeff is the Father of James Jefferson "Jimmy", Jr., Leonard Henry, and Stephen Walker (deceased). The boys lost their Mother, Martha, October 1, 1957 from an automobile accident. Jeff married M. "Bea" Behrea December 13, 1958, and they had a son, Robert Edward.

Jimmy was a coach at Leon High School and remains in the school system. Leonard worked for Jeff at the family upholstery business site on what is now MLK Jr. Boulevard. Robert operates Sauls Signs at that site now.

When the State bought the block on which the Sauls family homes were situated to build the Carlton Building, Marvin's family moved out on the Jacksonville Highway (Highway 90 East). They lived in the same neighborhood as future wife Jane.

Mamie's sons, Carl and Victor, moved Mamie out the Perry Highway (Apalachee Parkway) just beyond the truck route (Capital Circle SE). She had a gorgeous brick home, but it did not have the wrap-around porch. Not as many people went there to visit as when she lived downtown. She died not many years thereafter, possibly of a broken heart from being moved from her home and friends and family that made her life. Mamie was the tie that bound the Sauls family and the Elmer McPherson family.

Submitted by Dorothy Lee "Dotty" McPherson 24236 Lanier Street, Tallahassee, FL 32310

McPherson — Raised by the Gatlins

Wright T. Gatlin (1854-1930) was the son of Richard R. Gatlin (1812-1898). Wright married one of the Hopkins girls, Lucinda "Lou" Hopkins (1869-1944). Martha Hopkins Sauls, wife of James Dewitt Sauls is Mother of Annah Leona "Annie" Sauls. Annah is wife of Charles A. McPherson and Mother of Elmer and Charles and Mildred.

The Gatlins, Hopkins, McPhersons, and Sauls are related by marriage.

When the wife of Charles A. McPherson, Sr., Annah Leone "Annie" Sauls McPherson, became ill, he depended on the Gatlins to raise their children. Elmer often told his daughter, Dorothy Lee "Dotty" McPherson, about Lillie or Lilla Gatlin raising them. The Gatlins were farmers, hunters and fishermen at Bloxham and Lake Talquin. Elmer and Charles learned those skills well.

Marjorie Sauls and Dotty McPherson by the cannon at the Old Capitol

Elmer McPherson and his brother-in-law, Bill Hunnicutt

Elmer was a very successful gardener. He grew Texas Big Boy tomatoes at his homes - first on Bass Street and then on Gadsden Street. His yield was so big, he would weigh them by bagfuls and allow Dotty, his daughter, to sell them door to door to their neighbors in Menlo Park, through which Gadsden Street ran and ended at South Magnolia Drive. The Gadsden Street home was due east downhill from the FRM Feed Store that fronted on South Monroe Street.

At an earlier home on Bass Street, Elmer grew bananas, oranges, kumquats, gorgeous Dahlia flowers, cone flowers, ginger flowers, and giant Elephant Ears. He also grew hot peppers.

Bass Street was a great place to grow up with the Bass, Hodges, Gilmer, Trotman, Wilder, Davis, Horne, and Whitaker families, amongst others. Some were like extended families for Dotty.

Written and Submitted by Dorothy Lee "Dotty" McPherson
24236 Lanier Street, Tallahassee, FL 32310

Robert Skip Montgomery-Prince Skip of the Movie Industry

Robert Skip Montgomery was born to a Movie mega Family, So, you might say; he was born to Act. This movie industry family is well known for their Royal involve men in community affairs in the United States; Skip provided his talents to Tallahassee, Florida in 1993, just seven years before the famous actor's death. He produced and taught acting classes at Florida State University. Robert Montgomery, Jr. was born February 15, 1936 in Los Angeles, California to actors Robert Montgomery Sr. (1904-1981), and former stage actress, Elizabeth Allen (1904-1992). Robert is the Montgomery's third child, the second born is daughter Elizabeth Montgomery, of the hit TV show "Bewitched" (1933-1995). The first born was daughter, Martha Bryan (1930-1931).

Robert, or Skip, as he was known, was raised in the height of the Hollywood's era. Summers were spent in the Montgomery farmhouse in Patterson, New York. In 1939, Skip became the youngest lifetime honorary member of the Screen Actors Guild, chiefly due to his father's roll as president of the Guild. In 1945 Skip attended a private school in Arizona until 1952, when he attended St. Mark's High School in Southboro, Massachusetts. Skip benefited from his father's career in the movie industry when he landed small parts in the school plays. For Skip this was all in preparation for his career in the movie industry. In 1958, 22-year-old Skip decided, with much encouragement, to follow in the footsteps of both his parents and his sister by beginning his own acting career. He also became a father that year when his wife, socialite Deborah Chase gave birth to a son, Robert Montgomery, III.

By 1959, Skip found minor rolls in many feature films, "Say One For Me" and "A Private's Affair" as well as roles on television including "The Loretta Young Show" That year Deborah gave birth to a daughter, Deborah Elizabeth Montgomery. His vast exposure to the movie industry made him more in demand for leading rolls like; "The Gallant Hours" (1960), "12 to the Moon" (1960), and "The Tall Man" (1961), just to name a few. Skip continued his acting career through 1962 with roles in both films and television. But, in 1963 Skip abandoned his acting career and headed for the financial arena. For twenty years he worked for the firm of Hayden, Stone & Co. as a stockbroker on Wall Street. After raising his children Skip started working on his production career in 1983.

Not much is know about Skip's career between 1983 and 1994 but, he maintained a New York address and a Tallahassee residentce during this time. He met and married Melanie Griffith, an actress in 1984 and they settled in Leon County permanently to raise their family. In 1994 Skip moved to Tallahassee Florida where he became a Liaison between the Community and the Florida State University Graduate Film Conservatory School. He formed the "Sleepy Actors Group" in 1995 which provided Housing to Graduate student6 working on their Master's Degree in Film production. And in 1998 he became

Executive Producer for an Independent Film company where he produced the film "Roses"

On February 7, 2000, Skip was diagnosed with cancer. The prognosis for recovery was favorable. However, a few months later on April 28, 2000, Skip unexpectedly passed away at the age of 64, leaving behind a widow, Melanie and, his minor children: Michael, Meghann, and Sarah. The funeral for Skip was large with numerous celebrities from around the world. He was cremated and his ashes were given to his family here in Leon County Florida. Skip is gone but not forgotten by everyone, especially the people here in Leon County due to his vast contributions to this community.

Written by: Melanie G. Montgomery

Stewart Nelson

Born in Virginia, raised in Europe and a resident of Tallahassee, FL since 1979, Stewart Nelson received a BA in Photography from the University of Alabama and has explored his vision of fine art photography ever since. His images combine traditional photography using 35mm or 110 film cameras with computer imaging. In this technique of Digitalism, work is created with a computer as one of the critical tools in producing fine art.

Nelson also explores the process of digital image capture, using a flatbed scanner to create art from found objects such as leaves, fruit and crushed cans. The use of a scanner to capture an image for manipulation is often referred to as scanography and is the digital equivalent of one the earliest forms of photography, the photogram, which was used at the turn of the century in America.

As a former painter, Nelson's sense of color and texture pushes his photography beyond realism with the manipulation of color and light, changing their relationship and creating an altered reality more evocative of dreams or fading memories. These distinct moments gain importance through this exploration to create the final image, an image far removed from the original moment of capture. His award-winning work is displayed in galleries and museums worldwide.

Submitted and written by: Stewart Nelson 3224 Yorktown Drive Tallahassee, FL. 32312 850-567-5138
stew@snelsonphoto.com

Dr. Leedell Neyland

Leedell Wallace Neyland was born in Gloster, Amite, Mississippi in 1921 to Gammell Neyland (1885-1950) and Estelle Wallace (1899-1983); he was the youngest of 6 children to this union. Leedell was always curious about life and set out at an early age to discover the true meaning behind the phrase of the United States Constitution: "Every man is Free to Life, Liberty and the Pursuit of Happiness." After his educational pursuits Leedell met and married Della L. Adams, a teacher from Florida A & M University High School in 1955. They have three children: Beverly, a pediatrician; Keith a lawyer; and Katrina, Coordinator of Special Services at Florida A & M University.

Leedell received his early education at Amite County Training School in Mississippi. He received his Bachelor of Arts from Virginia State University in 1949 and a Master of Arts in 1952 from New York University. While working on his doctoral degree, he worked as a teacher under the Danforth Grant and his doctoral major was in Modem American History, and obtained his Ph.D from New York University in 1959. Dr. Neyland has held many prestigious positions at colleges and universities all over the South. Some of Dr. Neyland's titles were: Professor of History, Dean of the Arts and Sciences College, and Vice President of Florida A & M University. He has written four books so far and contributed his thoughts to many professional and scholarly journals. Dr. Neyland was an active member and elder of the Trinity United Presbyterian Church in Tallahassee, Florida and was always active in many professional associations, civic societies and religious organizations in Leon County. Dr Neyland has retired from his civic duties and moved in with his daughter who lives in Nevada. He now enjoys spending time with his grandchildren, and family.

In honor of

Dr. Leedell W. Neyland

Dr. Neyland's dedication and service while at Florida A&M University an art gallery on the campus was named after him in 2006. The rich collection of the University's history is dedicated to Leedell W. Neyland, who served FAMU for more than 45 years. Neyland served Leon County for half a century, but states his greatest satisfaction has come from preserving FAMU's history. The idea to open the gallery and dedicate it to Neyland was suggested by Larry Reese, vice president for administrative and fiscal services, and by Provost Larry Robinson, vice president for academic affairs. Earl Murell Dawson, director of the Southeastern Regional Black Archives Research Center and Museum at FAMU, made the idea a reality.

When asked his feelings on the dedication, Neyland said, "I am honored by the dedication, but if we could learn from our past and sincerely appreciate the historical lessons they teach, then we will make firm foundations upon which to build our future. This will enable us to look towards the future with hope and greater expectations for our life."

Written and Submitted by: Dr. Leedell Neyland 2128 Bliss Comer Street Henderson, NV 89044 (702) 616-8799

Nicks' Descendants Honored as Fallen Heroes of Florida

Two sons of Frances Fair and James Rinaldo Nicks lived into the 20th Century. They were William Richard and Robert Henry R. Nicks. William lived with his parents at Lake Iamonia, Leon County, Florida around 1833 until they moved to Hernando Co. in 1853, where his youngest brother, Henry R. Nicks was born in 1852.

William Nicks married Sophronia Mitchell in 1855 and their daughter, Mary Ann married Daniel O'Berry and had seven children. Mary's son, William Henry Nicks-O'Berry became a Deputy Sheriff for Pasco County, Florida. He was killed in the line of duty in 1926. In 2004, Lt. (now Capt.) Mike Shreck of the Pasco Co. Sheriff's Dept. began research on O'Berry's "end of watch." He was honored in May, 2004 at the Pasco Law Enforcement Memorial Service in Dade City, Florida. A niece attended in his honor and a rose was placed at the site alongside other fallen officers.

Henry R. Nicks married Alatha Frances Jane Hope in 1873 in Hernando County. Their son, Sheldon S. Nicks, was born in January of 1886. On the 1900 Census he is listed in his parent's household at Spring Lake and also in his brother-in-law's home in Hudson. Nicks' descendants knew that Henry R. Nicks was a Town Marshal for Fivay, Pasco County, FL and that on May 9, 1909, he went to arrest a fugitive with his son, Sheldon S. Nicks. The fugitive fired a shot at them, and Sheldon leaped in front of his father. The bullet passed through Sheldon's body, killing him instantly and lodged in his father's shoulder, where it remained until his death in 1928.

Not one of the Nicks' descendants knew that Sheldon was actually a Deputy Sheriff until years later. Local New Port Richey researcher Jeff Miller discovered a newspaper article and brought it to the attention of Nicks' relatives, the Sheriff's Department, and the St. Petersburg newspaper. Reporter Bill Stevens wrote a story about the discovery, and it was Captain Mike Shreck who once again took up the cause of adding Sheldon's name to the Pasco Co. Fallen Hero's Memorial. Once approved, they honored Sheldon's picture with a rose on May 1, 2009.

Sheldon's niece, Frances Clark Mallett placed the rose flanked by grand nephews, Charles Blankenship, Butch Mallett and Steven Hancock at the site. On May 3rd and May 4th, 2009, Sheldon was again honored at the State Capitol in Tallahassee. His grand nephew, Charles Blankenship and wife, Tisha (former residents of Tallahassee) attended both ceremonies.

The Pavilion between the Old and New Capitol buildings was a fitting site for the memorial, since Sheldon's paternal grandfather, J.R. Nicks, had served in the House of Representatives from 1856-1959 and his mother's maternal great grandfather, Michel Garrison, had served the same position in 1845.

Neither lawman had any direct descendants. Sheldon's wife, Ruby Eugene Clark Nicks, remarried and had a daughter who is still living. Sheldon's sister Lonnie Lee Nicks Clarks' daughter is still living. Both knew the story of Sheldon's demise, but neither knew he was actually a Deputy until old newspaper items were brought to their attention. They will be honored each year, forever in Dade City and Tallahassee, Florida with other brave lawmen who have kept Florida safe for all.

Written by: Charles Blankenship; Submitted by: Tisha A. Blankenship 55 Country Club Cove, Jackson, TN 38305

Descendants of Sarah Ann Nicks

Sarah Ann Nicks (aka Sarah Ann Sauls) was born in downtown Charleston, SC in 1819. Her parents were Joseph De Witt Nicks and Elizabeth Harrison by her second marriage. Elizabeth, widow of Richard Fair, boot and shoemaker of Charleston, SC, remarried Joseph after Richard's death in 1817. They had three children, including Sarah, Martha and James W. Nicks. In 1828, James died. He was buried in Charleston's Bethel Methodist Cemetery.

After the death of her husband, Joseph, Elizabeth moved to Leon Co., FL where her children by Richard Fair had relocated before her. On the 1840 U.S. Census for Leon Co., Fl, four families (James R. Greene, James R. Nicks, Richard Van Brunt and Celete Sauls) were close neighbors on the western edge of the Strickland Arm of Lake Iamonia. They remained there until the early 1840s. In 1842, Sarah Ann Nicks witnessed an indenture for her brother-in-law, James R. Greene.

Sarah's mother, Elizabeth Nicks, moved to Columbus, Muscogee Co., GA. Martha and Sarah were still with her. The Greene and Sauls families also moved and on January 4, 1843, Sarah Ann Nicks married Celete Greene-Sauls and Daniel Sauls' son, James D. Sauls. Several deeds, a marriage record and other material for James and Sarah Nicks Sauls exist in Muscogee Co., GA records.

The Sauls family lore has it that James D. Sauls, on hearing about some unmarried girls in South Georgia, went there from his home in North Florida and met Sarah Galbraith. They married in Leon County, FL and had a son, James Robert Sauls. Sarah died soon after, and James took his son to Columbus, GA, where his mother lived, and there he met and married Sarah Nicks. Eventually her mother moved across the river to Girard, Russell Co., Alabama, where she died in 1845. James and Sarah moved north into what was still Russell Co. at the time to Opelika, Alabama. They were still there on the 1850 Census enumeration. Their children were Robert (James Robert), James D., Absalom D., Elizabeth, Frances, Walter D. and William Sauls.

The same 1850 Census still had most of Sarah's siblings living close by in Opelika, including Mary Ann Greene, Sophia Burr and Joseph Fair. Ten years later in 1860, Sarah and James D. had moved back to Columbus, GA. The enumeration of their household included James D. (15), Absalom D. (14), Elizabeth (10), Frances (9), Walter D. (7) and William (7). James' eldest son James Robert moved on, eventually settling in West Virginia where the town of Saulsville was named or him. James D. Sauls' family moved back to Florida and settled in Quincy, Gadsden County, FL. Sarah died before 1868 as James married for the third time to Martha Black on March 30, 1868. His four children with Martha were: Florida, William, Martha Eleanor, and Ellen. To this day, Sauls' descendants continue to live in Wakulla and Leon counties.

Written by: Charles Blankenship; Submitted by: Shirley and Charles Sanders 309 Sweetbriar Dr. Tallahassee, FL 32312 850-385-0403

Descendants of Martha Nicks

Martha Nicks, the youngest daughter of Elizabeth Harrison Fair Nicks and Joseph DeWitt Nicks was born c. 1825 in downtown Charleston, SC. Her mother and two uncles (James and Robert) came from Cavan County, Ireland around 1794 with her grandmother, Ann (?) and John Harrison. Elizabeth's first marriage was to boot and shoemaker, Richard Fair. (See Fair - Nicks' sibling sketches)

Martha's father, Joseph Nicks, was a teacher who most likely tutored the Fair children and after the death of Richard Fair in 1817, married Elizabeth. They had three children, including Sarah Ann, James and Martha. She too grew up in Charleston until the extended family began their outward migration. After Joseph's death, the family ventured toward Thomasville, Thomas Co., GA where Elizabeth's oldest daughter, Mary Ann married James R. Greene in June of 1832.

Soon after, in 1833, Elizabeth witnessed an Indenture of a Deed of Gift in Leon Co., FL. Mrs. Eleanor (?) Greene Nicks in Trust to her son, Benjamin Greene of Screven Co., GA gave about 200 acres of land to her daughter-in-law, Frances Fair Nicks and her children. The land was located on the northern side of Lake Iamonia just west of today's Strickland Arm.

Elizabeth's sister, Frances Fair had married James Rinaldo Nicks, son of Eleanor and William Nicks of Screven Co., GA. Eleanor was probably a stepmother to Joseph Nicks and his father was most likely William Nicks by an earlier marriage. Elizabeth and Eleanor had a mutual friendship for several years when their daughter and son married. Several Indentures written in GA, AL and FL were in favor to several of the Fair and Nicks' children by their mothers.

The 1840 U. S. Census enumerated four families who were related and living in the Lake Iamonia, Leon co., FL area. They included Richard Van Brunt and wife, Elizabeth Jane Fair; J R. Nicks and wife, Frances Fair, and J. R. Greene and wife, Mary Ann Fair. Nearby was Greene's sister, Celete Greene Sauls and her son, James D. Sauls married to Martha's sister, Sarah Ann Nicks.

Martha and her mother and sister were most likely in the Richard Van Brunt household for the 1840 census. They remained there until the Sauls and Greene families moved toward Columbus, GA in the early 1840s. Sometime after May 1844, Martha married John Mizell. He and Martha's half sister Sophia Fair's husband, Allen Burr, had a firm in Girard, AL. He died in October and Martha inherited twothirds of his estate. Elizabeth Nicks was also living in Girard where she died in 1845. After John Mizell's death, both Burrs and Martha moved up to Opelika, AL. Martha met and married James Pinckard Durr in December 1845. They lived in the area until 1860. At that time, she moved to Jefferson, Marion Co., TX by way of New Orleans, LA. About the same time or shortly thereafter, Martha's half-brother, Joseph Harrison Fair moved his family to Jefferson also.

Martha and James Durr continued to live in Jefferson, TX for the remainder of their lives. They appear on the 1860 Census with their family. Strangely, in 1870, Martha was not counted on the census, but in 1880, she is again in her husband's household with her daughters.

The six daughters of James and Martha Durr included Lizzie, Mary Ann, Kitty, Jennie, Sarah Greene and Johnny Alice. Johnny Alice Durr (1856-1944) married Francis Erwen Adams and lived in Cleburne TX. Their descendant, Jacqueline Holt Wright, published a book titled *Meet Your Ancestors* in 1944. The book compiles the Harrison-Fair and subsequent Harrison-Nicks families of Charleston, SC and their outward migration from SC through GA and into Leon Co., Fl in the 1830s. They moved out in the early 1840s, first to GA and then AL. By 1860, the Nicks-Durr line moved to TX.

The short history of the Harrison-Fair-Nicks corrects the two books by Charles E. Fair in that the parents of the Fair children were Elizabeth Harrison and Richard Fair. It also adds to Frank Hawthorne's Greene-Fair by adding three "...Lost Cousins," Martha Nicks, Sarah Ann Nicks and Frances Fair.

Martha Nicks-Durr

Except for two siblings (Robert Richard Fair and James W. Nicks) the Fair and Nick's siblings lived in Leon Co., FL when it was part of the Territory of Florida. Most of the siblings moved out of Florida before Statehood. Only Elizabeth Jane Fair Van Brunt and Francis Fair Nicks remained.

The Lake Iamonia land is within 2-3 miles of the Tall Timbers Plantation. The history of the plantation should know these people were there before those who came after. They are part of the history of Leon County, Florida. The descendants living in Florida would do well to be introduced to their kin.

Written by: Charles Blankenship for Jacqueline H. Wright, 7774Creekridge Rd., Citrus Heights, CA 95610

Descendants of James Rinaldo Nicks

James R. Nicks, son of William Nicks and Eleanor (?) was most likely born in Screven Co., GA. His mother was previously married to Revolutionary War veteran, Benjamin Greene. Their land lay along the Savannah River, north of Briers Creek. After Benjamin's death, Mrs. Eleanor Greene signed a marriage settlement protecting her children by Benjamin and married William Nicks. James Nicks was born around 1808.

He grew up in Screven Co. and is twice listed as a Georgia Land Lottery winner for 1827 and 1832. Around 1828, his mother purchased land located in Leon Co., Fl as did her son Benjamin Greene. The lands located in Township 1N and Range !E was located on the north side of Lake Iamonia in Section 13, Lots 4 and 5 amounting to almost 200 acres.

Sometime in 1832, James married Miss Frances Fair of Charleston, SC. In August 1833, Eleanor Nicks, by a Deed of Gift in Trust to her son Benjamin, gave the two lots of land to Frances Nicks and her children. James and Frances lived in Leon Co. for the next twenty years. They appear on both the 1840 and 1850 U. S, Census years. The 1850 census lists William R., Frances (Francis) R., Benjamin R., Susan A. and James R. (Jr.) who when compared with 1852 Chancery Court records for Leon Co. are listed as their known children.

That same Chancery Court record of equity was to claim the land for Frances Nicks and her children after the death of James' half-brother, Benjamin Greene of Sceven Co., GA. Their reason for leaving was because the land was worn, no educational facilities for the children, and health concerns for the younger ones.

One other child, Robert Henry R. Nicks, was born November 1852 in Leon Co. just before his parents moved south to Hernando Co., FL. He would live until 1928 and help establish the small town of Port Richey in Pasco Co. Because of his vision that someday, residents would not have a place to launch their boats to get into the Gulf of Mexico, he deeded property to the City of Port Richey. Today, that property is known as H. R. Nicks Park and he as "The Father of Port Richey."

After James Rinaldo Nicks settled on Lake Iamonia land, he welcomed his wife's siblings to join them in close proximity to their household. His brother-in-law, James Russell Greene and Mary Ann Fair purchased land just west of James. Later, another brother-in-law, Richard Van Bruntand Elizabeth Jane Fair bought land that today, much of it is inside the "Tall Timbers" land. The 1840 Census enumerated four families almost together including J. R. Nicks, J. R. Greene, Richard Van Brunt and Celete Sauls.

Other siblings living within the households included Sophia Fair and also the mother of the Fair children and two more daughters by her second marriage (Martha and Sarah Nicks) were embedded in sibling households. The families broke up between 1840 and before 1845 moving north to Columbus, GA, later to Girard, AL, and finally to Opelika, AL.

During the years J. R. Nicks lived in Leon, Co., he was appointed as a Justice of the Peace and served as Election Inspector for the 1845 Florida Statehood Election. Later, he attended the Democratic Conventions as a delegate. He paid taxes in Leon Co. for the twenty years and has several indentures filed with Leon Co. Deed Records. Both his mother and mother-in-law have records for 1833 and 1844 too.

After moving to Hernando Co. around 1853, James Rinaldo Nicks never really left Leon Co. In 1856, he was elected to serve as State Representative from Hernando Co. to the Florida General Assembly. The Florida House Journals for 1856, 1858 and partially in 1859 depict his time served and committees appointed to for his served terms. Upon leaving in 1859, Governor Madison S. Perry appointed J. R. Nicks to serve as Commissioner of Portage for the Port of Bayport in Hernando, Co.

James' wife, Frances Fair, was the daughter of Elizabeth Harrison and Richard Fair. Both parents emigrated from Cavan County, Ireland to Charleston, SC before 1800. They married in 1804 and their children born thereafter were first generation Irish-Americans who grew up in downtown Charleston. Frances was given a small Day Book with her name "Miss Frances Fair" and a date of June 14, 1831 written inside.

Her Day Book contains poems of poets for the 1800s. One is from Thomas Moore's *Irish Melodies* and another from Shakespeare's *Twelfth Night*. Her sister, Mary Ann Fair, and Richard Van Brunt's names are in the book. On the very first page, she had records of her sister, "E. J. VB" borrowing sugar and other items. Another page listed her girl schoolmates for Charleston. In 1864, her son, Francis R. Nicks, penned a letter to his Company Captain Saxon in July. That letter was asking for more time at home to recuperate from his illness while serving in the Civil War.

The letter indicates the stark reality of Francis and his brother, Benjamin, but also gives some insight as to his mother "feeling very low."

James R. Nicks died 1861 and Frances Fair Nicks c. 1864. The DeSoto Masonic Lodge in Brooksville drafted a Resolution for their deceased brother mason and signed the same on January 25, 1862.

Three brothers-in laws, J. R. Greene, Richard Van Brunt and Joseph Fair honored James Rinaldo Nicks by naming sons "Rinaldo." Neither of James two surviving sons, William R. and Robert H. R. Nicks named their sons by their father's middle name. For years, descendants of H. R. Nicks thought the "R" in the five sons of James and Frances was for Rinaldo, but in fact, the 1852 Leon Co. Chancery record revealed William R. Nicks' full name included Richard for Frances Fair's father, Richard Fair.

Submitted by: Charles Blankenship for Jack Bates, Jr. (in honor of Grace Clark Rossi) 6311 Emerson Dr., New Port Richey, FL 34653-1711

Nancy Norman

Nancy Norman started out as a Florida Cracker, born and bred in Sanford, Florida, 88 years ago. And now she is back in Florida, here in Tallahassee and First Baptist Church.

In the intervening years Nancy graduated Stetson, qualified to teach at the university and in public schools, teaching English and Drama in Junior High and High Schools.

Nancy met her husband Bill in what today would be considered an unusual way. Her mother and his mother graduated college together and kept in touch, even after they both were married. Husband Bill's momma, from Gainesville, visited Nancy's momma in Sanford, and, as mommas tend to do, did a little match making, exchanging photos and stories over the years.

When Bill was a student at the University of Florida he and his friends would throw football parties, and all of the other guys would invite their girlfriends to stay over at Bill's house, where his mom would keep an eye on everything, while feeding a bunch of hungry guys and gals. All the other guys except Bill had girls. He was always just "too busy" with classes, work assignments and such, to develop a close relationship. At least that's what he SAID! All of his friends though felt that good ole' Bill was making moves on their girls, so they got rather insistent that Bill get a girl of his own! But, in spite of the "Good Ole' Mom Network" Bill and Nancy didn't match up until a Baptist Students Retreat at O'Leno Campground near Ft. White in 1940.

When it finally happened though, it was the marriage of a lifetime. The couple exchanged vows in Sanford in March of 1945. The State of Florida was so impressed with their union that they took that opportunity to join in the occasion by declaring that this would henceforth ALSO be known as the 100th anniversary of the admission of Florida to the United States. Nancy and Bill were united for 63 years.

While most of Nancy's life has been spent in Florida, there was a thirty-six year period in the middle where the Norman family spent six months in Washington, D.C. and six months in Jacksonville, bounced around by Bill's job as a Congressional Aide. In all this chaos Nancy nurtured and raised their four children; two boys and two girls.

While in D.C., Nancy began a fifty-two year odyssey as a volunteer teacher for International students, an effort that she continued here at First Baptist Church for many, many years. Nancy was awarded the prestigious Daughter of the American Revolution "Community Service Award" for her special teaching efforts.

Accepting Christ as her Savior as a young teen in First Baptist Church in Sanford, Nancy has kept the flame of her faith alive and glowing with her Bible study and her unwavering faith in the simple truth of her favorite Bible verse, John 3:16.

Besides becoming a Christian, Nancy feels her best times and her worse times revolve around her loving husband, Bill; the best times, when they met and married, the worst time, when she knew that she had lost him to a heart attack, ten years ago.

When asked what she thought was the biggest change in our country that she remembers Nancy chose the deteriorated condition of the nation's economy. Having lived in Washington, D.C., and been around the workings of government, she sees the lack of standards there as part and parcel of the whole sad mess.

On her wall in her home is one of Nancy's most treasured mementos. It is a simple one dollar bill that her husband, Bill was presented by the man he worked for in Washington, U.S. Representative Charles Bennett.

One day, while putting a lowly dollar bill in his wallet, Bill Norman noticed that the bill did not say, "In God We Trust". He remembered from his studies that, in the past, that motto had been on the nation's currency.

Bill took his discovery to his boss, Representative Bennett, a true American and a patriot. The two men worked together, jumping through all of the congressional hoops, dotting all of the "I"s and crossing all the necessary "T"s, until a bill was passed, approved and signed by the President of the United States.

"In God We Trust" once again graces our currency. That simple, unassuming, humble one dollar bill on Nancy's wall is the second dollar bill off the U.S. Treasury Department's presses to proudly display that noble phrase.

Written by Carol Ann and Bill Boydston © 1639 Twin Lakes Circle, Tallahassee, FL 32311; Submitted by: Nancy Norman

Colonel Herbert Gerald Parker (Retired), Ph.D.

An officer, leader, athlete, singer and volunteer, this multifaceted gentleman has been an integral part of the Tallahassee community since moving here in 1973 to head Florida A&M University's Army ROTC unit. During his thirty~year stint in the military, he rose from the grade of Private to the rank of Colonel. While in the military this foreign area specialist served with emphasis in Far Eastern Affairs. His military training included Command and General Staff College, the United States Army Airborne School, Ranger School, Leadership School and Infantry School.

Commanding Airborne, Ranger and Special Forces Units included all Special Forces in the Delta of South Vietnam in 1968-69. He also served in the 82nd and 101st Airborne Divisions. His distinguished career included Commandant of the Army's Civil Affairs School and as Professor of Military Science (PMS) at North Carolina A&T State and Florida A&M Universities.

His twenty-six military awards include the Silver Star for Gallantry in Action, two Bronze Stars for Valor, the Purple Heart, and the Meritorious Service Award in addition to two Legion of Merit Awards for his outstanding professionalism and significant contributions to the United States Army. Community involvement is one of his volunteer hallmarks. A difference maker is evidenced in his exceptional volunteer work. With its first Silver Star award, the Tallahassee Senior Center also recognized his being a person who really set the standard for positive aging.

Acknowledging his dedicated and continuous leadership and outstanding achievements in the pursuit of victims' rights earned him the James Fogarty annual award. His leadership as President of Capital Rotary Club was acknowledged in his receiving Rotary International's Four Avenues of Service--club, vocational, community and international services- award. He is the first African American president among Tallahassee's then four, now six, Rotary Clubs and a Level 2 Paul Harris Fellow.

Mentoring young males and being scholarship chairman of several organizations are some of his interests. He has chaired such local boards as Tallahassee Senior Center Foundation and Tallahassee Urban League, and served on numerous others to include Capital Chordsmen, Salvation Army, and Neighborhood Justice Center Advisory Board.

Colonel Herbert Parker (Retired) in his military uniform - 2002

He was Florida's first Executive Director of its Crimes Compensation program, subsequently becoming Chief of the Bureau of Crimes Compensation and Victim/Witness Services for the State of Florida. Later he became Treasurer, then President of the National Association of Crime Victim Compensation Boards.

Being an avid golfer is one of his passions. With his storehouse of stories and ability to liven up the setting, he is sought as master of ceremonies for local and regional affairs. "Super" for which he is best known, epitomizes his positive outlook on life. A steward and class leader at Bethel African Methodist Episcopal Church, he founded the church's male chorus and a quartet. He was a member of several church choirs. An officer and gentlemen, this proud family man acknowledges his wife, Florida, daughter, Christie Smith, and his grandson, Matthew Smith.

Written and submitted by: Florida Fisher Parker 3510 Tullamore Lane Tallahassee, Florida 32309 850-893-2671

Mary Patton

Sometimes it seems that there are as many ways to come to Christ as there are people. For Mary Patton the way to salvation was through her beloved grandfather. He was a Baptist preacher in North Georgia and would often sit and talk about Christ Jesus with the young Mary. What a vivid memory Mary has, of being just eight years old and walking down the long church aisle, to where Grandpa was waiting to take her by the hand and gently lead her to God's saving grace.

The simple but powerful story of John 3:16 has always been Mary's hope and promise; "For God so loved the world that he gave his only begotten Son that whosoever believeth in him should not perish but have everlasting life".

Mary's youth was spent in the rolling hills around Athens, Georgia. She attended the University of Georgia High School where she met her husband-to-be, Rudell (Pat) Patton through a friend. Pat took Mary to the High School Senior Dance. Their mutual attraction grew and they were married in 1942. Mary also completed her education at the University of Georgia, earning a four-year degree in Education.

Mary and Pat's marriage was blessed with two children, a boy and a girl. She feels that the birth of her children is her greatest blessing and the most wonderful thing that has happened to her. The kids also gave Mary a chance to excel at her children's school where she served as President of the PTA, and was rewarded with an award of recognition for her volunteer work with that organization.

Mary worked for many years with her husband in their Athens paint and body shop. But Pat's poor health forced the sale of the shop and a move to Tallahassee, where he bought Hughes Alignment and renamed it Patton Alignment, a company that grew to become a landmark on South Adams Street.

When the Pattons arrived in Tallahassee they began a search for a new church home. All of their lives in Athens, Georgia they had been members of small churches, feeling at home with the close-knit feeling a small congregation brings. But their son, who was a student at FSU, had begun attending First Baptist, through our active college student program and he finally convinced his parents to try FBC. They did, and never looked back. They found here the friendly closeness and Christian commitment they were seeking.

The death of Pat was a dark time in her life, but Mary kept on, running the business that they had built in Tallahassee. Eventually, she was able to lay that burden down, selling the company to a trusted employee and settling down into a quieter, calmer life.

When asked what she saw as the biggest change in her lifetime Mary harkened back to the days of World War II. The people of America in those days were trying to make the world a better place, fighting against tyranny, sharing the load of rationing and shortages, supporting each other, and pulling together for the good of all. Nowadays, she says, young people don't seem to respect that world conflict or our present war. They don't seem to know or understand what sacrifice, "for the good of all" is all about.

Written by: Carol Ann and Bill Boydston ©, 1639 Twin Lakes Circle, Tallahassee, FL 32311;
Submitted by: Mary Patton

Harvey Paulk

Farming is as important to American life as any other vocation and more important than most. Farming is part art, part skill and part science, with a lot of good ole common sense thrown into the mix. What could be more satisfying than growing up on a farm, going to college to learn more of the science of fanning, and then spending a lifetime helping other fanners make the most of their efforts? That is just what Harvey Paulk has done.

Raised on a farm in Jackson County, near Campbellton, Harvey learned the art and skill of farming as a youth and young man. He graduated from Campbellton High School in 1940 where he was honored as Salutatorian of his senior class. Harvey earned a Bachelors Degree in Agriculture from the University of Florida in 1943. He served in the U. S. Air Force for 3 ? years after graduation until war's end. Mustering out in 1946 with the rank of Captain.

Harvey returned to Malone in North Florida after the war, taking a position as a Vocational Agriculture teacher. It was at a Malone School Teachers Faculty meeting that he met a beautiful brunette elementary teacher with the loveliest brown eyes; two features that Harvey says "seemed to be of his liking". She was Miriam Tuten.

The young couple had a lot in common. Each was from a farming family. Each had seven siblings. Both came from staunch Southern Baptist families who were active in their churches. It just seemed natural that Harvey and Miriam found each other. A year later they were married and they have shared a wonderful life together. They had two children, a boy and a girl.

Harvey continued as a Vocational Agriculture teacher for ten years in Malone. During that time be completed his thesis and was awarded a Masters of Agricultural Science Degree from U of F in 1952. This degree opened new doors for Harvey. He soon became an Assistant County Agriculture Agent worked with the Cooperative Extension Service in Madison for six years, in Blountstown for eleven years and then for nine years in Tallahassee, retiring as the Leon County Extension Director, after thirty-six years of serving the farning community of North Florida.

Harvey bas been retired for twenty-seven years. He and Miriam have seen their family grow to include their children's spouses and five lovely granddaughters, all Christians, all living strong and active Christian lives.

The worst that has happened to Harvey has, after many years, become his biggest and best blessing. His youngest granddaughter was born twenty-four years ago with a heart condition that has continually threatened her life. Two heart surgeries, the first at six months and then at 2 years kept her alive but last year a third and final operation corrected the problem for good and now see is living a full, healthy life. Harvey is certain that this is a miracle, an answer to a lot of prayers!

John 3:16 has always been an anchor in Harvey's life, and the strength and promise of those words continue to support him and Miriam is their Christian walk together.

Harvey is distressed over today's weakening of family institutions. The loss of moral values and the persecution of Christians by the news media, government rules and regulations and tism is foreboding. But he is also comforted by the words of his favorite Bible verse, "…that whosoever believeth in Him shall not perish, but have everlasting life".

Written by Carol Ann and Bill Boydston © 1639 Twin Lakes Circle, Tallahassee, FL 32311; Submitted by: Harvey Paulk

Pearsons, Wilkinsons and Andrews

I am not sure what brought my dad, Lawrence Murray Pearson, to Tallahassee. He had a brother, James Clayton Pearson, that lived here also with his wife Rudy Dale Cutchens Pearson and daughter, Geneva, my Uncle Shorty, as we called James Pearson, worked for Baker Alford as an auto mechanic back when it was down where the city bus station is now. He then worked for the Dodge dealer. After that, he opened up his own gas stations back when they did mechanical work. My dad, Lawrence Pearson, held a number of jobs. The first I remember was he worked for Rams Radio and TV downtown, as were all the businesses and government back in the early 1960s.

My mother is Frances Andrews Pearson. She came to Tallahassee with her mother, Mary Rebecca Wilkinson Andrews, and father, Darrell Haisley Andrews, from Bay County during the Great Depression. He had lost his job at a bank in Panama City during the Depression. His brother, Charles Oscar Andrews, had several high ranking jobs with the state and was a U.S. Senator and helped him get a job here in Tallahassee with the state.

My grandmother, Mary Rebecca, had moved to the Woodville area with her dad, John Lawrence Wilkinson, and mother, Eugenia Rebecca Kite Wilkinson, in 1903. She was a

Mother-Bertha Pearson with Children: Kent, Nell, lna, Ken, Stuart, Woodrow, Winston, Lawrence, and Thad

schoolteacher and taught school over in Bay County. I am guessing that is what took her to Bay County. My grandmother had several brothers and sisters. The oldest was Lawrence Wilkinson who moved his family out West. Two of her brothers were Henry and Broadus. Uncle Broadus was a postmaster in Woodville and taught school at Fort Braden School. He and Uncle Henry ran a store on the corner of the Wilkinson farm at what is now 1907 S. Adams Street, one mile due south of the Capitol building after they both became crippled. Her sisters were Frankie Mae and Ruby Jane Wilkinson. She also had a brother and sister that died when they were 17 years old. They were Idolene Wilkinson and Ben Hill Wilkinson.

Most of my Wilkinson ancestors mentioned here are buried in Woodville Cemetery behind White Church. My mother's brother was John Andrews. He too worked for the state. He also had a part-time job downtown at the "American Opinion Bookstore". It was next door to where the Leon County Library was on Monroe Street. He had two daughters, Linda Andrews Sumner Babies and Brenda Andrews Lovern Gaines. My mother and dad had four children, Andrew Blane

Pearson, Merry Lauren Pearson, Shawn S. Pearson and Dana Prince Pearson. My mother still lives in Leon County as do I. My oldest brother, Blanc, lives over in Crestview, he married Sandy Strong. My sister, Lauren, lives over in Chipley, she married Doug Owen. My brother, Shawn, lives in Wakulla County just a few miles from where my great granddaddy, John Lawrence Wilkinson, had a farm. He married Sallie Eubank of Amherst, Virginia.

Written and submitted by: Dana Pearson (Granddaughter of Bertha Pearson) 12089 Waterfront Drive, Tallahassee, Florida 32312

John Penrod's Wood Vessels

John P. Penrod is a full-time wood-turner who produces a wide variety of wooden vessels and art objects. Each piece is an original and is turned on a wood lathe using hand-held gouges, scrapers, boring bars, and skews. Most of his work consists of whole-log, end-grain turning. Some pieces have additional carving applied following turning.

The majority of his wood-turnings are made from subtropical woods, including Norfolk Island Pine, Grapefruit, Royal Poinciana, Jacaranda, and West Indies Rosewood. With the exception of decorative wood accents nearly all of his turnings are fashioned from "recovered" or "found" wood. He specializes in turning vessels from palm trees including Sabal, Queen, Washingtonia, Royal, and Canary Island Date Palm. Each turning is created in a way that shows the wood's finest features and every item produced is designed, turned, carved, and finished solely by him.

Wood has a natural warmth and beauty that sets it apart from other media. Although it is greatly appreciated visually, wood is a truly multi-sensory medium and more fully enjoyed using visual, tactile, and olfactory senses. It is very rewarding to take a piece of a stately old tree, destined to rot or become an addition to the firewood pile, and give it new life by turning it on the lathe to create an object to be cherished and enjoyed for many years. It is the thrill of exposing the beautiful patterns and designs hidden within each piece of wood and the creation of an item representing new life from an old tree that makes wood-turning so gratifying.

Written and submitted by: John P. Penrod, 2786 Pecan Rd. Tallahassee, FL 32303

The Phillips Family, Three Generations of Volunteers in Leon County

Martha Elaine Milton-Phillips (1936-2002) was born in Phillips County Arkansas to Maple Jordan (1916-1945) Pend Reverend Mack 111 Milton (1907-1977). Martha was the fourth child of six children who were raised to believe "improving your community enriches your life." Martha remembered her southern hospitality teaching even through she was raised in the North by continuously volunteering her services whenever she could. She was in charge of the Shut-in program at her church, which made visits to the sick and elderly in her community. She continuously volunteered at the Cook County Hospital children's ward in Chicago for over a decade. After Martha married Howard Phillips of Birmingham, Alabama in 1955, she raised her children to believe "To receive an enriched life, you must be of service to others." Martha also volun-teered at the Senior Center while living in Tallahassee during the winter months.

Carol Denise Phillips-Johnson is Martha and Howard Phillips' fourth child of seven children.

Carol moved to Tallahassee, Florida in 1994 and she has continued to volunteer at the Capital Area Chapter of the Red Cross, Mothers in Crisis, The Salvation Army and Civic functions like the Unity in the Community festival.

Lexius Marquee Phillips- Stone born Jan 19, 1995 is Carol's youngest daughter of two children and was born in Tallahassee, Florida. Lexius has carried on the family tradition of volunteering to enrich her life and others. Presently Lexius is a member of the Four-H Club, the Toys for Tots program during Christmas

Martha Elaine and daughter, Carol Denise Phillips, 1996 "Clean-Sweep" Volunteers

school break, the Senior Center of Tallahassee during the summer breaks and many other after school projects in Leon County.

In 1996 Martha and Carol volunteered during the Clean Sweep Project to help keep the city clean. Mother Martha., Daughter Carol, and Grand-daughter Lexius have lived a normal life while living in Leon County, Florida: but under their mild mannered demeanor lives three generations of heroes.

Their contributions to the community have made them heroes because they give not only their money to non-profit organizations but also their time and energy into making Leon County what it is today, "One of the Best places to live in the United States." When asked; why do they volunteer? Martha replied: "The most rewarding work I have ever done is when I am helping others." Carol says; "Volunteering gives me the opportunity to meet new people and it keeps me informed on current events in Leon County." Lexius states, "I like seeing new places in and around Leon County." For the Phillips Family, volunteering is the best family activity they know and when they hear some one say; "Thanks for your help", to them it's worth its weight in gold. Being involved in community affairs also allows these three generations to continue their family tradition of "Sharing is Caring" Daughter and Grand-daughter of Martha E. Phillips continue to serve the community today. That's three generations of Phillips giving back to the Leon County community that welcomed them in as family. Carol states; "I know my grandfather, Reverend Mack Milton, is very proud of his legacy of volunteers."

Written by: Carol D. Phillips-Johnson; Submitted by: Norma Phillips- Henry

Carol D. Phillips-Johnson

Carol Denise Phillips-Johnson was born and raised in Chicago, Illinois. She is the fourth of six children born to Martha Elaine Milton (1936-2002) of Arkansas and Howard Minter Phillips of Alabama. Her maternal grandparents are Maple Ann Jordon (1916-1945) from Arkansas and Reverend Mack Milton (1907 - 1977) from Louisiana. Her paternal grandparents are Sallie Owens (1902-1932) from Georgia and James Roy Phillips (1892-1978) from Alabama. Carol has two daughters, Linda and Lexius. She first married Jerry Moody in 1977, and one child was born to this union, Linda Moody. In 1984 she married Bernard Fleming, no children, and in 1998 she married Michael Johnson (1955-2005), no children. Carol's youngest daughter, Lexius Marque Stone (1995-Present) was born in Tallahassee, Florida and her father is Jeffrey Stone of Madison, Wisconsin. Carol attended Saint Joseph Grade School (1973) IL, Marshall High School (1978) IL, Phillips College (1983) IL, Miami Dade College (1993) FL and Florida A &M University (2005) FL. Carol maintains an knowledgeable level of Education by attending different vocational studies, for example Clerk-typist-Dawson institute, Office Administrator - Tallahassee Community College, Electrician Apprentice-International Brotherhood of Electrical Workers (IBEW), and Computer Operator-Miami Dade College. She has worked for many state agencies and private companies in recent years to supplement her incomefor traveling.

Carol recalls her youth, "when I was growing up I remember traveling to different states to visit relatives. My godfather, Reverend James McCoy of New Mount Pilgrim MBC, would let me

Carol D. Phillips-Johnson

live with them during the summer months from the age of eight years old until I turned thirteen and we went everywhere in Chicago. Everyday there was a social function he was involved in and I got a chance to meet a lot of people from different walks of life. He would not only help the sick and the young, but he attended many businesses meeting with political figures in the city. When I wasn't with him, I went shopping with his daughters. I did not know it then, but I think I was some kind of chaperone for them. While I was in Catholic school we took many trips around the state to visit Nunneries. I was encouraged to join, but I had other plans and couldn't wait to graduate. I believe this is where I got my interest in traveling. Carol was raised as a

Baptist and christened as a Catholic but does not follow any religious doctrine today.

Carol has spent many years traveling throughout the United States and Europe. She states, "I enjoy seeing new place and cultures; it enriches my life and helps me to relate to people's situations: " She has worked for numerous temporary agencies, which allows her to further her travel experiences. Carol's hobbies include: Volunteer for The American Red Cross Disaster Services, The Salvation Army Thrift Store, Genealogy, Leon County Community events, she has also spent time on different Committee Projects for the Tallahassee Genealogical Society. Carol hopes her future will be as blissful as her past. She plans to finish her degree and looks forward to spending more time with her granddaughter Leah.

Written and Submitted by: Carol D. Johnson, 214 North Columbia Drive B-13, Tallahassee, Florida 32304

Donalee Pond-Koenig

Donalee Pond was born in 1946 in Rochester, New York where she attended the Columbia School for Girls. After High School she attended the Pratt Institute in Brooklyn, New York where she obtained a Bachelor of Arts Degree (BFA) by 1967. In 1968 she met and married Peter A. Koenig and they had one daughter, Moya Pond-Koenig. When Moya grew up she married Warren P. Huff and they had a daughter named Mia Lynn Huff. Donalee's daughter and her family all reside in Tallahassee, Florida.

When Donalee's family came to Tallahassee, Florida in 1977 their daughter had just turned one. They bought a new house under construction. Fortunately, they were able to make some construction changes that suited their needs. Unfortunately, a studio was not in the plans, but she managed to set up a small art space. After settling in, one of Donalee's priorities was to set out to find an Art Center within the community. She found the Lemoyne Art Foundation and was excited by its quaint old building style that stood on Gadsden Street. There was an art function going on and she was able to meet the director, some of the local artists and other members of the community. Lemoyne was a haven for her to assimilate into the community through her artistry.

Donalee's husband, Peter, was getting settled at Florida State University in the Art Department for Interior Design. She remembers being thankful for the FSU Newcomers Club, where she began meeting artists in the University community. Later, she became the President of that club and started her other most important need, finding a play group for her daughter, Moya. But this was harder than her previous task, so she started "Mom and Tots" which the arrangement of mothers and children meeting for a play time in morning. It was very successful then and now. Throughout the years of exhibiting her work in Tallahassee, Donalee has established a repu-tation for herself from the many articles published about her art work in the *Talla-hassee Democrat* newspaper.

Donalee's jobs have all been related to the Fine Arts with exhibits in Galleries all over the United States. She has provided some private teaching and was an adjunct Professor at Florida State University and Tallahassee Community College. She has worked on various art-related committees to benefit the arts and she has won the Volunteer of the Year Award 2001 in the Arts, Tallahassee, Florida. Donalee is now a member of many clubs and galleries for example: Artists' League, FSU Museum, Lemoyne Art Foundation, National Women in the Arts Council, Southern Watercolor Society.

Donalee Pond-Koenig

Donalee says "It is hard to believe that thirty-three years have passed since I arrived in Leon County. Peter is retiring this summer, and we now have an adorable granddaughter. I find it hard to believe that now we live out in the country in a house and studio my husband designed, on a pond with all the natural beauties that Tallahassee has to offer. We are grateful for living in such a good, rich community like Tallahassee, and we finally feel like we are home."

Written and Submitted by: Donalee Pond-Koenig, 7605 Broadview Farms Lane Tallahassee, Florida 32309

Jackie Pons, Leon County Superintendent of Schools

Jackie Pons was born in Leon County, and he is the greatgreat- great-great grandson of the pioneer family of Pons, who opened a hardware store on the corner of Adams and Jefferson in 1922-1950. Leon County School Superintendent, Jackie Pons, has spent the past 25 years in the educational field. He has earned an extensive and diverse experience base in educational leadership within the Tallahassee community.

He holds a BS in Physical Education from FSU and an MS in Administration and Supervision from FAMU. He began his teaching career at North Florida Christian School in Tallahassee and Robert F. Monroe High School in Quincy FL. He has served as a basketball coach at both schools and later as an assistant basketball coach at Florida State University, where he also taught as an adjunct professor.

In 1987, Professor Pons came to the Leon County School Board joining the faculty at Rickards High School. At Rickards, he worked his way from the classroom as a teacher to an administrator, an Athletic Director to Dean of Students, and finally to Assistant Principal. His next assignment took him to Godby High School as an Assistant Principal, and in early 1999, he was promoted to Principal of Deerlake Middle School. In November of 2006, he was elected to his current position as the Superintendent of,Leon County Schools.

Superintendent of Schools for Leon County, Jackie Pons

Among his many honors, Pons was named Leon County Schools' Principal of the Year for the year of 2000. In 2005, he led Deerlake Middle School to the much-coveted recognition of a National Blue Ribbon School of Distinction.

Written by: Carol D. Johnson; Submitted by: John Pons (Father), Velda Woods Dr., Tallahassee, Florida 32309

Virginia Porter Rounds

Virginia Porter Rounds was born in Albany, GA. Because of circumstances of her birth mother's health, she was raised by her dad's sister, Jewel Porter Ford in Tallahassee, Florida. Virginia's father was Roy Porter.

Her birth mother moved to Perry, Florida and Virginia visited her during the summer months. Her sister Catherine, who was 20 months old when Virginia was born; graduated from Perry High School and married Roy Fite. Virginia's birth mother lived to be 89 years old.

Virginia attended school in Tallahassee: kindergarten and elementary at the old Caroline Brevard School on South Calhoun Street and she graduated from Leon High School.

While at Leon High School, Virginia was a member of the vocal ensemble "The Triple Trio," which was later named "The Melodears." She was a soloist with the high school Glee Club and won one second place (Excellent) and two first place (Superior) awards at the "'Florida State Music Educators Association's" vocal competition.

Miss Ollie Reese Whittle, Virginia's mentor and friend, said; "Virginia's group was the best class she has ever had." Miss Whittle started "The Melodears" when she was choral director at Leon High School.

Virginia married M. Alvin Middleton in 1942 during WWII, and lived at Eglin Field. They divorced and she moved back to Tallahassee, Florida where she met and married Paul Rounds in the late 1940's. Her daughter Anita Rounds was born in 1950 and Pam Rounds, her second daughter, was born in 1954 in New Jersey.

Virginia worked in the Treasurer and Comptroller's Office for the State of Florida before retiring in 1983. She sang in the Trinity United Methodist Church choir and sang solos

Virginia Porter Rounds with her dog in 2009

for special choir programs. Since retirement, Virginia has lived at The Cherry Laurel Retirement Home, and enjoys visits from her children.

Submitted by: Virginia Porter Rounds, 514 Gunter Street Tallahassee, Florida 32308; Written by: Mary L. Marchant, 2901 Springfield Drive Tallahassee, FL 32309-3274

William and Emmie Sills Powell

During the 1930s and 40s, my grandparents William and Emmie Sills Powell lived on the corner of Boulevard and Jefferson Streets in Tallahassee. My sister and I visited them in the summer and they saw that we had a good time. We went swimming at Lake Bradford and Dog Lake which was followed by a picnic supper. They took us swimming at Wakulla Springs so that we could see the diving bell used in filming a Tarzan movie. They gave us our first airplane ride over the City of Tallahassee. We saw the first showing in Tallahassee of *The Wizard of Oz* at the State Theater on College Avenue.

Granddaddy Powell was a Justice of Peace and held court at the City Hall, which was on Park Avenue at the time. One day our Uncle Wilson took us to court to see Granddaddy at work and how his court was run.

Granddaddy Powell was well known and was called Judge Powell by people in town. Granny called him Will and his friends called him Bill. Granddaddy came home for lunch which was always ready, because Granny was a good cook and housekeeper. As a young girl she had been to the Vashti School in Thomasville, Georgia, where she learned the attributes of a good wife, which she was.

Between her household chores she managed to make great peanut butter fudge and cookies for us. She taught us to crochet, embroider and play many card games. We played Chinese checkers, Jacks, Bingo and put together puzzles. When the ice cream truck came by, Granny gave us money for treats. Those cool Popsicles tasted so good on a hot day, and it was hot in Tallahassee in the summer. After supper we would sit on the front porch to cool off or go chase fireflies in the field in front of the house. Granddaddy would be inside reading the paper or listening to the radio.

Some Sunday afternoons we would go to Live Oak Island to visit their friends, other times we would go to baseball games at Centennial Field, because Granddaddy and his friends were big baseball fans. Granny liked to take walks and took us to the Old City Cemetery and told us stories of people buried there such as Prince and Princess Murat. She knew a lot about Leon County history as her Sills family, from North Carolina, were in Leon County before 1840. Her grandmother Lucinda Wellford/Wilford married Solomon Sills. Most of Lucinda's family died in the yellow fever epidemic of 1841. Granny's grandparents raised her after her mother died. Granddaddy Powell's family came to Leon County from Llano County, Texas in 1888 and established a dairy farm near Chaires, Florida. His parents James (born in VA) and Nancy Elizabeth Lackey Powell (born in MO) were victims of the flu epidemic, and are buried in Pisgah Church Cemetery.

Judge William Powell

Submitted by: Barbara (Powell) Boynton 1806 Sunset Lane Tallahassee, Florida 32303

William Stanley (Sandy) Proctor

William Stanley Proctor was born and raised in Tallahassee, Florida. Sandy continues to live there today with his wife, Melinda. They raised three children, Stanley Jr., Stewart, and Peggy. Sandy has enjoyed working, in the past, with his son, Stan, and currently with his daughter, Peggy, as they manage his career and business. Sandy attended Washington and Lee University in Virginia before pursuing an internship in Washington D.C, by working for a Senator from Florida. Eventually, he began working with his father and brother in their family business in Tallahassee, Florida while he raised his children.

Sandy's painting hobby began to take more and more of his time as people became increasingly interested in his artwork. The constant support of his wife and family motivated

Sandy to begin his career as a painter, and eased his transition into three dimensional artwork as he carved alabaster and marble. In the beginning Sandy was a self taught painter, working in watercolor, oils, and acrylic. As a child and young man, Sandy sketched and painted what he knew and what inspired him. His love of the outdoors; birds, flowers, trees, landscapes and animals provided Sandy with myriad subject matter, which helped him increase his ability to capture an identifiable essence and realism in his artwork.

His paintings were chosen by many juried shows including the Southern Watercolor Society Show and Florida Watercolor Society Show. Additionally, his paintings traveled to shows at the Smithsonian Museum in Washington D.C., the British Museum of Natural History, and the Royal Scottish Academy in Scotland. Now, W. Stanley Proctor has a national reputation as a professional sculptor of the highest caliber. Prior to concentrating in bronze sculpture, Sandy was an accomplished stone carver whose work has been displayed at museums of national and international recognition. After more than 30 years as a professional artist, the State of Florida commemorated Sandy and his contributions to the arts by inducting him into the Florida Artists Hall of Fame in March 2006, and in 2004 he was selected as the American Artists Professional League Award recipient for the best work depicting traditional realism at the juried National Sculpture Society 71st Annual Awards Exhibition in New York. Sandy is a member of the National Sculpture Society, and recently, he completed a larger than life-size sculpture commemorating integration at Florida State University entitled: "Integration: Books, Bats and Beauty.

" Sandy explains what motivates his artwork: "An individual's face, hands, hair, gestures and body posture are as identifiable as a name or symbol and usually convey more of the essence of the person. The human form, from the freedom of childhood to distinguished seniority, has always moved me. I strive to capture the emotion, personality, grace, and honor of all my subject matter and have been fortunate to be chosen to sculpt many private and public monuments. While I am studying a subject, using photographs, measurements and conversation, I am constantly looking for the hand gesture, the slight wink, the curl at the mouth, the "thing" that makes them unique. If I am able to distinguish and recreate those identifying and unique characteristics, then I have done my job, for it is the person that lived the life that should be seen and remembered in the sculpture. With research, patience, photos and memories, my job is to sculpt "that person" to be uniquely and immediately identifiable and known."

Sandy recalls what makes his artwork unique: "When I am commissioned to create a sculpture of a person whose face and body are or were known over many years, I describe it as looking at the scrapbook of one's life from infancy to present day, and choosing just one photo that captures that life. It is a very difficult task, but it is a challenge I eagerly pursue. The unique things rarely change over a person's life, because their energy and essence are always the same. After long consideration of any and all available information, I chose recurring images to create a conceptual vision and eventually the sculpture reveals that result. In order to see and know which images are unique and full of information, I must first get to know the person I am supposed to create in clay. Whether I am able to talk with them, or if I need to research or study photographs, there is a significant connection that I must make with the subject.

W. Stanley (Sandy) Proctor, Sculptor

That connection and relationship guides the sculpting process, as I must above all honor the person and the image that I am creating."

Recently, Sandy has installed numerous public and private commissions of monumental and portrait bronzes. His completed commissions include: a monumental sculpture of two Navy Seals, killed in the line of duty, entitled, "The Guardians" for the Veteran's Memorial Park in Cupertino, California, which was dedicated in November 2007 by Secretary of the Navy, Donald Winter; "Head Bust" of Football Coach Bobby Bowden for Florida State University's Doak Campbell Stadium; the "Trojan" sculpture for Lincoln High School in Florida. Other works by

Sandy include a large installation at the Florida Governor's Mansion Children's Park and the Leon County Courthouse in Tallahassee. He also has pieces on display at the White House, the Polk Museum of Art in Lakeland, Florida, and Tallahassee Memorial Hospital. Sandy's family continues to celebrate his success as his career in bronzed sculptures grows to express the artist's inner talents.

Written and Submitted by: Peggy Proctor, Daughter of Sandy 1844 Chardonnay Place Tallahassee, Florida 32317 wspbronzes@nettally.com

Ramsey-Steed-The Perfect Wedding Venue

It took months for us to decide on a wedding date. Since we both like the holiday season but knew Christmas Eve and Christmas Day would be out of the question, I suggested to Robert that we have the wedding on December 31. He said, "Why not. Just think of the anniversary parties we could have!"

Now that we had established the date, we had to select the venue. We were new to the Tallahassee area, and had no idea where to begin. We were looking for a natural beauty setting-- something unique--one that would require little or no additional decoration. For some strange reason we were drawn to an outdoor vs. an indoor location. We looked at Maclay Gardens, Lake Ella, and Wakulla Springs to name a few. I know an outdoor wedding in December does not sound feasible but remember Florida typically has very mild winters. Maclay Gardens are beautiful year round. In December the camellias are in full bloom. Lake Ella is as charming. During the holiday season the lanterns are adorned with wreaths and the gazebo is outlined with garland and lights. During the holidays Wakulla Springs lodge is always nicely decorated for their annual New Year's Eve Gala. One Saturday, just weeks before the wedding, we set out determined find a venue. While driving around looking for ideas, we drove by the Old Capitol and I made the comment how beautiful the Christmas decorations were and Robert said, "Wouldn't it be neat, if we could have the wedding there! How many couples can say that they were married on the Capitol grounds?" I responded, "Now that would be a story to tell our grandchildren! Stop; let's go inside."

Once inside, I was overwhelmed with the beautiful Christmas decorations and I stated, "This is the place." We have to find out how to hold the wedding here!" We spoke with the receptionist and asked her how to go about getting permission to hold an event on the grounds. She gave me a contact person's name and number and told me to give her a call on Monday. I could hardly wait. First thing that morning I gave her a call. I explained what I wanted and she responded, "What a great idea! When is the wedding?" When she realized that it was only a few weeks away, she said in a hesitant voice, "Normally we need a six month notice." I then began to plead my case. After hearing how excited I was, she told me she would send me the application and see what she could do. I promptly completed and returned the application and waited for a response. Would you believe around 4:45 p.m. that same day she called and said, "You are one lucky bride. They gave you permission to hold your wedding on the Capitol grounds."

Robert Steed with his new bride Deanna Ramsey

The Capitol will always hold an extra special place in our hearts. Each year on our anniversary we stroll the grounds and reminisce looking forward to the day we can share the story of our wedding with our grandchildren.

Submitted by: Deanna Ramsey, 6504 Kingman Trail, Tallahassee, FL 32309. looking4family@gmail.com

Rask-My Childhood Playgrounds

In the *Tallahassee Democrat* newspaper dated August 5, 2005, the headline read, "Hiroshima-60 Years After the Bomb". My memory of the day — August 15, 1945, as a five year- old girl, was of a hot summer day. My sisters Bette Ann and Anita, our friend and neighbor Joan Tomberlin, and I were climbing the big old oak tree in front of our house on North Jackson Street when the noise — bells, car horns, people calling to each other. My mother was in the house and we jumped from the tree to ask what the commotion was. My mother tearfully replied, "The war is over!" Joan, who was two years older than I, understood and she started crying. We all started walking down to the next block to her aunt's house and I asked why everyone was crying? Then, I was too young to understand, but this memory makes me cry now.

I grew up on North Jackson Street in the 1940s. In those days it was not dangerous to walk anywhere in Tallahassee, day or night. It was a normal thing — great exercise, too!! Our family walked a lot-to the movies uptown sometimes, the ice cream shop on Monroe and Fifth Avenue, the Jitney Jungle Grocery Store on Monroe, between Sixth and Seventh Avenues. We three girls, all under five-years-old, trailing Mama like little ducklings.

Daddy put up great swings in our yard that hung, from a high limb in the big oak tree. We'd swing way above the rooftop, as our yard was greatly sloped. We did a lot of tumbling in our backyard. We'd camp-out in Daddy's big army tent there, too. There were a lot of kids to play with in the neighborhood.

Daddy and Mama took us swimming in the summertime before 'the pool' (Levy). At first we rode the city bus to Lake Bradford-a wooden boardwalk around the swimming area with changing rooms and a diving board. There was a covered dance floor, a jukebox and a snack bar.

After we got a car we'd go further-to Silver Lake and Campground Lake, west of town. There we'd explore the surrounding woods to a clear spring trickling out of the ground, passing sometimes turtle nests filled with unhatched eggs. We were taught never to bother them.

We often swam in the sinkholes-Big and Little Dismal, Riversink, Cherokee and Blue Sink. Wakulla Springs and Alligator Point were fun, too.

We went to Sealey Elementary School about seven blocks from home, walking there and back "uphill both ways". It's now the Tallahassee Police Department on Seventh Avenue. What a great school. We had wonderful teachers!!

Those were the "Good Ol' Days!!!"

Submitted by: Helen Barrett Rask, 5996 Ponder Lane, Tallahassee, FL 32309

Sherry Reams Burch, Tallahassee Lassie

My roots, like the big oak tree here, spread strong and wide. My great grandparents moved here in the 1930s; my mother and grandparents moved here in the 50s, and my mom and dad raised their family here since the 60s. My husband I started our family in 1980. We had a son in 1980 and daughter in 1990 both born here. I was born and raised in Tallahassee and will always call this beautiful city home.

When my grandparents moved here with my mother, little did they know how many wonderful lives they were starting. I am the oldest of three, my sister and I were born at TMH, my brother in Monticello. All three of us and our children had the same pediatrician. We moved into a home my grandmother Chandler purchased on Rexwood Drive. My mother still lives there today.

As kids, we went to exciting places, and did many things. Climbing the tall oak trees, making crowns with moss while fighting the red bugs, and hiding eggs in the sand on the beach on Easter morning, were the most memorable. I also remember watching the Jerry Lewis Telethon with the live cuts to the Tallahassee Mall. We got to make beds in the living room and watch T.V. with mom, and eat what ever we wanted all night. We laughed and cried at these times. We never missed the North Fla. Fair. I can still remember the smells in the air.

Burch children

We picked sugar cane and went to cane grindings to make homemade syrup. From getting swamp cabbage from what looks like a palm tree, to many visits to the junior museum, boy has it changed today. The best for me was the fireworks over Lake Ella each July 4th, we saw friends and family there we hadn't seen all year.

I married my childhood sweetheart who moved in our neighborhood in 1972. We married under the big oak tree at the courthouse still there today. Our son is a graduate of Godby High School, which is the same school we both attended. He is now a graduate from F.S.U. with a bachelor's degree in accounting and works for our great state at the Dept. of Education Comptrollers office. He has given us two grandchildren born here in 2002 and 2009.

Our delightful daughter lived here for nine years, and attended our middle school Belle Vue.

"All grown up": Danny, Mom, Sherry (me), and Jody at the home we grew up in

She will start her first year of college this year majoring in Education at Eastern Ky. University in Richmond, Kentucky.

I have always treasured the pleasure of saying I was born in Tallahassee, and now I'm back for good. Seeing the first sign of moss in Thomasville, gives me a smile each time indicating that I am getting closer to home. Also seeing the big oak tree at Lake Ella that so many children have played and climbed, even my children and grandchildren and yes, even I have climbed a couple of times myself.

I remember the excitement of getting to the top level of the Capitol to see all over Tallahassee, with my mom and siblings, to field trips with my children and now my grand-children will see a whole different Tallahassee from the same view. This is my Tallahassee story.

I can say I've been and will always be a Tallahassee Lassie and have the blessing of being a true Floridian.

Submitted by: Sherry Reams Burch, 2931 Rexwood Drive, Tallahassee, Fla. 32304

Jody Reams Davis

I was born and grew up in Tallahassee, now I'm raising my son here. I attended Godby, and have worked for Comcast for many years. My mom moved here as a child, moved away, then moved back to stay and raise her family. My father's family goes back many years in the history of this area. I enjoy hearing of my family history, and talking about it. I learned a lot from my father's, aunts' and uncles' stories. We spent a lot of time with family and friends.

There's no way to write this without starting with my dad's great-grandfathers. Both of them were in the Civil War, and raised large families. Some of both families did business and lived in Tallahassee over the years.

My dad's mother's granddad, Joseph B. Carroll, moved to this area in the 1870's. He was a 2nd Lieutenant in the 4th Florida Infantry. While he was in "The West Florida War" in 1864, he met Robert Russ, who later became his brother-in-law when he married Fannie Russ from Vernon, FL.

Soon after the war they moved to Thomas County, then to Jefferson County where they lived until they died, Joseph in 1890, Fannie in 1901. During the time they lived there they raised seven children, and became a very prominent family. Joseph was in the Senate in 1879; he is mentioned in *The History of Jefferson County* and *The Bourbon Era*

One of his sons, Roland J. Carroll followed in his dad's footsteps, and was in the Senate in 1918-1919. He is also mentioned in *The History of Jefferson County*. I have heard that Fred Carroll started the Ice House in Tallahassee many years ago, and I know he had a "Farmers Peanut Company" in Cairo, Ga. Now I know why we stopped at the Ice House so often and why we always had so many peanuts. Roland's funeral in 1942 at Culley's on 210 East Pensacola St. cost a whopping $555.00 total. That included moving him from the Johnson's Sanitarium at 805 N. Gadsden St. that charged $6.00 a day, 50 cents for a special nurse, $4.00 for oxygen, and $3.50 for medicine. Dr. M. R. Clements, M. D. at the Western Union Building in Tallahassee charged $25.00 to go to Lamont because Dr. Walker was not available. Mr. Fred Carroll who lived at Meridian Hts. In Tallahassee was the administrator of Roland Sr.'s estate.

My great-great-grandfather, Calvin Joshua Reams, was in Camp Leon also. He enlisted in 1862 into Company D 5th Florida Infantry and died in 1863 at the General Hospital #11 in Richmond, Va. He raised his family in the back woods on the Aucilla River. My grandfather was born and raised not far from

My dad, Bennie Joe Reams with his brothers and sisters at his birthday fish fry in 1976. Left to right in back: Willie Draydon Reams, Bennie Joe Reams, Carroll Brinson Reams, Agnes Reams Watson, and Eloise Reams Jenkins

My family now: (back to front) Cameron Davis (my son) Kassidy Hopkins (Lee's daughter); Lee Hopkins, Jody Reams Davis Snoop

Ream's Landing, and Rocky Ford Church. His dad, Robert Draydon Reams, was one of the founders. My grandparents and many others in our family are buried there. Robert Draydon is pictured on the Rocky Ford Cemetery website.

My great-grandfather Willie T. Carroll was the youngest son of Joseph B. and Fannie Carroll's children. He went to work for the South Georgia Railroad. The railroad sent him to El Paso, Texas. where he met Hilda Eloise Pickering. They married and had Fannie Carroll in Texas. Then they moved to Jefferson County, and had their second daughter, Maudie Carroll. The girls grew up in Lamont. The *Monticello News*, which is now at the State Archives in Tallahassee, told many stories of their family. We have read the *Lamont News Section*, and the Carrolls were mentioned in many, some when Mr. Carroll motored up to Tallahassee or other places with Miss Fannie and Miss Maudie, his daughters. It tells of family gatherings, fish frys, and complaints of the road conditions. It mentions them as scholars, and both girls became teachers, Fannie in school, Maudie in music. It also tells of Miss Fannie going to church with Mrs. Amanda Reams, and they believe wedding bells will ring soon.

The wedding bells did ring when Miss Fannie Carroll married Mr. Reuben Benjamin Reams, the youngest son of Robert Draydon and Martha Aman Donaldson Reams. My grandparents had five children that lived. When they first married they lived not far from where my grandfather was raised. They had their first child there. Later they moved to Lamont and raised their family. My dad had two sisters, and two brothers; he was the second to youngest. They lost their mom during childbirth when my dad was four years old. Later their dad remarried and raised his other five children in the same home with them. The family grew up the old fashioned country way of living.

We went to family reunions, where I loved to listen to the many stories. Everyone seemed to know everyone; and all their business. They did tell a lot of history there, which I wanted to learn about. It was fun and interesting to hear some of the comments they made about each other. My mom would talk all the way home about what she had found out. Once in awhile my dad would have some news she'd missed, and she'd ask lots of questions, and he'd say, "I've done told you all I know." By the next day she'd find out from somebody, and we'd all know the whole scoop before the sun went down.

My parents kept the three of us with them, and took us where they went, no babysitters for us. My mom loved being a mom, and having a family to care for. We always had a pool, we had our own refrigerator, so we could have water, drinks, and snacks. There always seemed to be some of our friends and family at our house, or with us. We did a lot of family things like camping, fishing, picnics, going to the beaches, historical sites, fun places, cane grindings, picking blackberries, going to church and family reunions. Sometimes we'd slip off by ourselves, and no one could find us. When we got back there would always be someone who had tried to find us but couldn't. It was funny because they'd act like we had done them wrong by not letting them be with us.

I'm glad to be from this area, and have always enjoyed living here.
Submitted by: Jody Reams Davis, 2232 Pineland Dr. Talla. Fl. 32308 jody.davis@cable.comcast.com

Kathryn Elizabeth Reece

Kathryn Reece was born in 1899 in North Carolina to hard working parents of modest means. Her father had a hardwood specialty business making shuttle-blocks for textile mills and both parents worked small farms. The family moved every few years to areas where hardwood was available. In 1918, the family moved to Tallahassee to a home on College Avenue, a block from the Florida State College for Women campus. The family built a shuttle-block mill on Gaines Street and purchased a 75-acre farm on Park Avenue east of Magnolia Drive.

Kathryn Reece Haun

Growing up, Kathryn impressed family and friends with her singing voice, intelligence, and personality. She sang at many church, school, and family events. She attended FSCW from 1919-1921 graduating with a special diploma in voice. Kathryn had a beautiful coloratura soprano voice. She attended the Cincinnati Conservatory of Music on scholarship from 1921-1924 graduating with a Masters Degree in voice.

Kathryn married Ewald Haun in 1924. He was on the faculty of the Conservatory, and a renowned flutist, composer, arranger, and conductor for various orchestras.

In 1925, Kathryn was awarded a scholarship to study at the Julliard School of Music in New York. Soon after, her Broadway debut was as Phyllis in Gilbert and Sullivan's opera *Iolanthe*. Other works she appeared in include: *Pirates of Penzance*, *H.M.S. Pinafore*, and *Enchanted Isle*. In 1928, she and Ewald sailed to Australia. Kathryn was cast as lead in the musical *Princess Charming* and he conducted the musical *Rose Marie* being presented there. They continued their trip by sailing to Europe and on to New York arriving in early 1929 completing their round-the-world trip. Ewald saved Kathryn from being kidnapped in the Suez Canal.

Kathryn appeared in the movie *Animal Crackers* with the Marx Brothers in 1930. She continued performing over the next few years in Canada, England, and the United States in various Gilbert and Sullivan operas, *Peggy Ann*, *Blossom Time*, and other musicals. She performed at FSCW for the Artist Series. In 1936, Kathryn and Ewald traveled to Germany to settle the estate of Ewald's aunt. They attended the Berlin Olympic Games and saw Hitler. They traveled all around Germany and parts of Europe for several months before returning to New York in 1937 to resume their careers.

Ewald died in 1939 from heart disease. Later that year, Kathryn became an instructor at the Cincinnati Conservatory Drama Department and later joined the faculty at Western College in Ohio. During WWII, she sang at many benefits and fund raiser events. She had leading and supporting roles in several Gilbert and Sullivan productions across the USA from 1943 to 1946. She last appeared on Broadway in 1944. The young Beverly Sills was her understudy in several productions and they became friends.

Kathryn moved back to Tallahassee in 1946. She helped found the Tallahassee Little Theatre and appeared in many TLT productions over the years. She became a real estate agent, taught private voice lessons, and became an accomplished portrait, still-life, and landscape oil painter. Kathryn traveled extensively to Europe and the Far East with friends and family. Beverly Sills visited Kathryn at her home when Ms. Sills performed in Tallahassee in the late 1960's.

Kathryn cared for her aged parents from the mid-50s until her father passed in 1969 at age 99. Kathryn herself passed away in 1994 one day before her 95th birthday. She is buried in the Oakland Cemetery in Tallahassee

Written by: William Whitfield

Eluster Richardson

Born and raised in Tallahassee, Florida, Eluster began painting as a child in the third grade. All through high school Eluster practiced his craft; there was never a doubt in his mind as to what he wanted to do with his life. His works have won numerous awards in Florida and are exhibited in the Bethune-Cookman College fine art gallery in Daytona Beach, Florida and the Zora Neale Hurston Museum in Eatonville, Florida. He was the Visual Arts director for Tallahassee's 1998 Harambee Festival. Some of Eluster's works are exhibited at several fine art galleries around the United States, but currently Eluster maintains his studio in Tallahassee, Florida.

When asked why he chose painting,

Eluster Richardson

Eluster replies: "We search for a way to make sense out of life, wondering what to do, and yearn for a call that will take us beyond ourselves and show us the reason for our existence. My work primarily encompasses people and their expressions, so my paintings tend to reflect their emotions on canvas. I work primarily in watercolor, which is an additional chal-lenge, but I do work in other mediums such as oil on canvas and pencil sketches." Uplifting, inspiring, and educational are often the words heard when speaking of Eluster Richardson's art. Eluster's drawings, oils and watercolor paintings show special interest in the depiction of historic personages and scenic beauty in the North Florida region, particularly around Leon County.

Eluster is the Artist-in-Residence at the Riley House Museum in Tallahassee and The Resource Center for African-American History and Culture in Orlando, Florida, which is the home for a collection of historical works by Eluster. These works have also been displayed in several Leon County area museums. Eluster prefers painting people instead of landscapes stating: "People are such a challenge when trying to capture their emotions." He especially enjoys children as a subject because of their curiosity about life, making his daughter, Jasmine, a source of many paintings. He is adept in oil and especially pencil but his medium of choice is watercolor.

Written and Submitted by: Eluster Richardson, 7056 Bradfordville Road, Tallahassee, Florida 32309 eluster7@embarqmail.com

Elsie Elizabeth Richbourg Belk

Elsie Elizabeth Richbourg, daughter of (Caswell) Joseph Tobin Richbourg and Elizabeth "Bettie" Johnson Richbourg, was born September 15, 1911 in Woodville, Leon County, Florida. Her father farmed and worked in the timber industry at Woodville. The family later lived in Hosford, Liberty County, Florida, and eventually moved to Clearwater, Pinellas County, Florida.

On October 28, 1933 in Panama City, Bay County, Florida, Elsie married William "Billy" Brady Belk, born, born August 15, 1901 in Monroe, North Carolina. Their son, Ronald "Ron" Kent Belk was born March 1, 1935 at St. Andrew in Bay County. For some 30 years the Belk family lived in West Palm Beach, Florida, where Billy owned and operated a lumber business. Ron, a successful Palm Beach architect, designed the Tiara and the Phoenix Twin Towers, ocean front condominiums located on Singer Island and Riviera Beach. The design of Palm Bay Towers in Miami brought prestigious national recognition to his work.

William "Billy" Brady Belk died in West Palm Beach on October 6, 1984 and was buried at Royal Palm Memorial Gardens. Ronald "Ron" Kent Belk died February 16, 1996 at

In West Palm Beach, Elsie attained membership and held various offices in the Margaret Mitchell Chapter, United Daughters of the Confederacy, proving her descent from Noah (Noel) Johnson, her maternal grandfather. Noah (Noel)Johnson served in Company H, First Florida Infantry, CSA, and later lived at Eoodville. Pembroke, Georgia. He and his wife, Matilda Dixon Johnson, are buried in the White Primitive Baptist Church Cemetery at Woodville. A Confederate marker honors his memory.

Elsie was also a member of the Confederate Salt Works Chapter, United Daughters of the Confederacy, in Panama City. In addition, she was an active member of the Southern Dames of America. During the years in West Palm Beach she was a member of Northwood Baptist Church and later a member of Pembroke Baptist Church in Pembroke, Georgia. An expert seamstress, she often created lovely additions to her wardrobe and decorative accessories for her gracious home. She excelled in public speaking and dramatic presentations, entertaining family and other groups where she was often invited to speak. She combined her love of family history and her talent for writing when she published *Grandmother and Me,* a collection of humorous short stories.

Elsie Elizabeth Richbourg Belk is currently a resident of Blountstown, Calhoun County, Florida. Her speech is articulate, and her demeanor is

Billy, Ron, and Elsie Belk Chester Lee Richbourg

regal. She welcomes visitors with dignity, grace and charm, characteristics which have defined her throughout her entire life. Note: Elsie passed away July 8, 2011. She is buried in Pembroke, GA.
Submitted by: Elsie Richbourg Belk, Written by: Judith Richbourg Jolly, 11541 Arlhuna Way, Dade City, Florida 33525

Chester Lee Richbourg

Chester Lee Richbourg, son of (Caswell) Joseph Tobin Richbourg and Elizabeth "Bettie" Johnson Richbourg, was born February 1, 1890 in Castleberry, Conecuh County, Alabama. In the mid-1890s, his family moved to Woodville, Leon County, Florida. Lee attended school at the Woodville School and spent his childhood and youth in the Woodville community. Sometime after 1911, the family relocated to Liberty County.

On July 3, 1917, he married Mattie Lee Dykes (March 7, 1898-March 8, 1978), daughter of William Henry and Sarah Alice Mims Dykes of Jackson County. In addition to his work as a barber, Lee and Mattie followed the fruit picking season in south-central Florida. Chester and Mattie divorced July 20, 1929 in Bay County. They were parents of three children. (1) Daisy Lee Richbourg was born May 15, 1918 and married (1st) Steadmon Hobbs. She married (2nd) Daniel Alexander Engelhardt. Daisy died April 11, 2004 in Palm Harbor, Florida. (2) Horace Mitchell Richbourg was born February 5, 1920 and married Nettie Ruth Cook. Horace died December 10, 2003 in Marianna, Florida. (3) Adrian Dee (A.D.) Richbourg was born April 21, 1923 and married Mildred Elizabeth Penton.

On September 16, 1929, Chester Lee Richbourg married (2nd) Dora Lee Canterbury (August 27, 1908-February 12, 1989), daughter of James Loudy and Allier Ineta Wesson Canterbury. Their son, Wilson Wesson Richbourg, was born December 9, 1948. On April 14, 1979, he married Sonja Nowell Wilson.

Chester Lee Richbourg

Chester Lee Richbourg died September 12, 1978 in Panama City, Florida and was buried at Evergreen Memorial Cemetery.
Submitted by: Mildred Penton Richbourg, 3909 West 16th Street, Panama City, FL; Written by: Judith Richbourg Jolly, 11541 Arlhuna Way, Dade City, Florida 33525; Source: Richbourg...A Sequel by Mildred Penton Richbourg

(Caswell) Joseph Tobin Richbourg

(Caswell) Joseph Tobin Richbourg, former Woodville resident, was the son of William Middleton Richbourg (CSA) and Rebecca Nettles Richbourg (daughter of Benjamin Nettles and Mary Varner Nettles). His great-great-great grandfather was the French Huguenot minister, the Reverend Claude Philippe de Richbourg, who sailed with other refugees on the ship *Mary Ann* from England to Virginia in 1700. They reached the James River on October 20 and traveled to Manakin Town, about 20 miles from present-day Richmond. They later went to North Carolina and eventually settled in South Carolina at Jamestown on the Santee River.

Joseph Tobin Richbourg was born September 28, 1865 in Muskogee, Escambia County, Florida. About 1885, he and his sister, with their widowed mother, moved to Conecuh County, Alabama to be near extended family. On July 13, 1887 in Conecuh County, Joseph T. Richbourg married Elizabeth "Bettie" Johnson, daughter of (Noel) Johnson (CSA) and Matilda Dixon Johnson. Joseph Tobin and Bettie Richbourg remained in Castleberry, Conecuh County, until the mid-1890s when they moved to Woodville, Florida. The 1900 Leon County census lists J.T. Richbourg as a sawmill laborer and the 1910 Leon County census lists him as a foreman in a turpentine camp. It is likely that C.J. Richbourg, enumerated in the 1910 Wakulla County census as a night watchman in a convict camp, was Joseph Richbourg. About 1911, the family moved to Hosford.

According to their youngest son,

(Caswell) Joseph Tobin Richbourg, 1926

Wilson Emmet Richbourg, Joseph Tobin was a businessman in Hosford and owned a store and oyster bar. He also had a grist mill on the south side of Marianna and ran logs on the Chipola River. A hard worker, he possessed the stamina necessary to log, fish, farm, and work in turpentine, timber, and sawmills. Per his daughter, Elsie Elizabeth Richbourg Belk, he was also a man who loved to be with and entertain his family when the day's work was done. The children would gather in the evening for his stories and jokes and would laugh with delight. Once in a while Bettie would softly chide, "Now, Toby."

It is known that Joseph Tobin Richbourg removed Tobin from his name on legal documents sometime between 1900 and 1920. He added Caswell, the name of a deceased brother, in place of Tobin and became Caswell Joseph Richbourg. Family members can only speculate why. Son Wilson, born December 18, 1915, only knew father as Caswell Joseph. Yet, Bettie continued to call her husband Toby.

About 1920, the Richbourg family moved to Clearwater in central Florida, and on August 20, 1925, he and Bettie sold their Hosford property to their oldest daughter, Leila Richbourg Hardee. In Clearwater, (Caswell) Joseph Tobin Richbourg truck farmed in citrus and produce, harvested oysters, and caught and smoked mullet from the bay. He died in Clearwater on February 16, 1928. He was buried in the old Clearwater Municipal Cemetery around the corner from the family's Grand Central Avenue home. His tomb stone is engraved with his name, "Caswell J. Richbourg."

Submitted by: Carol Richbourg Matthews, 109 Maplewood Avenue, Clearwater, Florida; Written by: Judith Richbourg Jolly, 11541 Arlhuna Way, Dade city, Florida 33525

Elizabeth "Bettie" Johnson Richbourg

Elizabeth "Bettie" Johnson Richbourg, former Woodville resident, was born August 16, 1871 in Conecuh County, Alabama. She was the daughter of Noah (Noel) Johnson (CSA) and Matilda Dixon Johnson. Her maternal greatgrandfather, Jeremiah Dixon, (about 1764-July 26, 1835) served in the North Carolina State Line during the American Revolution. He and his wife, Elizabeth Goff, arrived in Alabama by 1816 and eventually settled in Covington County where they bought land on the Conecuh River on December 29, 1823. Their son, Captain Rufus Wiley Beauregard Dixon and his wife, Elsie Permelia Helen May, (daughter of James David May, Sr.) were Bettie's maternal grandparents. Bettie's paternal grandparents were Nicholas Johnson and Nancy Rachels who married October 9, 1834 in Warren County, Georgia.

On July 13, 1887 in Conecuh County, Elizabeth "Bettie" Johnson married Joseph Tobin Richbourg. With affection, she called him Toby and with affection, he called her Betsy or Bets. Their children remember that no unkind words were ever spoken between them. They lived in Castleberry until the mid-1890s when they moved to Woodville. They later moved to Hosford sometime after the 1911 birth of their daughter, Elsie Elizabeth, and remained in Hosford for several years.

Elizabeth "Bettie" Johnson Richbourg was a warm and loving wife and mother, and she and Joseph Tobin were blessed with eleven children. Bettie was a talented seamstress who made lovely dresses for her daughters. She was untiring, creative, and resourceful. Said her daughter, Elsie Elizabeth Richbourg Belk, "My mother, a pretty woman, worked magic with what little my father could earn to raise their large family." Bettie was a devout Christian and a member of the Baptist church. Sometime during the early 1920s, the Richbourg family moved south to Clearwater in Pinellas County.

Bettie cared for her husband during his extended illness and was with him when his earthly life ended. She then knew the struggles of life as a widow with two children still dependent on her. She took boarders into their home to make ends meet. Eventually, when that was not enough, her home was one of the many casualties of the tragic years of the Great Depression. On October, 7 1929, it sold to the highest bidder on the steps of the Pinellas County Courthouse. Nonetheless, she remained steadfast and resilient and became an example to

Elizabeth Johnson Richbourg

her family of not giving up in bad times. She taught them that love and family loyalty were far more important than material possessions.

From her home with her daughter Allie Mae Richbourg Gatlin in Clearwater, Bettie often returned to Hosford for extended visits with family. She died May 24, 1941 in Hosford during a visit with her daughter, Leila Frances Richbourg Hardee. After services conducted by the pastor of Calvary Baptist Church in Clearwater, she was buried in the newer section of the Clearwater Municipal Cemetery across the road from where her husband, (Caswell) Joseph Tobin "Toby" Richbourg was laid to rest in 1928. Her memorial marker reads "Safe in the arms of Jesus."

Submitted by: Patricia Richbourg Stephens, 44 23 E. Brandon Drive, Marietta, Georgia; Written by: Judith Richbourg Jolly, 11541 Arlhuna Way, Dade City, Florida 33525; Sources: Heritage Books of Covington, Alabama, Escambia, Florida, and Liberty, Florida; military, vital, and family records

Allie Mae Richbourg Gatlin

Allie Mae Richbourg Gatlin, daughter of (Caswell) Joseph Tobin Richbourg and Elizabeth "Bettie" Johnson Richbourg, was born November 10, 1906 in Woodville, Leon County, Florida. Her family lived in Hosford, Liberty County, Florida for several years and then moved to Clearwater, Pinellas County, Florida about 1920.

About 1925, Allie married Dan Gatlin, Jr., son of Daniel Gatlin, SR. and Laura Jean Adams Gatlin. Don Gatlin was born February 2, 1905 in Opp, Covington County, Alabama.

In the early years of their marriage, Allie Mae Gatlin worked in a citrus plant in Clearwater and packed oranges and grapefruit for local and out-of-state sales. She was a member of Calvary Baptist Church and taught children in Sunday School. Dan, an entrepreneur, was a hard worker. He owned and operated Dan Gatlin Paving Company and later was coowner of ABC Terazzo, a business partnership with his brother-in-law, Wilson Emmet Richbourg.

Allie Richbourg Gatlin

Allie Mae Richbourg Gatlin died November 23, 1953 in Clearwater, and Dan Gatlin died August 4, 1958 at Duke Hospital in Durham, North Carolina. Both were buried at Sylvan Abbey Memorial Park Cemetery in Clearwater. Two daughters were born to Dan and Allie Gatlin, each named for a grandmother.

(1) Betty Lou Gatlin was born May 20, 1926. On June 15, 1947 in Clearwater, she married John Harvey Meek, Sr., son of John Henry Meek and Nellie Pearl Pauley Meek. John Harvey Meek, Sr. was born March 16, 1919 in Garfield, Hancock County, Indiana. Betty Lou Gatlin Meek died June 27, 2001 and was buried at Sylvan Abbey Memorial Park Cemetery near her parents. John and Betty Gatlin Meek were parents of two sons, John Harvey Meek, Jr. and Daniel Lee Meek, both born in Clearwater.

(2) Laura Jean Gatlin was born October 28, 1928 in Clearwater. Following high school graduation she served in the U.S. Air Force and was stationed for a time at Eglin Air Force Base in Fort Walton Beach, Florida. In 1954 at McDill Air Force Base in Tampa, Florida, she married (1) Robert Lykins. She married (2) David Kool. Laura Gatlin Kool died November 20, 1976 at Bay Pines Veterans Hospital in St. Petersburg, Florida. Her ashes were placed between her mother and father at Sylvan Abbey Memorial Park Cemetery.

Submitted by: Juliet Jolly, 10910 Mansker Road, Dade City, Florida 33525; Written by: Judith Richbourg Jolly, 11541 Arlhuna Way, Dade City, Florida 33525

Nancy Pearl Richbourg Melvin

Nancy Pearl Richbourg, known as Pearl, was the daughter of (Caswell) Joseph Tobin Richbourg and Elizabeth "Bettie" Johnson Richbourg. Pearl was born September 20, 1902 in Woodville, Leon County, Florida. She died May 11, 1959 in Bethesda, Maryland and was buried in Arlington Cemetery, Virginia.

She married Golden Ernest Melvin, son of Murdock Merrit Melvin and Sydney Cornelia Lane Melvin. He was born December 28, 1899 in Aycock, Florida and served in France during World War I. He died November 16, 1962 in Marianna, Florida and is buried at Arlington Cemetery.

They were parents of two daughters. (1) Lollee Elizabeth Melvin was born April 5, 1921 in

Pearl Richbourg (right) with (l-r) Maude, Bettie. Wilson, Allie

Millville, Bay County, Florida. On December 8, 1945, she married James "Bo" Barr Doster, son of James Parker Doster and Minnie Frances Powell Doster. Bo Doster was born October 4, 1920 in Florala, Covington County, Alabama. Bo and Lollee were parents of five children: Diane, Debora, James Barr "Jim Bo", David Powell and Dorothy "Dodie" Elizabeth.

(2) Ann Lee Melvin was born July 17, 1927 in Marianna, Florida. On September 19, 1947 at Coronado, California, she married John Randolph Conner, son of Charles Lester Conner and Amy Alta Jones. He was born July 13, 1923 in Bay, Alaska and died August 5, 1994 in Bartlesville,Oklahoma. Ann and John were parents of six children: Jenny Lynn, Janice Lee, Justin Melvin, James Edward, and Nancy Amy.

Submitted by: A.D. Richbourg, 3909 West 16th Street, Panama City. Florida; Written by: Judith Richbourg Jolly, 11541 Arlhuna Way, Dade City, Florida 33525; Source: Richbourg...A Sequel by Mildred P. Richbourg, 1994

Richbourg Children

(Caswell) Joseph Tobin Richbourg and Elizabeth "Bettie" Johnson Richbourg, early residents of Woodville, were parents of eleven children.

(1) Leila Frances Richbourg was born May 26, 1888 in Castleberry, Alabama. On August 13, 1905, she married A.G. "Shady" Hardee. A.G. died June 24, 1941, and Leila died September 1, 1958. They are buried in Hosford Cemetery.

(2) Chester Lee Richbourg was born February 1, 1890 in Castleberry , Alabama. He married (1) Mattie Lee Dykes and (2) Dora Lee Canterbury. He died September 12, 1978 and is buried in Panama City, Florida.

(3) Hosea Richbourg was born in February 1892 in Castleberry, Alabama. He died between 1900 and 1910 in Woodville, Leon County, Florida, and is buried at the White Primitive Baptist Church Cemetery in Woodville.

(4) Bertha (Lebertha) Richbourg was born July 15, 1894 in Castleberry, Alabama. On May 10, 1915, she married Robert Emmett Galloway. He died in 1922. She married (2) L. Shelton Stanaland. Bertha died November 17, 1925 in Clearwater, Florida and is buried at the Clearwater Municipal Cemetery.

(5) Thomas Radford Richbourg was born in April 1897 in Woodville, Florida. On January 1, 1927, he married (1) Laurie Foster. He married (2) Lennie Delk. He died January 30, 1967 in Blountstown, Florida and is buried in Hosford Cemetery. (See separate story.)

(6) A child of unknown gender was born and died before 1900.

(7) Nancy Pearl Richbourg was born September 20, 1902 in Wood-ville, Florida. About 1920, she married GoldenErnest Melvin. She died May 11, 1959 in Bethesda, Maryland and is buried at Arlington National Cemetery in Arlington, Virginia.

(8) Allie Mae Richbourg was born November 10. 1905 in Woodville, Florida. About 1925, she married Daniel Gatlin, Jr. She died November 23, 1953 and is buried at Sylvan Abbey Memorial Park in Clearwater, Florida.

(9) Vera Maude Richbourg was born in 1909 in Woodville, Florida. About 1925, she married Benjamin Franklin Sanders. She died in 1953 in Ocoee, Florida and is married in the Ocoee Cemetery.

(10) Elsie Elizabeth Richbourg was born September 15, 1911 in Woodville, Florida. On October 28, 1933, she married William Brady Belk. Elsie is a resident of Blountstown, Florida.

(Front) Joseph Tobin, Allie, Maude, Bettie holding Elsie; (Back) Pearl, Bertha

(11) Wilson Emmet Richbourg was born December 18,1915 in Marianna, Florida. On June 30, 1938, he married Sarah Bragg. He died May

15. 1989 in Blountstown, Florida and is buried in Hosford Cemetery.

Submitted by: Jennifer Jolly Rothschild, 5287 South Parkhill, Springfield, Missouri 65810; Written by: Judith Richbourg Jolly, 11541 Arlhuna Way, Dade City Florida 33525; Sources: Family and vital records; Richbourg ...A Sequel by Mildred Penton Richbourg 1994

Thomas Radford Richbourg

Thomas Radford Richbourg was born in Woodville, Leon County, Florida. He was the son of (Caswell) Joseph Tobin Richbourg and Elizabeth "Bettie" Johnson Richbourg and was known as Tom by friends and family. Per the 1900 Leon County, Florida census, Tom was born in April 1897. Later records cite October as the month of his birth.

The family remained in Woodville for several years and then moved to Hosford sometime after the 1911 birth of Tom's sister, Elsie Elizabeth Richbourg. It was in Hosford that Tom (as Tommy Richberg) registered for the World War I draft in September 1918. Military records describe him as 6 feet tall, slender, with blue eyes and light hair.

Tom Richbourg

Tom moved with his family to Clearwater, Florida in the early 1920s.

On January 1, 1927, he married Laurie Foster. On June 10, 1939, he married (2nd) Lennie Delk. Tom was a housepainter by trade. A meticulous craftsman, his work was his art, a trait characteristic of many of the Richbourg family.

Tom eventually moved back to Hosford and bought property in 1950. He died January 30, 1967 in Blountstown. Following services at Corinth Baptist Church, where he was a member, he was laid to rest near family in the Hosford Cemetery. His grave, to the left of his brother, Wilson Emmet Richbourg, remains unmarked today.

Submitted by: Tom Matthews, 2833 Eagle Run Circle South, Clearwater, Florida 33760; Written by: Judith Richbourg Jolly, 11541 Arlhuna Way, Dade City, Florida 33525

Virginia Reynolds Smith Robbins

Virginia Freda Reynolds was born in Crescent City, FL in 1921. Her parents were Fred Otis (Ote) and Ethel Lynch Reynolds.

Ote was well liked in Crescent City, having been a volunteer fireman, running a taxi service to the train station 3 miles out of town and barbering with his brother John Reynolds.

Virginia had one sister, Dorothy Dixon Reynolds, and no brothers.

Ote died in Crescent City at age 32 of pneumonia, leaving his wife, who never remarried, with 2 young daughters to raise.

In her single days during WW II, Virginia was a "General" in the "Victorettes," meeting at the Servicemen's Club on Calhoun St. in Tallahassee.

After taking a Florida Merit System exam in Daytona Beach, she received an offer by telegram from Tallahassee, for a position with the Florida Industrial Commission-a big adventure for a country girl like her, who grew up in the little town of Crescent City, Fl. She then became Secretary to the Parole Officer at the Federal Correction Institution for two years. Later she worked for an attorney and when his brother, Dick Ervin was elected as Attorney General, she worked for Frank Heintz, one of the Assistant Attorneys General.

Virginia in April 2010

Virginia married her three children's dad, L. G. (initials only) Smith in 1947. Her three children are Karen, Lawrence (Larry) and Ivy Jo Smith. Larry was the only one born in Tallahassee and the only one who still lives here. Karen was born in Tampa, and Ivy Jo in Daytona Beach.

Virginia resigned her job to follow her husband with two young children, all over the country, later working for a law firm in Miami. After the birth of her third child, Ivy Jo they moved back to Tallahassee where she worked for 19 years as Staff Assistant for the Director of the Division of Securities.

L. G. deserted the family when Ivy was 2 years old; many years later he died in Portland, Oregon (probably in 1982) according to his sister, Aline Apthorp.

After all three of her children were grown and married, and during the time she worked for the Division of Securities, she took a trip with her mother to visit her Aunt Freda. As they passed through Crystal River, her mother suggested that they visit the Museum, and that's where she met her future husband, Tom Robbins. They were married on an Indian Mound in the Crystal River Archaeological Site overlooking the Crystal River. They sailed to Dunedin, FL in their Venture 21 Fiberglass sailboat, "Cacique" which means Indian King. Halfway to their destination they went aground on "Red Rock" which was marked by a very small post that they didn't see. They spent the night on "Red Rock" waiting for the tide to come in. They moored in Dunedin Marina and then were hosted by the Dunedin State Park staff and given a ride in a motorboat to nearby Caladesi Island, where they enjoyed a Jeep tour of the Island.

Written and Submitted by: Virginia Reynolds Smith Robbins robbinsnest42@brmemc.net; Paraphrased by: Mary J. Marchant

Roberts-Theus Family

Samuel Theus, a forty year old widower and his second wife, Mariah, moved to Leon County from the Charleston, South Carolina area in 1829. His family originally emigrated from Ems, Switzerland in the 1700's. He purchased 160 acre for the beginning of their large farm on what is known today as Roberts Road in the Centerville community. In 1830 he built their home, which still stands and is the oldest existing Leon County residence. It was originally located on the hill northeast of its current location. In 1862 the west section (Defined by adz hewn beams.) was moved by oxen team to the present location and two large rooms, center hall, detached kitchen and Carolina porches were added.

Samuel and Mariah were listed as founding members of Pisgah Methodist Church in 1830. Samuel died in 1844 and his wife, son William and two grand-daughters, Mary Jane and Elizabeth Ann Cook, divided his estate of 360 acres. In 1850 the farm produced 900 bushels of corn, 600 pounds of rice (11% of Leon County's), and forty-seven bales of cotton along with peas, beans, sweet potatoes, butter, cane sugar and 80 gallons of syrup, forty pounds of beeswax and honey.

Elizabeth Ann Cook, sixteen, married Thomas Jefferson Roberts, son of William Roberts, in 1832. The Roberts came to Leon County from Georgia in 1825 and were livestock farmers (200 cattle, 300 sheep, 215 hogs).

By 1855 Eliza and Thomas had amassed 393 acres and they produced 3,000 corn bushels and seventy-two cotton bales. By 1863 the holdings were 487 acres and in 1866 were 840, with some coming from the Theus estate. By 1873 the farm reached its maximum size of 1,560 acres.

Eliza died in 1870, leaving three children: Philip and twins Leila and Willie. Thomas remarried in 1872 to Sarah Harley of Thomasville.

In 1875 Thomas and Sarah provided the lumber needed and deeded five acres at the intersection of Bradfordville/Roberts/Centerville Roads to St. Phillips African Methodist Episcopal Church, (Until the war ended the AME members were part of Pisgah Methodist Church.) The family had also built a one-room school on the same property to serve the African-American children of the neighborhood. The school, named "Roberts School," remained active until the 1940's. The name was revived with the dedication Of Roberts Elementary School in 2004.

Following the Civil War Thomas continued to be an active farmer. He was elected director of the Agricultural Society to encourage experiments in methods, machinery, fertilizers and crop diversification. He ran a profitable farm, seldom seen in post-war Florida. But in the 1870's hard times were felt when cotton prices bottomed and 1,153 acres were in bankruptcy. By 1880 all land had been re-purchased and he paid taxes on 1,200 acres; in 1890, 1,600 acres. In 1884 he produced 2,000 bushels of corn, 1,500 bushels of oats, 250 cotton bales, 50 bushels of cow peas, 1,800 bushels potatoes and 2,000 pounds of tobacco. His products were valued at $13,925 and he employed 14 people to run his steam-powered cotton, grist and sugar mills, giving him an additional profit of $2,025.

The *Thomasville Times* published the following description of the farm in August 1887: "I have been spending a short time in Centerville, surveying the lands of T.J. Roberts and ex-Governor Walker. The latter plantation is cultivated by renters who exhibit little skill. On Mr. Roberts' place you can see a spirit of energy and enterprise unequaled in our county. He has what he calls "wages hand," hired by the year, with whom he has cultivated corn, cotton, and…other crops. His labormen are all cheerful and full of life. As they are justly and kindly treated, all show a willingness to do all they can to please their employer. Would that we had more such planters in our county."

In 1886 he and son Phillip purchased the down town block bordered by Duval, Adams, Pensacola and Jefferson streets. He established a livery and stocked horses and mules and sold four-and six-seat carriages, surreys, hacks, buggies, phaetons, wagons, harnesses, etc. By 1890 it had expanded into a food, feed and general mercantile store.

While Phillip ran the downtown properties, the younger son, Will, ran the farm, ginning cotton, selling cotton seed, wholesaling crops, shipping foodstuffs north by train and operating a commissary and the mills. Among items the commissary sold were: sardines, candy, cigars, snuff, bluing, soap, flour, coffee, tin buckets, tin pans, meat and syrup along with overalls, shoes, and later, soft drinks. The grist mill ground corn meal and grits for the neighborhood until the mid-1950s.

In 1897 T.J. Roberts purchased "The Columns" and Union Bank building located on the corner of Adams Street and Park Avenue and it was occupied by his wife "Aunt Sally" and him as their home. It served as a popular gathering for the Roberts' children, offspring, and friends until she sold it in 1925.

Upon T.J. Roberts moving to town, the farm house became the home of his son Will and his bride, Lillian Taylor of Monticello. Lillian's family arrived in America from Kenardiston, England circa 1635 and was descended from several New England area governors and Revolutionary War soldiers. In 1898 Will was deeded 560 acres, one-third of the farm.

Thomas Jefferson Roberts died in 1901. His life spanned much of the 19th Century and epitomized the changes in agriculture. His acreage at his death totaled 1,005 acres: Will purchased Sallie's and Leila's interest in the farm and tenant farmers cultivated many of the 900 acres in cotton, corn, peavine hay, velvet beans and peanuts. Tenant houses were furnished for them with one, built in 1925, still standing on the Lang portion of the farm.

Will continued his father's interest in progressive farming. He experimented with shade tobacco in 1906 and tung trees in 1909 and had a producing orange tree. He built a windmill in 1910 which made it possible for the family to have one of the first indoor bathrooms in rural Leon County. In 1914 a Fairbanks-Morse engine converted the gristmill to kerosene from steam and provided electricity for the home.

The Roberts purchased one of the first cars in Leon County in 1911. Will and his son Charles, (my father), traveled to Thomasville to get "the first car off the train" and spent the full day coming home because they had to stop every few mils to add water and oil to the cooled engine. Their arrival was eventful; when they reached the closed gate at the entrance to the farm, Will yelled, "Whoa"…and the car didn't stop.

In 1914 Lillian Roberts became the first Leon County home demonstration agent. My father, Charles, remembers going with her all over the county in the car which was fitted out with canning jars for her food preservation demonstrations.

Will and Lillian Roberts had eight children: Mary (died as an infant), Gladys, Thomas Jefferson, William, Charles, Lillian, Phillip and Jimmy. All the neighboring rural families took turns entertaining each other and the wide hall at the Robert's home was the site of many parties during the 1920s.

Gradually Will sold parts of the farm, and when he died in 1937, there were 386.5 acres remaining. Lillian continued to farm, assisted by her sons Jimmy, Charles and Phillip. Upon her death in 1963, the farm was divided between T.J., Charles, Phillip and Jimmy with the house property going to Jimmy, who lived with her for twenty-two years.

In settling her estate, it was discovered that the land given to St. Phillip's AME Church, the school and road right-of-way had never been properly deeded. The family then "regifted" the property to the church and county. T.J.(married Ruth Whitehead) sold his acreage to Willie and Lou Gutsch, but the remainder remained in the family. Charles' farm (married Martha Bradford) went to Mary Alma Roberts Lang (see Roberts/Richard Bradford and Lang history); Phillip's (married Marguerite) to daughters

Phyllis (deceased) and Harriet; Jimmy's (married Agnes Hartsfield, Doris Hoge) to sons Jim, Bill and Steve. The farm was awarded "100 Year Pioneer Farm" recognition and the home and farm were placed on the National Historic Site Register.

During their lifetimes the brothers continued to raise beef cattle and corn as well as many vegetables to share with family and friends, but after their deaths pine trees have become the main crop except for one herd of cattle. It is our hope that the family home can be restored one day to its former glory as the center of family and community.

Submitted by: Mary Alma Roberts Lang, 6025 Roberts Road, Tallahassee, FL 32309

Barbara Pearlman Rosen

Barbara Pearlman Rosen was born in the Bronx, New York, not quite a "baby boomer," but she was born during WW II, and raised in Monticello, New York, a very small town in the Catskill Mountains, 85 miles NW of New York City. She was fortunate to attend elementary, junior and high school all in the same building with the same friends from kindergarten through high school graduation. She still remains in close contact with those classmates. In fact she is getting ready to celebrate her 50th high school reunion in August 2010.

Barbara attended a local community college and always expected to be in some aspect of the medical profession, because, at the age of fifteen she recalls going to work for her family physician, while taking medical technology courses in college. Even now she continues to work for a physician part time.

At age 14 suddenly and unexpected she started to write poetry. Both her grandfather and grandmother were very artistic, so she felt fortunate to get that gene. Barbara was married and her children were all born near Monticello, N.Y. She used to live about 15 miles from where the Woodstock Musical Festival happened, and she drove a wonderful Volkswagen van to the site the day before it began as people were starting to fill the site. When she returned a few days after the event, the countryside was stripped of grass, and the stages were still coming down. Unfortunately, she never made the event as they had two young children and she was pregnant with the 3rd child.

In 1971 Barbara left NY and moved to Miami, Florida. She heard it said, "You are born with either a city soul or a country soul." There is no doubt she has a country soul and never quite adapted to the hectic pace of Miami, nor the crime rate. Somehow they stayed until Hurricane Andrew came and at that time their kids were all at FSU in Tallahassee, Florida. Although the storm didn't level their home, it did affect her husband's travel to and from work in South Miami.

In 1993 we decided to leave our long-held jobs and head to Tallahassee and help our sons get their business going. Since day one we have found Tallahassee to be a great place to live, with just enough small town environment to suit us, and large enough to have all the conveniences. I continued my crafting, and eventually started to make patchwork quilts. I had to keep my hands active.

We've always dreamed of having a second home either in the mountains or by the shore. Luckily in 1998, before the housing market took off like a rocket, we found a perfect place on Alligator Point, Florida. My husband of 45 years, David Rosen slices wood, cuts gourds, drills holes, takes me into the woods to find the really long pine needles, and pulls over to the side of the road, so I can cut tall grass to include in my designs. My son Michael slices dry wood branches from his yard that are perfect for centerpieces. My son Peter brings friends to my booths and manages to purchase several baskets for gifts. Our daughter Julie orders baskets for gifts for teachers and her friends.

Life is good here on Alligator Point. We still keep a small apartment in Tallahassee since I continue to work 2 days a week there. Pine needle baskets are ancient and mostly a lost art here in the USA. American Indians continue to make them, also in South America, Central America, and Africa. They are made mostly for sale to tourists. Since I am self taught from the old book, I try to allow this art to just evolve from ideas I come up with. I try not to be influenced by other artists. Although I do like to include centers that are made and traded from other artists, I can't do it all and I don't try to do it all. I love what I do and am grateful for whatever source this art/skill comes from. I had my baskets shown at the Leon Co. Library Branch on Thomasville Rd the entire month of July, 2010. I am very fortunate.

Submitted by: Barbara Rosen, Alligator Point, FL 32346

Jean L. Rosenau, Tallahassee's Scottish Piper

Jean Louise Aitkenhead was born January 18, 1922 in Moscow, Idaho. She is the oldest daughter of William C. and Lillian L. Aitkenhead. For a time Jean and her family lived in Russia, where she learned she had a flair for mastering different languages. She used this skill to her advantage by graduating from the University of Colorado with a major in Languages in 1943. After, graduation she joined the Marine Corps and completed Aerographers School to become a weather observer.

After serving for two years, Jean met her future husband of 62 years, Jack C. Rosenau and they were married September 6, 1945 in Santa Ana, near the El Toro Marine Corp Air Station, California. After the War, Jean and Jack moved to Michigan, where she started her graduate studies in Geology at the Michigan State College. But upon the birth of their first child in 1946, Jean placed her studies on hold to raise her children. They have seven children: Andrew, Ann, James, Robert, David, Steven, Sandra; sixteen grandchildren, and two great-grandchildren.

A few years after their last child was born in 1958, Jean and her family traveled for a number of years before settling in Tallahassee, Florida in 1969. In 1972, Jean decided to complete her studies by earning her Master's Degree in Library Science from Florida State University. Jean was active in numer-ous organi-zations in Florida and Leon County for over 25 years, but her greatest love was her children, education and playing the bagpipes.

Her love for bagpiping started in the mid 1970s, when Jean spotted an article in the *Tallahassee Democrat* that a South Florida clergyman had moved to Tallahassee and was seeking potential students interested in learning to play the bagpipes. Both Jean and Jack had Scottish family backgrounds and were members of the Talla-hassee Saint An-drew's Society. They also were part of a small group of Scottish country dancers. Jean had a solid musical foundation, so the opportunity to learn to play the bagpipes was quickly pursued.

Jean Louise Aitkenhead-Rosnau at home in 1989

Jean enjoyed playing the pipes and her favorite location for practicing was their front porch. Neighbors could hear her playing at anytime between 1975 through 1995. It was Alzheimer's disease that stopped her from playing and ultimately took her life in 2007. A year or so ago Jack chanced upon meeting their former postman, Mr. Terrell Hovan, who mentioned how he and others had heard Jean playing the pipes when they were in the area and how much they missed the soothing melody she provided. Jean was also a good teacher with a natural enthusiasm that started others in bagpiping; among them was her oldest son, Andrew Rosenau and one of Jean's former students, Joe Ashcraft.

Joe is now an excellent piper and leader of the "Tallahassee Pipe Band" and he also teaches bag piping. Joe was the piper at Jean's funeral service in 2007 and again at her memorial, a year later at her gravesite. Their son Andrew is still an active piper and takes his pipes where ever he goes for business or pleasure. Jean is remembered as a woman who gave much with her love of music.

Written-Submitted by: Jack C. Rosenau, 1177 Old Fort Drive Tallahassee, FL 32301

Lt. Colonel Jack C. Rosenau

Jack Clayton Rosenau was born on October 26, 1919 in Detroit, Michigan. He is the oldest son of Arthur Henry Rosenau (1900-1980) and Florence Muriel McNeally (1896-1993). The Scot-Irish McNeally family migrated to London, Ontario, Canada in the 1890s where Florence McNeally was born to Louisa L. Stevenson and Robert J. McNeally. Jack's grandparents are Gottliebe Pannick and Gottfried Rosenau, who migrated from Germany to Canada in the 1880's.

While growing up in Detroit, Jack recalls the many summer trips he went across the Detroit River into Canada to visit his Canadian relatives. Jack has two sisters, Muriel and Betty, and a brother, Robert Rosenau, who all attended Detroit schools. Jack graduated in January 1939 from Cass Technical High School's Aeronautical Curriculum, but joined the United Marine Corps Reserve in 1937, while still a high school student.

His fighter squadron was called to active duty in December, 1940, and Jack served as weather forecaster for the First Marine Air Wing

Division in the South Pacific. Upon his return to the States in 1943, and now a Master Technical Sergeant, Jack's assigned responsibilities included operation of the weather office at El Toro Marine Corps Air Station in Santa Ana, California.

He found his future wife, Sergeant Jean L. Aitkenhead a weather observer stationed at this base. They were married September 6, 1945 by Naval Chaplain, Lieutenant Head and they subsequently received honorable discharges in late November before heading home to Michigan.

Jack and Jean spent their first Christmas as man and wife with his parents in Detroit, and later traveled to East Lansing Michigan, where he enrolled in Michigan State College for a degree in Geology. Jack and Jean's family includes two girls and five Eagle Scouts, thanks to his great wife, Jean Aitkenhead-Rosenau.

Jack graduated in 1949 with an army commission in field artillery. His commission was transferred to the air force effective 1948. Jack obtained employment with the Michigan Geological Survey Division and later worked for the State of Michigan until hired by Mr. D. B. Steinman, Consulting Engineer, as Resident Geologist (1952-1955) for construction of the Mackinac (pronounced Mackinaw) straits bridge that joined the upper and lower part of Michigan. On completion of the bridge work, Jack was hired by the Federal Geological Survey Division's ground water branch to investi-gate and report on ground water conditions in New Jersey (1956-1961), Hawaii (1961-1969), and North Florida (1969-1985).

Jack is a member of several scientific organizations including the Geological Society of America, due to his strong aviation interests. While in the Marine Corps Jack flew many military aircraft including the famous S.B.D. Dive Bomber. He earned his private pilot certificate in March 1964, from flying out of Wheeler Field, Oahu, Hawaii. His Instrument Rating Certification was earned in north Florida in 1978. He received a promotion to Lt. Colonel on Dec 3, 1970 and retired on October

Jack Rosenau and Jean Rosenau

26, 1979 after almost 30 years of military service.

After an exciting career in aviation, Jack's remaining interests include membership in the Military Officer Association of America, the Marine Corps League, and the Saint Andrew's Society. The United States Coast Guard Auxiliary was a special organization for Jack and Jean Rosenau. They joined the "Flotilla 13" at Shell Point, Florida in April 1974 and offered their aircraft, [1968 model, Cherokee 150 (N-192FC)] for use in patrolling from Shell Point to the Coast Guard Station of New Orleans. Patrols were mostly flown on weekends for search and rescue of individuals and boats. Jack flew with an observer, usually Jean, or other members of the flotilla to help when possible.

Over a span of twenty-five years Jack has flown 550 patrols out of Tallahassee's airport. In appreciation for this dedication and having the safest flight record among Florida's pilots, the city of Tallahassee inducted him into their "Aviation Wall of Fame" on March 23, 2006.

Written by: Jack Rosenau; Submitted by: Robert Rosenau (son) 2634 Street Fair Lane Tallahassee, Florida 32317

Philip and Jennifer Rothschild

Philip Clayton Rothschild and Jennifer Lee Jolly Rothschild, current residents of Springfield, Missouri, lived in Tallahassee from 1991 until 1996 while Philip was a graduate student at Florida State University. He was a teaching associate and adjunct professor and earned a Ph. D in Organizational Communication/Management in 1996. Philip and Jennifer were members of Celebration Baptist Church in Tallahassee.

Philip, son of David and Diane Roesel Yates, was born November 22, 1963 in Melbourne, Brevard County, Florida. Jennifer, daughter of the Rev. Lawson and Judith Richbourg Jolly, was born December 19, 1963 in Clearwater, Pinellas County, Florida. They met during student days at Palm Beach Atlantic College in West Palm Beach, Florida and were married August 9, 1986 at First Baptist Church of Dade City, Pasco County, Florida, where Jennifer's father was pastor.

Philip served as Director of Student Development (1985- 1988) and Assistant Professor and Program Specialist (1988-1991) at Palm Beach Atlantic College. He earned a Master of Education degree in Human Resource Development at Florida Atlantic University in 1987. From 1996-1999, Philip was Assistant

Professor of Management and Business and Industry Outreach Liaison at Oklahoma Baptist University in Shawnee, Oklahoma. Philip is currently Tenured Assistant Professor of Management and Director, Entertainment Management Program at Missouri State University, College of Business Administration in Springfield.

During the years they lived in Tallahassee, Jennifer's career as a speaker and recording and concert artist placed her in many churches, conferences and events in Leon County and the surrounding area. Jennifer, a 1986 graduate of Palm Beach Atlantic College, is a nationally known personality with multiple television appearances and has been a featured guest of Women of Faith events. She currently hosts her own Fresh Grounded Faith conferences around the country. In addition, she is a prolific writer, having authored several books, including *Lessons I Learned in the Dark*, recently featured by the

Philip, Jennifer, Clayton and Connor Rothschild

Billy Graham Association. Her latest video series based on her book *Self Talk, Soul Talk* was released in early 2009.

Jennifer's loss of sight began when she was a young teenager in Miami, Florida. Her courage and achievement in the face of blindness have inspired and encouraged thousands. Her life is grounded and lived in the scripture promise, "We walk by faith and not by sight." In addition to a demanding speaking and writing schedule, Jennifer also maintains an online ministry through the publication of two monthly newsletters.

Jennifer and Philip are parents of two sons. Philip Clayton Rothschild, Jr. was born October 10, 1989 in West Palm Beach, Florida and is currently a freshman at Baylor University in Waco, Texas. Connor Lawson Rothschild was born December 9, 1998 in Shawnee, Oklahoma and is a fourth grade student at Wanda Gray Elementary School in Springfield.

Submitted by Philip Clayton Rothschild, Jr., Baylor University, Texas;
Written by Judith Richbourg Jolly, 11541 Arlhuna Way, Dade City, Florida 33525

Ruffin - Childhood Memories of Leon County

We moved to Bloxham around 1929 when I was about 5 years old, and lived in Leon County for about 10 years. Because my father, Claude Ruffin, was working on the completion of the hydroelectric power plant on the Ochlocknee River and Lake Talquin, we lived in housing provided for the workers at "Jackson's Bluff". Lake Talquin was named that because it was between the towns of Tallahassee and Quincy. My mother, Pearl Chennault Ruffin, had a fir over the housing, because the walls were not finished, there was no indoor plumbing and water had to be heated in a reservoir attached to the wood stove and drained from a spigot into a wash tub.

Mother grew tired of these living conditions, and we moved into the town of Tallahassee on Gaines Street near the Capitol building. I attended Caroline Brevard School, now known as The Bloxham Building. On "May Day", we spent the day at the city park where there were speeches and music. We children dressed as pioneers in colorful dresses and danced around the maypole using ribbons that matched our dresses.

The day the Barnum & Bailey Circus came to town we got up before dawn to see the animals brought off the train. There was no school that day, and we parked our car along the route as close to the ditch as possible so the wagons could pass by. We had an 'A' Model Ford but the isinglass curtains were missing so that the windows were open. The elephants sniffed us as they passed by, and I was afraid they would push our car into the ditch. The steam calliope shook the ground as it passed. We made "skateboards" by attaching roller skates to boards and skated on the sidewalks in town. At night the children sat under the street lights and told ghost stories.

Written by: Florence Moore, 14421 W. Seashell Court, Crystal River, FL 34429;
Submitted by: Mary Ann Machonkin, 19 Cupania Court, Homosassa, FL 34446

Anne Mae (Russell) Cavanaugh

Anne Mae Russell was born in Springhill, Florida on May 5, 1897. She joined the American War Mother (A.W.M.) organization in 1941. The

Anne Mae Russell-Cavanaugh in 1975, wearing her American War Mothers Sash

AWM was founded in 1917 during WWI by Alice Moore French. This National Organization was for mothers of young men and women who were in the armed forces. Her son, John had joined the army and later was a POW. In May near Mother's Day the ladies would distribute carnations to the public much like the American Legion Auxiliary distributes red poppies and the Veterans of Foreign Wars Auxiliary distributes blue poppies.

During WWII, she served as an airplane observer in 1941 through 1942. She lived on a high hill on Old Bainbridge Road, and could see a full sky from East to West, which made it an excellent spot for observing aircrafts. Long after the War she remained involved with the AWM, and from 1942 thru 1972. She held many offices within the organization. She was also a member of the American Legion Auxiliary Unit # 13 and served as the Civil Defense and National Security Chairperson for a few of those years. This unit is still active today and includes many of our family members who remain involved in its operations. Other organizations she was active in included the Junior Museum Guild, the Murat House Association, Democratic Women's Club, and The United Daughters of the Confederacy, The Tallahassee Garden Club, and The Christian Women's Club of Tallahassee. She was a long standing member of the First Baptist Church on College and Adams Street in Tallahassee.

In 1961 and 1962 she was Vice President and President for the State of Florida Chapter # 1 0 of The American War Mothers. During these years she was instrumental in organizing AWM Chapters in Miami (#17), and in Pensacola (#18). She also held the Presidential post at the AWM State Convention, but left this position on Oct 16, 1962. She became the National AWM Chaplain in 1965 and went on to be nominated the 4th Vice President in 1968 at the 26th annual National convention, and was endorsed by her local chapter (#10) in conformity with the national by-laws. Her local chapter presented her with the American Honor Award in 1968 for her life-long dedication.

At the age of seventy-five in 1972, she resigned as National second vice president of the American War Mothers. She was elected as the Committee Woman for the precinct #25 Leon County on the 10th of September 1974. Ann Cavanaugh remained active in her other organizations, as previously listed until around 1977. She left this life in 1984 at the age of eighty-seven. Everyone noticed she was gone and had taken all her good practices with her, but she will never be forgotten in the hearts and minds of this nation.

Submitted by Beverly Ashby 7764 Christy Cary Lane Tallahassee Fl 32304; Written by: Carolyn Losey (Maternal-granddaughter of Anne- Mae) 3379 Lakeview Drive, Tallahassee, Florida 32310

Vera Maude Richbourg Sanders

Vera Maude Richbourg, known as Maude, was the daughter of (Caswell) Joseph Tobin Richbourg and Elizabeth "Bettie" Johnson Richbourg. She was born in 1909 at Woodville, Leon County, Florida. Her family later moved to Hosford, Liberty County, Florida, and about 1920, to Clearwater, Pinellas County, Florida.

Maude Richbourg was married to Benjamin Frank "Sif" Sanders, son of Wilks and Mary Sanders. Frank was born December 2, 1899. Per his World War I draft registration, he had brown eyes, brown hair, and was of medium height and build. He was a farmer by occupation.

Maude Richbourg Sanders died in 1953 and Benjamin Frank Sanders died in 1959. They are buried at Ocoee Cemetery in Orange County, Florida. Their son, Charles Franklin "Sonny" Sanders, was born July 8, 1926 and died January 27, 1978. He and his wife, Frances Marion Holloway Sanders, were parents of two daughters, Candace Ann and Marsha Lynn.

Maude Richbourg (right) with sister, Allie, and brother, Wilson

Submitted by: Dr. Heyward Mathews, 109 Maplewood Avenue, Clearwater, Florida; Written by: Judith Richbourg Jolly, 11541 Arlhuna Way, Dade City, Florida 33525

The Sapronetti Artists

If you visit downtown Tallahassee on Saturday, you often find a host of artists displaying their works in the park (along Park Avenue). Many, such as the Sapronetti's, are local artists specializing in a wide range of art forms. The Sapronetti Artists have become known for their North Florida landscape & wildlife paintings and for their Native American jewelry. By 2009, some of their works had been featured in *GOD, St Marks Calendar*, the *TCC International Photo Calendar*, and *The Best of Florida Artist Series*. They had also won numerous contests including the *FSU International Calendar* in 2008. Most do not realize this husband & wife team are long-time Tallahassee residents who have contributed much to preserve the local history and capture our unique habitat.

Eric Anthony Sapronetti, born 1962 in Akron, OH, to parents Nancy A. Windows Sapronetti Shoaps and Richard Lee Sapronetti. He has a rich Italian heritage through his grandparents. Paolo "Paul" Sapronetti, was born in 1890 and immigrated from Acqapendente, Italy to New York City in 1907. Paul then moved to Akron, OH, and in 1922 he married Mary Jean Antonucci (born 1907). Eric's family moved from Ohio to Tallahassee, Florida in 1980. He graduated from Leon High School and from Florida State University with a BA in Art Education. His artistic talents first received recognition in the early 80's in the area of photography and later for his paintings.

Susan Patricia Howard was born' in 1965 in Tallahassee, FL and she married Eric in 1983. As the daughter of Franklin Delano Howard and Mary Frances Halley Howard (from Blountstown, FL), Susan has a Native American Muskogee Creek ancestry and is very passionate about preserving her heritage through art. Susan is a multi-talented artist with skills in photography, painting, beadworks and jewelry making. After graduating from Leon High School, she received a degree in Photography from Lively Vo-Tech and attended college art classes. She was a member of the Apalachee Archaeological Society and she has been published in *The Florida Anthropologist* {Volume 41.3,9/88). Her artistic talents first received recognition in the late 70s in

Eric and Susan Sapronetti, 2009

photography and acrylic paintings, and later for her Native American beadwork.

Both are members of the FSU Artists' League and have taken active roles in preserving local history, especially the St. Marks Lighthouse. On Lighthouse Day you can find them giving historical presentations. During the first years of their marriage, they photographed many of the old regional tobacco barns which have now been destroyed. Over the years, they have continued to tour the North Florida area and capture its beauty and uniqueness in photographs and paintings.

Susan's animal paintings have a fine attention to detail and realism and her landscapes are rich with Florida beach and woodland scenes. Susan gets inspiration for many of her pieces from studying Native American motifs. She is very versatile in her techniques for beading with a number of different stitches including brick, gourd, ladder and loom-work.

Eric's paintings are prized for their vivid colors and detail. As a Christian, Eric derives great inspiration from God's creations. He considers God to be the Ultimate Artist. Eric's painted scenes of the North Florida coastline incorporate a mixture of coastal flats, mossy oaks, pines and palms as well as sandy beaches. He has a passion for saltwater fishing and loves to paint the subjects he catches.

Over the years they have worked together on many jobs, including portrait photography, photographing houses for *Homes and Land Magazine*, as well as selling art in the park at the Downtown Market and at the cannery in Havana/FL. To learn more, visit their website www.littletownmart.com/activecreations.

Written and submitted by: Marie and Julia Sapronetti, 2640 Stonegate Rd., Tallahassee/ Fl 32308

Eric Anthony Sapronetti

Eric A. Sapronetti was born Sept 19, 1962 in Akron, OH. His parents are Richard Lee Sapronetti and Nancy Alice Windows-Sapronett Shoaps. Eric graduated from Leon High School in Tallahassee, Florida in 1981.

He joined the Army National Guard and was stationed at Fort Leonard Wood, Missouri from January 1982 until March of 1982. From April 1982 through July 1982 he was stationed at Fort Sam Houston, Texas. His unit was deployed from there to Camp Blanding in Stark, Florida and then to Fort Bliss in El Paso, Texas for his annual summer training. He served in the 494th medical detachment for the Florida National Guard, where he continued to serve until his honorable discharge in 1987.

Eric Sapronetti in his military service uniform in 1982

He married Susan Howard in 1983. They now have three children.

Submitted by; Eric Sapronetti, 2918 Pearl Dr., Tallahassee, Florida 32312

The Sauls Family of Old Tallahassee

James Dewitt Sauls homesteaded in Wakulla County, FL (1839). Upon learning a group of young women in Thomas County, GA were looking for husbands, he went, met, and married Sarah Galbraith. She died in 1842 giving birth to James Robert Sauls. James Dewitt served in the Florida Light Artillery, Dyke's Company, during the War Between the States. His entire adult life, he farmed in Wakulla County. He married twice again, and fathered nine more children.

His second wife bore Lee (1845), James Dewitt, Jr. (1847), AB (1849), Carrie (1851), and Elizabeth (1853) and his third bore William (1856), Ellen (1858), Mattie (1860), and Florida (1862).

James Robert Sauls (1842), first son of James Dewitt Sauls, Sr. was born in Crawfordville, FL. He was enlisted in the 1st Florida Infantry (1861); later listed on the Muster Roll, Company M, 1st Regiment, Florida Regulars, Army of Tennessee, CSA; taken prisoner, but allowed to 'go home to plant crops'; and discharged from service at Point Lookout, MD, 1865.

In West Virginia, he married Manerva A. Clay (1862), daughter of Henry Clay and Martha Miller. Manerva's family included well-known statesmen and politicians, including 2nd cousin Senator Henry Clay of Kentucky. James became a logger/lumberman and they raised their children, James Martin (1863), Henry LeRoy, Mary C., Mary Martha Staunton (adopted), William Reilly, Martha Elizabeth, Charles Edward, John Albert, Gilbert Arthur, Walter, George Paris (a/k/a Gerald P.).

They brought first son James Martin and Charles Edward and William Reilly with their families to Crawfordville, FL (1903). After the winter of 1904, they moved east of Tallahassee to Magnolia Heights (East Park Avenue, now). James Martin built a house there (still standing in 1998).

In 1905, William Reilly and family returned to West Virginia. Manerva returned to Saulsville, W.VA.

James Robert lived with Martin until 1907 and was buried in Crawfordville alongside his Father,

James Dewitt. James Martin and Charles Edward died in Tallahassee. James Dewitt Sauls, Jr., married Martha Ann "Mattie" Hopkins about 1869. Their children were Annah Leone "Annie" (1873-1950) and Henry R. (1874-1945). They are first cousins to James Martin Sauls. Annah married Charles A. McPherson.

Henry R. Sauls and Fannie Hill (1877-1918) begat Clyde R. (1907-1940). Clyde married Ruby [1908-c.1980]). Clyde was a Leon County Deputy Sheriff. He and another Deputy were killed serving a warrant on McComb Street in Tallahassee.

Henry and Fannie begat Lawrence Patrick (1918-1981), who married Arlene Hicks [c.1920]). Their infant, L. P., died at childbirth (1946).

Henry married Mattie Gilbert (c. 1900-c. 1965), and their infant, H.R., died 1923.

James Martin Sauls (1863-1937, Tallahassee) married Mary Ann Chafins in West Virginia (c.1883). She bore his son, Gerald Edward (1886-1950) and another son. He married Willie Jane (Mamie) Jarrell about 1890 in West Virginia, a descendant of John Fitz Jerrell who emigrated to Virginia from Ireland in the late 1600s. Her parents were Callows Jarrell and Harriett Toney (Jarrell).

While young, Martin was an advance man for the circus (speculated to be Buffalo Bill's Wild West Show) setting dates, arranging sites, and advertising. He traveled to Florida and San Francisco, from whence he got employed on a ship going to London and back to New York.

Martin moved Mamie and their children to Florida in 1903, farmed for a year, and then worked as a carpenter until 1914. He worked for the State Drainage Board (1914- 1926), digging flood control canals about the Everglades. He owned an automobile repair garage 1927-1937. He served in the Florida National Guard.

Martin and Mamie produced eight children: Paul "Pap" Vane (1891), Pauline Bennett (1894), James Robert (1896), Claude Lorraine (1899), Victor Hugo (1901), Frank Black (1904), Charles Edward (1908), and Alfred Carl "Cooter" 1902).

Martin Sauls had a farm in 1910. He was featured in the *Florida* newspaper for having a 2-headed cow born on his farm.

When Martin sailed Cape Horn, he wrote a Journal for Mamie - in an exquisite handwriting, with many flowers he drew. Some of his writings appear to be poems or songs. On March 7, 1885, the title *The Girl I Left Behind* was drawn into a vine of flowers; 4 numbered verses followed. On the next page, he wrote *Little Log Cabin in the Larre*. And page 90 shows *Popular 0 Sing to me robin*, viz: "0 sing to me robin the bright sun is shining ... " He signed the bottom of that page James M Sauls.

Martin and Mamie's son, Paul Vane "Pap" Sauls, married Florence Rose Ellis (1912). They begat Paul Vane Sauls, Jr., who, with Jessie Lee Strickland beg at Marvin Francis Sauls (Married County Commissioner Jane Carolyn Grissett Sauls), Marjorie Ann Sauls (Married Ronald Hartsfield, Jr.), and Carl Dallas (Deceased/Married Nancy A. Basile).

At 18 years of age, Pap substituted for his father, Martin, as a Watchman for the Post Office January 8, 1910. Two men intending to rob the Post Office got into a gun battle with Pap. One of the bandits was Garber "Tennessee Dutch" Moore, a Clarksville, TN, native with a long police record. Pap got a flesh wound in the arm, and had a hand-to-hand struggle with Garber, but came out the hero by killing both robbers. President Woodrow Wilson recognized Pap for his heroism.

Pap was a carpenter/foreman on the forest service's Silver Lake project. Silver Lake was the site of many summer camps and a popular swimming site out Highway 20 West.

Martin and Mamie's son, Claude Lorraine Sauls, was a World War II hero for whom the local American Legion Sauls-Bridges Post 13 is named. Corporal Sauls was with Company C 6th U.S. Infantry, 5th Division A.E.F. He was killed in action at St. Michel France, September 14, 1918, at the age of 19. He joined the army after graduating from Leon High School (1917). He is buried in the Sauls family plot in the Old City Cemetery north of Brevard Street.

Martin and Mamie's son CharlesEdward Sauls received special honors as an inductee into the Leon High School Hall
of Fame. He was a member of the Old Tallahassee City Baseball Team in 1927. He played ball with Bob Parrimore [sic], Charlie Paulus, Ralph Powell, Alex Howard, Jac Yeager, Paul Appleyard, Ralph Swatts, Leon Langston, Buddy Walker, Sam Register, and Felix Walker, and a couple other young Tallahassee men. Ed also was a member of the University of Florida 1928 Championship Football Team. He was a Leesburg High School principal, a football coach, and School Superintendent in Lake County, FL.

Sister of Paul Vane, Jr., is Enid Gwendolyn (1913-1995) who married Benjamin Bond Stoutamire (1909-1966). Their daughter is Benita Gail (1939).

Written and Submitted by: Dorothy Lee (Dotty) McPherson 24236 Lanier St., Tallahassee, FL 32310; Sources: 20 Faces and Places, A History of the People of Highway 20 and the Ochlocknee River Area and numerous documents at the Florida Archives, South Bronaugh St,

John Archibald Sanders/Saunders

John Archibald Sanders/Saunders was born 21 November 1871 and died 21 February 1953. His family emigrated from Greene County, NC to FL in 1847. Josephus Starkweather, his wife, Martha (Deal/Deale), and their four children settled in Leon County. Their fifth child was born there. The only census in which his father,

John Durance Sanders/ Saunders, is listed is 1870 Wakulla Co., FL. He was age 40, born in

FL. His wife Phoebe (marred December 21, 1865 in Leon County), and daughters, Annie Eulalia and Eunice Unarell, are included.

John Durrance enlisted 6 May 1862 in Milton's Light Artillery, Santa Rosa County, FL. He was present on roll July and August 1864, the last on file. At the close of the war, he was at home sick. No more is known by his compiler of John Durrance Sanders' parents, siblings, etc. John Archibald knew his father only three years before he passed October 7, 1874. Phoebe, a master seamstress, supported her family by walking to and from Tallahassee to sew her clients.

Eunice (16 Oct 1868-21 Sept 1920) married 9 January 1887 in Leon County William J. Dykes (c 1854-15 Feb 1918). To them nine children were born. William and Eunice are buried in Rhodes Family Cemetery, north of Woodville in Leon County. Eulalia Ann (8 Nov 1866-31 Mar 1924) married 23 December 1885 in Leon County Perry Lee Boatwright (April 1866-October 1912). To them five children were born. Annie and Perry are buried in the Old City Cemetery in Tallahassee.

After attaining adulthood, John went to Jacksonville where he met and married Miss Maude E. Dye on Christmas Day 1895. She was one of two known daughters of Jasper Newton and Catherine Elizabeth (possibly Riles) Dye. John and Maude's first child, Ruth L., was born 15 September 1896, presumably in Duval County. A son, Jasper Durant, was born 12 August 1898 according to the 1900 US Federal Census for Leon County and his headstone in Rhodes Family Cemetery. He was born in Tallahassee. His death certificate and World War I Military File give 12 July 1898 as his date of birth. Ruth apparently died before the 1900 census as Maude said she had two children and only one living. No grave has been found for Ruth, and the family is not sure when John and Maude left Jacksonville for Leon County. On 7 July 1900, a second son, Clarence Homer, was born in Leon County. Unfortunately, Maude died 19 January 1901. She is buried in Rhodes Family Cemetery. No Florida death certificate for 1900, 1901 or 1902 has been found.

Son Jasper was a Private 1st Class in the US Army in World War I. He served overseas 7 October 1918-27 April 1919. He enlisted in the National Guard in Duval County 6 July 1917 and was honorably discharged 12 May 1919. He married Maude D. Smith 24 July 1920 in Duval County. Their issue: daughter, J. Deanie, born c1924, and son, Jasper Durant Saunders, Jr., born 18 August 1925, both presumably in Duval County. Nothing more is known of Deanie. Jasper, Jr. died 10 September 1996 in Broward County, FL. Jasper, Sr. was killed 18 June 1930 in Duval County by a gunshot to the abdomen. The incident was ruled a homicide, and an autopsy was performed. He is buried in Rhodes Family Cemetery with a military headstone supplied by the Federal Government. The Headstone Application was signed 25 June 1930 by Mrs. Maude Saunders of 3834 Jean Street, Jacksonville, Duval County, FL.

Clarence Homer (or Homer Clarence) was born 4 July 1900. In the 1920 Duval County Census he was employed by the Jacksonville Ship Yard as a Pipe Fitter. He later worked at the Claude Nolan Cadillac dealership in Jacksonville. His first wife, Lotteese Maria (Ritter), daughter of Duval County Commissioner and Mrs. W.R. Ritter, Sr., was born 6 March 1897 in Jacksonville and died 29 May 1972. She rests in Evergreen Cemetery in Jacksonville. They were married in Duval County 24 August 1918. Their only known child, Harold Ritter Saunders was born 31 October 1919, Jacksonville, and died 13 August 1971. He also lies in Evergreen. His second wife was Mazie Passut. They married 3 February 1921 in Duval County. Clarence was killed 9 June 1922 in an automobile accident near Evergreen Cemetery. He is buried in Rhodes Family Cemetery.

John moved his sons to Duval County, worked for S.B. Hubbard Company as a Tinner, and preached in area Baptist churches. At one church he sang a solo, and the young lady

John A. Saunders

playing the piano later became his bride. Alma Victoria Parrish (12 April 1894-9 Jan 1984) was only 15 when she became his wife on 2 January 1910 and the mother of two young boys, ages 10 and 12. They were married in her parents' home in Whitehouse, Duval County.

When his health began to fail, the doctor suggested he leave the "big city" and move to the country. About 1923, the family moved from the Westconnett area of Jacksonville to Middleburg, Clay County, FL. They purchased 10 acres and began truck farming; but, he just wasn't a farmer. He was a preacher and, he followed this vocation. He was ordained 8 October 1908 in Woodlawn Baptist Church in Jacksonville and was instrumental in organizing several Baptist churche in the Duval/Clay areas. He preached when and where he could and often took his firstborn son to weddings, funerals and services he performed. He pastored Wesconnett Baptist Church from October 1910 to September 1912 and was their fourth pastor. He also pastored Middleburg Baptist Church for many years.

At age 82, while eating dinner, he choked on a piece of meat and died soon thereafter in Dr. Bergh's Clinic in Orange Park. He is buried next to his parents, first wife and their two sons in Rhodes Family Cemetery. Together, John and Alma reared his sons by Maude and their seven children with love, discipline, compassion, hard work, family values and a deep love of God.

Submitted by Patricia Ann Parkinson, Granddaughter, 19106 Player Park Drive, Humble, TX 77346; Sources: Census, Cemetery, and Legal records; Westconnett Baptist Church Archives

Rev. John A. Saunders

My grandfather, a Baptist minister, was a tireless worker for God and his beliefs. He was well-liked and well-respected throughout the community.

For many years he was pastor of the Middleburg Baptist Church in Clay County, Florida. Following his death the Memorial Committee of the church wrote a beautiful tribute to his life and ministry. It is lovingly included here.

"God in His infinite wisdom saw fit to remove from our midst our brother in Christ, Rev. J.A. Saunders, Feb. 21, 1953.

"In his death we lose a devoted Christian and believe our loss is his eternal gain.

"We pray that his life of leadership and counsel may be an inspiration to all who knew him.

Brother Saunders was born Nov. 21, 1871 at Woodville, Florida. He was converted and united with the Woodville Baptist Church at an early age. He came to Jacksonville, Florida about 1890 and married Miss Maude Dye in 1895. To this union three children were born. He and his family returned to Tallahassee and lived for several years. During this time his wife died, in the year 1900.

"He became a licensed minister, working in the churches of Leon County. He married Miss Alma Parish in 1910 and to this union seven children were born.

"He was ordained at Woodlawn Baptist Church, Jacksonville, Florida, October 8, 1908. Brother Saunders was instrumental in organizing several churches in and near Jacksonville.

"He moved to Middleburg, Florida in December 1921. He was a member of the Middleburg Baptist Church and served as pastor for many years. He was a member of Black Creek Association and served as a member of the Executive Committee.

"Brother Saunders was an outstanding man of our denomination, a Christian gentleman of highest rank and order, having faithfully, efficiently served the denomination in giving the best years of his life to his church.

John and Alma Saunders

"Therefore Be It Resolved:

"First, that we, the Memorial Committee for the Middleburg Baptist Church, do hereby express a deep sense of loss in the homegoing of this good servant of Christ. "Second, that a copy of these resolutions be included in our minutes of the Middleburg Baptist Church, a copy be published in the *Florida Baptist Witness* and a copy sent to the family.

"Submitted in Love, Mrs. H.A. Master, Mrs. L.C. Canova, Jr. and Mrs. Galdys Mann."

My grandfather was the father of ten and the Shepherd of many. We are saddened not to known him longer.

Submitted by: Patricia Ann Parkinson, Granddaughter, 19106 Player Park Drive, Humble, TX 77346; Source: Florida Baptist Witness, March 1953

Daniel Seitz, Native American Engineer

Daniel (Dan) Seitz was born October 30, 1939 in Columbus, Franklin County, Ohio. He is the only child of William Charles Seitz (1913-1955) and Helen Jeretta Holden (1913-1962). Daniel has two half brothers from his father's second marriage: Donny (FL) and Billy (TX), with whom he maintains close ties. Dan's mother, Helen H. Seitz has eleven siblings and is a Native American, daughter of Chief Whitehead of the Blackfoot tribe. Dan's father, William is of German decent, has four brothers, and his surname means "glassmaker" in German. The Seitz are considered to be related to the Zsar of Russia family.

Daniel Seitz, 2009

As an only child Dan spent a lot of time alone, so he spent most of his time tinkering with small engines. His family found him to be mechanically inclined and saw that he could fix almost anything that ran with a motor. As he grew up, his family encouraged him to use this gift to further his career.

Dan graduated from John Burrow Grade School (1954), West High School (1956), and Ohio State University (1968). After spending two years in college Dan joined the army in 1963 to receive more vocational training in mechanics from the Army Officer's Candidate School (OCS). After completion he was promoted to the rank of Captain. With an honorable discharge under his belt, Dan returned to Ohio State Univer-sity, where he received his BS in Electri-cal Engi-neering. His first job was with Owen Coming's Fiberglass Company in Newark, Ohio. With his career well established, Dan met and married Patricia Fulk in Florida and they had two children, Stacy and Daniel, Jr. His second marriage was to Sarah Harvey and they had two children, Joseph and Sarah, plus Dan adopted her three children from a previous marriage. Today Dan has a total of seven children, twenty-two grandchildren and three great grandchildren. During the 70s and 80's Dan moved his family around gaining a vast amount of experience in mechanical engineering, and ended up living in Lakeland, Florida in 1987 with his second family. In 1995 he moved to Mobile/Alabama and worked for different engineering contractors for over 10 years, until he was forced to retire due to health in 2005. Due to the effects of hurricane Katrina, Dan arrived in Tallahassee during the later part of 2005 and has found unlimited opportunity to practice his mechanical skill during his retirement years by volunteering his services in repairing the mechanical problems of his church, repairing his neighbors' cars; and giving advice on mechanical problems to strangers. He is well known in the community for always being willing to give a hand to stranded motorists. Dan enjoys living in Leon County's tempered climate, and the warm heart of his new neighborhood has made living here more satisfying. He also enjoys spending time with his grandchildren and visiting with his family on the holidays. He is a member of the Wildwood Presbyterian Church. His .hobbies include fishing, hunting, and mechanics. Because Dan has been a true friend and reliable neighbor, we all wish him long life and prosperity.

Written by: Carol D. Johnson; Submitted by: Dan Seitz, 214 Columbia drive # A-1, Tallahassee, FL 32304

Shackleford-Dowery

Most of my Shackleford ancestors are from Greene County, North Carolina, where many relatives currently live. However, this story is about me, Evelyn Faye Shackleford Dowery, and my little family unit which is well grounded in Tallahassee. My daughter, Sharma Adiya Shackleford, was almost two years old when we moved to Tallahassee in 1984. It was just the two of us. We were moving from Ft. Rucker, Alabama, transitioning from military life to civilian life. Although I was born and raised in Snow Hill (Greene County), North Carolina, I went out of state to attend college (Hampton Institute in Virginia). After graduating, I accepted a commission as an officer in the Army Medical Specialist Corp. I had grown accustomed to relocating about every three years and assumed that, most likely, Tallahassee would be a temporary location. It reminded me of the small-town, rural life, and southern hospitality that I grew up with and that we enjoyed in the

Evelyn Shackleford and Sharma Shackleford, 1984

communities surrounding Ft. Rucker. I had not anticipated the events or milestones that would shape our lives and result in us making Tallahassee our home.

Other than my daughter Sharma, I knew one other person in Tallahassee. That individual was Mr. Bert Boldt, owner of Tallahassee Physical Therapy and Rehab Services. During a job interview, he assured me that not only was Tallahassee a beautiful city, but it was also a great place to raise children. I accepted the job with his company as a physical therapist and began the process of settling down in Tallahassee.

The very first church that Sharma and I visited was University Church of Christ on Thomasville Road (currently Capital City Church of Christ). I studied the Bible and was baptized as a disciple of Jesus Christ, according to what I had gleaned from my studies. I became a Christian in Tallahassee and have been a part of the same church family for 25 years. Sharma was a long-time participant in the *Kingdom Kids* program. She studied the Bible as a teenager and became a Christian in Tallahassee. Sharma attended public schools in Leon County. She entered kindergarten at Killearn Lakes Elementary School, and was later re-zoned for DeSoto Trail Elementary. She went to Deerlake Middle School, and completed the International Baccalaureate Program at Rickards High School in 2000.

Russell and Evelyn Dowery, FSU Graduation 1994

After touring about 8 or 9 colleges from Michigan to states along the Atlantic seaboard, she enrolled at Florida State University. Sharma had a wonderful experience at FSU and graduated in August 2003 with a B.S. degree in Mass Media. She left home to attend graduate school at the University of Central Florida where she graduated with a Master's Degree in Communications in December 2004. We have always enjoyed learning, and seemingly could not stay away from the classroom! During the years that Sharma was enjoying grade school I was enrolled in graduate school at FSU. With the help of the Lord, I received the Doctor of Education degree in Higher Education in 1994 in Tallahassee.

Family photo: Russell, Evelyn Dowery Shackleford and Sharma, 1997

When Sharma was 10 years old her life changed dramatically, as she has often said. In 1990, Russell Dowery became a Christian at the same church that Sharma and I attended. We were married on June 13, 1992, at Tallahassee (formerly University) Church of Christ and, from the perspective of a 10-year-old, she was losing her mom. She later grew to understand that she had actually gained a father. Russell was a retired Army Chief Warrant Officer whom I met while completing a tour of duty at Landstuhl Army Medical Center in Germany in 1979. He was born and raised in Charlotte, North Carolina, prior to joining the Army at age 17, and lived in El Paso, TX for many years. Sharma was actually born in El Paso. However, this city is very special to us because we became a family, in Tallahassee.

Written and Submitted by: Evelyn S. Dowery, 3445 Paces Ferry Road Tallahassee, Florida 32309
dowery@comcast.net

Richard Alexander Shine, Builder of Tallahassee

Richard Shine was one of Tallahassee's leading pioneers. He is listed as voter number 58 for Tallahassee in 1829. He built Tallahassee literally, politically, militarily and religiously. He was Tallahassee's leading builder of homes and civic buildings, in the 1830s to 1860s. He served in the 1840s on the city council. He also served in the Territorial Legislature as well as the State House after statehood as a member of the Whig party. Richard served as captain in the Leon Riflemen and was an elder in the First Presbyterian Church in the 1840s.

Richard had a large brickyard in Tallahassee. Best that I can determine, using vague descriptions, the brickyard was located between Leon High School and Goodwood Plantation. This area also has the clay needed for making bricks. He supplied bricks for building the First Presbyterian Church and the capitol building built in 1845. He was contractor on several of the downtown historic homes extant as well as for Goodwood Plantation. The historic marker in front of the Bloxham House at 410 N. Calhoun St. lists him as the builder. The Chittenden House on Park Ave., then 200 Foot Road, is said to have been built by Richard with materials from the Capitol building that was torn down. One of his most notable engineering feats is the "deep cut" or "long cut" for the railroad where it runs under Magnolia Dr. by the Tallahassee Democrat. This was done in the late 1850's and early 1860's just before the War Between the States. He also engineered and rebuilt the railroad to St. Marks. In 1843 most of downtown Tallahassee burned. It was determined that rebuilding should be done using bricks. Richard Shine supplied most of the bricks in this rebuilding effort. Richard, also had losses during this fire. He was part owner in buildings that housed businesses on the west side of Monroe street. They were A.M. Hobby, M.L. Baker, Sentinel Office, Ward and White's law office, Ward and May's Saddlery. He was also part owner in buildings that housed businesses on Clinton Street (now College Ave.); Thompson and Hagner's law offices, F. Flagg's watch shop and Life and Trust Bank.

Richard Alexander Shine (courtesy of Florida Photographic Collection)

Richard Shine also helped build the population of Tallahassee. He and his wife, Mary Ann had 10 children. His son, R.A. Shine, Jr., was a local business man and a county tax collector. His son, William Francis Shine, was a prominent surgeon for the Confederate Army during the War Between the States. His son, Francis Eppes Shine, was also a doctor. Three of Richard Senior's sons married 3 of Francis Eppes' daughters. Francis Eppes was the grandson of Thomas Jefferson and the founder of what was to become Florida State University, and was six times mayor of Tallahassee both before and after statehood. Richard Shine Senior's direct descendants are full of medical doctors, with some buried at Monticello, the Jefferson home in Virginia. Richard Shine Senior is buried in the Old City Cemetery. His tomb along with his wife and other family members is on the "Walking Tour" and is featured on the front of the Walking Tour brochure. These tombs are very distinctive in that they are double arched and have carved tablets for the enclosures. These tombs are just inside the gate as you enter the cemetery off of Martin Luther King Blvd.

My lineage with Richard Shine is through my 6th great granddad, Maj. Daniel Shine born 1690. He was Richard Shine's great granddad. Richard's granddad was John Shine born 1725.

Richard Shine tomb. on walking tour Old City Cemetery (courtesy of www.findagrave.com)

His dad was Frances Stringer Shine born 1760. My line, of course, is more lengthy. My mother is Mary Frances Andrews Pearson. She came to Tallahassee with her mother and father back in the 1930's. Her mother was Mary Rebecca Wilkinson Andrews. Mary Rebecca was the daughter of John Lawrence Wilkinson, CSA. He moved to Wakulla County in 1903 from Sumter County, Georgia.

His children attended the school in Woodville. His line follows the Shine line through his mother, Elizabeth Jane Miller Wilkinson. Her mother was Sarah Williams Shine Miller. Sarah's father was John Shine, born 1759, who served in the Revolutionary Army. His dad was Daniel Shine born 1729. His mother was Barbara Franck who was friends with George Washington and had him in her home when he toured the States. Daniel Shine, born 1729, and his dad was Maj. Daniel Shine born 1690.

My own personal history in Tallahassee starts when I was born at Tallahassee Memorial Hospital in 1956 to Lawrence Murray Pearson and Mary Frances Andrews Pearson. I attended Leonard Wesson School and Tallahassee Christian Schools. I lived at 112 Polk Drive until I went off to school in Lynchburg, Virginia in 1973. There I met my wife the former Sallie (Penny) Pendleton Eubank. When Penny and I first met, my sister Lauren asked her when was her birthday, she said Feb. 22, 1956. This being my birthday as well, my sister thought she was fooling around. When we compared our birth certificates we found out she was born an hour and 33 minutes before me. We moved back to Tallahassee after being married June 12, 1976, the U.S.A. bicentennial year. After about four months we moved to Wakulla Station in Wakulla County. My history with Tallahassee does not stop there. I have continued to work in Tallahassee ever since. My son Kent and daughter Carrie were both born at Tallahassee Memorial Hospital. My daughter is now attending TCC and working in Tallahassee as well. My mother still owns the house I grew up in on Polk Drive and still lives in Leon County. My youngest brother Dana also still lives in Leon County.

I am proud to know that my family has not only been a builder of Tallahassee but of our nation as well. I have at least 2 ancestors that fought in the Revolutionary Army. My 6th great grandparents were the first settlers of New Bern, South Carolina from Germany and my Andrews ancestors were pioneers to Holmes County, Florida.

Submitted by: Shawn Pearson, 4521 Bloxham Cut Of Road, Crawfordville, Florida 32327

Superintendent Owen Smith (1909-1981)

Superintendent Owen Smith was born July 9, 1906 in Samson, Alabama. He was the second child born to the late Judge and Beretta Artery-Smith. When he was five years of age, there were many things he could see that his parents could not see. When he was seven years of age, his father moved to a small town called Glendale, Florida. He married when he was young to Miss Earnestine Green in Crestview, Florida. He became the father of one son, Richard Lee Smith

Superintendent Smith lived the life of a sinner until 1933. In that year he had a vision and saw 27 years of his life wasted, so by 1940 he gave his life to God and he was saved and baptized with the Holy Ghost and fire on April 18, 1933 about 1:30 a.m. He spoke in tongues according to Acts 2:4. Another part of his life that he would never forget was how God saved him from drowning three times. This too made him want to be a Christian. He used to say; "I wish I could tell the world what God has done for me though His power and the Holy Ghost."

In 1934, God called him to minister, and he heard the call, but would not answer. He waited until 1940, and God called on him again; then he answered the call in the city of Tallahassee, Florida. After moving to Tallahassee, Florida and soon afterward he began pastoring. While he had his health and strength, he served as Pastor of both Watson Temple Church of God in Christ for 3 years and Midway Church of God in Christ for 11 years. He continued to try to pastor the two churches, but his health was failing. He had to give up the churches in Midway and Tallahassee before God could heal him.

In 1953, the Lord led Supt. Smith to build Him a house of worship. The Lord blessed this work to be completed, which was called University Church of God in Christ located at corner of Poppy Street and Osceola Street. Supt. Smith pastured there for 29 years. He also worked with the Southern Leadership Conference and served as Chaplain for Florida A&M University Hospital. Elder Smith was an active member of the Tallahassee Urban League, the

Superintendent Owen Smith

Interdenominational Ministerial Alliance and the National Association for the Advancement of Colored People (NAACP).

Supt. Smith is known to the Leon County Big Bend area as "Granddaddy", and his legacy still lives on in the Smith- Williams Center on Pasco Street and in numerous Lambs that are now Rams such as Barbara Hines, P Ed., of First Baptist Church in Tallahassee, Michael Moore, Esquire, Charles E. Richardson, MD, Judge Joseph Lewis Jr. and many others.

Written and submitted by: Barbara Hines, 735 Bob Miller Road Crawfordville, FL. 32327

William Godfrey Smith

Tributes to the life of Godfrey Smith can be found in the *Tallahassee Democrat* during the city's mourning of Godfrey's death. Just two months before his demise on November 9, 1999, the Capital City Rotary Club allowed Mr. Smith the opportunity to hear what his life had been all about — his integrity, his honesty, and his banking professionalism. A standing ovation surrounded this 85 year-old individual who was considered the most influential person for the city's growth in the last half century. This civic organization bestowed upon Godfrey Smith the honor of being the first recipient of the Bill Duggar Professional Integrity Award. Godfrey's family did not have to wait until his death to have these attributes be recognized and once again be brought to the community's attention. This award did so. He was so widely admired for his modesty, down-to-earth nature, and warmth to people from all walks of life.

William Godfrey Smith was born in Tallahassee on March 18, 1914, in a home at the northwest corner of Gadsden Street and Virginia Street. It was about 1915 when the family moved into their home on Park Avenue. A brother Julian was born into the family soon after. Godfrey's father died in 1928, and his mother Fannie Wilson Smith maintained this home. His son Bill and wife Paula presently live at the residence.

Trinity Methodist Church records reveal Godfrey's baptism on May 16, 1915. Caroline Brevard was his elementary school. A favorite story he would tell about elementary school was that lots of boys wanted to go home with him for lunch because he had "meat between the bread". As times were so tough during the depression, he said that friends would bring a sweet potato to school for lunch. Godfrey was the mainstay of the offensive line on the Leon High football team, playing the center position at 150 pounds.

William Godfrey Smith, Captain, U.S. Army

He graduated from Leon, then went to the University of Florida. While at the University, Godfrey was a member of Florida Blue Key and president of Kappa Alpha fraternity. On the day of his graduation in 1937 he received a job offer by way of a phone call from Sam Teague, bank president at the time. Work began the next day!

During World War II he entered the Army as a second lieutenant. As aide to General Kastin, who was the Chief of Finance for the Army Air Corps, Godfrey was stationed at the Pentagon. His rank progression proceeded rapidly, and after fewer than five years in the Army he returned home a Lieutenant Colonel.

He met Patricia Louise Hill at the Tallahassee Woman's Club at a wedding reception for one of her sorority sisters. They were married November 9, 1946, in Jacksonville (Patty's hometown) at the Christian Science Church on Riverside

William Godfrey Smith, 1999

Avenue. Godfrey and Patty built a home in 1950 on Magnolia Drive where they raised two sons, William Godfrey Smith, Jr., and Robert Hill Smith.

Written and submitted by: E. Lynn McLarty, 2102 Olivia Drive Tallahassee, Florida 32308

Lydia Suzannah Stafford

Lydia Suzannah Stafford was born 1806 in Leon County, Florida, the daughter of Ellis Stafford, an original land owner under the Spanish rule of Florida. She married Edward Lemuel Howard in Tallahassee, Leon County, Florida in 1827. She had two children with him, Andrew Jackson Howard and a daughter who was said to have been killed during an Indian raid.

Edward Lemuel Howard was a sailor (who had been a powder monkey during War of 1812), but was "accidentally" drowned on the Ocella River in 1832. He was killed when a wooden oar hit him on the back of head while he was in a boat. Lydia remarried a second time in Thomas County, Georgia to Esom Davenport Franklin. He died in 1842. She then remarried a third time to James Younger, a stevedore born in New York and they appeared on the 1850 Census in Franklin County, Florida. Lydia's son, Andrew Jackson Howard married Martha Ann Franklin (daughter of Esom D. Franklin) in 1857 in Liberty County, Florida.

Andrew and his family appeared on the 1860 Census in Wakulla County, Florida as a carpenter (who helped build and lived in the lighthouse there). They appeared on the 1870 Census of Gadsden County, Florida, but migrated to Anacoco, Vernon Parish, Louisiana, where they appeared on the 1880 Census, with Lydia Franklin living with them. So, it seems that Lydia disappeared from the 1860 and the 1870 Censuses and it is said that she had remarried twice more, to a Thigpen and a Thomas, but I can find no proof of that. She applied for 1812 widow's pension from both her first two husbands, in 1887 in Anacoco, Vernon Parish, Louisiana, but was denied the pension for both as she had remarried after them. Lydia disappeared again after 1880, and is said to have died in Anacoco, Vernon Parish, Louisiana at the age 104. Some say she lived to be 110 years old, but no matter how old she was, she had quite the life filled with adventures and romance. (Lydia's pension applications are posted on www.usgenweb.org ; under Vernon Parish La. Archives)

Lydia Howard, at 104 years old, while living in Louisiana

Written and Submitted by: Leatha A. Betts Woods Cross, Utah

Bertha Richbourg Galloway Stanaland

Bertha Richbourg, also known as Lebertha, daughter of (Caswell) Joseph Tobin Richbourg and Elizabeth "Bettie" Johnson Richbourg was born July 15, 1894 in Castleberry, Conecuh County, Alabama. Her family moved to Leon County, Florida shortly after her birth and lived for several years at Woodville. The family moved to Hosford sometime after the birth of Bertha's sister, Elsie Elizabeth, in 1911.

On May 10, 1915, in Liberty County, Bertha married Robert Emmett Galloway, son of William J. Galloway and Martha "Mattie" Catherine Dubose Galloway. Robert Emmett Galloway was born October 1, 1891 in Darlington County, South Carolina.

The 1910 census recorded his family in Walton County, Florida, where he and his father were both working in a sawmill. Brothers and sisters were Jesse Olin (March 29, 1893-May 18, 1958), Ransom, Rozelle, and Leona. Robert Emmett Galloway registered for the World War I draft as a Hosford resident and noted that he was a mechanic for Graves Brothers Lumber Company in Hosford. His physical description was medium height, medium build, with light hair.

Their first child Voncille Marion Galloway, was born about 1917, presumably in Hosford. By 1920, the young family had moved to Darlington County, South Carolina where Robert Emmett was employed as a mechanic. They lived with his paternal grandparents. A second daughter, Sue Nell Galloway, was born October 21, 1921 in Hartsville, South Carolina. Robert Emmett Galloway, age 32, died July 18, 1922 in Hartsville while at work. He was buried in Hartsville.

Bertha's brother, Tom Richbourg, went to Hartsville and brought Bertha and her young daughters back home to Clearwater, Florida, where her family lived after they moved from Hosford. Bertha and her daughters lived with her parents until Bertha married L. Shelton Stanaland

and then lived only a few houses away on Jeffords Street. Bertha died in childbirth in 1925 in Clearwater. She and her infant were buried together in an unmarked grave in the old Clearwater Municipal Cemetery on Myrtle Avenue.

Voncille Marion Galloway, first daughter of Bertha and Emmett Galloway, married Joseph O'Dell McIntyre. She died May 7, 1963. She and her husband are buried in Grove Hill, Alabama.

Sue Nell Galloway, second daughter of Bertha and Emmett Galloway, married Talmadge "Tal" Leon Moss. Their children were Robert Clarence Moss, George Edward Moss, Talmadge Leon Moss, Jr., and Richard Derek Moss. Sue Nell died July 23, 2006 in Mobile, Alabama.

Submitted by: David Wilson Jolly, 19417 Gulf Boulevard, Indian Shores, Florida 33785; Written by: Judith Richbourg Jolly, 11541 Arlhuna Way, Dade City, Florida 33525; Sources: Census and vital records; Richbourg...A Sequel by Mildred Richbourg, 1994.

Reverend Charles Kenzie Steele

Charles Kenzie Steele was born in Bluefield, West Virginia on February 17, 1914 and lived until August 19, 1980. His father Charles K. Steele, Sr. worked as a miner in Gary, West Virginia and his mother, Lydia Steele, raised her children to believe in justice for all. Charles graduated from Gary High School for Colored in West Virginia, and after graduation felt the calling of the Lord to preach at his local church at the age of fifteen. In 1938 he attended Morehouse College in Atlanta, GA, and after graduation spent fourteen years preaching at numerous churches in Georgia, Alabama and Florida. In 1941, while living in Montgomery Alabama, he met and married Lois Brock (1924-1983), and they had six children: Rochelle Eunice, Charles Kenzie, Jr., Henry Marion, Clifford Nathaniel, Darryl Keith, and Derek Maurice Steele.

In 1952 Reverend Steele moved his family to Tallahassee, Florida, where he became pastor of Bethel Baptist Church and his wife, Lois Steele after raising her children, became a guidance counselor at Leon High School in the late 1980s. During his time in Tallahassee the town was segregated and many feared a race riot was near. Rev. Steele felt the calling of his people, and began organizing passive resistance movements to the Jim Crow practices. While the whole country was concerned with the Vietnam War, the Cold War and the Kennedy-Nixon debates, Rev. Steele was concerned with the 1954 outlawing of segregation in schools, the bus boycotts of 1955 and 1956, the Brown vs. Board of Education in 1957, the wave of sit-ins at lunch counters and theaters, raising his children and teaching his congregation the morals of true Christianity.

Reverend Charles Kenzie Steele, 1970

Many felt he had an unusual kind of rendezvous with destiny, because he came at a time when men abused other men and he saw as an evil that needed to be attacked by a "Warrior Bold and Gentle." While maintaining his friendship with Rev. King, Sr. and Jr., Reverend Steele became one of the five founders of the Southern Christian Leadership Conference (SCLC), and its first Vice President. He organized marches for equality in Virginia, Alabama and Florida. While preaching and caring for his family, Rev. Steele carried the fight for equality through the 1960s and 70s. Many people in Tallahassee felt his activities were for the general good of the city.

During his lifetime, Rev. Steele received numerous awards, proclamations, plaques and a statue of him stands on the property of the City Bus Terminal. In 1979 he received an Honorary Degree from Florida A&M University for over 25 years of campaigning for human equality and a citation from Governor Askew. Rev. Steele was quoted as saying: "We won't have reached Utopia, but we will be further along than we are today, and if I don't see that day, I hope my efforts have brought people together in a strong organization determined to obtain for all people an equal share of justice and equality." Under the facade of being humble and quiet, he was aggressive and outgoing, "A Warrior, Bold and Gentle", but thank God we heard him.

Written by: Carol D. Johnson; Submitted by: Rochelle Steele-Davis 3021 Southshore Circle Tallahassee, Florida 32312

Pearlease Desiree Stephens-Lowery

Pearlease Desiree Stephens-Lowery was born in Quincy, Florida to Lillie Wright (1931-1971), and Bishop Virgil Centenial Stephens, Jr. (1927-1984). They were married at the Gadsden County Courthouse in 1954. Lillie Mae's oldest child is Patricia A. Screen who was raised by her grandmother Rose and her mother's sisters. Pearlease is the oldest of nine of her ten siblings by Virgil C. Stephens, Jr. Her maternal grandparents are Rose and Sam Wright of Decatur County, Georgia and her paternal grandparents are Mattie Woodberry (1908-1959) and Virgil Stephens, Sr. (1899-1929) of Quincy Florida. Pearlease is the namesake of her father's sister, Pearlease Woodberry-Mack. She met and married James Lowery in 1991 in Florida while on one of her many travel excursions.

While growing up, Pearlease attended school at Stevens Elementary. Her family spent many hours working in the fields of the Blake Plantation. After graduating from Shanks High School in Quincy, Florida, Pearlease obtained her first real job at the local Greyhound Station. She recalls; "All I did was go into the station one time and I was hired on the spot. Things were different then; they didn't ask for identification or a social security number." While working for Greyhound, Pearlease took advantage of the discount travel fares. She often traveled to different states to learn the customs of the area.

Pearlease recalls the lessons learned during her childhood: "I learned the whole process of raising shade tobacco when I was nine years old in 1964. During the summer when school was out and sometimes after regular school days, I helped my mother and grandfather in the fields. I helped out with everything from looping, wrapping, priming, to carrying, packing, and stringing the shade tobacco. I watched my mother and my grandfather work in the fields from sunup to sundown, and I wanted to earn money too. My daddy owned his own painting company and was considered a city boy. He didn't want his children working in the fields, but my mother always had the last word. She made the final decisions and she let me, my oldest sister and my oldest brother start working in the fields when we were small children.

Pearlease Lowery

I carried tobacco from the primer to the packer that put the tobacco on a long wooden wagon and they used the mules to pull the wagons to the barns. It was hard work for the men who plowed the fields to make room for the tobacco plants. Pushing that plow connected to the mules up and down the long rows all day was hard work, but we somehow made it work. I remember standing in line to get my little brown envelope; it would be about $1.75 for a whole week's work. Mother would take a dollar and give me the seventy-five cents. Back then you could get a soda for five cents, candy was only one cent and you could get an ice cream cone for five cents. I was in child heaven. When we got to the fields early in the mornings the shade tobacco would be soaking wet from the morning dew. Sometimes they would have the sprinklers on all night, so we would get wet from head to toe. We didn't stop working just because we were soaking wet and our clothes dried on our bodies by lunch time.

Pearlease Lowery

After the shade tobacco would be cured in huge barns that would be closed up tight with kerosene heaters in them, they were kept hot every night until the tobacco dried as it hung from the ceiling cord. These barns would be sometimes five stories high and men had to start from the top and work their way down to the bottom tier. My grandfather, Sam was a "Straw Boss," they call it, and he gave orders and seemed to enjoy his job. He had to push up the tobacco that had been strung and that green tobacco was heavy because I tried it, and I couldn't move it.

Several people lived on the plantation. There were old wood houses sometimes two bedrooms like what we lived in with ten people in that little house, and the house had no bathroom, electricity, or indoor plumbing. We had to use an outhouse, which was one small wood hut, with just enough room to sit on the wood seat, and it was made out of a piece of plywood, with a round hole in the middle. The hut sat on a small foundation over a hole dug in the ground for human waste. It smelled awful and it was one of the scariest experiences I ever encountered as a child.

We were tenant farmers who lived on the Blake Plantation, but we paid no rent. During the winter time when we couldn't work in the fields, the farm owners would be very generous when it came to lending money. It was routine for families to borrow so much money during the winter months that they had to work almost all summer just to pay their debts. It was somewhat of entrapment or form of slavery, because you couldn't leave the farmland owning the farm owner, so you would be stuck. I learned a lot during those years about being responsible, working hard, and I must admit it has made me stronger to this day."

Written and Submitted by: Pearlease Desiree Stephens-Lowery, 749 Basin Street Apt #9, Tallahassee, FL 32303

Marie Preclik Stoeff

We lived in Buffalo, New York when we decided to migrate to Florida as pioneers. In September of 1925 we set out from New York for the "Promised Land" in Leon County, Florida. My sister Emilie was age 6 when the thought of this adventure appealed to me. My father Chris bought a Ford for $60.00 and a high-bred German shepherd female puppy for $75.00.

We piled our few belongings into the car and headed south. It turned out to be a true adventure making at most 200 miles a day, taking 7 days to get there, and without a clear idea on how to get there without a map. We found ourselves on a country road that seemed to lead nowhere, yet it was the main highway to Florida. We headed for Tallahassee, the capital of Florida, thru many small towns. Though we were sleepy and hot over a dusty, clay road we were very excited to go. We arrived at our destination Thursday afternoon, when stores were closed and not many people were about. Deserted it seemed.

We tried some kind of business with another promoter in a dancing hall, but lost our money. Dad tried carpentry, but it paid too little to live off. Things looked terrible that spring of 1926. Though we didn't want to, we had to plan on going back to New York because we were down to our last nickel. It was as if you had to be driven good and tight against a wall before your luck changed. Ours did just that. A man sent for my father, Chris. He wanted someone to run his store for a year. There was nothing to pay for the privilege and all profits from the store were ours. A little 2x4 hut with dirt floors near a depot was all we had to work with, but we stocked it with groceries, fruits, and drinks and we were in business.

After the year was over the gasoline company built our store or at least paid for the lumber and we were in our own business building, located along a busy highway about 200 yards from our house which was located on a slope, with pretty surroundings. We really began to feel that we were working for ourselves when we worked 16 hours a day, every day of the year. We pumped gas, sold 15 cent bunches of bananas on Saturday and Sunday, and sold crates of soda, groceries, and cigarette smokes. The new store stood under a sprawling oak shaded spot and people in cars, all the way from Atlanta, Georgia liked to stop in the cool shade and refresh themselves. Our dog was a special attraction too, because she was a strange breed of wolf and everybody wanted a puppy from her. We walked our feet off on weekends, but we were happy in doing it while prospering. This store was located on South Adams Street just north of the Florida A&M University.

Written by: Marie Preclik Stoeff (Mrs. Kristo Stoeff); Submitted by: Christopher John Frano (Marie grandson)

Roy Strickland

In the summer of 1937, Robert Jordan, Circulation Manager for the *Daily Democrat*, gave me my first real job. I was eight years old and excited to become a paper boy for the *Daily Democrat* (actually the paper was published six days a week. There was no paper on Saturday). Paper boys, as distinguished from the older boys who had routes and delivered to homes, hawked the papers on the downtown streets of Tallahassee. We would roam the streets calling

LeRoy Strickland on his 80th Birthday on October 19, 2008

"*Daily Democrat*" along with the headline of the day. Although my father owned a shoe store, I went barefoot every summer and would hurry across the hot asphalt streets from one corner to the other searching for customers.

The first day I sold papers the headline was an "Extra" and involved a local lynching. There are conflicting dates as to when this occurred. Some sources say July 20, 1937 and others say August 2, 1937.

Sometime after midnight (probably July 20th, 1937) Tallahassee police officer Vernon Kelly was making his rounds when he found the door to George Demetree's restaurant unlocked. He discovered two black men, Richard Hawkins and Ernest Powders (or Ponder), inside. Officer Kelly was stabbed several times in the left side and his face was gashed. He managed to make it to the nearby police station and survived. Richard Hawkins was later picked up and admitted the crime but said Ernest Powders did the stabbing.

Sometime later, after Officer Kelly's stabbing, Sergeant Harry Fairbanks was taken from the Tallahassee Police Station at gunpoint by a group of masked men and forced to hand over the prisoners at the jail. Hawkins and Powders were later found shot to death without benefit of a trial.

This sad story was my introduction to selling papers. Robert Jordan told me I sold the most papers of anyone that day. The papers sold for 5 cents each. The *Democrat* received 3 cents and the paper boys 2 cents. I soon found a way to supplement my income. There was a man from Monticello, Florida who boiled peanuts and sold them on the streets of Tallahassee. You could hear the cry, "Fresh Monticello boiled peanuts," echoing in the downtown streets. He gave me a job selling his peanuts for 5 cents a bag. Like the *Democrat*, I received 2 cents a bag and he received 3 cents. So, I would yell "*Daily Democrat*" and in the next breath, "Fresh Monticello boiled peanuts".

By selling both papers and peanuts I was able to at least double my income. I think sold more peanuts than papers. But being the young entrepreneur, I was not happy giving up 3 cents a bag on the peanuts I sold. My younger brother Don and I came up with the idea of buying our own peanuts and having our mother boil them. We would purchase the peanuts at the Curb Market located on Boulevard Street (now Martin Luther King). This was only a block from our home at 310 W. Lafayette Street. We would purchase the small sacks from a grocery and bag our own peanuts. Our profit was more than 2 cents a bag.

Sometime in the late 30's or early 40's I was promoted to a paper route. I had several different routes, but my favorite started in downtown Tallahassee and ended at Clarks Auto Court on North Monroe Street. One of my customers was Miss Ruby Diamond. She lived on the second floor of the old Floridan Hotel. I would deliver her paper to her room. She was very gracious and always remembered me at Christmas. Another customer I remember was White's Rooming House located at the intersection of N. Monroe and Thomasville Road. Clarks Auto Court, later Bowman's and finally Albertsons were located at the very north end of Tallahassee. Beyond it was woods, pastures and rural Leon County.

Papers were delivered Monday through Friday in the afternoon. There was no paper on Saturday and Sunday's paper was delivered early on Sunday morning. It cost 25 cents a week to subscribe to the *Daily Democrat*. The route boys

LeRoy Strickland at age 14, ID second from the left. Photo taken August 23, 1942, of the boys who were the war bond winners. Left to right: Harris Riley, Roy Strickland (age 14), Don Strickland, Colonel James P. Doharty, Dean Scruggs, Dewitt Miller, Bobby Mears and W. B. Keaton.

received 5 cents and the *Democrat* 20 cents. We used Saturdays to collect from our customers.

This was the time of WWII and the *Democrat* carriers (all papers were delivered by boys on bicycles) were assigned the task of selling war bonds to their customers. Those who sold the most were rewarded with a visit to Dale Mabry Field (Army Air Force training field in Tallahassee for fighter pilots) where they reviewed the troops, toured the field and lunched in the Officers' Mess.

Submitted and Written By: Roy Strickland, 133-C Villas Ct., SE, Tallahassee 32303

Roy Strickland's Home

It was 1934 and I was five years old when my family moved from 1119 North Duval Street to 310 West Lafayette Street. This was our home until 1940. The street began on Adams Street at the rear of the old Capitol. It was flanked on the north by Pensacola Street and on the south by St. Augustine Street. The first two blocks of West Lafayette were paved with sidewalks. After crossing Bronough Street at the end of the 200 block you entered a different world. This was "the other side of the tracks". The 300 block of West Lafayette was on a steep hill with an unpaved street of red clay with deep ditches.

Our home was a modest frame house sitting on brick pillars that allowed my brother Don and me to stand up under portions of the house. There were no TV or computer games in the 1930's so we played mainly outside. A favorite game was cowboys and Indians. Underneath the house served as the corral for the broom stick horses the cowboys rode. In the dry dirt underneath the house were funnel holes created by ant lions (doodle bugs). Drop an ant into the hole and the struggle of the ant to climb out of the loose sand would cause the ant lion, which lived at the bottom of the hole, to grab him. Don and I spent many an hour playing with the "doodle bugs" and ants.

The steep hill in front of our house, with its deep ditch, provided for another fun game. We would pretend our little red wagon was a stagecoach and ride it down the hill. We would jump off just before allowing the wagon to run over the "cliff" into the ditch. The stagecoach running over the cliff idea was inspired by the cowboy movies we would see at the State Theatre on Saturday mornings. The movies cost 10 cents

Theater across from Strickland's Store

and the theatre located on College Avenue was an easy walk.

At the bottom of our block at the intersection of Boulevard Street (now MLK), and Park Avenue was a rooming house with several colorful characters. I recall a round little man walking down the hill with a sack full of beer in bottles. In those days (1930's) there were no six packs with handles. Beer was stuffed in paper bags. Mr. Roly Poly was a little tipsy and lost his footing on the slick clay. Beer bottles flew everywhere and our tipsy neighbor rolled into the ditch. This doesn't sound funny on paper, but it was hilarious to the two young boys who witnessed it.

Our Lafayette Street house faced south. The back of the house had steep steps coming down from a screened-in back porch into a small back yard. On the east side of the back yard was a one-car tin garage and on the west side was a low brick wall. On the north side, facing Pensacola Street was a wire fence separating us from our neighbors, a black family. Branches from a pear tree growing in our neighbors' yard hung over our side of the fence. Don and I enjoyed playing baseball with an old broom handle as a bat (one of our broom stick horses) and pears as baseballs. Hitting a pear over the brick wall was a homerun. One day our mother watched us playing and evidently felt sorry for us. She bought us a real baseball and bat. Baseball in the back yard was never as much fun after that.

The tin garage served as a backstop for our baseball games. A tree grew at the back of the garage. The roof of the garage was our "secret place". We could easily climb the tree to the top of the garage and survey the Lafayette Street neighborhood. From our perch we could see the back of Leon County Sheriff Frank Stoutamire's impressive home on Bronough Street and our landlady Mrs. Harper's home on Bronough. From our secret place we could "telephone" our friend James Phillips (Jimmy remains a close friend to this day) who lived on the corner of Bronough and Pensacola streets.

Our telephone was two tin cans joined together with a long string coated with Octagon soap. It really worked and was much more fun than today's cell phones. In the summer Don, Jimmy, and I explored the deep ditches and culverts that were being installed on the surrounding streets. Some of the sewer pipes were large enough for us to stand erect. Others we had to crawl through and unable to turn around we would back out. All this we did barefooted and suffered many cuts and bruises, but we would never consider wearing shoes in the summer. Another summer activity was hitching rides on the back of mule-drawn ice wagons. The cooling ice was better than today's air conditioning and the ice slivers quenched our thirst.

Roy's tin phone

From our front door we could see the back of L.C. Yeager's "mansion" located on the "better side of the tracks" at the southwest corner of Bronough and Lafayette. On the "Other side of the tracks" at the southwest corner of Boulevard and Lafayette was an African-American church. A short distance from our Lafayette Street home on Boulevard (now MLK) was Hines' grocery store. Mr. Hines was a white man with an impressive white handlebar moustache. Further south on Boulevard was Speed's Store. The Speeds were an influential black family. The curb market was also located on Boulevard. Ours was a very diverse neighborhood.

My brother Don and I first started to school from Lafayette Street. Although we had a tin garage, I don't recall us having a car so we walked to school. The school was located on the campus of the Florida State College for Women (now FSU) on the corner of Copeland and Call streets.

The first through the sixth grades were called the Demonstration School. The seventh through the twelfth grades were known as Florida High School. Although FSCW was an all girl's school, the Demonstration and Florida High Schools were coed. The schools were designed to train teachers in a real live environment. They were called practice teachers and were supervised by the regular classroom teacher.

Walking to school was an adventure. The school was located several blocks west of our Lafayette Street home. Sometimes we would walk the College Avenue route and other times choose the Park Avenue path. Some days dogs would chase us, but we were never bitten. Friends who lived along the way would join us. Among them were Corbett "Buddy" Dean and his sister Carol who lived on Park Avenue.

The Dean family had lived at 310 West Lafayette just prior to our moving there. Their father was an employee of the *Tallahassee Democrat*. He was in charge of the presses. I had a crush on a girl named Deryl Brumbalow who lived on College Avenue. We sometimes attended "Prom Parties" and played "spin the bottle". If you spun the bottle and it landed facing a certain girl, the two of you had to walk "promenade" around the block. Maybe you got a kiss or maybe not. In 1940 we moved from "the other side of the tracks" to 223 North Adams Street and attended Leon High School. (That is another story to be told at a later time.) Sometime after we moved, many of the homes on West Lafayette were demolished to make room for the Florida Supreme Court and other state buildings. The old 100, 200 and 300 blocks no longer exist, but boyhood memories of 310 West Lafayette Street still live in the pages of this octogenarian's mind.

Written and Submitted by: Roy Strickland, 133-C Villas Court SE, Tallahassee, FL 32309

Roy Strickland – Adams Street

It was 1940 and I was twelve years old when my family moved from 310 West Lafayette Street to 223 North Adams Street. Like our Lafayette Street address, the Adams Street location was only a few blocks from downtown Tallahassee, but we were closer to Leon High School. My brother Don and I switched from Florida High School to Leon High. Our new home was a two-story building with four apartments. It was located on the southeast corner of Adams and Tennessee Streets. Several of my schoolmates lived on Adams Street; among them were Wilda Larson, who was to teach English at Leon High for 41 years. Another good friend was Freddie Ley who, many years later, moved back to his boyhood home in the 500 block of North Adams. Next door neighbors were Ronald, Leonard and Lindy Melton. Ronald and Leonard played on the first Florida State University football team. My cousin Harris Riley lived two blocks away on Virginia Street.

The block across Adams Street from us is now taken up by the C. K. Steele City Bus Terminal. In the 1940's a duplex apartment was located on this block. One of the apartments housed long-time Leon County school teacher Kate Sullivan and her sister. Dr. William Robison was to later open a dentistry office in one of the duplexes. In the next block on North Adams there were two stately old homes with beautiful grounds. The home of Mary Whitfield was located

LJohnston Manor, NW corner of Adams and Tennessee Streets, 1939

on the SW corner of Adams and Virginia. On the NW corner of Adams and Tennessee was the Johnston home. These homes were to eventually be destroyed and replaced with an A&P Grocery Store, Trailways and Greyhound Bus Stations. The Greyhound Station still stands at the location of the old Johnston mansion. The Trailways building still remains but the company was sold out and the A & P building is no longer located on this block.

On the SW corner of Adams and Call Streets was Register's Fruit Stand. Mr. Register allowed me, my brother Don and Cousin Harris to sell peaches door to door. Peaches were 25 cents a basket. We would keep 5 cents for each basket sold. In addition to selling peaches, the three of us had *Democrat* newspaper routes. Once I accompanied my cousin Harris on his route.

Harris had two dogs: Prince a German shepherd mixed and Spot was a small mutt. These dogs knew the route as well as Harris and would run ahead of him as he delivered his newspapers.

Adjacent to the lot was a garage apartment. It seems Prince, on previous occasions, had been chasing the owner's cat and this day she called the police. Patrolman Barney Gatlin arrived and confronted us in the vacant lot. He was preparing to shoot Prince, but as he unholstered his pistol, I stepped in front of him begging that he not kill Prince. Somehow in all the commotion, Prince disappeared and lived to run another day.

My friends and I were seldom inside. We traveled all over Tallahassee on our bikes. A favorite destination on hot summer days was Diehl's Pool. Today, if you travel out East Call Street until it dead ends past the railroad tracks you will see to the north a thickly wooded area sitting between Call Street and the tracks. In the 1940s there was a small spring-fed pool located in these woods. I, my cousins Sylvan Strickland and Harris Riley, along with others, enjoyed skinny dipping in the cool spring water until one day we climbed out of the pool to find ourselves covered with leeches. That was our last visit to Diehl's Pool!

LeRoy Strickland, 2009

In the fall and winter we played tackle football on the weekends. We would gather up our team and arrange to meet another group at Lafayette Park or some other location. We had no uniforms or protective gear and no referees. I don't recall anyone getting seriously hurt and we always seemed to settle any arguments. One Sunday in December of 1944, our team met the Sunnyland team at a vacant lot beside the old Armory (now the Senior Center). There were eight men on each side. Our lineup consisted of Francis Smith, Audie Stanaland, Tommy Reynolds, Wallace Martin, Harry Mullikin, Harris Riley, David Bingham and myself. The Sunnyland eight were Louie Sutton, Skeets Strickland, Ernest

Williams, J.W. Grimsley, Ricou Browning, Jim Tully, Bobby Tully and Bob Foster. Our team won 30 to 12.

Other players I remember who participated in our weekend games are Sylvan Strickland, Harry Ryder, Ed Ranew, Gene Fitchner, Tom Ellis, J. Hall, Dougald McMillan, Frank Gray, Leo Crutchfield, and Earl Cawthon. I can't play football on a vacant lot next door to the old Armory anymore, but I am eligible to participate in the activities of the Senior Center.

Written and Submitted by: Roy Strickland, l33-C Villas Court, SE Tallahassee, FL 32303

Sylvan Strickland

The Great Depression caused me to move to Tallahassee in August 1940 at age 13. I came from Ewell, Alabama, a tiny crossroads community located five miles east of Ozark. I attended elementary school in Ewell and the 7th and 8th grades in Ozark. I entered the 9th grade in Leon High School in Tallahassee in September 1940.

Tallahassee was a small town but large in comparison to Ozark. It took me a while to adjust but I grew to love the school and the city. Leon High was like new, having been built four years before I arrived. Until 1936 it had been located in the 200 block of West Park Avenue, on the site where the county library was built.

My father, Fred, my stepmother, Edna, and I lived at 1408 Green Street. At that time Edna was a student in a local beauty school. In due course she was graduated and got a good job. She was a member of a large farm family named Tyus in Grady County, Georgia, near Cairo. Fred's job took him into Wakulla County two days per week. I went with him a few times. His route included Wakulla Springs, Crawfordville and Ivan (or Arran, or both). In 1942 he became a deputy clerk of circuit court for Leon County and had a 26-year career there, the last years of which were as county finance director. Fred's older brother, L. M. Strickland, and L. M.'s brother-in-law, Pitt Riley, owned a shoe store at 115 East College Avenue. L. M. bought Pitt's interest in 1945.

I did not have a bicycle in Ewell. I bought a used one from Bobby Bennett for $8. I could ride that bike from home to any place in town in 10 minutes (or it seems) without fear of being hit by a car. On my bicycle I delivered newspapers, the *Daily Democrat* and the *Florida State News*, afternoon and morning respectfully, published by the same company, in the 100 block of South Adams Street, which was paved with bricks in that area. Newspapers were not delivered by car in those days. My route was part of Thomasville Road and all of Glendale. One early morning in September 1941 while I was delivering newspapers the

Sylvan Strickland, 1969

fringe of a hurricane brought strong winds and rain to Tallahassee. I rode the bike through wind and rain, not knowing the severity of the situation, and when I finished my route and turned the corner from 7th Avenue onto Green Street, Fred and Edna were standing on the front porch watching for me.

Later I got the Los Robles route. The first house on the route was at Thomasville Road and Calhoun Street. The customer was Jerry Carter, a member of the Public Service Commission.

I became an usher at the Florida Theater on my 16th birthday, October 31, 1942. Ushers carried flashlights and escorted customers to seats. I don't know when theaters discontinued ushers. I parked my bicycle beside the theater for 21 months without locking it and without fear of theft, and it was never stolen. I rode my bicycle to school every day for four years, hot or cold, rain or shine.

Written and submitted by: Sylvan Strickland, 3423 John Hancock Dr., Tallahassee, FL 32312

Paul Tamanian

Paul Tamanian is a Florida native and holds a degree in interior design from State University. He came to art relatively late, in his mid-thirties, after working in a variety of fields. He was even co-owner of an automobile business at one time. He discovered an affinity for clay by attending a pottery class at a local community center. He moved rapidly from basic skills to technical innovation. Since his first exhibit at a small gallery in Havana, Florida in 1992, he has gone on to show and sell his artwork across the United States. He has been invited to display his works in the company of some of America's foremost craftsmen and artists. Currently his two and three-dimensional works are exhibited and sold in various cities across the United States, and his work is part of many corporate and private collections around the world.

Tamanian started his career in the arts as a ceramicist. Unlike most ceramic artists though, he did not settle on one style with a limited set of shapes with similar glazes. He is, instead, an intrepid experimenter. An examination of his work over the past ten years reveals movements from small slab built vases to larger organic forms, including his highly successful "Tusks", and then on to even larger vessels that are three feet or taller. His works became more sculptural than nominally utilitarian. The one constant over these years has been his emphasis on surface over form. As appealing as his shapes may be, they serve primarily as "canvases" for a remarkable variety of finishes including traditional glazes, industrial fabric dyes, automobile paints, chemicals that alter texture, color, and other materials and techniques that produce a constantly changing collection of surfaces and styles.

Paul Tamanian

"I spend endless hours researching new forms and finishes for my ceramics and experimenting with techniques to create movement for my paintings. My work is constantly evolving, and I am always striving to reach some ineffable, impossible state of perfection," said Paul.

Elegant, fluid and often very sensual forms and shapes that sometimes seem to defy gravity are the trademark of Paul Tamanian's style. Using a variety of mediums and glazes he creates sculpture and paintings that are truly unique. Tamanian rolls, pounds, scrapes, sands, fires, glazes, paints, sandblasts and stains each piece until it meets his expectations. Each pieced of artwork is a result of years of research and experimentation with glazing clay, and aluminum bodies firing techniques. There are even techniques not normally associated with ceramic or metal works among his art pieces. His artwork is ever evolving and is a refection of his constant effort to extend, and experiment with unique artistry he has already achieved.

Submitted and Written by: Paul Tamanian, 6393 Fitz Lane, Tallahassee, Florida 32311

Philip Sheridan Taylor

Philip Sheridan Taylor was part of the well-known "Taylor's of Tennessee," nearly every generation occupied high office — senators, governors, and Commissioner of Indian Affairs. He was born in 1884 in East Tennessee, near Johnson City. Phil S. Taylor graduated from Marysville College in Tennessee. His wife graduated from Hardin College in Missouri. He moved to Tallahassee, FL in 1926, accompanied by his wife, Willie Blanch Hook Taylor, and daughters, Betty Ann and Susan Jane.

Phil S. Taylor at age 20

Paul worked for Nathan Mayo, Commissioner of Agriculture. His office was on the first floor of the capitol building. He was state supervising inspector for the Florida Department of Agriculture. Because he was an excellent speaker, he toured the state for Nathan Mayo to speak at a variety of meetings. During World War II he called square dances at the local U.S.O.

He was a "lay preacher" at Trinity Methodist Church, andoften led the evening worship service at FAMU At the church, he taught the men's Bible class, and he helped organize the Wesley Foundations at F.S.C.W. The men enjoyed a breakfast once a month; there, he said, "No loyal son of Wesley ever shirks his table duty."

All of the Taylor men were bald by their 30th birthday. When he felt a hair on his head, he yelled, "Sanna Jane-- quick! Get the tweezers; I have a hair on my head."

When he died in 1955, the presiding minister described "Mr. Phil" by reading the First Psalm:

Blessed is the man, Who walks not in the counsel of the ungodly, Nor stands in the path of sinners. Nor sits in the seat of the scornful; But his delight is in the law of the Lord, And in His law he meditates day and night...For the Lord knows the way of the righteous, But the way of the ungodly shall perish.

His grandson, Walter A. DeMilly, III, is a writer living in Key West. "Walt" also has published two books, and worked for Monroe County's "Child Abuse and Domestic Violence" agency. He earned his "God and Country" award and was an Eagle Scout. He was elected as most valuable member of Leon High's chorus. He graduated from Emory University in Atlanta with a degree in psychology and philosophy.

Phil's granddaughter, Sanna Kay DeMilly Davis, graduated from Presbyterian College in Clinton, SC where she majored in art, as did her Grandmother Taylor. She taught at "Thornwell Home for Children," and has enjoyed living in Clinton with her husband, Tommy, and their children, Taylor and Thomas. Thomas and his wife, Jordan Trotter, recently become parents of Audra Ann Davis. Taylor has his master's in childhood psychology for disabled children. She will marry Tift Mitchell in October.

I, his daughter, thanks to my parents, have faith in God. In 1945, I graduated from F.S.C.W. with a degree in speech and literature. I am able to give Bible studies, offer oral prayers and console friends in trouble. For all the above, I attribute to the grace of God.

Submitted by: Sanna Jane Taylor DeMilly, 4434 Meandering Way, Apartment 101, Tallahassee, FL 32308

The Thompsons of Leon County

Oda C. Thompson waited expectantly in the car under the spreading limbs of a huge oak. It was 1940 in Tallahassee on the campus of Leon High School. His 34-year-old son, Romulus Thompson, was interviewing for the position of band director. The Leon County School Board had decided they wanted to hire a band director who would be on the faculty of Leon High School.

When Romulus emerged from the school with a big smile, Oda knew his son had gotten the job. For the next ten years, the Leon band would become one of the most popular institutions in Tallahassee. The band in its red and white uniforms, modeled after the West Point uniform that Romulus so revered, thrilled audiences whenever they appeared in parades, concerts and half-time shows.

Leon High home football games were played at Centennial Field located at South Monroe and Blount Streets. One of the most exciting shows featured the band standing at the goal post in formation. The open strains of *William Tell Overture* were heard. As the band marched forward the music segued into *Tallahassee,* a song made popular by Bing Crosby: "When you see land kind of green and grassy...you know you are in Tallahassee." Well, that brought everyone to their feet.

Rom, as he was sometimes called, brought with him to Tallahassee his wife, Rachael Cawthon Thompson and son, Carl Wayne. In 1941, their daughter Judy was born, Rachel returned to her profession of teaching elementary school, first at Prince Murat and later at Kate Sullivan Elementary until her retirement in the early 1970s.

Carl, their son, graduated from Leon High where he played the French horn in the band. When he returned from service in the Air Force in the 1950s, he was with the US Post Office in Tallahassee.

When their daughter Judy turned five years old, she decided she wanted to march out in front of the Leon band with those girls who twirled the "silver sticks." After an unsuccessful effort to quiet her begging at one of the rehearsals, Rom said, "Okay. Get out there and I'll show you that you can't keep up!" Well, what did he know? Judy took her baton, stood behind the head majorette, Jean Andrews, and not only kept up

JoAnn Hutto, Romulus Thompson, Judy Thompson Leon Band c. 1948

with the band, but she knew every stop, every turn, and stepped as high as the majorettes. A career was born as the majorette mascot of the Leon High Band.

In 1950, Romulus Thompson resigned as band director, and Judy "resigned" her mascot position now that she was getting older. She later was head majorette in 1959. Romulus and Rachael lived on in Tallahassee until their deaths, Rom in 1996 at age 89 and Rachael in 2000 at age 95.

As of this writing in 2008, Carl and Judy live in Tallahassee, expanding their families by five children and six grandchildren between them.
Submitted by Judy Thompson Goodwin, 3970 Meandering Way, Tallahassee, FL 32308

Walker – Life on Holton Street in 1969
It is 1969 and my parents Annie Rose Walker and Herman Walker were no longer together as husband and wife. All I knew was that we now lived in a different place than my father.

The way it looked to me, a four year old, we'd moved into a nice apartment. The buildings were pretty red bricks, looked new and were scattered about with a playground in the middle of them next to the laundromat. The people were pleasant. Inside the apartment, the walls appeared to be huge white rectangles stacked on top of each other, kind of offset. The floors were made of large squares (linoleum).

Ms. Annie Rose, as she was called, moved to Holton Street Apartments (The Projects) with all five of her daughters. Her only son, Johnny, the oldest child, lived right up the street from us with his wife, Carolyn, and children. "The Projects" was full of moms and their children. The families that moved there were women and innocent children. Many of the moms came from broken marriages and others who never made it to marriage with the baby's daddy. Looking back on it, I'm saddened by the concrete life created by ill will and poverty. At the same time, I am content and warm because that was home, the best days of my life. The value of a good home is priceless, and my mom gave us so much love that I didn't even know at the time that we were "poor".

Ms. Annie Rose made G140 our home. She was a churchgoing woman with strong faith and clear views on morality. She taught her children. Daddy, Herman, was a regular part of our lives, spending every Friday with us after work and celebrated holidays with us, as though any other time of the year, he was just away at work. He loved his children. The Projects afforded my mom the ability to provide a home for her children that included him, even though they chose not to maintain a marital relationship. For that I am grateful.

I remember Fridays sitting on the small porch with my Daddy learning, at four years old, that words are amazing. Yes, my Daddy, Herman, taught me to spell words, big words, like Czechoslovakia, Wewahitchka, and so forth. Feel the way the words make your mouth feel when you say them, look at how they are spelled. How do you get "check" from C-z-e-c-h? He made it all so interesting to me.

I remember feeling happy and safe all the time. Ms. Annie Rose was short, but had the strength and character of a lion, always observant and careful, yet highly capable of defending and being courageous in the face of adversity. She did the things that mothers should do. She talked the talk and walked the walk.

Holton Street holds many more memories, too many to recount in this limited space. Perhaps I'll pick up the memories in another place.
Written and Submitted by: Ivy Shivers, 9798 South Salt Road Lamont, FL 32336

Charles Walker
There is nobody at First Baptist Church with a more positive attitude than Charles Walker, and why not? For just shy of 65 years he's been married to Lois, the prettiest gal in the church. He has spent all of his professional life on one college campus or another, starting back when he was a lowly plebe at Carson Newman College; then a Masters candidate at George Peabody College for Teachers in Nashville, as Registrar at Cumberland University, Registrar at FSU and Registrar and Dean of Students at Miami/Dade College. Having come up from Fordsville, Kentucky, (a town so small that they attach the "Welcome To" and "You Are Now Leaving" City Limit signs to the same pole), Charles has made the most of his love for people. His ability to communicate and his love of doing it has garnered him more friends and acquaintances than all of the rest of us, put together.

It was in Kentucky, at the age of eleven that Charles accepted Christ and began his lifelong worship of and friendship with his Savior. Since that early beginning, John 3: 16 has always been in his heart. He has been happiest in his life with Lois and their three children, living and growing in the serene setting of campus life. Their idyllic life together began almost the first day he arrived as a freshman at Carson Newman, where he met and fell in love with his soul mate Lois. They met at a new-student mixer, paired up and have been together ever since. They were married in Knoxville, TN in 1944.

It took World War Two and the U. S. Army to keep Charles and Lois apart. Charles saw the horrors of war first-hand. His saddest, most heart-wrenching experiences were seeing men he knew killed, and later, when he returned home, visiting the families of those who died. After the war he was back home with Lois, picking up his studies, completing his degrees, getting a job, settling down with family and friends. After a year as Registrar at Cumberland University, in 1948 Charles came to Tallahassee and FSU where he spent twelve years, first as Assistant Registrar, then Acting Registrar and then ten years as Registrar. It was early on during this time that Charles and Lois joined First Baptist. He had heard about the church, tried it on and found it was a "perfect fit". That was in 1948 when he whole heartedly embraced Dr. Harold Sanders' vision of a "Second Century Church".

Charles and Lois were happy in Tallahassee. But when opportunity called from South Florida Charles took on the position of Registrar and Dean of Students at what became one of the nation's largest institutions of higher education, the sprawling Miami/Dade College. Thirty-three years in the land of palm trees and parking lots were all that the Walkers could tolerate. They longed for the rolling hills and Spanish moss of Tallahassee. So in 1993 Charles and Lois returned to First Baptist. They wrapped themselves in the music and great fellowship of the church, with Charles becoming President of First Joy Choir, Chairman of the Church's 1999 Sesquicentennial Celebration, Chairman of the Deacons and co-winner of the 2004 "Senior of The Year" Award.

So you see where this is going. Charles was valedictorian of his high school class, naturally the winner of the 1950 "Courtesy" award at FSU, President of the Southern Association of Collegiate Registrars and Admissions Officers along with other honors already mentioned. The, folks from Fordsville, Kentucky should be mighty proud of this native son. In fact, they ought to consider adding one more sign to their City Limits post, "Home of Charles Walker, Good Christian, Outstanding Educator and Allaround Great Guy".
Written by: Carol Ann and Bill Boydston, 1639 Twin Lakes Circle, Tallahassee, Florida 32311; Submitted by: Lois Walker

Lois Walker

Her personal ministry is music. Music for us…music for the churches she has belonged to. Lois' heart is full of piano and organ music. It overflows into her lovely eyes and spreads around the room to everyone who is near to her.

This wonderful Christian belongs to God for sure. And, whenever God frowns about the goings-on down here, I'll bet He thinks of Lois and smiles again.

Lois was born in a little town near Knoxville, Tennessee called Fountain City. When she was five years old her mother, worried no one would teach Lois at that age, talked the piano teacher into taking the little girl. She started playing at five. At 16 years old a new organ came to the church in Fountain City and her piano teacher taught her that, too.

Lois accepted Jesus as her Savior when she was 13 years old. Her favorite Bible verse to this day is Proverbs 3:5-6: "Trust in the Lord with all thine heart; and lean not unto thine own understanding. In all thy ways acknowledge him, and he shall direct thy paths".

In High School she won her first award for typewriting and later won an award for good citizenship from the Daughters of the American Revolution. She attended that beautiful school in the hills: Carson-Newman College in Jefferson City, Tennessee.

She was in her sophomore year when her future husband, Charlie applied for a job at the same time she did. He had to come through her office to get to his work and as the story goes ... they lived happily ever after. They were married in 1944 at the Central Baptist Church in Fountain City, Tennessee.

Lois had two daughters and then a son and was a stay-at home mom until the children were in college. Then she taught school for 13 years: 5 years in the Head Start Program and 8 years as a first grade teacher. After retiring from teaching she became the State President of WMU for five years and was also Vice President of the National Board of WMU.

The place she has lived the longest was 35 years in Miami where she played the organ and piano in her church there, as well. She has lived in Tallahassee for a total of 27 years, now. She says it is a beautiful place and nearer than Miami to her children since they all live out of state.

Lois says there are two most wonderful things that have happened to her. One was becoming a Christian and the other was meeting Charlie. One of the worst things is experiencing falls. Falling has been scary and worrisome to her. Lois thinks the biggest change in her lifetime is a man walking on the moon. This wondrous event made a lasting impression on her life.

If you see Lois Walker, just say thanks. Because thanks is all she will accept for the hours and hours of piano and organ playing she does for all the events and all the choirs. And she deserves a million thanks.

Written by Carol Ann and Bill Boydston ©. 1639 Twin Lakes Circle, Tallahassee, FL 32311; Submitted by: Charles Walker

Colonel George Taliaferro Ward

Colonel George Taliaferro Ward was assigned to the 2nd Florida Infantry of the Confederate States of America in 1825. During that time the Ward family arrived from Kentucky and settled south of Chaires, establishing "Southwood" Plantation. There were two sons: George Taliaferro Ward, who had graduated from Transylvania University, Lexington, Kentucky in 1824, and William Seymour Ward, who attended West Point in 1823 through 1825.

In 1839 William's friend and fellow cadet, Eliakim Parker Scammon, visited the Wards at Southwood. At that time no one could have imagined that these friends would become enemies 21 years later. In October of 1862, Scammon, who was a Union Volunteer, was promoted to Brigadier General of the United States Army regiment.

On February 8, 1844, George Ward married Sarah Jane Chaires. The Ward's

Colonel George Taliaferro Ward, Owner of Southwood Plantation 1860s

"Southwood Plantation" and the Chaires' "Verdura Plantation" were adjoining land and according to documents, Sarah received property from her family which increased the size of the Wards' Southwood Plantation.

George Ward was not only a planter, but also a banker, a politician and a Colonel in the Confederate States of America army. He led his regiment in Virginia through some victories, but on May 5, 1862, at the Battle of Williamsburg, he lost his life after a fatal gunshot wound. Interment was held the following day at Bruton Parish Church in Williamsburg, VA. That same year, the Ward family received the Confederate Battle flag for his service to his country. San Marcos de Apalachee at St. Marks, Florida, was renamed Fort Ward in honor of George T. Ward.

Submitted by: Dorothy C. Spence, 3982 Chaires Cross Road, Tallahassee, Florida 32317

The Watson Family of Leon County

As far as I know, relatives of the original Watson family are deceased. I would think that they were a pioneering family, who lived preceding 1890. Henry Watson had a family before marrying Susan, my grandmother. They were parents of Benjamin, David, John, Caroline, Emma, and Susan. Their spouses were Faith, Ada Mae, Harry, Nathaniel, and Robert.

Susan and Robert Watson always lived on the homesteads. The first homesteads' addresses were 1815 and 1821 Thomasville Road, The next homesteads were 1555 and 1557 Payne Drive. Off-springs were few: John's daughter, Geraldine was the mother of Charles J. Adams and Martin Langston Watson Adam; Emma's daughter, Joyce was the mother of Kirk N. Evans and Clanese J. Evans.

Benjamin and his wife, Faith lived away from the homestead. The relatives living on Meridian Road were Alex and Annie Mae Macon, developers of the Macon community, including the Macon cemetery. This property was later sold to the City for the construction of I-10. Other relatives' names escape me now, however, there were others who lived in the community, but moved to other places as time went on. I spent summers in Tallahassee from as far back as I can remember until the age of eighteen.

My cousin Charles and his brother Martin, now deceased, spent summers in Tallahassee from age five until their high school years. Charles completed undergraduate work at Florida State

University. From my childhood, I remember the grown folks talking and close friends visiting. John (Uncle Boots) lived in a wooden house in the back of the original homestead and took his meals in our kitchen, when his sister Susan or Aunt Poss called him. Uncle David had a shower stall outside the back porch of his house. There was a cellar that had potatoes, etc. stored in it. Many vegetables were grown on this land. I remember shelling peas, shucking corn, etc. I also remember seeing beautiful rose bushes and azaleas in this yard.

When the property on Thomasville Road was sold to make way for a shopping center, movie theater, etc., a road was made at the back of the property and named Payne Drive. The main house and Uncle David's house were moved and had an empty lot in between them. Uncle Boots' house was built on the far edge of this property. Another person important to our family was Jimmy and two others whose names I can't recall.

Of the original family, Charles J. Adams and me, Joyce S. Guarine are alive along with our offsprings. Charles Adams, Sr. is the father of Daniel and Charlea Adams. Memories living in Tallahassee are many and great! More than ten family members are buried in the Macon Cemetery. My cousin and I conclude it was a great time to be alive and visiting Leon County, Florida.

Submitted by: Alyce Joyce S. Guarine, 147 Apple Valley Road, Macon, GA 31217-5554 ajguarine@cox.net

The Bert and Ina Watson Family of Woodville

Elgin Bertis (Bert) Watson was born in Wade, MS on November 1, 1903. He was the seventh of ten children and the second of four sons born to Henry Cornelius Watson (b. Jan. 12, 1861; d. Feb. 7, 1947) and Mary Ellen Faggard Watson (b. Apr. 28, 1873; d. Jan. 29, 1957). A family Bible record shows that Henry's father, Cornelius Thomas Watson, was born in the Tallahassee area in 1827. Cornelius lived in Leon and Wakulla Counties and was a Confederate Conscript during the Civil War. Henry had been born in the Tallahassee area, grew up in Wade and attended high school there. In the fall of 1922, Henry decided to leave Mississippi and move back to the Leon-Wakulla County area. Bert was among the four younger children who moved to Florida with their parents. Bert recalled that the family loaded their furniture aboard the coastal steamer Tarpon in Mobile and sent it on to Carrabelle, where Henry's older brother Kilby Matthew Watson lived. The family made the trip from Pascagoula, Mississippi to Tallahassee, Florida by train on October 22, 1922. The family first settled in Vareen, a small farming community in northern Wakulla County. But within two years they had moved onto a small farm located in Leon County about a mile northwest of Woodville.

When they first arrived in Florida, Bert and his brother Neil worked on a large farm in Wakulla County for George Russ. But after getting settled in the Woodville area, the boys began doing carpentry work, a profession in which Bert became very proficient and in which he remained all of his working career. But like many other folks of that age, he also became a part-time farmer and every year had a fine garden. Later he took advantage of the open range law and had hogs and cows. Sale of these animals greatly supple-mented his income during the depression years when carpentry work was scarce. After moving to Woodville, Bert spent many years living on rented farms in the area. In 1928 he married Ina Rosemond Chester (b. Mar. 29, 1907; d. Dec. 13, 1979). Ina, a native of Concord, Florida had obtained a teaching certificate in Quincy, Florida and was a teacher in Woodville School in 1926 and 1927. Some of her students were nearly her age! (See Photo 1. In this enclosed picture, Ina is in the center of the front row.) In 1935 they rented and moved onto the 110-acre Revells farm a mile west of Woodville. In 1939, he and Ina purchased a home on the west side of Woodville so the family could be near their church, the local school and the stores. In 1946 he purchased the Revells farm. Still later he purchased the adjoining 40-acre Wiley Lawhon

Ina Rosemond Chester and her Woodville School Students, circa 1926.

Bert and Ina Watson, at home in Woodville, circa 1950

farm. In 1969 he and Ina moved back onto the farm, where they remained for the rest of their lives.

Ina gave up teaching when her first male child was stillborn in 1928. During the following two decades seven other children were born to Bert and Ina, a daughter and six sons. They were Mary Lillian (b. Sept. 20, 1930; m. Joe L. Wright; three children: Joey, Susan Elaine and Mary Ellen): Thomas (Buddy) Cornelius (b. March 1, 1932; m. 1st, Anna Jane Hendren; m. 2nd, Mary Lou Watts; and m. 3rd, Betty Estelle Watson; no children); Donald (Don) Eugene (b. August 31, 1934; m. 1st, Annette Smith; no children; m. 2nd, Patsy Rouse; one child, Donald Eugene, Jr.; m. 3rd, Carol Sheffield; no children) ; Edward Wilke (b.July 20, 1940; d. April 1, 1960; m. Sharon Gibson; one child, Sherril Elaine); Jerry Wayne (b. August 15, 1942; m. Carol Ann Johnston, 1963; no children); and Maurice Randall (b. December 29, 1948; m. Mary Faye Martin, 1969; two children, Timothy Randall and Edward Todd). The grandchildren of Bert and Ina, named above, number eight. There are seven great grandchildren. (Photo 2 is a photograph of Bert and Ina in the yard of their Woodville home, circa 1950.) Bert was a master carpenter and except during the most severe years of the depression was able to find work in and around Tallahassee. Some of the builders and contractors he worked for were Wilson Construction Company, Dan Carter Cabinet shop located first in Woodville and then in Wakulla County just above Wakulla Station. Bert helped in the construction of beach homes at Wilson Beach in Franklin County for Ross Hannon, George Nesmith and Edwin Culbreath. Like so many other carpenters in the area, he made the long ride on a bus morning and night for several months to help construct the barracks and other buildings at amphibious base Camp Gordon**Error! Bookmark not defined.** Johnston near Carrabelle in Franklin County during the early part of WWII. Once he was hired for several months in the mid 1940s by some federal agency to teach carpentry to the inmates at the Federal Correctional Institute in Tallahassee.

His team actually built a small frame house on the prison property. Though carpentry work was sometimes hard to come by, the Bert Watson family never went hungry. Like so many others during the depression period, Bert supplemented his income by farming part time and by raising hogs and cows. He always had a milk cow or two and planted peanuts to fatten hogs which provided all the meat the family needed. And he sold both hogs and cows at the stock market in Monticello. Whenever he got into a bind for money, he would gather up a load of hogs and haul them off to market.

Bert and Ina's family had more than their fair share of illnesses and attendant expenses. Bert lost the function of one kidney to a massive kidney stone in the early 1930s and was bedridden for six months. Thomas contacted polio at the age of three and was hospitalized in Umatilla, Florida for almost two years. At the age of eight, Don had a ruptured appendix, double pneumonia and the mumps all at one time. And their son Edward was killed in an automobile accident in 1960. Somehow Bert and Ina coped with all these difficulties and managed to keep going. In the 1950s when all the kids were in school, Ina worked part time at the Woodville post office. The family was blessed by Ina's Uncle Wilke McElvy coming in the early 1940s to live with them for a decade or so. He took over the farming and gardening for Bert. Uncle Wilke was an outdoors type guy and took the Watson boys on memorable hunting, fishing and camping trips in the local area.

In 1969 Bert and Ina moved into a mobile home on the Revells farm. Bert continued raising corn crops and gardens as long as he was physically able. All their children remember fondly the pea shellings, fish frys, and the Thanksgiving and Christmas family gatherings that were held on the farm. Three of the sons, Billy, Jerry and Maurice, have built lovely homes on the property and continue to live there. Ina died of a heart attack in the winter of 1979. Bert continued living on the farm with the aid of his

children and grandchildren until his death in 1985. The success the children of Bert and Ina Watson have enjoyed in life can be attributed in large measure to the love, guidance and inspiration afforded by their adoring parents.
Submitted by: Thomas C. Watson, 2043 Queenswood Drive, Tallahassee, FL 32303

The Ira Bell Watson Family of Woodville

Ira Bell Watson (b. Sept 10, 1898; d. Feb 1, 1974) was the oldest son of Henry Cornelius and Mary Ellen Faggard Watson of Wade, MS. He was born and grew up in Wade MS and finished high school there. As a young man, he worked initially in the sawmill and timbering business. During and shortly after WWI he worked as a carpenter at Ingalls Shipyard in Pascagoula, MS. In Wade he met Lois Lillian Cochran (b. June 21, 1898; d. Sept 30, 1984) and was married to her on Dec 26, 1922 in Escatawpa, MS by a Rev. Hulbert. After marrying they moved and lived a short time near Atlanta, GA where Ira worked as a carpenter. But Lois insisted they both move back to Wade to be near her family before their first child, Lillian Iris Watson, was born (b. Oct 25, 1923; d. Mar 27, 1975). In 1927 they moved above Woodville, FL to be near his parents who had moved to Florida in 1922. In 1930 Ira and his father built Ira and Lois's home about three miles north of Woodville. Ira and Lois Watson's second child, Henry Wesley Watson (b. May 9, 1930; d. Sept 14, 1999), was born in a Tallahassee hospital. Iris and Henry grew to adulthood in their little home beside the Woodville highway. Photo 1 is a 1959 photo of the family.

Like his father before him, Ira was an expert carpenter and was usually able to find work in and around Tallahassee. He spent many years on the maintenance crew at Florida State College for Women, now Florida State University. Lois was a dedicated housekeeper and devoted her life to making a home for Ira and looking after the two children. But she found time to teach private students piano and to play the piano at the Woodville Methodist Church for many years. Iris was a precocious child and Lois taught her early on to play the piano. Ira had a good quality voice and the family traveled to nearby communities where he led various choirs and church groups in singing gospel songs. Lois and Iris played the piano and organ at some of these sing fests. Iris was so sufficiently talented that in the 1940s, she appeared on a weekly radio show in Tallahassee playing the piano for half an hour.

Henry and Ira Watson, Quail Hunters – 1969

Ira Bell Watson Family of Woodville, FL – 1959

Ira and Lois Watson's second child was Henry Wesley Watson. Henry's childhood was a happy one centered around outdoor activities. He and Ira spent many days fishing, quail hunting and deer hunting together throughout Henry's childhood and into his adult life. Henry grew up sharing these outdoor passions with his father. Even in MS as a young man, Ira owned good pointer bird dogs and was widely known for his bird hunting. Henry's family always had many bird dogs and deer hounds. See Photos 2 and 3. Lois, also, was hooked on freshwater fishing and in the spring and summer months, they fished weekly in the nearby ponds, lakes and rivers. Fish fries were a common occurrence at the Watson's home.

Ira's life came to a tragic end on Feb 1, 1974. As they had done for many years, Ira and Lois went fishing on the Six Mile Pond, just a couple miles above their home and adjacent to the Woodville Highway. Somehow they managed to turn the boat over and Ira suffered a massive heart attack and died on the spot when trying to right the boat in deep water. Lois clung to the boat and shouted for help. Miraculously someone heard her and she was rescued. She lived on another decade, mostly in poor health, and died in a Tallahassee nursing home on September 30, 1984.

In the early years of WWII many military pilots trained at Dale Mabry Field in Tallahassee. Iris was smitten by one of these pilots, Allan A. Lathan (b. July 11, 1918; d. Oct 6, 1997) and they were married June 30, 1942 in West Palm Beach, FL. Allen made the US Air Force a career and became a full Colonel before retiring in Fort Worth, TX in the 1970s. The couple was stationed all over during their married life: NY, AL, LA, AK, NE, and TX. The marriage produced three children: Linda Kay (b. May 4, 1945), Barbara Jo (b. Oct. 5, 1948) and Scott Adale (b. May 21, 1952). Before Allan retired, they built a lovely cottage on Panama City Beach, FL. Iris's brother Henry designed and drew the blue prints for the small two-story beach house. The family and various relatives spent many happy summers and holidays vacationing at this little retreat.

Henry Watson, Deer Hunter – 1974

Henry joined the US Army in the mid 1950s and was stationed in Germany. There he met and married Rosemarie Martha Muller. Henry returned from overseas bringing Rosemarie with him to settle in Woodville. Henry was trained as a draftsman and followed that line of work for twenty years. Rosemarie died of a heart ailment in April of 1958. The next year on 15 August 1959 Henry married Betty Estelle Sanford (b. Mar 1, 1937), a young woman from Largo, FL who was about to obtain a degree at FSU and then launch a thirty-two year career teaching math in various Leon County schools. Henry became employed by the Leon County School Board and worked at school building design and maintenance for over twenty-two years. Early on they adopted two children, Mark (b. June 4, 1964) and Leann (b. July 5, 1966). In 1984 Leann married Kirk Brewer (b. Sept 8, 1962), a native of Tallahassee. They have two lovely children: Leanna Kirklynn (b. Mar 22, 1997) and Cole Wesley (b. Aug 24, 2000). Photo 4 is a photo of the Kirk Brewer family. Henry developed lung cancer and died on Sept 14, 1999.

Kirk and Leann Brewer Family – 1999

On Jan 11, 2003 Betty married Henry's first cousin, Thomas C. Watson (b. Mar 1, 1932). They are thoroughly enjoying living in Tallahassee near Lake Jackson next to Leann, Kirk and the two grandchildren, Leanna and Cole.

Compiled by: Leann Brewer, 2045 Queenswood Drive, Tallahassee, FL 32303

Nancy and Harry Waugh

This is how Nancy Stowers Waugh and Harry Montgomery Waugh, Jr. came to Tallahassee from West Virginia. Nancy Stowers was born in 1927 in Bluefield, W VA, where she grew up and where she graduated from HS. She had 3 brothers and 1 sister: Eugene Stowers, Jr., Richard, Harry and Sue. Nancy's parents were Iva Metcalfe and Eugene Stowers. Her parents were natives of VA, her dad from Bland Co, VA and her mother from Graham, VA. Her dad was an automobile dealer. Her paternal grandparents, Julia and Frazier Stowers came across the mountain from Bland Co, VA. Her grandparents were early settlers of Bluefield where her grandfather Frazier served as Sheriff and Mayor

Nancy Waugh and Emily Waugh

and where a street, Stowers Street, was named in his honor.

After graduating from Bluefield High School, and Hollins College in Roanoke, VA, Nancy met Harry M. Waugh, Jr. in Bluefield, where he also lived. His parents were Gertrude Sleadd and Harry Montgomery Waugh, Sr. Harry, Jr. graduated from Bluefield, W VA HS and Tulane University in New Orleans, where he received his degree in Finance. The reason he attended Tulane was "He wanted to know what the other side of the mountain looked like." Although he started Tulane without a track scholarship, he later earned one after he got there. He had three brothers younger than he was, so the scholarship was a blessing. They were Edgar, Goree and Phil. Goree served in the Naval Air Corp. Unfortunately he was shot down in 1943 while on a mission off the coast of Brazil. All four Waugh brothers served in WWII.

Nancy and Harry were married in 1956 in Bluefield. They lived in Charleston, W VA for ten years. They had two children, Emily and Harry III. Homes and the schools were high on the mountain tops in WV, but work was down in the valleys where the air was smoggy and unclean. They felt they needed to find another climate in which to live. Harry met a friend at a Southeastern Banking Conference who encouraged him to apply for a job in Tallahassee at Tallahassee Bank and Trust. When Harry flew down to Tallahassee and was offere a job here, he took it. He said the trees were beautiful, the air was clean, and there was plenty of land. So the family decided to make Tallahassee their permanent home. They arrived here in 1967.

The family became involved in the community. Harry volunteered with the US Tennis Association and served as Treasurer for the Florida Tennis Association for 17 years. Nancy volunteers with Tallahassee Music Guild, United Methodist Woman, Trinity United Methodist Church, Violet Garden Circle, and the Tallahassee Garden Club. She has enjoyed two years in Senior Chimes at Trinity UMC. Harry, Jr. passed away Oct 30, 2007 and is buried in Roselawn Cemetery in Tallahassee. Their son, Harry Waugh III, lives in Madison Co. AL and has 2 children: Harry IV and Scott. Daughter Emily lives in Tallahassee and is a lawyer.

Submitted by: Nancy Stowers Waugh, 414 Vinredge Ride, Tallahassee, FL 32303

Major Edmund Cottle Weeks 1829 - 1907

He was Commanding Officer of the 2nd Florida Cavalry at Cedar Key, FL (1864-1865); Lieutenant Governor of Florida (1870); Leon County Commissioner (1871-1874); Leon County Sheriff (1874-76); State Representative, Leon County (1876-1878); Postmaster, Tallahassee (1879-1890); US Marshall of Florida (1890-1903); and Surveyor General of Florida (1903-1905).

Major Weeks was honored on Memorial Day 2011 at a dedication ceremony of the Veterans Administration Civil War Memorial Stone in the Old City Cemetery. The dedication was sponsored by Camp 5, E.A. Carr Department of Florida, Sons of the Union Veterans of the Civil War in conjunction with The Tallahassee Historical Society. Honored guests included the Murphy family of Tallahassee, descendents of Major Edmund C. Weeks; Roy Thomas Dye, Major Edmund C. Weeks historian; Claude Kenneson, President, Tallahassee Historical Society; Wayne Britt, Director, Tallahassee City Cemeteries; and Re-enactors from the 2nd USCT Infantry, 54th MA Infantry, SUVCW Veterans Reserve, and Sons of Confederate Veterans.

Submitted by: Mary J. Marchant, 2901 Springfield Drive, Tallahassee, FL 32309-3274

Edmund Cottle Weeks, Leon County's Marshall, Sheriff and Post Master

Edmund Cottle Weeks was born in Massachusetts in 1829. His father, Hiram Weeks, was a sea captain. Growing up he sailed with his father to South America, Africa, and England. He spent 3 years at medical school in New York. Then, in a fit of rebellion, he quit medical school and signed on as a seaman. After 3 years he advanced to the rank of Master. By 1860 he married Mary Jones of England and worked as an accountant in Boston.

Weeks applied for a

Edmund C. Weeks, 1879

commission in the US Navy after the attack on Fort Sumter. He was given the rank of Acting Master on the *USS Pensacola* in Admiral Farragut's fleet. In the Union naval attack on New Orleans, the Pensacola was struck 9 times by Rebel shells, sustaining heavy damage and many casualties. With the Pensacola in ruins, Weeks served on a captured Rebel steamboat, and commanded troops on land in an amphibious operation at Franklin, LA.

After sick leave in 1863, Weeks was assigned Executive Officer on the USS Tahoma of the East Coast Blockade Squadron in Florida. Weeks continued to gain a good reputation commanding ground operations, including an assault on a salt works at Saint Marks, Florida. This ability to conduct ground operations came to the attention of General Daniel Woodbury at Key West Army Headquarters. Lt. Weeks was promoted to Major, and was the commanding officer of the 2nd Florida at Cedar Key. The new regiment consisted of Southern Unionists, Confederate deserters, and a few convicts and criminals. When these men enlisted, their families were moved to Cedar Key and received protection and provisions. Weeks felt discipline was lax, and many of his troops enlisted simply to feed themselves and their families, and/or steal government supplies. So, out of disappointment with his troops, he returned to a desk job in Key West, Florida.

In September of 1864, Major Weeks returned to Cedar Key. On board the *USS Harriet*, he and the captain drank in celebration of his return. When Weeks left ship, sentry James White challenged him, and Weeks struck him. White fell off the pier onto the beach and Weeks grabbed the private's rifle as he fell. White got up to run away. Weeks called "Halt!" twice, but White kept running. Weeks shot him through the leg from 25 feet.

Junior officers placed Weeks under arrest. White died 2 weeks later, and Weeks was court martialed in Key West on November 1, 1864. The trial lasted over 3 months. Weeks hired 2 Boston lawyers. Testimony revealed the arresting Captain Strickland was a former Confederate officer, the arresting guards were deserters from the Rebels, and one man was a convicted cattle rustler. The post doctor was found negligent in treating White's leg wound, thus causing his death. Weeks' lawyers built a good case of conspiracy within the camp, including a plot to assassinate Weeks. Captain Weeks was acquitted on all counts, and Captain Strickland was decommissioned to private.

In early 1865, Weeks planned a return raid on St. Marks, in preparation for an assault on Tallahassee, the only Confederate state capital held by Rebels throughout the war. Weeks attacked with 3 companies from the 2nd Florida Cavalry and 3 from U.S. Colored Troops. They were unable to cross the St Marks River, as bridges had been captured and burned by the Rebels. Learning of Natural Bridge, the Union forces headed there, but were repulsed by Confederate General Sam Jones.

After the Civil War, Weeks made Florida his home and bought land near Tallahassee, notably the plantation Tuscawilla. Weeks leased the property, paid the taxes, and allowed the family to maintain control. But without the former 300 slaves to run the place, a plague of caterpillars, and cotton prices down to nine cents a pound, Weeks would spend the next twenty years paying his farm debt.

However, Weeks remained friends with powerful Republicans in Tallahassee, including future Governors Harrison Reed and Ossian Hart. Governor Reed appointed Weeks to Lt. Governor after the office was vacated by an election dispute. Being a former Union officer, and having fought alongside Black troops, he was not liked by the Democrats. At the opening of a session of the Senate, Weeks walked to the podium, grabbed the gavel, and called the Senate to order. One Senator was enraged and a vote was taken to have Weeks arrested, until two Black Senators protested, and he was permitted to retire "in good order." Later, the State Comptroller refused to pay Weeks, but he won his pay from a Court order within a week.

In 1874 Governor Hart appointed Weeks as Leon County Sheriff, because of Leon County's large Black population support of him. Weeks served 2 terms as state representative for Leon County in the 187's, and was appointed Tallahassee Postmaster in 1879. The 1880s were particularly hard on Major Weeks' family; his son Edmund Jr. contracted measles, and died from typhoid fever, his brother Wallace and his mother Mary both died from respiratory ailments. But Edmund carried on, with his stepdaughters Katherine, Josephine, and his son, Mason Weeks. Edmund remarried Elizabeth H. Crafts in 1890, widow of Gilbert Crafts, who had also moved to Tallahassee after the War. By this time the

Weeks-Murphy Home, built 1890 on Park Avenue in Tallahassee

Wilson/Whitfield home – 502 s. Adams c. 1934

Democrats succeeded in intimidateing and disqualifying the black's vote, and the Republicans were no longer a force. Soon Florida's U.S. Marshal resigned and Major Weeks was nominated to replace him, but despite a smear campaign from Democrats, President Benjamin Harrison hired Weeks as US Marshall for the Northern Florida District and his name appeared on the 1900 Census for Florida. He was the right man for the right job. He had military experience, law enforcement experience, and was committed to Blacks' voting rights. His reputation had grown in Florida to that of a stern, fearless and well respected individual. Even the Democrats congratulated him in the Tallahassee newspaper.

As Marshall, he set out to bring law and order to Florida. He served arrest warrants on those accused of civil rights violations, murders, and voter fraud. With his limited resources, Weeks could not stop all the voting violations or lynching. He was not deterred by threats which made his office a sanctuary for freedmen and Republicans from mob violence. Major Weeks was buried in 1907 at the Old City Cemetery.

His home still stands, where his daughter, Josephine Murphy's descendants now own.
Written-Submitted by: Dr. Bill Hopkins, 900 W. Chippewa Street, Cadott, WI 54727 doch609@aol.com

Richard Gittings Welford and Matilda Elaeanor Smith Yellow Fever Epidemic – 1841

My Great Great-grandfather Richard Gittings Welford married his sweetheart Matilda Eleanor Smith in Tallahassee in late August, 1841. They honeymooned at a clapboard hotel at Bel-Air, a settlement south of Tallahassee on the shores of a sandy bottom lake. About 10 days after their wedding, Richard received word that his entire family in Tallahassee had contracted yellow fever and was very ill. Both Richard and Matilda rushed back to Tallahassee to help. Richard's parents and two brothers were very ill. After caring for them Richard became infected as well. After a while Richard, his parents, and two brothers all died within days of each other in late September and early October. The entire family was buried in a mass grave in the Old City Cemetery in Tallahassee without a headstone.

Matilda survived and soon realized she had become pregnant during the short honeymoon. My great grandmother Mary Richard Welford was born in May, 1842. Matilda's parents, residents of Tallahassee, were not touched by the Yellow Fever Epidemic. They provided support to Matilda and since her father was a medical doctor Matilda family escaped the epidemic. Aside from the emotional trauma from Richard's death, Matilda did well. She and her daughter inherited Richard's estate and the estate of Richard's family. She took

Mary Richard Welford with three grandchildren c. 1909

Mary Richard to Maryland to meet and visit her cousins, aunts, and uncles on Richard's side. After a normal mourning period, Matilda married Samuel Woodberry, a Methodist minister her age, and had three children with him. They lived in Quincy, Monticello, Madison, Live Oak, and Tallahassee during their time together. Samuel died in the mid 1880s and Matilda in 1888. Both are buried next to Matilda's Daughter Mary Richard Welford in the Old City Cemetery of Tallahassee.
Submitted by: William Whitfield, 1417 White Star, Tallahassee, Fl 32312, billnans@embarqmail.com

Mary Richard Wellford Wilson

Mary Richard Wellford was born in Tallahassee, Florida, on April 29, 1842. She was the daughter of Richard Gittings Wellford and Matilda Eleanor Smith Wellford. Richard died on October 6, 1841, from yellow fever during the devastating epidemic that occurred in Tallahassee in September and October, 1841. Richard and Matilda had married August 24, 1841.

Mary was raised by her widowed mother in sparsely populated Tallahassee-a town of clapboard houses and businesses along dirt streets surrounded by cotton plantations, woods, and swamps. Tallahassee, the capitol of Territorial Florida, was relatively isolated geographically. It was slow to change after Florida became a state in 1845.

Matilda was able to support herself and Mary from the estates of her husband and his family. Mary was educated as females were at that time by her mother, her mother's parents, and by semi-trained teachers in homes. Matilda took Mary to Maryland and Virginia in the early 1850s to meet and visit with Richard's extended family. Soon after, Matilda married the Reverend Samuel Woodberr who was a Methodist minister. Children were born to Matilda and Samuel and the family occasionally moved within the Methodist Conference to parishes in Madison, Tallahassee, and Quincy.

Joseph Wilson and Mary Richard Welford in 1865

Mary and Children of Joseph "fighting Joe" Wilson in 1885

Mary met Joseph David Wilson when he returned from his Confederate naval service in June, 1865. They were married a few weeks later in July and eventually raised 8 children. The family bought a home on South Adams Street in Tallahassee directly across the street from the State Capitol building (and now the site of the new Capitol building).

Joseph became a railroad engineer. He was killed in a railroad accident near Madison on November 30, 1880. Mary supported herself and her children by taking in boarders. She also had a small pension from Joseph's military service. Mary continued to live in their home where she died on December 8, 1910. The home remained in the family until 1948 when it was bought by the State for capitol expansion.

Mary and Joseph are buried side by side in the Old City Cemetery in Tallahassee next to Matilda and Samuel. The family placed a monument in the 1990s to memorialize the 5 members of the Wellford family who died in the 1841 yellow fever epidemic. The Wellford family and many other yellow fever victims were hurriedly buried in the same cemetery in an unmarked and now lost common grave.
Written by: William Whitfield, 1417 White Star Lane, Tallahassee, Florida 32312, billnans@embarqmail.com

Sandra Lee Blankenship Werner

Sandra moved to Tallahassee; Florida in 1942 from her birthplace of Lake City, Florida. Her father, George W. Blankenship, had been an administrative clerk with the CCCs since 1934, and they were transferred to the War Department for the duration of WWII. Her mother, Frances

Fair Clark, was a seventh generation Floridian. Frances' grandfather was born near Lake Iamonia in northern Leon County in 1852 and his parents, Frances Fair and James Rinaldo Nicks had lived here since 1833 before moving to Hernando County in 1853.

During the time Sandra and her two brothers, Charles and George Francis, lived at Dale Mabry Heights, they became aware of the State Capitol and the importance of government. Many years later, Sandra would become involved in the same and returned many times to Tallahassee. Her maternal ancestors (James Nicks and Michael Garrison) had served as State Representatives. The Nicks voted to change the town of her birth from Alligator to Lake City in the middle 1850s and Michael Nicks served the first year Florida gained Statehood in 1845.

During 1943, the family moved down to Camp Gordon Johnston and lived in the Pickett Apartment until the end of WWII. They remained there until around 1946 before moving to Carrabelle Beach Florida. In early 1948, Sandra moved away from Florida, first to New Mexico, and then to Virginia. In 1949 she moved to Kingsport, Tennessee. During Sandra's senior year of high school, she moved back to Florida. Because of a Florida school requirement to complete a biology science course, she stayed another year in high school at Gulf High in New Port Richey. Her extra courses enabled her to become acquainted with the State laws and eventually allowed her to enter politics.

Sandra Werner-(Blond) and Sylvia Young in 1982

Before 1980 Sandra worked in a local law firm, and became an assistant for an U. S. State Representative to Congress, plus she attended the Republican Convention in 1976 as a delegate. From her gained experience in politics, Sandra was elected (along with Sylvia Young) as the first female county commissioners for Pasco County.

Sandra Blankenship-(Blond) at age six in 1938 at Mabry Field

She served in that capacity for four years and returned to Tallahassee many times. Two projects were most important to her: one was the acquisition of a State park, now named; Werner-Boyce Salt Springs Run State Park, named after her late husband, Gene Werner and his partner, Bill Boyce; two was the project to fight for the Sheriff's budget in 1981.

After leaving office, Sandra still remained involved in local politics and until just recently served as Pasco County Planning Commission Vice Chairperson. She served in that capacity for ten years. Sandra has three sons and one daughter. One son, Paul Nessler, Jr., has been a lawyer since 1983 and her daughter, Frances Katherine Werner since 1998. When her brother Charles moved back to Tallahassee in 1985, Sandra visited and the two became interested in their Florida heritage. In 1986, they proved their maternal Florida ancestors came to Florida in 1762, before the English Possession period, and their Fair-Nicks line arrived in 1833.

Written by: Charles Blankenship; Submitted by: Riley Watkins (Sandra's Daughter), 4932 Marlin Dr., New Port Richey, FL 34652

Thomas Kent "T.K." Wetherell

Dr. Wetherell is married to Virginia Bacon-Wetherell, who was appointed by Governor Chiles as Secretary of the Florida Department of Environmental Protection from 1991 to 1998. She previously served as a state legislator representing Pensacola. She currently is president of Wetherell Consulting Services. They are the parents of three children: Kent, Blakely, and Page. They are the proud grandparents of Emily and Tyler. Wetherell's personal interests include outdoor recreation, travel and aviation.

Dr. Thomas Kent "T.K." Wetherell became the 13th president of Florida State University on January 6, 2003. He is the first university alumnus to serve as president of Florida State. A career educator with more than 30 years of experience in the State of Florida's educational system, Dr. Wetherell is also the only FSU president with experience in all four major divisions within higher education, having held positions in the offices of academic affairs, student services, business affairs, and college development. He has held leadership positions in two-year as well as four year colleges, and he has served as a faculty member in both public and private institutions of higher education.

Dr. Wetherell is recognized as a high-energy, student-oriented president. He is an innovator who challenges faculty, staff and administrators to set high professional and personal standards. Dr. Wetherell established the "Pathways of Excellence" program designed to enhance Florida State University's stature as a public graduate research university. Dr. Wetherell is an outstanding advocate for higher education

Thomas Kent "T.K." Wetherell

and has been called the state's most "politically astute president." In addition to his political insight, Dr. Wetherell is an expert in resource development and has led the university to successfully complete Florida State's second major capital campaign. During the campaign Dr. Wetherell gave the largest gift a seated president of a public research university has ever given to an institution in the United States. As President, Dr. Wetherell has also been the university's most vocal advocate for a community service program as part of a student's college experience.

Dr. Wetherell has been inducted into Florida State University's Hall of Fame and was the recipient of the prestigious Moore-Stone Award, the Circle of Gold Award and the university's Distinguished Service Award. In addition, he has also been awarded an honorary Doctorate of Letters from Flagler College.

Dr. Wetherell served in the Florida House of Representatives from 1980 to 1992, the last two years as Speaker of the House. During his tenure in the House he served as chairman of the appropriations committee and the higher education committee. A third-generation Floridian, Dr. Wetherell was born on December 22, 1945 in Daytona Beach, Florida. He attended Port Orange Elementary School and Mainland Senior High School, where he was active in service clubs, student government and athletics. He attended Florida State University on a football scholarship and played on the 1963-67 football teams. He still holds the record for the longest kickoff return in Florida State University history. He earned his bachelor's and master's degrees in social studies education from FSU in 1967 and 1968 respectively. He earned a doctorate in education administration from FSU in 1974.

Written and Submitted by: Jill Elish, 2888 East Capp Hwy, Lunt, FL. 32311

McPherson Extended Families – Growing Up with the Wilders

The home of Andy and Louise Wilder was on Bass Street across from Elmer McPherson, his wife Thelma Lee, and Dotty. Andy worked at Sears and was a preacher for Sunny Hill Primitive Baptist Church on Crawfordville Highway. Louise was a Sunday School Teacher. Dotty called them Uncle Wilder and Aunt Wilder. The whole Wilder family had deep and lasting effects in the shaping of Dorothy Lee "Dotty" McPherson.

Daughters Mary, Ruby, Sadie, and Katie were like sisters to Dotty, as Dotty was an only child. They included Dotty when they helped pick the chickens after Uncle Wilder wrang their necks. She helped with household chores. She ate many a meal with them. They went to Sunday school and church on Sunday mornings, and church again Sunday and Wednesday nights.

One time when washing dishes after Sunday dinner, the girls were dancing to music in the kitchen. Aunt Wilder caught them and in her high-pitched but melodic, passive voice scolded "You're gonna go to the Devil...You're gonna go to the Devil."

As teenagers, Mary, Ruby, and Dotty dated Max, Gilbert, and Tommy Lawhon, respectively. Their dates mostly centered around church activities, singing in the choir, having dinners on the ground, and going to Sunday School. But they

almost always ended up at the Wagon Wheel or the Corral for a Strawberry and 7-Up Float.
Written and Submitted by: Dorothy Lee "Dotty" McPherson, 24236 Lanier Street, Tallahassee, FL 32310

Freeman Williams

Why do you suppose so many farm boys become aviators? Maybe it's because they want to be able to look down and see the family farm from the air. Well, Freeman Williams had plenty of opportunities in his lifetime to fly over the farm he was born to in Pembroke, Georgia, outside of Savannah. After a stint as a photographer in Savannah, Freeman answered the call to serve as a Navy gunner aboard a torpedo bomber in World War Two. He liked flying, so after the war he took a job as a civilian flight instructor and aircraft engine mechanic for two years.

But the call to serve his country was strong. In 1948 he rejoined the military, in the U. S. Air Force Aviation Cadet Program. Freeman became a bomber pilot, staff officer and later, an engineering officer. He served the air force for many, many years as a pilot, bombardier, and radar officer. At one time Freeman was Director of Safety for the Air Division for three years.

Because of the many opportunities the Air Force offered to expand on his education, Freeman attended several colleges across the country, working toward a degree in engineering. Although he never completed his course of study he was able to use what he had learned to become Director of Engineering at the airbase on Guam, where he was responsible for providing facilities and base maintenance to keep those big B-52's in the air over Southeast Asia. After his years with the military Freeman left the Air Force and moved to an architectural engineering firm in Coral Gables, where he ultimately retired as Vice President with eighteen years service.

But we all know that there is more to life than work. For Freeman, the highs and lows of his life centered around two wonderful women. His first wife, Ann he met while he was a young bachelor officer in Savannah. She was his roommate's girlfriend. They met, he took her to the beach, and that was that! They were happily married in 1949. He was a smooth operator. But life has a way of bringing you up short. His wife died. Freeman spent many years alone, while his daughter Susan was in college. That was until 1976, when Baptist Church friends in Coral Gables invited him to dinner. There he met Nancy, a lovely woman who, this time, charmed him into marriage.

His wonderful daughter Susan was a strong comfort when his second wife passed away. It is Susan who prompted Freeman to come settle in Tallahassee. She had graduated from FSU, earned a Masters from Northwestern and a Doctorate from the University of Arkansas in Fayetteville. She took a position in Tallahassee and Freeman came here to settle near her. Freeman bought a place across the street from Jack and Barbara Nix. One Sunday morning they gathered him up and brought him to First Baptist. The combination of our fine folks and the preaching of Doug Dortch have kept him here ever since. Having been a believer since he was an eight-year-old farm boy in Georgia, Freeman recognized a strong Christian home here. With the Lord's Prayer as his guide he struggles to make the most of his health challenges, while keeping his quick wit and friendly smile for all he meets.

As an engineer Freeman has watched the runaway growth in transportation, electronics and medicine with interest and understanding, His hope for us all is that the rapid growth in these fields will be matched with the personal and spiritual growth that will help turn these advances to the good of all mankind.
Written by: Carol Ann and Bill Boydston©, 1639 Twin Lakes Circle, Tallahassee, FL 32311; Submitted by: Freeman Williams

Minnie Lucile Wynn Williams High School Days

I came to Tallahassee to attend Lincoln High School in 1933, after finishing the tenth grade from Dunbar Junior High School in my hometown, Apalachicola.

My ride to Tallahassee was on the Luke's Bus Lines and, because there was no bridge over

Lincoln High School Graduating Class of 1935 with Principal, C. H. Walker

the Apalachicola Bay, the bus had to cross on the ferry. When we reached Tallahassee, the bus driver stopped at the bus station to check in and unload some passengers before taking me to my destination.

The bus station was on Adams Street behind the post office, which was on the corner of Park Avenue and Adams Street facing north – where the Doubletree Hotel now stands. The bus driver took me, with my trunk, to my destination on the Old Bainbridge Road where I would live for two years with Mrs. Mamie Newborn, a widow who lived around the corner from the school which was on Brevard Street.

Mrs. Mamie Newborn had been recommended to my mother by a friend of hers who she met when they attended the Florida A. and M. College. The friend, Mrs. Viola Hunter, was a teacher in the elementary department of Lincoln. Other teachers that had been friends of my mother while in school were Miss Henrietta Williams and Miss Jeannette Twine who taught in the elementary department and Miss Lillian Hardin, one of my teachers in the high school.

I, a teenager now attending a school much larger than I was accustomed to, found the school week exciting, met many new friends, and thought the teachers were the best. There was our principal, Mr. Cecil H. Walker, a dapper young man who expected the best of his students. There were Rev. E. W. Spearman who taught history; Miss Lillian Hardin, English and Literature; Mr. W. H. Robinson and Mrs. Harpie Adams, Mathematics; Miss Thelma Jiles, French; Mrs. Jennie Stewart Robinson, English and Music; Mr. A. J. Robinson, Science; and Mr. Breaux Martin, Physical Education.

Among the teachers of the elementary school that I recall were Miss Amy Jackson, Mrs. Daisy Hall, Mrs. Paralee Philpot, Mrs. Ruby Washington, Mrs. Letisha Byrd, Mrs. Pottsdamer, Mrs. Victorine Blake, and Mrs. Alma Littleton.

There were few people that I knew before coming to Tallahassee, but I found delight on Sundays attending Bethel A. M. E. Church on the corner of Virginia and Duval Streets where the Reverend N. Z. (Noah Zachariah) Graham was pastor. He had been my father's pastor at St. Paul A. M. E. Church in Apalachicola and I always was greeted by him as one in the family. I knew his children Laura Anna, Ruth Sophia (So-fi' -a), Nellie Mae and William Franklin.

Also, I was greeted warmly by Rev. W. M. Burns and Mrs. Austine Bums when on alternate Sundays I attended Bethel Baptist Church on the corner of Boulevard and Tennessee Streets. Rev. Burns had been my mother's pastor at Mt. Zion Missionary Baptist Church in Apalachicola.

Then there was Rev. Watson, pastor of the Church of God in Christ, who was my father's distant cousin. My first cousin, Lula Belle Wynn, lived with the Watsons while we both attended Lincoln.

I often visited the Casanas family around the corner in the last block of Copeland Street. Their daughter, Aquilina who was one grade ahead of me, and I became lifelong friends.

Regarding sites that reflected a different Tallahassee, on the corner of Gaines and Monroe Streets, facing Gaines where the Fletcher Building now stands, the family that later would become my in-laws lived. Also, behind them on Monroe Street where a state garage now stands, my classmate, Dorothy Walker lived with her mother, Mrs. Maggie Walker. They had a huge pecan tree in their backyard from which they shared with me many bags of pecans.

Submitted by: Minnie Lucile Wynn Williams, Retired Educator who has spent most of her life in Tallahassee. 2114 Broad Street Tallahassee, Florida 32301

Jessie Willis Locating my Great-Great Grandfather

Just got back from our month-long driving vacation around the country through the southwest, southern California, then up the Pacific coast to Mt. Vernon, WA, then across to St. Louis via Yellowstone, then down to Tennessee, then on home with many kinfolk and friend visits along the way. My cousin, Mark Beasley, and I have been working on my brick wall, great-great-grandpa, Jesse Willis, ca 1810-1868, born inGeorgia then moved to Dale County, Alabama about

My Great-Great-Grandfather, Jesse Willis

My Great-Grandfather, Iverson Asbury Willis

1839.

We located my grandfather, Jonathan Willis and then my great-grandfather, George Willis, Jr., and finally my great great grandfather, George Willis Sr. This line came down to Robeson County, North Carolina from Virginia, and before that, Devonshire, England.

Jonathan and his father, George Willis, came to Leon Co., FL in the 1830's and Jonathan bought 360 acres in the northeast Tallahassee area: in Section 1, T2N, R1E and in Section 6, T2N, R2E. He must have sold his land here in Tallahassee because a few years later he shows up on the 1840 Dale Co., AL federal census with his son, Jesse Willis. Jesse's grandfather, George Willis, apparently died in Leon County before 1840 because he does not show up on the Dale County census with Jonathan and Jesse Willis.

Here is some census data on my Willis line that came from Virginia to NC to GA to Tallahassee, to Dale County, AL. Then my grandfather, George Washington Willis (grandson of Jesse), moved to Bagdad, FL in 1917 to work in the big sawmill there. That's where I was born. It was a Happy Day for Rodney E. Willis.

I began my genealogical research in the 1990s upon the death of my father. My parents are Mary Willis and Jake Willis. I have one brother, Jesse and two sisters, Ann and Beth. I moved to Tallahassee to attend FSU in 1949.

Submitted by: Rod Willis (aka, Rodney Earl Willis), 5386 Back Forty Road, Tallahassee, FL 32303 bagdad34@comcast.net; Sources: NC, GA, & AL Census Records 1790-1850

Rodney Earl Willis Talented Tallahassean

Rod was born across Blackwater River from Bagdad, Florida, in 1934, the youngest son of John Ollie Willis (1903-1979) and Edna Mae Collinsworth (1910-1943). Growing up in the country enabled Rod to maintain a limber and athletic form, which served him well at Milton High School, where he played 4 years of basketball, baseball and football. Following graduation on June 2, 1953, he joined the Marine Corps. After 10 weeks of boot camp at Parris Island, South Carolina, he served at Camp Lejeune, North Carolina, with side trips to Vieques Island, Puerto Rico, for further training, then on to Japan and Okinawa for a year before mustering out at Treasure Island, California, on September 1, 1956. He recalls putting his seabags on a train in Oakland and riding his thumb down Route 66 through Texas. He then veered southeast toward the family home in Milton, Florida, and made it in less than 72 hours.

As many veterans did after they were discharged, Rod enrolled at Florida State University on September 10, 1956. A mere one week later he met his future wife, Carolyn Elvidge, at the water fountain backstage in Ruby Diamond Auditorium on freshmen's Talent Night, circa September 15, 1956. She was dancing a jazz number and he was singing Elvis songs. People thought he was talented enough to warrant a Flambeau article, which mentioned how he became a state celebrity with his singing. It also talked about his hopes and dreams for his newfound singing career. It seems that all his athletic training paid off during this rock and roll era. The record sold about 50,000 copies, not enough to stay in business, so he went back to school, married Carolyn, and graduated with a BS in Business. Shortly hereafter Rod went to work for the State of Florida (13 years in the Governor's Budget Office), bought 80 acres in Northwest Leon County, moved to "The Back Forty" community and never left. Rod and his wife have 5 children, 19 grandchildren, including 3 sets of twins and one set of triplets, and one great grandchild.

Rod got interested in genealogy when he retired from the State in 1988. Carolyn retired from the Florida Senate in 1994. They both have served as

Rodney E. Willis Singing in 1958

Treasurer for the Tallahassee Genealogical Society for about a three-year span. Those were "Happy Days" for Rodney E. Willis.
Written by: Rod Willis (aka, Rodney Earl Willis), 5386 Back Forty Road, Tallahassee, FL 32303 Bagdad34@comcast. Com
Submitted by: Robert Willis (Brother of Rod), 6807 Aegean Drive, Milton, FL 32583 Rwillis627@aol.com

"Fighting Joe" Wilson

Joseph Wilson was born in Tallahassee in 1840. He was appointed to the United States Naval Academy in 1857. Wilson resigned from the Academy in 1861, and reported to the Confederate Navy Department. Wilson was commissioned a Midshipman and ordered to report to Captain Rafael Semmes aboard the *CSS Sumter*.

The "Sumter" ran the blockade in summer, 1861, and intercepted and destroyed Yankee commercial vessels for nine months from Cuba to Brazil to Spain. The ship was worn out by April, 1862. Semmes turned the *Sumter* over to the British. The Confederacy arranged for the construction of a warship in England. The warship was commissioned the "CSS Alabama" in August, 1862 with Semmes commanding. Wilson was promoted to Lieutenant. His duties included being gunnery officer, boarding officer, and Officer of the Deck.

The *Alabama* was a sailing ship and steamer. It began its attack on Yankee commercial vessels in September in the North Atlantic. It cruised in the West Indies and Gulf of Mexico, and near Brazil, and South Africa. The *Alabama* was well received by the British at Capetown. During one shore visit, Wilson and several officers went big game hunting.

Semmes took the "*Alabama*" to the East Indies. The *Alabama* docked to spend Christmas, 1863, at Singapore. On Christmas Eve, Wilson and fellow officers went ashore and encountered a group of Yankee naval officers. Words evolved into a fistfight. The authorities were called. The British ordered the *Alabama* to leave. Thereafter, Wilson was known as "Fighting Joe".

The *Alabama* was in need of overhaul and the aged gunpowder was losing potency from dampness. The ship sailed to India to Capetown and back to Europe. The *Alabama* docked at Cherbourg, France in June, 1864. It caused a sensation. Many came to see the ship, including Confederate and Union operatives stationed in France. The nearby *USS Kearsarge* was notified and it soon blockaded Cherbourg.

Joseph Wilson – 1862 in Navel uniform during the Civil War

The naval battle between the *Alabama* and *Kearsarge* occurred June 19, 1864. International law prevented Semmes from adding additional officers and crew, and fresh gunpowder. Outgunned and outmanned, the *Alabama* was sunk. Wilson commanded an 8" cannon. This gun was hit by a shell and several crewmen were killed. Wilson was not seriously injured. Many "Alabama" shells failed to explode.

Wilson was the ranking officer captured. Semmes and other officers escaped to England. The *Kearsarge* resumed its patrol with the officer captives aboard. A month later, the U.S. ambassador to Britain, requested the *Kearsarge* captain to parole Wilson at Dover, England. Wilson was paroled but the other officers were taken to a U. S. Naval prison.

One may wonder why Wilson was paroled. One reason might be that Union operatives could follow him to Confederate operatives. Wilson was ordered to return to the Confederacy. He took British ships to Halifax and Bermuda where he boarded the *Condor*, a blockade runner. A fellow passenger from England was Rose Greenhow, the famous Confederate operative returning home after diplomatic efforts in Europe.

The *Condor* ran aground near Wilmington. All took to lifeboats. Greenhow's lifeboat capsized and she drowned. Wilson swam to shore. Wilson was assigned to the James River Squadron near Richmond. The CSN had ships to prevent the Union Navy from attacking Richmond via the James River. Semmes was the commanding officer.

On April 2nd, Lee's army evacuated Richmond. Semmes ordered the destruction of the ships to join Lee, but Lee's army had already left. Semmes' men commandeered a train to Danville. Semmes organized the Semmes Naval Brigade as a part of the Confederate Army. They surrendered and were paroled soon after Lee surrendered. Wilson traveled home with the Semmes party. Wilson had served with Semmes longer than anyone. He left the travel party near Columbus, Georgia, and walked home arriving early June.

Wilson became a civil and a railroad engineer. He married Mary Welford in 1865. They had 8 children. Their home was located on the site of the new Florida State Capitol. He was killed in a railroad accident near Madison in 1880. He is buried in the old Tallahassee City Cemetery.

Wilson's Ship the *Sumter* took 18 U. S. vessels and the "Alabama" 69 including one Union warship. Most captured vessels were burned with prisoners released. These ships and other CSN commerce raiders seriously disrupted Yankee shipping forcing most commercial vessels into port. It forced the Union to send warships worldwide in an effort to safeguard commercial shipping. The *Alabama* was the most successful of the Confederate commerce raiders and almost caused war between the United States and Britain.

Written and Submitted by: William Whitfield, 1417 White Star Lane, Tallahassee, Florida 32312

The Mark Turner Winchester Family of Old Tallahassee

My father, Mark Turner Winchester, with my Mother, Bernice Thompson Winchester, returned from World War II and opened Winchester's, a grocery and service station on Old Perry Highway (Hwy 27 South), which is now Apalachee Parkway. It originally was where Governor's Square Mall is located. The restaurant next to the station was well known for his barbeque. Three adjacent cabins were rented to travelers.

They drove a black Packard then. Gas was 28 cents a gallon.

When the road was 4-laned, they moved Winchester's Grocery And Market across the road to LafayetteStreet, where it becomes Old St. AugustineRoad. The building remains today. TheAlley behind the building was named Winchester Lane. Locals visited the store to talk about news and especially politics. Being downhill from the Capitol, county, and state buildings, men would head to Winchester's to unwind and drink a beer before heading home.

Winchester's Restaurant (top) Grocery (middle) and cabins (lower)

My father was a butcher and cut and stored wild game local hunters brought him. He was known for his smoked sausage, which he smoked in the smokehouse out back. He shipped sausage all over the United States. I'm the oldest of their eight children and we all grew up working in the family business. Good thing he had a grocery store to feed all of us.

Written by: Jesse Winchester; Edited and Submitted by: Dorothy Lee McPherson, 24236 Lanier Street, Tallahassee, FL 32310

Winterle – Wartime Memories

The World War II years stand out in memory: rationing coupons, spotting airplanes on cold winter nights on Vason's hill, near where Tallahassee Nurseries is now, military convoys, Camp Gordon Johnston, Dale Mabry air training base, soldiers, pilots – many of whom ranked up to colonel visited in the Winterle home. How they appreciated visiting in a home, or sitting around a supper table.

The most fascinating experience for our family was a friendship with a group of Chinese pilots who came to Dale Mabry Field from

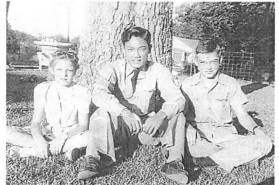
Irene Winterle, Joseph (Evans) Chao-Pin Mao, and Joe Winterle

Phoenix. They were young, handsome, vivacious, and courteous. Some had Barry Goldwater as a flight instructor in Phoenix. Our dad, Fred, met some of the pilots when they got off the bus at the Gulf Oak Service Station, then on the corner of Pensacola and Adams where there was a large live oak and where the Supreme Court is now. He owned the Gulf Oil Agency and knew the owners of various car dealerships, and he helped some of the fellows get used cars - including David Huang and Joseph (Evans) Chao-Pin Mao (kin to Chairman Mao, but not communist himself). Friendship grew fast through our family and the Chinese. How far away from home they were and they were so grateful to visit in our home. Occasionally the family and their new friends would go swimming at Lake Hall and then come back home where Mother had a delicious meal! Before the squadron left for their port of embarkation in Charleston, SC, David and Joseph asked our family to go with them to P.W. Wilson's to buy gifts to take back to China. As Mrs. Cook waited on them and showed linens made in China, David and Joseph would chat in Chinese and sort of giggle. This was puzzling. After making their purchases all went to our home for lunch. The gifts were brought from the car and presented to our mother! Wow! We missed them so much, so our dad saved gas coupons. He loaded the trunk of the car with safe containers of gas, and we headed to Charleston in the middle of the night during the least traffic. We had so much fun at the beach with the Chinese pilots. One of the fellows convinced Dad to buy a 16 mil. Movie camera while in Charleston: we have movies of our dear friends having fun at Folly Beach.

A humorous thing happened to Joe, who loved aviation and who soloed at age 18. He was asked to move an old P-51 (no globe over the cockpit) that the military had given Lively Vocational Technical School at Park Avenue and Duval Street. When asked how he moved the plane from the base to Lively he said he taxied it down Pensacola Street! When he arrived, the young pilot was given an arousing welcome. High excitement there– the motor stopped. Joe got out of the plane. The Lively group and Joe were close to the plane in extreme jubilation when all of the sudden there was a huge bang; everybody had a shock! That was the nature of a liquid cooled engine instead of air cooled – Joe's glory was interrupted.

Submitted by: F. Irene Winterle Yerger and Joe Winterle, 606 Plantation Road, Tallahassee, FL 32303

Winterle- Yerger
Memories of our Neighborhood

In the late thirties the Fred Winterle family moved to Tallahassee from Lynn Haven, Ocala, and first Atlanta where Joe and Irene were born. Our dad traveled as a sales-man for Gulf Oil Corporation. We lived in a new home off Thomasville Road rented to us by H.L. Jones, who lived a few yards north of us, where he and his wife had a small grocery store (later called Nesmith's Nursery) and gas station combined. They were located across the road from where Books-A-Million is now, and we were located just south of Mr. Jones where McDonalds is now – across from the I-10 flyover. Joe and Irene rode their bikes on the two lane concrete highway (there wasn't much traffic there). An occasional huge log truck would come by. When we heard the trucks coming we moved fifteen feet off into the Bahia grass! We visited Raymond Diehl and the Turners where Nell Turner Carlyle lived. Their home would be in the middle of I-10. The Diehl home was about where Metropo-litan Boulevard is now and had a driveway bordered with beautiful glossy-leafed camellias.

In our yard were four large live oaks, Two were in the front near the fence – the others were at either end of the teardrop-shaped driveway left of the house. The area inside the drive was full of Formosa Indica Azaleas. They smelled marvelous when they blossomed. Irene would ride her tricycle and later her bicycle round and round. She doesn't know who was happier, she or the big bumblebees that were in heaven among the flowers. The area became a macadam parking lot for McDonalds much later.

While living there a mean hurricane hit Tallahassee. The heavy lawn chairs tumbled across the front yard like cardboard. The yard and highway were a disaster. For two weeks there was

H. L. Jones house rented to the Winterle family on Thomasville Road

no electricity and thus no water because we had an electric water pump. Our mother, Laura, filled the bathtub full of water and Mr. Jones loaned us a two-burner kerosene stove. He also had a hand water pump in the front of his store where we got fresh water. When Dad was finally able to get to town for a block of ice, Mother used the easy-washing machine for an icebox.

One summer was very lonely for us - that was during a polio epidemic. Our mother who was a retired nurse would not let us leave the yard, nor would she permit anyone to visit us, but we were spared polio.

Submitted by: F. Irene Winterle Yerger, 4140 Covenant Lane, Tallahassee, FL 32308

Woodard – The Colonel

At the end of World War II, Tallahassee was a small town with the promise of future growth. With the closing of Dale Mabry Field, many young military men moved on to begin their future lives elsewhere; but a handful stayed on in Tallahassee to endeavor in their careers.

A.P. Woodard

Some were doctors who became the founders of Tallahassee Memorial Hospital; some were lawyers who set up their practice, as well as other professions. One such entrepreneur was Albert P. Woodard, an architect who went on to later preside as president of the Florida chapter of the AIA.

Mr. Woodard, or as many people still referred to him as "the Colonel" until his death in 1970, set up practice and designed many office buildings, churches, sorority and fraternity houses at FSU, as well as many private homes in Tallahassee and the surrounding area.

Along with his friend and apprentice, the talented Mr. Jack Buckley, he left his stamp on the beautiful architecture enjoyed by Tallahasseans. Most of the structures still stand today.

Submitted by: Carol Woodard Sheffield, 1844 Talpeco Road, Tallahassee, FL 32303

A History of Woodward Avenue in Tallahassee, Florida

It is little known that Woodward Avenue that runs north and south at the west end of Jefferson Street was named for the Woodward families that occupied the land from the year 1850 until about 1935.

My sister, Mary Ellen Mays Bryson, and I, Julia Mays Wood, are the daughters of Frances Woodward Mays and Hugh Leston Mays of Tallahassee, Florida.

Our mother was born in the old Woodward plantation home that was at the end of a lane which later became West Jefferson Street. Our mother's father, our grandfather, Frank Papy Woodward, named the road Woodward Ave. when it was opened up south to Gaines Street. Later the avenue was extended north to Tennessee Street.

About the year 1910 the Woodward home was moved about 100 ft. south to make way for Jefferson Street to be extended west and curve around to connect to the road that became Pensacola Street.

In the beginning, these Woodward lands were bought by our great-great-grandfather, Judge Alfred LePaire Woodward, Sr. He moved to Tallahassee from Jackson County, Marianna, Florida, in 1850. He bought lands that were bounded on the south and west by the railroads. He owned land east to where the Sweet Shop is today, as well as some

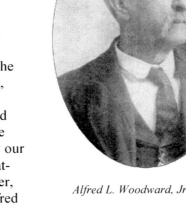
Alfred L. Woodward, Jr., 1907

land on the north side of the lane that became West Jefferson Street. Today the Florida State University stadium is built on what was Woodward land, bounded by railroads.

Alfred L. Woodward, Sr., a judge, lived in Tallahassee on his plantation from 1850 until his death on September 7, 1882. He left two sons, Alfred L. Woodward Jr. (our greatgrandfather) and William Woodruff Woodward, and one grandson who was our mother's father, Frank P. Woodward. These families are all buried in the old City Cemetery.

In 1914 Dr. Josier (J.B.) Game arrived to teach language at the Women's College (forerunner to FSCW). He bought the old Woodward home that had been moved in 1910, and several acres. Dr. Game also helped the college to acquire much of the Woodward property east of Woodward Avenue. The lands were eventually sold by the sons, except for the northeast corner of Woodward Avenue and

Monument to the Signers of Florida's First Constitution in Port St. Joe, FL

Jefferson Street. Another Woodward home and a small house were built on this land. I was born in 1923 and lived in the small house with my parents until I was eight years old. We moved to East 6th Ave. when my sister Mary Ellen was born.
In June of 1973, a gift collection of Woodward materials was made to the Florida State Archives and Records Management, Department of State. This collection was to be known as the Frank Papy Woodward Collection, who saved and preserved the papers.

My grandmother, Julia Collins Woodward, was the first wife of Frank Papy Woodward. She died in 1920. There were two daughters and a son from the first marriage: Mildred, Frances (my mother), and William.

My grandfather's second marriage was to Sara Ambrose Lee. They had a son and a daughter, Frank P. Woodward, Jr., and Sara Lee Woodward. Sara Lee Woodward Holloway is a writer now living in Cookeville, Tennessee. She organized the Woodward papers in 1973 and made the preparations to give them to the Florida State Archives.

Our great-great-grandfather, Judge Alfred L. Woodward, Sr., is important to us because he was a judge in Marianna, FL and was sent as a delegate from Jackson County to the first Constitutional Convention. It was held at St. Joseph, Florida (Port St. Joe) from December 3, 1838 to January 11, 1839. The convention delegates drew up the first Constitution in order to be approved to join the Union. Florida, however, did not become a state until March of 1845.

A monument was established in the park at St. Joseph, Florida (Port St. Joe) with recognition of all the signers of that first Constitutional Convention. My husband and I drove to Port St. Joe several years ago to take a picture of the monument.
Written by: Julia Mays Wood; Submitted by: Mary Ellen Mays-Bryson 1022 McLendon Dr. Tallahassee, FL 32308

Woodward – Heald – An FSU Family

While neither I nor any of my family was born in Tallahassee, we have had connections here for four generations. My maternal greatgrandparents moved to Vero Beach from Illinois around 1920 to farm in a more moderate climate. My grandfather's sister, Frances Woodward (DuBose), graduated from Florida State College for Women (FSCW) in the early 1920s.

My mother, Dorothy Woodward (Heald), graduated from FSCW in 1932 with a degree in Library Science. She lived in Broward Hall her first year, and roomed with Hope Anderson (Yeuell) and Josephine Herring (Jones), forming a lifelong friendship. Mother also lived in Reynolds Hall. She kept a small scrapbook in which she pasted pictures, concert programs, party invitations, notes and letters from boyfriends, report cards, and encouraging telegrams from her father in Miami. One of my favorite telegrams is "Don't give up the ship. You'll make it .. Dad". She even kept "notices", small slips noting callers or messages.

A favorite weekend outing was Thomasville, GA, for dances at The New Russell Hotel. On Sundays they would drive to the Herring's house in Miccosukee for dinner. One

"Excuse for Absence" note cites "due to conditions of roads" as an excuse for Monday, Oct. 8, 1928.

Mother was an "Even", meaning she would graduate in an even numbered year, and she kept a pamphlet called "Even Spirits" containing songs and cheers for the "Green and Gold" of '30 and '32.

Social activities included movies like "The Jazz Singer", starring Al Jolson. The Artists' Series of 1929 included the Prague Teacher's Chorus and Palmer Christian, Organist. Sketches on scrap paper diagrammed football games (1929- "Tech - Fla"). Mrs. Luella Knott presented her with an autographed copy of her 4-H songbook for her participation. When Josephine played piano for the Women's Club, she went along.

My mother's sister, Helen Woodward (Curry), only attended FSCW for a year, but she's proud of her membership in "F" club. Her son, Charles Curry, Jr. graduated in 1961 and married Patricia Schmidt in the Church of the Advent.

When I was young, we visited Tallahassee. We stayed at the Lake Ella Motel. Once my grandfather bought a cane pole to fish in Lake Ella. My father fished with shrimp in Miami, so I was not thrilled with using live worms!

Charles and Pat were active in the Episcopal Student group, and we went to the Episcopal camp ground at the beach. They loved to tell "ghost" stories about the pirates who still rolled casks up the beach at night in search of water.

I earned 2 graduate degrees, my first when the Library School was in the basement of Strozier Library. Studies in the new Louis Shores building were aided by one of the first Macintosh computers, which quickly became the favorite! Hospitality students liked the Graphics course because they could design fancy menus, and they brought goodies to the weekly social hour.

Four younger cousins followed and completed undergraduate degrees, giving the family a total of 10!

Submitted by: Donna Heald, PO Box 1074, Tallahassee, FL 32302

Wrenn – Moving to Woodville

My family moved to Leon County on Monday the 4th of July in 1955. I moved from Freeport, Walton County, Florida to Woodville, Leon County, Florida on the rainiest days I had ever experienced. That was one of the most exciting and saddest days of my young life. I was leaving the only life that I had ever known and entering a new and unfamiliar life in a different world. My father, Clarence Russell Wrenn, worked with Bay Oil Company and had been transferred to the St. Marks terminal from Freeport, Florida. This was also my mother, Bessie Lou Boudreaux Wrenn's, first time away from her home. My mother and I spent the night with her sister, Eddie Pearl Bergeron Spence, in DeFuniak Springs, Walton County, Florida, the night before we left Walton County.

As we drove from DeFuniak Springs, I tried to imagine what my new life would be like. I remember thinking that we wouldn't make it because it was raining so hard, so hard at times that you couldn't see the road for the rain. As we pulled into the driveway of our new house on the corner of Woodville Highway and Natural Bridge Road in Woodville, I was so happy to have a house with an indoor bathroom. My first "real" bathroom. We had to wait, I believe it was the next day, until the rain stopped to unload the van that had our furniture on it.

Bessie L and Clarence R. Wrenn, 50th Anniversary

As we were unloading, a young man about 7 years of age came to the door and asked my mother if there were any boys in the family. As she told him no, that she only had a daughter. He looked very sad and let down. He may have been let down at that time, but we became good friends then and are still friends today, some 54 years later.

I grew up living across the street from Woodville Elementary School and attended school there from the 4th grade until the 8th. After that I went to Cobb Jr. High (Middle School) and then to Leon High in Tallahassee and graduated in 1964. I feel privileged to have lived in Woodville as a child and as an adult. I married John Michael (Mike) Harvey in the First Baptist Church of

Woodville in 1965. Riley Russell and Wrenn Michael Harvey, our sons, were born while we lived in Woodville.

I started my career with the U.S.P.S. in 1973 and worked in the Woodville Post Office until my retirement in 2003. I became Postmaster of the Woodville Post Office in 1990 and it was a privilege to serve the people of Woodville for 30 years. I also wish to say that I had the best parents in the world. They celebrated their 50th wedding anniversary in 1995. I lost my Father in 1996 and my Mother in 2006, but they will never be forgotten.

Submitted by: Carolyn Wrenn Harvey, 102 Lonnie Raker Lane, Crawfordville, FL 32327

Emily Zlotnicki

It doesn't matter when you hear God's call to salvation, it only matters that you hear it. That is why Emily Zlotnicki is such a blessing to us all. There is nothing like a new Christian, and Emily's enthusiasm and excitement is infectious.

Just three years ago Emily agreed to accompany her good friend Nancy Norman to a Sunday morning service at First Baptist Church. She came, she saw, she heard, she felt the conviction and at eighty-six years of age, she was baptized and committed her life to Jesus.

In these past three years she has read the Bible through and through three times, and is beginning her fourth trip through the Word. She buys and passes out Bibles to those she meets, spreading her faith and commitment to all she can.

Emily has chosen the 23rd Psalm as a biblical passage that offers special comfort in her life. "The Lord is my shepherd . . . He restoreth my soul. . . I will fear no evil . . . surely goodness and mercy shall follow me all the days of my life, and I shall dwell in the house of the Lord forever"; words of comfort and serenity for Emily.

Emily was horn in Bridgeport, Connecticut in 1919. She spent most of her life just down the road in Stamford, Connecticut, only moving to Tallahassee twenty years ago. She has been around "religion" most of her life, as her familiarity with the old hymns that she plays on the piano for us in Sunday School attests. It just didn't take until her visit to First Baptist.

She met and married her first husband, Bill, in Stamford in 1940. She claims she found him on the street and he followed her home. Emily and Bill had a son and a daughter and settled into married life. Sometimes what seems a perfect match doesn't work out. Emily and Bill were divorced.

After the divorce, Emily earned her way as an office worker and raised her children by herself. In 1960 she drove into a filling station for a tank of gas and drove off with Ben, her second husband.

Ben was the happiest and the saddest thing that ever happened to her. They were married twenty-six years before Ben passed away and she eventually found her way to our city.

Emily loves Tallahassee and the good friends that twenty years here have brought her. "Boots", as they call her at the American Legion Hall, loves to dance. You will find her there at least twice a week, kicking up her heels and cutting the rug on the Legion Hall dance floor.

What Emily has is what we used to call "spunk". It is a mixture of enthusiasm, cleverness, a joy of life and an impish spirit that puts a twinkle in her eye, boots on her feet and butterflies in her hair.

Although she sees her monies shrinking from inflation and a weakening economy, Emily "doesn't sweat it". She faces life and tomorrow head-on, with a strong faith in God and a funny little smile of happiness on her face.

Written by: Carol Ann and Bill Boydston ©, 1639 Twin Lakes Circle, Tallahassee, FL 32311
Submitted by: Emily Zlotnicki

INDEX

Abernathy, 91
Abner, 65
Abraira, 41
Absalom, 232
Adams, 3, 13, 17, 22, 46, 60, 65, 80, 92, 121, 122, 130, 131, 154, 202, 225, 230, 233, 253, 276, 278, 279, 286, 287, 294, 298
Adcock, 60
Aitkenhead, 259, 260
Alam, 217
Alford, 64, 238
Allen, 51, 52, 63, 97, 146, 147, 158, 159, 168, 171, 179, 180, 212, 229
Ammons, 85
Anderson, 1, 56, 100, 101, 108, 173, 304
Andrews, 19, 42, 72, 85, 86, 238, 270, 271, 283
Antonucci, 263
Appleyard, 265
Apthorp, 44, 86, 87, 256
Archer, 105
Archibald, 266
Argyle, 212
Aronovitz, 204
Arthur, 87, 88, 264
Asbury, 92, 100
Ashby, 262
Ashcraft, 259
Ashmore, 14, 35
Atkinson, 121, 206
Ausley, 13, 101
Austin, 21, 65
Avery, 203, 220
Ayres, 185
Babies, 238
Bailes, 10
Baird, 72
Baker, 270
Ball, 53, 127
Ballard, 58
Bannerman, 45, 94, 95
Barineau, 137
Barnard, 226, 227
Barnes, 9, 29, 65, 66, 114
Barnett, 79
Barr, 254
Barren, 145
Barrentine, 185

Barrett, 10, 74, 77, 83, 88, 89, 246
Basile, 265
Bass, 2, 75, 76, 78, 229
Batchelor, 46
Battles, 137
Baum, 33
Baxley, 128, 129
Bazzell, 113
Beasley, 298
Beaudoin, 26
Beck, 91
Behrea, 228
Belcher, 55
Belk, 250, 252, 254
Bell, 173, 224
Bellagh, 91
Bellah, 91
Belton, 89
Bennett, 235
Bernard, 12, 89, 90, 108, 109
Betton, 66, 80, 91, 173
Betts, 273
Beyers, 10
Biletnikof, 41
Billingly, 44
Billingsley, 223, 224
Bingham, 280
Black, iii, 36, 57, 65, 74, 81, 91, 92, 93, 94, 119, 157, 176, 181, 188, 231, 232, 267
Blackburn, 12, 51
Blackstock, 190
Blair, 45
Blake, 12, 29, 89, 90, 107, 108, 175, 275, 298
Blankenship, 82, 94, 95, 96, 141, 143, 144, 146, 147, 171, 172, 181, 220, 231, 232, 233, 235, 294, 295
Blanton, 54
Blount, 44, 45
Bloxham, 207
Blumenstock, 37
Blunt, 224
Boatwright, 266
Boen, 101
Boggs, 14
Boldt, 269
Bonney, 103
Booth, 63

Boudreaux, 305
Bowden, 40, 41, 42, 96, 193, 244
Bowdoin, 218, 219
Boyd, 33, 56, 96, 97, 98
Boydston, 89, 98, 99, 100, 117, 161, 162, 172, 177, 193, 199, 201, 235, 237, 238, 285, 286, 297, 306
Boyer, 64
Bradford, 27, 28, 49, 58, 89, 90, 100, 101, 108, 109, 131, 147, 207, 257
Bramlett, 211
Branch, 58, 66, 101, 131
Branden, 198
Brandon, 17, 194, 253
Brandt, 101, 102
Bray, 92
Brevard, 35, 61, 62, 78, 89, 102, 103, 108, 109, 115, 119, 121, 122, 151, 175, 242, 260
Brewer, 290
Bridges, Jr, 57
Bristow, 54
Britt, 291
Brogaw, 103
Brokaw, 103, 104, 203, 222
Brooks, 16, 37, 135, 209
Brown, 10, 44, 47, 73, 104, 105, 106, 118, 197, 209, 274
Browning, 225, 281
Bruce, 1, 2, 40, 133
Brumbalow, 279
Bryan, 106, 107, 108, 229
Bryant, 65, 66, 96, 170
Buford, 77
Bullard, 141
Bums, 6, 298
Burch, 246
Burdette, 61
Burke, 47
Burney, 9, 30
Burney II, 9
Burns, 121, 298
Burr, 141, 146, 147, 171, 179, 180, 232, 233
Burt, 195
Bussard, 35
Butler, 159
Butterworth, vii, 68, 101, 108, 109
Byrd, 12, 29, 30, 31, 35, 88, 89, 90, 91, 107, 108, 109, 175, 183, 298
Cain, 110, 111, 112
Calhoun, 65, 80, 91, 103, 108, 119, 121, 175, 242, 255
Call, 23, 56, 66, 80, 101, 102, 125, 174, 175
Callahan, 95, 118

Cameron, 165, 169, 203
Camp, 62, 82, 95, 113, 114, 122, 163
Campbell, 28, 41, 43, 54, 99, 114, 173, 206, 208, 225
Canova, 267
Canterbury, 251, 254
Cantor, 118
Cappelman, 41
Carlisle, 114, 115
Carmine, 33
Carpenter, 215
Carr, 28, 175, 291
Carroll, 167, 247
Carswell, 115, 205
Carter, 37, 39, 44, 45, 77, 80, 281
Caruthers, 185
Carvalho, 115, 117
Case, 27
Cassels, 58, 117
Cates, 56
Cavanaugh, 117, 118, 261, 262
Cawthon, 19, 281
Cay, 54, 130, 131
Chaires, 22, 32, 33, 34, 54, 105, 118, 119, 157, 243, 286
Chandler, 64, 80, 119, 246
Chapman, 55
Charles, 19, 29, 34, 37, 54, 82, 94, 96, 109, 113, 115, 125, 130, 131, 143, 144, 146, 147, 164, 171, 179, 181, 201, 226, 233, 235, 264, 268, 272, 286
Charlie Crist, 127, 128, 154
Chase, 229
Chason, 60, 178, 213
Chester, 287
Clark, 14, 95, 125, 134, 135, 144, 203, 231, 235, 295
Clarke, 33
Clay, 264
Clements, 247
Clifford, 16, 25, 26, 120, 274
Clifton, 90, 101, 109, 131, 142, 175
Clinton, 154
Coates, 2
Cobb, 35, 59
Cochran, 37, 289
Cocke, 210
Coe, 44, 45, 120, 121, 122
Cohens, 65
Coldwell, 74, 75, 81, 82, 84, 93, 94, 182, 189
Cole, 9, 181
Coles, 12
Collier, 169

Collins, vii, 20, 23, 24, 25, 31, 38, 39, 45, 65, 123, 124, 125, 207, 225, 304
Collinsworth, 299
Colwell, 99
Cone, 77, 140, 205, 207
Conley, 63
Conner, 254
Convery, 61, 125, 126
Cook, 1, 251, 256
Cooley, 13, 147
Cooper, 33, 34, 117, 137
Costa, 44
Cotton, iii, 33, 90, 137
Council, 4, 17, 61, 65, 85, 241
Cowan, 130
Cowart, 77
Cowger, 65
Cox, 18, 50, 81, 126, 127, 166
Crafts, 292
Craig, 50, 92
Crane, 137
Crist, 154
Croft, 1
Cromer, 14, 15
Cromer, Jr, 14
Croom, 66, 107, 108
Cross, 198
Crow, 163, 274
Cruce, 128, 129
Crutcher, 44
Crutchfield, 281
Culberson, 175
Culbreath, 288
Culley, 98, 122, 133
Cunkle, 167
Cunningham, 37
Cupp, 130
Curry, 305
Daniels, 149
Darby, 102, 225
Davidson, 188, 225
Davis, 28, 40, 45, 54, 79, 114, 119, 130, 134, 189, 194, 202, 229, 247, 248, 274, 283
de Soto, 69
De Soto, 60, 69
Dean, 279
Dean Hansen, 67
DeAngelis, 208
Decoteau, 49, 50
Deeb, 57, 78
Degaultiers, 60
Delk, 254, 255
DeLong, 166

Demetree, 277
DeMilly, 64, 101, 130, 131, 134, 135, 283
DeMillys, 130, 131
Denham, 12
Densmore, 1
Dewitt, 264
Diamond, 93, 127, 131, 132, 277, 299
Dickson, 198
Diehl, 16
Dixon, 194, 196, 252
Dodd, 203
Donaldson, 18, 135, 248
Donalson Fain, 15, 135
Dorch, 199
Dorr, 114
Dortch, 297
Doster, 254
Douglas, 106, 135, 136
Dowery, 268
Doxsee, 17
Doyle Carlton, 224
Dozier, 91
Drake, 136, 137, 158
Drennon, 6
Driscoll, 47
DuBose, 13, 104, 145, 304
Duden, 87
Dugan, 65
Duggar, 137, 138, 272
Dughi, 138, 139
Duhart, 65
Dukes, 225
Dunaway, 43
DuPree, 33
Durant, 266
Durham, 40, 253
Durr, 180, 233
Durrance, 266
Duzer, 114
Dye, 266, 291
Dykes, 251, 254
Dzialinski, 132, 134
Eaton, 204
Eckland, 78
Edenfield, 225
Edge, 31
Elias, 163
Elliott, 139, 140, 176
Ellis, 176, 265, 281
Englert, 43, 122
Ensley, 25, 26, 69
Eppes, 27, 28, 37, 101, 158, 197, 270
Estock, 96

Eubank, 271
Eubanks, 121
Evans, 286
Fain, 15, 16, 134, 135, 225
Fair, 39, 42, 95, 140, 141, 142, 143, 144, 145, 146, 147, 170, 171, 178, 179, 180, 181, 231, 232, 233, 234, 260, 295
Fairbanks, 277
Falkinburg, 149, 151
Fallier, 49
Farr, 92
Farrell, 125
Farrior, 144
Farris Bryant, 3
Favier, 13, 147
Ferrell, 34, 156, 157
Firestone, 12, 46
Fisher, 148, 236
Fitchner, 281
Fite, 242
Fleming, 240
Fletcher, 54, 149, 150, 151, 152, 153
Flowers, 198
Flynn, 118
Folsom, 185
Foster, 36, 153, 154, 254, 255, 281
Fox, 55, 80, 191
Frances, 190, 232, 234
Franck, 271
Franco-Crist, 154
Franklin, 29, 51, 129, 144, 214, 219, 225, 226, 268, 273
Frano, 74, 75, 82, 84, 93, 94, 182, 189, 276
Free, 155
French, 36, 48, 51, 72, 74, 77, 91, 159, 160, 262, 298
Friensehner, 6
Frojen, 54
Frost, 92
Fuller Warren, 199, 214
Funderburk, 155
Gabordi, 25, 96
Gaines, 35, 71, 108, 187, 238
Galbraith, 264
Gallimore, 65
Galloway, 254, 273, 274
Galt, 56
Gamble, 54, 159
Game, 304
Gandy, 226
Gannon, 69
Gardner, 21, 22, 156, 157
Garfein, 131, 132, 133, 134

Garrison, 144, 231, 295
Gatlin, 158, 209, 228, 253, 254, 280
Gavalas, 20
Gavin, 18
Gehan, 35
Gendron, 188
Genetin, 151, 153
Gerrell, 34, 51, 158, 159
Gibbs, 16, 77, 90, 159, 160
Gibson, 7, 163, 288
Gilbourne, 228
Gilbreath/Galbreath, 179
Gilchrist, 3, 37, 149, 160, 161, 162
Gillespie, 164, 165, 166, 204
Gilmer, 229
Glick, 35
Glidewell, 224
Godby, 42, 43, 78, 120
Goff, 34, 194, 196, 252
Golden, 120, 125, 172
Goldwater, 302
Goodwin, 163
Gordon, 62, 65, 72, 82, 95, 120, 122
Gracida, 61
Graddy, 19, 82
Graham, 64, 80, 99, 132, 163, 164, 188, 205, 217, 261, 290, 298
Gramling, 11, 40, 122
Granberry, 165
Grant, 166
Grantham, 159
Gray, 47, 56, 57, 78, 135, 158, 167, 168, 261, 281
Green, 169, 271
Greene, 28, 40, 140, 141, 142, 143, 145, 146, 147, 170, 171, 178, 179, 180, 202, 232, 233, 234, 265, 268
Griffin, 17, 45, 65, 122
Griffing, 105
Griffith, 229
Grimsley, 121, 172, 281
Griscom, 24, 28, 101
Grissett, 181, 265
Grubaugh, 167
Guarine, 287
Guercia, 125
Gunn, 172, 173, 209
Gutsch, 173, 174, 257
Gutting, 40
Gwynn, 174, 175
Hacker, 36, 37
Hadley, 175, 176
Hagood, 158
Haley, 125

Halford, 158
Hall, 3, 4, 34, 44, 51, 64, 85, 121, 122, 175, 194, 281, 298, 304
Halley, 189
Hamer, 159
Hamilton, 35, 190, 195
Hamlin, 34
Hammond, 41
Hancock, 77, 92, 231, 253, 281
Hand, 65
Hanes, 176
Hanna, 31, 57
Hannon, 34, 127, 288
Hardee, 177, 196, 252, 254
Hardin, 298
Harley, 256
Harper, 279
Harrelson, 177
Harris, 65, 145, 171, 236, 280
Harrison, 45, 141, 142, 143, 145, 146, 147, 178, 179, 180, 232, 233, 234, 293
Harsanyi, 6
Hart, 292
Hartsfield, 139, 168, 258, 265
Hartz, 115
Harvey, 31, 34, 74, 81, 83, 84, 93, 94, 118, 123, 181, 193, 238, 268, 305, 306
Haskin, 38, 41
Hatton, 121
Haun, 249
Hawkins, 277
Hawthorne, 146, 179
Hay, 182
Hayden, 220
Hayes, 171
Haynes, 104, 184
Hazelton, 162
Heald, 305
Hebert, 89
Heintz, 255
Henderson, 145, 171, 184, 221
Hendry, 44
Henry, 19, 31, 48, 65, 66, 72, 85, 87, 90, 100, 101, 105, 126, 144, 231, 240, 274, 289
Herold, vii, 29, 31, 32, 184, 185
Hicks, 158
Hickson, 205
Hiers, 50
High, 160
Hightower, 35
Hilaman, 35
Hill, 21, 31, 32, 33, 36, 88, 90, 101, 125, 130, 157, 177, 185, 186, 225, 264, 272, 274

Hills, 32, 65, 66, 118
Hilsenbeck, 208
Hines, 43, 272
Hinson, 6
Hirschberg, 133
Hobby, 222, 270
Hoch, 186
Hodges, 166, 219, 229
Hoge, 258
Holcomb, 179
Holland, 27, 170
Homer, 266
Hood, 17, 186, 187, 188
Hoose, 6
Hope, 144, 231
Hopkins, 66, 74, 81, 84, 158, 182, 188, 228, 264, 293
Horne, 8, 49, 229
Houck, 158
Hough, 77
Hovan, 259
Howard, 189, 263, 265, 273
Howell, 65, 88, 145
Huang, 302
Huff, 41, 53, 80, 190, 191, 192, 241
Hugh, 54, 93, 94, 303
Hugon, 61
Hulbert, 289
Humphrey, 32, 175
Hunter, 298
Hurst, 8, 85
Husbands, 192
Hutchins, 141
Hutto, 11
Hyatt, 45, 73, 193
Ingalls, 31
Ingram, 130, 185
Ireland, 193
Isler, 34, 194
Ivory, 198
Jackson, 23, 27, 35, 49, 59, 60, 82, 95, 96, 103, 107, 108, 131, 138, 146, 147, 149, 181, 185, 219, 225, 273, 298, 304
Jacob Wuest, 48
Jacqmein, 114
James, 225
Jeb Bush, 128
Jefferson, 3, 27, 37, 90, 101, 121, 122, 131, 146, 160, 179, 180, 202, 228, 248, 270, 285, 304
Jenkins, 19, 65, 137
Jerrigan, 226
Jiles, 37, 298
Jimenez, 7

John Branch, 27, 100, 131
Johnson, vii, 11, 14, 15, 18, 22, 25, 28, 37, 45, 48, 53, 54, 59, 62, 63, 65, 66, 99, 101, 103, 122, 136, 139, 145, 147, 156, 157, 167, 186, 193, 194, 195, 196, 197, 198, 199, 210, 219, 225, 239, 240, 241, 242, 250, 251, 252, 253, 254, 255, 262, 268, 273, 274
Johnston, 62, 80, 82, 95, 137, 138, 197, 280, 288
Jonas, 47
Jones, 34, 65, 66, 69, 168, 215, 220, 254, 291, 292, 302, 303, 304
Jordan, 277
Jordon, 240
Kastin, 272
Kates, 199
Keller, 17
Kelly, 277
Kendrick, 53, 80
Kenneson, 61, 199, 200, 291
Khoury, 163
Kidd, 200
Kilcrease Light Artillery, 51
Kilpatrick, 59
Kimber, 201, 202
Kindon, 164, 202, 203, 204
King, 274
Kirby, 61, 75
Kirk, 145, 290
Knott, 305
Koenig, 241
Kool, 253
Kottkamp, 204, 205
Krentzman, 55
Kuralt, 38
Kutz, 114
Ladd, 213, 222
Lafayette, 27, 28, 59, 64, 66, 78, 80, 103, 278
Laing, 44, 75
Lamb, 183, 205, 224
Landingham, 151
Landrum, 131
Lane, 205
Lang, 205, 206, 207
Langston, 17, 18, 34, 158, 265, 286
Langstons, 166
Laster, 65
Lastinger, 182
Lathan, 290
Law, 73, 85, 105, 208, 217
Lawhon, 34, 137, 287, 296
Lawrence, 65, 81, 238
Lawson, 159, 201, 209, 260, 261
Layfield, 224

Lee, 2, 9, 12, 14, 16, 19, 20, 44, 45, 46, 53, 57, 59, 73, 74, 75, 76, 78, 79, 81, 82, 85, 86, 87, 127, 130, 138, 142, 145, 157, 158, 162, 165, 166, 175, 183, 185, 209, 210, 224, 225, 226, 227, 228, 229, 231, 254, 264, 265, 296, 297, 300, 301, 304
Lehr, 26
Lehrman, 159
LeMoyne, 55, 148
Leonard, 9, 43, 44, 130, 131, 176, 228, 280
LeRoy, 264
LeRoy Collins, 3, 12, 43, 124, 125, 192
Lester, 27, 213
Levy, 59, 88, 121
Lewandowski, 132
Lewis, 9, 14, 31, 34, 51, 65, 92, 101, 114, 119, 137, 138, 175, 210, 211, 222, 272
Lice, 44
Lincoln, 9, 190
Lindley, 25
Lindquist, 87
Littleton, 298
Livingston, 79, 191
Lloyd, 24, 90, 129, 218
Locastro, 47
Logan, 37, 163, 174
Lomas, 65
Lomax, 36
Long, 86, 101, 109, 121
Longsdon, 14
Lonnbladh, 54
Losey, 262
Loudy, 251
Love, 15, 31, 56, 77, 83, 135
Lowe, 91, 92
Lowery, 194, 196, 275, 276
Luke, 182
Lykins, 253
Lyman, 149, 150, 151
Lynne, 80
Mabry, 41, 48, 49, 50, 55, 64, 65, 82, 95, 104, 122, 211, 212, 222, 303
Macbeth, 47
Machonkin, 261
Mack, 20, 111, 112, 128, 239, 240, 275
Macon, 286
Madden, 212, 213
Mahaffey, 101
Mallett, 144, 213, 214, 231
Mann, 267
Marchant, vii, 4, 5, 6, 7, 11, 15, 17, 18, 20, 22, 23, 24, 26, 35, 36, 38, 40, 42, 43, 54, 57, 59, 69, 76,

78, 96, 103, 115, 120, 125, 156, 160, 186, 195, 212, 214, 215, 216, 243, 256, 291
Marks, 182, 216, 217
Marsh, 218, 219
Martin, 22, 56, 61, 69, 77, 82, 122, 125, 142, 200, 213, 221, 264, 280, 288, 298
Mash, 60
Massey, 14, 219, 220
Master, 267
Mathews, 263
Matthews, 86, 252, 255
Maxwell, 44, 105
May, 252
Mayfield, 220, 221
Mayhew, 19
Mayo, 39, 282
Mays, 33, 34, 102, 221, 222, 303, 304
McAlister, 158
McCaa, 207
McCall, 181
McCants, 60
McCarthy, 91
McCarty, 207
McCord, 15
McCormick, 186
McCoy, 240
McCranie, 159
McCullough, 163
McDaniel, 198
McDonald, 6, 210, 224
McDougald, 92
McDougall, 222
McElvy, 222
McElvy, 223, 288
McGorty, 65
McGrotha, 25, 26
McInnis, 158
McKinnis, 65
McLarty, vii, 166, 204, 272
McLin, 224
McIver, 181
McMillan, 60, 281
McMullen, 224, 225
McNeally, 259
McPherson, 2, 12, 14, 16, 19, 20, 44, 46, 53, 57, 59, 73, 74, 75, 76, 78, 79, 81, 82, 158, 225, 226, 227, 228, 229, 264, 265, 296, 297, 301
Mears, 201
Meek, 253
Meeks, 157
Meggs, 43, 163, 172
Melton, 167
Melvin, 253

Mendes, 132
Mercer, 178
Merryman, 126
Messer, 48, 50, 55, 212
Metcalfe, 290
Middleton, 242, 251
Miller, 40, 44, 56, 103, 149, 231, 264, 272
Milton, 240
Mitchell, 22, 45, 65, 80, 144, 145, 149, 157, 207, 224, 231, 251, 283
Mizell, 144, 146, 180, 233
Mock, 64
Modesitt, 163
Monroe, 13, 16, 22, 43, 46, 48, 54, 61, 72, 73, 74, 75, 77, 78, 79, 80, 81, 82, 88, 108, 109, 119, 122, 160, 183, 221, 242
Montford, 30
Montgomery, 229, 230
Moody, 240
Moore, 41, 49, 57, 60, 176, 178, 234, 261, 272
Moorer, 6
Moran, 102, 139
Morell, 48
Morgan, 43, 72
Morris, 9, 115, 131, 134, 158, 159, 167, 213
Morris Jr., 9
Morrison, 163
Morse, 54
Moss, 274
Mrs. McKenzie, 44
Muller, 290
Mullikin, 280
Mullins, 186
Mullryne, 205
Mumford, 101
Murphy, 293
Musgray, 65
Nam, 115
Napier, 35
Nasby, 65
Nelson, 6, 230
Nettles, 56, 81, 251
Newborn, 298
Neyland, 230, 231
Nickolaidi, 5
Nicks, 94, 95, 140, 141, 142, 143, 144, 145, 146, 170, 171, 172, 178, 179, 180, 231, 232, 233, 234, 295
Nix, 297
Nixon, 222
Norman, 306
Nugent, 40
Nunez, 58

O'Berry, 171, 231
O'Sullivan, 61
Ogbourn, 158
Olin, 273
Olmstead, 47, 70
O'neill, 16
Oumano, 154
Owen, 239
Owens, 14, 158, 240
Page, 34
Palmer, 19, 59, 72
Pannick, 259
Parish, 29, 60, 61, 90, 108, 109, 267, 273, 286
Parker, iii, 9, 29, 55, 66, 101, 126, 148, 236, 254
Parrimore, 265
Parrish, 266
Parsons, 26, 126
Partch, 127
Passut, 266
Patrick, 91, 131
Patterson, 33, 169
Patton, 236
Paulk, 237, 238
Paulus, 265
Payne, 77
Pearson, 10, 18, 72, 80, 81, 238, 239, 270, 271
Penrod, 239
Penton, 251
Pepper, 78, 99
Perkins, 29, 31, 43, 175
Perrin, 106, 107
Perry, 195, 206
Peterson, 41, 96
Peurifoy, 63
Phillips, 194, 239, 279
Pichard, 17
Pickett, 158
Pierson, 19
Plant, 53, 109, 117
Poag, 92
Pollitt, 6
Ponce de Leon, 47, 165
Ponder, 41, 246, 277
Pond-Koenig, 191
Pons, 242
Poole, 35
Pope, 14, 215
Popp, 185
Poppell, 45
Porter, 65, 219, 242, 243
Pottsdamer, 298
Powell, 243, 254, 265
Pratt, 103

Pringle, 205, 207
Pritchard, 55
Proctor, 11, 21, 22, 56, 59, 221, 243, 244, 245
Proctor III, 22
Proctor, Jr, 22
Putnam, 11, 55
Raa, 189
Rachels, 252
Ragsdale, 48, 49
Ramsey, 245
Randolph, 54, 102, 254
Raspberry, 91
Reagan, 91
Reams, 246
Reece, 248
Reed, 292
Reese, 231
Reeves, 121
Register, 28, 32, 34, 54, 58, 265
Rehwinkel, 14
Reilly, 264
Rentsch, 184
Revells, 158, 166
Reynolds, 255, 280
Reynolds III, 65
Rhodes, 29, 34, 45, 103, 168, 266, 267
Richardson, 250
Richberg, 255
Richbourg, 177, 178, 194, 196, 197, 250, 251, 252, 253, 254, 255, 260, 261, 262, 263, 273, 274
Riley, 280
Ring, 31, 44, 120
Ritter, 266
Roach, 37
Robbins, 256
Roberts, 14, 16, 19, 42, 49, 62, 63, 72, 101, 137, 157, 166, 167, 174, 197, 207, 256, 257, 258
Roberts., 14, 28, 62, 72, 137, 157, 166
Robertson, 201
Robinson, 9, 181, 231, 298
Robison, 34, 280
Rocco, Jr, 77
Rodgers, 194
Rogers, 47, 124, 196, 220
Rosen, 258
Rosenau, 55, 56, 58, 59, 259, 260
Rosenblum, 140
Ross, 101, 125
Rothschild, 255, 260, 261
Rounds, 242
Rudd, 158
Ruffin, 261

Rumsey, 114
Russ, 247
Russell, 44, 117, 141, 142, 143, 145, 146, 179, 180, 232, 234, 261, 269, 305, 306
Ryder, 40, 281
Ryerson, 80
Sanders, 60, 232, 254, 262, 265, 266, 285
Sanford, 290
Sapronetti, 190, 263, 264
Sauls, 56, 57, 142, 145, 146, 158, 170, 171, 179, 180, 226, 227, 228, 232, 233, 234, 264, 265
Saunders, 85, 265, 266, 267
Saxon, 12, 13, 143, 234
Scammon, 286
Schmidt, 215, 305
Schreeder, 114
Scott, 149
Sederquist, 60
Sellers, 39, 41, 158
Semmes, 300
Sessions, 45
Shackleford, 54, 268, 269
Sharp, 50
Shaw, 4, 14
Shearer, 35
Sheffield, 221, 288, 303
Shellahamer, 7
Shelley, 175
Shepard, 149, 194
Sherwin, vii, 3, 5, 21
Shine, 269, 270
Shivers, 284
Shoaps, 263, 264
Shreck, 231
Sikes, 55, 207
Sills, 243, 249
Simmons, 54, 163
Sims, 219
Skagfield, 23
Skiber, 36
Skipper, 55, 213
Slade, 30
Slosek, 62
Slusser, 202
Small, 65
Smith, 13, 16, 23, 24, 25, 29, 37, 41, 48, 53, 54, 64, 66, 90, 137, 148, 166, 171, 175, 198, 199, 221, 222, 224, 236, 255, 256, 266, 271, 272, 280, 288, 293, 294
Smith, Jr., 13
Smoak, 106
Snyder, 55
Southall, 126

Spearman, 298
Spence, 220, 305
Spurgeon,, 6
Stafford, 273
Stanaland, 254, 273, 280
Stanley, 37, 120, 122, 123, 134, 178, 182
Starkweather, 265
Starrett, 129
Steed, 245
Stephens, 275
Sterk, 14
Stevens, 65, 114, 231, 275
Steverson, 61, 62
Stewart, 13, 14, 230, 298
Stinson, 114
Stoeff, 276
Stoutamire, 118, 158, 265, 279
Stowers, 290
Strickland, 11, 13, 44, 45, 77, 95, 115, 117, 142, 143, 170, 184, 197, 217, 219, 232, 265, 276, 278, 279, 280, 281, 292
Strong, 55, 65, 239
Sullivan, 61, 64, 114, 122, 134, 249, 280
Sullivans, 80
Summer-Clark, 14
Sutton, 280
Swatts, 265
Sykes, 158, 177
Tait, 14
Tamanian, 281
Tanner, 61, 154
Tapers, 24, 25
Tatum, 103
Taylor, 12, 62, 91, 109, 131, 221, 224, 257, 282, 283
Teague, 31, 272
Tew, 225
Tharpe, 205
Theus, 256
Thigpen, 273
Thomas, 4, 12, 18, 37, 44, 48, 89, 90, 93, 100, 101, 105, 106, 108, 109, 121, 126, 141, 186, 213, 273, 289
Thompson, 20, 31, 33, 65, 72, 77, 78, 270, 283, 284, 301
Thornton, 54
Thorton, 168
Tibbitts, 203
Tilden, 12, 91, 101
Tillman, 227
Tison, 106
Todd, 119, 126, 178, 288
Tomberlin, 149, 245

Touchton, 80
Townsend, 23, 24, 33, 141
Trammell, 222
Travis, 50
Tribble, 80
Trotman, 229
Trull, 47
Tryon, 55
Tucker, 19, 25
Tully, 281
Turnbull, 29
Turner, 75, 77, 88, 164, 165, 168, 206, 301, 302
Turners, 81
Tuten, 237
Twine, 29, 298
Upchurch, 13, 33
Van Brunt, 31, 101, 109, 122, 140, 141, 142, 143, 145, 146, 170, 175, 178, 179, 180, 232, 233, 234
Van Weller, 36
Vane, 265
VanZant, 12, 167
Vaughn, 17, 65
Vause, 167
Waeckel, 216
Wagner, 155
Wahnish, 56
Waite, 131
Waldron, 9
Walker, 17, 59, 92, 95, 136, 161, 174, 175, 188, 228, 247, 257, 265, 284, 285, 286, 297, 298
Walston, 56
Ward, 41, 42, 105, 150, 168, 213, 270, 286
Wardman, 185
Washington, 173, 298
Watkins, 34, 141, 295
Watson, 34, 223, 224, 286, 287, 288, 289, 290, 298
Watt, 193
Watts, 80, 191, 288
Waugh, 290
Weeks, 291, 292, 293
Weinke, 41, 42
Weissmuller, 53
Weldon, 22, 23
Welford, 293, 301
Wellford/Wilford, 243
Werner, 96, 141, 294, 295
West, 213
Wetherell, 41, 295, 296
Wetherell,, 41, 295
Whidden, 12
Whitaker, 100, 134, 229

Whitcomb, 39
Whitehead, 257
Whitfield, 66, 249, 280, 294, 301
Whittle, 242
Wiggins Gerrell, 51
Wilbanks, 107
Wilder, 44, 45, 79, 81, 229, 296
Wilds, 206
Wilfong, 14
Wilke, 288
Wilkes, 118
Wilkinson, 10, 34, 72, 238, 270
William, 12, 19, 36, 56, 62, 65, 73, 86, 87, 90, 92, 109, 117, 139, 144, 164, 165, 171, 172, 175, 182, 190, 202, 232, 264, 268, 272, 273, 294, 301, 304
Williams, 11, 22, 27, 37, 47, 52, 53, 65, 66, 120, 132, 134, 137, 141, 142, 146, 157, 192, 214, 281, 297, 298
Williamson, 34, 41, 81
Willis, 298, 299, 300
Wills, 26
Wilson, 56, 78, 110, 112, 160, 175, 185, 194, 198, 224, 251, 254, 265, 274, 294, 300, 301, 302
Winchester, 36, 301
Winn, 99, 131
Winterle, 167
Winthrop, 56, 66, 80, 157
Wise, 112, 113
Wood, 1, 38, 98, 114, 123, 128, 221, 222, 303, 304
Woodard, 129, 303
Woodberr, 294
Woodberry, 54, 115, 275, 294
Woodbery, 33
Woodbury, 292
Woodrow, 218
Worrell, 15
Wrenn, 305, 306
Wright, 177, 196, 275, 288
Wynn, 298
Yaeger, 130
Yarbrough, 29
Yates, 260
Yeager, 265
Yellowhair, 28
Yerger, 302, 303
Young, 1, 29, 36, 62, 76, 90, 105, 197, 229, 295
Youssef, 83
Yunis, 121
Zappone, 145
Zeigler, 222
Zimmerman, 43